ROUTLEDGE HANDBOOK OF SOUTHEAST ASIAN POLITICS

Now available in paperback, this Handbook provides a comprehensive analysis of the major themes that have defined the politics of Southeast Asia. It provides a comprehensive and cutting-edge examination of this important subject. The introductory chapter provides an overview of the theoretical and ideological themes that have dominated the study of the region's politics and presents the different ways the complex politics of the region have been understood. The contributions by leading scholars in the field cover a range of broad questions about the dynamics of politics.

The Handbook analyses how the dominant political and social coalitions of the region were forged in the Cold War era, and assesses the complex processes of transition towards various forms of democratic politics. How institutions and systems of governance are being forged in an increasingly global environment is discussed and whether civil society in Southeast Asia has really evolved as an independent sphere of social and political activity. The Handbook examines how national governments are dealing with growing tensions within the region as matters such as labour, human rights and the environment spill beyond national boundaries, and how they are establishing a place in the new global framework.

By engaging the Southeast Asian experience more firmly with larger debates about modern political systems, the Handbook is an essential reference tool for students and scholars of Political Science and Southeast Asian studies.

Richard Robison is Emeritus Professor at the Asia Research Centre, Murdoch University, Australia. His research is concerned with the political economy and the politics of markets with a special focus on Indonesia. He is the author and editor of many publications on Southeast and East Asian Politics, including *Reorganising Power in Indonesia: The Politics of Oligarchy in an Age of Markets* (co-authored with Vedi Hadiz, 2004), also published by Routledge.

ROUTLEDGE HANDBOOK OF SOUTHEAST ASIAN POLITICS

Edited by Richard Robison

LONDON AND NEW YORK

First published in paperback 2014

First published 2011
by Routledge
2 Park Square, Milton Park, Abingdon, Oxon OX14 4RN

Simultaneously published in the USA and Canada
by Routledge
711 Third Avenue, New York, NY 10017

Routledge is an imprint of the Taylor & Francis Group, an informa business

British Library Cataloguing in Publication Data
A catalogue record for this book is available from the British Library

Library of Congress Cataloging in Publication Data
Routledge handbook of Southeast Asian politics / edited by Richard Robison.
    p. cm.
  Includes bibliographical references and index.
  1. Southeast Asia–Politics and government–1945- I. Robison, Richard, 1943-
  DS526.7.R68 2011
  320.959–dc23
            2011022318

ISBN: 978-0-415-49427-4 (hbk)
ISBN: 978-0-415-71651-2 (pbk)
ISBN: 978-0-203-15501-1 (ebk)

Typeset in Bembo
by Taylor & Francis Books

Printed and bound in the United States of America
by Edwards Brothers Malloy

CONTENTS

Contents

LIST OF TABLES

CONTRIBUTORS

Editor

Richard Robison is Emeritus Professor at the Asia Research Centre, Murdoch University, Australia. His research is concerned with the political economy and the politics of markets with a special focus on Indonesia. He is the author and editor of many publications on Southeast and East Asian politics, including *Reorganising Power in Indonesia: The Politics of Oligarchy in an Age of Markets* (co-authored with Vedi R. Hadiz, 2004), also published by Routledge.

Editorial Board

Richard Doner, Emory University, USA
Jeffrey A. Winters, Northwestern University, USA
Kevin Hewison, University of North Carolina at Chapel Hill, USA
Chua Beng Huat, National University of Singapore
Pasuk Phongpaichit, Chulalongkorn University, Thailand
Vedi R. Hadiz, Murdoch University, Australia
Edward Aspinall, Australian National University
John Sidel, London School of Economics, UK
Meredith L. Weiss, University of Albany, USA

Contributors

Edward Aspinall is a Senior Fellow in the Department of Political and Social Change, College of Asia and the Pacific, Australian National University, Canberra. His research focuses on Indonesian politics and on issues of democratization, nationalism and ethnic politics. His publications include *Islam and Nation: Separatist Rebellion in Aceh, Indonesia* (Stanford University Press, 2009).

Chris Baker is an independent scholar and long resident in Thailand, who writes on Thai history and politics. Together with Pasuk Phongpaichit he has written *A History of Thailand* (Cambridge University Press, 2005) and *Thaksin* (Silkworm Books, second expanded edition 2009), and recently published a translation of the Thai epic, *The Tale of Khun Chang Khun Phaen* (Silkworm Books, 2010).

Chua Beng Huat is Provost Professor and Head, Department of Sociology, National University of Singapore. His recent research is on Singapore politics and on the regionalization of pop culture in East Asia. He is a founding co-executive editor of the *Inter-Asia Cultural Studies* journal. His publications include, as editor, *Elections as Popular Culture in Asia* (Routledge, 2007).

Richard Doner is Professor in the Department of Political Science at Emory University in Atlanta, Georgia, USA. His research is on the political economy of economic development in Southeast Asia, with special emphasis on the roles and origins of institutions. His publications include *The Politics of Uneven Development: Thailand's Economic Growth in Comparative Perspective* (Cambridge University Press, 2009).

Michele Ford is Associate Professor in the Department of Indonesian Studies at the University of Sydney, Australia. Her research interests focus on social activism in Southeast Asia and the Indonesia–Singapore borderlands. Michele's publications include *Workers and Intellectuals: NGOs, Unions and the Indonesian Labour Movement* (NUS/Hawaii/KITLV 2009).

Martin Gainsborough is Reader in Development Politics in the School of Sociology, Politics and International Studies at the University of Bristol in the United Kingdom. His research is on the politics of development, with an area specialism on Southeast Asia, and expertise on state theory, governance and corruption. His publications include *Vietnam: Rethinking the State* (Zed Books, 2010).

John Gillespie is Professor of Law and Director of the Asia Pacific Business Regulation Group, Department of Business Law and Taxation, Monash University. His current research focuses on non-state regulation of land and markets as well as law and development in socialist East Asia. His most recent book is *Law and Development and the Global Discourses of Legal Transfers* (with Pip Nicholson, eds, Cambridge University Press, 2012).

Vedi R. Hadiz is Professor of Asian Societies and Politics at the Asia Research Centre, Murdoch University and an Australian Research Council Future Fellow. He is currently researching the political economy of Islamic populism. His most recent book is *Localising Power in Post-Authoritarian Indonesia: A Southeast Asia Perspective* (Stanford University Press, 2010).

Natasha Hamilton-Hart is an Associate Professor at the University of Auckland Business School. Her research is in the fields of political economy and international relations, with a particular focus on Southeast Asia. She is the author of *Hard Interests, Soft Illusions: Southeast Asia and American Power*, forthcoming with Cornell University Press.

Kevin Hewison is Professor in the Department of Asian Studies and Director of the Carolina Asia Center at the University of North Carolina at Chapel Hill. His current research is on precarious work in Asia and the political economy of Thailand. He is co-editor of the *Journal of Contemporary Asia*.

Caroline Hughes is Director of the Asia Research Centre and Associate Professor of Governance Studies in the School of Social Sciences and Humanities at Murdoch University. Her research interests focus on two related questions: the politics of post-colonial state-building in Southeast Asia; and the politics of post-conflict reconstruction and international aid policy. Her publications include *Dependent Communities: Aid and Politics in Cambodia and East Timor* (Cornell SEAP, 2009).

Paul D. Hutchcroft is a Professor in the Department of Political and Social Change in the ANU College of Asia and the Pacific. He is a scholar of comparative and Southeast Asian politics who has written extensively on the Philippines. He is currently completing a manuscript entitled 'The power of patronage: capital and countryside in the Philippines from 1900 to 2010'.

Jane Hutchison is Senior Lecturer in Politics and International Studies and a Fellow of the Asia Research Centre, Murdoch University, Perth, Western Australia. She researches social and political change in the Philippines, focusing on labour and the urban poor. With Andrew Brown, she edited *Organising Labour in Globalising Asia* (Routledge, 2007).

Lee Jones is a lecturer in the School of Politics and International Relations at Queen Mary, University of London, UK. His research focuses on state–society relations, sovereignty and international intervention. His book, *Sovereignty and Intervention in Southeast Asia: Beyond the Myth of the 'ASEAN Way'*, will be published by Palgrave in late 2011.

John McCarthy lectures in the Australian National University's Crawford School. John carries out research into issues to do with agrarian change, land tenure, environmental governance and natural resource policy. He has carried out various assignments with agencies in Australia and Indonesia including AusAID and the Centre for International Forestry Research (CIFOR). He is the author of *The Fourth Circle: A Political Ecology of Sumatra's Rainforest Frontier* (Stanford University Press, 2006) and has published in *World Development*, *Development and Change*, the *Singapore Journal of Tropical Geography*, the *Journal of Peasant Studies*, *Human Ecology*, the *Journal of Southeast Asian Studies*, and other journals.

Moira Moeliono is a senior associate with the Forest and Governance Programme of CIFOR. She has a long experience with community involvement in natural resource management, with a special interest in forest tenure and conservation issues. She has contributed to works on decentralization, community-based conservation and tenure issues. More recently, she has been involved in research on national–local policy linkages in forest governance in the context of reducing emissions from deforestation and degradation (REDD).

Helen E. S. Nesadurai is Associate Professor at the School of Arts and Social Sciences, Monash University (Sunway Campus, Malaysia). Her research focuses on the politics and political economy of global and regional governance arrangements, with an emerging interest in non-state, soft law governance regimes. Recent publications include on 'Economic surveillance as a new mode of regional governance: contested knowledge and the politics of risk management in East Asia', *Australian Journal of International Affairs* (vol. 63, no. 3, 2009).

Pasuk Phongpaichit is Distinguished Professor of Economics at Chulalongkorn University, Bangkok. Her research has been on corruption, the illegal economy and social movements. Her current project concerns inequality.

Richard Robison is Emeritus Professor at the Asia Research Centre, Murdoch University, Perth, Western Australia. His research is on political economy and the politics of markets with a special focus on Indonesia. His publications include *Reorganising Power in Indonesia: The Politics of Oligarchy in an Age of Markets* (co-authored with Vedi R. Hadiz, Routledge, 2004).

Joel Rocamora is Chairman of the Board at the Institute for Popular Democracy and Lead Convenor of the National Anti-Poverty Commission. He has written extensively on Indonesian and Philippine politics.

Garry Rodan is an Australian Professorial Fellow of the Australian Research Council and Professor of Politics and International Studies at the Asia Research Centre, Murdoch University, Australia. His thematic research interest is in the relationship between capitalist development and political regime directions in Southeast Asia. Attempting to characterize and explain dynamic and durable forms of authoritarian rule has been a particular focus, including through his book *Transparency and Authoritarian Rule in Southeast Asia* (Routledge, 2005).

Andrew Rosser is Associate Professor in Development Studies at the University of Adelaide. His research focuses on the political of development with a particular focus on Indonesia and Timor Leste. His recent publications include 'The politics of corporate social responsibility in Indonesia' (with Donni Edwin), *Pacific Review* (March 2010).

Henk Schulte Nordholt is Head of Research at the Royal Netherlands Institute of Southeast Asian and Caribbean Studies (KITLV) in Leiden and Professor of Southeast Asian Studies at the VU University in Amsterdam His research interests focus on Balinese history, political violence, the anthropology of colonialism, the making of an audiovisual archive of everyday life, and contemporary politics in Indonesia. His publications include *Renegotiating Boundaries: Local Politics in Post-Suharto Indonesia* (with Gerry van Klinken, KITLV Press, 2007), *Bali: An Open Fortress 1995–2005 – Regional Autonomy, Electoral Democracy and Entrenched Identities* (NUS Press, 2007) and *Indonesie na Soeharto: Reformasi en Restauratie* (Bert Bakker, 2008).

Meredith L. Weiss is an Associate Professor in the Department of Political Science at the University at Albany, State University of New York. Her research addresses political mobilization and contention, civil society, nationalism and ethnicity, and electoral politics, with a particular focus on Malaysia and Singapore. Her publications include *Universities and Students in Malaysia: Crucible, Mirror, Sideshow* (Cornell SEAP/Singapore, 2011) and *Protest and Possibilities: Civil Society and Coalitions for Political Change in Malaysia* (Stanford University Press, 2006).

Ian Wilson is a Research Fellow at the Asia Research Centre and a lecturer in the School of Social Sciences and Humanities, Murdoch University. Western Australia. His research focuses on gangs and organized crime, political violence, the urban poor and informal street politics in Indonesia. He has published in journals such as *Critical Asian Studies* and *Nationalism and Ethnic Politics*, and collaborated with organizations such as Indonesian Corruption Watch.

Jeffrey A. Winters is a Professor of Political Economy at Northwestern University, Chicago, USA. His research focuses on oligarchy, elites and the politics of democracy without law. He is the author of *Oligarchy* (Cambridge University Press, 2011) and *Power in Motion: Capital Mobility and the Indonesian State* (Cornell University Press, 1996).

ACKNOWLEDGEMENTS

Volumes such as this, with a large number of authors and extensive planning, communications and editorial work, require substantial support. This was provided in large part by the Asia Research Centre at Murdoch University. A Murdoch University Strategic Research Grant made it possible for the editor to discuss the chapters directly with several of the authors. Tamara Dent of the Asia Research Centre organised the copy-editing of drafts and communication with authors related to this process as well as formatting the manuscript. Together with Ros Lumley she kept the project on schedule, particularly in the more frenetic period as deadlines drew closer. Because the volume itself and my own chapter covered such a vast scope of topics and literatures I sought the time and advice of colleagues. I received very helpful and thoughtful comments about my ideas for the structure of the volume and who might be approached for the different papers from a number of colleagues. Among these were Edward Aspinall, Jeffrey Winters, Garry Rodan, John Sidel, Chua Beng Huat, Vedi Hadiz and Kevin Hewison. Later, Jane Hutchison, Garry Rodan, Kevin Hewison and Caroline Hughes gave me thoughtful comments on my own chapter.

Richard Robison
Perth
28 February 2011

INTRODUCTION

Richard Robison

This collection provides an authoritative and comprehensive overview of the major themes and issues that have defined the politics of Southeast Asia in the modern period. It brings together scholars who have influenced the way the politics of the region has been understood over several decades and others who are opening new and innovative ways of looking at things.

It seeks to engage the Southeast Asian experience more firmly with larger debates about how modern political systems and modern states are formed and how countries and regions are drawn into the global system. The chapters will be relevant to larger, comparative and theoretical debates as well as providing solid empirical investigations.

The central themes and issues of the volume

Understanding the complex politics of Southeast Asia is made especially difficult because they are played out in circumstances that have differed substantially from one country to another. It is true that political analysts everywhere can point to the special nature of particular histories that make general conclusions and comparisons difficult within regions and even within countries. But in Southeast Asia the artificiality of the region is particularly stark. Malaysia, Thailand, the Philippines and Indonesia share important characteristics because they are to varying degrees defined by a system of state authority forged within economies driven largely by private interests and where the boundaries of private and public power is often confused. But these similarities are somewhat limited by other factors. In the Philippines, politics is largely defined by the dominance and authority of a complex oligarchy with historical roots in a rural landowning elite; it resembles a form of patronage politics more typical of Latin America. At the other extreme, Indonesia has been defined by a highly bureaucratized and central state apparatus and rapacious private interest wrapped in nationalist and corporatist ideology that evokes stark parallels with the rise of similar regimes in North Africa and the Middle East, including Mubarak's Egypt.

Elsewhere, the differences are even greater. In Vietnam, for example, while the politics of the South in the 1950s and 1960s had important resonances with those of other countries in the region, it was the dominance established by a communist party that has defined politics since then. Given this dominance, the central political question in Vietnam has been how a communist party state is managing the incorporation of a market economy without surrendering its political hegemony, making comparison with China more relevant than with other countries in

1

the region. And the case of Singapore appears to fit more easily into the pattern of political authority and state-managed capitalism that has been so prominent in Northeast Asia. Elsewhere, the progress of political regimes in Cambodia and Burma are defined more specifically by issues of violence and the crude imposition of state authority and the early stages of state building and what Marx understood as 'primitive accumulation'.

Given these realities, any study of the politics of Southeast Asia must confront the problem of dealing with quite fundamental differences as well as seeking out meaningful comparisons.

The book is organized into six sections that deal with very broad questions about the dynamics of politics: power, states and regimes, markets and governance, society and participation, violence and authority, and regional and global accommodation. These are preceded by a chapter that provides a context for the study, looking at how the big questions and the main interpretations have been constructed by scholars.

Chapter 1: Interpreting the politics of Southeast Asia: debates in parallel universes

This chapter by Richard Robison examines the main theoretical and ideological paradigms within which the politics of Southeast Asia have been understood and asks how these have been established and consolidated over time. Specifically, it focuses on three big questions about the politics of the region that have been critical in shaping the literature: why have democracies often been so fragile and authoritarian regimes so resilient? How does market capitalism influence the institutions of politics and governance and the configuration of power? Does political and administrative decentralization and democratic reform open the door to a progressive and self-reliant civil society as a major player in the politics of the region?

In the context of these questions, the chapter examines the rise and fall (or transformation) of different theoretical and ideological approaches. It asks whatever happened to modernization theory and dependency theory, so dominant in the 1960s and 1970s and so clearly the products of the Cold War. It looks at the way neoliberal ideas have redefined the political problem as one of providing efficient administration through public policy, good governance and efficient institutions, constructing a new orthodoxy in political analysis from the 1980s. It asks how modernization theory has been reconstituted in different institutional approaches and in new ideas about social movements and the politics of identity. It asks how critical theories of politics that explore state and class have addressed changing circumstances.

Section I: The changing landscape of power (Chapters 2, 3 and 4)

Here the book explores the genesis of power in Southeast Asia and the way economic and global changes have reshaped the forces that now dominate the political and economic life of the region. In Chapter 2, Kevin Hewison and Garry Rodan examine the changing nature of political opposition, from the radical Left in the Cold War era to the rise of a middle class and bourgeois opposition in the modern period. Jane Hutchison, in Chapter 3, asks why organized labour has been such a weak political force and explains why none of the social democratic accommodations that were a feature of capitalism in Europe have emerged in the region, or any liberal pluralist polities within which labour might compete. On the other side of the coin, in Chapter 4 Jeffrey Winters looks at the big end of town. He examines the ways in which large oligarchies have emerged and concentrated political and economic power within complex alliances and within broader global relationships.

Section II: States and regimes (Chapters 5, 6, 7, 8 and 9)

It is significant that political regimes have taken such different forms across the region. How do we explain why the varieties of democratic politics that have emerged in the region are so heavily influenced by populist ideas, and in what situations have money politics dominated the parties and parliaments of the region rather than coherent ideologies or policy agendas? To what extent are new models of consultation and participation really new forms of authoritarianism attempting to bypass representative and competitive forms of democracy? Have the middle classes and business been a progressive or a conservative force in Southeast Asian politics? In Chapter 5, Vedi R. Hadiz looks at the way democratic transformation in Indonesia has produced a form of money politics, while Pasuk Phongpaichit and Chris Baker, in Chapter 6, explain the populist roots of the recent challenges to the establishment in Thailand. Paul Hutchcroft and Joel Rocamora explain in Chapter 7 the democratic deficit in the Philippines and the patronage-based dynamics of that system. The contrasts with Singapore could not be greater, and in Chapter 8 Garry Rodan explains how a form of consultative authoritarianism has emerged in that country to embed society within its agendas. In Chapter 9, Martin Gainsborough looks at the way the regime in Vietnam deals with the task of accommodating emerging social forces and capitalist markets within the party-based structures of a communist political system.

Section III: Markets and governance (Chapters 10, 11, 12 and 13)

The politics of Southeast Asia have been dramatically changed with the rise of markets and the increasing integration of the region into global economic structures. One of the most interesting questions is why the models of economic growth and institutional change in the region have differed from the paths set down by the developmental states of Japan and South Korea. Richard Doner examines this critical puzzle in Chapter 10. This is related to the broader question of the impact of market capitalism on the models of governance in the region, from what are generally considered neo-patrimonial systems to regularized systems defined by rule of law. Because the Asian Economic Crisis was seen by many to be the consequence of cronyism and corruption within the governments of the region itself, these were subjected to intensive pressures to reform their institutions and build effective public institutions. In Chapter 11, Andrew Rosser asks how organizations like the World Bank and the IMF (and local technocratic officials) have struggled with the twin, and often competing, pressures to impose 'good governance' and those to ensure 'country ownership' in framing their policies for institutional reform. In Chapter 12, John Gillespie's study of the difficulties faced in attempts to judicialize market regulation demonstrates that the construction of rules and institutions is far from a technical matter and is embedded in the world of politics. Chua Beng Huat steps away from the close-up world of governance, politics and technocratic contestation in Chapter 13 with his analysis of the dramatic reshaping of Asia's new global cities. Here, he foregrounds highly structural forces at work as different capitalist economies move from being industrial and domestically oriented towards a more global orientation based around information, services and headquartering. Thus the new Asian mega city is absorbed by showcasing these aspects in the global arena rather than being a centre for production.

Section IV: Civil society and participation (Chapters 14, 15 and 16)

With the fall of some authoritarian regimes and increasing decentralization and democratization, there have been expectations that Southeast Asia is witnessing the rise of civil society as an independent sphere of progressive social and political activity outside the control of powerful states. Liberals expected that progressive political movements and ideas would find their way into social movements and NGOS and that middle classes would become a force for liberal trans-formation along the lines of Fukuyama's end of politics argument. Yet, despite programmes of decentralization and democratization it appears that vigorous social movements have made few inroads into the power of oligarchies and large political parties often backed by the state or by big business. As enthusiasm has been tempered by disappointment, Edward Aspinall and Meredith Weiss in Chapter 14 and Henk Schulte Nordholte in Chapter 15 explain some of the complex processes where civil society and social movements collide with entrenched interests and the state and how this has transformed the nature and tactics of many CSOs. In Chapter 16, John McCarthy and Moira Moeliono illustrate these difficulties in the case of the forestry sector CSOs by examining the frustrating process of legislating and enforcing new regulations in the Indo-nesian forestry industry and the constant counter-moves by vested interests to circumvent these.

Section V: Violence and state authority (Chapters 17 and 18)

Extra-legal forms of coercion and violence have long been a part of Southeast Asian politics in cases where the authority of the state has been circumscribed or where the state has found these instruments valuable in its own service. Caroline Hughes' study of Cambodia and Timor in Chapter 17 looks at the problems of constructing state authority in post-conflict situations where the state's survival depends on drawing together political constituencies in highly volatile cir-cumstances. In contrast, Chapter 18 sees Ian Wilson examine those long-standing cases where governments have had complex relationships with militias, vigilantes and private security orga-nizations and the often highly ambiguous status of these groups in the ongoing consolidation of state power.

Section VI: Forging regional and global accommodations (Chapters 19, 20, 21 and 22)

A vast literature has been assembled to look at the emergence of institutions established to advance regional co-operation, notably in strategic, political and economic co-operation. Whether these have indeed created a new dimension of regional power and influence has been the centrepiece of interminable debates. In this book, however, we will approach this question from the bottom up, looking at the underpinnings of various accommodations or retreats from new global and regional realities. In Chapter 19, Michele Ford looks at some of the more difficult accommodations that confront the nations of the region in the fluid and volatile politics of labour migration. It is at this level where conflicting interests cannot so easily be contained. And rather than looking at accommodations with the global economy and with global powers from a realist or liberal perspective, these are considered in the context of contending domestic interests, ideas and perceptions. Helen Nesadurai examines, in Chapter 20, how the complex interplay of domestic interests influences trade policy in Southeast Asia at the regional level and in its accommodations globally. Natasha Hamilton-Hart argues in Chapter 21 that positive perceptions of American power prevail across the region despite popular critical rhetoric because, in the final analysis, American ascendancy is essential to those strategic sectors that are the main beneficiaries of ongoing economic growth and political order. In Chapter 22, Lee Jones explains the con-struction of security policy and relations within the countries of the region, not in terms of perceived national interest but in terms of the subtle shifts and manoeuvring of political forces within the domestic arena.

1

INTERPRETING THE POLITICS OF SOUTHEAST ASIA

Debates in parallel universes

Richard Robison

Among the critical questions that have defined debates about the politics of Southeast Asia, three have been especially enduring. One of these asks why liberal politics has proven so fragile across the region and why various forms of authoritarianism or electoral politics based on one-party rule or money politics have been so pervasive. A second question is concerned with the relationship between market capitalism and political institutions and ideas; in particular why various forms of interventionist state and predatory systems of governance have survived and flourished despite the embrace of market capitalism. A third is concerned with more recent patterns of decentralization of authority, the spread of democratic reforms and the participation of social movements and local actors in the political arena. It is a matter of contention whether these developments signal the long-awaited rise of a progressive and self-reliant civil society or the consolidation of new social and economic oligarchies and mechanisms for control on the part of the state.

This chapter examines how these important questions have been addressed within different schools of thought and how they have themselves been consolidated and transformed over time.

What has driven the debate? The parallel universes of political analysis

The politics of Southeast Asia has been explained and understood within three main ideological and scholarly traditions. These include:

- American political science, in both its pluralist and behavioural aspects and its structural functional dimensions, especially as this is constituted within modernization theory.[1]
- Political economy in the British and European tradition, especially as this is influenced by Marxist ideas about the relationship of capitalism, state power and class interest.[2] This will be referred to in this chapter as critical political economy.
- Public choice/rational choice political economy and New Institutional Economics.[3]

Several subsidiary approaches have emerged from these traditions.

- A new pluralist political sociology and cultural politics emphasizing the critical importance of civil society, social movements and the politics of culture and identity in the transformation of political systems. It does not always accept modernization assumptions of a necessary grand convergence of markets, democracy and good governance.

- The new pluralism has also merged with ideas that recognize the transformative capacity of institutions and the pathways of possibilities they establish for political and economic reform.[4] In this approach, institutional reform can be a prelude to broader democratic and liberal consolidation by means of negotiation between conservatives and reformers.[5]
- A departure from more mainstream ideas about class and state emerged in the 1970s and 1980s in the form of dependency theory, emphasizing the primacy of global relations of exploitation and dependence in shaping the dynamics of politics and power in developing economies.

These boundaries are porous in some respects. Behavioural, organic and institutional approaches thread their way across both modernization theory and rational choice political economy. And it is recognized across all schools of thought that institutions matter, although their primacy is contested and there is disagreement about where institutions come from. We also find that many of the same questions are at the heart of debates within all the theoretical camps. Is civil society a progressive or a reactionary force? Are there substantive relationships between democratic political institutions, markets and civil society? Or can markets be incubated in illiberal and authoritarian systems?

Nevertheless, it is true to say that the literature has proceeded in three largely parallel universes, insulated by institutional as well as ideological factors. Rational choice political economists dominate the research factories of the World Bank and associated policy institutions, as well as economics departments in most universities. Behavioural and pluralist approaches are institutionally and ideologically rooted in the US political science academy while critical political economy is found mostly in universities in the UK and Australia. The intellectual cores of the three main schools and their understandings of such key concepts as the 'state', 'civil society', governance and class, the transformative possibilities of institutions and markets and the possibilities of agency are hardwired in such fundamentally different ways there is little room for compromise. Thus, a central argument here is that theoretical debates about the politics of the region have taken place almost entirely on the basis of collisions and disputes within the main paradigms themselves.

What, then, causes the rise and fall of the different schools and their influence? The unravelling of democratic politics and the expectations of middle-class power in post-colonial societies and the rise of authoritarianism dealt a blow to liberal pluralist approaches. As Western powers placed an increasing primacy on political order and social control in the Cold War, studies that could conflate authoritarian rule with the process of institutional and behavioural modernity flourished. A second fundamental shift in the larger context of economic and political power took place in the 1980s and 1990s. The ending of manufacturing-based social democracy in the West and the rise of neoliberalism under Thatcher and Reagan meant that the political agenda now moved to transforming society and politics in the image of the market by embedding its principles and values. It was this that incubated the rise of rational choice political economy, methodological individualism and a new political economy of institutions where techno-managerial forms of authority and 'good governance' would contain the predatory impulses of society and the destructive potential of representative and competitive politics.

The very same dynamics meant that critical political economy and history now operated in a framework where social democracy was on the retreat and its influence in the policy-making institutions of the state diminishing. At least in Britain and to a lesser degree in Australia, its influence in some media and intellectual institutions has proven resilient for the time being.

Perhaps the important question is whether these paradigms will continue or whether there is a new and fundamental change in the wind. Will a new post-neoliberal phase drive a revitalization of pluralist politics or critical political economy? The possibilities are not simply intellectual. Such changes will also need to overcome the institutional arrangements that cement the orthodoxies within in the academies and their funding bases and journals and in organizations such as the World Bank and the various national development assistance agencies. I will discuss this further in the conclusion.

The 1950s to the 1980s: explaining the fragility of the liberal experiments and the rise of authoritarian rule

There was an initial mood of optimism among Western observers of Southeast Asia after the Second World War and the unravelling of colonial rule. Seemingly vigorous democracies emerged in several countries and middle classes appeared to play an increasingly influential role in political life. It was also widely felt that countries like the Philippines, Thailand, Malaysia and Burma in particular, with their export agricultural industries, were better placed to emerge as modern economies than those of Northeast Asia. Yet in the decades from the 1950s to the 1970s most of the new democracies established across the region were progressively undermined by conflicts within elites over the spoils of power and by the rise of populist movements, some supported by military and by quasi-fascist alliances and others by rural-based insurgencies organized and led by communist parties. It was a period defined by a trend towards authoritarian rule, one-party states, military politics, corporatist and nationalist ideals, often resting on direct state intervention in the economy.

Formal institutions of parliaments and elections often proved useful mechanisms for distributing patronage and power among powerful propertied oligarchies, as was the case in the Philippines. In other cases, they did not embody ideals of representation and the rights of critics and opponents. In Singapore and Malaysia, these were systematically curtailed on the grounds of maintaining social order or providing economic growth. In both countries, internal security acts were introduced to control political activity and in Malaysia a New Economic Policy, introduced following the race riots in 1969, effectively tied the Malay community to what was to become the effective state political party, the United Malay National Organization.

In several cases, democratic regimes were dismantled. In the Philippines, an authoritarian interregnum was introduced by President Marcos, allegedly to sweep away the ongoing corruption of democratic government. And, less than a decade after its establishment, Indonesia's seemingly vigorous parliamentary system was replaced by a system of 'Guided Democracy', argued by President Sukarno to replace the bickering of vested interests and the residues of feudalism and imperialism with a particularly Indonesian form of politics. Representative politics gave way to populist ideas and corporatist institutions and the authority of the state was enhanced by a vast bureaucratic apparatus as well as state-sponsored political organizations and state-owned corporations (see Reeve 1978/9). In Thailand, a right-wing military dictatorship under General Sarit in 1957 ushered in an era of authoritarian politics that would last for almost two decades.

For most modernization theorists, the resurgence of authoritarianism and centralized populism were the logical political expressions of traditional cultural values and patrimonial political and economic behaviour. In the Philippines, Marcos' authoritarianism was seen as the resurgence of an institutional tradition set down in colonial times (Hutchcroft 1991; Sidel 1999) or the inevitable centralization of patronage politics (Doronila 1985). In Thailand, authoritarianism was argued to be the manifestation of the tradition of bureaucratic polity where the state and its officials maintained a political monopoly and engaged directly with society, generally through systems of patronage and networks of clients (Riggs 1966). Similarly, Sukarno's 'Guided Democracy' was explained as the resurgence of ideas of the state laid down by the Dutch (McVey 1982) or as a victory of the politics of cultural symbolism and neo-patrimonial relationships over the politics of pragmatism and modernity (see Feith 1962: 79–97; Wilner 1973: 517–41).

As the Cold War deepened, it is not surprising that we find in this period a reassessment of authoritarianism among Western political scientists and policy-makers. Thus, for Samuel Huntington (1968), authoritarianism could be understood as a necessary functional response to disintegrative tendencies that emerged in the process of modernization and which required more government, not less. In other words, the political problem was one of establishing order; a task unsuited to many democracies. In particular, it was argued, the military could provide the advance guard of modern values and could play the historical role of the middle classes in the interregnum prior to the establishment of their own political hegemony (Huntington 1968: 222). At the same time, revolutionary challenges could be explained as pathologies of dysfunction rather than real conflicts over the way power and wealth was distributed.

Nevertheless, the portrayal of authoritarian regimes as the advance guard of modernity was highly selective. While some modernization political scientists saw Soeharto's New Order as a manifestation of neopatrimonial practices and culture (Crouch 1979), others saw its military leadership in particular as a modernizing force (Jackson and Pye 1978). Neo-classical economists recognized it as nothing less than a victory of rationality over politics (Arndt 1967). This was not because it was any less corrupt or repressive in its practices or any less nationalist in its rhetoric or that it relinquished state ownership of the commanding heights of the economy. It did, however, now ally itself to the West in the Cold War and was more receptive to private capital investment and to the advice of Western-trained economic technocrats. It is also significant that governments across the region were themselves quick to seize onto the idea that authoritarian rule could be legitimized in terms of the tasks of political order, national integration and, most important, economic development (Moertopo 1973).

For critical political economists and for many historians, these views of politics as conflicts between traditional and modern cultures or as a choice between order and disorder were seen as masking the real struggles over power (Wertheim 1959). Revolutionary wars and conservative counter-revolutions of this period were seen more in terms of conflicts that emerged from deeper shifts in economic and social power (Mortimer 1969; Race 1972; Scott 1976; Kerkvliet 1979). One of the difficulties for these scholars was to explain why capitalist transformation had failed to produce the social democratic outcomes that had transformed Europe. Why did capitalist transformation, in important instances, appear to sustain authoritarian states, and why were the commercial bourgeoisie or the rural or urban petty bourgeoisie so often reactionary rather than progressive in their attitudes, supporting despotism rather than liberal transformation?

In one way, this intellectual/theoretical problem was resolved by the proposition that politics now operated within a system of global exploitation and dependence that transferred wealth from the peripheries of the global economy to the centres and reduced the bourgeoisie to the role of compradors. Developed with the Latin American experience in mind, dependency theory became an important alternative explanation for the rise of various authoritarian and predatory political regimes across Southeast Asia through the 1970s (Levine 1969; Mortimer 1973; Stauffer 1974; Bello et al. 1982; Hawes 1987).

For others, the problems were to be found in the increasingly powerful position of the bureaucrats as they extended their authority over the apparatus of the state and were able to operate autonomously of social forces and interests. Ben Anderson emphasized the importance of the enduring interests of the corps of officials of the state themselves and how these were able to transcend and adapt to different political and economic circumstances and the idea of a 'state qua state' in understanding the powerful position of the state in Indonesia (Anderson 1983). Other scholars saw despotism in Bonapartist terms: flourishing where a weak and disorganized bourgeoisie were, initially at least, unable to organize politically to protect their own interests although, at the same time, structurally forced to guarantee the general interests of capital and to protect them from populist challenges (see Robison *et al.* 1993: 30–4).

But why did state officials in these cases not act more thoroughly like those of Bismarck's Germany, for example, or, for that matter, Lee Kuan Yew's Singapore, to insulate their institutional power from the influences of powerful economic and social alliances? These questions led to an increasing focus on understanding the internal construction of ruling classes and oligarchies and on the ambiguous intersections linking the state, its officials and private interests and more generally on the state as a social order (Robison 1986: 70–105; Anderson 1988, 1998; Hewison 1989; Gomez and Jomo 1997; Pasuk and Baker 2004; see also Winters 1996 and this volume).

This ongoing question about how political regimes are constructed and why liberal politics had stumbled in Southeast Asia was rejuvenated in the 1980s and 1990s by the ending of state socialism in Europe and transitions towards democracy, beginning in Southern Europe and Latin America and spreading to Asia, including South Korea, Taiwan and Thailand. The same players were to be involved. These will be considered later. In the meantime, the big debates about the politics of Southeast Asia became increasingly concerned with relationships between politics and markets.

Political economy, politics and markets: the concerns of the 1990s

By the 1980s levels of investment and growth in Southeast Asia began to accelerate, aided by a vast relocation of investment in low-wage export manufacturing from Northeast Asia. Southeast Asia became a region of growing economic interest to investors and global policy-makers and a site for conflict over the rules that governed capitalist markets. In this context, neo-classical economists within the World Bank and other international financial and development institutions assumed increasing influence in shaping the region's economic policies and as analysts of the region's politics. Not surprisingly, they were less interested in whether regimes were liberal or authoritarian than in whether governments could provide an effective environment for investors. Because they initially assumed that the establishment of market economies and the imperative of efficiency would be enough in itself to bring to an end the practices of predatory rent-seeking and corruption that sustained various predatory regimes,[6] their efforts were focused on establishing 'good' policy: economic deregulation, fiscal austerity, privatization and monetary restraint specified in the so-called Washington Consensus (see Williamson 1990).

However, the battleground would soon shift as the Bank began to accept that the efficient management of increasingly complex economies required a framework of institutions and 'good governance' that would restrain arbitrary and predatory behaviour (World Bank 1981, 1991). Exactly how such institutions would be constructed and by whom was not so clear. Early theoretical explanations had assumed institutions would be created as rational individuals and firms responded to changing problems of transaction costs and information asymmetries (North 1994). At the same time, theorists in the rational choice (public choice) school also recognized that it was entirely rational for coalitions to organize collectively for the purposes of making raids on the state rather than to establish the institutional basis for collective goods that made markets work (Bates 1981).

9

Thus, the World Bank was forced to accept that the state would necessarily play a key role in the process of development (World Bank 1997). Yet, within what we might broadly call the neoliberal camp, the state was itself no less defined by predatory behaviour than society; neo-liberals had arrived at a point where neither state nor society could be trusted. It is in this context that they turned to the idea that reform must be provided by enlightened technocrats operating above the demands of politics (Williamson 1994; see Grindle 1991). In this techno-managerial approach, distributional coalitions could be neutralized by institutional engineering designed to alter the incentives shaping the choices and preferences of individuals (see Bates 2006; Levi 2006).

The idea of 'good governance' as a means of enforcing market-enhancing institutions and protecting them from the rationality of politics became the focal point in designing the new market state (World Bank 1991, 2002). This belief that technocratic forms of rule could potentially offer unique advantages for markets is exemplified for neoliberals in the Singapore model which regularly appears at the top of tables for economic freedom produced by various market-oriented foundations (see Rodan 2006). In practical terms, these ideas about the proper operation of government were reflected in the way the World Bank and major Western gov-ernments sought alliance with various groups of technocrats within the economic departments of the public bureaucracy of most Southeast Asian governments. Replacing politics with 'good governance' became a central focus for political analysts and was driven through the 1980s and 1990s by economists, mainly within the World Bank but also within economic departments of universities, most notably at the Australian National University through the pages of the *Bulletin of Indonesian Economic Studies*. There were some convergences between the ideas of neoliberals and some modernization theorists. Liddle (1991, 1992) argued that the rational ideas of tech-nocrats could converge with the more instrumental interests of politicians as it became clear that the market could deliver the social order and economic prosperity important to the survival of regimes.

Historical institutional theorists also believed that rational bureaucracies and systems of governance were essential pre-requisites for modern economies and societies.[7] However, they departed from neoliberal assumptions that these could be established through voluntarist technocratic interventions and institutional transplants. Instead, they argued that deeply rooted historical institutional pathways constrained and limited the opportunities to make fundamental changes in institutions (Zysman 1994). For Paul Hutchcroft (1998: 45–64) building good gov-ernance in the Philippines was difficult where a political regime based on patronage suited the interests of highly organized business interests dependent upon the rent-seeking opportunities it offered. He compared this to cases where cohesive regimes faced disorganized business interests and argued that such circumstances offered the potential to generate organized and regulated markets. On the other hand, Doner et al. (2005) argued that the 'impressive capacities' of developmental states of Northeast Asia emerged not from their autonomy from society but from an interactive condition of 'system vulnerability' that required the delivery of side payments to restive popular sectors. By contrast, elites in Southeast Asia could uphold political coalitions with much less ambitious state-building efforts (Doner et al. 2005: 327).

Critical political economists shared with historical institutional theorists the assumption that capitalism could survive and even flourish in different institutional forms and that market institutions were the result of conflicts over power rather than any technocratic search for efficiency. However, they placed less emphasis on the transformative capacities of institutions and the disciplines of historical institutional pathways. What mattered were the kinds of social and political forces that emerged from the advance of capitalism and how they organized poli-tically around different social agendas, whether as supporters of technocratic ideals of good governance or populist and nationalist grabs for protective arrangements or within predatory political cabals (Robison 1986, 1988; Rosser 2002; Jayasuriya and Hewison 2006). In this view, the neoliberal idea of 'good governance' was simply an attempt to establish the normative preferences of neoliberals and to legitimize attempts to neutralize forces opposing market agendas within a form of technocratic and managerial rule that constituted, as Jayasuriya (2000) argued, a new 'liberal authoritarianism'.

The debate about the politics of the region entered a new phase with the Asian economic crisis of 1997/8. For some neoliberals, the crisis meant the end of governments that refused to accept the rules and the disciplines of global capital markets and that failed to deregulate their economies. Within the IMF in particular, the crisis was blamed on cronyism and weak institutions that had led to over-investment and over-borrowing and to highly vulnerable financial systems (see Camdessus 1998). How could it be explained that many of the regimes now accused of cronyism and corruption had so recently been championed and defended by the World Bank and others, even as the crisis broke, as exemplary leaders of efficient market reform? The neoliberals were presented with a dilemma (Jayasuriya and Rosser 2001). If the problem lay not with the seemingly discredited regimes of the region, it could only lie with the international financial system and, in the case of Indonesia, on imprudent decisions by governments to float currencies (Garnaut 1998; McLeod and Garnaut 1998; Hill 2000).

While any serious reform of the international financial systems was clearly out of the question, neoliberal policy-makers saw the road ahead in even more and cleverer programmes of institutional engineering and capacity building designed to reshape incentives for individuals that would inhibit corrupt behaviour (see World Bank 2003; Fritz et al. 2009). Yet institutional answers and fixes proved difficult. It was often in the very finance and economic ministries and in the judicial systems, where capacity building and training of staff had been most rigorously implemented, that predatory behaviour proved to be most damaging and persistent (see Lindsey 2000; Hamilton-Hart 2001; Gillespie 2006). The question was raised among some neoliberal economists and political scientists whether the decline of authoritarian rule and the rise of less cohesive democratic systems meant formerly predictable and organized predatory practices now became increasingly disorganized and chaotic, and whether the benefits of accountability of rulers were offset by the problems of capture by vested interests (MacIntyre 1999; McLeod 2000; Duncan and McLeod 2007).

For critical political economists, the significance of crises and their aftermath was not to be found in the lessons they provided for policy and institutional reform but their impact on the configuration of power and whether they strengthened entrenched political and economic oligarchies or reformist coalitions. In particular, it was critical whether neoliberal reformers could now mobilize effective political alliances around the market agenda.

Seen in these terms, the emergence of Thaksin Shinawatra was explained as a political response to threats posed to powerful domestic business interests by the unleashing of global markets, at least until they had consolidated their capacity to deal with the new challenges (see Hewison 2005; Pasuk and Baker 2008). In Indonesia, far from destroying the system of predatory politics and the main political and business players within, it was argued that the various neoliberal administrative reforms and the establishment of democratic politics were not inimical to the interests of oligarchies who successfully reorganized their power within the new structures (see Robison and Rosser 1998; Robison and Hadiz 2004; Felker 2008). Within this process, the neoliberal enterprise contained important paradoxes. Because market capitalism provided the property rights necessary for the privatization of public wealth and opened access to highly unstable banking and financial institutions, it was highly suited to the consolidation of various forms of authoritarian and predatory regimes and to political–business oligarchies that

11

relied on extra-economic relationships. Ironically, the very forces that had provided the political muscle for market reform in the first place, sweeping away opposition from the Left and from social democrats, now stood as the main obstacles to liberal political reforms and 'good governance' where these threatened their political ascendancy (Robison 2009).

After the crisis: the rise of civil society and the possibility of new forms of politics

In different ways, the new millennium seemed to open the door for a new era of politics in Southeast Asia. The 1998 election of President Estrada in the Philippines appeared, albeit briefly, to mark a shift away from the entrenched oligarchic politics towards a neo-populist model. In Indonesia, the long-standing Soeharto regime collapsed, to be replaced by a remarkably open and highly competitive electoral democracy and a robust public media. A new constitution in Thailand in 1997 appeared to signal the demise of a regime dominated by localized political and economic oligarchs and characterized by weak political parties, money politics and unstable coalition governments. It was replaced by a populist regime led by business tycoon Thaksin Shinawatra, based upon a tactical alliance of new business and the rural poor. In Cambodia, as Hun Sen consolidated his rule, the central political task in that country turned from one aimed at securing military control to one of state building in its wider sense.

Although none of the formal political systems of other countries experienced comparable dramatic changes, it seemed clear that civil society, however understood, was increasingly important in the world of politics. Social movements and non-government organizations were becoming engaged in battles over the social welfare, the environment, corruption and transparency, civil and legal rights and property rights. Even the government in Singapore, that most entrenched and organized system of centralized authority, began to engage in different, albeit highly controlled, programmes of participation involving citizens. Several countries in the region, notably the Philippines, Thailand, Indonesia and Cambodia, also underwent important political and administrative decentralization resulting in a reconfiguration of local politics and power.

Yet the rise of civil society and its influence for politics was understood quite differently across the ideological and theoretical spectrum. Among hard-core neoliberals, an increasingly strident civil society represented a potential assault by vested interests intent on diverting public resources from efficient private investment into rents or collective goods. It is significant that, from Hayek to the Cato Institute, neoliberals remained suspicious that democracy could be an ideal incubator for the rise of these predatory interests. Their main concern was not whether governments were democratic or authoritarian but whether they protected markets and the idea of property rights (Hayek 1967; Dorn 1993).

Against this view, there was a liberal mainstream across the neoliberal camp and within modernization and historical institutional theory for which the apparent rise of civil society represented, in a Toquevillian sense, the inevitable upsurge of a progressive and entrepreneurial middle class and free associations of citizens straining against the restrictions of the state (see Alagappa 2004). Several political scientists had argued that private business had played a critical role in the construction of effective economic institutions (Anek 1992; Doner 1992; MacIntyre 1994). Within the World Bank it was also argued that civil society represented a potential repository of entrepreneurial energies. Social movements and NGOs were considered potential allies against governments, bureaucracies and elites that had persistently resisted market reforms and 'good governance' (World Bank 2000). Thus, within the terms of its Poverty Reduction Strategies established in the 1990s, the World Bank and other development organizations increasingly sought to bypass recalcitrant governments and parties and to deal directly with social movements and organizations at the local level to improve the implementation of programmes. Ideas that progressive 'drivers of change' and the 'demand for governance' could come from civil society were increasingly taken seriously by development agencies (DFID 2004; Hout 2009).

For the World Bank and other development organizations, unlocking the progressive potential of civil society requires both the construction of social capital (values, networks and associations) and administrative and political decentralization to liberate society from the constraints of centralized state authority (see Manor 1999).[8] The World Bank and the IMF built decentralization policies into agreements with governments in the region following the Asian economic crisis, especially in Indonesia and Thailand. In Cambodia and East Timor, decentralization was also a key element in post-war reconstruction strategies. There was apprehension that decentralization could also release local warlords, criminals and tribal or clan associations that were also part of civil society and were unruly and unpredictable. These could be de-politicized by programmes of capacity building – creating the networks and values of social capital – to enable individual citizens to mobilize on behalf of market agendas. Strategies of hyper-decentralization could also get below these dark elements to the real grassroots of atomized individuals via programmes including micro-credit and small-scale participatory infrastructure creation (Cliffe et al. 2003).

The rise of civil society and the increasing role of social movements also meant an increasing interest in the politics of the region by political sociologists, for whom the contest between progressive and reactionary elements was manifest in issues of culture and identity as much as in the politics of class interest or in conflicts between technocrats and self-seeking vested interests. Most writing on political Islam, for example, explained the volatile course of Islamic politics as collisions involving doctrine and religious cultures that pitted inherently anti-modern and anti-liberal traditions against more 'moderate' streams able to co-exist in a secular political system (Hefner 2000: 4).

For most pluralist social theorists, emerging civil society brought with it a challenge to old forms of authority, not least through the growing political influence of progressive student and middle-class social movements and NGOs (Aspinall 2005; Weiss 2005). They were attracted to the idea that democratic reform and the shift of administrative and political weight to local and regional arenas might offer spaces for such progressive social alliances to politically organize themselves. However, neo-pluralists quickly became disillusioned as expectations of a Toque-villian flowering of progressive associational politics often gave way to recognition that civil society could be uncivil and reactionary (Schulte Nordholt and van Klinken 2007; Meitzner and Aspinall 2010; Schulte Nordholt this volume, Chapter 15).

What, then, would determine whether progressive or conservative and reactionary forces triumph, given that pluralism, by definition, does not embody any larger structural theory of power? For pluralists, factors of agency are critical, including the charismatic appeal of reformers and their ability to provide leadership and to organize politically or build institutions or to negotiate pacts. These ideas were also clearly influenced by the literature on democratic transitions which emphasized both negotiations and the internalization of specific behavioural and institutional features as the driving forces of change (Linz and Stepan 1996). The collateral damage of this process was that seemingly progressive movements and NGOs could be co-opted by the state, or their leaders bought out (Aspinall and Fealy 2003; Weiss and Hassan 2003; Aspinall and Weiss this volume, Chapter 14). Thus, the triumph of progressive social movements might require that they establish themselves within the mainstream of political parties and formal political organizations (Aspinall and Weiss this volume, Chapter 14).

For critical political economists, however, and for sociologists and historians taking similar approaches (see King 2008), agency was limited by the way power was organized within large structural relationships. Attempts to reform or regulate the apparatus of the state, including within the judiciary and in the finance sector and the forestry and mining areas (Hamilton-Hart 2001; Gillespie 2006; Gellert 2009), had always been complex processes. This was because reformers confronted, in the view of critical political economists, not simply a jumble of opportunistic vested interests but forces operating in defence of a deeper social and political order. This is a view in which civil society is an arena for conflicts over power and wealth mediated or imposed by the exercise of state authority.[9]

Thus critical sociologists and political economists see World Bank programmes of decentralization, 'good governance', 'participation' and 'ownership' as part of a larger struggle to reconstitute social and political power in market terms (Hatcher 2009; Rosser and Simpson 2009; Carroll 2010). In her assessments of post-conflict Cambodia and East Timor, Caroline Hughes (2009) argued that the design of development assistance has been important in determining how society was being re-shaped. Such key programmes as micro-credit, for example, are focused on creating individual opportunity and have the effect of atomizing societies rather than building political communities, leaving the political space to the state party and undermining cohesive civil society. At the same time, strategies of capacity building and institutional reform (including property rights) have avoided measures that would upset existing power relations and ignored the way embedded power relations actually underpinned poverty and marginalization (Hughes 2009: 1–23).

In the case of the Philippines, open and seemingly unencumbered involvement of social movements and NGOs in political life and the periodic spectacular displays of people power on the street suggested a political system where civil society is progressive and influential. This is questioned by Eva-Lotta Hedman (2006), who proposes, in a Gramscian analysis, that both social movements and people power are effectively used by elites as a means of controlling the realm of the state. Jane Hutchison (2006 and this volume, Chapter 3) has also argued that progressive civil society organizations have found it difficult to build fundamental reforms where the state is neither strong nor responsive and democracy is based on shifting and short-term populist coalitions. And the susceptibility of social movements to co-option has also been emphasized by Nathan Quimpo (2009), who has argued that social movements and NGOs are amenable to co-option. The claim that social movements and NGOs were rarely able to escape the control of governments and powerful elites is made also in the Thai case, where many ended up carrying substantially moderate agendas that reflected the official policy (Kengkij and Hewison 2009).

And the relationship between democratic transition and civil society was also confused. Although modernization theorists had assumed there were social pre-requisites for democracy, pluralist political scientists had become attracted to the idea that transition to democracy could be negotiated between declining and rising political elites, even where such pre-requisites were not in place, in a process where institutional design, leadership, strategy and chance played a key role. While this understanding was different from neoliberal arguments that institutions could be designed by technocrats and simply imposed in a managerial process, it nevertheless shared the belief that, once in place, institutions could themselves provide both the incentives and constraints that would enforce specific pathways to wider social and political change (see, for example, O'Donnell and Schmitter 1986; Linz 1997). The belief in the wider transformative capacities of democracy shaped the work of many political scientists of Southeast Asia (Uhlin 1997; Tornquist 2000).

However, it was apparent that the creation of democratic institutions did not always lead to liberal outcomes. Behavioural political scientists accepted that democracies could be defined by resilient neo-patrimonial ideologies and culture (Webber 2006). And these could be measured in quantitative surveys of electoral behaviour or party support (Liddle and Mujani 2007). Other pluralist political scientists explained the difficulties of democratic consolidation in terms of stalled process of institutional reform where liberal forces jostled with conservative residues to produce hybrid democratic regimes (Crouch 1993; Case 1996, 2001). However, attempts to explain the persistence of repressive or predatory politics within formal democracies as a problem of hybrid formations was rejected by critical political economists. They argued that democratic formal structures with limited representative politics and civil rights were not simply institutions stalled on their way to somewhere else, but could be complete in themselves and designed to serve specific entrenched and stable interests.[10]

Democracies inherited the social legacies of reactionary regimes, and these were often heavily populated with violent and criminal forces, vigilantes and militias as well as reactionary religious and xenophobic sentiment (Trocki 1998; Sidel 1999, 2006; Wilson 2006). At the same time, critical political economists and other scholars have argued that the support of the bourgeois and the middle classes for democracy, particularly in its liberal form, has been highly contingent. Their periodic alliance with authoritarian regimes and conservatives against the demands of popular forces or the threat to economic rents is considered historically important (Robison and Goodman 1996; Bellin 2000; Robison and Hadiz 2004: 18–39).

The contingent nature of this relationship has been most recently illustrated in the recent conservative counter-revolution in Thailand. But the highly capricious nature of the bourgeois position has always been important in explanations of the volatile history of Thai politics by critical political analysts. Thus, the resurgence of electoral politics in the 1980s was seen to suit the Thai bourgeoisie, enabling them to bypass the state bureaucracy and more directly influence and access economic policy and patronage through the world of party politics, and to consolidate pork-barrelling and patronage (Anderson 1990; Hewison 1993). On the other hand, the lurch towards a neo-populist form of democracy under the political leadership of Thaksin Shinawatra has been argued to reflect the political interests of a national business class seeking respite from the economic restructuring advocated by the IMF and their allies among market-oriented middle classes. Populist politics and programmes of economic redistribution in the rural areas became, in this context, an ideal means of mobilizing allies among the rural poor and bypassing the old party gatekeepers and their middle-class and conservative allies. The subsequent overthrow of Prime Minister Thaksin and the civil disorder that followed was regarded by some in the neoliberal camp as a 'good coup' that constituted the victory of rationality over vested interests. Among critical political economists and historians, it was seen as a virtual counter-revolution by a tactical alliance of political conservatives and various elements of the bourgeoisie and middle classes (see Pasuk and Baker 2004; Hewison 2005; Connors and Hewison 2008).

Similarly, the unravelling of the Soeharto regime and the subsequent democratic transition in Indonesia after 1999 was argued by Robison and Hadiz (2004) to be a process where social and economic oligarchies found themselves no longer able to rule in the old way and forced to reorganize their power within new democratic or decentralized institutions. While new reformist political forces struggled to make gains in electoral contests, old power relationships proved resilient as business interests easily shifted their alliances from the bureaucrats and despots of a centralized regime into the new political parties, and the parliaments and the political entrepreneurs that inhabited these institutions. Together with democratic reform, decentralization also opened the door for new political players. In his extensive study of decentralization in Indonesia, Hadiz (2010) explained the ongoing struggles for control in the new provincial and regional legislatures and bureaucracies as ones where oligarchic power was ultimately reorganized and reformulated, drawing in new allies from business and the shadowy world of extra-legal coercion.

Critical political economists also directed their fire at neoliberal attempts to establish new forms of democratic governance within which civil society could be engaged. This was concentrated especially in studies of Singapore, Vietnam and Malaysia, where state-orchestrated deliberative democratic political practices suggested the beginnings of a loosening of political control. Institutions for political and administrative participation and accountability were introduced that included consultative boards, watchdog and monitoring organizations, feedback units, state-sponsored cultural bodies, ombudsmen, social investment funds and participatory budgeting. These were argued to be less an opening of the door to a vibrant civil society than a new means of co-opting and controlling opponents or pre-empting social unrest and resentment. Specifically, these new forms of participation were understood as mechanisms to replace representative politics with functional concepts of citizenship and with technocratic ideals of management and 'governance' that embraced society in a highly controlled agenda of anti-politics.[11]

Conclusion: where to now?

It has been proposed here that the study of Southeast Asian politics has been undertaken within schools of thought rooted in larger ideological, theoretical and political structures. Given the fundamental nature of their differing understanding of politics, economic and society, these have operated as parallel universes. Their progression has been driven, not by intellectual debate across the divisions, but by upheavals within that are the consequences of larger conflicts over social and economic power. Thus, the remarkable rise of rational choice political economy and quantitative political science mimicked market fundamentalism within the economics profession in the era of Thatcher and Reagan and reflected a reordering of intellectual priorities as Western economies were restructured towards a globalized financial and services capitalism (Harvey 2003). Rational choice/positivist/neoliberal ideology has been dramatically consolidated in the institutions of the political science academy, especially in the US where the political science departments of many universities and an increasing majority of political science journals have become the bastions of quantitative methodologies.

This advance of rational choice political studies and quantitative methodology, generally involving mathematically measured correlations and survey-driven data collection and analysis, is clearly a threat to political studies of Southeast Asia under the umbrella of area studies in the US (Emmerson 2008).[12] It is not surprising that apprehension over this methodology-driven ideological assault has become a central concern among many American political scientists dealing with Southeast Asia, even if the full implications are not addressed (Kuhonta et al. 2008). There have been collaborations between neoliberal and behavioural pluralist political scientists, and some institutional political scientists sail close to the flagship of new institutional economics. Yet neoliberal approaches have been applied to the study of Southeast Asia mainly by economists in the World Bank and in university economics departments rather than by political scientists.

Outside the US, the grip of quantitative and neoliberal approaches in political science departments has not been so thorough. The social democratic tradition remains stronger generally. Several important politics journals in the UK remain showcases for studies in critical political economy field, and this is where much of the critical discipline-based (as opposed to area studies) literature on Southeast Asia appears. Some political analysts of Southeast Asia now operate in departments and journals outside the political science disciplinary mainstream, in fields such as geography, development studies, cultural studies and sociology.

There has been some interesting interaction between critical political economy, historical institutional approaches and social theory in research programmes of some development agencies, particularly the UK Development Agency, DFID. These have attempted to understand why institutional and policy fixes that focus on market and institutional reform, good governance and capacity building have not worked as well as hoped. Studies aimed at explaining how politics shapes the possibilities of governance and institutional reform and how this factor might be accommodated in development policy has opened the door for a wider debate (see Leftwitch 2009; Unsworth 2009).

Yet even here, the threat to critical political economy, sociology and other areas is growing. Some of the same forces at work in the US political science academy are being manifested, for example, in Australia as the surge to metrics, driven by new public policy attempts to measure efficiency in universities, threatens a new institutional orthodoxy based on science models.

Notes

1 The key element in modernization theory is the notion of evolution from tradition to modernity, whether understood as a cultural or behavioural in nature or as processes of increasing functional complexity in social and political structures. A key text is Almond and Powell (1966) and among overviews and analysis are Randall and Theobold (1985: 12–64) and Higgott (1983).

2 Many of these ideas and themes are illustrated in the collection of seminal articles by Colin Leys (1996). More recently, and in reference to Southeast Asia, see the review of this theory by Rodan et al. (1997).

3 For a broad overview of the New Institutional Economics and its public choice and other neoliberal roots, see Harriss et al. (1995). This collection includes a key chapter by Douglass North (1995), a defining figure in this approach. See also Evans (1995: 21–73).

4 See Doner 1991; Zysman 1994; Hall and Taylor 1996.

5 O'Donnell and Schmitter 1986; Diamond 1994.

6 For an overview see Toye (1987: 47–74).

7 See the influential thesis of Evans et al. (1985) that was focused on 'bringing the state back in'. See also Lange and Rueschemeyer (2005).

8 A comprehensive analysis of the attachment of the World Bank and other development organizations to policies of decentralization can be found in Hadiz (2010: 1–39). Interestingly, Kurt Weyland (1996) finds important affinities between neoliberal preferences for a system of governance that bypasses representative coalitions and the neo-populist regimes of Latin America under Fukuyama and others.

9 For general statements of this idea of civil society see Wood (1990), Rodan (1996) and Harriss (2002).

10 For an early sceptical view of democratization promotion programmes see Gills and Rocamora (1992) and their notion of 'low intensity' democracies.

11 This argument is most comprehensively established in Rodan and Jayasuriya (2007).

12 See also the debate between Robert Bates (1997) and Chalmers Johnson (1997).

References

Alagappa, M. (2004) 'Civil society and political change: an analytical framework', in M. Alagappa (ed.) *Civil Society and Political Change in Asia: Expanding and Contracting Democratic Space*, Stanford, CA: Stanford University Press.

Almond, G. and B. Powell (1966) *The Politics of Developing Areas*, Princeton, NJ: Princeton University Press.

Anderson, B. (1983) 'Old state, new society: Indonesia's New Order in comparative historical perspective', *Journal of Asian Studies* 42 (3): 477–96.

——(1988) 'Cacique democracy in the Philippines: origins and dreams', *New Left Review* 169: 3–31.

——(1990) 'Murder and progress in modern Siam', *New Left Review* 181: 33–48.

——(1998) *The Spectre of Comparisons: Nationalism, Southeast Asia and the World*, London: Verso.

Anek Laothamatas (1992) *Business Associations and the New Political Economy of Thailand*, Boulder, CO: Westview.

Arndt, H. (1967) 'Economic disorder and the task ahead', in T.K. Tan (ed.) *Sukarno's Guided Indonesia*, Brisbane: Jakaranda, pp. 129–42.

Aspinall, E. (2005) *Opposing Suharto: Compromise, Resistance and Regime Change in Indonesia*, Stanford, CA: Stanford University Press.

Aspinall, E. and G. Fealy (2003) 'Introduction: Decentralization, democratisation and the rise of the local', in E. Aspinall and G. Fealy (eds) *Local Power and Politics in Indonesia: Decentralization and Democratisation*, Singapore: Institute of Southeast Asian Studies, pp. 1–14.

Bates, R. (1981) *Markets and States in Tropical Africa*, Berkeley: University of California Press.

——(1997) 'Area studies and the discipline: a useful controversy', *PS, Political Science and Politics* June: 166–9.

——(2006) 'Institutions and development', *Journal of African Economies*, AERC Supplement, 15 (1): 10–61.

Bellin, E. (2000) 'Contingent democrats: industrialists, labour and industrialisation in late developing countries', *World Politics* 52 (January): 175–205.

Bello, W., D. Kinley and E. Elinson (eds) (1982) *Development Debacle: World Bank in the Philippines*, San Francisco, CA: Institute for Food and Development Policy.

Callahan, M. (2007) *Political Authority in Burma's Ethnic Minority States: Devolution, Occupation and Coexistence*, Policy Studies 31, Washington, DC: East–West Centre.

Camdessus, M. (1998) 'The IMF and good governance', address at Transparency International, Paris, 21 January.

Carroll, T. (2010) *Delusions of Development: The World Bank and the Post-Washington Consensus*, Basingstoke: Palgrave.

Case, W. (1996) 'Can the "halfway house" stand? Semi-democracy and elite theory in three Southeast Asian countries', *Comparative Politics* 28 (4): 437–64.

——(2001) 'Malaysia's resilient pseudo democracy', *Journal of Democracy* 12 (1): 51–65.

Cliffe, S., S. Guggenheim and M. Kostner (2003) 'Community-driven reconstruction as an instrument in war-to-peace transitions', CPR Working Paper 7, Washington, World Bank Social Development.

Connors, M.K. and K. Hewison (2008) 'Thailand's "good coup": the fall of Thaksin, the military and democracy', *Journal of Contemporary Asia* 38 (1): 1–10.

Crouch, H. (1979) 'Patrimonialism and military rule in Indonesia', *World Politics* 31: 571–87.

——(1993) 'Malaysia: neither authoritarian nor democratic', in K. Hewison, R. Robison and G. Rodan (eds) *Southeast Asia in the 1990s: Authoritarianism, Democracy and Capitalism*, Sydney: Allen and Unwin, pp. 133–58.

Department for International Development (DFID) (2004) *Drivers of Change*, Public Information Note, London: Department for International Development, available at: www.gsdrc.org/docs.open/DOC59.pdf (accessed 17 September 2010).

Diamond, L. (1994) 'Rethinking civil society: toward democratic consolidation', *Journal of Democracy* 5 (3): 4–17.

Doner, R. (1991) 'Approaches to the politics of economic growth in Southeast Asia', *Journal of Asian Studies* 50 (4): 818–49.

——(1992) 'The limits of state strength: towards an institutionalist view of economic development', *World Politics* 44 (3): 398–431.

Doner, R., B. Ritchie and D. Slater (2005) 'Systemic vulnerability and the origins of developmental states: Northeast and Southeast Asia in comparative perspective', *International Organisation* 59: 327–61.

Dorn, J. (1993) 'Economic liberty and democracy in East Asia', *Orbis* 37 (4): 599–619.

Doronila, A. (1985) 'The transformation of patron–client relations and its political consequences in postwar Philippines', *Journal of Southeast Asian Studies* 16: 99–116.

Duncan, R. and R. McLeod (2007) 'The state and the market in democratic Indonesia', in R. McLeod and A. MacIntyre (eds) *Indonesia: Democracy and the Promise of Good Governance*, Singapore: Institute for Southeast Asian Studies, pp. 73–92.

Emmerson, D. (2008) 'Southeast Asia in political science: terms of enlistment', in E. Kuhonta, D. Slater and Tuong Vu (eds) *Southeast Asia in Political Science: Theory, Region and Qualitative Analysis*, Stanford, CA: Stanford University Press, pp. 302–24.

Evans, P. (1995) *Embedded Autonomy: States and Industrial Transformation*, Princeton, NJ: Princeton University Press, pp. 21–73.

Evans, P., D. Rueschemeyer and T. Skocpol (eds) (1985) *Bringing the State Back In*, Cambridge: Cambridge University Press.

Feith, H. (1962) *The Decline of Constitutional Democracy in Indonesia*, Ithaca, NY: Cornell University Press.

Felker, G. (2008) 'Southeast Asia and globalisation: the political economy of illiberal adaption' in Erik Martinez Kuhonta, Dan Slater and Tuong Vu (eds) *Southeast Asia in Political Science: Theory, Region and Qualitative Analysis*, Stanford, CA: Stanford University Press, pp. 174–301.

Fritz, Verena, Kai Kaiser and Brian Levy (2009) *Problem Driven Governance and Political Economy Analysis: Good Practice Framework*, Washington, DC: World Bank.

Garnaut, R. (1998) 'The financial crisis: a watershed in economic thought about East Asia', *Asia Pacific Economic Literature*, May: 1–11.

Gellert, P. (2009) 'The politics of governance of Indonesia's forest Industries: progress and regress in a neo-liberal age', in W. Hout and R. Robison (eds) *Governance and the Depoliticisation of Development*, London: Routledge, pp. 107–20.

Gillespie, J. (2006) *Transplanting Commercial Law Reform: Developing a Rule of Law in Vietnam*, Aldershot: Ashgate.

Gills, B. and J. Rocamora (1992) 'Low intensity democracy', *Third World Quarterly* 13 (3): 501–23.

Gomez, E.T. and Jomo, K.S. (1997) *Malaysia's Political Economy: Politics, Patronage and Politics*, New York: Cambridge University Press.

Grindle, M. (1991) 'The new political economy: positive economics and negative politics', in G. Meier (ed.) *Politics and Policy Making in Developing Countries*, San Francisco, CA: International Centre for Economic Growth.

——(2010) *Localising Power in Post-Authoritarian Indonesia*, Stanford, CA: Stanford University Press.

Hadiz, Vedi R. (2010) *Localising Power in Post-Authoritarian Indonesia: A Southeast Asian Perspective*, Stanford, CA: Stanford University Press.

Hadiz, Vedi R. and Richard Robison (forthcoming 2012) 'Political economy and Islamic politics: insights from the Indonesian case', *New Political Economy*.

Hall, P. and R. Taylor (1996) 'Political science and the three new institutionalisms', *Political Studies* XLIV: 936–57.

Hamilton-Hart, N. (2001) 'Anti-corruption strategies in Indonesia', *Bulletin of Indonesian Economic Studies* 37 (1): 65–82.

Harriss, J. (2002) *Depoliticising Social Development: The World Bank and Social Capital*, London: Routledge.

Harriss, J., J. Hunter and C. Lewis (eds) (1995) *The New Institutional Economics and Third World Development*, London: Routledge.

Harvey, D. (2003) *The New Imperialism*, Oxford: Oxford University Press.

Hatcher, P. (2009) 'The politics of entrapment: parliaments, governance and poverty reduction strategies', in W. Hout and R. Robison (eds) *Governance and the Depoliticisation of Development*, London: Routledge, pp. 123–36.

Hawes, G. (1987) *The Philippine State and the Marcos Regime: The Politics of Export*, Ithaca: Cornell University Press.

Hayek, F.A. (1967) 'The principles of a liberal social order', in *Studies in Philosophy, Politics and Economics*, Chicago: University of Chicago Press.

Hedman, E.-L. (2006) *In the Name of Civil Society: From Free Election Movements to People Power in the Philippines*, Honolulu: University of Hawai'i Press.

Hefner, R. (2000) 'Islam, state and civil society: ICMI and the struggle for the Indonesian middle class', *Indonesia* 56: 1–35.

Hewison, K. (1989) *Bankers and Bureaucrats: Capital and the Role of the State in Thailand*, Yale University Southeast Asian Monographs 34, New Haven, CT: Centre for International and Area Studies.

——(1993) 'Of regimes, state and pluralities: Thai politics enters the 1990s', in Kevin Hewison, Richard Robison and Garry Rodan (eds) *Southeast Asia in the 1990s: Authoritarianism, Democracy and Capitalism*, Sydney, Allen and Unwin, pp. 159–90.

——(2005) 'Neoliberalism and domestic capital: the political outcomes of the economic crisis in Thailand', *The Journal of Development Studies* 41 (2): 310–30.

Higgott, R. (1983) *Political Development Theory*, London: Croom-Helm.

Hill, H. (2000) 'Indonesia: the strange and sudden death of a tiger economy', *Oxford Development Studies* 28 (2): 117–39.

Hout, W. (2009) 'Development and governance: an uneasy relationship', in W. Hout and R. Robison (eds) *Governance and the Depoliticisation of Development*, London: Routledge, pp. 29–43.

Hughes, C. (2009) *Dependent Communities: Aid and Politics in Cambodia and East Timor*, Cornell, NY: Southeast Asia Program Publications.

Huntington, S. (1968) *Political Order in Changing Societies*, New Haven, CT: Yale University Press.

Hutchcroft, P. (1991) 'Oligarchs and cronies in the Philippine state: the politics of patrimonial plunder', *World Politics* 43 (3): 414–59.

——(1998) *Booty Capitalism: The Politics of Banking in the Philippines*, Ithaca, NY: Cornell University Press.

Hutchison, J. (2006) 'Poverty of politics in the Philippines', in G. Rodan, K. Hewison and R. Robison (eds) *The Political Economy of Southeast Asia: Markets, Power and Contestation*, Melbourne: Oxford University Press, pp. 39–73.

Jackson, K. and L. Pye (eds) (1978) *Political Power and Communication in Indonesia*, Berkeley: University of California Press.

Jayasuriya, K. (2000) 'Authoritarian liberalism, governance and the emergence of the regulatory state in post-crisis East Asia', in R. Robison, M. Beeson, K. Jayasuriya and Hyuk Rae Kim (eds) *Politics and Markets in the Wake of the Asian Crisis*, London: Routledge, pp. 315–30.

Jayasuriya, K. and K. Hewison (2006) 'The antipolitics of good governance: from global social policy to global populism', in G. Rodan and K. Hewison (eds) *Neoliberalism and Conflict in Asia After 9/11*, London: Routledge, pp. 161–79.

Jayasuriya, K. and A. Rosser (2001) 'Economic orthodoxy and the East Asian crisis', *Third World Quarterly* 22 (3): 381–96.

Johnson, C. (1997) 'Pre-conception versus observation, or the contributions of rational choice theory and area studies to contemporary political science', *PS: Political Science and Politics*: 170–4.

Kengkij Kitirianglarp and K. Hewison (2009) 'Social movements and political opposition in contemporary Thailand', *Pacific Review* 22 (4): 451–77.

Kerkvliet, B. (1979) *The Huk Rebellion: A Study of Peasant Revolt in the Philippines*, Quezon City: New Day Publications.

King, V. (2008) *The Sociology of Southeast Asia: Transformations in a Developing Region*, Honolulu: University of Hawai'i Press.

Kuhonta, E., D. Slater and Tuong Vu (2008) 'Introduction: The contributions of Southeast Asian political studies', in E. Kuhonta, D. Slater and Tuong Vu (eds) *Southeast Asia in Political Science: Theory, Region and Qualitative Analysis*, Stanford, CA: Stanford University Press, pp. 1–29.

Lange, M. and D. Rueschemeyer (eds) (2005) *States and Development: Historical Antecedents of Stagnation and Advance*, Houndsmill: Palgrave.

Leftwich, Adrian (2009) *Drivers of Change: Refining the Analytical Framework, Part One: Conceptual and Theoretical Issues*, York: University of York. Available at: www.gsdrc.org/docs/open/DOC103.pdf (accessed 3 September 2010).

Levi, M. (2006) 'Why we need a new theory of government', *Perspectives on Politics* 4 (1): 5–19.

Levine, D. (1969) 'History and social structure in the history of contemporary Southeast Asia', *Indonesia* 7: 5–19.

Leys, C. (1996) *The Rise and Fall of Development Theory*, Nairobi: EAEP, Oxford: James Curry, Bloomington: Indiana University Press.

Liddle, R.W. (1991) 'The politics of development policy', *World Development* 20 (6): 793–807.

——(1992) 'The relative autonomy of the Third World politician: Soeharto and Indonesian economic development in comparative perspective' *International Studies Quarterly* 35 (4): 403–27.

Liddle, R.W. and Saiful Mujani (2007) 'Leadership, party and religion: explaining voter behaviour in Indonesia', *Comparative Political Studies* 40 (7): 832–57.

Lindsey, T. (2000) 'Black letter, black market and bad faith: corruption and the failure of law reform', in C. Manning and P. van Dierman (eds) *Indonesia in Transition: Social Aspects of Reformasi and Crisis*, Singapore: Institute for Southeast Asian Studies, pp. 278–92.

Linz, J. (1997) 'Some thoughts on the victory and future of democracy', in Axel Hadenhuis (ed.) *Democracy's Victory and Crisis*, Cambridge: Cambridge University Press, pp. 404–26.

Linz, J. and Alfred Stepan (1996) *Problems of Democratic Transition and Consolidation: Southern Europe, South America and Post-Communist Europe*, Baltimore, MD: Johns Hopkins University Press.

MacIntyre, A. (ed.) (1994) *Business and Government in Industrialising Asia*, Ithaca, NY: Cornell University Press.

——(1999) 'Political institutions and economic crisis in Thailand and Indonesia', in T.J. Pempel (ed.) *Politics of the Asian Economic Crisis*, Ithaca, NY: Cornell University Press, pp. 143–62.

McLeod, R. (2000) 'Soeharto's Indonesia: a better class of corruption', *Agenda* 7 (2): 99–112.

McLeod, R. and R. Garnaut (eds) (1998) *East Asia in Crisis: From Being a Miracle to Needing One*, London: Routledge.

McVey, R. (1982) 'The Beamtenstaat in Indonesia', in B. Anderson, and A. Kahin (eds) *Interpreting Indonesian Politics: Thirteen Contributions to the Debate*, Ithaca, NY: Cornell Modern Indonesia Project, pp. 84–91.

Manor, J. (1999) *The Political Economy of Democratic Decentralization*, Washington, DC: World Bank.

Meitzner, M. and E. Aspinall (2010) 'Problems of democratisation in Indonesia: an overview', in E. Aspinall and M. Meitzner (eds) *Problems of Democratisation in Indonesia: Elections, Institutions and Society*, Singapore: Institute of Southeast Asian Studies, pp. 1–20.

Moertopo, A. (1973) *The Acceleration and Modernisation of 25 Years Development*, Jakarta: Centre for Strategic and International Studies.

Mortimer, R. (1969) 'Class, social cleavage and Indonesian communism', *Indonesia* 8: 1–20.

——(1973) 'Indonesia: growth or development?', in R. Mortimer (ed.) *Showcase State: The Illusion of Indonesia's Accelerated Modernisation*, Sydney: Angus and Robertson.

North, D. (1994) 'Economic performance through time', *American Economic Review* 84 (3): 359–68.

——(1995) 'The new institutional economics and Third World development', in J. Harriss, J. Hunter and C.M. Lewis (eds) *The New Institutional Economics and Third World Development*, London: Routledge.

O'Donnell, G. and P. Schmitter (1986) 'Tentative conclusions about uncertain democracies', in G. O'Donnell, P. Schmitter and L. Whitehead (eds) *Transitions from Authoritarian Rule: Prospects for Democracy*, Baltimore, MD and London: Johns Hopkins University Press, pp. 3–72.

Pasuk Pongpaichit and C. Baker (2004) *Thaksin: The Business of Politics in Thailand*, Bangkok: Silkworm.

——(2008) *Thai Capital After the 1997 Crisis*, Chiang Mai: Silkworm.

Pepinsky, Thomas (2009) *Economic Crises and the Breakdown of Authoritarian Regimes: Indonesia and Malaysia in Comparative Perspective*, Cambridge and New York: Cambridge University Press.

Quimpo, N. (2009) 'The Philippines: predatory regime, growing authoritarian features', *Pacific Review* 22 (3): 335–53.

Race, J. (1972) *War Comes to Long An*, Berkeley, CA: University of California Press.

Randall, V. and R. Theobold (1985) *Political Change and Underdevelopment*, Houndsmill: Macmillan.

Reeve, D. (1978/9) 'Sukarnoism and Indonesia's "functional group" state: developing "Indonesian democracy"', *Review of Indonesian and Malayan Affairs* 12 (2): 43–94 and 13 (1): 53–115.

Riggs, F. (1966) *Thailand: The Modernisation of a Bureaucratic Polity*, Honolulu, HI: East West Centre Press.

Robison, R. (1986) *Indonesia: The Rise of Capital*, Sydney: Allen and Unwin.

——(1988) 'Authoritarian states, capital owning classes and the politics of newly industrialising countries: the case of Indonesia', *World Politics* 41 (1): 52–74.

——(2009) 'Strange bedfellows: political alliances in the making of neo-liberal governance' in Wil Hout and Richard Robison (eds) *Governance and the Depoliticization of Development*, London: Routledge, pp. 15–28.

Robison, R. and D. Goodman (eds) (1996) 'The new rich in Asia: economic development, social status and political consciousness', in R. Robison and D. Goodman (eds) *The New Rich In Asia: Mobile Phones, McDonald's and Middle Class Revolution*, London: Routledge.

Robison, R. and V.R. Hadiz (2004) *Reorganising Power in Indonesia: The Politics of Oligarchy in an Age of Markets*, London: Routledge.

Robison, R. and A. Rosser (1998) 'Contesting reform: Indonesia's New Order and the IMF', *World Development* 26 (8): 1593–609.

Robison, R., K. Hewison and G. Rodan (1993) 'Political power in industrialising capitalist societies: theoretical approaches', in K. Hewison, R. Robison and G. Rodan (eds) *Southeast Asia in the 1990s: Authoritarianism, Democracy and Capitalism*, Sydney: Allen and Unwin, pp. 9–38.

Rodan, G. (1996) 'Theorising political opposition in East and Southeast Asia', in G. Rodan (ed.) *Political Oppositions in Industrialising Asia*, London: Routledge, pp. 1–39.

——(2006) 'Neo-liberalism and transparency: political versus economic liberalism', in R. Robison (ed.) *The Neoliberal Revolution: Forging the Market State*, Houndsmill: Palgrave.

Rodan, G. and C. Hughes (forthcoming 2012) 'Ideological coalitions and the international promotion of social accountability: the Philippines and Cambodia compared', *International Studies Quarterly*.

Rodan, G. and K. Jayasuriya (eds) (2007) *Beyond Hybrid Regimes*, Special Issue of *Democratisation* 14 (5).

Rodan, G., K. Hewison and R. Robison (1997) *The Political Economy of Southeast Asia*, Melbourne: Oxford University Press; later editions in 2001 and 2006.

Rosser, Andrew (2002) *The Politics of Economic Liberalisation in Indonesia: State, Market and Power*, Richmond: Curzon.

——(2009) 'The ownership agenda: will it enhance aid effectiveness?' Policy Brief No. 3, Asia Research Centre, Perth: Murdoch University.

Rosser, A. and A. Simpson (2009) *The Ownership Agenda: Will It Enhance Aid Effectiveness?* Policy Brief 3 (January), Perth: Asia Research Centre.

Schulte Nordholte, H. and G. van Klinken (eds) (2007) *Renegotiating Boundaries: Local Politics in Post-Soeharto Indonesia*, Leiden: KITLV Press.

Scott, J. (1976) *The Moral Economy of the Peasant: Rebellion and Subsistence in Southeast Asia*, New Haven, CT: Yale University Press.

Sidel, J. (1999) *Capital, Coercion and Crime: Bossism in the Philippines*, Stanford, CA: Stanford University Press.

——(2006) *Riots, Pogroms, Jihad: Religious Violence in Indonesia*, Ithaca, NY: Cornell University Press.

Stauffer, R. (1974) 'Political economy of a coup: transnational linkages and Philippine political response', *Journal of Peace Research* 3: 161–77.

Tornquist, O. (2000) 'Dynamics of Indonesian democratisation', *Third World Quarterly* 21 (3): 383–423.

Toye, J. (1987) *Dilemmas of Development*, Oxford: Basil Blackwell.

Trocki, C. (ed.) (1998) *Gangsters, Democracy and the State in Southeast Asia*, Ithaca, NY: Cornell University Press Southeast Asia Program.

Uhlin, A. (1997) *Indonesia and the Third Wave of Democratisation: Indonesian Pro-Democracy Movement in a Changing World*, Richmond: Curzon Press.

Unsworth, S. (2009) 'What's politics got to do with it? Why donors find it so hard to come to terms with politics, and why this matters', *Journal of International Development* 21 (6): 883–94.

Webber, D. (2006) 'Consolidated patrimonial democracy? Democratisation in post-Soeharto Indonesia', *Democratisation* 13 (3): 396–420.

Weiss, M. (2005) *Protest and Possibilities: Civil Society and Coalitions for Political Change in Malaysia*, Stanford, CA: Stanford University Press.

Weiss, M. and S. Hassan (eds) (2003) *Social Movements in Malaysia: From Moral Communities to NGOs*, London: RoutledgeCurzon.

Wertheim, W. (1959) *Indonesian Society in Transition*, The Hague: van Hoeve.

Weyland, K. (1996) 'Neopopulism and neoliberalism in Latin America: unexpected affinities', *Studies in Comparative International Development* 31 (3): 3–31.

Williamson, J. (1990) 'What Washington means by policy reform', in J. Williamson (ed.) *Latin American Adjustment: How Much has Changed?* Washington, DC: Washington Institute for International Economics, pp. 7–20.

——(1994) 'In search of a manual for technopols', in J. Williamson (ed.) *The Political Economy of Policy Reform*, Washington, DC: Institute for International Economics, pp. 11–28.

Wilner, R. (1973) 'The neo-traditional accommodation to political independence: the case of Indonesia', in J. McAlister (ed.) *Southeast Asia: The Politics of National Integration*, New York: Random House, pp. 517–41.

Wilson, Ian (2006) 'Continuity and change: the changing contest of organised violence in post-Suharto Indonesia', *Critical Asian Studies* 38 (2): 265–97.

Winters, J. (1996) *Power in Motion: Capital Mobility and the Indonesian State*, Ithaca: Cornell University Press.

Wood, E.M. (1990) 'The uses and abuses of civil society', *The Socialist Register*: 60–84.

World Bank (1981) *Accelerated Development in Sub-Saharan Africa: An Agenda for Action*, Washington, DC: World Bank.

——(1991) 'Managing development: the governance dimension. A discussion paper', Washington, DC. Mimeo.

——(1997) *World Development Report: The State in a Changing World*, Washington, DC: Oxford University Press.

——(2000) *Working Together: The World Bank's Partnership with Civil Society*, Washington, DC: World Bank.

——(2002) *World Development Report: Building Institutions for Markets*, Washington, DC: Oxford University Press.

——(2003) *Combating Corruption in Indonesia: Enhancing Accountability for Development*, Jakarta: East Asia and Pacific Region Poverty Reduction and Economic Management Unit.

Zysman, J. (1994) 'How institutions create historically rooted trajectories of change', *Industrial and Corporate Change* 3 (1): 243–83.

SECTION I
The changing landscape of power

2

SOUTHEAST ASIA

The Left and the rise of bourgeois opposition

Kevin Hewison and Garry Rodan[1]

There can be little doubt that conservative elements associated with the political Right have been the dominant political influence in Southeast Asia since the end of colonial rule in the 1950s and 1960s. It is true that the Left and related progressive forces have exerted important influences at particular times. However, it is apparent that their agendas of radical social, economic and political transformation have been subordinated to those promoting capitalist economic development, essentially conservative politics and hierarchical social structures as specified in various other chapters of this volume.

In this chapter we seek to outline the significance of the Left as well as its political demise following a period from about the 1930s to the early 1980s when socialist and communist parties were most active and significant. For the more recent period we outline how the political space occupied by these movements has come to be occupied by broad social democratic movements. In this category we include a range of liberal social movements, civil society organizations (CSOs), community-based organizations (CBOs) and non-governmental organizations (NGOs) that have promoted a politics associated with human rights, environment, media freedom, rural livelihoods and other causes directly or indirectly championing citizenship rights of one sort or another.

In other words, from a period where Left and progressive politics was associated with radical socio-economic and political transformation, this has been replaced with activism that is supportive of enhanced protection for civil and individual rights and collective goods such as the environment. Whereas progressive politics was once opposed to conservative or reactionary ideologies and sought to oust conservative and military governments, in contemporary Southeast Asia, the NGOs noted above are more likely to operate without seeking to fundamentally transform the established political order. In Southeast Asia, over most of the period we discuss, progressive politics opposed colonialism, held generalized notions about egalitarianism and social solidarity, and worked against authoritarian and military-based regimes. While socialists and communists generally adopted class analysis when analysing society and sought to oppose capitalism, bourgeois activists were more interested in reforms that brought classes together within the capitalist economic system in a way that guaranteed certain rights. These basic definitions underpin the following discussion.

Socialist and communist movements had their greatest influence during the nationalist struggles from the 1930s and following the Second World War. In these struggles coalitions of workers, peasants and nationalists became indispensable elements of the anti-colonial movements.

In particular, the communists often provided organizational strength to the independence movements. While there were both links and divisions between the Left and other nationalist parties with, for example, the largest communist party in Asia in Indonesia, for a time the prospects for socialism in Southeast Asia seemed promising. However, as will be shown, despite taking power in Vietnam, Cambodia and Laos in 1974–5, the political influence of communist and socialist movements and ideas of egalitarianism have declined across the region. To a degree, the political gap left by this decline has been filled by a bourgeois, often liberal, opposition seen in the social democratic forces noted above.

Self-proclaimed Leftist political movements continue to exist as legal or underground groups or parties in the region, and some have even been revitalized in recent times, as in Thailand in 2009–10 (see below). However, as capitalist development deepens – even in Vietnam and Laos where communist parties remain in power – the Left has substantially declined.

In this chapter it is argued that the momentum for the expansion of a non-state political space was established through the activism of the organized Left.[2] This political space, and the influence of the Left, has ebbed and flowed as first colonial and then authoritarian states repressed political expression. The chapter examines this process through a broad historical account, focusing on the Left and a range of other non-state groups that have sought to extend the space available for political activity. This discussion follows a brief account of the theoretical underpinnings of the emergence of a 'politicized' civil society, not as any natural outcome or as an end point in a process of economic and political development, but as the product of a constantly evolving contest over the extent and nature of political space. Integral to this contest are competing preferences for who should be represented in the political process and how.

Civil society, political space and political oppositions

In the discussion of political space in Southeast Asia the emergence of 'civil society' is often seen as a recent phenomenon born of the development of middle classes. This position discounts the political struggles of earlier decades. Earlier contests for non-state or independent political space were usually repressed by colonial and post-colonial authoritarian governments, but re-emerged, reinvigorated. In short, contemporary civil society in Southeast Asia is neither new nor the result of an evolutionary transition from authoritarianism to democracy.

Civil society is no simple category. It has a meaning deeply rooted in the development of capitalism and the end of absolutism in Western Europe (Brook 1997: 19–20). The forces unleashed by these processes saw the rise of counter-elites that often sought to reduce the political weight of the state (see Bernhard 1993: 307–11). For Southeast Asia, this historical context is not without parallels, although the fit is not always straightforward. For example, Steinberg (1997) has observed that civil society has to be narrowly defined for contemporary Burma, where the military has ruled since 1962. He argued that civil society is:

> composed of those non-ephemeral organizations of individuals banded together for a common purpose or purposes to pursue those interests through group activities and by peaceful means. These are generally non-profit organizations, and may be local or national, advocacy or supportive, religious, cultural, social, professional, educational, or even organizations that, while not for profit, support the business sector, such as chambers of commerce, trade associations, etc.

Many analysts would accept this definition. Yet it may be too broad for the meaningful analysis of politics, political activism and regime change. For example, Ngok (2007: 10) has argued for attention to 'political society' while Thayer (2009) writes of 'political civil society'. This approach acknowledges the development of NGOs, CBOs and even government-sponsored civic associations. However, it turns analytic attention to essentially 'non-violent political, advocacy, labour and religious organizations and movements that seek to promote human rights and democratization in authoritarian states' (Thayer 2009: 1–2).

In this narrower context, Bernhard (1993: 307) provides a useful account, specifying that civil society 'constitutes the sphere of autonomy from which political forces representing constellations of interests in society have contested state power'. His emphasis on contesting state power is an important addition to these definitions. In any society there will be organizations that are relatively autonomous but which engage in activities that are non-political. Examples of such civic organizations include sporting clubs and charitable associations. At the same time, the emphasis in Thayer's definition on non-violence and activism against authoritarian states is unwarranted. The struggle for political space, whether with authoritarian or democratic regimes, will at times be violent.

Groups that are politically active usually include political parties and organizations, trade unions, employer and professional associations, women's groups, student organizations, peasant and ethnic associations, politically activist NGOs, CBOs and social movements. Groups such as these are seeking to create what Bernhard (1993: 308) identifies as a 'public space'. He emphasizes that, in the European context, these groups were able to 'autonomously organize themselves outside the dominant official political sphere and to compel the state through political struggles to recognize and respect their existence'. It would be rare for such groups to be spawned by the state but by their activism they exist in a relationship with the state.

As indicated by Steinberg (1997), claiming that civil society is politically organized is itself controversial. Several well-cited authorities conceive of civil society as *any* organization that exists outside the state. This is most commonly seen in modernization perspectives (see Pye 1990; Huntington 1991). This approach presumes a causal link between economic development and political change, arguing that a breakdown of authoritarian rule was inevitable – even if protracted and mediated by assorted factors – as economic growth promoted the growth of middle and business classes that would eventually mean the development of a vibrant civil society. These changes meant an unavoidable conflict with authoritarian states that would eventually see democracy take root.

This equation of capitalist development with a more lively civil society has been a common assumption for Southeast Asia (for example, Girling 1988). However, as the cases of Singapore and China suggest, a strong capitalism does not always see the emergence of a strong civil society or political democracy. This failure has resulted in modifications to the modernization perspective that seek to explain the emergence of civil society in terms of 'social capital' and 'networks' being prerequisites for the emergence of a 'trust' that is assumed necessary for CSOs to emerge (Richmond 2006: 18–19). This approach leads to a political archaeology that seeks to reveal the cultural prerequisites of democratization and civil society.

This approach also results in a romantic view of civil society. Where civil society emerges, it is seen as the natural domain of individual and group freedoms, contrasted with the state's coercive institutions and relationships. However, as Rodan (1996) has argued, civil society is not a socially atomized entity, for it is reflective of the divisions that exist in any society. Because civil society is divided, a site of struggles over power, and is linked to state power, CSOs are likely to reflect these divisions and contests. This means that civil society groups will not all seek to advance liberal or democratic political positions.

A further misleading implication of this modernization approach is that a 'strong state' must mean a 'weak civil society', thus diminishing the range of possible configurations of state–civil society relations. Likewise, there is an unwarranted perception that the emergence of civil society is an historical end point. As will be shown below, political space is variable and a product of the interplay of political activism, the state and the classes that dominate it. CSOs can expand political contestation beyond narrow bases in formal political structures but as Rueschemeyer and colleagues (1992: 49) observe, where 'powerful and cohesive upper classes' dominate CSOs, they may 'serve as conduits of authoritarian ideologies, thus weakening democracy'. For all of this, it is true that autonomous activism remains critical for organizing the strength of subaltern classes as they struggle against the hegemony of dominant classes and state. This is precisely why there has been a privileging of certain types of CSOs in state–society engagements involving various regimes in Southeast Asia, in an attempt to enhance political participation while reducing contestation (Jayasuriya and Rodan 2007).

CSOs must have a relationship with the state. As Bernhard (1993: 326) points out, CSO autonomy must be legally sanctioned by the state. It is the state that establishes the boundaries that define the relatively autonomous space for political organizing. These boundaries are meant to protect that space from the state's own interference. Hence it is the state that defines what is to be considered 'political' and 'legitimate' even if this process involves considerable contestation. In return for the granting of independent political space and the protection it affords, the organizations occupying it must engage in self-discipline. This might mean eschewing the harnessing of class-based mass organizations (Rodan and Jayasuriya 2009) and, in capitalist societies, results in bourgeois political activism.

It is clear that the emergence of 'civil society' cannot be understood as a natural opposite to an authoritarian state or as being separated from capitalist relations of exploitation and domination (Wood 1991: 74). Social pluralism does not invariably translate into political pluralism and democracy and activist organizations can co-exist with authoritarian regimes (Bernhard 1993: 326). Independent and organized political activism is but one form of political space that may be able to accommodate greater social pluralism. Increasingly, authoritarian regimes develop creative institutional and ideological initiatives to expand political space *within* the state (Rodan and Jayasuriya 2007; Rodan 2009).

In the following discussion of Southeast Asia, rather than equating the birth and development of civil society with the coupling of capitalism and democracy, the analysis is of the ebb and flow of independent political space generated by extended political struggle as it is shaped by the state and class forces. This approach permits attention to history and to the role of Left political movements in expanding independent political space.

A brief history of political space in Southeast Asia

The emergence of independent political space or civil society is usually considered to be either a late colonial or modern phenomenon. For the pre-colonial period, it is argued that there was a unity of state, society and economy as rulers sought to maintain order and security through the control of the symbolic and spiritual (for example, Taylor 2009: 67–83). This view of an unchanging pre-colonial period ignores ubiquitous class and status conflicts. Even so, it is clear that imperialism and colonialism confronted indigenous political structures with new ideas about science, economics and politics that challenged the old orders. Importantly, colonial rule resulted in new ideas about how society could be organized and managed.

Some of these ideas involved socialism, communism and nationalism, often in combination, and organized into ideologies that drove anti-colonial movements. For Marxists, the rise of nationalism was both a challenge and an opportunity. For example, Lenin's *Imperialism* proved a powerful document for those opposing colonialism. Writing in 1913, Lenin recognized the potential for revolution in Asia (see Gafurov and Kim 1978: 385). Marxism arrived in Southeast

Asia by numerous routes, involving internationally linked labour organizations, intellectuals and organizing by international communists like Ho Chi Minh and Tan Malaka.

It is not possible, in a short chapter, to provide a full account of the ebb and flow of independent political space in five countries of Southeast Asia over a period of some eight decades. Rather, broad slices will be made through the modern history of Southeast Asia, beginning from the 1920s.

Anti-colonialism and political space

In the century up to the 1920s, the colonial governments of Southeast Asia and the (colonial-like) Thai state instituted centralized and bureaucratized administrations, roughly marked out the geographic boundaries of colonies and future nation-states, and established imperial systems of law and order (Ileto 1999; Trocki 1999). There was considerable opposition to the economic and political changes associated with colonialism. For example, as the British took Upper Burma in 1886, there was widespread rebellion resulting in ruthless repression and a large-scale relocation of people. Such events saw the rise of 'patriotism' as an oppositional form (Myint-U 2001: 200–4). With colonial structures developing in place of, on top of and around indigenous structures, further political changes saw the emergence of insistent demands for new political space. This space was sometimes granted by the colonial state but was always limited and carefully policed.

In the era of high colonialism, local economies had been reoriented to the demands of mercantilism, with trade in commodities dominating the economic relationship with the West. An important requirement of colonial rule was for a new, largely indigenous, administrative class. This was the class of 'essential collaborators', schooled in the colonial system, that some of the more radical nationalists came to see as 'bloodsuckers' (Owen 2005: 210, 212). There was a related emergence of 'middle class' occupational groups associated with economic change and political activity became focused on urban areas and a flowering of civic organizations. Throughout Southeast Asia a large number of usually urban-based civic associations emerged to further the interests of local people as well as the large immigrant communities of Chinese and Indians (see Owen 2005: 259–60 on Burma; Skinner 1958 on Siam; and Weiss 2003: 19–22 on Malaya). These groups were not usually overtly political, attending to social and cultural affairs, but could become politicized and were often utilized by the state in managing immigrant communities. Overtly political organizations also developed. According to Taylor (2009: 156), the Karen National Association, formed in 1881, was the first 'Western-style voluntary political organization in Burma's history'. It was probably the first nationalist political association in Southeast Asia.

Much of the political activism that emerged challenged the inequities and contradictions inherent in colonial policies and administration. The governments of the time were unrepresentative, either as an absolutist monarchy in Thailand or as colonial administrations. By the 1920s, a political renaissance resulted in considerable ferment and activism. Labour organizing expanded, newspapers and magazines expanded and nationalist agitation persisted. This tumult saw concerted demand for expanded political space and independence (Pluvier 1974: 15–21, 72–9, 121).

Nationalist ideas took hold everywhere. In British Burma, the Young Men's Buddhist Association became the General Council of Burmese Associations in 1920, and agitated against colonialism across the country (Kratoska and Batson 1999: 282–3). In the Dutch East Indies (Indonesia), a plethora of associations were politicized, especially student groups and religious organizations. Several religious groups in Dutch Indonesia and British Malaya were influenced by the anti-colonial sentiment of Islamic reform movements in the Middle East (Steinberg et al.

1971: 275–8, 326). Colonial regimes reacted in various ways including co-opting, allowing limited political development and, as often as not, repression.

As capitalism developed, separate employer and employee organizations tended to split ethnic Chinese communities. Labour activism increased substantially, some of it associated with political change in China (on Malaya, see Stenson 1970; on Thailand, see Brown 2004). Worker organization was particularly threatening for colonial administrators, with Trocki (1999: 85) noting that the creation of various 'security forces, secret police organizations and spy networks' was to suppress unions and other political movements. Colonial and Thai authorities viewed labour unions as especially threatening when linked with socialist, communist and republican opposition. While unions remained small, they operated in critical economic sectors such as ports, transport and mills.

From the early 1920s, socialist and communist organizations gained strength. For example, the Communist Party of Indonesia (later, Partai Kommunis Indonesia, or PKI) was formed in 1920. In concert with developments in Vietnam and China, communist organisations were soon founded throughout the region, and many trade unions came under Left influence (van der Kroef 1980: 4–7; Cribb 1985: 251). Some of this early communist activity was related to the establishment of the Third International (Comintern) in 1919 and Soviet foreign policy. The Comintern had debated the relationship between communist parties and anti-colonialism, with Lenin calling for alliances with nationalist movements. Arguably, though, local conditions played a more significant role in developing the Left. The PKI adopted a revolutionary strategy that emphasized the anti-colonial struggle (Knight 1985: 53–9). Other communist and socialist parties followed suit.

The period saw considerable labour organizing and activism. In Thailand, labour activists established a workers' newspaper during a strike in 1923. The workers behind the strike and the newspaper soon became active in broader political struggles seeking to unseat the absolute monarchy (Brown 2004: Ch. 2). Labour movements were often embedded in an ethnic division of labour, and when labour, ethnicity and organized communism converged, the colonial and Thai states felt most threatened. For example, vernacular Chinese schools throughout the region were caught up in the political movements in China and became important recruiting grounds for the Left (Kasian 2001). The Communist Youth League in Singapore was established in 1926, with a strong base in schools. A similar pattern was seen in Thailand and Malaya, where authorities closed Chinese schools for political reasons.

The Left's political fortunes were boosted during the Great Depression. In Singapore, the Comintern-inspired South Seas General Labour Union, established in 1926, gained political traction during the economic downturn. The Malayan Communist Party (MCP), established in 1930 with a Singapore base, found the downturn in mining and plantations provided its affiliated unions with considerable impetus. A campaign to mobilize labour saw the Malayan General Labour Union formed in 1934 as the unions became a base for political activism (Starner 1965: 223). In the Philippines, the opposition and independence movements expanded during the depression. The Socialist Party formed in 1929 with a nationalist stand and its own labour organization. Supporting peasants and workers, the Party ran in elections and increased its support between 1933 and 1937. The Communist Party (Partido Komunisat ng Philipinas, or PKP) was established in 1930, but went underground when banned in 1931. In 1938, the Socialist and Communist parties merged in an anti-fascist front (Kerkvliet 1977: 1–60; Richardson 1993: 386). Similar patterns of Left-oriented political activism were seen throughout Southeast Asia.

By the late 1930s, the communist and socialist movements that had emerged were all influenced by, and influential on, growing anti-imperialist movements and shared a distrust of

Western liberalism and capitalism (Golay *et al.* 1969: 18). The Left had contributed to and benefited from the independent political space of the 1920s and 1930s. However, as World War II approached, authorities attempted to curtail political activism. In Thailand, the military was in control and moved closer to fascist regimes in Europe and Japan. The colonial state in Singapore and Malaya, threatened by communism, crushed the CPM in 1931, but soon faced communist-led worker opposition in the mid-1930s (Starner 1965: 237).

One important element of the anti-colonial movement in Indonesia was that of Islamic traders and landowning classes under threat from Chinese business. They blamed the colonial government in part for this situation, demanding protection and subsidy for domestic/indigenous business. Another important element was that of middle-class professionals in the PNI who mobilised mass support and led the anti-colonial war in the 1940s.

Post-war/Cold War

During World War II, while some nationalist movements accepted Japanese attacks on Western colonialism and lined up with them in opposing colonial masters, the communists generally opposed the Japanese. In several places, including Malaysia and Vietnam, the Allies supported the communist resistance against the Japanese. The early defeats inflicted on the Western colonial masters by the Japanese gave strength and impetus to anti-colonial movements. The Japanese also vigorously suppressed communist movements. In Malaya, Singapore, Indochina and the Philippines, communists led or were major elements of anti-Japanese movements (Pluvier 1974: 286–311). In Burma, the Anti-Fascist People's Freedom League was founded in 1944 as an anti-Japanese resistance force encompassing Aung San's Burma National Army, the Communist Party and what became the Socialist Party (see Hewison and Prager Nyein 2010). The communists gained credibility by leading anti-Japanese movements. At the end of the war these movements were in a strong and popular position, and the link between nationalism and communism was well-established.

Following the war, Southeast Asia experienced a short period of relative political openness, with nationalists and the organized Left leading the drive to independence. Decolonization was generally supported by the United States and the USSR. However, while the British were decolonizing in South Asia, they seemed keen to re-establish colonial regimes in Southeast Asia. Not only did they do this in their own colonies, but they supported the re-establishment of colonial regimes in Indochina and Indonesia (Stockwell 1999: 353). For nationalists, and this included most on the Left, anti-colonialism was the major political issue, with a strident anti-Western tone.

Further, the increased international influence of the USSR was cause for optimism on the part of Southeast Asian communists. As a founding power of the United Nations, the USSR provided political support to local communists. For example, when Thailand wanted to join the UN in 1946, it required Soviet support. The USSR sought and received the repeal of Thailand's anti-Communist laws (Insor 1963: 90). Many communists were also heartened by the progress of communist parties in Indochina and China. Another support for the Left was the impetus given to centralized economic planning by Soviet economic and war success and, ironically, the Marshall Plan for reconstruction in Europe. The Left had long argued for industrialization through government investments, and planning and economic nationalism became a central pillar of industrialization strategies (Golay *et al.* 1969: 453). This was seen in Burma, Indonesia and, in a more limited way, Thailand, Malaya and the Philippines (Golay *et al.* 1969: 119–24).

The socialist movement – much of it anti-communist – also made gains. Calling for an 'Asian socialism', Burmese Prime Minister U Ba Swe called for 'revolutionary democratic Socialist methods to improve the standard of living of the masses' in Southeast Asia. Opposed to capitalism because of its links with colonialism and to communism as a form of totalitarianism, 'Asian socialism' was nationalist, supported state social welfare and saw itself as 'democratic, egalitarian and fraternal' (Josey 1957).

By 1950, the broad Left of socialists and communists in Southeast Asia must have felt that the tide of history was in their favour. The Philippines and Indonesia had gained their independence, albeit by quite different routes, the Chinese communists were in power, the situation in Indochina was in the balance; communists had launched armed struggles or rebellions in Malaya and Singapore, the Philippines (the Hukbalahap movement), Indonesia, and Burma (see van der Kroef 1980: 25–32). In Indonesia, the PKI believed that 'the national movement, and later the national state, might be captured by Marxism through peaceful means and, having been captured ideologically, would naturally admit Marxists to positions of power' (Cribb 1985: 259). Meanwhile, in Malaya, the Communist Party had abandoned peaceful and constitutional opposition to the reinstitution of colonialism and had embarked on armed struggle. In other places, the Left had made political gains as worker and peasant unrest developed. By 1947, for example, MCP-dominated unions controlled three-quarters of the organized work force in Singapore, while in Thailand labour organization increased, and a new generation of leaders, influenced by Marxism and close to the Communist Party of Thailand (CPT), emerged. The PKI also had strong links with labour (Golay et al. 1969: 198–99; Stenson 1970: 11–80; Hewison and Brown 1994).

The success of labour organizing can be seen as a part of the rise of a more generalised Leftist discourse in the region. As Reynolds (1987: 25) has observed for Thailand, 'there was a distinctly Left orientation in Bangkok public discourse for a decade or so after World War II'. In Malaya and Singapore, radical unions played a critical role in mobilizing a broad movement of students, workers and formal political parties. Leftist discourse, especially in labour circles, employed concepts of class, class struggle and exploitation, challenging capitalism, colonialism and bourgeois nationalism. As labour activism deepened, governments sought to curtail certain forms of political representation and mobilization and targeted key socialist and communist organizations. Anti-communist laws became increasingly draconian. For example, in Thailand, the 1952 Anti-Communist Act prevented criticism of the private enterprise system and outlawed acts defined as 'creating instability, disunity, or hatred among the people, and taking part in acts of terrorism or sabotage' (Reynolds 1987: 28).

From this time, the fortunes of the Left became increasingly entangled with the geo-politics of the Cold War. The US and other Western powers, shocked by the 'loss' of China and Eastern Europe and the war in Korea, moved quickly to confront communism everywhere, including in Southeast Asia. The Cold War political agenda meant support for pro-Western and pro-business governments. Throughout Southeast Asia the US supported anti-communists. In Thailand, it supported Right-wing generals in the police and army. In Indochina, the US supported the French against the Viet Minh, before becoming militarily involved. Likewise, in Malaya, it supported the British in their anti-communist war. In Indonesia, the US championed the military against Sukarno and the PKI while it supported the nationalists in the Philippines against the Huk rebellion. At the same time, in Burma and Cambodia, the US undermined governments it considered 'dangerously neutral'.

This support for repressive political structures resulted in a remarkable narrowing of political space, even for democrats and nationalists. This anti-communist turn had a neat fit with authoritarian domestic agendas and often brutal repression. The organized Left was identified as 'alien' and as a 'fifth column' movement and found its organizations suppressed by authoritarian regimes that jailed and killed political opponents. Huge amounts of US aid supported this repression.

Challenging Cold War authoritarianism

By the end of the 1960s, almost all of the countries of the region were ruled by post-colonial regimes that were authoritarian and repressive. At the same time, communist-led armed struggles in the Philippines and Thailand were gaining strength, while the US intervention in Indochina was drawing to an inevitable close. The eventual victories for the communist movements in Indochina initially gave considerable impetus to the broad Left. In addition, political opposition to authoritarianism developed, much of it related to anti-imperialism and demands for new economic models.

In Singapore, for example, there was a short-lived revival of the student movement. University students had an agenda that included supporting workers and promoting civil liberties. The government cracked down, having student leaders arrested for 'unlawful assembly' and 'rioting', and putting student union funds under the control of the university and Ministry of Education. The student union was then prevented from engaging in political affairs. The involvement of students in struggles for expanded independent political space was a pattern throughout the region between 1968 and 1975. The breakaway Maoist Communist Party of the Philippines was formed by student leaders and intellectuals in 1968 and students were especially active until the introduction of martial law in 1972. In Indonesia and Thailand, students protested against Japanese economic imperialism. Joining peasants protesting falling prices, students in Malaysia demonstrated against the government in 1974, being subject then to considerable state repression (Ali 2008: 26). The most remarkable student activism was in Thailand, where students and intellectuals brought tens of thousands into the streets to overthrow a military dictatorship in 1973, only to be crushed by the military and Rightist forces in 1976 (see Morell and Chai-Anan 1981).

In part, student activism resulted from the massive expansion of tertiary education and the enormous social and economic changes taking place as a consequence of growth generated by import-substituting industrialization (see Anderson 1977). As noted above, radicalism suggested to authoritarian governments that students were manipulated by the Left. The result was repression and attempts to take control of student organizations. Of course, students did not operate in a political vacuum. They established solidarity groups with workers, peasants and the downtrodden and developed relationships with both the legal and underground Left. Thailand in 1973–6 is an example. Student–Left alliances succeeded in expanding political space but also prompted violent Rightist and state retaliation. In alliance with developing capitalist classes, governments again closed the political opening, and repressive regimes dominated the political stage throughout the late 1970s and into the 1980s.

For the Left, facing increased repression, a glimmer of hope was seen in the self-declared socialist governments of Laos, Vietnam and Cambodia and the expansion of communist-led rebellions in Thailand and the Philippines. But this came to nothing. In Cambodia, the Pol Pot regime embarked on a hyper-nationalist reign of terror which, while initially supported by some on the Left, was only concluded when Vietnam invaded in late 1978. One outcome of this was a brief but bloody war between China and Vietnam in 1979, which threw most of the organized Left in Southeast Asia into ideological confusion (see Evans and Rowley 1984). This confusion was amplified when the US and ASEAN began supporting their former enemy in the murderous Khmer Rouge against the forces that had thrown out the Pol Pot regime (Vickery 1986).

These intra-communist clashes had important impacts for communist movements in Southeast Asia. The CPT, which had been able to claim more than 15,000 fighters in its armed struggle, imploded. Allied to China, the CPT supported the Khmer Rouge and China, thereby losing support from Vietnam and Laos. When it also lost China's support as the Chinese leadership decided to support capitalist and repressive regimes in the region, the CPT was dead (see Chai-Anan *et al.* 1990). Armed struggle died out and it was really only in the Philippines that it continued, albeit with numerous splits amongst those on the Left (Reid 2000).

Changing patterns of international production also had a major impact on the nature of government in the region. The increased mobility of international capital saw a relocation of production to East and Southeast Asia. This movement was fostered by a shift from import-substitution to export-oriented and low-wage manufacturing. Keeping wages low and workers docile meant that unions were attacked and broken, further weakening the Left. Three other events contributed to this weakening: first, the move to capitalist production in China; second, the political and economic collapse of Eastern Europe; and third, the growing economic success of many of the capitalist Southeast Asian countries, while maintaining repressive political environments. By the mid-1980s, the future for Left and progressive forces seemed bleak.

Civil society and bourgeois politics

During the late 1980s and prior to the 1997–8 Asian economic crisis, further changes in the global political economy saw high-growth capitalist development further undercut socialism's potential appeal in the region, providing low-paid production jobs (see Rodan *et al.* 2006). As the region became integral to global production chains, increased competition between economies, companies and workers developed. Significantly, in many countries, capitalist development has been achieved while maintaining political authoritarianism. Indeed, authoritarian political leaders in the region used economic success to boost political regime legitimacy and to justify repression.

In this context of a declining Left and a seemingly triumphant capitalism, progressive politics increasingly became associated with bourgeois reformism, seeking a capitalism that at least evidenced some concern for the weakest and poorest but where notions of egalitarianism, collectivism and revolution became fringe ideas. The result was a growing interest in limited political goals associated with human rights, liberty and representative forms of government – comparatively progressive ideas in a region where authoritarian governments remained politically repressive.

The growth of bourgeois reformism coincided with social and economic transformations that involved the expansion of capitalist and middle classes (see Robison and Goodman 1996). Capitalist development saw an ever more complex bourgeois class engaged in diverse domestic and global accumulation strategies. This generated new political aspirations and demands but did not necessarily result in progressive or even liberal politics. While modernization theorists had anticipated expanded political space, not all political space was independent space and nor was it equally meaningful for different societal forces. While some argued that the development of business and professional organizations moved political power away from the state, structures emerged that limited rather than expanded political space, often involving the business elite and sections of middle class having close relations with the state and the organizations of the capitalist class (MacIntyre 1991; Anek 1992).

Meanwhile, the revitalization of NGOs and CSOs meant that, in some places, there was a push for an expanded political space. The demarcation of non-state political space should make political contestation more likely – even if, in order to avoid proscription and co-optation, confrontation is avoided. The most significant manifestation of contemporary political activism is seen in the NGOs that assign to themselves the representation of the 'underprivileged'. At various times and locations, these organizations have been important mechanisms for expanding independent political space, engendering considerable enthusiasm for the political potential of

NGOs (see Clark 1991). However, over the past two decades, authoritarian states have been able to resist, co-opt or accommodate these reformist demands.

In authoritarian Singapore, from the 1980s, some groups emerged in the narrow space that existed. Notable were the Law Society, lay religious organizations, the Nature Society, the Association of Women for Action and Research, and the Association of Muslim Professionals (Rodan 1993). The evolution of these groups reflected a perception that existing political structures inadequately accommodated distinctive interests. It is clear that, since then, the Singapore government has embarked on a strategy to expand state-sponsored and state-controlled political space as an alternative to concessions on the extent and nature of independent civil society space. This has involved a range of new mechanisms for political consultation and feedback, inside and outside parliament, all of which are premised on acceptance of one-party rule (this 'consultative authoritarianism' is discussed in detail in Chapter 7). Meanwhile, tolerance for independent organizations has been conditional on their political roles remaining overt and limited, something that has generally been abided with. Like business organizations, the possibility of co-option and corporatism has meant that it is sometimes difficult to distinguish state and non-state organizations.

In military-run Burma, there was considerable optimism that, following Cyclone Nargis in 2008, developing NGOs and CSOs might be able to pry some limited political space away from the regime. However, not only did some of these organizations demonstrate a willingness to work closely with the regime, but the military regime continued to control all political space in the run-up to rigged elections in 2010 (see Hewison and Prager Nyein 2010).

Such examples do not exhaust the range of political activism undertaken by NGOs and social movements in Southeast Asia. In circumstances less authoritarian than those in Singapore and Burma, such organizations are operating outside the realm of party politics and in ways that distinguish them from the influence or lobby groups that are central in pluralist theory. They are activist and marshal support from a range of groups and classes in society. That such organizations can be oppositional to authoritarian regimes has been demonstrated in the Philippines in 1986, where NGOs played a role in overthrowing the Marcos regime, and in Thailand, where they had a role in the 1991–2 events that led to the demise of a military-backed government.

When politics has been more open, as in the Philippines since 1986, Thailand from 1992 to 2006 and Indonesia from 1998, NGOs and CSOs have tended to act as a loyal opposition outside parliament. Significantly, though, many NGOs found that they needed to continue to challenge elected governments, supporting the poor and arguing for better representation and participation in policy making. This involved the building of oppositional coalitions between unions, development groups, women, religious groups and environmentalists. A good example of successful activism is seen in Malaysia, where the range of NGOs and CSOs has included steadfastly oppositional politics (Weiss and Hassan 2002; Weiss 2006).

At the same time, the social embeddedness of NGOs and CSOs was demonstrated in political events that followed the 1997–8 economic crisis. In the Philippines and Thailand, the economic downturn saw the emergence of political leaders who doubted the efficacy of the neo-liberal economic recovery prescriptions demanded by the IMF, World Bank, international corporations and Western and Japanese governments. In the Philippines, Joseph Estrada was elected president in a landslide in 1998 and touted anti-poverty policies and other 'populist' and pro-poor measures (De Castro 2007). In Thailand, Thaksin Shinawatra gained the country's biggest ever election victory in 2001 and introduced similar 'populist' policies that were so popular that he was re-elected in a landslide in 2005 (Hewison 2010a). Both elected leaders were opposed by middle-class and business groups and accused of corruption. Thaksin was also accused of human rights abuses. In both cases, NGOs and CSOs joined with the elite and urban middle class in mounting street protests to bring down these elected and popular politicians. In Thailand, some of these organizations espoused elitist and anti-democratic politics, arguing for limited political rights that disadvantaged their own grassroots constituents (see Kengkij and Hewison 2009). The lesson of these events is that political action and contestation is built on class interests. Especially when lower classes challenge elite rule, the class nature of the organizations of civil society become apparent.

There is a tendency for analysts to view NGOs as naturally 'anti-state' because they are 'non-state'. This is naïve. In the Philippines, Indonesia and Thailand, NGOs have regularly been incorporated within the structures of local government and as service agencies (Jayasuriya and Hewison 2004; Reid 2005). This co-option by the state and international agencies like the World Bank has led to a debate over independence and political location (see Petras 1999). Class factors are at work, with most NGO leaders being drawn from urban intellectuals and middle-class groups, and while these leaders may work with the poor, this does not mean they are natural class allies of the downtrodden. NGO ideology may emphasize empowerment for the poor, disorganized and disenfranchised, their methodologies might claim to value participation, representation and collective action, and strategies that might expand political space, but NGOs inevitably reflect the class nature of the society in which they are embedded (see Petras 1999).

The most remarkable demonstration of the impact of class location has been in Thailand in 2009–10. Not only did many NGOs and CSOs oppose electoral outcomes that they deemed 'inappropriate', but they supported the repression of political movements associated with the poor and marginalized. In Thailand, these groups and their middle-class leaders campaigned with royalists, the military and a range of Right-wing groups to overturn electoral outcomes and then defeat the United Front of Democracy against Dictatorship (UDD), a movement that had the support of workers and small farmers. At the same time, Right-wing social movements formed to support elite rule and the defeat of electoral victors through street protest. The class antagonisms were dramatically demonstrated when the UDD began to mobilize around issues of inequality, injustice, class struggle and opposition to an 'aristocratic elite'. Many NGOs and CSOs rejected such rhetoric and expressed considerable opposition to grassroots organizing that they labelled as Left-wing or even communist (Kengkij and Hewison 2009; Hewison 2010b). They feared the UDD and its radical position, preferring that the UDD operate locally, dealing with local politics and local-level issues such as corruption (see Jacques-chai and Chanida 2010). This is about a reformism that tames and depoliticizes the UDD and its supporters.

Conclusion

In the early twenty-first century, it might have been hoped by liberals that the rapid maturation of capitalism would have delivered benefits sufficient to have made redundant the class-based politics of the Left in Southeast Asia. On the contrary, the social contradictions of market relations that manifest themselves in political contestation have become increasingly evident in recent years. Many of the ongoing conflicts in the region are fundamentally about the economic exploitation and political oppression maintained by political and economic elites. The resentment of the monopoly of economic and political power by the privileged classes is evident throughout the region. In this sense, while the social and economic contexts are vastly changed, many of the basic political conflicts remain focused on issues recognized by the Left decades ago.

The struggle for increased independent political space continues unabated, and in various countries this space remains remarkably narrow. Many of the emerging non-state organizations have a class position predisposing them to limited forms of contestation with the state that entrenches political and economic privilege. In essence, these organizations promote reform of the existing political system rather than its transformation. Yet while the organized Left may barely exist in present-day Southeast Asia, the issues that have energized it for decades remain at the core of contemporary political and economic struggles. The historical development of capitalism in Southeast Asia has fostered powerful coalitions of interest institutionalized through state power, but that institutionalization requires continued refinement to ensure limits to political opposition are reproduced.

Notes

1 Research for this essay by Garry Rodan was supported by Australian Research Council funding for a Discovery Project (1093214), 'Representation and Political Regimes in Southeast Asia', for which the author is grateful.
2 For our earlier treatment of the Left and political development in Southeast Asia see Hewison and Rodan (1994).

References

Ali, S. (2008) *The Malays: Their Problems and Future*, Petaling Jaya: The Other Press.
Anderson, B. (1977) 'Withdrawal symptoms: social and cultural aspects of the October 6 coup', *Bulletin of Concerned Asian Scholars* 9 (3): 13–31.
Anek Laothamatas (1992) *Business Associations and the New Political Economy of Thailand*, Singapore: Institute of Southeast Asian Studies.
Bernhard, M. (1993) 'Civil society and democratic transition in East Central Europe', *Political Science Quarterly* 108 (2): 307–26.
Brook, T (1997) 'Auto-organization in Chinese society', in T. Brook and B.M. Frolic (eds) *Civil Society in China*, Armonk, NY: M.E. Sharpe, pp. 19–45.
Brown, A. (2004) *Labour, Politics and the State in Industrializing Thailand*, London: RoutledgeCurzon.
Chai-Anan Samudavanija, Kusuma Snitwongse and Suchit Bunbongkarn (1990) *From Armed Suppression to Political Offensive*, Bangkok: Chulalongkorn University, Institute of Security and International Studies.
Clark, J. (1991) *Democratising Development: The Role of Voluntary Organizations*, London: Earthscan.
Cribb, R. (1985) 'The Indonesian Marxist tradition', in C. Mackerras and N. Knight (eds) *Marxism in Asia*, New York: St Martin's Press, pp. 251–72.
De Castro, R. (2007) 'The 1997 Asian financial crisis and the revival of populism/neo-populism in 21st century Philippine politics', *Asian Survey* 47 (6): 930–51.
Evans, G. and K. Rowley (1984) *Red Brotherhood at War*, London: Verso.
Gafurov, B. and G.F. Kim (eds) (1978) *Lenin and National Liberation in the East*, Moscow: Progress Publishers.
Girling, J. (1988) 'Development and democracy in Southeast Asia', *Pacific Review* 1 (4): 332–6.
Golay, F., R. Anspach, R. Pfanner and E.B. Ayal (1969) *Underdevelopment and Economic Nationalism in Southeast Asia*, Ithaca: Cornell University Press.
Hewison, K. (2010a) 'Thaksin Shinawatra and the reshaping of Thai politics', *Contemporary Politics* 16 (2): 119–33.
——(2010b) 'Rebellion, repression and the red shirts', *East Asia Forum Quarterly* 2 (2): 14–17.
Hewison, K. and A. Brown (1994) 'Labour and unions in an industrialising Thailand', *Journal of Contemporary Asia* 24 (4): 483–514.
Hewison, K. and S. Prager Nyein (2010) 'Civil society and political oppositions in Burma', in Li Chenyang and W. Hofmeister (eds) *Myanmar: Prospect for Change*, Singapore: Select Publishing, pp. 13–34.
Hewison, K. and G. Rodan (1994) 'The Decline of the Left in Southeast Asia', in R. Miliband and L. Panitch (eds) *The Socialist Register* London: Merlin Press, pp. 235–62.
Huntington, S. (1991) *The Third Wave: Democratization in the Late Twentieth Century*, Norman: University of Oklahoma Press.
Ileto, R. (1999) 'Religion and anti-colonial movements', in N. Tarling (ed.) *The Cambridge History of Southeast Asia*, Vol. 2, Part 1, *From c. 1800 to the 1930s*, Cambridge: Cambridge University Press, pp. 193–244.

Insor, D. (pseud.) (1963) *Thailand: A Political, Social and Economic Analysis*, London: Allen and Unwin.

Jacques-chai Chomthongdi and Chanida Chanyapate (2010) 'Aftermath of the battle: picking up the pieces', *Focus on the Global South*, 25 May; available at: www.focusweb.org/content/aftermath-battle-picking-pieces (accessed 26 May 2010).

Jayasuriya, K. and K. Hewison (2004) 'The antipolitics of good governance: from global social policy to a global populism?' *Critical Asian Studies* 36 (4): 571–90.

Jayasuriya, K. and G. Rodan (2007) 'Beyond hybrid regimes: more participation, less contestation in Southeast Asia', *Democratization* 14 (5): 773–94.

Josey, A. (1957) *Socialism in Asia*, Singapore: Donald Moore.

Kasian Tejapira (2001) *Commodifying Marxism*, Melbourne: Trans Pacific Press.

Kengkij Kitirianglarp and K. Hewison (2009) 'Social movements and political opposition in contemporary Thailand', *Pacific Review* 22 (4): 451–77.

Kerkvliet, B. (1977) *The Huk Rebellion: A Study of Peasant Revolt in the Philippines*, Berkeley: University of California Press.

Knight, N. (1985) 'Leninism, Stalinism and the Comintern', in C. Mackerras and N. Knight (eds) *Marxism in Asia*, New York: St Martin's Press, pp. 24–61.

Kratoska, P. and B. Batson (1999) 'Nationalism and modernist reform', in N. Tarling (ed.) *The Cambridge History of Southeast Asia*, Vol. 2, Part 1, *From c. 1800 to the 1930s*, Cambridge: Cambridge University Press, pp. 245–320.

MacIntyre, A. (1991) *Business and Politics in Indonesia*, Sydney: Allen and Unwin.

Morell, D. and Chai-Anan Samudavanija (1981) *Political Conflict in Thailand: Reform, Reaction, Revolution*, Boston, MA: Oelgeschlager, Gunn and Hain.

Myint-U, Thant (2001) *The Making of Modern Burma*, Cambridge: Cambridge University Press.

Ngok, Ma (2007) *Political Development in Hong Kong: State, Political Society, and Civil Society*, Hong Kong: Hong Kong University Press.

Owen, N. (ed.) (2005) *The Emergence of Modern Southeast Asia: A New History*, Honolulu: University of Hawai'i Press.

Petras, J. (1999) 'NGOs: in the service of imperialism', *Journal of Contemporary Asia* 29 (4): 429–40.

Pluvier, J. (1974) *South-East Asia from Colonialism to Independence*, Kuala Lumpur: Oxford University Press.

Pye, L. (1990) 'Political science and the crisis of authoritarianism', *American Political Science Review* 84 (1): 3–19.

Reid, B. (2000) *Philippine Left: Political Crisis and Social Change*, Manila: Journal of Contemporary Asia Publishers.

——(2001) 'The Philippine democratic uprising and the contradictions of neoliberalism: EDSA II', *Third World Quarterly* 22 (5): 777–93.

——(2005) 'Poverty alleviation and participatory development in the Philippines', *Journal of Contemporary Asia* 35 (1): 29–52.

Reynolds, C. (1987) *Thai Radical Discourse: The Real Face of Thai Feudalism Today*, Ithaca: Cornell University Studies on Southeast Asia.

Richardson, J. (1993) 'Review article: The millenarian–populist aspects of Filipino Marxism', *Journal of Contemporary Asia* 23 (3): 382–95.

Richmond, J. (2006) 'Promises, prospects, and prognostications for a civil society in Burma', *LBJ Journal of Public Affairs* 18 (2): 17–26.

Robison, R. and D. Goodman (eds) (1996) *The New Rich in Asia: Mobile Phones, McDonald's and Middle Class Revolution*, London: Routledge.

Rodan, G. (1993) 'Preserving the one-party state in contemporary Singapore', in K. Hewison, R. Robison and G. Rodan (eds) *Southeast Asia in the 1990s*, Sydney: Allen and Unwin, pp. 75–108.

——(1996) 'Theorising political opposition in East and Southeast Asia', in G. Rodan (ed.) *Political Oppositions in Industrialising Asia*, London: Routledge, pp. 1–39.

——(2009) 'New modes of political participation and Singapore's nominated members of parliament', *Government and Opposition* 44 (4): 438–62.

Rodan, G. and K. Jayasuriya (2007) 'The technocratic politics of administrative participation: case studies of Singapore and Vietnam', *Democratization* 14 (5): 795–815.

——(2009) 'Capitalist development, regime transitions and new forms of authoritarianism in Asia', *Pacific Review* 22 (1): 23–48.

Rodan, G., K. Hewison, and R. Robison (eds) (2006) *The Political Economy of South-East Asia: Markets, Power and Contestation*, Melbourne: Oxford University Press.

Rueschemeyer, D., E. Stephens and J. Stephens (1992) *Capitalist Development and Democracy*, Cambridge: Polity Press.

Skinner, G.W. (1958) *Leadership and Power in the Chinese Community of Thailand*, Ithaca, NY: Cornell University Press.

Starner, F. (1965) 'Communism in Malaysia: a multifront struggle', in R. Scalapino (ed.) *The Communist Revolution in Asia*, Englewood Cliffs, NJ: Prentice-Hall, pp. 221–55.

Steinberg, D. (1997) 'A void in Myanmar: civil society in Burma', *The Burma Library*; available at: www.burmalibrary.org/docs3/Steinbergpaper.htm (accessed 25 September 2009).

Steinberg, D., D. Wyatt, J. Smail, A. Woodside, W. Roff and D. Chandler (1971) *In Search of Southeast Asia: A Modern History*, New York: Praeger.

Stenson, M. (1970) *Industrial Conflict in Malaya*, London: Oxford.

Stockwell, A. (1999) 'Southeast Asia in war and peace: the end of European colonial empires', in N. Tarling (ed.) *The Cambridge History of Southeast Asia*, Vol. 2, Part 1, *From c. 1800 to the 1930s*, Cambridge: Cambridge University Press, pp. 1–58.

Taylor, R. (2009) *The State in Myanmar*, Singapore: NUS Press.

Thayer, C. (2009) 'Vietnam and the challenge of political civil society', *Contemporary Southeast Asia* 31 (1): 1–27.

Trocki, C. (1999) 'Political structures of the nineteenth and early twentieth centuries', in N. Tarling (ed.) *The Cambridge History of Southeast Asia*, Vol. 2, Part 1, *From c. 1800 to the 1930s*, Cambridge: Cambridge University Press, pp. 75–126.

van der Kroef, J. (1980) *Communism in South-East Asia*, Berkeley: University of California Press.

Vickery, M. (1986) *Kampuchea: Politics, Economics and Society*, London: Pinter.

Weiss, M. (2003) 'Malaysian NGOs: history, legal framework and characteristics', in M. Weiss and S. Hassan (eds) *Social Movements in Malaysia*, London: RoutledgeCurzon, pp. 17–44.

——(2006) *Protest and Possibilities: Civil Society Coalitions for Political Change in Malaysia*, Stanford, CA: Stanford University Press.

Weiss, M. and S. Hassan (2002) 'Introduction: From moral communities to NGOs', in M. Weiss and S. Hassan (eds) *Social Movements in Malaysia*, London: RoutledgeCurzon, pp. 1–16.

Wood, E.M. (1991) 'The uses and abuses of "civil society"', in R. Miliband, L. Panitch and J. Saville (eds) *Socialist Register 1990*, London: The Merlin Press, pp. 60–84.

3

LABOUR POLITICS IN SOUTHEAST ASIA

The Philippines in comparative perspective

Jane Hutchison

A feature of Southeast Asian politics is the comparative weakness of organised labour. Activist trade unions are present in all but the most tightly controlled countries; however, they are fragmented, have very low worker-coverage and lack links to major political parties. This matters for studies of politics because labour's capacity for disruptive collective action makes it a key social actor, and therefore a target of mobilisation or control by others. In Southeast Asia, organised labour is comparatively weak because economic and political elites have successfully contained labour's collective activism as a part of broader projects to limit social representation and dissent. When and where alliances with other social classes and sectors have formed, they have contributed to political disruption and even regime change without strengthening labour significantly as a result. There are structural reasons for this: conditions associated with the timing and forms of capitalist industrialisation and globalisation have inhibited labour's collective activism, leaving it relatively marginalised during important political and economic transformations (Deyo 2006). However, structural factors are not independent of political projects as often their impacts are amplified by the nature of the political spaces for legitimate labour organising.

At one level, the political spaces for labour union organising are set by the laws and institutions which govern industrial relations, since these formally establish the organising forms which are state-sanctioned. Collier and Collier (2002) argue that the initial shift from state repression of labour to state control by legal and institutional means constitutes a 'critical juncture' in the development of national polities. The shift need not be total for it to shape the course of state–labour relations thereafter, by institutionalising certain patterns of accommodation and conflict during the early phases of modern-state formation. In this regard, this chapter focuses on the Philippines, with some additional commentary on Indonesia, Thailand and Singapore. However, notwithstanding the significance of the spaces for labour organising which are formally constituted, at no point is it argued that labour's weakness in the Philippines is in fact reducible to these. There are three main reasons for this – each of which highlight the overriding impact of the nature of struggles for state power and recognition more broadly.

First, for workers' legal rights and protections to be effective, they depend on state enforcement vis-à-vis employers. When enforcement is weak or absent, these formal rights and protections become sites of struggle and are constituted in fact as much by power balances involved as by the law itself (Woodiwiss 1998; Chang 2009). Second, state controls over labour are not limited to those which are specifically prescribed by industrial relations law, as for example when mayors and provincial governors impose their own forms of control over workers and their organisations as a part of local development strategies to attract investment (Kelly 2001). Conversely, labour activism can also assume forms that are not prescribed within industrial law, as for example when NGOs and religious are involved directly in worker advocacy and organising (McKay 2006; Ford 2009). Third and finally, the political spaces for labour organising are also shaped by the ideologies of state–labour relations and the attendant social and political alliances and perceptions of the legitimacy of workers' grievances and tactics. Because the Philippine labour movement is deeply divided on ideological grounds, within shared structural and legal constraints, the constituent federations operate very differently in relation to the state.[1] Whereas the conservative federations tend to be incorporated politically via patronage and tripartite channels, others are more independent, with some of these belonging to leftist movements with radical change agendas. Thus, in so far as they impact directly on the power and legitimacy of the state, the political spaces for labour organising are at their most variable.

The chapter begins with an account of the initial controls over labour organising in the Philippines in the early decades of modern-state formation and independence, prior to the Pacific War. Thereafter, the chapter covers further major turning points in state–labour relations, against the background of broader political and socioeconomic continuities and transformations. There are sections on the Cold War, export-oriented industrialisation and authoritarian rule, democratisation and globalisation. Throughout we will see that nowhere in the region have there emerged the social democratic modes of accommodation that have featured in Europe. By the same token, nor do we see the kind of pluralist polities that liberal modernisation theorists predict will emerge with capitalist industrialisation.

Initial controls

Southeast Asian trade unions generally trace their origins to early capitalist development and the rise of wage labour in the late nineteenth century, principally in export agriculture and related processing, manufacturing, transportation and printing. Whilst the first unions had limited worker coverage, the political milieu of their emergence meant that all experienced state repression of different intensities and duration. In the Philippines, repression by the colonial authorities came earlier and had less lasting consequences than in the Dutch East Indies, now Indonesia, for example (see Hadiz 1997). This is because the United States had quickly promised Filipinos independence and so circumvented the formation of a nationalist movement that might have otherwise brought the interests of the masses closer to those of the elite. In the early 1900s, prominent labour leaders were arrested and jailed for 'subversion'; but within a few years they were drawn into election campaigns by the independence process having moved to the formal political arena (Kerkvliet 1992). However, because property and literacy requirements had denied most workers the vote, it did not follow from the leaders' political involvement that links were established between unions and new political parties.[2] In the critical early stages of modern-state formation in the Philippines, political participation was thus the preserve of an economic elite with established social control within their local bailiwicks (Simbulan 2005).

Hutchcroft argues that the United States colonial authority's twin policies of sequencing initial elections 'upwards' (from local to provincial and then national levels) and giving 'greater attention to elections and legislative institutions than to the creation of a modern bureaucratic apparatus' (Hutchcroft 2010: 426) had major long-term consequences because it established the conditions for an *elected* elite to control and wield state power in their own interests, essentially unchecked. In other words, the American period set in train a number of state features that survive to the present. More immediately, it paved the way for greater state control over labour organising following independence.

During the American period, trade unions were officially tolerated industrially, but as they were also 'not specifically protected or encouraged' (Carroll 1961: 227–8), their growth was contained by employer opposition and the small size of the wage labour force. Communism had some influence in the movement in the 1920s, but a state crackdown on leftists in the early 1930s meant this was at an end by independence (Wurfel 1959; Carroll 1961; Kerkvliet 1992). When cuts to wages in industry and agriculture and growing unemployment increased worker militancy, it was mostly unorganised and so not an indicator of growing movement strength (Kunihara 1945: 65).

Nevertheless, at the founding of the Philippine Commonwealth in 1935, labour was 'obstreperous enough to elicit a reaction from the political elite' (Wurfel 1959: 586). This reaction was centred on the intensification of state power to control union formation and industrial unrest. Unions were now able to apply for legal recognition; however, the application process was so rigorous that only a minority of unions were successful (Carroll 1961). Meanwhile, a new industrial relations court was established with wide powers to compulsorily arbitrate all major industrial disputes. A 'social justice' programme was also passed, enacting worker protections that included an eight-hour working day and minimum wage. But without attendant state enforcement – and with workers simultaneously allowed very limited political space to demand this – the formal protections were intended to be little more than 'palliative' (Kunihara 1945: 28). The nomenclature of social justice was itself a fiction as it was applied to capital and labour as if equals in fact – in other words, as if there did not exist inequalities between them that required just interventions to correct (Kunihara 1945: 27).

In summary, before the Pacific War labour unions in the Philippines were established but industrially weak and politically marginalised. The same was true across Southeast Asia (Thompson 1945). In Dutch East India (Indonesia) in the early 1920s, the colonial authorities used repression to control labour activism. The harshness of their actions caused labour to be effectively eliminated from the anti-colonial struggle: thus, whilst 'unions continued to exist into the 1930s, their political role in the nationalist movement was largely negligible' (Hadiz 1997: 45). In Thailand in the same period, labour unions became aligned with other social forces 'intent on challenging the [then absolute] monarchy' (Brown 2004: 35). With regime change in the early 1930s there was consequently a brief period during which workers' legal rights and protections were increased; however, within a short time this favourable political space was again contracted, now by the rise of the military and anti-labour social forces (Brown 2004). There were many structural – and in some cases ethnic – factors limiting labour's emergence as a social force in capitalist Southeast Asia up to the 1940s. Nevertheless, as already indicated, critically, there were additional, political dynamics involved.

Post-war, Cold War

The Philippine political elite survived the period of Japanese occupation between 1942 and 1945. Spared the consequences of collaboration by the United States, they also benefited greatly from the aid, trade and military assistance that the United States soon provided (Simbulan 2005). The military assistance was needed to help to crush the peasant army that won favour by resisting the Japanese, but in peacetime looked to threaten the socioeconomic order that the political elite wanted restored. Rather than immediately make some reform concessions, both the elite and United States officials set about stressing the threat posed by the peasant movement, labelling it both 'dangerous and communistic' (Kerkvliet 1979: 117–18). In fact, the Partido Komunista ng

Pilipinas (PKP) – formed in 1930 – 'did not inspire or control the peasant movement' (Kerkvliet 1979: 264). In the late 1940s, the PKP moved in and out of alliance with the movement as the goals of each were 'frequently out of phase and sometimes in conflict with each other' (Kerkvliet 1979: 265). By the early 1950s the peasant rebellion was defeated.

The PKP had stronger roots in the urban labour movement yet was far from controlling that either. The Congress of Labor Organizations (CLO) – formed in 1945 – included communist officials, 'but they were by no means alone' (Kerkvliet 1992: 112). The CLO fractured internally over ideological differences in 1950, the government then dealing 'the fatal blow' by closing the organisation down as a 'communist front' a year later (Kerkvliet 1992). In the CLO's place, the secretary of labour sponsored a rival federation under his direct control (Wurfel 1959). This was heralded as a high point of state intervention in the Philippine labour movement. Whilst the government's powers were not formally greater than they had been before the Pacific War, the same powers were now used more often and discriminately, for example to deregister the unions considered subversive (Wurfel 1959).

Significantly, after leftist forces in the movement had been appreciably defeated, the political space for labour organising was formally transformed with the introduction of enterprise-based, employer–employee bargaining under the Industrial Peace Act of 1953. Earlier, a United States crisis mission to the Philippines had recommended there be greater 'freedom' from state intervention in industrial relations. The change originated from this, but there was also no domestic political opposition strong enough to scuttle it. Elite interests generally did not consider it a threat, given the weakened state of labour organising. Some of the stronger, conservative unions also 'thought they could do better with bargaining' (Shalom 1986: 134) – and the whole labour movement wanted to limit the powers of the secretary of labour.

Under the new Industrial Peace Act, the role of the old industrial relations court changed from dispute resolution to law enforcement (Ramos 1990). Union registration requirements were retained but made less onerous and less discretionary. The number of authorised unions increased thereafter, directly as a result of these procedural changes rather than a substantive improvement in labour's organising capacities (Wurfel 1959). But, without proper state enforcement of workers' rights and protections, matters of union recognition and harassment were effectively shifted from the state to employers. Consequently, the actual political space for labour organising in the Philippines in the 1950s and 1960s was 'not changed as sharply as a reading of the Industrial Peace Act alone would indicate' (Wurfel 1959: 605). In the lead-up to martial law, most unions 'did not in fact conform to a model of labor relations based on collective bargaining' (Snyder and Nowak 1982: 48–53). Only a minority of unions had successfully negotiated collective bargaining agreements and the majority of these agreements delivered no more than was already the legal minimum (Snyder and Nowak 1982). At the same time, most of the cases before the industrial relations court involved employers' breaches of the law with respect to recognition of workers' rights of association (Wurfel 1959). Thus, enterprise unionism was – and continues to be – as much an achievement of labour organising as a space for organising that is simply guaranteed by law.

Liberal modernisation theorists expect and prefer that labour organising will unfold in accordance with the growing social pluralism of industrialising societies. Thus they consider this organising will take the form of trade unions whose reason for existence is the collective interests of their members, strictly as workers (Martin 1989). In line with this thinking, industrial relations theorists in the post-war period often compared the goals and strategies of 'economic unionism' with the aberrant broader, social change goals of 'political unionism'. In the 1950s and 1960s, the relative prevalence of political unionism in developing countries was variously explained by: colonisation and labour's involvement in attendant nationalist struggles;

industrialisation and modern-state formation being in their early stages; and structural conditions weakening labour industrially (Sharma 1985). However, during the Cold War, modernisation theory conceptions of the legitimate form of labour organising were also ideological justifications for the favoured treatment of 'economic' modes of organising that were perceived as not threatening the established order. There was extensive US funding of labour education in the 1950s and 1960s to explicitly promote economic unionism over other forms (Shalom 1986). Notably, in the 1970s, during martial law, this extended to assistance to the government-sponsored Trade Union Congress of the Philippines (TUCP).

Nevertheless, in the 1950s and 1960s the political space for labour organising in the Philippines was also shaped by ideological and leadership divisions within the movement itself. To the extent that there was in fact a movement, it was beleaguered by 'constantly shifting alignments, affiliations and disaffiliations' (Carroll 1961: 244–5). Under law, unions formed at the enterprise level but were able to federate and/or directly join a peak labour centre. Historically, this happened haphazardly, mostly around the career interests of particular leaders as against the logic of trade or industry organising (Kimura 1990). Heavy reliance on the old industrial relations court had meant that, following independence, many of the labour leaders were not originally workers who had advanced through the ranks of their organisations, but rather 'outside' lawyers who took up their positions as the legal advocate of groups of workers. Accordingly, the federations they established were run to all intents and purposes as their own firms, with all the resulting concerns not to lose fee-paying clients to competitors.

In a patronage-based polity, it was also good for business for the labour lawyer leaders to participate politically via their own personal links with a range of state officials and politicians (Snyder and Nowak 1982). In elections they would thus commonly endorse a number of different party candidates to be sure to increase the likelihood of ending up on the winning side (Kimura 1990). Sometimes individual leaders also ran as independents or 'guest candidates' of major parties; however, very few were ever successful in provincial and national contests (Snyder and Nowak 1982; Kimura 1990). This shows that, whilst there were labour leaders with links into the political mainstream, none were in fact able to mobilise a significant labour vote. As such, prior to the declaration of martial law in 1972, Snyder and Nowak argue that 'political unionism with broad and long-range ideological goals was simply not in evidence' (Snyder and Nowak 1982: 46) in the Philippines. As we will soon see, from the late 1960s there was renewed communist activism: however, this did not have a significant labour presence until the 1980s.

In Indonesia after the Pacific War, there was a resurgence of labour organising in the context of heightened nationalist struggles. Even given these radical tendencies, Hadiz maintains that 'the political environment was highly favourable for organised labour' (Hadiz 1997: 46) in the early post-colonial period. However, in the course of the 1950s 'the tide distinctly turned' (Hadiz 1997: 39) as state power was consolidated behind social forces opposing radical labour and through the military. In the mid 1960s, the suppression of communism was more lasting than in the Philippines, clearing the way for the shift to 'exclusionary corporatist' modes of control under President Suharto (Hadiz 1997). In Singapore, the political marginalisation of communist forces was not as bloody but still no less complete. Communist trade unionists were members of the People's Action Party (PAP) when it took power in an election in 1959; but within two years they had split from it, leaving the Lee Kuan Yew faction to establish a 'one-party state' (Rodan 1989: 53–72). State powers were then used against independent labour activism, such that by the mid 1960s 'militant trade unionism was finished in Singapore' (Rodan 1989: 93) – the political space for organising being thereafter limited to corporative structures of the state.

In the Philippines in the late 1960s, communist forces were expanding via the recruitment of a new generation of nationalist, often young student, activists. In 1968 when some of these activists broke from the PKP to form the new Communist Party of the Philippines (CPP), they were particularly condemnatory of the parliamentary struggle (Weekley 2001). In the same period Catholic and Protestant religious leaders were also stepping up community organising among the rural and urban poor. On the industrial front, strikes were more frequent, but were again more reflective of mounting economic grievances than an indicator of growing labour movement strength (Snyder and Nowak 1982). Under these circumstances – and approaching the end of his constitutional time-limit in office – President Marcos declared martial law in 1972.

Authoritarianism and export-oriented industrialisation

In line with the spread of authoritarian rule, in capitalist Southeast Asia over the 1960s and 1970s there emerged a group of state-sponsored labour centres with a monopoly on political access through corporatist and tripartite channels. Compared to pluralist modes of representation, in which a range of interest groups act autonomously to pressure the state, corporatism institutionalises the incorporation of privileged groups into policy-making processes. In short, it is deliberately 'geared to facilitate the control and demobilisation of society-based organisations and movements' (Hadiz 1997: 27).

In the Philippines, following the declaration of martial law, there was direct control of labour's collective activism by the state. For example, the right to strike was initially withdrawn completely. Although subsequently the ban applied only to 'vital industries', in other areas there were additions to the process of applying for the right to lawfully strike, making it more onerous, leaving workers unprotected from employer harassment for a longer period. Compulsory arbitration of industrial disputes was re-introduced through the establishment of a new National Labor Relations Commission (NLRC) with powers exceeding those of the old industrial relations court that existed prior to the Industrial Peace Act of 1953. Enterprise unionism was retained, yet significant sectors of the waged labour force – including all those employed in the public sector – were barred from union membership. What is more, unfair labour practices (union busting) were downgraded from a criminal to an administrative offence (Villegas 1988).

Significantly, however, sections of the existing, anti-communist labour leadership were politically incorporated through tripartite decision-making in the public agencies that covered industrial disputes, wage setting, employment and training, and social security. After the Employer Confederation of the Philippines (ECOP) was formed, officials from the more conservative federations were generally keen to establish a counterpart labour body – the Trade Union Congress of the Philippines (TUCP). In the end, not all these labour leaders brought their federations into the TUCP – and some withdrew shortly thereafter – so the body did not in fact unite the non-leftist blocs in the labour movement. Nevertheless, whilst the federations remaining independent were still allowed to operate, the TUCP 'enjoyed privileges not available to other federations' (Institute for Labor Studies 1989: 11). The mode of incorporation of anti-communist labour leaders was consistent with Marcos's more general concern to strengthen his political control through centralising patronage resources (Hutchcroft 2010). The spoils for labour were relatively minor but they did ensure a period of loyalty that bolstered his regime's legitimacy internationally.

Dependency theorists explain the imposition of tighter, often corporatist-style state controls over labour as an effort to secure a cheap and compliant workforce for foreign investment and export competitiveness (Crowther 1986; Villegas 1988). As such, they see a direct, causal connection between the export-oriented industrialisation (EOI) and state repression of labour organising. Yet, in countries like the Philippines, Indonesia and Singapore, we have seen that state formation followed the path of labour containment before EOI strategies were introduced. Moreover, the motivation was political and not tied to a particular national development strategy. That, in the Singapore case most particularly, the earlier political controls came 'to fuse nicely' (Rodan 1989: 84) with the later requirements of EOI does not alter this fact. We have seen that, in the Philippines, despite some growing activism in the late 1960s, the labour movement remained weak and incapable of making the sort of wage demands that would seriously threaten employers and investors (Snyder and Nowak 1982). Indeed, the Marcos regime was not unambiguously behind an EOI strategy anyway: the presidential cronies had interests in virtually all sectors of the economy except export manufacturing – the sector the regime was supposed to favour (Snow 1983: 33). On the other hand, EOI expanded manufacturing and brought new entrants into the urban workforce. Dependency theorists widely portray women workers in export factories as the hapless victims of EOI, but through the 1980s and 1990s they were often an important source of independent labour organising in the Philippines and Indonesia (Hadiz 1997; Hutchison 2001). Nevertheless, the perception of foreign dominance of the economy was a strong element in leftist organising.

In 1980, a new national labour centre, the Kilusang Mayo Uno (May First Movement, KMU), was formed. It was a part of the legal movement that was nevertheless linked to the CPP and National Democratic Front (NDF).[3] In addition to organising within the formal arena of enterprise bargaining, the KMU sought to overcome the strictures of this by building *alyansas* (alliances) to connect unionised workers with non-unionised workers and community supporters around specific actions. Legally, these *alyansas* could not act as a bargaining unit; they nevertheless often *de facto* performed this function by intensifying the pressure on employers in a particular location, industry or firm (King 1985). However, militancy is never a guarantee of industrial strength. The KMU also raided rival unions for members and their disposition towards strike action did not mean that the outcomes were necessarily good for the workers concerned – if employers retaliated by relocating, striking workers could simply lose their jobs (King 1985; Hutchison 2001). The structural conditions for collective organising were prohibitive, no matter what the ideological orientation of leaders. Half the workforce was not in wage labour and many who were worked in small and micro enterprises and/or had only temporary or seasonal employment contracts. Further, from the mid 1970s there was a surge in the number of male and female Filipino workers finding contract employment overseas, in Asia, the Middle East, the United States and Europe.

Nevertheless, the KMU's militancy was an important spearhead in the political opposition to Marcos during the 1980s. Its radicalism achieved greater social legitimacy in the midst of the broader challenges to authoritarianism than it did after the restoration of democracy (West 1997). When the KMU did not abate its social and political disruption objectives, it became significantly marginalised and eventually split acrimoniously in the early 1990s.

Democratisation

Transitions to democracy generally entail greater labour activism, in association with broader social mobilisations (Valenzuela 1989). However, as Valenzuela further explains, labour's future political position relies in part on the leaders' own preparedness and capacity to show restraint to avoid additional disruption. This is not only further contingent upon labour's unity and strength; it also depends upon the political inclinations of other leading social forces behind the transition

(Valenzuela 1989). For a brief period before and after the fall of Marcos, the Philippine labour movement was relatively more politically unified as, on the one hand, the radical left was drawn closer into the mainstream and, on the other hand, its opponents in the TUCP were able to remain in the mainstream by adroitly switching their political allegiances.

Without a doubt, martial law grew the political influence of the CPP and NDF. This was 'the biggest, best-organized, and most militant force within the broad anti-Marcos movement' (Quimpo 2008: 58–9). As we have seen, on the labour front the KMU was an important part of this. However, by the mid 1980s, most of the TUCP affiliate federations had also joined the social opposition to the Marcos regime. When the regime fell in early 1986, the TUCP leaders were thus ready, despite regime change, to position themselves to retain their privileges through state incorporation, especially as the KMU remained committed to further radical change.

The new Aquino administration initially established a forum through which labour broadly could be consulted. Within months, however, the political space for radical socioeconomic agendas was narrowing significantly. In May 1987, leftist candidates were 'badly thrashed' in the first national elections post-Marcos as much of the traditional political elite were returned to their dominant position in Congress (Quimpo 2008: 59). In the same year, the KMU held several successful 'people's strikes' and there was an increase granted in the official minimum wage. However, by October President Aquino was committing publicly to a further crackdown on labour militancy. In 1989, a second official minimum wage rise was achieved, but immediately the national political space for labour activism over wages was effectively closed by the process of wage setting being devolved to regional boards. Notably, amendments to the Marcos Labor Code – sponsored by a former TUCP leader, now Senator – were directed mainly at containing labour militancy. There were extensions of the right to freedom of association to groups of workers previously excluded – for example in the public sector. However, no easing of the procedures for union registration and undertaking protected strike action has left workers still very vulnerable to employer harassment.

National democrats had 'played a critical role in the restoration of democracy in 1986' (Quimpo 2008: 75). Paradoxically, this achievement came to expose the 'undemocratic features' of the CPP movement (Quimpo 2008: 75–8). Whilst the party leadership was still focused on the seizure of state power, other progressive groups were prepared to go down the path of policy and legal reform, in and through the spaces denoted as 'civil society'. This produced internal divisions in the CPP that were also reflected in the KMU splitting in 1992. To this day, the CPP cadres retain a capacity for organising that generally exceeds that of other progressive groups; however, its vanguardist stance is a barrier to the formation of a Philippine broad left (Quimpo 2009: 350).[4] Within the labour movement, the CPP-aligned elements are still estranged from their social democratic counterparts. In other words, in the post-Marcos era the political space for labour organising has remained tightly contained. On the one hand, this is because polity has retained critical features from the American period which are an obstacle to reform (Hutchcroft 2010). On the other hand, however, this is also because divisions on the left have contributed to the continued 'segmented collectivism' of progressive organising which act as a barrier to interest aggregation politically (Roberts 1998: 54). This has been amplified by the party-list mode of political participation. Since 1998, under this system, 20 per cent of House of Representatives seats are allocated to the representatives of marginalised social sectors on a proportional voting basis. Party candidates must secure a certain portion of the total vote to be successful, but also a concomitant limit on the number of winnable seats has encouraged the proliferation of parties from the same bloc. Indeed, the very principle of sectoral party representation is a barrier to the development of progressive mass parties. The major labour groupings have their own party-list party (or two); however, the conservative ones are yet to win a seat.

The TUCP has survived as the peak labour confederation. Caraway (2008) argues that, in addition to the inherited advantages that such a body possesses – in terms of membership, resources and institutional openings – the officials' capacity to forge political links with the new regime and 'the quality of competing unions' are important survival factors. On the TUCP leadership's part, they have always tended to favour political incorporation through established channels. This is shown in the pragmatism of their adaptation to political regimes of different types. However, it needs to be stressed that labour's political incorporation in the post-Marcos era has been limited essentially to individual leaders' participation as labour representatives in a large number of tripartite and multi-sectoral bodies. Not only have TUCP officials continued to have a stranglehold on these positions, their selection and appointment have lacked transparency as there are very few stipulated rules and procedures around nomination and selection, divestment requirements, salaries and other benefits, term limits and so on (Institute for Labor Studies 2004). What is more, there is little or no accountability to the individual's organisation: no reporting back requirements are in existence and there are no set standards by which performance in the position can be assessed (Institute for Labor Studies 2004).

Post-Marcos, the mode of labour's state incorporation is selective in fostering the monopoly position of one labour grouping. It is also overtly demobilising. The tripartite structure of the channels of participation mean the state is only committed to acting on the decisions on which both labour *and employer* participants are in agreement. It is significant that the TUCP is not able to exert any influence over congressional debates and legislative reform. This again reveals that the leadership is not able to mobilise a labour vote.

In Indonesia, the 1998 fall of Suharto saw the dissolution of state corporatism. New labour laws allowed for independent unionism, but at the enterprise level, thus encouraging persistent fragmentation (Caraway 2006). There was a resultant 'explosion' in the number of independent trade unions, yet their actual worker coverage 'remains negligible' (Ford 2009: 161–4). The coincidence of regime change and a major economic crisis increased labour's organising difficulties due to rises in unemployment and informal employment. The government-sponsored peak body split and was reorganised, but remains the largest and 'most widely recognised confederation internationally' (Ford 2009: 165–6). The leftist grouping is more marginalised. Labour's collective activism has 'not threatened to become the basis of stronger coalitions with more than a limited section of the middle class opposition' (Robison and Hadiz 2004: 135). This has diminished the political space for progressive and 'more radical' political projects of reform (Robison and Hadiz 2004). As a result, Indonesian workers 'have continued to organize under difficult conditions – ... without much recourse to broader political alliances' (Robison and Hadiz 2004: 138).

Democratisation in Thailand has similarly seen labour politically marginalised and in a weakened position industrially. From 2001 to 2006, the government of Prime Minister Thaksin Shinawatra worked to maintain 'the political subordination of labour, while also mobilizing workers and their organisations behind the restructuring of Thailand's economic and political regime of accumulation' (Brown and Hewison 2005: 354). A new social contract was developed that addressed employment and training matters and unemployment benefits to ameliorate some of labour's concerns. Reforms to the labour ministry also aimed to improve services to workers, both locally and overseas. However, critically, these new political openings are designed to rule out collective activism (Brown 2007). Since Thaksin's ousting, royalist, business and middle-class forces have sought to marginalise the rural poor and urban working classes further (Hewison 2007).

Globalisation

Globalisation has produced significant economic restructuring across Southeast Asia for some time. For labour, a current key concern is an associated increase in the contractualisation of employment leading to larger numbers of temporary, casual and self-employed workers who are not covered by rights of association laws or otherwise are difficult to organise (Sibal *et al.* 2008; Chang 2009). The growth in contracting out, for example, means that many of the 'functions and services previously handled directly by corporations have been transferred to the self-employed' (Chang 2009: 172) causing labour controls to shift from industrial law to commercial agreements. Otherwise, changes to global trade rules have affected industrial and employment structures, most obviously in the garment and textile industry with the end of preferential market access under the Multi-Fibre Agreement (MFA) (Ofreneo 2009). As well, since the late 1990s, regional and global financial crises have in general pushed labour onto the industrial back foot, in an attempt to preserve jobs and or legal entitlements (Brown and Hewison 2005).

We have seen that dependency theorists see a direct causal connection between export-oriented growth and foreign investment and a national regime of tight labour controls. I have already noted that this overlooks the political history of state–labour relations in Southeast Asia. However, it is also worth noting that control regimes linked to globalisation and contemporary restructuring in fact exist 'at multiple scales' and involve various public and private actors (Kelly 2001: 2). In the Philippines, these include: 'village, municipal, provincial, and national governments; the families of workers; industrial estate managers; and recruitment agencies' (Kelly 2001: 2; also McKay 2006). This reflects the enduring territorial dispersal of state power as much as the processes of formal administrative decentralisation since the early 1990s (Hutchcroft 2010).[5]

Globalisation has nevertheless also further opened up some possible transnational political spaces for labour organising and advocacy. Since the 1990s, this has been facilitated particularly by links and alliances with labour NGOs, both domestic and international. A number of related campaigns have invoked media scrutiny and new trade rules to force governments to adopt and/or properly enforce the International Labour Organisation (ILO) conventions in particular. In Thailand in the early 2000s, for example, there were 'concerns expressed by some politicians, people and officials [that] Thailand's poor record on labour standards could negatively impact on foreign investment and access to developed country markets' (Brown and Hewison 2005: 368). However, the resultant reforms paid more attention to child labour than to freedom of association and collective bargaining rights for workers in general (Brown and Hewison 2005). In Indonesia, ILO pressure was also brought to bear in influencing the direction of post-Suharto era labour laws (Caraway 2006). In the Philippines as well, labour federations have lobbied the ILO over government violations of freedom of association and collective bargaining conventions and related human rights abuses. In all those cases, the carrot of securing trade preferences into the US market was an important influence on government decision-making.

However, in the last twenty years, transnational campaigns have also moved from 'regulation by ILO convention' – targeting national governments – to governance via codes of conduct targeting the reputation risks from adverse publicity for firms and industries (Hassel 2008). These private governance regimes are generally developed, monitored and enforced by NGOs and businesses for the purpose of influencing consumer and investment behaviours directly, as a part of wider corporate social responsibility (CSR) agendas (Hassel 2008).[6] The debate centres then on the quality of monitoring and enforcement. Berik and van der Meulen Rodgers (2010) argue that, in Cambodia, trade incentives produced better monitoring and 'modest' improvements in working conditions in the garments industry but also undermined union organisation and ignored political violence against union leaders. They maintain that this link was crucial and superior to alternative systems, which lacked a link to preferential trade. However, in the shrinking Philippine garments and textile industry, there is little evidence that similar corporate social responsibility campaigns have had any impact; most particularly failing to shift anti-union strategies of firms in the industry (Ofreneo 2009). There is also no impact on the non-tradable sectors.

Responding to their own parlous state, a number of labour federations and centres in the Philippines have turned to 'social movement unionism' as a strategy to organise the unorganised in the workforce – informal, contract and domestic workers who sit outside the formal definition of employer–employee relationship in industrial relations law (Aganon et al. 2008). However, based on different ideological orientations, there is significant variance in the ways in which the strategy is actually conceptualised and applied. For conservative groupings this has involved a focus on the provision of alternative livelihoods, through cooperatives, micro-credit and small enterprise development. Social democratic unions, on the other hand, tend to have a clearer view of social movement unionism as a vehicle of mass mobilisation for achieving broader 'social transformation' (Aganon et al. 2008: 33). In short, in different ways across the labour movement, there are attempts to forge new spaces for organising beyond the industrial relations system. This is simply because, by the formal standards of this system, labour organising is at historical lows. There is some growth in the number of registered unions, but worker coverage is declining. By the measure of having negotiated a collective bargaining agreement, only 2 per cent of the workforce is effectively organised – and then most of these agreements deliver little more than is already the legal minimum (DOLE 2009).

Conclusion

As this chapter shows, in the case of the Philippines, during the course of early modern-state formation, certain patterns of political accommodation and conflict were established which, despite significant capitalist development and regime change since, have contributed strongly to labour's relative weakness as a key social actor to the present day. Rather than attempt to mobilise labour support, in different ways, emerging elites moved to contain the disruptive potential of workers' collective activism. As this occurred in association with wider limitations on social representation and dissent, parliamentary oppositions did not emerge to reflect socioeconomic cleavages more broadly within the polity. In short, although I have acknowledged the often adverse structural conditions for labour organising, the focus of the chapter has been on labour politics in relation to struggles for state power and recognition. The formal political spaces for labour organising have been especially covered, but from the perspective of how they in fact operate: to sanction and protect – or to frustrate and proscribe – particular expressions of worker discontent. Accordingly, attention has also been paid to ideological and career leadership divisions within the movement, and how these have in turn shaped the political spaces for state incorporation on the one hand and independent militancy on the other. The point has been to argue that state formation processes are integral to the issue of labour's comparative weakness in Southeast Asia.

Notes

1 Structural constraints are very much shared at the enterprise level. Thus, the differences in the outcomes from local organising by rival federations are often not as great as their rhetoric suggests (see Hutchison 2001: 77–8). Note, there are currently about ten competing national labour centres and 130 federations covering 70 per cent of local unions in the Philippines (DOLE 2009).

2 Property, literacy and sex limitations on the franchise kept the electorate to less than 3 per cent of the population. 'Even three years after the elimination of the property qualification in 1916, the electorate was less than seven per cent of the population' (Simbulan 2005: 42). The politically active labour leaders were not from the rank-and-file; some were indeed factory owners and employers (Kerkvliet 1992).

3 The NDF is the revolutionary grouping within the broader national democratic movement. It consists of the CPP and its allied organisations, both in the underground and in legal arenas (Quimpo 2008: 58).

4 This is demonstrated in the party-list election results for National Democratic parties such as Bayan Muna.

5 See also Sidel (1999) on 'bossism' in the Philippines.

6 Private governance is 'market based, based on incentives and information rather than prohibitions, largely voluntary, carried out in a number of partially overlapping networks that consist of public policies and civil society organizations (CSOs), and in cooperation with business' (Hassel 2008: 233).

References

Aganon, M.E., M.R. Serrano, R.C. Mercado and R.A. Certeza (2008) *Revitalizing Philippine Unions: Potentials and Constraints to Social Movement Unionism*, Philippines: Friedrich Ebert Stiftung and University of the Philippines School of Labor and Industrial Relations.

Berik, G. and Y. van der Meulen Rodgers (2010) 'Options for enforcing labour standards: lessons from Bangladesh and Cambodia', *Journal of International Development* 22: 56–85.

Brown, A. (2004) *Labour, Politics and the State in Industrializing Thailand*, London and New York: Routledge Curzon.

——(2007) 'Labour and modes of participation in Thailand', *Democratization* 14 (2): 816–33.

Brown, A. and K. Hewison (2005) 'Economics is the deciding factor': labour politics in Thaksin's Thailand', *Pacific Affairs* 78 (3): 353–74.

Caraway, T. (2006) 'Freedom of association: battering ram or Trojan Horse?' *Review of International Political Economy* 13 (2): 210–32.

——(2008) 'Explaining the dominance of legacy unions in new democracies: comparative insights from Indonesia', *Comparative Political Studies* 41 (10): 1371–97.

Carroll, J. (1961) 'Philippine labor unions', *Philippine Studies* 9 (2): 220–54.

Chang, D. (2009) 'Informalising labour in Asia's global factory', *Journal of Contemporary Asia* 39 (2): 161–79.

Collier, R.B. and D. Collier (2002) *Shaping the Political Arena: Critical Junctures, the Labor Movement and Regime Dynamics in Latin America*, Notre Dame, IN: University of Notre Dame Press.

Crowther, W. (1986) 'Philippine authoritarianism and the international economy', *Comparative Politics* 18 (3): 339–55.

Department of Labor and Employment (DOLE) (2009) *Bureau of Labor and Employment Statistics*, July, Manila: DOLE.

Deyo, F.C. (2006) 'South-East Asian industrial labour: structural demobilisation and political transformation', in G. Rodan, K. Hewison and R. Robison (eds) *The Political Economy of South-East Asia: Markets, Power and Contestation*, Melbourne and New York: Oxford University Press, pp. 283–304.

Ford, M. (2009) *Workers and Intellectuals: NGOs, Trade Unions and the Indonesian Labour Movement*, Singapore: NUS Press.

Hadiz, V.R. (1997) *Workers and the State in New Order Indonesia*, London and New York: Routledge.

Hassel, A. (2008) 'The evolution of a global labor governance regime', *Governance: An International Journal of Policy, Administration, and Institutions* 21 (2): 231–151.

Hewison, K. (2007) 'Constitutions, regimes and power in Thailand', *Democratization* 14 (2): 928–45.

Hutchcroft, P.D. (2010) 'Dreams of redemption: localist strategies of political reform in the Philippines' in Y. Kasuya and N.G. Quimpo (eds) *The Politics of Change in the Philippines*, Manila: Anvil, pp. 418–54.

Hutchison, J. (2001) 'Export opportunities: unions in the Philippine garments industry', in J. Hutchison and A. Brown (eds) *Organising Labour in Globalising Asia*, New York and London: Routledge, pp. 71–89.

Institute for Labor Studies (1989) *Situationer on the Philippine Trade Union Movement*, Manila: Department of Labor and Employment.

——(2004) *Labor Representation in Government Institutions in the Philippines*, Manila: Department of Labor and Employment.

Kelly, P.F. (2001) 'The political economy of local labor control in the Philippines', *Economic Geography* 77 (1): 1–22.

Kerkvliet, B.J. (1979) *The Huk Rebellion: A Study of Peasant Revolt in the Philippines*, Quezon City: New Day Publishers.

Kerkvliet, M.T. (1992) *Manila Workers' Unions, 1900–1950*, Quezon City: New Day Publishers.

Kimura, M. (1990) 'Philippine peasant and labor organizations in electoral politics: players of transitional politics', *Pilipinas* 14 (Spring): 29–78.

King, A. (1985) 'A confused state of industrial relations', *Philippine Journal of Industrial Relations* 7 (1–2): 81–91.

Kunihara, K.K. (1945) *Labor in the Philippine Economy*, Stanford, CA: Stanford University Press.

McKay, S.C. (2006) 'The squeaky wheel's dilemma: new forms of labor organizing in the Philippines', *Labor Studies Journal* 30 (4): 41–63.

Martin, R.M. (1989) *Trade Unionism: Purposes and Forms*, Oxford: Clarendon Press.

Ofreneo, R. (2009) 'Development choices for Philippine textiles and garments in the post-MFA era', *Journal of Contemporary Asia* 39 (4): 543–61.

Quimpo, N.G. (2008) *Contested Democracy and the Left in the Philippines*, Monograph 58, New Haven, CT: Yale University Southeast Asian Studies.

——(2009) 'The Philippines: predatory regime, growing authoritarian features', *The Pacific Review* 22 (3): 335–53.

Ramos, E.T. (1990) *Dualistic Unionism and Industrial Relations*, Quezon City: New Day Publishers.

Roberts, K.M. (1998) *Deepening Democracy? The Modern Left and Social Movements in Chile and Peru*, Stanford, CA: Stanford University Press.

Robison, R. and V.R. Hadiz (2004) *Reorganising Power in Indonesia: The Politics of Oligarchy in an Age of Markets*, London and New York: Routledge.

Rodan, G. (1989) *The Political Economy of Singapore's Industrialization: National State and International Capital*, Basingstoke: Macmillan.

Shalom, S.R. (1986) *The United States in the Philippines: A Study of Neocolonialism*, Quezon City: New Day Publishers.

Sharma, B. (1985) *Aspects of Industrial Relations in ASEAN*, Occasional Paper No. 78, Singapore: Institute of Southeast Asian Studies.

Sibal, J.V., M.S.V. Amante and M.C. Tolentino (2008) 'The Philippines: changes at the workplace', in S. Lee and F. Eyraud (eds) *Globalization, Flexibilization and Working Conditions in Asia and the Pacific*, Geneva: International Labour Office and Oxford: Chandos Publishing, pp. 279–312.

Sidel, J. T. (1999) *Capital, Coercion, and Crime: Bossism in the Philippines*, Stanford, CA: Stanford University Press.

Simbulan, D.C. (2005) *The Modern Principalia: The Historical Evolution of the Philippine Ruling Oligarchy*, Quezon City: University of the Philippines Press.

Sinay-Aguilar, M.V. (1990) 'Regional wage fixing and labor in the context of Philippine development', *Philippine Journal of Labor and Industrial Relations* 12 (1): 8–15.

Snow, R. (1983) *The Bourgeois Opposition to Export-Orientated Industrialization in the Philippines*, Third World Center Papers no. 39, Quezon City: University of the Philippines.

Snyder, K.A. and T.C. Nowak (1982) 'Philippine labor before martial law: threat or non-threat? Studies', *Comparative International Development* 17 (3–4): 44–72.

Thompson, V. (1945) 'Labor organization in Southeast Asia', *Far Eastern Survey* 14 (8): 101–3.

Trade Union Congress of the Philippines (TUCP) (1987) 'Trade Union Congress of the Philippines (TUCP): an organizational profile', unpublished memo, TUCP, Manila.

Valenzuela, J.S. (1989) 'Labor movements in transitions to democracy: a framework for analysis', *Comparative Politics*, July: 445–72.

Villegas, E.M. (1988) *The Political Economy of Philippine Labor Laws*, Quezon City: Foundation for Nationalist Studies.

Weekley, K. (2001) *The Communist Party of the Philippines 1968–93: A Story of its Theory and Practice*, Quezon City: University of the Philippines Press.

West, L.A. (1997) *Militant Labor in the Philippines*, Philadelphia, PA: Temple University Press.

Woodiwiss, A. (1998) *Globalisation, Human Rights and Labour Law in Pacific Asia*, Cambridge, New York and Melbourne: Cambridge University Press.

Wurfel, D. (1959) 'Unions and labor policy in the Philippines', *Industrial and Labor Relations Review* 12 (4): 582–608.

4

OLIGARCHS AND OLIGARCHY IN SOUTHEAST ASIA

Jeffrey A. Winters

This chapter examines a set of cases in Southeast Asia from the perspective of oligarchs and oligarchy. It should be noted at the outset that an emphasis on the power and influence of small groups at the top of a social formation does not deny the power of other actors, nor imply that social mobilization is pointless or that electoral democracy is a sham. It is, rather, a recognition that certain extreme concentrations of minority power in society can exist under a variety of regimes ranging from authoritarian to democratic. Oligarchic power in advanced industrial contexts, for instance, is almost universally fused to procedural democracy. Although it is impossible to focus on all the cases in the region of Southeast Asia, Indonesia, the Philippines, and Singapore have been selected for the ways in which they help develop oligarchic theory and for how the theory helps illuminate important aspects of the cases. We begin with a brief discussion of oligarchs and oligarchy, since the terms are widely used but also highly muddled conceptually.[1]

Following Aristotle (1996 [350 BCE]), many misinterpret oligarchy simply to mean rule by the few, as opposed to by the one or the many. But for Aristotle, oligarchs were not just any powerful "few." His definition was materialist, not numerical. He was referring specifically to the wealthy, who happen always to be the few.[2] From Aristotle's time until the rise of the modern state, oligarchs played a direct role in ruling—including when only one unusually dominant oligarch from among their ranks held the highest formal position of power. In addition to focusing specifically on the power of wealth, the theory of oligarchy also emphasizes the political challenges associated with concentrating so many resources in the hands of so few against so many. Wealth throughout history has always attracted threats, whether from below, laterally from other oligarchs, or from organized states once these emerged apart from direct oligarchic rule. The politics of oligarchy is the politics of wealth defense that inevitably accompanies extreme material stratification.

Oligarchic theory is most useful when it is focused on the material power resources of *individuals*.[3] It does not refer to the power of institutionalized collectivities such as corporations, and is not limited to any time period or mode of production, such as modern capitalism.[4] It is also important not to confuse oligarchs with elites. Like oligarchs, elites can exercise minority influence over societies. But their power resources are not material. Elites have highly concentrated power at the individual level based on such power resources as official position, coercive power, and mobilizational capacities. Oligarchic power is distinct because it is materially based. Oligarchs can sometimes blend their material power with other power resources (such as high political office), making them simultaneously oligarchs and elites. But pure elites lack material power resources they can deploy personally. Corrupt elites who use their government positions to amass large personal fortunes can certainly become oligarchs by virtue of their new-found material power. But they were simply elites until they became personally wealthy. Oligarchs might be entrepreneurs, but neither in the contemporary period nor throughout history is this a requirement. Individuals who control massive resources by virtue of their official positions (in corporations, government ministries, or large organizations) are not oligarchs. Take away the positions and the resources disappear as well.

Oligarchs are defined in a way that is constant across history. Those with significant fortunes have always been uniquely empowered. But they have also been uniquely threatened because of their wealth. Oligarchy is not simply a collection of oligarchs. If the definition of oligarchs is constant, oligarchy is, by contrast, a highly variable phenomenon. This is because oligarchy describes *how* oligarchs in any particular context or era manage the threats to their wealth and position. In the face of chronic contestation and threats for oligarchs, their central political problem is wealth defense. There is a great deal of variation in the solutions to the wealth defense problem, and thus oligarchy assumes several forms. There are certain key factors that allow us to categorize these forms into ideal types. The first factor concerns coercion and enforcement, which lie at the base of all property claims and rights, and without which oligarchs and their fortunes could not exist. Related to this is the fact that coercion can be supplied individually or collectively, personally or impersonal-bureaucratically. This yields four basic forms of oligarchy throughout history—warring, ruling, sultanistic, and civil.[5] All of these forms have existed in Southeast Asia over the centuries, but the twentieth and twenty-first centuries have been dominated by the ruling, sultanistic, and civil forms.

The cases of Indonesia, the Philippines, and Singapore are examined in greater detail in this chapter to illustrate how these forms have been manifested in the region. Suharto in Indonesia and Marcos in the Philippines both ruled sultanistic oligarchies, but the oligarchs they dealt with were very different. There was no significant stratum of Indonesian oligarchs prior to Suharto's New Order. They arose while the dictator was in power. An electoral ruling oligarchy was established in the wake of the Suharto regime. The Philippines had a well-established stratum of oligarchs during late Spanish colonial rule. Under the Americans the oligarchs became institutionalized into an electoral ruling oligarchy. This was disrupted by Marcos's imposition of a sultanistic oligarchy. When he was overthrown, an electoral ruling oligarchy again emerged— but in a radically different form than had existed during the decades before martial law.

Singapore takes the discussion in a different direction. It is a particularly interesting case because, like the United States or Australia, it is a civil oligarchy in which the armed state and the country's legal regime defend concentrated property and wealth, while oligarchs are fully disarmed and routinely submit to the rule of law. It is uncommon to group a non-democratic country like Singapore with longstanding democracies. But this serves to underscore the point that the varying forms of oligarchy can coexist (or not) with electoral systems of government. Indonesia and the Philippines today are reasonably functioning electoral democracies. There is contestation among candidates through multiple parties, voting is secret, the press and speech are reasonably free, and the outcomes are not fully known in advance. And yet, ruling oligarchs thoroughly dominate the political processes in both cases and in neither do oligarchs submit to the rule of law. Oligarchs are more powerful than the laws, and wealth is routinely used to block or bend legal outcomes or thwart enforcement. This is a key part of wealth defense for these oligarchs.

In Singapore, virtually none of the freedoms or processes associated with democracy is present (see Rodan, this volume Chapter 8). And yet Singapore's legal system is strong and it routinely adjudicates oligarchs. The establishment of firm and impersonal legal institutions regulating property, contracts, and securing wealth is what qualifies Singapore as a civil oligarchy in the same category as the US and the UK. The case underscores the point that although civil oligarchy is fused to electoral democracy in many places, it can function over extended periods without it (just as electoral democracy captured by oligarchs can function for decades despite a weak legal regime). The only two forms of oligarchy that are absolutely incompatible with democracy are warring and sultanistic oligarchies. With these preliminary definitions and comparisons in place, the discussion now turns to a closer examination of these three cases through the lens of oligarchic theory.[6]

Indonesia

Among those with concentrated minority power, Indonesia's many local elites held positions of great influence, from the Dutch colonial period until the end of the Sukarno regime. But for centuries the archipelago had no significant stratum of oligarchs who wielded power based on their accumulated wealth. The pitched struggles in the 1950s and 1960s among party leaders with mass followings, members of the intelligentsia, religious figures, and armed actors in the military were all among elites. The Dutch had blocked the emergence of a wealthy domestic element (even among the tiny ethnic Chinese population—most of whom were well off but did not have massive fortunes), and the period from 1945 to 1965 was far too chaotic politically and economically for oligarchs to emerge, much less flex significant political muscle (Robison 2008 [1986]).

The story of oligarchy in Indonesia not only commences with the Suharto regime, but the dictator Suharto must himself be credited with creating the nation's oligarchs. It is not that Suharto necessarily intended this outcome. But it was the direct consequence of how he organized the extraction of wealth in the archipelago for purposes of strengthening and stabilizing his rule. The first decades after independence saw important developments that set the stage for the emergence of oligarchs and oligarchy in Indonesia. Three key things occurred that were to have profound consequences. First, the Java–Outer Island struggle was decisively settled in favor of Java. This meant that when oligarchs did arise, they would be entirely Java-based, and mostly in Jakarta. Had the regions won early battles for more autonomy and power-sharing with Java, the geographic spread of the nation's oligarchy would have been quite different—and it is likely a figure like Suharto would have had a harder time establishing his sultanistic rule. The oligarchs that did eventually arise seized control over skimming and extracting operations that extended across the islands, but they were never actors based in the regions in any political or economic sense.

The second development was the shifting of Dutch firms into the hands of the military and then the state as government-owned enterprises. This was significant because these firms served as important nodes of engorgement for oligarchs. And the third development was the massacre in 1965 and 1966, which set the stage for a property regime in Indonesia in which threats to oligarchs would not come from below. Instead, they would come from each other or from above—from a sultanistic figure like Suharto or from the ruling oligarchic state that operates in part on its selective predations on oligarchs.

As these important events were unfolding and the property regime in Indonesia was being shaped, there was also a process of aggressive institutional incapacitation underway. Nowhere was this more evident than in the legal infrastructure. Had Indonesia's oligarchy emerged in a context where the strength and independence of the legal institutions was high, it is much more likely that they would have been "tamed" impersonally rather than through sultanistic rule. Indonesia had the rudiments of such institutions at the end of the colonial era and for much of the first decade of independence. But they had already been severely weakened *before* Suharto came to power (Lev 1985, 2007).

When Suharto took control of the country in the closing months of 1965, the situation was fragile. President Sukarno was damaged politically. But he was not lacking in reserve capacities to mobilize an angry reaction to the military regime that was taking over in stages. In addition, there was, during the first seven to ten years of the Suharto regime, significant resistance within the armed forces that he needed to co-opt or crush. Many generals and other officers had been elevated to high positions through decisions made by Sukarno, and they were wary of the prospect of Suharto making sweeping changes that could end some careers and stall others. No one was more emblematic of this resistance than General Soemitro, who was not sidelined decisively until 1974 (Crouch 1988; Soemitro and Ramadhan 1994).

Suharto's preferred method of consolidating his power and network was to invoke the Indonesian political custom of *bagi-bagi*, which translates in this context as "sharing the spoils." During the most stable periods of oligarchy in Indonesia, the system of shared theft and enrichment has worked remarkably smoothly. Because oligarchs are disarmed and do not directly defend their wealth with coercion, accepting the norms of *bagi-bagi* has also been largely voluntary in the sense that those who become fabulously rich understand that a condition of securing property involves spreading gains to others who could be dangerous if not satiated. Suharto began the process of creating Indonesian oligarchs by bestowing opportunities for enrichment on elite figures across the armed forces, often in partnerships with ethnic Chinese entrepreneurs who had the skills to turn monopolies and concessions into cash. This was the only precarious stage in which emerging material power had any links to coercive capacities.

If the first stage in the development of Indonesia's sultanistic oligarchy was the military–Chinese phase, stretching from 1965 to 1974, the second might be termed the indigenous period. This enlargement of the oligarchic stratum involved the deliberate inclusion and enrichment of Muslim-Malay actors (*pribumi*), who had grown critical and restless because they were left out of the deals cut in the first phase. The second stage was strangely institutionalized, though not in the ordinary state-building sense of the term. It is also striking that part of Suharto's control over indigenous oligarchs was personalistic, and yet through bodies that operated semi-bureaucratically. These institutions were little more than complex extensions of Suharto's hand. Particularly prominent in this role were agencies like Bulog, Pertamina, and Team 10 operating from within the State Secretariat (Winters 1996). This gave the expansion of Indonesia's oligarchy greater institutional coherence without creating independent institutions. Suharto's dominance was never in doubt. There were countless decisions taken that were on institutional "autopilot" across the government and the archipelago, but no decisions taken at any level could stand if they conflicted with things Suharto cared about or opposed.

Suharto created this oligarchy and also ruled it as the first among the group. He had little interest in luxuries and fancy living. For him wealth was power, and he accumulated it at a furious pace as he enriched and inevitably empowered those around him. The source of wealth defense for oligarchs was Suharto himself and the coercive capacity he commanded. A politics of proximity to Suharto determined precisely how much protection and access to further wealth an oligarch could reasonably expect. The further one's proximity from the man himself, and the more layers of intermediaries through which one had to operate, the more likely it was that a larger share of one's resources would have to be expended through *bagi-bagi* to achieve a comparable degree of predictable safety. The politics of proximity also played a key role in diminishing horizontal conflicts between oligarchs. Suharto doled out benefits and punishments. He did not have to jail or execute those who displeased him. Simply cutting off access was among the harshest penalties he could inflict on an oligarch because this signaled to other oligarchs and predatory elites in the state ministries that it was open season on this individual, their family or business. While the politics of proximity mediated most politics at the upper levels of the social formation, the slaughter in the mid-1960s and the military-intelligence apparatus installed afterward muted all threats from below.

The third stage in the evolution of sultanistic oligarchy under Suharto might be termed the family phase. This began in the early 1980s, and then accelerated toward the end of the decade. The maturation of Suharto's offspring into adulthood not only commenced a new chapter in Indonesia's oligarchy, it also triggered its most radical and destabilizing transformation. When his own children began staking a claim to oligarchic wealth, and did so in a highly predatory manner, the politics of proximity changed. With it changed the calculus of wealth defense across the entire oligarchy. Suharto's key achievement, and an important element in the long-evity of his regime, was that his method of rule-by-access tamed the country's oligarchs as effectively as laws could—the system was coherent, logical, operated predictably, and had its own internal integrity and justice. Investment and growth flourished despite the absence of the rule of law. This is because oligarchs do not demand laws, only a strong system of wealth defense. Laws are but one means to achieve that outcome.

What changed with the emergence of Suharto's children was that the system of predation and recourse had been altered in ways that deeply unsettled the country's oligarchs. No existing or future oligarch could match the proximity and access of Suharto's own offspring. Their addition to the mix of Suharto's sultanistic oligarchy subverted his capacity to reliably deliver certainty of property and contract. The spirit and practice of *bagi-bagi* was being increasingly violated by Suharto's children. Most alarming of all, by the mid-1990s it had become apparent that Suharto was grooming some of his progeny for succession. For Indonesia's oligarchs, this meant that the turbulence the children were creating threatened to become a permanent fixture of the system rather than a temporary irritant.

In the 1960s and 1970s, the complaints about the country's rising oligarchy—its theft, its grabbing of the country's wealth, and the corruption that pervaded the process—came largely from without. Criticisms arose from students, intellectuals, the media, activists, and some *pribumi* players who had not yet received a share of the oligarchic largesse. But by the 1980s and with even greater force in the 1990s, the criticisms were coming from *within* Indonesia's oligarchy. An article appearing in the *New York Times* in 1990 (Erlanger 1990) was the first shot over the regime's bow. Suddenly the whispers and withering criticisms that had been heard for several years in polite oligarchic circles were splashed into the open. The article quoted a series of unnamed figures in prominent positions within Suharto's New Order—a cabinet minister, top Golkar officials—complaining about Suharto's children and asking aloud if the ageing dictator might step down in 1993. The article mentioned that even within the army, all that remained were disgruntled loyalists.

Interviews this author conducted with a range of oligarchs since the 1990s offer deeper insights into what, precisely, was so disruptive to Indonesia's oligarchy about the rise of the children. A first problem was that they fought among themselves, often involving other oligarchs in family conflicts that proved treacherous to navigate. This became a source of uncertainty, as saying "no" to Suharto's children was nearly impossible and oligarchs found themselves pulled into the fray. Many oligarchs simply tried to lie low—which contradicted the logic of the politics of proximity to Suharto himself. The family increasingly became a disruptive package deal with all former avenues of recourse blocked. A second matter was that the children took much larger cuts of deals and were directly predatory on the operations of established oligarchs. In return they offered very little. Having grown up under a system of relative peace and stability, they had no appreciation for the finer points of Indonesian *bagi-bagi*. They were spoiled, fearless, and largely incompetent, whereas their father had been hardened, shrewd, and yet cautious and systematic.

When serious problems arose for oligarchs, caused directly or indirectly by his children, the aggrieved actors did not dare complain to the father about his own kids. General Benny Moerdani, one of the most powerful military figures during the New Order, spoke directly and bluntly to Suharto about the difficulties his children were creating, and he quickly saw his power and positions cut. The signal was clear that Suharto's capacity to provide security to the oligarchs had been compromised by the onset of his children as the newest addition to their ranks. "As long as his children are not involved, the president makes very rational economic decisions," noted one cabinet minister in a 1992 interview. "But when the kids get involved, rationality loses. Then it's the father that speaks, not the president" (quoted in Schwarz 2000: 146).

When the regime was hit by a financial crisis in 1997 and 1998, it was not that the country's oligarchs overthrew Suharto politically. It was more that they and the rest of the elite visibly stood aside and withdrew support. This was a reversal of the politics of proximity that had served Suharto so well. Actors across the country's elite and oligarchy sent a signal that their commitment to Suharto was weak, and that if the rest of the family was part of the deal (which everyone understood they were), their posture was one of outright hostility. The message was not lost on activists and students who rose up to challenge the regime. The response by the once fearsome New Order apparatus was suddenly fragmented and hesitant. When Suharto handed the commander of the armed forces a signed presidential instruction empowering him to establish martial law and use any means necessary to restore order, he left it up to the general to decide if he wanted to carry out the order. The commander ignored it and Suharto stepped down within forty-eight hours (Wiranto 2003).

This prompted two transitions in Indonesia—one much commented upon and the other largely ignored. The first and most obvious was the transition from authoritarian rule to an electoral democracy. Indonesia has steadily risen in the Freedom House (www.freedomhouse.org) rankings and the country has held numerous regional and national elections which, although flawed in myriad ways, have been widely judged as free and fair. The second transition has been from a tamed to a wild oligarchy, which is a direct consequence of Suharto's fall but entirely unrelated to the rise of democracy that followed. This second transformation is in many ways as important as the first—although with decidedly negative consequences. Suharto inherited a debilitated legal system and damaged it even further during his presidency (Lev 1985, 2007; Pompe 2005). All wealth defense, as well as all order and security for oligarchs, flowed from Suharto's sultanistic rule, not from the laws. When Suharto was removed, there was a functioning electoral democracy in the sense of a system for selecting political leaders. But there was no strong, independent, or functioning legal infrastructure in place to subdue the country's powerful oligarchs—who were now quite numerous and varied in their composition (Robison and Hadiz 2004). Some were ethnic Chinese, some *pribumi*, some on Java, others based more regionally. What all of these oligarchs have in common is that they are individually and as a group more powerful than the laws and the system of legal enforcement. They are able to use their material power resources to block, deflect, or minimize the impact of the system of laws. They secure their property, contracts, and fortunes not by taking matters to court on their merits, but by spending their uniquely oligarchic resources to win conflicts—whether with actors in the state, with each other, against foreigners, or those below them (Winters 2011).

This has rendered the Indonesian political economy vastly more uncertain, and the costs to oligarchs have risen while security has declined. Much greater and more constant expenditures must be made to maintain the kind of security that was routine when Suharto served as mafia don among an array of capos and underbosses. The transformation of the oligarchy also inter-sects with the democratic transition itself. In addition to going from being tamed to untamed, the oligarchy also went from being sultanistic to a ruling oligarchy—in this instance an electoral ruling oligarchy. In the process, there was a bifurcation of roles based on race and ethnicity. *Pribumi* oligarchs, as members of the majority, not only emerged as the dominant players in the parties and in major organizations, but political positions themselves became instruments for threatening wealth and property, as well as a means of wealth and property defense.

Ethnic Chinese oligarchs, unable to defend themselves directly through rule and political positions, have been left to engage in wealth defense primarily through carefully calibrated payoffs to political actors, parties, candidates and others who could potentially cause devastating damage if not mollified with money. With no figure like Suharto to tame not just the oligarchs but powerful elites who can attack their fortunes, oligarchs now confront a torrent of predations from the police, prosecutors, judges, and other officials who are supposed to be upholding the law—but who instead treat their positions as opportunities to take a share of a now more vicious game of *bagi-bagi*. The result is "criminal democracy" in Indonesia in two senses—first, it is a robust democracy without the strong rule of law, and second, the political contestation at the heart of this vibrant democracy has been captured by oligarchs who routinely engage in corruption and other criminal acts to defend their wealth and by powerful elites who abuse their government positions in the hope of becoming major oligarchs as well.

The Philippines

Like Suharto, Ferdinand Marcos ruled over a sultanistic oligarchy in the Philippines. But his tenure in the role of sultanistic ruler was half the duration of Suharto's, and his authority from the outset was always more contested. One obvious reason for this is that Marcos did not create the stratum of oligarchs in the Philippines (though he arguably reshaped it significantly).[7] Rather, Marcos himself emerged from within an electoral ruling oligarchy that he eventually displaced and sought to dominate through the advantages of the state's coercive apparatus. There are four prominent differences between the cases of Indonesia and the Philippines. First, Marcos faced a fully matured oligarchic stratum that was based in Manila but also distributed widely across the major islands, and had been in a dominant position politically and economically for a century. Second, from the outset these ruling oligarchs played a direct role in the coercive aspects of wealth defense—particularly in the countryside. At no point from the late Spanish period forward have Filipino oligarchs ever been fully disarmed, and many retain significant private armies or can quickly hire defense and attack forces as needed.

Third is that splits among Filipino oligarchs do not follow racial or ethnic lines to the degree that Indonesian oligarchs are split as *pribumi* and ethnic Chinese. This made it harder for an outside power like the Spanish or the Americans (or Marcos) to manipulate a favored segment of the oligarchs against the rest. And finally, peasants and workers have been under almost constant attack in the Philippines. But they had never been dealt the sort of death-blow deliv-ered to mass popular forces in Indonesia in the 1960s. As a consequence, oligarchs have faced significant contestation and threats from below and they have deployed ferocious private coercion backed up by government troops and paramilitary forces.

The Philippines represents an odd combination of political violence and democratic long-evity. One of the reasons for this is that the country's ruling oligarchy channeled their domination through electoral institutions and practices founded during the American colonial period early in the twentieth century (Hutchcroft 2000). The catch was that they retained significant private

59

coercive capacities (largely in the form of personal armies) for wealth defense even as they organized their conflicts and cooperation within democratic forms. It helped that the United States upheld and enforced these institutions and practices in the formative decades. This gave electoral democracy considerable staying power after World War II as American intervention remained significant but became less direct. Ruling oligarchy in the Philippines confronted two challenges: how to manage lateral threats from semi-armed members of the oligarchy, and how to prevent the sultanistic takeover of a modern coercive state by one ambitious oligarch among the group occupying the position of president.

From ancient Athens and Rome through to the Philippines of the twentieth century, maintaining a ruling oligarchy has involved oligarchs themselves attempting to manage intra-oligarchic competition, avoiding major outbreaks of violence within the ruling stratum, keeping the power of office rotating among members of the oligarchy so that no single actor or subset can take over their collective apparatus of state, all while defending the rules and norms that make this balancing act possible. For many years, oligarchic deference to these self-imposed rules gave the appearance of the rule of law in the Philippines. But strong and impersonal legal institutions that have consistently been able to impose their will in an indifferent manner over Filipino oligarchs have never existed. There have been periods when oligarchs were tamed. During the zenith of their pre-Marcos ruling oligarchy phase they were largely self-tamed. And under Marcos they were mostly tamed by the repressive forces the dictator could unleash. But significantly, they have been untamed and unable to restore self-regulation since Marcos's overthrow.

Given the powers of modern presidents and prime ministers, oligarchic rotation is a particularly sensitive matter for electoral ruling oligarchies (Thompson 1995). A Philippine president was simultaneously commander in chief and oligarch in chief (Anderson 1988). One of the most significant indicators of effective intra-oligarchic management was the fact that presidential succession in the Philippines had always been regular and rapid. Indeed, Marcos was the first in a long line of presidents to win a second term. Oddly, this was a danger not only to the rest of the oligarchy but also to Marcos himself. Staying in office overly long afforded him more time to concentrate his power—both coercive and material. But it also made handing over power more treacherous. Succession depended vitally on an oligarch being able to leave office safely with a minimum of angry fellow oligarchs who might retaliate once the president was exposed. Both factors played a role in Marcos imposing martial law in 1972 and hanging on until he was deposed in 1986.

Had Marcos followed the single-term pattern of succession in place from Quezon in 1935 until Marcos's own election in 1965, it is unlikely anyone around the world would know his name, or that of his colorful wife Imelda. His second victory in 1969 proved to be too much for the electoral ruling oligarchy to sustain. He drew liberally and corruptly upon financial resources of the state to win, and, most ominously, he made extensive use of the coercive capacities of the Philippine armed forces and police. Marcos had alienated broad swaths of the country's oligarchy through these tactics, and he raised the dangers to himself and his corrupt family if he were to honor the law on term limits and surrender the presidency in 1973. Clinging to power increased the need to cling to power (Thompson 1995).

What changed most when Marcos imposed martial law and founded his sultanistic oligarchy was the basis of wealth defense for all oligarchs. In place of a collective ruling oligarchy that defended property and wealth through shared norms, Marcos as a sultanistic ruler amassed enough power to be able to threaten even the most wealthy and influential oligarchs in the nation (McCoy 2009). But the fact that Filipino oligarchs had been entrenched for decades, and also remained at least partially armed in the provinces, meant that Marcos faced significant contestation. He could hold most of the nation's oligarchs at bay through threats to their wealth and property—and sometimes personal threats of violence (something Suharto never did)—but he never fully subdued this stratum of society. Marcos was openly opposed by oligarchs before, during, and after his authoritarian inclinations became evident in 1969. And oligarchs played a direct and active role in his overthrow and exile to Hawaii in 1986. The fact that Suharto stepped down and quietly went home to his private residence, never fearing for his personal safety or that of his family, contrasts sharply with the risks Marcos faced when he boarded US helicopters to flee Malacañang Palace. Indonesia's oligarchs were always grateful to Suharto, their generous creator—they just did not appreciate the threats posed by the rest of his family. To resolve the problem of the children, the father had to go.

Marcos was also compelled by powerful forces at the top of society to lift martial law long before he was overthrown. The electoral challenges he faced from competing oligarchs and their party vehicles were significant during his sultanistic rule. Suharto faced no parallel electoral threats during the ritualistic voting that occurred during his thirty-two years as president. Indeed, the Golkar Party existed primarily as an organizing structure for oligarchs and patronage. And there were no oligarchs in the other parties. By contrast, Senator Benigno Aquino was easily the single most important indicator of the relentless resistance Filipino oligarchs posed to Marcos. Aquino was a strong contender for the presidency on the eve of martial law in 1972, he was arrested, sent into political exile in the US, and when he dared to return in 1983 to challenge Marcos's presidency one last time, he was shot in the head by state forces as he was escorted off a plane at Manila's international airport. Political murder was hardly new in the Philippines. It is one of the most dangerous functioning democracies on earth for political candidates—mainly because the process is a form of ordered competition among armed and wealthy oligarchs, with the degree of violence increasing the lower the level involved. But the assassination of an oligarch at Aquino's level was unprecedented and sent shockwaves throughout the polity—but especially among the most powerful. It was a step too far, and the act briefly united an otherwise fragmented stratum of oligarchs who were determined to see Marcos deposed.

The arrangements and norms of power-sharing from earlier in the century defied restoration in the decades following Marcos's overthrow. Oligarchs thoroughly dominate what has re-emerged as an electoral ruling oligarchy in the Philippines. Individuals with massive personal wealth are the prime contenders for power at all levels (or candidates of modest means are directly backed by a handful of oligarchs). But partly because Marcos activated and politicized armed forces that had been under firm civilian rule for decades, the mix of violence, coups, and the rise of elites with significant coercive power (who usually dream of becoming oligarchs) has rendered the system incapable of self-taming. And there are no powers external to the oligarchs—either sultanistic–authoritarian or impersonal–legal—to impose restraints. The result is that democracy has been restored to the Philippines, but for the first time it is dominated by a wild rather than tamed ruling oligarchy. In this sense, Indonesia and the Philippines are more similar to each other at the beginning of the twenty-first century than they have ever been in their modern histories.

Singapore

Singapore is the only civil oligarchy in Southeast Asia. The single most important factor that gives it this status is that the city-state's legal institutions and system of enforcement are stronger than its oligarchs. The hallmark of a civil oligarchy is that oligarchs are tamed by laws, not by persons. But equally important, property and wealth are also guaranteed impersonally by the same system of laws. This is the trade-off for oligarchs historically. Nowhere do laws tame oligarchs unless they also guarantee property. The conundrum for observers has been that Singapore has both the rule of law and yet remains non-democratic.

It is a case of what Jayasuriya (2002) has termed "authoritarian legalism," which is the obverse of Indonesia's criminal democracy. Authoritarian legalism is perplexing for analysts because a strong and independent judiciary is supposed to be one of the most crucial pillars of liberal freedom. It seems impossible for a single legal system to function in so bifurcated a manner. The same police, prosecutors, judges, and court rooms that reliably and fairly adjudicate matters of vital importance to oligarchs—the enforcement of property and contracts—also adjudicate politically motivated defamation cases that intimidate critical voices in the opposition. Some critics have attempted to argue that, on these grounds, judicial independence does not exist in Singapore.[8] An oligarchic perspective would lead to different conclusions and explanations for the contradiction.

Although Singapore is dominated by a large state-owned or controlled sector, the nation has long had a stratum of citizens with highly concentrated wealth—a pattern that has only intensified during the era since World War II. The average net worth of the fifty richest Singaporeans in 2009 was $977 million. Eleven of them were billionaires. The combined fortunes of the top fifty was $49 billion. Out of a population of only 4.8 million Singaporeans, this ultra-rich group at the top represents 1/1000th of 1 percent, but own 5 percent of all wealth.[9] Wealth is six times more concentrated at the top in Singapore than in the United States.[10]

Singapore has a distinction among states in that it gained full national independence by expulsion against its will.[11] It was perhaps the most unhappy independence day on record, with Prime Minister Lee Kuan Yew crying on live national television on the first evening of separation from Malaysia in 1965. It was fear for Singapore's security that made the man who would lead the country so resistant to having the island fly solo.[12] Singapore is a small enclave of predominantly ethnic Chinese citizens and small Indian and Malay minorities, with no natural resources, no countryside, and a domestic market too small to sustain the economy. The city-state was surrounded in 1965 by two far larger states, Malaysia and Indonesia, that had majority Islamic Malay populations, and both countries were hostile toward Singapore.

Singapore was a nation born into a condition of paranoia and fear, and significant external threats and dependence placed its national survival in serious doubt. This produced not only a powerful drive for what Woo (1991) writing on South Korea terms "defensive industrialization," but also operated as a strong constraining force among the most powerful strata inside Singapore itself. There were no assurances that the city-state would emerge as a hub for trade, production, and finance in Asia. In the 1950s and 1960s, the island was beset by drug operations, corruption, gambling, and deadly Triads. Oligarchs themselves were not only untamed, but faced a range of threats to property and person from violent criminal elements in society. There were more than 10,000 youths organized into 360 gangs that clashed in the streets using knives and clubs. It was not uncommon for Singaporean millionaires and their children to be kidnapped and held for large ransoms. Those who resisted or failed to pay were butchered (*Time* 1960). Singapore could easily have become a mafia-infested haven like Macao rather than a paradise for oligarchs.

The combination of domestic and external threats Singapore faced generated a posture of "total defense," which would prepare the city-state for "total war."[13] The mindset among the leadership in 1965 was that economic strength would be the linchpin of national defense and resilience. Lee Kuan Yew possessed a tremendous amount of power in 1965 and could have fashioned himself into a sultanistic oligarch. But he and those in his inner circle were convinced that only by creating a strong and institutionalized system of laws regarding property could Singapore attract the capital it needed to be viable over the long term. Global capital flowing to countries like Indonesia or China to exploit natural resources or large domestic markets might tolerate a great deal of uncertainty over property and contracts, including a stratum of wild and predatory local oligarchs. Singapore's lack of resources and markets placed tremendous constraints on how Lee Kuan Yew could attract investments. It also meant that the legal system and bureaucracy inherited from the British, which was rudimentary and corrupt, had to be rapidly strengthened. The institution chosen to carry out this task was the Corrupt Practices Investigation Bureau (CPIB)—which under the British had been focused on petty crimes among the lower ranks of the civil service.

Prime Minister Lee made the deliberate decision to focus the CPIB on the highest levels of power—the elites and oligarchs (Quah 1982; Lee 2000). This was the start of the process of taming Singapore's oligarchs by impersonal institutions and the law, rather than through the interventions of a sultanistic ruler. Civil oligarchy was in formation from the 1960s forward. Lee used his dominant position within the People's Action Party (PAP) to push new rules through the parliament that greatly expanded the power and scope of the CPIB. And the body was placed directly under the prime minister's office. Over the next fifteen years, on a case-by-case basis, the CPIB developed a formidable reputation for pursuing powerful figures, both oligarchs and elites, who engaged in corrupt practices and used material power to distort the system. After being exhaustively investigated, these individuals, including cabinet ministers, were taken to court, tried, and punished. Despite being personally close to the prime minister, in some cases for decades, the accused were pursued relentlessly. When powerful figures within the ruling PAP were ensnared, Lee repeatedly stepped aside and let them fall in disgrace.

The most spectacular case was that of Teh Cheang Wan, the Minister of National Development. In 1986 he was investigated by the CPIB on charges of accepting bribes from Singaporean oligarchs. When he attempted to bargain with senior CPIB officials to get the case stopped, they instead reported the efforts to Lee and mentioned that Teh had asked to see him. Lee refused to meet until the investigation was finished and Teh's guilt or innocence had been determined by a court. Teh ended the process prematurely by committing suicide through a drug overdose and left a personal note for the prime minister saying that it was only right that he should "pay the highest penalty" for his mistake (Lee 2000). The signal this series of cases sent to oligarchs in Singapore was that the law was being made not only strong, but impersonal. It did not matter that many of these prominent cases, all splashed in lurid detail in the state-controlled press, involved figures with excellent political connections. Prime Minister Lee was putting in place the antithesis of Suharto's politics of proximity.

This process of taming paid high dividends for Singapore among investors. The city-state was a pure price-taker internationally and needed to attract regional and global capital to flourish. But this would be impossible if local elites and oligarchs were untamed. By the 1980s Singapore enjoyed a reputation for a strong legal system, low corruption, and extremely secure property arrangements for private owners. By the 1990s Singapore regularly topped global polls that rated countries on their good governance and absence of corruption. But as living standards rose at a rapid pace and Singapore became one of the most vibrant and trusted locations in Asia for binding international arbitration, abysmal ratings for democracy and freedoms of speech, assembly, and the press placed Singapore near the bottom of the rankings. The country had achieved civil oligarchy without civil rights—demonstrating that the rule of law has two distinct spheres. One is focused on fair and impartial adjudication in the material realm. This is the sphere that is of greatest significance to oligarchs. And providing justice over property claims and conflicts was a pre-condition for oligarchs submitting to the broader legal structure. The other sphere centers on liberal freedoms.

The International Bar Association (IBA 2008) produced a major critique of Singapore's legal system in 2008. It acknowledged that Singapore "ranks highly in international recognition of its economic competitiveness, liberal trade policies, property rights, legal efficiency and business standards." But also pointed out that PAP officials have "initiated a series of defamation suits that have been won against opposition figures," and that "no PAP leader has ever lost a defamation suit against an opposition figure in court." The IBA concluded that Singapore's judicial system lacks "objective and subjective independence" because "its rankings are very low regarding its recognition and implementation of human rights and democracy." Paradoxically, the IBA analysts were arguing that a single legal structure could somehow be both independent and prostrate.

The IBA dealt with the obvious contradiction by redefining the scope of the rule of law. For a judicial system and the rule of law to be "strong and robust," the IBA claimed, it requires a "respect for and protection of democracy, human rights—including freedom of expression and freedom of assembly—and an independent and impartial judiciary." This simply denies the fact that there are different spheres of judicial impartiality—one that protects oligarchs and property, and one that protects everyone else. The IBA also tried to sow concerns among oligarchs that partiality in the realm of civil liberties could threaten impartiality in the realm of property. This concern was first raised two decades earlier by a fact-finding mission by the New York Bar, but it has thus far failed to cause serious alarm among local oligarchs or international investors.[14]

Conclusion

The cases presented in this chapter attempt to place the power of those controlling concentrated material resources into a framework that operates comparatively across countries, historical periods, forms of the polity, and modes of production. Although all three cases discussed are embedded within global capitalism during the periods covered, the theory and accounts offered here do not follow from capitalism itself. Nor is the focus on how wealth is extracted and accumulated. The emphasis is, instead, on how wealth is defended—whatever the system of extraction and accumulation. Oligarchs have sometimes been armed and ruled directly to solve their wealth defense needs. In other cases, a single sultanistic ruler has reliably provided the defense. And in still other cases, oligarchs have been fully disarmed and do not rule the armed states that secure property under impartial and impersonal legal guarantees. The cases here show that these different solutions to wealth defense have highly variable connections to democratic freedoms. They also help untangle how places like Indonesia and the Philippines can be democratic and yet have almost no rule of law applying to oligarchs, while cases like Singapore can be non-democratic and yet the rule of law over and for oligarchs is undeniable.

Notes

1 For a much fuller treatment of the concept and its application in a variety of cases and historical contexts, see Winters (2011). A review of relevant literatures on oligarchy is available in Winters and Page (2009).
2 Aristotle (1996) writes that:

> whether in oligarchies or in democracies, the number of the governing body, whether the greater number, as in a democracy, or the smaller number, as in an oligarchy, is an accident due to the fact that the rich everywhere are few, and the poor numerous.
>
> (III, viii, 1279^{b}35–39)

3 This is an adaptation of Korpi's (1985) work on power resources.
4 This differs in important ways from the pioneering work of Robison and Hadiz (2004) on oligarchs in Indonesia, as well as that of Rodan and Jayasuriya (2009) and Jesudason (1996)—all of whom place the political economy of contemporary capitalism in the analytical foreground and embed their arguments about oligarchs within that context.

5 These forms are elaborated in Winters (2011). But briefly, in a warring oligarchy, oligarchs are armed, play a direct role in coercion and enforcement to defend property and wealth. But they operate individually and rule their own realms. All oligarchs face threats from below. But in warring oligarchies, lateral threats are particularly prominent. In a ruling oligarchy, oligarchs operate more collectively to defend stratification and concentrated wealth. Oligarchs range from being semi-armed to fully disarmed, but the management of coercion is a key factor in the stability of a ruling oligarchy. Oligarchs are directly engaged in rule, though not all of them are necessarily involved. A subset of oligarchs can defend the group's vital property interests. In a sultanistic oligarchy, one oligarch emerges as more powerful than all the others to enforce the regime of wealth and property claims. Other oligarchs in the system tend to be fully disarmed, though sometimes they maintain a private coercive role, especially if they are landed oligarchs and are based outside the capital. The sultanistic ruler protects the interests of oligarchs in general, though predations on individual oligarchs frequently occur. Rule is individualistic and personalistic. Much of the politics in a sultanistic oligarchy is focused on how oligarchs navigate around these dangers and maintain their security. The last type is a civil oligarchy. Oligarchs in a civil oligarchy are fully disarmed, they do not rule (if they hold office it is not *as* or *for* oligarchs), and property and wealth are enforced by an impersonal bureaucratic state. This is the only oligarchic form in which there exist property rights under law rather than property claims (which oligarchs always play a role in enforcing). In a civil oligarchy, the legal regime is more powerful than oligarchs, and they routinely submit to its constraints.

6 The material–oligarchic approach adopted in this chapter differs fundamentally from the mainstream perspectives emphasizing modernization, behavioral–pluralist, public choice, and neoliberal institutionalist optics for understanding power that have been prominent in the literature on Southeast Asia. For a critical survey of this scholarship, see Hewison *et al.* (1993).

7 Important works on oligarchs and minority power in the Philippines include Anderson (1988), Hutchcroft (1991, 1998, 2000, 2008), Larkin (1982, 1993), McCoy (2009), Sidel (1999, 2004), Thompson (1995). This section relies heavily on this excellent scholarship.

8 See in particular the work of Rodan (1993, 1996).

9 Statistics on wealth and incomes in Singapore are from Forbes Asia (2010), CapGemini World Wealth Reports (2008 to 2010), Singapore Department of Statistics (2010), and Boston Consulting Group (2010).

10 Singapore also has about 880 ultra High Net Worth Individuals, each of whom has at least $30 million in non-home investable assets, and nearly 100,000 millionaires with an average of $4.5 million in non-home net worth. They make up a startling 2 percent of the population, the thickest stratum of millionaires in the world, and own about 47 percent of the nation's private wealth. The net worth of the average millionaire in Singapore is about 110 times the income of the median citizen, while the net worth of the average member of the fifty richest is about 24,000 times the median income.

11 The city-state was granted partial independence from the British in 1959, but then became a state within the Federation of Malaya in 1963.

12 Lee Kuan Yew's memoir (2000) is a useful source for the 1950s and 1960s.

13 On Singapore's concept of total defense and total war, see www.totaldefence.org.sg and www.ne.edu.sg.

14 The mission visited Singapore and Malaysia in 1989 and issued their report in 1991. See Frank *et al.* 1991. Local oligarchs and foreign actors concerned with property rights and the independence of the Singaporean judiciary were not perturbed when it was the Finance Minister and the Monetary Authority of Singapore, and not the fearsome CPIB, that investigated allegations that condominiums purchased at a discount by Lee Kuan Yew and members of his family were improper. For a thorough treatment of the case, see Seow 2006.

References

Anderson, B. (1988) "Cacique democracy in the Philippines: origins and dreams," *New Left Review* 169: 3–33.

Aristotle (1996) *The Politics and The Constitution of Athens*, ed. Stephen Everson (original translation by Benjamin Jowett), Cambridge: Cambridge University Press.

Boston Consulting Group (2010) "Regaining lost ground: resurgent markets and new opportunities," Global Wealth 2010, June; available at: www.bcg.com (accessed 15 August 2010).

Capgemini (2008) "World wealth report," Capgemini and Merrill Lynch, Inc.; available at: www.us.capgemini.com (accessed 4 July 2010).

——(2009) "World wealth report," Capgemini and Merrill Lynch, Inc.; available at: www.us.capgemini.com (accessed 4 July 2010).

——(2010) "World wealth report," Capgemini and Merrill Lynch, Inc.; available at: www.us.capgemini. com (accessed 4 July 2010).

Crouch, H. (1988) *The Army and Politics in Indonesia*, revised edition, Ithaca, NY: Cornell University Press.

Erlanger, S. (1990) "For Suharto, his heirs are key to life after '93," *New York Times*, 11 November; available at: www.nytimes.com/1990/11/11/world/for-suharto-his-heirs-are-key-to-life-after-93.html? pagewanted=all (accessed 15 June 2010).

Forbes Asia (2010) "Singapore's 40 richest," 28 July; available at: www.forbes.com/lists/2010/79/ singapore-10_Singapores-40-Richest_Rank.html (accessed 3 August 2010).

Frank, B.S., J.C. Markowitz, R.B. McKay, and K. Roth (1991) "The decline in the rule of law in Malaysia and Singapore: Part II—Singapore, a report of the Committee on International Human Rights, January/February," *Record of the Association of the Bar of the City of New York* 46 (1): 7–85.

Hewison, K., R. Robison and G. Rodan (1993) *Southeast Asia in the 1990s: Authoritarianism, Democracy and Capitalism*, London: Allen and Unwin.

Hutchcroft, P.D. (1991) "Oligarchs and cronies in the Philippine state: the politics of patrimonial plunder," *World Politics* 43: 414–50.

——(1998) *Booty Capitalism: The Politics of Banking in the Philippines*, New York: Cornell University Press.

——(2000) "Colonial masters, national politicos, and provincial lords: central authority and local autonomy in the American Philippines, 1900–1913," *Journal of Asian Studies* 59 (2): 277–306.

——(2008) "The Arroyo imbroglio in the Philippines," *Journal of Democracy* 19 (1): 141–55.

IBA (2008) "Prosperity versus individual rights? Human rights, democracy and the rule of law in Singapore," an International Bar Association Human Rights Institute Report, July; available at: www. world-rights.org/singapore/07_2008_July_Report_Singapore-Prosperity_versus_individual_rights.pdf (accessed 8 August 2008).

Jayasuriya, K. (2002) "The rule of law and governance in East Asia," in M. Beeson (ed.) *Reconfiguring East Asia: Regional Institutions and Organisations after the Crisis*, New York: RoutledgeCurzon, pp. 99–116.

Jesudason, J.V. (1996) "The syncretic state and the structuring of oppositional politics in Malaysia," in G. Rodan (ed.) *Political Oppositions in Industrializing Asia*, London: Routledge, pp. 128–60.

Korpi, W. (1985) "Developments in the theory of power and exchange," *Sociological Theory* 3 (2): 31–45.

Larkin, J.A. (1982) "Philippine history reconsidered: a socioeconomic perspective," *American Historical Review* 87 (3): 595–628.

——(1993) *Sugar and the Origins of Modern Philippine Society*, San Francisco: University of California Press.

Lee, Kuan Yew (2000) *From Third World to First: The Singapore Story, 1965–2000*, New York: HarperCollins.

Lev, D.S. (1985) "Colonial law and the genesis of the Indonesian state," *Indonesia* 40: 57–74.

——(2007) "The state and law reform in Indonesia," in T. Lindsey (ed.) *Law Reform in Developing and Transitional States*, New York: Routledge.

McCoy, A.W. (ed.) (2009) *An Anarchy of Families: State and Family in the Philippines*, Madison: University of Wisconsin Press.

Pompe, S. (2005) *The Indonesian Supreme Court: A Study of Institutional Collapse*, Ithaca, NY: Cornell Southeast Asia Studies Publications.

Quah, Jon S.T. (1982) "Bureaucratic corruption in the ASEAN countries: a comparative analysis of their anti-corruption strategies," *Journal of Southeast Asian Studies* 13 (1): 153–77.

Robison, R. (2008 [1986]) *Indonesia: The Rise of Capital*, London: Equinox Publishing.

Robison, R. and V.R. Hadiz (2004) *Reorganising Power in Indonesia: The Politics of Oligarchy in an Age of Markets*, London: RoutledgeCurzon.

Rodan, G. (1993) "Preserving the one-party state in contemporary Singapore," in K. Hewison, R. Robison, and G. Rodan, *Southeast Asia in the 1990s: Authoritarianism, Democracy and Capitalism*, Sydney: Allen and Unwin.

——(1996) "State–society relations and political opposition in Singapore," in G. Rodan (ed.) *Political Oppositions in Industrialising Asia*, London: Routledge.

Rodan, G. and K. Jayasuriya (2009) "Capitalist development, regime transitions and new forms of authoritarianism in Asia," *Pacific Review* 22 (1): 23–47.

Schwarz, A. (2000) *A Nation in Waiting: Indonesia's Search for Stability*, Boulder, CO: Westview Press.

Seow, F.T. (2006) *Beyond Suspicion: The Singapore Judiciary*, Monograph 55, New Haven, CT: Yale Southeast Asian Studies.

Sidel, J.T. (1999) *Capital, Coercion, and Crime: Bossism in the Philippines*, Palo Alto: Stanford University Press.

——(2004) "Bossism and democracy in the Philippines, Thailand, and Indonesia: towards an alternative framework for the study of 'local strongmen'," in J. Harriss, K. Stokke, and O. Tornquist (eds)

Politicising Democracy: The New Local Politics of Democratisation, Basingstoke: Palgrave Macmillan, pp. 51–74.

Singapore Department of Statistics (2010) "Key household income trends, 2009," Occasional Paper on Income Statistics, February, available at: www.singstat.gov.sg/pubn/papers/economy/op-s16.pdf (accessed 15 June 2010).

Soemitro and K.H. Ramadhan (1994) *Soemitro: Dari Pangdam Mulawarman Sampai Pangkopkamtib, Petikan dari Memoar: 1965–1976*, Jakarta: Pustaka Sinar Harapan.

Thompson, M.R. (1995) *The Anti-Marcos Struggle: Personalistic Rule and Democratic Transition in the Philippines*, New Haven, CT: Yale University Press.

Time (1960) "Singapore: how to catch a millionaire," *Time* magazine, 15 August; available at: www.time.com/time/magazine/article/0,9171,939750,00.html (accessed 23 May 2010).

Winters, J.A. (1996) *Power in Motion: Capital Mobility and the Indonesian State*, New York: Cornell University Press.

——(2011) *Oligarchy*, Cambridge and New York: Cambridge University Press.

Winters, J.A. and B. Page (2009) "Oligarchy in the United States?" *Perspectives on Politics* 7 (4): 731–51.

Wiranto (2003) *Witness in the Storm: A Memoir of an Army General*, Jakarta: Delta Pustaka Express and Centre for Globalisation and Social Studies.

Woo, Jung-en (1991) *Race to the Swift*, New York: Columbia University Press.

SECTION II
States and regimes

5

DEMOCRACY AND MONEY POLITICS

The case of Indonesia

Vedi R. Hadiz

From centralized authoritarianism to decentralized money politics

For three decades the 'New Order' in Indonesia had epitomized the kind of rigidly centralized authoritarian rule that gave little room for autonomously developing civil society-based organizations, and where oppositional political parties and the press were all but hamstrung, while highly orchestrated general elections provided a smokescreen for systematic coercion and brutality. By stark contrast, Indonesia today easily ranks among the most democratic countries in Southeast Asia, along with the likes of the Philippines and Thailand (the overthrow of Thaksin Shinawatra in 2006 notwithstanding). There is notable vibrancy in Indonesian civil society, while a multitude of political parties contest national and local elections regularly and vigorously. In spite of numerous potential threats against it, the Indonesian press thus far remains remarkably free. Furthermore, Indonesia's experiment with administrative and political decentralization has been lauded for its 'radical' nature (Betts 2003; Rohdewohld 2004), and in yet another break with the past, the Indonesian military has been forced to take a back seat role in formal politics, although it continues to jealously guard economic interests through involvement in a range of informal political alliances, notably at the local level (Honna 2006). The relative economic and political stability of the second half of the last decade, moreover, has largely overshadowed earlier, much exaggerated, fears of Indonesia being overwhelmed by communal violence, terrorist activity or descending into state failure.[1]

A further characteristic of New Order rule that remains relevant today, however, was that it made possible the development of a particularly rapacious and predatory form of capitalism. In fact, the New Order constituted in part a highly centralized network of patronage, through which a range of predatory business, military, bureaucratic and political interests interlocked, extending from President Soeharto's Cendana Palace all the way down to the provinces, cities and villages (Robison and Hadiz 2004: 43). From within this vast network of patronage there emerged wealthy, mainly ethnic Chinese, business conglomerates like that of the Salim Group, as well as powerful political-business families best represented by the Soehartos themselves, who benefited tremendously from direct access to or control over state power and resources. Initially on the basis of foreign aid and investment, then windfall oil profits, and later still, greater incorporation into the world economy through low wage manufacturing exports and selective liberalization of particularly the trade and financial sectors, the Indonesian economy almost consistently grew at admirable rates until it went bust during the Asian economic crisis of 1997–8. The political-business families and business cronies formed the core of an oligarchy that wielded unrivalled power and grew fabulously rich during this high growth period before the collapse of the New Order.

In spite of the extraordinary changes Indonesia has experienced since 1998, the legacy of the New Order cannot be ignored: it has arguably helped to entrench a distinctly money politics-fuelled kind of electoral democracy in the post-Soeharto era. As also suggested by Robison and Hadiz (2004), the social underpinnings of Indonesia's predatory form of capitalism has remained largely intact in spite of the institutional unravelling of the centralized and authoritarian New Order, and its replacement by a highly decentralized democracy. The collapse of the New Order was *not* in fact accompanied by the substitution of old predatory interests by a cohesive coalition of reformist interests. This is crucial, as the former quickly resurfaced in new coalitions of power and took control of Indonesia's post-New Order social and political institutions; in other words they essentially hijacked Indonesia's fledgling democracy by reinventing themselves as democrats. Moreover, such old interests have continued to latch on to newer diffuse, competing and decentralized networks of patronage, no less predatory than that which constituted the New Order, through which the spoils of power are now distributed – mediated in part by electoral processes dictated by the logic of money politics. Certainly, there have been new-comers: for example, former students or NGO activists who have joined the variety of political parties made possible by democratization. However, these have mainly been forced to play by the rules established by more entrenched and powerful interests.

Against this background, 'matter of time arguments' at least partly based on rather simplified notions of democratic 'transitions' and 'consolidations' (as developed by authors like O'Donnell and Schmitter 1986 and Linz and Stepan 1996) are quite evidently insufficient to explain the Indonesian trajectory (Hadiz 2003).[2] In their most facile form these notions as applied to Indonesia hold that the country will gradually outgrow its money politics orientation and develop a more accountable form of democracy. Schneier (2005), for example – writing for a major international organization specializing in democratization issues – argued that the key is setting up the right institutions, which will then develop and impose their own logic on political life as they mature. This purportedly happened in the USA, where the institutions of governance ensure that democracy thrives in spite of a Constitution originally written by property-owning elites. But no matter how one assesses the nature of contemporary American democracy, there is no reason to assume that its experience will be emulated in Indonesia. Arguably, the trajectory of the former American colony, the Philippines, beset with money politics following more than two decades of democracy after the Marcos era, is far more relevant and instructive than that of its one-time colonizer.

It should be noted that 'matter of time arguments' were incorporated into 'transitology' most prominently in relation to the early *reformasi* period as far as Indonesia is concerned. But the fixation with democratic transitions exhibited by authors like Ghoshal (2004) and many others, ignored the possibility that the basic form of Indonesia's post-Soeharto democracy had already been established and become more or less entrenched (Hadiz 2003). This is because of the nature of the constellation of interests and power prevailing at the onset of *reformasi*. Conceptualizing a linear process of democratic 'transition' and 'consolidation' resulting from benign 'elite pacts' and the like can only be analytically misleading, from this point of view.

A small minority of authors have taken a different tack and resorted to re-applying the long-held neo-patrimonial view of Indonesian politics onto the analysis of Indonesian democracy. A recent expression of this is found in Webber (2006), who holds that the greatest obstacle to Indonesia's successful transition to democracy is found in a deeply rooted cultural disposition initially best exhibited by pre-colonial Javanese rulers and which remains quite resilient in the democratic era. The propensity to blur the difference between public and private property in Indonesia is reputed to be based on innate cultural tendencies, and thus the corruption of the Soeharto regime, according to Webber, is due to it having been modelled on the rule of the old Javanese kings (a view he puts forward via a quote from no less than an old Soeharto ally, Singapore's Lee Kuan Yew). Interestingly, in a throwback to old 'modernization' theory, Webber suggests that Indonesian neo-patrimonialism may be on the verge of breaking down – under the weight of a modern electoral democracy that forces leaders and parties to behave in a more accountable and rational manner. But as we shall see in the discussion below, electoral competition is actually helping to develop very different kinds of political parties and elections than Webber has in mind, though the reasons for this are not primarily cultural.

By contrast, Slater's (2004) conceptualization of contemporary Indonesian politics as rule by 'cartel' is among the more insightful of those currently available. He suggests that Indonesia is being run by political elites who have collectively developed an interest in sustaining coalitions that co-opt major parties, marginalize smaller ones and effectively deny the possibility of political opposition. However, his analysis is weakened by a lack of attention to the dimension of political economy, in spite of a stated aim to show the structural and systemic roots of cartel rule. Slater's conceptualization of 'rule by cartel' – borrowed from a very specific interpretation of the driving forces of European political party life – takes too little account of the context of, and imperatives deriving from, the particularly predatory logic that has driven Indonesian capitalism since the New Order. Even if cartelization were to be outwardly found in both the Indonesian and European experiences, it is obvious that political parties operate in these societies in ways that are vastly and fundamentally dissimilar. It is only by accounting for the different political economy (and social–historical) trajectories of Europe and Indonesia that this could be explained at all.

The political economy dimension is emphasized in Robison and Hadiz (2004) in their analysis of the reorganization of power in post-New Order Indonesia alluded to earlier. Extending such an analysis to the local level of politics, Hadiz (2007, 2010) argues that the main beneficiaries of Indonesia's democracy have been those previously placed at the lower rungs of the New Order's system of patronage, and relatively ignored by analysts during the zenith of centralized authoritarian rule.[3] These are the local level politico-bureaucrats and entrepreneurs who now harbour big ambitions, the operators and fixers of any number of carefully cultivated 'mass organizations' from which the New Order had regularly recruited apparatchik, as well as the deposed regime's formidable army of informal enforcers – local-level thugs and 'youth organization' activists – who migrated *en masse* into a host of new political parties or their militia groups at the start of the democratic era. All of these had been cultivated within the New Order's predatory capitalism, by which private wealth was accumulated through systematic and privileged access to, or control over, public resources and institutions. All of these are also well placed now to continue to pursue their predatory aims within the format of democratic competition.

The limits of technocratic reform

The resilience of predatory interests in spite of a range of institutional reforms in fact remains one of the most enduring problems of Indonesian political economy. Why haven't the pressures for 'good governance' reforms emanating from within and outside Indonesia hindered them more seriously? More basically, one could legitimately ask where the reformist impulse might be found in Indonesia, if at all. In truth, reformers have always been around in Indonesia and are located easily within NGOs, labour and student movements and the like. But these have remained fragmented and plagued with seemingly perennial political incoherence, partly as a legacy of severe disorganization during the authoritarian New Order.

Others may look elsewhere, to reformers of the more technocratic kind, who could be more realistically expected to exert greater and longer-lasting influence on the political economy.[4] During the Soeharto period, after all, there was the famous so-called Berkeley Mafia that almost regularly filled the majority of economic positions in various New Order cabinets. Today, the heirs of the Berkeley Mafia are certainly represented in the corridors of power but, as always, their presence is felt mainly in Jakarta, where they are able to maintain crucial links with representatives of the international community of technocrats, ensconced in the modern office buildings where the headquarters of international development organizations can be found. In the provinces, districts, cities, towns and villages, the allies of these ideological free marketeers remain scarce, demonstrating the absence of a broad social base to underpin the technocratic agenda outside of the capital city.

Not surprisingly, the present technocratic agenda of good governance and free markets (formulated with the assistance of a number of international development organizations in the immediate post-Soeharto period) is constantly supplanted by politico-bureaucratic and business interests unconstrained by abstract economic dogma and which are furthered by such concrete weapons as money politics. Indeed, for all the talk about providing the institutional framework for the 'rational' operations of free markets, Indonesia's technocrats have hardly been able to prevent the usurpation by predatory interests of the policies they advocate – something which represents a continuation of a trend already present during the Soeharto period. Decentralization, for example, was initially championed by way of technocratic ideas promoted by such organizations as the World Bank (e.g. White and Smoke 2005) – but it appears now that locally situated predatory interests have been able to latch on to the language of good governance while muscling their way into newly more powerful – and lucrative – political and administrative positions at the local level. Nothing is more suggestive of the continuing lack of technocratic power than the Bank Century scandal of 2009, which came to embroil two of Indonesia's most respected economists in some very murky affairs involving the bail-out of a small, failing private bank. Critics of President Susilo Bambang Yudhoyono – known simply as SBY to the Indonesian people – claim that the bank was used for embezzlement purposes and as a conduit for secret money required to fund his 2009 presidential election campaign (*Tempo* 21–27 December 2009: 133–7, 28 December 2009–3 January 2010: 27–9, 15–21 February 2010: 34–6).

It is notable that SBY had won that election soundly with more than 60 per cent of the popular vote against two formidable opponents: his own vice-president, top New Order-era businessman Jusuf Kalla – whose running mate was a former top New Order general – and former President Megawati Soekarnoputri, who also ran with a former top New Order general (no less than Soeharto's own former son-in-law). Of course, SBY himself is a former senior general of the New Order era. Yet he had somehow emerged from the Soeharto era with a reputation relatively untainted by allegations of either direct involvement in corruption or violation of human rights, and had gone on to key ministerial posts in several post-Soeharto cabinets before winning the presidency for the first time in 2004.

It is also noteworthy that, as part of his re-election strategy, SBY had cultivated an image as an incumbent who was on a serious crusade against unbridled corruption in the country. He did this partly by demonstrating what seemed to be unwavering support for the then pro-active Anti-Corruption Commission. He was seen to have not impeded the work of the commission even when it prosecuted a close family member who had held a senior position at the Central

Bank. Following this victory, however, the new SBY government was seen to be siding with a number of institutions, including the police force and the attorney general's office, to weaken the Anti-Corruption Commission (*Tempo* 28 December 2009–3 January 2010: 99–101, *Forum Keadilan* 28 December 2009–3 January 2010: 20–1), which had ruffled many feathers for its surprising level of aggression. A particular annoyance was to occur when Indonesian social scientist George Aditjondro published a controversial slim book which purported to show how SBY had built social foundations, run by trusted allies, whose function was to secretly mobilize funds for murky intentions (Aditjondro 2010). Though the accusation was staunchly rejected, it nevertheless brought back memories of how President Soeharto had used an array of family and crony-controlled social foundations to mobilize illicit money for a variety of purposes.

Accusations of corruption and misappropriation of power thus came back to haunt SBY at the start of his second term in office, underlining the fact that his government, much like previous ones, inevitably accommodates a range of predatory interests, old as well as newer. As mentioned, these have been remarkably resilient throughout the institutional changes that have taken place in Indonesia since 1998, and no less so than at the local level of politics, as we shall see.

Money politics, decentralization, democracy

Prior to democratization in Indonesia, the cases of the Philippines and Thailand had already provided much material to reflect on the significance of money politics in recently emerged democracies in the region. In all three countries, there has developed an election industry of considerable size and extent and which has become significant in the operations of the democratic system. Of course, one may suggest that the same exists in most democracies, whether established or more recent. But in these Southeast Asian cases, the elections industry blurs the realm of the legal and illegal, the above- and under-ground, by its intrinsic nature. It comes replete with campaign consultants, rally organizers, pamphleteers, as might be expected, but also typically with private security forces, rent-a-crowds and available-for-purchase local notables. It covers not just advertising (on television, radio and in the printed press), or producing T-shirts, banners, 'souvenirs' for supporters – but activities all the way to intimidation and outright vote-buying.[5]

As in Indonesia, democratization in Thailand and the Philippines was accompanied by administrative and political decentralization. Therefore, much attention has been devoted by analysts to the workings of money politics at the local level. In an exemplary work on Thailand, Arghiros (2001) details how vote buying and mobilization takes place systematically at the local level of politics, while noting how the cost of winning elections has continued to grow at incredible rates. The same could be said for the Philippines, where the operations of illegal lotteries known as *jueteng* involving large sums of money play a critical role in funding the escalating campaign costs borne by politicians (Balgos 2001: 86–9; Co *et al.* 2007: 171). The point to be made here is that the imperatives of money politics ensure that contesting elections, national as well as local, has become the purview of those with access to considerable sums of money, notwithstanding the formal rules governing and limiting the use of campaign funds in these recent democracies. In effect, newer patterns of social and political exclusion and inclusion have been entrenched in these democracies through the link between predatory power and money politics.

Similar to Thailand and the Philippines, the cost of running election campaigns has skyrocketed in Indonesia since the country's first democratic parliamentary elections in over four decades in 1999. By the time the second elections beckoned, it was reported that the PDI-P (Indonesian Democratic Party for Struggle) of Megawati Soekarnoputri was charging individuals several hundred millions of rupiahs to be listed as an official party candidate for provincial and national parliamentary seats. Golkar, the former electoral vehicle of New Order power-holders, was carrying out the same practice, according to the news report (*Media Indonesia* 2003).[6] Being registered as a party candidate for district or municipal-level seats had also cost a relatively hefty sum by then. Though notionally less prestigious, such seats are coveted because decentralization has meant that much authority, including over local budgets and projects, has been shifted to district and municipal-level governments.[7] Moreover, it must be remembered that much greater sums of money would be required to actually win elections once nominated.

A significant change did occur in 2005, however, which influenced greatly the operations of money politics in Indonesia. Prior to this year, governors, mayors and district heads had been elected by members of their corresponding parliaments. The consequence was that vote-buying had been largely confined to parliament houses. Under such a system, the period leading up to Election Day would be typically accompanied by feverish negotiations involving monetary transactions (and acts of intimidation) but these would mainly engage candidates, local political party officials, parliamentarians – as well as the media – rather than the population at large. But Governmental Regulation no. 6/2005 instituted a system by which governors, district heads and mayors would be elected on the basis of the popular vote. Choi (2005) observed that the reformed electoral system served to further strengthen the hand of political party branches and their executive bodies because only a party or coalition of parties in control of 15 per cent or more of seats had the right to nominate candidates, thereby making local party chiefs more crucial gatekeepers than ever before. Reinforced, therefore, was a veritable auction house-like arrangement, which of course favours those capable of putting up the highest bid. It is no wonder that Mietzner (2006) quickly noticed the high proportion of businessmen (along with bureaucrats) represented as candidates in recent local elections in Indonesia.[8]

The auction-house arrangement can result in some rather surprising outcomes, however, because the relationship between political parties and their candidates becomes very ad hoc in nature. Under the arrangement, prospective candidates can negotiate 'prices' with various parties before a 'sponsorship' deal is struck. Because of this, political parties often throw their support behind moneyed 'outsiders' rather than their less financially endowed cadres. This means that such cadres will be encouraged to jump ship with little thought whenever convenient to do so. Writing on electoral contests in Gowa, South Sulawesi, Buehler and Tan (2007: 65) conclude that '[a]s a rule, candidates originated from outside the parties that nominated them.' Undoubtedly, such an observation would not be out of place in most parts of Indonesia.

An obvious consequence of this arrangement is the absence of party loyalty – a tendency which is bolstered by the fact that political parties are best described as essentially representing shifting and competing networks of patronage, rather than clear groupings based on programme or ideology. Interestingly, the same observation can be applied equally to so-called 'secular nationalist' parties (like the PDIP, Golkar or SBY's Democratic Party) and to those that have chosen to embrace Islam as a distinguishing characteristic. Though some may suggest that the relatively successful Islamic-oriented Partai Keadilan Sejahtera (PKS; Justice and Prosperity Party) is more ideologically driven than others, there are reasons to question this assumption. First of all, as a matter of national party policy, the PKS has pragmatically retreated from overtly promoting the Syariah, and substituted it for good governance promotion (Rahmat 2008) in the hope of appealing to a broader electorate. In this regard, the PKS seems to have tried to emulate the model of the far more successful AKP in Turkey, which had won government in 2002. Furthermore, as the PKS expands and more party members experience dealing with the actual demands of being in coalitions of power, including at the sub-national level of politics, ideological compromises have had to be made for practical purposes.[9]

Given all the above, it is not surprising that political campaigns in Indonesia are hardly ever fought according to competing election platforms. Candidates and political parties are usually difficult to distinguish on the basis of policies that they endorse. This would be a familiar sight for anyone well informed on the nature of political parties and electoral politics in Thailand and the Philippines.[10]

Another important consequence of the advent of direct local elections has been the rise in the overall cost of winning local office. Anecdotal evidence abounds which suggests that candidates can easily spend ten billion rupiahs or more of their personal money and still lose a local election.[11] Furthermore, the cost of seriously contesting the mayoral position, say in major industrial and commercial cities like Medan in North Sumatra and Surabaya in East Java, will definitely cost more than in a relatively peripheral town or district.[12] Being district head in areas greatly endowed with natural resources is also a greater prize than those poorly endowed – and therefore a candidate would be pushed to invest more to secure victory. Again, all these tendencies clearly favour those with access to large sums of money, whether or not ill-gotten, and furthermore induce election winners to recoup their investment during their incumbency, plausibly leading to engagement in corrupt activity while in office. As a corollary, fewer people may be able to afford to lose expensive electoral contests in the future. It has been widely reported in the Indonesian media that financial ruin has in fact already befallen many of those defeated in recent local electoral contests and who have not, as a result, enjoyed the opportunity of seeking a return on their investment.

It does not follow, however, that contests for local office will be less intense in economically less strategic areas. Local politicos in these places will still have an interest in carving out a realm of autonomous power given the obvious advantages of having direct control over local budgets and local revenue-generating activities. Vel (2005) observes, for example, that all the candidates in a local election in the district of East Sumba were involved in money politics. She also suggests that the 'position of district head has become a very attractive and powerful bureaucratic post', and 'that candidates for the post can attract investors who hope to profit from their loyalty in the future' (Vel 2005: 106). Describing an easily generalized phenomenon, she notes the role of the local business community in providing the required funds for the game of money politics to be played in this district found on the economically marginal island of Sumba.

It does not follow either that those individuals who spend the most money will always emerge victorious. Credible reformers have been known to win contests, although, predictably, this is a rare occurrence. The case of the gubernatorial election in West Sumatra in 2005 is often cited as an exceptional case, where a candidate who had won widespread respect in his previous position as a district head defeated a Jakarta-based candidate seen to be endowed with greater material resources as well as political connections.[13] Also often seen as exceptional cases, though more problematically so, are the results of district-level elections over the years in Kebumen, Bantul (both in Java) and Jembrana (Bali). In spite of their rather stellar reputations, 'reformers' who won elections in these cases have subsequently been accused of abuse of power to ensure re-election (in the case of Kebumen, see *Suara Merdeka* 2005), corruption (Bantul, see Savirani 2004), or of practicing 'strongman' politics (Jembrana, see Schulte-Nordholt 2007).

Why didn't the change to a decentralized democracy create the institutional incentives for the development of what might be called accountable good governance? After all, there is no reason to doubt that the technocratic architects of state policy genuinely believed that the direct election system, for example, would truly result in local governments that are more accountable to local citizenries and run in more transparent fashion, in spite of a probable instinctive preference for low intensity electoral contests. Furthermore, the reform accorded with the populist aspirations of local NGO activists who had been critical of the flaws of Indonesia's democracy, pointing to its elitist nature – epitomized before 2005 by the fact that local parliaments had sole power to elect governors, mayors and district heads. Direct local elections, in other words, accorded to some extent with the accountability and good governance rhetoric of the designers of state policy, while simultaneously satisfying the local community empowerment ideals of NGO-based critics.

However, the broader social terrain on which the electoral reform took place ensured that the objective of curbing money politics, or of creating local governments that are more accountable and responsive to the needs of local communities, would not be necessarily the outcomes of institutional change, no matter how well intended. Not only were the changed rules hijacked again by still-ascendant local predatory interests, they broadly conformed as well to the need of heads of local governments to be freed from the shackles imposed by over-dependence on their legislative counterparts (e.g. Lay 2002). Even this sort of friction has a tangible basis; it has been suggested that local government heads have to provide kickbacks to local legislators in order to ensure their support for policy initiatives. Such kickbacks also help to ensure that local legislative bodies do not reject the annual and end-of-term financial reports that heads of local governments are obliged to convey (see Kurniawan *et al.* 2003: 23). The newer system enhances the bargaining position of local heads of government vis-à-vis local legislative bodies, simply because their ascent to office is no longer dependent on legislative support.

Another institutional innovation – the introduction of 'independent' non-party candidates in 2007 (with strict eligibility criteria) – is unlikely to result in great changes in the foreseeable future. At best the innovation may end up allowing local bigwigs who have enough personal resources and stature to attempt to by-pass the political parties. Instead of paying off these parties to get on a formal ticket, they might choose to spend more money on direct vote-buying or on co-opting local notables. In any case, independent candidates have yet to become a prominent feature of local elections.[14]

Indonesian lessons

The Indonesian experience since 1998 reiterates the necessity of reassessing conventional renderings of electoral politics and of political parties. It is hardly useful to label Indonesia's political parties as 'immature', 'irrational' or 'neo-patrimonial' on the basis of idealized notions of party roles in Western liberal democracies. In the context of post-authoritarian societies like Indonesia, political parties as they exist currently – able to utilize money politics and even political thuggery when necessary – are quite suited for the purposes of the range of predatory interests that dominate them. It may be said that there is an internal logic to political party life and electoral competition that does not make internal transformations very likely in the foreseeable future. In fact, given the experience of democracies which have emerged in recent times, such as those in Southeast Asia, the liberal pluralist model associated with the Western experience may become increasingly exceptional.

All the above does not suggest that electoral politics cannot meaningfully take place in Indonesia. After all, national and local direct elections have now been successfully implemented in the country for over a decade. Most have taken place quite smoothly, though it is true that conflicts arising over the actual counting of poll results have frequently led to outbreaks of violence. The level of violence, however, has not been alarming in the majority of cases; certainly it has yet to lead to political assassinations (Buehler 2009). Indeed, overt acts of violence and intimidation now seem to be a less prominent feature of local elections than they had been in the earlier part of the post-Soeharto period, when cases such as the mayoral election in

Medan in 2000 came to the fore.[15] Even in areas previously torn apart by ethnic or religious strife, such as North Maluku, Poso in Sulawesi, and West Kalimantan, elections have regularly taken place in a relatively orderly manner.

Buehler (2009) suggests a hotchpotch of mainly institutional reasons for the comparative lack of overt violence in Indonesia in comparison to the Philippines (or Thailand). Among these is the fact that large numbers of candidates have reasonably good bureaucratic jobs to fall back on in case of electoral defeat; also that heads of local governments in Indonesia have less time in office than in the Philippines because of stricter limits on terms in office. Such reasons, he suggests, make local office in Indonesia not attractive enough for candidates to resort to violence to attain them. But almost every local election demonstrates that scores of holders of local bureaucratic power covet direct political power, and for obvious reasons. Moreover, they are not exempt from having to distribute large amounts of money to have a realistic hope of attaining it. Since their outlay is not going to be covered by their meagre official salaries and pensions, having less time to recoup investment on electoral campaigns only provides greater pressure to make the most of more limited time in office. Buehler's institutional fetish overlooks the more likely possibility that local elites have developed an interest in the relatively peaceful running of elections in order to safeguard the legitimacy of the political process that ensures their privileged social position. This is not a new discovery: as early as 2005, Barron *et al.* (2005: 11) had pointed out that, in many places, local elites had quietly appealed to supporters to refrain from practising open violence against each other.

Reflecting such a trend, members of the Pemuda Pancasila 'youth' organization in North Sumatra claimed in that year that they had been asked by no less than the candidates they were backing to adopt a lower than usual public profile. This included the exhortation to abstain, where possible, from appearing in their menacing organizational colours when assisting in the organization of rallies or other shows of public support (author interview 2005b, 2005d). The obvious intent of the request was to avert large-scale clashes between groupings of enforcers supporting rival candidates and parties. This was a significant development given that local politics in this province has been so notoriously rough and tumble in nature, perhaps most prominently so in the capital city of Medan. But such developments do not imply that violence and intimidation no longer have a place in local politics, as those specializing in providing the service of political thuggery are well aware. The availability of instruments of coercion remains useful in pursuing decidedly predatory aims while in office, as members of 'youth' or gangster organizations realize as they contemplate their evolving place in Indonesia's democracy (author interview 2005b).

More specifically, it might be said that local politicos have developed a general interest in preventing situations that might provide the opportunity for the military to regain some of the political space it has had to concede over the last decade. They are obviously cognisant that major outbreaks of violence could lead to the type of disorder that would not only damage the standing of Indonesian democracy – which has greatly facilitated their social advancement – but also allow the military extra leverage as the institution poised to restore order. There is certainly little point in inviting a situation that would necessitate sharing more of the spoils of power with the still feared military. It is for this reason that a statement on the potential disruption caused by local elections made by a senior Indonesian general in 2008 must have been so scary for local politicians to hear. Not only did the general suggest – in true New Order form – that Indonesians weren't ready for democracy, but he also warned that the military would take decisive action if national unity and stability were ever threatened by conflict arising from electoral contests (*Kompas* 2008).

79

Given the foregoing discussion, the Indonesian lesson is clearly not about successful transition and then linear entry into the 'consolidation' stage of democracy as some analyses would have it (Barron *et al.* 2005). It is about how predatory interests originally incubated within a centralized authoritarian regime, including those ensconced at the local level of politics, have been able to adroitly maintain and even further their social ascendance through the institutions of democracy and through the mechanisms of money politics. In a nutshell, the Indonesian lesson is ultimately about how social power almost always trumps institutional reform.

Notes

1 Indonesia's economy grew by more than 6 per cent in 2008 and continued to do relatively well in spite of the global economic crisis.
2 Another influence was the idea of the 'third wave of democratization' that had been introduced by Samuel Huntington (1991) in one of his pre-'clash of civilizations' incarnations.
3 Among the exceptions were Malley (1999), Schiller (1996) and Antlov (1995).
4 An early example was MacDougall (1975).
5 In Indonesia for example, the *serangan fajar* or 'raid at dawn' typically takes place on polling day where massive operations take place on behalf of individual candidates to disburse gifts and money to voters at their homes before polling booths actually open.
6 A sum of, say, Rp 400 million would amount to well over USD 40,000. To place this in context, according to the World Bank, Indonesia's Gross National Income per capita in 2005 was USD 1,250. See World Bank (2009).
7 Author interview (2003).
8 Businessmen constituted 28 per cent of the candidates, while bureaucrats constituted 36 per cent, according to Mietzner.
9 During fieldwork in North Sumatra, I found instances of PKS-sponsored candidates for local office cavorting politically with known thugs or apparently engaged in money politics. The PKS has also nominated candidates who are clearly not party cadres, suggesting involvement in the behind-the-scenes wheeling and dealing that is typical of other political parties.
10 Ufen (2006), for example, notes how political parties in Indonesia are coming to resemble those in the Philippines in their character. Also see Rocamora (1998) on the Philippines or Shatkin (2003) on Thailand.
11 E.g. author interview (2005a) with Helifizar 'David' Purba, failed candidate for district head of Serdang Bedagai, North Sumatra. A contractor who hails from the local branch of the New Order-era youth/gangster organization the Pemuda Pancasila, he is a feared and respected local notable. He was defeated by the businessman brother of a late former governor of North Sumatra, a senior New Order-era general.
12 The re-election campaign of Mayor Abdillah of Medan in 2005 involved a campaign war chest of allegedly up to Rp 50 billion, according to a member of his 'success team', Medan legislator Yunus Rasyid (author interview 2005c). The Indonesian Anti-Corruption Commission pursued a case against Abdillah in 2008 (*Waspada*, 7 January 2008), which ultimately resulted in a conviction and jail term for him and his former deputy on charges of misappropriating public funds.
13 This is the case of Gamawan Fauzi – former district head of Solok in West Sumatra. Before finishing his term as governor, he was appointed to the position of Minister of Home Affairs by SBY.
14 Though some press reports suggest that this situation is about to be altered. See, for example, 'Tiga Calon Independen Bakal Ramaikan Pemilihan Bupati Situbondo', *Tempo Interaktif*, 9 February 2010.
15 In this case, local parliamentarians attached to the PDI-P famously had their lives threatened by politically connected thugs before they received a relatively small amount of money to support one of the mayoral candidates, a local businessman with interests in construction. See Sumatera Corruption Watch (n.d.).

References

Aditjondro, G.J. (2010) *Membongkar Gurita Cikeas: Di Balik Skandal Bank Century*, Yogyakarta: Galangpress.
Antlov, H. (1995) *Exemplary Centre, Administrative Periphery: Rural Leadership and the New Order on Java*, NIAS Monographs no. 68, Richmond: Curzon Press.

Arghiros, D. (2001) *Democracy, Development, and Decentralization in Provincial Thailand*, Richmond: Curzon.

Author interview (2003) 'Akhyar Nasution', member of Medan local parliament for the PDI-P, 15 December.

——(2005a) 'Helifizar "David" Purba', failed candidate for district head of Serdang Bedagai, North Sumatra, 15 June.

——(2005b) 'Hendra DS', Patriot Party and Pemuda Pancasila official, Medan, 16 June.

——(2005c) 'Yunus Rasyid', Medan legislator, 16 June.

——(2005d) 'Sahat Simatupang', Ikatan Pemuda Karya official, Medan, 18 June.

Balgos, C. (2001) *Investigating Local Governments: A Manual for Reporters*, Quezon City: Philippine Center for Investigative Journalism.

Barron, P., N. Melina and B. Welsh (2005) 'Consolidating Indonesia's democracy: Conflict, institutions and the "local" in the 2004 legislative elections', Social Development Papers, Conflict Prevention and Reconstruction, No. 31, December.

Betts, I.L. (2003) 'Decentralisation in Indonesia: a review of decentralisation policy and the problems and issues that have faced businesses and investors since the implementation of regional autonomy in Indonesia', *Indonesian Business Perspective Online, Harvest International's Journal for Decision Makers* 5 (5) June–July; available at: www.harvest-international.com/perspec/Jun_Jul03/special.htm (accessed July 2003).

Buehler, M. (2009) 'Suicide and progress in modern Nusantara', *Inside Indonesia* 97 (July–September); available at: www.insideindonesia.org/edition-97/suicide-and-progress-in-modern-nusantara (accessed 20 June 2011).

Buehler, M. and P. Tan (2007) 'Party–candidate relationships in Indonesian local politics: a case study of the 2005 regional elections in Gowa, South Sulawesi province', *Indonesia* 84 (October): 41–69.

Choi, Nankyung (2005) *Local Elections and Democracy in Indonesia: The Case of the Riau Archipelago*, Working Paper No. 91 (November), Singapore: Institute of Defence and Strategic Studies.

Co, E.E.A., M.O. Lim, M.E. Jayme-Lao and L.J. Juan (eds) (2007) *Philippine Democracy Assessment: Minimizing Corruption*, Manila: Friedrich Ebert Stiftung.

Forum Keadilan (2009/10) 28 December 2009–3 January 2010: 20–1.

Ghoshal, B. (2004) 'Democratic transition and political development in post-Soeharto Indonesia', *Contemporary South East Asia* 26: 506–29.

Hadiz, V.R. (2003) 'Reorganising political power in Indonesia: a reconsideration of so-called "democratic transitions"', *Pacific Review* 16 (4): 591–611.

——(2007) 'The localization of power in Southeast Asia', *Democratization* 14 (4): 873–92.

——(2010) *Localising Power in Post-Authoritarian Indonesia: A Southeast Asia Perspective*, Stanford, CA: Stanford University Press.

Honna, J. (2006) 'Local civil–military relations during the first phase of democratic transition, 1999–2004: a comparison of West, Central, and East Java', *Indonesia* 82 (October): 75–96.

Huntington, S.P. (1991) *The Third Wave: Democratization in the Late Twentieth Century*, Oklahoma: University of Oklahoma Press.

Kompas (2008) 24 January.

Kurniawan, L., A. Charisudin, N. Hadi, A. Khariri and B. Bachtiar (2003) *Menyingkap korupsi di daerah*, Malang and Surabaya: In-Trans and YSPDI.

Lay, C. (2002) 'Eksekutif dan legislative di daerah: Penelitian tentang potensi konflik antara dprd dan birokrasi di daerah', research report, Ministry of Research and Technology of the Republic of Indonesia and the Indonesian Institute of Sciences, Jakarta.

Linz, J.J. and A. Stepan (1996) *Problems of Democratic Transition and Consolidation: Southern Europe, South America and Post-Communist Europe*, Baltimore, MD: Johns Hopkins University Press.

MacDougall, J. (1975) 'Technocrats as modernizers: the economists of Indonesia's New Order', unpublished thesis, University of Michigan.

Malley, M. (1999) 'Regions: centralization and resistance', in D.K. Emmerson (ed.) *Indonesia beyond Suharto: Polity, Economy, Society, Transition*, New York: M.E. Sharpe, pp. 71–105.

Media Indonesia (2003) 21 December.

Mietzner, M. (2006) 'Local democracy: old elites are still in power, but direct elections now give voters a choice', *Inside Indonesia* 85 (January–March): 17–18.

O'Donnell, G. and P.C. Schmitter (1986) *Transitions from Authoritarian Rule: Tentative Conclusions about Uncertain Democracies*, Baltimore, MD: Johns Hopkins University Press.

Rahmat, M.I. (2008) *Ideologi Politik PKS: Dari Masjod Kampus ke Gedung Parlemen*, Yogyakarta: LKiS.

Robison, R. and V.R. Hadiz (2004) *Reorganising Power in Indonesia: The Politics of Oligarchy in an Age of Markets*, London: RoutledgeCurzon.

Rocamora, J. (1998) 'Philippines political parties, electoral system, and political reform', *Philippines International Review* 1 (1); available at: www.philsol.nl/pir/JR-98a.htm (accessed 3 June 2010).

Rohdewohld, R. (2004) 'Building capacity to support decentralisation: the case of Indonesia (1999–2004)', paper presented at Tokyo International Symposium on Capacity Development, Tokyo, 4–6 February.

Savirani, A. (2004) 'Local strongman in new regional politics in Indonesia', unpublished Master's thesis, University of Amsterdam.

Schiller, J. (1996) *Developing Jepara: State and Society in New Order Indonesia*, Melbourne: Monash University Asia Institute.

Schneier, E. (2005) 'The role of constitution-building processes in democratization', Case Study Indonesia; available at: www.idea.int/cbp/upload/CBP_indonesia.pdf (accessed 15 June 2010).

Schulte-Nordholt, H. (2007) 'Bali: an open fortress', in H. Schulte-Nordholt and G. van Klinken (eds) *Renegotiating Boundaries: Local Politics in Post-Suharto Indonesia*, Leiden: KITLV Press, pp. 387–416.

Shatkin, G. (2003) 'Globalization and local leadership: growth, power and politics in Thailand's eastern seaboard', Urban and Regional Research Collaborative Working Paper Series No. 03–05, University of Michigan.

Slater, D. (2004) 'Indonesia's accountability trap: party cartels and presidential power after democratic transition', *Indonesia* 78: 61–92.

Suara Merdeka (2005) 13 June.

Sumatera Corruption Watch (n.d.) 'Kronologis Kasus Money Politics Pemilihan Walikota Medan', leaflet.

Tempo (2009/10) 21–27 December 2009: 133–7; 28 December 2009–3 January 2010: 27–9, 99–101; 15–21 February 2010: 34–6.

Tempo Interaktif (2010) Available at: www.tempointeraktif.com (accessed 9 February 2010).

Ufen, A. (2006) 'Political parties in post-Suharto Indonesia: between *politik aliran* and "Philippinisation"', GIGA Working Papers no. 37, GIGA, Hamburg.

Vel, J. (2005) 'Pilkada in East Sumba: an old rivalry in a new democratic setting', *Indonesia* 80 (October): 81–107.

Waspada (2008) 7 January.

Webber, D. (2006) 'Consolidated patrimonial democracy? Democratization in post-Suharto Indonesia', *Democratization* 13 (3): 396–420.

White, R. and P. Smoke (2005) 'East Asia decentralizes', in R. White and P. Smoke (eds) *East Asia Decentralizes: Making Local Government Work*, Washington, DC: World Bank, pp. 1–23.

World Bank (2009) 'World Development Indicators database', September; available at: http://ddp ext.worldbank.org/ext/ddpreports/ViewSharedReport?&CF=1&REPORT_ID=9147&REQUEST_TYPE=VIEWADVANCED&HF=N&WSP=N (accessed 10 October 2009).

6

POPULIST CHALLENGE TO THE ESTABLISHMENT

Thaksin Shinawatra and the transformation of Thai politics

Pasuk Phongpaichit and Chris Baker

Starting in the years around the millennium, the word 'populism' began to appear in Asia (Mizuno and Pasuk 2009).[1] In the Philippines, Joseph Estrada was dubbed a populist after he won election as president in 1998 as a hero of the poor. In Thailand, a Thai translation of the word 'populist' was created to describe Thaksin Shinawatra's 2001 electoral success on a platform of rural reforms and his subsequent commitment to work 'for the people' (Pasuk and Baker 2009: 8). In South Korea, Roh Moo-hyun's rise to the presidency in 2002 against the opposition of the established political elite was explained in terms of his nationalist and populist appeal. Similarly in Taiwan, the success of Chen Shui-bian, son of a poor tenant farmer, in capturing the presidency against the party which had ruled Taiwan since its foundation, was attributed in part to his populist appeal. In Japan in 2001, the surprising rise of the maverick politician, Jun'ichiro Koizumi, to head the ruling party and the government, excited comment about his populist allure (Calder 2001). A few years later, S.B. Yudhyono's campaign for re-election as president in 2009 was described as a populist innovation in Indonesian politics (Wahyu 2010).

'Populism' is a notoriously slippery word. Often it is used as a term of abuse. Some analysts argue its meaning is too imprecise for the term to be useful, and others that its use should be confined to certain places and eras where its meaning is clearer, especially late nineteenth-century USA and Latin America since the 1930s. Yet an alternative view is that the appearance of the word in a particular context signifies something and is worthy of analysis. Several scholars have argued that it is pointless to tie the term to a particular ideology, or a particular form of political organization, or a particular social equation. Where the term 'populism' was once criticized constantly for being 'vague', the broadness of the term is now seen as an asset. Especially in the work of Ernesto Laclau and his associates, populism has been identified as a *form of political practice* that could appear in varied contexts (Laclau 2005; Panizza 2005).

Kenneth Roberts (2006) summarized 'the essential core of populism' as 'the political mobilization of mass constituencies by personalistic leaders who challenge established elites'. Sabatini and Farnsworth (2006: 63, n. 2) point out that 'populism' is used to describe any movement that 'mobilises those who feel themselves to be disadvantaged by socioeconomic and political dislocation, as well as a leadership style that draws on a sense of disaffection from the established political system and elites'. Margaret Canovan (1999: 3) stressed that populist movements 'involve some kinds of revolt against the established structure of power in the name of the people. Populists claim legitimacy on the ground that they speak for *the people.*'

The appearance of populism in Asia was bound up with the Asian economic crisis of 1997 or, more broadly, with the trends within globalization that conspired to create the crisis, and with the social impact left in its wake. The crisis came after an unprecedented boom in Northeast Asia and Southeast Asia. Over a generation, Japan was established as the world's prime manufacturing economy. Korea and Taiwan grew at rates that even surpassed Japan in its heyday. Southeast Asian countries seemed to be readying themselves for a similar surge. New wealth, new aspirations and new pride were created across the region. Against this background, the financial disarray of 1997 was a crisis not only for economies but for ruling oligarchies, and for the state itself.[2] Korea, Thailand, Malaysia, the Philippines and Indonesia faced not only dramatic reversals in economic growth, but intrusions by the IMF on their economic sovereignty, and wholesale denigration of their economic strategies and political systems at the hands of western analysts.

As existing political elites were discredited, people looked for someone to rescue them from hardship and restore their pride and aspirations. The stage was thus set for the rise of political leaders who had strong personal appeal and an ability to present themselves as somehow different from an old elite. The 1997 crisis also created pools of discontent, especially among urban labour, peasant farmers and migrant workers who often bore the brunt of the downturn in the form of unemployment and falling real incomes. There was discontent also among urban middle classes that had become accustomed to rising prosperity, and had often allowed their aspirations to race ahead of reality. Populist leaders rose on the support of coalitions of discontent. In the five years following the financial crisis, virtually every Northeast Asian and Southeast Asian country with an open economy experienced a jolting political disjuncture of some kind.

The political career of Thaksin Shinawatra in Thailand belongs to this wave of Asian populism. He rose to power in the immediate aftermath of the crisis by focusing discontent against the old political leadership. He became the bearer of the hopes of many and varied groups. Like most of the other Asian populists of this wave, he was brought down when he failed to deliver against many of those hopes, and when the old establishment rallied in self-defence. But perhaps more than the others, Thaksin exposed the rifts that had been opened in society by prior decades of uneven development and limited distribution of power. His career sparked a mobilization of mass forces on a scale not previously seen in Thai politics. Although he and most of the other Asian populists were driven from power and replaced by the conservative forces they had challenged, Thai politics has been fundamentally changed.

Oligarchy and resentment

Thailand's political history through the twentieth century was characterized by evolution rather than disjuncture. There was no nationalist movement against colonial rule, or any other successful mass mobilization for change.[3] With no disruption from below, the state was dominated by an oligarchy which constantly evolved, incorporating new groups and power centres, and building internal bonds through networks, patronage ties and deals. At the core of this oligarchy was a new bureaucracy modelled on colonial patterns and grafted onto the old feudal system from the late nineteenth century onward. After the absolute monarchy was converted into a constitutional monarchy in 1932, the military rose to take a dominant position for most of the next fifty years. Under US patronage during the Cold War, the monarchy entered into a close relationship with the military to resist communism. Several analysts of this era, including Fred Riggs (1966), described Thailand as ruled by a small coterie of civil and military officials.

After an upsurge of protests by students, workers and farmers in the 1970s, there was a partial shift. The ruling elite resolved to promote 'democracy with the King as head of state', meaning that democratic institutions would have a growing role in response to popular demand, but that the monarchy would be strongly promoted as the focus of political loyalties (Connors 2003). Parliament, which had existed fitfully since 1932 but been overshadowed by the military, now became more permanent and more important. Elected MPs gradually replaced bureaucrats and generals as ministers. But this parliament represented only a narrow minority of the population. Local businessmen invested heavily in getting elected, ensuring money was a key qualification. In the 1990s, around 70 per cent of MPs were drawn from the ranks of male business owners who make up less than 3 per cent of the population.[4] In effect, parliament was a mechanism for drafting business leaders into the ruling oligarchy. The generals withdrew from the political front line but retained considerable influence, status, and independence. Top bureaucrats negotiated a new distribution of power with elected politicians for mutual benefit.

By the last years of the century, however, there were growing pressures to revise these cosy arrangements. Economic growth was transforming the society. Over the last quarter of the century, average per capita income tripled. A quarter of the population was transferred out of agriculture to urban work. Rising incomes brought new aspirations and increasing demands on government. In addition, this new prosperity was not evenly distributed, leading to growing inequality, especially between urban and rural, the capital and the periphery, the few in the globalized formal economy and the mass still in declining agriculture or a swelling urban informal sector of casual labour and petty enterprise. In the 1990s, these pressures fed into a growing trend of protest politics, social movements, NGOs and public demonstrations (Praphat 1998; Missingham 2003). These movements focused on specific issues, particularly growing competition over resources of land and water, declining agricultural prices, corruption and over-centralization. This trend came to a climax after the 1997 financial crisis when the economic pain was quickly transferred onto the lower social echelons, particularly through unemployment and declining farm prices (Pasuk and Baker 2000: 69–106). These pressures did not feed into parliamentary politics since the parliament was perceived to be a captive reserve of the rich business elite.

Sensing the growing demands for change, a liberal segment of the elite promoted reforms to bring the political system into line with changing social realities. A new constitution introduced in 1997 was designed to strengthen the parliament and executive so that government would be more effective, while strengthening checks and balances on the abuse of power. A decentralization act redistributed power and budget to elected local bodies. Whereas the mass of people had earlier voted only once every few years for a parliament that seemed remote from their lives, they now also elected senators, village and sub-district heads, local mayors and members of various local government bodies. In the more intimate arena of local government, people quickly learnt the potential of the vote to bring material changes which directly affected their own lives. From there it was only a small step to transfer the same awareness to the value of the vote at the national level (Somchai 2008; Walker 2008).

The rise of Thaksin Shinawatra

Thaksin Shinawatra became the vehicle whereby this pressure for change was channelled into national-level parliamentary politics. However, this prospect was far from apparent when he launched his bid for power in the late 1990s. Thaksin hailed from an established business and political family from northern Thailand. After a short career in the police, he made a spectacular fortune from a government-granted concession on mobile phones. He was initially drawn into politics in the early 1990s in order to protect his semi-monopolistic business from competition.[5]

Thaksin launched the Thai Rak Thai (Thai loves Thai, TRT) party in July 1998 in the pit of the downturn after the financial crisis. He promised to overhaul the bureaucrat-dominated government that had led Thailand into the crisis and that was seen by domestic business to have cooperated with the IMF's disastrous policy packages, resulting in massive damage to Thailand's larger corporations (Natenapha 2008). He appealed especially to business leaders by promising to rescue them from the crisis, to transform the bureaucracy into a business-friendly system, and to drive growth so that Thailand accelerated to an OECD-level economy. In the confused post-crisis atmosphere, Thaksin attracted a wide spectrum of support from groups that imagined such an avowed reformer would promote their own particular agenda. Many NGOs and pro-test groups gave their endorsement. A prominent radical academic dubbed him 'a breath of fresh air' (Kasian 2002: 339). His TRT party won just short of a majority at elections in 2001, and many politicians who had resisted his appeal now rushed to join his party.

Throughout this rise, Thaksin had shown little interest in the underdog, and had made no commitment to promote dramatic social changes. However, he had recruited a small number of former student activists because of their skills in political organization. These activists had crafted an election platform for the rural areas promising debt relief, local development funds and cheap universal health care. The platform attracted scant attention at the time since voters perceived such platforms as mere window-dressing. But shortly before the election, Thaksin was put on trial for corruptly concealing some of his immense financial assets under the names of his rela-tives and household servants. To fight these charges, he sought popular support. In striking new rhetoric, he declared, 'Nothing will stand in my way. I am determined to devote myself to politics in order to lead the Thai people out of poverty' (*The Nation* 2000). After his election victory, he launched a weekly radio programme where he chatted to listeners about his work, and made sure he dominated the television news. He also accelerated the implementation of his policy platform.

This strategy worked. His personal popularity rating rose from 30 per cent before the elec-tion to 70 per cent on the eve of the court verdict. He survived the court case on a split verdict, and won huge popularity for his policies, especially the medical scheme which brought health care within reach of millions for the first time, significantly reducing the numbers remaining below the poverty line.

Still, Thaksin's main focus as premier was on transforming Thailand in the interests of business. He packed the cabinet with business colleagues, and put economic policy under an academic who believed a country could be run like a corporation. The project which unfolded over his early years in power can be summarized in the following way. Have the country run by businessmen using business principles, rather than bureaucrats (or bureaucrat-minded politicians) using bureaucratic methods. Accelerate the economy by protecting and promoting domestic capital while maintaining Thailand's attraction as a site for multinational companies. Spread the benefits more widely through a 'new social contract' (Hewison 2004), meaning more state welfare available to all as a right, and accessible microcredit schemes to broaden and deepen the involvement of all in the capitalist economy. Establish a single dominant political party, financed by big business, able to stay in power for the long term. Centralize authority within the government, especially over the budget. Ensure 'quiet politics' by controlling the media, dispersing civil society and delegitimizing independent intellectuals. Discipline the society through cultural campaigns, especially emphasizing national unity and national goals.

Early opposition

Thaksin set out to relocate power in the hands of a democratically elected leader and a more centralized and national political party at the expense of the various fractions of the old oligarchy. This ambitious programme provoked fierce opposition from old centres of power.

Unsurprisingly, senior bureaucrats saw Thaksin as a threat, not just because of his attempt to reform officialdom, but because of the way his personal popularity and party dominance was shifting power away from the bureaucracy to the parliament. Royalists drew attention to incidents when Thaksin's flaunting of his personal popularity seemed to intrude on political space they believed was reserved for the monarch. At his annual birthday speech in December 2001, the King took the unusual step of criticizing the prime minister in front of the live television audience, and was again critical in the same speech two years later.

As part of the same power complex, the old guard in the military bridled at Thaksin's growing power. They were further provoked when Thaksin tried to get a grip on the army hierarchy by accelerating the promotions of his old colleagues from the military cadet school, and even inserting his poorly qualified cousin as army chief (McCargo and Ukrist 2005: 121–65).

Segments of the business community also became hostile, particularly after the benefits of Thaksin's rule seemed to accrue to a small inner circle of Thaksin's friends, and especially to his own family companies. One of these companies continued to dominate the mobile-phone market, despite efforts at market liberalization, and others extended into property, airlines, television and other areas with all too obvious assistance from government agencies. In addition, Thaksin reneged on his promises to roll back the IMF-mandated reforms which had crippled many Thai businesses. He courted foreign investment and actively sought free-trade agreements – both moves which distressed insecure local entrepreneurs – while his vaunted programmes to boost domestic capital came to very little.

Activists and NGOs also stampeded towards the opposition. The hopes that Thaksin would assist many individual causes were quickly dashed. Political activists became hostile as it became clear that Thaksin hoped to install a virtual one-party system and remain in power for at least two decades on the model of Mahathir Muhammed or Lee Kwan Yew. They also bridled when Thaksin poured scorn on concepts of democracy, human rights and the freedom to criticize. As he became more authoritarian in manner and action, the press generally became hostile.

By 2004, Thaksin's personal popularity was still strong, but he was coming increasingly under fire from this vocal minority in the old oligarchy, big business and civil society. This criticism focused on his personal corruption and abuse of power for profit, and on his growing authoritarianism.

From modernist to populist

Against this background of growing criticism, Thaksin transformed himself into a more thorough-going populist as elections approached in 2005.

He launched a series of tours covering all regions of the country, giving instant approval for local projects and budgets. He focused his mission on eradicating poverty in a very short space of time – 'Four years ahead, there will be no poor people. Won't that be neat' (Thaksin 2005). For his party's platform at the approaching elections, he spilled out new schemes including an extension of the village funds, land deeds for every landholder, a government pond dug for anyone prepared to pay a small fuel cost, four new cheap loan schemes, free distribution of cows, training schemes for the poor, cheaper school fees, special payments for children forced to drop out of school because of poverty, an educational gift bag for every new mother, care centres for the elderly, more sports facilities in urban areas, cheaper phone calls, an end to eviction from slums, more cheap housing, lower taxes, increased investment in the universal health scheme, and a nationwide scheme of irrigation.

His public appearance and speech underwent a makeover in this period. He shed his business suit in favour of shirtsleeves with buttons open at the neck, sometimes all down to his waist, and his hair lightly tousled. He stopped littering his speeches with English to denote internationalism and modernity, and instead used dialect and earthy humour. He stopped quoting Bill Gates and similar international figures, instead often mentioning his own family and sex life.

His exposure on the media increased (Nualnoi 2009). He dominated news on the government-owned television channels, and featured in several special programmes including a televised cabinet meeting and visits to schools. The format of his weekly radio show underwent a subtle change: instead of commenting on current issues, Thaksin related the events of his week like a diary, allowing listeners *into* his life. A pilot project for poverty eradication ran all day on live television as a form of 'reality show'. The upcountry tours provided opportunities for Thaksin to be photographed in homely situations – emerging from a village bath-house in a common man's lower cloth; transported on a village tractor; riding a motorbike down a dusty village street; accepting flowers from toothless old ladies.

His rhetoric underwent another shift. Particularly in speeches leading up to the 2005 election, he presented himself as a unique instrument for translating the will of the people into action. He poured scorn on the parliamentary process, judicial system, open debate and any kind of opposition as obstacles against him fulfilling this mission. He told NGOs that they no longer had any role because there was no need for intermediaries between the leader and the people (see, for example, Thaksin 2005). His party slogan was replaced with the intensely populist, 'The heart of TRT is the people.' He now constantly distinguished himself from an old guard of top bureaucrats, politicians and intellectuals who he claimed had never 'worked for the people'.

At polls in February 2005, the TRT party won an overwhelming victory. On the 'party list', a national vote by party, it won 61 per cent of valid votes and occupied 67 of the 100 seats. In the territorial constituencies it won 310 of 400 seats. The result was extraordinary. No previous elected premier had survived a full four-year term, let alone been re-elected. No party had ever won a simple majority of house seats, let alone three-quarters. The result came about partly because of Thaksin's personal popularity, and partly because so many local politicians had flocked to his party to survive.

Thaksin openly boasted of the '19 million votes' (on the party list) as a personal endorsement. He spoke of remaining in power for twenty or twenty-five years. He was more openly contemptuous of liberal democratic processes, and of the 'old guard' of bureaucrats, opposition politicians, activists and intellectuals.

Counterattack

The legitimacy provided by such an overwhelming electoral victory made Thaksin appear as an even more dangerous threat to other centres of power, especially the components of the old oligarchy. Open opposition to Thaksin was now spearheaded by royalists, top bureaucrats, some senior military figures and social activists. In different ways, these various groups appealed to the power of the monarchy as a counterweight to the democratic legitimacy, populism and popularity of Thaksin.

Immediately after the election, three members of the King's Privy Council[6] publicly criti-cized Thaksin over his policy towards the far south, where a lingering insurgency among Malay Muslims had flared up over the previous year. Over the following months, several privy councillors gave public speeches criticizing corruption in government, and often quoting the past words of the King, such as a 1969 speech saying, 'order depends on our strong support for good people, who must be given the opportunity to rule the nation, control and prevent bad people from seizing power and causing trouble' (*Bangkok Post* 2005a).

Bureaucratic resentment against Thaksin became focused on the case of Jaruvarn Maintaka, who had been dismissed from the post of auditor-general on a technicality after pursuing cases of political corruption. Jaruvarn resisted the dismissal, claiming, 'I don't think anyone can move me except a royal decree' (*Bangkok Post* 2005b). An order appointing a successor was sent for the final royal signature but never returned. A former Ministry of Interior official penned a book entitled *Royal Powers*, citing the Jaruvarn case and making extensive claims for the scope of the royal prerogative (Pramuan 2005).

In late 2005, Thaksin and the military old guard locked horns over the military reshuffle. When the list finally returned from the palace, Thaksin's candidate for army chief and several other key posts had been rejected. Over the coming months, General Saprang Kalyanamit, newly appointed head of the Third Army, talked often in public, saying that his soldierly duty was to protect the King and he would happily die in that defence.

In mid-2005, Sondhi Limthongkul, a media entrepreneur who had been an enthusiastic supporter of Thaksin but now figured among the growing ranks of apostates, was thrown off television and decided to continue his programme as a weekly public rally, broadcast more widely on satellite television. He gave space on his stage to many of the activist groups that opposed Thaksin's policies. Sondhi also publicized the book *Royal Powers*, and echoed royalist claims that Thaksin had infringed on the King's prerogative. He and his followers dressed themselves in yellow, a colour associated with the King, and swathed themselves in slogans claiming they were defending the monarchy and saving the country. In November 2005, Sondhi called on the King to remove Thaksin for corruption and immoral rule (Pasuk and Baker 2009: 252–6).

The privy councillors, bureaucrats and generals would regularly repeat the nostrum that the monarchy was above politics. Yet all in different ways invoked the authority of the King to contest the power which Thaksin had achieved in the parliamentary system.

Mass mobilization 1: the Yellow Shirts

To this point, the conflict was confined within a familiar world of parliament, the media and political activists in the capital. But over the next three years, the opposition between the King as a source of moral authority and Thaksin as a product of a parliamentary system expanded into two competitive mass mobilizations and a fierce ideological debate, quite unlike anything previously seen in Thai politics.

The first of these mass mobilizations was concentrated in (though not exclusive to) the urban middle class. Initially the middle class had been largely supportive of Thaksin. Bookshops overflowed with works lionizing his success in business and politics, and reproducing his words as advice in business and life. At the 2005 elections, 32 of 37 constituencies in Bangkok returned TRT candidates. In December 2005, polls gave Thaksin his highest popularity rating. Yet over the next month, this position changed dramatically. Thaksin's family sold their holding company to a Singapore government investment arm for US$ 1.7 billion without incurring any tax on the immense capital gain, and with many laws and regulations changed, bent or defied in the process (Ma Nok and Dek Nok Krob 2006). The sale evoked a gut reaction of anger and disgust, particularly among the tax-paying middle class.

Sondhi fanned this anger by portraying the middle class as a milch cow, milked by Thaksin for the super-profits of his business exploits, and for the taxes to pay for the populist schemes which kept him in power. Sondhi pitched his appeal at 'the middle classes ... who suffer most, whose rights have been infringed upon, who have been taxed to the hilt, who haven't been given a chance or opportunity to get what they deserve' (Crispin 2007). His weekly rallies swelled in size to tens of thousands. Many more became glued to Sondhi's ASTV television channel, which used the internet and satellites to evade Thailand's old broadcasting controls and was riveting if only because it was the first passionate political broadcasting in Thailand.

In February 2006, Sondhi again called on the King to remove Thaksin, and a royalist group presented a petition with the same demand. Sondhi further increased the royalist tone by accusing Thaksin and his TRT allies of plotting to overthrow the monarchy. At his rallies people wore T-shirts and headbands emblazoned with the slogans, 'We fight for the King.' Several social activists who had joined the earlier anti-Thaksin protests now peeled away, unable to tolerate this distinctly royalist turn (Kengkij and Hewison 2009). The anti-Thaksin coalition now included royalists, bureaucrats, the military old guard in the background, and large sections of the urban middle class mobilized by Sondhi. Some of those liberals who had promoted political reforms in the late 1990s took a prominent part in this opposition and openly regretted that the 1997 constitution had conferred too much power on the prime minister.

Assault on democracy

Thaksin responded by calling an election to reaffirm his mandate. The opposition boycotted the polls in April 2006, resulting in an unclear and contested result. The King called on the judiciary to sort out the mess, and the judges responded by invalidating the poll. Judges had hitherto played a very limited role in politics, but from this point they became an additional and important element of the anti-Thaksin alliance.

The parliamentary system entered the preliminary stages of limbo. Before another election could be scheduled, and in the midst of another wrangle over the military shuffle, the old guard in the army executed a coup on 19 September 2006. A few weeks earlier, General Prem Tin-sulanond, head of the Privy Council, had stated publicly that the 'real owners' of the military were the country and King, and that the elected government was a mere 'jockey'.[7] The soldiers manning the tanks which occupied the city wore yellow armbands. The generals cited cor-ruption, abuse of power, and affronts to the monarchy as justification for their coup. The junta appointed General Surayud Chulanont, a former army head and current member of the Privy Council, as prime minister. They pointed to the yellow-clad audiences of Sondhi's rallies as evidence of popular support for the coup. Although the generals claimed the coup had nothing to do with the King, the royalist tenor of the takeover was plainly evident. Thaksin and his supporters later accused General Prem of masterminding the coup.

Given the extremely open nature of the Thai economy, the generals knew they could not sustain a form of government that did not gain international approval. They undertook to restore parliament within a year, but used that time to enact a slew of conservative and repres-sive legislation that undid many of the advances of the prior two decades. As their first act, the coup junta tore up the 1997 constitution. Their replacement charter reduced the power of the parliament and executive in favour of the bureaucracy and judiciary. A hand-picked assembly passed an Internal Security Act which the parliament had been resisting for almost a decade, and also laws to control media, especially in cyberspace. The judges dissolved the TRT Party for malpractice at the failed 2006 election, and imposed a five-year ban on political activity by 111 of its members, including Thaksin.

The generals hoped to pass on power to an anti-Thaksin coalition headed by the Democrat Party. To achieve that end they invested considerable public money and resources in forming new political parties to act as the Democrats' coalition partners, intimidating Thaksin's bases of support, carrying out campaigns of dirty tricks and misinformation, and ordering military personnel and government servants to vote against pro-Thaksin candidates (Wassana 2008; Pasuk and Baker 2010). Yet these efforts were in vain. At polls in December 2007, the pro-Thaksin forces, now named the People's Power Party (PPP), won two seats short of a simple majority and were able to head a coalition government. A few weeks later Thaksin returned from self-imposed exile. The coalition government began manoeuvres to undo the work of the coup junta, including restoring all or part of the prior constitution, and rehabilitating Thaksin and other banned politicians.

The efforts of the anti-Thaksin coalition to block these moves became a broad attack on the institutions and theory of parliamentary democracy. As the military did not dare attempt another coup, the key weapons were the judiciary and Sondhi's mass mobilization, now named the People's Alliance for Democracy (PAD) and known colloquially as the Yellow Shirts. The judges harassed the government by removing various ministers, mostly on technical grounds. They also convicted both Thaksin and his wife of corruption and abuse of power, sending them back into exile to escape jail. Supporters heralded these moves as a new and virtuous judicial activism, while opponents dubbed them as politics by other means.

In mid-2008, the Yellow Shirts established a permanent protest camp in central Bangkok, defended like a military encampment. Nightly rallies, sponsored by business and personal donations, attracted prominent royalists, retired generals and large numbers of the Bangkok salariat. Speakers excoriated the government and heaped further charges of corruption and abuse on Thaksin. The Yellow Shirts also sent out detachments to harass ministers, and besieged Government House in an attempt to prevent the institution functioning. They also intermittently occupied airports, and finally closed down Bangkok's international airport for a week. This prompted the judges to another ruling which brought down the government, dissolved PPP and two other parties, adding another 109 names to the list of banned politicians. The generals were then able to craft a new ruling coalition, headed by the Democrat Party. Although several cases were brought against the Yellow Shirts for their disruption and harassment, somehow the cases never reached any conclusion.

The attack on parliamentary democracy also became ideological. Sondhi and other Yellow Shirt leaders argued that Thaksin's legitimacy based on election was void because votes were secured dishonestly by direct vote-buying or by populist lures. This situation was possible, they claimed, because the rural electorate was still uneducated and naïve, and hence a system of simple one-man/one-vote was inappropriate for the social conditions. In its place, they proposed Thailand should move to some other system, perhaps a majority of appointed MPs, or some form of franchise based on occupation. This argument undermined the first principle of elective parliamentary democracy.

Mass mobilization 2: the Red Shirts

The second mass mobilization took place among supporters of Thaksin, opponents of the military, and defenders of democracy embattled.

In the aftermath of the coup in late 2006, small groups of political activists protested against the return of the military to politics, some adopting red as the symbolic colour of dissent (Nostitz

2009: 14–15). During the Yellow Shirt campaigns in 2008, the pro-Thaksin government set up a television station where the key presenters adopted red as a uniform colour. All these various groups cooperated in occasional demonstrations, especially a rally at General Prem's house on 27 July, accusing him of masterminding the coup and the destruction of democracy. After the installation of the Democrat government in December, the group staged red-clad stadium rallies as shows of force. The television station adopted ASTV's model using the internet and satellites to avoid broadcasting controls. In addition the movement founded websites, local radio stations and magazines. Programmes broadcast through these media offered analyses of Thailand's politics that were more sophisticated and radical than anything heard on broadcast media for over thirty years. Especially in the northeast and north, and in the city among migrant workers, groups clustered around local radio stations formed building blocks of a movement. Some leaders circulated around the provinces, conducting political schools.

In early 2009, the Red Shirts (as they were now known) copied the Yellow strategy of establishing a permanent protest camp close to Government House. Supporters flocked in from the provinces to attend. Speakers demanded early elections, a return to the old constitution, an end to 'double standards' by the judiciary, and rehabilitation of Thaksin and other former TRT MPs. Thaksin appeared at these rallies through video-link from his exile in Dubai. At the approach of Thai new year in mid-April, the numbers swelled, Thaksin exhorted his supporters to achieve 'full democracy', taxi drivers began to contrive gridlock by blocking key city inter-sections, and groups travelled to nearby Pattaya to disrupt an ASEAN summit meeting. The army responded by bringing 10,000 troops into the city to disperse the demonstrations by an overwhelming display of force. Afterwards, the generals and Democrat leaders talked of moves to achieve 'reconciliation', but in fact resisted calls for elections or constitutional changes, and instead poured money into populist-like schemes in the hope of weaning support away from Thaksin.

In March 2010, tens of thousands of Red Shirts travelled from the provinces to the city in a massive display of support. The campaign had a single demand of immediate elections. For over a month, the rallies continued peaceably, gaining a great deal of sympathy among city dwellers, especially from rural migrants and the working class. The Democrat leaders offered negotiations which came to nothing. The demonstration moved from the official quarter into the com-mercial district, disrupting tourism and other businesses. Violent incidents increased, though whether these were instigated by the security forces to justify a crackdown or perpetrated by radical elements among the Red Shirts was never clear. Eventually on 19 May, the government ordered a crackdown which cleared the demonstration but left a total of almost a hundred killed and some thirty buildings torched in the finale. In three towns in the northeast, red sympathizers burnt down government offices.

In the aftermath, the government again talked about 'reconciliation', while arresting the Red Shirt leaders on charges of terrorism, closing down Red media, and sending soldiers into the north and northeast to suppress any further activity.

Conclusion

Since the late 1990s, participation in Thailand's national politics has penetrated deeper into the society and acquired a new intensity. Voting turn-outs have risen, new media have been founded to spread political messages, and political debate has become more widespread and more intense (Hewison 2010: 125). A nationwide survey in July 2009 found that 6 per cent of the adult population had participated in the Yellow Shirt activities, and another 6 per cent in the Red Shirt activities. In all, 18 per cent agreed with the Yellow Shirts, and 20 per cent with the Red Shirts.[8]

In other words, in the adult population of 50 million, there were around three million active participants and another seven million supporters for each side. The level of mass involvement in Thai politics has undergone a profound change.

Despite everything in his background, Thaksin became the instrument of a demand, bubbling up from below, for a fairer society and more open politics. The unprecedented popularity of Thaksin and the emotional support for the Red Shirt movement were mounted on demands rumbling up from society's lower ranks, not from the destitute, whose numbers had greatly diminished, but from those with rising incomes, rising aspirations and rising awareness of great inequalities and injustices. As Thaksin faced increasing opposition, he projected himself as a classic populist leader who was the instrument of the people's will, and the scourge of the old oligarchy. People not only found that Thaksin's populist programmes palpably improved their lives, but they also felt empowered by his offer to espouse their cause against the arrogant bureaucracy and old political elite.

Thaksin's combination of electoral legitimacy, great wealth and unprecedented personal popularity was perceived as a threat by all the major components of the old oligarchy. As a counterweight, they called on the moral authority of the monarchy. Although Thaksin never attacked the monarchy, he was accused of anti-monarchism because his personal power and popularity intruded on space hitherto reserved for the King. The cry of defending the monarchy served as a means to mobilize middle-class groups who felt insecure about their own weight in this emerging mass politics. Whereas the middle class and the old oligarchy had earlier seemed to welcome the development of parliamentary democracy, many changed their minds when power legitimated by the ballot box threatened to dramatically change the allocation of power and public goods. The Yellow Shirts argued that a democracy without checks and balances would be dangerous and unstable. They conjured up ideas of an alternative framework of politics based on law and morality rather than the electoral principle. When the generals and Yellow Shirts attacked both the idea and the institution of parliament, a counter-mobilization took place among Thaksin supporters and political activists dressed in red.

Support for the two mass mobilizations reflected multiple divisions within the society between rich and poor, centre and periphery, powerful and powerless. Support for Thaksin and the Red Shirts was focused in the lower ranks of society, especially among farmers and rural migrants. Support for the Yellow Shirts was focused among the old establishment and the middle class, especially in the capital.

But there was also a regional dimension. Support for Thaksin and the Red Shirts was strongest in the northeast and upper north. These two regions were poorer than the average, but also culturally distinct. They had been incorporated into Siam/Thailand in the nineteenth century and had been intermittently rebellious or politically truculent ever since. In these regions, support for Thaksin spread across the social spectrum, tapping a vein of cultural identity and resentment of central control that runs so deep it has largely been ignored. Support for the Yellow Shirts and the Democrat Party was based in the capital and the south. Unlike the other regions where the economy is based on peasant agriculture, the south is more urbanized, with an economy based on mining, plantations and tourism, and with a longer historical association with the capital.

In addition, support for Red or Yellow might cut across considerations of class or region and come down to ideological convictions about monarchy and democracy.

Thaksin's politics were very new in the Thai context, but very similar to movements and leaders that have been labelled as 'populist' in various other countries. Around the millennium the word 'populism' appeared in Asia for the first time. In five countries it was applied to describe regimes or leaders. In Japan, Korea and Taiwan, it was applied to leaders who in some way appealed to people for support against entrenched political machines. In Indonesia and Thailand, it was applied to leaders who focused the frustrations and demands of people who felt excluded by entrenched oligarchies.

The Japanese case was rather different from the others. Jun'ichiro Koizumi turned out in retrospect to be the trailer for a much larger change – defeat of the party which had ruled for 53 years. All of the other new Asian populists were driven from power, accused of corruption, and succeeded by the conservative forces which they had challenged. In the Philippines, Joseph Estrada was felled by street demonstrations in 2001, convicted and jailed for corruption, and replaced by Gloria Arroyo, a member of a prominent old family. In Korea, Roh Moo-hyun was conclusively defeated at election, accused of bribery, committed suicide in 2009, and was succeeded in power by the centrist party he had challenged. In Taiwan, Chen Shui-bian resigned in 2008 after his party suffered election defeat, was convicted on multiple counts of embezzlement and bribe-taking, and was succeeded by the KMT Party, which had dominated Taiwanese politics for half a century before his rise. In Thailand, Thaksin Shinawatra was removed from office by a military coup, convicted of abuse of power, and had his family assets seized on grounds of multiple cases of corruption and abuse of power. He was succeeded by the Democrat Party which he had characterized as part of the bureaucratic old guard.

Thaksin rose on the swell of a new mass politics generated by the rising prosperity and increasing social complexity over prior decades. Although Thaksin himself was removed by the classic devices of coup, corruption charges and exile, the support for Thaksin refused to die but instead ballooned into a mass protest and the biggest demonstrations seen since the mid-1970s. Although the conservative forces of the military and Democrat Party returned to power, they did not revoke Thaksin's 'populist' programmes but continued them, and embellished them with further social spending which they desperately branded as 'welfarist' rather than 'populist'.[9] Moreover, this conservative restoration could only survive through heavy support from the military and deployment of the repressive legislation passed in the aftermath of the 2006 coup – evidence that the social support for what Thaksin came to represent remains strong. In July 2011 the Thaksinite party, now called Phuea Thai (For the Thai), won 265 out of 500 seats at a general election, and Thaksin's younger sister, Yingluck Shinawatra, became Thailand's first female prime minister. The transformation of Thai politics is not yet over.

Notes

1 Of course, populist *appeals* had appeared earlier during anti-colonial struggles, but then they had been labelled as nationalist, not populist (see Anderson 2009).
2 Japan's slowdown and slump into a 'lost decade' came earlier but ultimately belonged to the same historical experience.
3 The communist insurgency from the 1960s to 1980s was confined to forests and hills in the periphery, and never sparked a mass mobilization.
4 This calculation is based on official declarations to the Election Commission of Thailand, and assumes that those who return their profession as 'politician' are also businessmen.
5 For a fuller account of Thaksin's career, see Pasuk and Baker (2009), McCargo and Ukrist (2005).
6 The King appoints the president and up to 18 members of the Privy Council who have a duty 'to render such advice to the King on all matters pertaining to His functions' (clause 12 of the 1997 constitution). Most of the members are retired generals, jurists and senior bureaucrats.
7 General Prem first made the statement on 15 July 2006, then repeated it to a foreign journalist in the week prior to the coup (Pasuk and Baker 2009: 279).

8 The survey, commissioned by the Thai Health Foundation, had a sample of over 5,000 which slightly under-represented farmers and manual labourers, possibly biasing the results a little. The results have never been published. Thanks to Anek Laothammatas.

9 In many contexts, 'populism' is a term of abuse, but in Thailand it was adopted by one post-Thaksin party as its slogan: 'Populism for a Happy Life'.

References

Anderson, B. (2009) 'Afterword', in Kosuke Mizuno and Pasuk Phongpaichit (eds) *Populism in Asia*, Singapore and Kyoto: NUS Press and Kyoto University Press.

Bangkok Post (2005a) 'Prem: social sanctions needed on the corrupt', 10 December: 3.

——(2005b) 'Jaruvan: I will return to office; auditor general vows to continue her fight', 5 September: 1.

Calder, K.E. (2001) 'Asian populism and the US security presence in Asia', transcript of an October 2001 roundtable in Washington DC, sponsored by the Sasakawa Peace Foundation; available at: www.spfusa.org/program/av2001/oct0301.pdf (accessed 3 December 2001).

Canovan, M. (1999) 'Trust the people! Populism and the two faces of democracy', *Political Studies* 47: 2–16.

Connors, M.K. (2003) *Democracy and National Identity in Thailand*, London: Routledge.

Crispin, S.W. (2007) 'Recollections, revelations of a protest leader', *Asia Times*, 27 April.

Hewison, K. (2004) 'Crafting Thailand's new social contract', *Pacific Review* 17 (4): 503–22.

——(2010) 'Thaksin Shinawatra and the reshaping of Thai politics,' *Contemporary Politics* 16 (2): 119–33.

Kasian Tejapira (2002) 'Post-crisis economic impasse and political recovery in Thailand: The resurgence of economic nationalism', *Critical Asian Studies* 34 (3): 323–56.

Kengkij Kitirianglarp and K. Hewison (2009) 'Social movements and political opposition in contemporary Thailand', *Pacific Review* 22 (4): 451–77.

Laclau, E. (2005) *On Populist Reason*, London: Verso.

Ma Nok and Dek Nok Krob (2006) *25 kham tham bueang lang dil tekowor shinkorp* [25 questions behind the Shin Corp takeover deal], Bangkok: Openbooks.

McCargo, D. and Ukrist Pathmanand (2005) *The Thaksinization of Thailand*, Copenhagen: NIAS Press.

Missingham, B.F. (2003) *The Assembly of the Poor in Thailand: From Local Struggles to National Protest Movement*, Chiang Mai: Silkworm Books.

Mizuno, Kosuke and Pasuk Phongpaichit (eds) (2009) *Populism in Asia*, Singapore and Kyoto: NUS Press and Kyoto University Press.

Natenapha Wailerdsak (2008) 'Companies in crisis', in Pasuk Phongpaichit and C. Baker (eds) *Thai Capital after the 1997 Crisis*, Chiang Mai: Silkworm Books.

Nostitz, N. (2009) *Red vs Yellow, Volume 1: Thailand's Crisis of Identity*, Bangkok: White Lotus.

Nualnoi Treerat (2009) 'Thaksin Shinawatra and mass media', in Kosuke Mizuno and Pasuk Phongpaichit (eds) *Populism in Asia*, Singapore and Kyoto: NUS Press and Kyoto University Press.

Panizza, F. (2005) 'Introduction: Populism and the mirror of democracy', in F. Panizza (ed.) *Populism and the Mirror of Democracy*, London: Verso.

Pasuk Phongpaichit and C. Baker (2000) *Thailand's Crisis*, Chiang Mai: Silkworm Books.

——(2009) *Thaksin*, Chiang Mai: Silkworm Books.

——(2010) 'The mask-play election: generals, politicians, and voters at Thailand's 2007 poll', Working Paper 144, Singapore, Asia Research Institute.

Pramuan Ruchanaseri (2005) *Phraratcha-amnat* [Royal powers], Bangkok: Sumet Ruchanaseri.

Praphat Pintobtaeng (1998) *Kan mueang bon thong thanon: 99 wan samatcha khon jon* [Politics on the street: 99 days of the Assembly of the Poor], Bangkok: Krirk University.

Riggs, F.W. (1966) *Thailand: The Modernization of a Bureaucratic Polity*, Honolulu: East–West Center Press.

Roberts, K.M. (2006) 'Populism, political conflict, and grass-roots organisation in Latin America', *Comparative Politics* 38 (2): 127–48.

Sabatini, C. and E. Farnsworth (2006) 'A "left turn" in Latin America? The urgent need for labor law reform', *Journal of Democracy* 17 (4): 50–64.

Somchai Phatharathananunth (2008) 'The Thai Rak Thai Party and elections in north-eastern Thailand', *Journal of Contemporary Asia*, 38 (1): 106–23.

Thaksin Shinawatra (2005) 'Thaksin Shinawatra, leader of the Thai Rak Thai Party, speech at Sanam Luang, 4 February 2005', unpublished audio transcript (in Thai).

The Nation (Thailand) (2000) 'I won't let NCCC crush me – Thaksin', 23 December.

Wahyu Prasetyawan (2010) 'The 2009 presidential election in Indonesia', unpublished paper.

Walker, A. (2008) 'The rural constitution and the everyday politics of elections in northern Thailand', *Journal of Contemporary Asia* 38 (1): 84–105.

Wassana Nanuam (2008) *Lap luang phrang: pathiwat prasat sai* [Secrecy, deception, camouflage: the sandcastle coup], Bangkok: Matichon.

7

PATRONAGE-BASED PARTIES AND THE DEMOCRATIC DEFICIT IN THE PHILIPPINES

Origins, evolution, and the imperatives of reform*

Paul D. Hutchcroft and Joel Rocamora

No country in Asia has more experience with democratic institutions than the Philippines. Over more than a century—from the representational structures of the Malolos republic of 1898 to the holding of regular elections for local and national posts under American colonial rule, from the *cacique* democracy of the postwar republic to the toppling of Ferdinand Marcos and the restoration of democracy in the 1986 People Power uprising—Filipinos know both the promise of democracy and the problems of making democratic structures work for the benefit of all. In the quarter century since the fall of Marcos, spirited hopes for democratic change have alternated with dispirited frustration over the character of the country's democracy. The past decade alone has witnessed dramatic ebbs and flows across three administrations. The 2001 downfall of President Joseph Estrada, via a second People Power uprising, was followed by new hopes in the leadership of President Gloria Macapagal-Arroyo. Her administration then degenerated into a crisis-ridden presidency remembered for corruption, electoral fraud, and authoritarian tendencies, and has been followed most recently by the emergence of extraordinary levels of trust in President Benigno S. Aquino III after he assumed the presidency in the middle of 2010.[1] As hopes are once again raised, there is no assurance that the country's political institutions will be able to respond to the needs of the Philippine citizenry—particularly the poor and the excluded mass of the population.

This chapter examines the country's longstanding democratic deficit, specifically how the enormous need for responding to pent-up demands and pressures from below is accompanied by the incapacity of the country's democratic institutions to do so with any degree of effectiveness. Although there are many ways in which this deficit might be filled, we argue that there is one crucial factor: the creation of more effective and cohesive political parties, oriented to programmatic rather than particularistic goals, policy rather than pork. Stronger parties can promote clearer choices to voters and help to structure political competition toward the realization of aggregate rather than particularistic interests.[2] Because institutional deficiencies bear the bulk of the blame for the many historical shortcomings of Philippine democracy, we argue, it is through institutional reform that the country can best begin to construct a democracy able to offer benefits to all.[3] Building on the many strengths that already exist in Philippine democracy, the key task is to ensure that popular demands can be channeled more effectively through the reform of democratic institutions—in particular through the creation of stronger political parties.[4]

When we speak of the alternating hopes and frustrations of Philippine democracy, it is important to emphasize that the fundamental values of democracy continue to command broad respect from all sectors of Philippine society.[5] The problems are manifested, rather, in the recurrent and dispiriting inability of democratic institutions to deliver the goods, specifically goods of a *public* character. One can note, most proximately, the failure of political institutions to resolve the 2000–1 impeachment crisis caused by the blatant corruption of the Estrada administration, and the Arroyo administration's equally blatant undermining of key institutions toward the paramount goal of regime preservation. From a broader perspective, it is essential to highlight a longstanding failure of the state to act on behalf of the public interest, extreme difficulties in controlling and regulating the means of violence (Lacaba 1995; Sidel 1999), deeply rooted obstacles to converting the country's rich human and natural resources into sustained development (Hutchcroft 1998), and a general lack of responsiveness to the needs of the majority of the population.[6]

While Philippine democracy has major difficulties delivering goods of a public character, those with favorable access to the state have countless means of milking the system for private gain. Rent-seeking activities tend to take place out of public view, but the phenomenon in general is widely acknowledged and breeds an increasing sense of cynicism with the practice of Philippine democracy. For ordinary citizens who derive few such benefits, explains economist Emmanuel de Dios,

> government is an abstraction, an alienated entity, whose only palpable dimension is the episodic patronage dispensed by bosses and politicians, which merely reinforces the poor's real condition of dependence. This same alienated condition causes the electorate in many places to repeatedly elect convicted criminals, underworld characters, and known grafters, simply because such behavior is *irrelevant* to the more advantageous local clientelist functions those persons discharge, whether this be of a material nature (e.g., the local privileges [given to the First Couple's home regions] ... under the Marcoses) or a symbolic one (for example, Estrada's image as champion of the masses).
>
> *(de Dios and Hutchcroft 2003: 265)*

At the same time, the failure of the state to deliver public goods leads many to seek to overturn the political system altogether. Alone among the countries of East and Southeast Asia, the Philippines has a more than four-decades-old communist-led insurgency—encouraged in large part by the immense gulf in levels of wealth and income between the elite and the millions of Filipino workers, urban poor, and peasants below them. In the south of the country, Muslim secessionist groups have been in rebellion for most of this same period. These insurgencies have elicited countermeasures that have led to persistent violations of human rights and limits to the exercise of political rights by organized groups of the poor.

In the first section of this article we provide a historical overview of Philippine political parties in the American years, with particular emphasis on the early colonial era under William Howard Taft (1900–13) and the Philippine commonwealth under Manuel Quezon (1935–41). We shall locate the origins of Philippine democracy's institutional deficiencies in the early American colonial period and explore how the type of patronage-oriented party that emerged in the first decade of the twentieth century persisted in the midst of many changes—both in the scope of democratic politics and in the structure of the overall political system. In the second section, we examine the continued evolution of patronage-oriented parties, from the emergence of a mass electorate in the early postwar years through the dictatorship of Ferdinand Marcos (1972–86). The third section focuses attention on the character of post-martial-law democracy, demonstrating how weak, patronage-based parties have endured amid very different styles of presidential leadership under Corazon Aquino (1986–92), Fidel Ramos (1992–8), Joseph Estrada (1998–2001), and Gloria Macapagal-Arroyo (2001–10). In conclusion, we argue the imperatives of political reform. When the debate over reform resumes, it should be undertaken with a clear understanding of the historical origins and evolution of the democratic deficit and proceed to identify mechanisms specifically geared toward the strengthening of Philippine political parties. The most important first step, we would suggest, is carefully designed reform of the electoral system.

The origins of modern Philippine parties: patronage politics in the colonial era

Following the conventional Western definition, the Philippine Omnibus Election Code of 1985 describes a political party as "an organized group of persons pursuing the same ideology, political ideas or platforms of government" (Leones and Moraleda 1998: 290). But nobody would accuse Philippine political parties of being such an animal. Carl Landé, perhaps the most influential student of postwar Philippine politics, explained in the late 1960s that

> the two rival parties in each province … are held together by dyadic patron–client relationships extending from great and wealthy political leaders in each province down to lesser gentry politicians in the towns, down further to petty leaders in each village, and down finally to the clients of the latter: the common [people].
>
> *(1969: 156)*

More recently sociologist Randolph David has described political parties as "nothing more than the tools used by the elites in a personalistic system of political contests" (2001: 24–25). Political scientist Nathan Quimpo provides perhaps the best description of contemporary Philippine political parties: "convenient vehicles of patronage that can be set up, merged with others, split, reconstituted, regurgitated, resurrected, renamed, repackaged, recycled, refurbished, buffed up or flushed down the toilet anytime" (Quimpo 2005: 4–5). Landé's description and those of David and Quimpo, it should be noted, are separated by some three decades, three constitutions, and fourteen years of Marcos's dictatorial regime in the 1970s and 1980s. The period before Marcos's declaration of martial law in 1972 was marked by the dominance of two major parties, the period after 1986 by what might be characterized as a multiparty system. While the parties themselves continue to be vehicles of elite interests lacking in ideological cohesion, there has also been significant change.

To understand the institutional deficiencies of modern Philippine democracy, one must begin with analysis of the institutional innovations of the early twentieth century.[7] Prior to American colonial rule, it is important to note, the Philippines had no significant experience with national-level democratic institutions or national-level political parties. American colonials— building on the residual architecture of the previous Spanish colonial state and responding to a very widely supported revolutionary challenge—established the foundations of the modern Philippine polity.[8] The key figure in the construction of American colonial rule is William Howard Taft, who between 1900 and 1913 (first as Philippine governor-general, then U.S. secretary of war, and later U.S. president) played a central role in the formulation of U.S. policy toward its largest colony. As part of Taft's so-called policy of attraction, the United States began to provide greatly expanded opportunities for *political* power to elites who had already developed a strong *economic* base throughout major regions in the latter decades of the Spanish era. Anxious to win over both a cosmopolitan *ilustrado* (educated) elite as well as a broader group of local *caciques* (chiefs) who had—particularly in the vicinity of Manila—given active support to the revolutionary effort, Taft and his associates drafted reforms that envisaged the creation of strong local governments and made longer-term plans for the convening of a national representative assembly (the promise of which was already formalized in the Organic Act passed by the U.S. Congress in 1902). There was nothing inevitable about this economic elite being transformed into a powerful *political–economic* elite; rather, this change came about through the very deliberate creation of new political institutions by the American colonial leadership. In other words, institutional rather than socio-economic factors are most important to understanding the stature that this elite came to possess during the early American period (and which this elite has, indeed, enjoyed ever since).[9] As Benedict Anderson explains, "It was above all the political innovations of the Americans that created a solid, visible 'national oligarchy'" (Anderson 1988: 11).

Although the efforts at "political tutelage" were proclaimed to be part of an effort to teach Filipinos the virtues of democracy, Taft and his fellow colonials made sure to limit the electorate to a very small, elite segment of the population based on the Americans' belief that "the masses are ignorant, credulous, and childlike" (Hayden 1942: 267; May 1984: 46, quoting a Philippine Commission report of 1900). In addition to limiting the rights of suffrage, the Americans actively discouraged any sort of popular mobilization that might threaten the political dominance of the elite. Even after the intensive military suppression of the Filipino–American war, nationalist groups could not organize themselves into parties because the Americans imposed an anti-sedition law declaring advocacy of independence a crime punishable by death (Banlaoi and Carlos 1996: 49).

Under the Americans, the political system was at the same time highly restricted and rapidly expanding. The electorate remained confined to a small elite, but the opportunities provided to this elite for political contention were extended to increasingly higher levels of government: municipal to provincial to national. As powers moved upward, and provincial governors came to be directly elected, Taft viewed provincial governors as a promising new source of Filipino leadership. The 1907 elections for the first national assembly (involving a highly circumscribed electorate through a U.S.-style single-member district plurality system) confirmed the shift toward provincial power. Two prominent former governors, Sergio Osmeña of Cebu and Manuel Quezon of Tayabas, emerged as the major figures in the newly formed Nacionalista Party, a purportedly pro-independence party that was to dominate Philippine politics for much of the next four decades. In contrast to many other provincial-based politicos, they had also been quick to see that it was possible to combine a *provincial* base with access to *national* power (Cullinane 2003: 167–71, 335–6). The provincial elites-turned-national politicos elected to the assembly very deftly responded to the new opportunities created by American colonials and achieved a level of political authority able to obstruct the goals of the U.S. governor-general (May 1984 [1980]: 57–73).

The Nacionalistas became in many ways the prototype for most subsequent twentieth-century Philippine political parties. While they consistently worked to consolidate their power at the national level, they were at the same time very responsive to allies in the provinces who desired a maximum degree of autonomy from colonial supervision. Because of their dominant role in the legislative leadership, the Nacionalistas can be described as a clear case of an "internally mobilized" party, defined by Martin Shefter as a party "founded by elites who occupy positions within the prevailing regime and who undertake to mobilize a popular following behind themselves in an effort either to gain control of the government or to secure their hold over it" (1994: 30).

In Shefter's framework, most "internally mobilized" parties will be patronage-oriented: because the parties occupy prominent roles *within the regime*, they have ready access to the patronage resources necessary to build a large following. There is one significant exception to the rule that an internally mobilized party will base its support on patronage resources, and that is the case of parties that have been established *after* the emergence of bureaucratic systems strong enough "to resist the depredations of patronage-seeking politicians."[10]

Because colonial regimes tend not to create effective representative institutions, and instead put major emphasis on the creation of powerful bureaucratic systems, one would not anticipate that internally mobilized parties would emerge in colonial settings. The political institutions of the U.S. regime in the Philippines, however, are highly unusual in the annals of colonialism. First, contrary to their counterparts elsewhere, U.S. officials gave far more attention to elections and the creation of representative institutions than to the creation of a modern bureaucratic apparatus. Second, because U.S. colonials not only held elections for elite political contestation but also established representative institutions with significant degrees of political authority, one finds the bizarre phenomenon of internally mobilized parties in a colonial state. Third, because representative institutions emerged *before* the creation of strong bureaucratic institutions, "the depredations of patronage-seeking politicians" quite easily overwhelmed the Philippine bureaucracy.[11] "As in the United States," explains Anderson, "civil servants frequently owed their employment to legislator patrons, and up to the end of the American period the civilian machinery of state remained weak and divided" (1988: 12).

The Nacionalista Party was home to those politicians who had the greatest access to patronage resources and who demanded reforms driven in large part by the desire for increased access to such resources. As the ideological divisions over how to respond to American colonialism receded into the past (see Cullinane 2003: 336–8), the logic of Philippine politics became driven to a very considerable extent by the politics of patronage: dividing the spoils among the elite and expanding the quantity of spoils available to the elite as a whole. In effect, American colonials successfully diverted the revolutionary quest for self-government into a simultaneous quest for increased local autonomy, expanded national legislative authority, and more extensive opportunities for patronage.

After 1913, as the goal of Philippine independence was given enthusiastic support by a Democratic governor-general, arenas for elite political contestation expanded further and the political reforms urged by the leading Nacionalista politicians at the end of the Taft era were to a large extent adopted. When the Philippine Commission (the small, American-dominated body that advised the governor-general) was replaced by the Senate in 1916, American colonials removed themselves entirely from the legislative branch of government. Governor-General Francis Burton Harrison "deliberately surrendered initiative to elected officials," leading to "an increasing measure of control over the executive departments and even the judiciary." Filipinization of the bureaucracy was rapidly accelerated, and all members of the cabinet except one were Filipino citizens. In 1918, the governor-general created the Council of State in which he shared executive authority with major legislative leaders, notably House Speaker Osmeña and Senate President Quezon (Stanley 1974: 252–4, quote at 252). Broad control over appointments and budgets gave the Nacionalista party leaders strong patronage links with the bureaucracy.

When Leonard Wood, the former general, become governor-general under a new Republican administration in 1921, he immediately set out to reassert executive authority after the diminution of its powers under Harrison. Even so, the Philippine legislature continued to be a major check on the authority of the American colonial executive.[12] Ironically, it was through a major step toward decolonization—the creation of the Commonwealth in 1935—that largely uncontested executive authority emerged in the colony. The new constitution, drafted mainly by Nacionalista party delegates, accorded Quezon, the commonwealth president elected in 1935, a potent range of powers in both the legislative and executive spheres.[13] In addition to acquiring the substantial executive powers formerly enjoyed by governors-general (Bolongaita 1996: 85), Quezon enjoyed a major advantage over those who had previously occupied the palace: through skillful dispensing of government resources, he was able to achieve considerable control over the Nacionalista party members that dominated the one-house legislature. Perfecting techniques that had emerged over the previous thirty years, Quezon centralized access to patronage and built what was arguably the strongest political party in Philippine history. As in earlier decades, however, the party remained thoroughly non-ideological. In the analysis of Alfred W. McCoy, Quezon became "the first Filipino politician with the power to integrate all levels of politics into a single system," as he directly manipulated provincial politics in order to challenge other national politicians' control over local vote banks; "Quezon once confessed to an aide that '90 percent' of his dealings with politicians involved the disposition of patronage" (1989: 120).

The vote banks of the 1930s were considerably larger than those of the early American colonial period. As the result of various reforms, the number of registered voters had risen steadily from 105,000 in 1907 (a mere 1.2 percent of the population) to 1.6 million in 1935. By 1940, after the 1937 enfranchisement of women, some 2.27 million Filipinos (14 percent of the total population) were registered to vote.[14] The expansion of the electorate, however, did not present any major challenge to those who had been put in control of the Philippine political system in earlier decades. In the Taft era, it will be recalled, those at the bottom were unable to vote (or to express their political views in other ways), whereas those at the top were provided with ever-expanding opportunities to enjoy political power. These opportunities came first in municipalities, then moved to the provincial level, proceeded to a new national assembly, and eventually reached the national executive (briefly tasted in the Council of State and thoroughly savored by Quezon in the Commonwealth twenty years later). By the time the electorate had been expanded to include non-elites, the dominance of the newly created national oligarchy was so well entrenched that challenges from below—motivated by deep social injustices—faced monumental odds. Such challenges became increasingly apparent in the late American colonial period, with more sustained political mobilization against landlords in protest against deteriorating conditions of tenancy. Quezon managed to contain the threats, for the time being, through calls for patience and tolerance and his 1937 proclamation of a sham "social justice" policy.[15]

Despite many changes in the structure of the political system from 1900 to 1941, one can note many enduring legacies of the political institutions established by the United States in the Philippines. Our analysis of Taft-era colonial democracy has highlighted not only the systematic exclusion of the masses and the emergence of elite-controlled democratic institutions but also the provincial basis of national politics, the decline of ideological differences within the elite, and the emergence of a patronage-oriented party that was to become the prototype for most subsequent twentieth-century political parties. The Quezon era continued all of these legacies and added new legacies of its own: the potential for authoritarian centralization of political patronage in the hands of a strong executive. Although it is indeed true that the Philippines is the Asian country with the most enduring experience with democratic institutions, one must also conclude that its democracy got off to a decidedly inauspicious start.

During the Japanese occupation, political parties were abolished and replaced with Kalibapi, a so-called mass party that was in fact led by "a charter member of the Nacionalista oligarchy," Congressman Benigno Aquino Sr. (Steinberg 1967: 61–2, 64, 184).[16] The most important new political formation, however, was the 1942 creation of the Hukbalahap (People's Anti-Japanese Army) to do battle against both the Japanese and their landlord collaborators. In response, there was a mass exodus of elites from the countryside to the relative safety of the cities (Kerkvliet 1977: 96). Wartime tensions between the Huks and U.S.-backed guerrilla forces worsened after General Douglas MacArthur's landing in October 1944, and the Huks (despite their frequent willingness to cooperate with U.S. forces) soon found themselves enemies of the state being reestablished by MacArthur and his many oligarchic friends (some of whom had collaborated with the Japanese during the war).

Post-independence political parties, 1946–86: elite hegemony, mass electorate, and authoritarianism

The war, and the countless intra-elite disputes that it engendered, destroyed the Nacionalista monopoly on political power. For the first time since the early years of the century, major cleavages emerged within an elite that was once again divided over how to relate to a new occupying power. Not surprisingly, one of the most important issues in postwar politics related to the major divisions between those who had collaborated with the Japanese and those who had not. Osmeña had assumed the presidency after Quezon's death in exile, but upon returning to the country he was soon challenged by a major rival from the old Nacionalista leadership. After being declared by MacArthur to be "free of wartime guilt," Manuel Roxas proceeded to form a new political party, the Liberals, and defeat Osmeña in the April 1946 elections (Steinberg 2000: 104–5).

The other major issue of early postwar democracy was mass challenges to elite hegemony. After the war, many on the left turned to parliamentary struggle and managed in the 1946 elections to have six members of its Democratic Alliance elected to the House of Representatives. In order to ensure the passage of a law granting parity rights for U.S. business, the Democratic Alliance representatives were barred from taking their seats. Meanwhile, repression of the peasantry grew worse in the countryside, and by late 1946 the Huk units were once again in full-scale rebellion (Kerkvliet 1977: 143–202; Shalom 1986: 1–69). The Huk Rebellion peaked between 1949 and 1951, after which counterinsurgency efforts began to achieve considerable success. Especially important was the role of U.S. advisers in cultivating Ramon Magsaysay, "America's boy" (Shalom 1986: 86–93). The major reason for the Huk decline, explains Benedict Kerkvliet, was that "peasants in Central Luzon liked Magsaysay, first as secretary of defense (1950–53) and then as president (1954–57), because he had personal contact with villagers and because the military became less abusive under his leadership" (Kerkvliet 1977: 238). Agrarian discontent was temporarily ameliorated through resettlement in Mindanao, and U.S. proposals for land redistribution were blocked; with the root causes of insurgency unaddressed, the left would eventually rise again (Shalom 1986: 84–5; Steinberg 2000: 26).

Throughout the period 1946–72 (since known as the period of pre-martial-law democracy), the Liberals and Nacionalistas alternated in power under the rules formally established by the 1935 constitution. Within a few years after the conclusion of the Pacific War, issues of Japanese collaboration had been eclipsed by other concerns, notably challenges from below and the never-ending struggles among political factions to secure their hold on the patronage resources of the state. Among the most important changes in the character of Philippine democracy resulted from an enormous increase in the size of the electorate. This was encouraged by the formal dropping of the literacy requirement (Rood 2002: 150) and far exceeded the substantial commonwealth-era growth rates already noted above. By 1951, the number of registered voters stood at 4.7 million (more than double that of 1940); this increased to 7.8 million voters in 1959 and 10.3 million voters in 1969 (Banlaoi and Carlos 1996).

Unlike in earlier years, therefore, political elites now had to convince non-elites to vote for them. At first, patron–client ties and deeply embedded traditions of social deference were sufficient. The organizational requirements of electoral campaigning remained relatively simple, as elites built factional coalitions in ascending order of complexity from the municipal level upward to the provincial and national levels. As Landé explains, local elite (often landholding) patrons used a variety of means—kinship, personal ties, and the offering of jobs, services, and other favors—to build a clientele composed of those from lower social classes. This clientele constituted a large vote bank, which could be exchanged for money and power from national politicians:

> Strong local roots and an ability to survive independently give the factions considerable bargaining power in their dealings with the national parties … Candidates for national offices need votes, which local leaders with their primary hold upon the loyalty of the rural electorate can deliver. Local leaders in turn need money to do favors for their followers, and this the candidates for high offices can supply [e.g.] … public works projects and … influence with the agencies of the central government … The result is a functional interdependence of local, provincial, and national leaders which promotes a close articulation of each level of party organization with those above and below it.
>
> *(Landé 1965: 24, 82)*

The "close articulation" of different levels of the party varied at different points of the four-year electoral cycle. Most presidents elected since independence in 1946 did not initially have working party majorities. Soon after each presidential election, however, enough members of the majority party shifted to the president's party in order to get in line for patronage and pork. By the middle of the president's term, the number of officials expecting patronage shares became so large that it was impossible to make everyone happy. Toward the end of the president's term, the unhappy politicians outnumbered happy ones, making it difficult for the president to get reelected. As Landé concludes, "The balance of power between higher and lower levels of party organization is an unstable one" (Landé 1965: 82; Thompson 1995: 15). This strange political system, neither centralized nor decentralized, links powerful presidents and powerful local bosses in a relationship that is both symbiotic and highly variable (depending on the stage of the political cycle). The effect of this system is illustrated in the fate of elected administrations that could not afford to alienate the local clans that controlled political factions (and often private armies) in the countryside.

In addition to being "loose federations … among independent factional leaders in the provinces," the two rival parties were also indistinguishable on ideological grounds (Landé 1965: 24). Not surprisingly, party-switching (known in the Philippines as "turncoatism") was rampant. One might expect that the relatively greater complexity of an economy formerly based almost entirely on agriculture would engender substantial new cleavages in a Philippine elite that had exhibited few substantial ideological divides throughout the century (with the exception, as noted above, of its responses to American and then Japanese conquest). Even with the diversification of the elite from agricultural into industrial and other ventures in the 1950s and 1960s, however, one can still not discern any sustained emergence of coherent cleavages within that elite. Beginning in the 1950s but becoming more obvious in the 1960s, there was instead a simultaneous process of diversification and homogenization: because it was so common for family conglomerates to combine ventures in agriculture, import substitution, banking, commerce, and urban real estate under one roof, major families continued to share a basic homogeneity of interests on major issues of economic policy. As in prewar years, there has been substantial consensus on big issues, and political battles were fought more exclusively over factional and personal issues that arise in the quest for the booty of state. One dominant segment of capital emerged and remains hegemonic to the present: the diversified conglomerates of oligarchic families (Hutchcroft 1998: 82–4).

The next stage in the development of political parties was set by the candidacy of Ramon Magsaysay in the presidential elections of 1953, briefly noted above. His major innovation was to supplement the traditional reliance on patron–client ties with direct campaign appeals to the people.[17] With the help of the U.S. Central Intelligence Agency, the popular former defense secretary formed the Magsaysay for President Movement and traveled extensively throughout the country. Political parties were affected not only by this new campaign style but also by the tendency of elite families to move beyond their simple prewar municipal party organization toward the construction of political machines "devoted primarily to the political support of its leader and the maintenance of its members through the distribution of immediate, concrete, and individual rewards to them." As municipal leaders built machines, there "was an increase in the importance of provincial and national considerations and a decline in the importance of local considerations in shaping the faction's character and its actions in all arenas" (Machado 1974: 525).

The continuing rapid growth of the electorate, combined with urbanization and the expansion of radio and television in the 1960s, amplified the impact of changes brought about by Magsaysay's direct appeals and the rise of more complex political machines. National campaigns now had to be organized on the basis of the segmentation of the vote into what can be called the "controlled vote" mobilized by local party leaders and that portion of the vote freer of such control and requiring increasingly elaborate media-oriented campaigns. The vastly increased financial requirements of national campaigns strengthened the national leadership vis-à-vis local party leaders, particularly to the extent that funds generated from the center (especially Manila) came to rival funds generated from the local economy (deriving in part from control over such activities as gambling, smuggling, and illegal logging). While local politicians still derived great power from their influence over the voters in their bailiwicks, they were more deeply integrated into national networks as compared to earlier years. In the midst of change, it must be emphasized, there was also continuity: the growing electorate, the use of media, and mass campaigns forced an elaboration of political party organization, but there was no corresponding differentiation between political parties. The logic of patronage remained central to understanding the strategies of both the parties and the politicians.

The framework most commonly used to understand pre-martial-law Philippine politics derives from Landé's work on factional networks and patron–client ties. In at least two major ways, however, this framework fails to capture important elements of political reality. Mark Thompson highlights the occasionally strong role of anticorruption and anti-electoral fraud movements in Philippine politics. Historically, there have been vocal, often middle-class elements of the Philippine electorate whose political participation is not primarily propelled by concrete material favors or stifled by *cacique* dominance but rather invigorated by outrage over authoritarian tendencies, corruption, and electoral abuses. As he explains, such appeals are closely related to anti-machine urban reformism in U.S. politics and were at the center of Ramon Magsaysay's campaign in 1953 (as well as Corazon Aquino's campaign against Ferdinand Marcos in 1986; see below).[18] Second, as the work of John Sidel convincingly argues, the patron–client framework also fails to give adequate attention to the role of violence and local monopolies in both Philippine electoral politics and social relations (i.e. the guns and the goons in the old troika of "guns, gold, and goons"). Throughout the archipelago, local bosses have enjoyed (and continue to enjoy) "monopolistic personal control over coercive and economic resources in their territorial jurisdictions or bailiwicks" (Sidel 1999: 141).

The elite dominance that Benedict Anderson describes as "cacique democracy" had its "full heyday" in the period 1954–72, when "the oligarchy faced no serious domestic challenges." Its genius, he writes, was its capacity to "[disperse] power horizontally, while concentrating it vertically." This *horizontal* dispersal of power, he continues, was able to "[draw] a partial veil over" the *vertical* concentration of power (Anderson 1988: 16, 33). Put somewhat differently, Philippine-style democracy provides a convenient system by which power can be rotated at the top without effective participation of those below. Because of the very substantial power of the president, explains Thompson, "a crucial but fragile rule of the political game was presidential succession" (Thompson 1995: 19, 23–4).

Ferdinand Marcos, elected president in 1965, steadily pushed the limits of this rule until he broke it entirely in 1972. Unlike his predecessors, who busted the budget only in election years, Marcos "ran deficits even in off years to fund a massive infrastructure program that was parceled out for maximum political advantage" (Thompson 1995: 34–5). He augmented the already enormous budgetary powers of the Philippine presidency with new discretionary funds that could be distributed directly to officials at the barrio level for "community projects." As Arthur Alan Shantz explains, the Marcos administration

> sought to broaden the flow of resources and executive contacts beneath the congressmen and into the municipalities, minimizing its dependence upon the political brokers in the legislative branch who have historically proven to be such a disappointment to incumbent presidents seeking reelection.
>
> *(1972: 148)*

Marcos also used the military in development projects and sent an engineering battalion to Vietnam in exchange for large, off-the-books payments from Washington (Hernandez 1984: 18–19; Bonner 1987: 75). Marcos became the first president to win reelection when, in 1969, he raided the public treasury and thereby hastened the arrival of the country's third major balance-of-payments crisis. As his defeated opponent grumbled, "[We were] out-gooned, out-gunned, and out-gold."

Determined to overturn the two-term limit prescribed by the 1935 constitution, Marcos declared martial law in 1972. As Benedict Anderson explains,

> from one point of view, Don Ferdinand can be seen as the Master Cacique or Master Warlord, in that he pushed the destructive logic of the old order to its natural conclusion. In place of dozens of privatized "security guards," a single privatized National Constabulary; in place of personal armies, a personal Army; instead of pliable local judges, a client Supreme Court; instead of myriad pocket and rotten boroughs, a pocket or rotten country, managed by cronies, hitmen, and flunkies.
>
> *(1988: 20)*

As Congress was disbanded and the judiciary cowed into submission, the United States rewarded martial law with very large increases in grants and loans (in exchange for unimpeded use of its military bases) (Wurfel 1988: 191). The absence of elections, combined with Marcos's monopoly of political power, left pre-martial-law political parties severely weakened. Marcos had no allegiance to the Nacionalista Party (on whose ticket he won the presidency in 1965 after a last-minute switch from the Liberal Party); neither did he show any inclination for creating a new type of highly institutionalized party such as those found nearby in authoritarian Indonesia and

Taiwan. It was not until 1978, in preparation for elections to the long-promised Interim National Assembly, that the Marcos regime launched its own ruling party, the Kilusang Bagong Lipunan (KBL; New Society Movement). The rhetoric of a "new society" notwithstanding, the old, informal patronage politics of the pre-martial-law years remained the fundamental basis of the KBL.

In at least three major ways, however, the emergence of the KBL represented a major break from pre-martial-law patterns. First, to a far greater extent than any Philippine president since Manuel Quezon and his Nacionalista Party in the 1930s, Marcos and his KBL achieved a masterful centralization of patronage resources (McCoy 1989). Throughout much of the country, politicians flocked to the KBL for the benefits that it could dispense. Local officials, who could be replaced at will by the regime, were particularly anxious to join the ruling party. The earlier "close articulation" of national, provincial, and local politics endured, but the balance of power came to be tilted much more decisively in favor of the national. Significantly, however, even Marcos could not attempt a full-scale assault on local power; he was able to restructure but not undermine the influence of clan-based factions in the provinces (McCoy 1993). Second, to a degree unprecedented in Philippine history, the ruling *family* lorded over all formal political institutions, the ruling *party* included. Third, there was considerable overlap between the structures of the ruling party and the crony abuses that defined the essential character of the Marcos regime.

The electoral exercises of the later Marcos years did bring forth new elite-led political parties seeking to challenge the KBL in elections, but by the late 1970s and early 1980s the major challenge to the regime came from an entirely new type of ideologically driven party: the Communist Party of the Philippines (CPP). Throughout the 1960s, Philippine students had become increasingly politicized and radicalized, provoked by campus issues, the presence of U.S. bases, the U.S. war in Vietnam and the deployment of Philippine troops there, inequitable social structures and the need for agrarian reform, and electoral fraud and demands for constitutional reform. The CPP was officially launched in late 1968, but it was not until after the declaration of martial law that it was able to build strong bases of support throughout many regions of the archipelago. Its New People's Army came to be the hope of many Filipinos across different social strata who desperately sought the demise of the Marcos dictatorship; the traditional politicians, by comparison, looked liked impotent has-beens.

With the assassination of Benigno Aquino, Jr. in 1983, the traditional elite increasingly abandoned Marcos and organized effective opposition efforts under the mantle of his popular widow, Corazon Cojuangco Aquino. Although these elites still lacked access to patronage, it was possible for them to build support based on opposition to rampant cronyism, human rights abuses, and economic decline. In the wake of the February 1986 "snap elections," anger over the regime's blatant electoral fraud and other abuses of the political system brought hundreds of thousands of people out into the streets in a huge display of "People Power" seeking both to defend a military uprising and support Aquino. The CPP, having chosen to boycott the elections, found itself on the sidelines. As Marcos and his family fled the palace for Hawaii, it was Aquino—a member of a very prominent oligarchic family—who was sworn into office at an elite club in Manila.

Philippine democracy after 1986: restoration and change

Cory Aquino's rise to power needs to be seen in the context of both the anti-dictatorship and social justice demands of the opposition to her predecessor, Ferdinand Marcos. Once in power, however, Aquino saw her primary duty as restoring the structures of pre-martial-law democracy.

To call this period a mere "restoration" of pre-martial-law democracy, however, only goes so far, given: (1) the degree to which the Philippine military had become a much more politicized force over the course of the martial-law years; and (2) the degree to which Philippine civil society was far more active and organized after 1986 than it had been prior to 1972.

The Philippines, of course, had changed a great deal during the twenty-one years that Marcos was in power. Aquino herself discovered this in her difficult relations with two new centers of power: the military and civil society. Disgruntled elements of the military launched a total of nine coup attempts against Aquino and, in two cases, came close to toppling her from office (McCoy 1999: 259). Philippine nongovernmental organizations (NGOs) began to mushroom in the 1980s, as thousands of groups formed to promote the interests of farmers, the urban poor, women, and indigenous peoples (Silliman and Noble 1998). Despite these major changes, the political system that Aquino reconstructed with the 1987 constitution restored many political institutions that can be traced to the 1935 constitution, most importantly a presidential form of government that went back to the political system built by the American colonial authorities and Filipino leaders. Aquino's difficulties, therefore, were not just those of moving from a dictatorship to constitutional democracy. They also arose because the political system she put in place continued to discourage the emergence of stronger, more programmatic political parties—and thus did not give room for the assertion of new political groups' ideas and interests.

The 1987 constitution reads like a completely different constitution from that of 1935. Many of the new ideas generated in the course of the anti-dictatorship movement found their way into the 1987 constitution. Among the institutional innovations were sectoral representation in local government councils and party-list elections for 20 percent of the members of the lower house (the remaining 80 percent of which were to remain under the single-member district plurality system of pre-martial-law democracy). As with many other progressive provisions in the 1987 constitution, however, implementing legislation was either not passed (as in the case of sectoral representation) or mangled beyond recognition (as in the case of the party list) (see Velasco and Rodriguez 1998). The effective reinstatement of pre-martial-law electoral and representational structures facilitated the restoration of the power of local clans, who through a variety of means have prevented significant political reform since 1986.[19] The so-called traditional politician, seen as the source of many national ills, became popularly known as *trapo* (meaning "dishrag" in Tagalog).

The old parties did not thrive, and the new parties that did emerge remained remarkably similar in their orientation toward patronage, reliance on coalitions of local elites, non-ideological character, and shifting membership. Given its poorly institutionalized character, the KBL did not survive the demise of its authoritarian leader, and neither the Nacionalista Party nor the Liberal Party recovered their former stature. Most dramatic is the shift from a two–party to a multiparty system. Because single-member district plurality systems are expected to yield a two-party system, the question arises as to why post-1986 Philippine politics has produced so many weak and unstable parties. Jungog Choi concludes that the provision of the 1987 constitution limiting presidents to a single term increases the number of candidates "because none of the individuals running has the incumbency advantage. Such a limitation significantly lowers the entry barrier for prospective candidates" (2001: 499). (Not surprisingly, given the weakness of Philippine parties, it is the number of candidates that tends to determine the number of political parties, not vice versa.) While this is a compelling argument, other factors are also important to consider (see Hicken 2008: 87–8 and Bevis 2001: 13, 28–9). Given the thoroughly unsystematic character of Philippine political parties, moreover, there are fundamental problems with the use of the term "multiparty *system*."

Because of the pressures Aquino faced from the military, and because her main goal appears to have been mostly to restore the system for mediating elite factional competition, she missed several other historic opportunities for both economic and political reform that were possible in 1986–7, including more radical agrarian reform and the negotiated repudiation of the more obviously corrupted international loans. The most innovative political reform during the Aquino years was the Local Government Code (LGC) of 1991, a decentralization initiative variously lauded as "the key to national development" (Pimentel 1993) and as a catalyst for greater local democratic participation. The Code gives greater authority and resources to a range of local politicians, some of whom have a genuine agenda of democratic reform (commonly in alliance with civil society organizations) and some of whom seek merely to further entrench their control of local authoritarian enclaves.[20]

Although promoted as a means of undermining patronage politics, the LGC can be viewed more cynically as a mere re-slicing of the patronage pie in favor of governors, city mayors, town mayors, and barangay captains. The most contentious element in the passage of the Code, and its most consequential outcome, was the guaranteed allotment of 40 percent of all internal revenues to provinces, cities, municipalities, and barangays. Despite all the fanfare to the contrary, one can conclude that the LGC has done little to alter the basic logic of Philippine politics or the basic character of Philippine political parties. "Assured revenue transfers," concludes de Dios, "have not weaned local politics away from the imperative of securing additional resources through typical networks of patronage and vertical transactions with the centre. The patronage relationship remains intact" (2007: 196).[21]

In addition to the provisions of the LGC, economic growth and diversification provide alternative resources to local executives who have long relied on some combination of funds from Manila as well as control over illegal economic activity at home. The least harmful of these activities are illegal gambling and smuggling, the more directly harmful illegal logging and more recently drugs and prostitution. The contest for control over these activities gives a premium to leaders with skills in manipulating illegality and the uses of violence. Since these contests are joined in elections, candidates with these skills, plus the money from these rackets, always have the advantage. Victory in elections means access to central government resources, control over police and to a lesser degree the military, and a level of influence over the judicial process (see Rocamora 2007). Greater resources in the hands of local politicians not only shifts the balance of power in their direction, but also encourages the further decentralization of political parties that were never strongly centralized in the first place.

Fidel Ramos came to power in 1992 with a much stronger reform impulse, but his reform initiatives were concentrated far more in the economic than the political realm. Ramos and his chief theoretician, former general Jose Almonte, blamed oligarchic groups for the country's laggard economic status and combined measures of economic liberalization, privatization, and infrastructure development with concerted attacks on "cartels and monopolies." At the same time, they asserted the need to build a more capable state and free the state of oligarchic influence. Ramos seemed better placed to do this than other politicians because, as former chief of staff of the armed forces, he had strong institutional backing from the military and could not be accused of being a traditional politician. Many in the business community, intelligentsia, and middle classes sympathized with the call for a stronger, more effective state.

The Ramos administration was proud to demonstrate the compatibility of development and democracy, but it consistently had to rely on old-style pork-barrel politics in order to promote new-style economics (Rocamora 1995). Little was done to try to improve the quality or substance of Philippine democracy. Without strong parties, policymaking was dominated by a process of deal-making that made it difficult to pass coherent bills (much less a series of interrelated legislation). Unfortunately for Ramos, his one major attempt at political reform was poorly managed. A conspicuously authoritarian draft revised constitution formulated by a team at the National Security Council was exposed by the media. By the time the charter change (immediately dubbed "Cha-Cha") campaign got going again, it was too close to the elections to effectively hide its term-limit extension goals.

Former movie star Joseph Estrada rode to overwhelming victory in 1998 with strong populist rhetoric and the enthusiastic support of millions of poor Filipinos, many of whom felt that Ramos had ignored their interests. It was, in the words of one Philippine political analyst, "the revenge of the masses. They are tired of being led by smart people." The victory of Estrada was part of a continuing post-1986 political trend for the electorate to reject the discredited traditional politician, or at least its stereotype. "Though possessing a long political career as a local official," explains Emmanuel de Dios, "the ex-actor Estrada's rise to prominence had bypassed the customary route of obvious patronage and horse-trading that typified the traditional politician's career at the national level, relying instead on media-driven national name-recognition" (de Dios and Hutchcroft 2003: 59). In essence, one can note the emergence of a new kind of patronage politics, as Estrada's media-generated populist appeals coexisted quite readily with much older styles of exchange between national politicians and local clan-based political machines.

As the politics of personality were expressed in new ways, party structures seem to have become even weaker and more marginal to the overall political process: throughout his term, Estrada relied on loose and ill-defined coalitions and did not even bother to build up his own political party. Redistributive rhetoric was expressed, concretely, through an antipoverty program that never took off and easily degenerated into a grab for patronage among local officials and privileged NGOs (Balisacan 2001). And the bulk of the redistributive effort, of course, benefited not the masses but Estrada's myriad cronies and multiple families. The poor would have been best served by the emergence of strong political parties able to give them a voice in a political environment long hostile to their interests; what they got instead, sadly, was a corrupt populist claiming to help the poor while he made himself rich.

Estrada quickly lost the support of key sectors of the elite and the middle classes when evidence emerged that he was taking protection money from illegal gambling syndicates, engaging in stock market scams, and brazenly siphoning off billions of pesos of public money to his private bank accounts (see Rocamora 2009). An attempt to remove him through a constitutionally mandated impeachment process failed not because he was acquitted but because his supporters in the Senate blocked the process. In response, a broad coalition (of civil society groups, segments of big business, media, and the Catholic Church, as well as reformers within the military and civilian bureaucracy) came forth in the January 2001 People Power 2, a huge four-day mass action that persuaded the military to withdraw support from the Estrada government. One could argue therefore that People Power 2 "unblocked" the constitutional process. Vice-president Gloria Macapagal-Arroyo was sworn in as president on 20 January 2001.

Estrada's cupidity had seriously damaged key institutions, including the police and the stock market and, of course, the presidency. At the time, it seemed that the removal of Estrada could halt the attacks on key institutions and reopen the political and economic reform process. Taken together, many analysts (including the present authors) believed that the popular removal of a corrupt incumbent president would contribute to advancing the democratization process in the Philippines—even if People Power 2 was, as a *method* for removing an elected president, clearly extraconstitutional. While the Supreme Court affirmed the legality of Arroyo's assumption of the presidency in several decisions, the mandate and authority of the Arroyo administration left much to be desired. The arrest of Estrada in late April brought forth a prolonged rally by his urban poor supporters, ending in a bloody, riotous attack that almost breached the walls of the presidential palace on 1 May. The rage that burst forth brought home the dangers inherent in a political system incapable of stemming the continued widening of the gap between the many poor and few rich. While former president Estrada sat in well-appointed jail, he and his allies challenged the Arroyo government with a combination of legal challenges, destabilization, and coup rumors. Beyond Estrada's culpability for the crime of plunder, his political maneuvers to avoid conviction illustrate the vulnerability of the political system to populist politics. "From the perspective of his poor supporters," explains Cynthia Banzon Bautista (2002: 33),

> Estrada's rise and fall from the presidency are conflated with their own long-standing struggle to lift themselves from poverty. Traditional politicians and Estrada himself used this view and the very real class divide to obfuscate the issues. They peddled his prosecution as an attack on the poor rather than on the very system of "old politics" that Estrada represents and which has, in large part, prevented the liberation of the poor.

Within months of coming to power, President Arroyo faced a national election in May 2001. The government's electoral vehicle, the People Power Coalition (PPC), seemed to carry the reform sentiments of People Power 2. In practice, PPC ran a traditional campaign in what was arguably the most fraud-ridden election in decades. Because neither the PPC nor the parties within it had significant mobilization capacity as parties, campaigning was mainly a matter of negotiating with local politicians who had vote-generation capability. After the election, PPC ceased to exist. Throughout the rest of her presidency, Arroyo did essentially nothing about the political system's main weakness, the absence of real political parties. At various points, she belonged, at least nominally, to three different parties.

In the initial two years of her presidency, Arroyo exhibited an inclination to engage with the reformers who had put her into power. This soon became overwhelmed, however, by larger concerns over legitimacy. The Supreme Court's imprimatur notwithstanding, significant portions of the population viewed Arroyo as a mere pretender—or at least not fully legitimate.[22] President Arroyo was determined to correct this at the ballot box, and in the 2004 elections the very considerable patronage powers of the Philippine presidency were skillfully deployed toward reelection by a margin of one million votes. There were many allegations of improper use of public funds and manipulation of government programs, as well as of tampering with the vote count, but election monitor groups (fearful of victory by her opponent, another movie star who was backed by Estrada) were generally happy to turn a blind eye and declare the results "free and fair."

One year later, these gains quickly unraveled with the release of tapes revealing that the president had been personally involved in colluding with election officials to ensure her decisive victory. These accusations produced a firestorm of anger against the Palace, the resignation of ten reform-inclined members of the cabinet, and widespread calls for her removal from office. In weathering the storm of controversy, Gloria Macapagal-Arroyo demonstrated an exceptional talent for regime preservation as she deftly garnered the support of local politicians and congresspersons (through ample provision of patronage resources), the top brass (skillfully rotating key military appointments as well as turning a blind eye to corruption and incompetence), and the hierarchy of the Catholic Church. In the process, she exhibited no qualms about further undermining the country's already weak political institutions. The resulting "Arroyo imbroglio" (see Hutchcroft 2008) involved on-going corruption allegations against the president and her husband; a failed coup-attempt-cum-popular-uprising in February 2006 leading to the declaration of emergency rule; concerted attacks on the press; an alarming spike in extra-judicial executions; repeated impeachment attempts; two major bribery scandals in late 2007, one involving the chief election officer and the other brazen cash payouts to congresspersons and governors at the palace; on-going military adventurism; a late 2009 election-related massacre of 59 persons in the Mindanao province of Maguindanao, for which close allies of Arroyo have been charged; and a Supreme Court packed—even up the final weeks of her term—with loyal minions. As the second-longest-serving president in Philippine history (exceeded in tenure only by Ferdinand Marcos) Arroyo should have had ample opportunities to bring forth measures of political reform. She instead left a trail of political destruction in her wake.

Not surprisingly, the May 2010 elections brought forth a widespread clamor both for change and for clean government. Following the August 2009 death of Cory Aquino, it was her son Senator Benigno S. "Noynoy" Aquino III who was lifted up by a wave of nostalgia to emerge as the candidate of the Liberal Party. Despite many years in the House and Senate, Noynoy had never been prominent on the national stage. He seemed happy enough to operate under the giant shadow of his parents, and many were drawn to him precisely because he was perceived as self-effacing and not overly ambitious. Reform elements of the Liberal Party had been reinvigorated in their opposition to the Arroyo administration, and in late 2009 they came to view Noynoy as the key to the party's electoral success.[23] Campaigning on the slogan "*Kung walang corrupt, walang mahirap*" (If no one is corrupt, no one is poor), Noynoy went on to obtain nearly 42 percent of the vote—the most decisive plurality since the fall of Marcos in 1986. His closest challenger was former president Joseph Estrada, who—now pardoned by Arroyo for his previous crimes of plunder—demonstrated his continuing appeal among many poor voters by capturing 26 percent of the total vote.

The May 2010 elections also heralded major change in the way ballots were cast. After multiple failed efforts in previous years, the country finally made the transition to electoral automation (replacing an antiquated hand-written ballot system in use for over a century). Despite numerous logistical difficulties, including last-minute fears that the elections would need to be postponed, the automation of the elections can be judged a truly significant step forward for Philippine democracy. Results for top national posts were known within days, thus removing many of the opportunities for wholesale cheating that had previously existed in the protracted process of manual counting. While retail cheating (i.e. individual vote buying) and intimidation by no means disappeared, their impact seems to have been primarily on local contests. Post-election surveys of voters and poll workers register substantially higher levels of confidence in the veracity of vote counts.[24]

Aquino's decisive victory raised obvious expectations, as confirmed in a June opinion survey in which 88 percent of respondents registered their trust in the incoming president.[25] These high expectations were inflated further in an inaugural speech proclaiming a new era in Philippine politics: "No more influence-peddling, no more patronage politics, no more stealing … no more bribes." Promising "to transform our government from one that is self-serving to one that works for the welfare of the nation," Aquino spoke with passion about the need for a new type of leadership. He has since attacked his predecessor's abuse of power, struck out at symbols of patronage politics (including the ubiquitous claims of personal responsibility for public projects), and proposed reform of some of the more egregious elements of the pork-barrel system. While there is no consensus on land reform or broader issues of asset reform, particularly given that the president's family owns a giant sugar estate in central Luzon, the administration has promised to enhance revenue generation and increase government spending on the delivery of education and health services to the poor.

At the same time, Aquino has thus far failed to articulate any vision of institutional change. Alongside his focus on a new style of leadership, close personal ties have influenced many key appointments (one notable example: the president's shooting buddy, a gun-shop owner, has been given oversight of the national police force). If he is to make any progress on his lofty goals, even in an incremental fashion, reform of the country's beleaguered political institutions is essential. This could begin, most concretely and with maximum short-term benefit, by back-stopping the reform impulses of key cabinet appointees with the support of reform-oriented elements from within the Liberal Party. While he speaks of carrying forth his parents' dedication to the causes of "democracy and peace," the fact is that Aquino only has one six-year term to promote change. If he is to sustain his reform goals beyond 2016, he must go beyond the personalism that has dominated most Philippine presidencies and give concerted attention to the strengthening and institutionalization of his political party. Beyond that, the country's longer-term prospects demand a more capable (and less corrupt) bureaucracy, judiciary, and military.

To summarize, post-Marcos hopes for a new system of politics have been largely undermined by the restoration of much the same institutional structure as that found in pre-martial-law politics. One can note four different styles of presidential leadership: Corazon Aquino as *elite restorationist*, with the primary objective of rebuilding the democratic institutions undermined by her authoritarian predecessor; Fidel Ramos as *military reformer*, concentrating more on issues of economic than political reform; Joseph Estrada as *populist self-aggrandizer*, building a strong following among the masses and then redistributing wealth in favor of himself, his families, and his friends; and Gloria Macapagal-Arroyo as the *great compromiser* (of herself and of national political institutions), willing to accommodate any political forces of influence that could help achieve her overarching goal of retaining the presidency. Benigno Aquino's leadership style is yet to be determined, but his talk of cleaner government and attention to the needs of the poor (combined with his self-effacing manner) once again raises hopes for change. Despite these differences in leadership, the logic of patronage remains central to understanding Philippine politics, and political parties remain weak, ill-defined, and poorly institutionalized.

The imperatives of reform

In this chapter, we have demonstrated how many of the major characteristics of Philippine democracy can be traced to the institutional innovations of the American colonial era: the exclusion of the masses and elite hegemony over democratic institutions; the provincial basis of national politics; the overarching dominance of patronage over ideology as the primary foundation of Philippine political parties; and a powerful presidency. These basic characteristics have endured and evolved across enormous transformations in Philippine politics since independence in 1946, including the rise and defeat of armed challenges to elite domination at mid-century, the creation of a mass electorate, the long nightmare of martial law, the reemergence of armed opposition in the countryside during the Marcos dictatorship, the toppling of Marcos via broad-based "People Power" in 1986, the growth of a vigorous NGO sector, the economic reforms of the 1990s, the populism of Joseph Estrada, the resurgent People Power uprising that forced Estrada from office in 2001, and the nine years under Gloria Macapagal-Arroyo.

Across the recurrent crises of the past decade, it has become clear—or at least it should be clear—that Philippine democracy can no longer ignore the interests and demands and resentment and anger of those at the bottom of society. For those inclined to downplay the extraordinary large class divides in Philippine politics, the popular uprising of May 2001 should serve as a high-decibel, cacophonous, and obtrusive wake-up call. While theorists explain that "democracy is a rather counterintuitive state of affairs, one in which the disadvantaged many have, as citizens, a real voice in the collective decision making of politics," Philippine democracy has done strikingly little to give the disadvantaged a voice. And while theorists further assert that "democracy takes on a realistic character only if it is based on significant changes in the overall distribution of power," Philippine democracy fails to give any substantive challenge to highly inequitable socio-economic structures (Rueschemeyer *et al.* 1992: 41).

Nearly a decade ago, we argued the following: "Because the institutional innovations of the early twentieth century bear much of the blame for the many shortcomings of Philippine democracy, the beginning of a new century is a particularly appropriate time to reform democratic structures and build a political system able to offer benefits to all" (Hutchcroft and Rocamora 2003: 284–5). Prior to the 2004 election, there did indeed seem to be hopeful momentum for constitutional revision, supported by the Speaker of the House, the President of the Senate, other influential opinion-makers, and even by the president herself. After the scandal related to the fixing of the 2004 elections, talk of constitutional change was hijacked—and thoroughly compromised—by a president seeking to divert attention from her own misdeeds and perpetuate herself in office. The new president, Noynoy Aquino, shows little interest in tampering with the constitution put in place under his mother's administration—and seemingly little awareness of how the perpetuation of weak political institutions will undermine his ability to satisfy the high expectations that have come forth with his strong electoral mandate.

While there is significant momentum for change in the new administration, there is not at this point any clear direction for institutional reform. We conclude our analysis by reiterating the imperatives of such reform. Just as different institutional arrangements could have induced different patterns of state–society relations in the colonial era, so can well-considered measures of institutional reform hold promise for improved governance in the decades ahead. While there is no silver bullet, it is our view that a number of specific electoral reforms could be useful in promoting the goal of stronger parties.[26] The most modest of these include a consolidated ticket for the election of presidents and vice-presidents and an option for straight-party voting. Two somewhat more ambitious electoral reforms, one for the Senate and one for the House of Representatives, could have much greater impact. The first would be to alter the current system in which senators are elected from one, nation-wide multi-member district. This ensures a great deal of intra-party competition, and forces each candidate to cut his or her own deals (typically involving the delivery of pork in exchange for the delivery of votes) with local powerholders throughout the archipelago. Far preferable from the standpoint of building stronger parties would be the election of senators from a nation-wide district through a proportional representational (PR) system of the closed-list type (meaning that political parties both choose and rank the candidates). This PR system could be further engineered to ensure gender and regional balance, specifically by requiring that party rankings of their senatorial candidates (a) alternate between women and men; and (b) ensure representation from Luzon, the Visayas, and Mindanao.

Second, in regard to the House, it is time to abolish the current party-list system through which 20 percent of the members of the House are selected. While most standard proportional representation systems require parties to achieve a certain percentage of the vote in order to have seats in the legislature, the Philippine party-list system is distinguished both by a very low floor (2 percent) and by the strange presence of a ceiling: quite incredibly, a single party is not permitted to have more than three seats in the legislature. This obviously entirely undermines the goal of aggregating interests under one party label. There has also been extensive interpretation and reinterpretation of what types of groups are eligible to form a party-list party; put a bit more bluntly, the Supreme Court has confused, and the Comelec corrupted, the process of accreditation of party list groups. Following the example of Japan and Korea, the Philippines could consider adopting a mixed system involving both single-member district seats and some element of a more standard PR system. As with the wholly PR system for the Senate, this partially PR system for the House could also be designed to promote gender and regional balance.

Regardless of the specifics, a primary goal of any electoral reform agenda should be the long-term cultivation of stronger and more programmatic political parties. Without a careful program of reform, parties and the electoral process will remain dominated by personalities rather than programs; legislative institutions will continue to be the domain of many of the same old political clans and *trapos*; and the legislative process will still be driven by the politics of pork and patronage. A major challenge—*the orderly attainment of which can only come through the long-term cultivation of stronger and more programmatic political parties*—is to insulate structures from particularistic demands (especially from the dominant oligarchy) and open them up to respond more effectively to collective pressures from societal groups whose interests have long been marginalized. In short, the creation of stronger parties is the most important way of closing the democratic deficit and making Philippine democracy more responsive to the citizenry as a whole. As a new administration struggles to meet high expectations, and comes up against the severe limitations imposed by the weakness of Philippine political institutions, there needs to be renewed attention to the imperatives of political reform. Once the debate resumes, clear priority should be given to the identification of institutional innovations that will work above all toward the strengthening of political parties.

Notes

* This is a significantly revised and updated version of an analysis that first appeared in the *Journal of East Asian Studies*, Vol. 3, No. 2, © 2003 by the East Asia Institute. Used with permission by Lynne Rienner Publishers, Inc. Thanks to Thuy Thu Pham and Jay Carizo for their research assistance, as well as to those who have provided comments. Any errors or omissions, of course, are ours alone.

1 Such ebbs and flows are reflected in two decades of opinion surveys measuring overall satisfaction with "the way democracy works." They were in the range of 41 to 70 percent between 1991 and 2000, with higher levels achieved after the 1992 and 1998 presidential elections and lower levels coming during the crisis of the Estrada presidency in 1999–2000. From 2001 to 2009, under the Macapagal-Arroyo administration, they were in the range of 28 to 54 percent, with the higher levels coming in the wake of the 2007 midterm elections that brought opposition victories in the Senate and the lower levels in the wake of an attempted military mutiny in July 2003. The most recent figures are 68 percent in June 2010, just after Benigno Aquino III was elected to the presidency and just prior to his inauguration, and 69 percent in September 2010. See the data of Social Weather Stations, http://www.sws.org.ph/.

2 As Gabriella Montinola (1999: 133) explains, "Meaningful social change has been inhibited because political parties have failed to structure political competition to allow for the representation of interests of the poor and marginalized sectors. … Quality of choice depends on political parties, the main organizations that structure political competition."

3 As is implicit in our analysis, we do not believe that institutional structures are merely derivative of larger socio-economic structures; they have a causal power of their own, able to influence and shape broader socio-economic realities in important ways. Even so, some readers may question why our focus is on institutional rather than deeper socio-economic change. More specifically, why the attention to electoral reform instead of, e.g., agrarian reform? While we wholeheartedly acknowledge the desirability of such deeper types of asset reform, we are skeptical of their feasibility in the short- to medium-term. At this point in history, institutional reform is not only feasible but also capable of fostering a broader set of political opportunities for poor and marginalized Filipinos. And, as we shall argue, such reform has the capacity to counteract the dysfunctional consequences of past institutional innovations.

4 The analysis of this article, we should explain at the outset, is more diagnostic than prescriptive. There has been much discussion in the Philippines about constitutional revision but surprisingly little analysis as to what the end goal (or goals) of reform should be. Through this examination of the origins and evolution of the country's "democratic deficit," we argue that the foremost goal of political reform should be the building of stronger parties. We do not provide comprehensive analysis of (1) the

specific institutional reforms by which this should be accomplished, or (2) the political dynamics of the process through which change of representational and electoral structures might be instituted. While these are extremely important issues they are, unfortunately, beyond the scope of this analysis.

5 In opinion surveys between 2002 and 2010, there was consistently strong preference for democratic over authoritarian government, albeit varying significantly in magnitude. Ratios of support for democratic over authoritarian government ranged from roughly 4.3:1 in late 2005 to roughly 2:1 in 2004 and 2010. See Social Weather Stations, http://www.sws.org.ph/. This faith in democracy is further evidenced by historically high turnouts in elections, despite the fact that voting is not compulsory. In the 2010 elections, voter turnout in the presidential race was 64.6 percent (36.32 million voters as a proportion of the total estimated voting age population of 56.21 million persons). Data from www.congress.gov.ph/halalan2010/viewpresboard_main.php and the National Statistical Coordination Board (www.nscb.gov.ph/factsheet/pdf10/FS-201005-PP2–01.asp).

6 We are not arguing, however, that democratic reform and the creation of stronger parties will resolve all problems of governance in the Philippines. Rather, these reforms are of a "necessary but not sufficient" character and must be supplemented by sustained attention to other elements of governance as well. First, the effective delivery of public goods also requires major improvements in the quality of the Philippine bureaucracy, at both the national and the local levels. Second, we are not ignoring the importance of wise policy choices once stronger democratic and administrative institutions have actually been put in place.

7 For fuller examination of this seminal period, see Hutchcroft and Rocamora (2003).

8 The following draws on Hutchcroft (2000).

9 The contrast with the Japanese conquest of Korea makes this point most clearly. There, the institutional innovations of the colonial power transformed a political–economic elite into a mere economic elite. The major foundation of this economic elite—landholding—did not translate into any significant degree of political power; in fact, the Japanese very much excluded Korean landholders from any substantial role in politics (see Hutchcroft 2011). Had the Japanese instead of the Americans become the colonial rulers of the Philippines in 1900, one might speculate, Japanese institutional reforms would have created a very different type of Philippine elite.

10 Shefter (1994: 28). In Shefter's second major category, "externally mobilized" parties are established by those outside the regime who do not have access to patronage and instead rely on ideological appeals in their quest for a mass following. Examples, he explains, are "socialist parties in Europe and nationalist parties in the Third World" (Shefter 1994: 30).

11 For further application of the Shefter framework to the Philippine political system, see Hutchcroft (2000: 282, 296, 298).

12 Meanwhile, after a major political showdown between Quezon and Osmeña in the early 1920s, Quezon emerged as the dominant figure for the remainder of the colonial era. (Golay 1998: 235–69, quote at 243). Hayden reports two points at which a two-party system began to emerge out of the Quezon–Osmeña rivalry: after their formal split in 1922, and again in the early 1930s when the two politicians feuded over the terms of the legislation establishing the commonwealth. "Upon each occasion, however, the transcendent issue of national independence was used to destroy the opposition as soon as it attained real strength" (Hayden 1942: 452).

13 In the legislative sphere, this includes what Bolongaita calls veto, initiating, summoning, and endorsement and delegated powers; in the executive sphere, great discretion over budgets, appointments of local government executives (and many others), and emergency powers (Bolongaita 1996: 99–100). Sergio Osmeña, Quezon's former rival, was elected vice president.

14 The 1935 constitution provided for literacy but not property requirements and lowered age limits from twenty-three to twenty-one (Hayden 1942: 825). Landé (1965: 28) notes that "growing laxity in the enforcement of literary requirements" and "the spread of literacy" expanded the size of the electorate in the early decades of the century, "in both absolute numbers and the percentage of the population that voted." The 1907 and 1935 data on absolute voters are from Banlaoi and Carlos (1996: 16, 17, 20, 34); 1907 and 1935 data on proportion of voters to total population from Salamanca (1984: 57); and Landé (1965: 29); and 1940 data from Hayden (1942: 204).

15 Kerkvliet (1977: 26–60); Ileto (1979); Golay (1998: 339–41, quotes at 339, 341); see also Hayden (1942: 376–400). In 1940, moreover, the pro-tenant Socialist Party registered strong gains in local elections in the province of Pampanga (Golay 1998: 400).

16 Aquino is the father of Marcos opposition leader Benigno Aquino, Jr., assassinated in 1983, and the grandfather of the current president.

17 The long-term weakening of patron–client ties had been an important factor in the rise of the Huks during the Japanese occupation and the renewal of armed struggle after the war (Kerkvliet 1977: 249–52).

18 Thompson (1995: 29–32). Eva-Lotta Hedman argues that strong movements for clean elections (in 1953, 1969, and 1986) coincided with recurrent "crises of authority" in which a "dominant bloc of social forces" not only protests authoritarian trends but also seeks to undermine extra-electoral challenges from below (2006: 176–7; see also 142–66).

19 One leading study describes the first post-Marcos legislature as "the return of the oligarchs." Eighty-three percent of the House came from elite families, 66 percent had previously participated in elections, and 22 percent had been elected to Marcos's legislative body in 1984 (Gutierrez et al. 1992: 162). Similar trends persisted in subsequent legislatures. See Gutierrez (1994: 4).

20 On the political dynamics of the passage of the LGC, see Hutchcroft (2004).

21 De Dios offers this analysis as part of a broader examination of the nature of local power in the Philippines. For the historical context of "localist strategies of political reform," see Hutchcroft (2010).

22 In 1986, Corazon Aquino had also come to power via People Power, but she was able to gain an invaluable post-People-Power mandate with the ratification of the 1987 constitution (the campaign slogan for which was "Yes to Cory! Yes to the Constitution!"). There was no such referendum for Arroyo.

23 In the election scandal of 2005, many of those who resigned from cabinet posts were associated with the Liberal Party. There emerged an intra-party split between anti-Arroyo vs. pro-Arroyo forces, and the subsequent exit of pro-Arroyo figures from the party bolstered the internal strength of reform forces.

24 See Mangahas 2010 and Rood 2010. According to a Social Weather Stations poll, 65 percent of voters and 94 percent of poll workers agreed that automation "lessened cheating in the counting of votes." At the same time, the polls recorded concern over long queues as well as technical glitches. Thirty-four percent of voters believed that there had been "cheating at some level, not limited to the precinct level." This is "still worrisome," as Rood notes, even if it does compare favorably with the 47 percent who held this belief in 2004.

25 See http://www.sws.org.ph/.

26 As the analysis of Allen Hicken suggests, institutional reforms should be crafted in such a way as to minimize unintended consequences (Hicken 2008: 94–6). Electoral reform, as compared to a wholesale shift from a presidential to a parliamentary system, conforms to this important goal.

References

Anderson, B. (1988) "Cacique democracy and the Philippines: origins and dreams," *New Left Review* 169: 3–33.

Balisacan, A.M. (2001) "Did the Estrada administration benefit the poor?" in A. Doronila (ed.) *Between Fires: Fifteen Perspectives on the Estrada Crisis*, Manila: Anvil.

Banlaoi, R.C. and C. Carlos (1996) *Elections in the Philippines: From the Pre-Colonial Period to the Present*, Manila: Konrad Adenauer Foundation.

Banzon Bautista, M.C.R. (2002) "People Power 2: 'The revenge of the elite on the masses'?" in A. Doronila (ed.) *Between Fires: Fifteen Perspectives on the Estrada Crisis*, Manila: Anvil.

Bevis, G.G. (2001) "Party time? The formation of programmatic parties in the Philippines," unpublished manuscript, Department of Political Science, University of Wisconsin–Madison.

Bolongaita, E.P. (1996) "The breakdown of Philippine democracy: a comparative institutional analysis," unpublished thesis, Notre Dame University.

Bonner, R. (1987) *Waltzing with a Dictator: The Marcoses and the Making of American Policy*, New York: Times Books.

Choi, J. (2001) "Philippine democracies old and new: elections, term limits, and party systems," *Asian Survey* 41 (3): 488–501.

Cullinane, M. (2003) *Ilustrado politics: Filipino Elite Responses to American Rule, 1898–1908*, Question City: Ateneo de Manila University Press.

David, R. (2001) "Political parties in the Philippines," in R. David (ed.) *Reflections on Sociology and Philippine Society*, Manila: University of the Philippines Press, pp. 110–28.

de Dios, E.S. (2007) "Local politics and local economy," in A. Balisacan and H. Hill (eds) *The Dynamics of Regional Development: The Philippines in East Asia*, Quezon City: Ateneo de Manila University Press.

de Dios, E.S. and P.D. Hutchcroft (2003) "Philippine political economy: examining current challenges in historical perspective," in A. Balisacan and H. Hill (eds) *The Philippine Economy: Development,*

Policies, and Challenges, Quezon City: Ateneo de Manila University Press; New York: Oxford University Press.

Golay, F. (1998) *Face of Empire: United States–Philippine Relations, 1898–1946*, Madison: University of Wisconsin Center for Southeast Asian Studies.

Gutierrez, E. (1994) *The Ties that Bind: A Guide to Family, Business, and Other Interests in the Ninth House of Representatives*, Metro Manila: Philippine Center for Investigative Journalism and Institute for Popular Democracy.

Gutierrez, Eric U., I.C. Torrente, and N.D. Narca (1992) *All in the Family: A Study of Elites and Power Relations in the Philippines*, Quezon City: Institute for Popular Democracy.

Hayden, Joseph Ralston (1942) *The Philippines: A Study in National Development*, New York: Macmillan.

Hedman, E.-L. (2006) *In the name of Civil Society: From Free Election Movements to People Power in the Philippines*, Honolulu: University of Hawaii Press.

Hernandez, Carolina G. (1984) "The role of the military in contemporary Philippine society," *Diliman Review* 32 (1) (January–February): 1, 16–24.

Hicken, Allen (2008) "Developing democracies in Southeast Asia: theorizing the role of parties and elections," in E. Kuhonta, D. Slater, and Tuong Vu (eds) *Southeast Asia in Political Science: Theory, Region, and Qualitative Analysis*, Stanford, CA: Stanford University Press.

Hutchcroft, Paul D. (1998) *Booty Capitalism: The Politics of Banking in the Philippines*, Ithaca, NY: Cornell University Press.

——(2000) "Colonial masters, national politicos, and provincial lords: central authority and local autonomy in the American Philippines, 1900–913," *Journal of Asian Studies* 59 (2): 277–306.

——(2004) "Paradoxes of decentralization: the political dynamics behind the passage of the 1991 Local Government Code of the Philippines," in M.H. Nelson (ed.) *KPI Yearbook 2003*, Bangkok: King Prajadhipok's Institute.

——(2008) "The Arroyo imbroglio in the Philippines," *Journal of Democracy* 19 (1): 141–55.

——(2010) "Dreams of redemption: localist strategies of political reform in the Philippines," in Y. Kasuya and N. Quimpo (eds) *The Politics of Change in the Philippines*, Manila: Anvil Press.

——(2011) "Reflections on a reverse image: South Korea under Park Chung Hee and the Philippines under Ferdinand Marcos," in Byung-Kook Kim and E.F. Vogel (eds) *The Park Chung Hee Era The Transformation of South Korea*, Cambridge, MA: Harvard University Press.

Hutchcroft, P.D. and J. Rocamora (2003) "Strong demands and weak institutions: the origins and evolution of the democratic deficit in the Philippines," *Journal of East Asian Studies* 3 (2): 259–92.

Ileto, R. (1979) *Pasyon and Revolution: Popular Movements in the Philippines, 1840–1910*, Quezon City: Ateneo de Manila University Press.

Kerkvliet, B.J. (1977) *The Huk Rebellion: A Study of Peasant Revolt in the Philippines*, Berkeley, CA: University of California Press.

Lacaba, J.F. (ed.) (1995) *Boss: 5 Case Studies of Local Politics in the Philippines*, Metro Manila: Philippine Center for Investigative Journalism and Institute for Popular Democracy.

Landé, C.H. (1965) *Leaders, Factions, and Parties: The Structure of Philippine Politics*, New Haven, CT: Yale University Southeast Asian Studies.

——(1969) "Brief history of political parties," in J. Abueva and R. De Guzman (eds) *Foundations and Dynamics of Filipino Government and Politics*, Manila: Bookmark.

Leones, E.B. and M. Moraleda (1998) "Philippines," in W. Sachsenröder and U.E. Frings (eds) *Political Party Systems and Democratic Development in East and Southeast Asia, Volume I: Southeast Asia*, Brookfield, VT: Ashgate.

McCoy, A.W. (1989) "Quezon's commonwealth: the emergence of Philippine authoritarianism," in R.R. Paredes (ed.) *Philippine Colonial Democracy*, Monograph No. 32, New Haven, CT: Yale University Southeast Asia Studies.

——(ed.) (1993) *An Anarchy of Families: State and Family in the Philippines*, Madison, WI: Center for Southeast Asian Studies.

——(1999) *Closer Than Brothers: Manhood at the Philippine Military Academy*, New Haven, CT: Yale University Press.

Machado, K. G. (1974) "From traditional faction to machine: changing patterns of political leadership and organization in the rural Philippines," *Journal of Asian Studies* 33 (4): 523–47.

Mangahas, M. (2010) "Acclaim for the automated elections," *Philippine Daily Inquirer*, 31 July.

May, G.A. (1984 [1980]) *Social Engineering in the Philippines: The Aims, Execution, and Impact of American Colonial Policy, 1900–1913*, Quezon City: New Day Publishers.

Montinola, G.R. (1999) "Parties and accountability in the Philippines," *Journal of Democracy* 10: 126–40.

Pimentel, A.Q. (1993) *The Local Government Code of 1991: The Key to National Development*, Manila: Cacho Publishing House.

Quimpo, N.G. (2005) "The left, elections, and the political party system in the Philippines," *Critical Asian Studies* 37: 1–29.

Rocamora, J. (1995) "The political requirements of economic reform," *Issues and Letters* 4: 1–4.

——(2007) "Equal opportunity violence," PCIJ; available at: http://pcij.org/i-report/2007/political-violence 2.html (accessed 10 February 2007).

——(2009) "Estrada and the populist temptation in the Philippines," in Kosuke Mizuno and Pasuk Phongpaichit (eds) *Populism in Asia*, Kyoto: Kyoto University Press.

Rood, S. (2002) "Elections as complicated and important events in the Philippines," in J.F.-S. Hsieh and D. Newman (eds) *How Asia Votes*, New York: Chatham House.

——(2010) "Citizens and poll workers declare first automated elections in Philippines a success, but flaws remain," available at: http://asiafoundation.org/in-asia/2010/08/04/citizens-and-poll-workers-declare-first-automated-elections-in-philippines-a-success-but-flaws-remain/ (accessed 9 September 2010).

Rueschemeyer, D., E.H. Stephens and J.D. Stephens (1992) *Capitalist Development and Democracy*, Chicago: University of Chicago Press.

Salamanca, B. (1984 [1968]) *The Filipino Reaction to American Rule, 1901–1913*, Quezon City: New Day Publishers.

Shalom, S.R. (1986) *The United States and the Philippines: A Study of Neocolonialism*, Quezon City: New Day Publishers.

Shantz, A.A. (1972) "Political parties: the changing foundations of Philippine democracy," unpublished thesis, University of Michigan.

Shefter, M. (1994) *Political Parties and the State: The American Historical Experience*, Princeton, NJ: Princeton University Press.

Sidel, J.T. (1999) *Capital, Coercion, and Crime: Bossism in the Philippines*, Stanford: Stanford University Press.

Silliman, G.S. and L.G. Noble (eds) (1998) *NGOs, Civil Society, and the Philippine State: Organizing for Democracy*, Quezon City: Ateneo de Manila University Press.

Stanley, P.W. (1974) *A Nation in the Making: The Philippines and the United States, 1899–1921*, Cambridge, MA: Harvard University Press.

Steinberg, D.J. (1967) *Philippine Collaboration in World War II*, Manila: Solidaridad Publishing House.

——(2000) *The Philippines: A Singular and a Plural Place*, fourth edition, Boulder, CO: Westview.

Thompson, M.R. (1995) *The Anti-Marcos Struggle: Personalistic Rule and Democratic Transition in the Philippines*, New Haven, CT: Yale University Press.

Velasco, D. and A.M.G. Rodriguez (1998) *Democracy Rising? The Trials and Triumphs of the 1998 Party List Elections*, Manila: Institute of Politics and Governance.

Wurfel, D. (1988) *Filipino Politics: Development and Decay*, Ithaca, NY: Cornell University Press.

8

CONSULTATIVE AUTHORITARIANISM AND REGIME CHANGE ANALYSIS

Implications of the Singapore case

Garry Rodan[1]

Introduction

It had been expected by earlier modernization theorists that social and economic transformations generated by rapid capitalist development would promote new aspirations, opportunities and functional governance pressures favouring liberal democracy (Huntington 1991). However, in Southeast Asia, while authoritarian regimes have collapsed in the Philippines, Thailand and Indonesia, they have proved durable in precisely the most economically advanced countries of Singapore and Malaysia. Such patterns in Southeast Asia and elsewhere led to analytical attention by transition theorists to the contingencies of political change (Diamond *et al.* 1997) – a focus that has both enriched the literature and also reinforced the limited nature of the problematic under investigation. Preoccupation with understanding the prospects of liberal democratic regimes has come at the expense of more open and fundamental questions. Where are political regimes headed, and why? What are the possibilities for the continuation of authoritarian rule and the forms this might take?

Answering these questions of Singapore reveals significant institutional and ideological changes challenging transition theory assumptions of liberal democracy as the natural regime partner of advanced capitalism. Indeed, Singapore's experience suggests the possibility that some authoritarian regimes may be able not just to survive advanced capitalism but to be modified and thereby strengthened in response to dynamics emanating from capitalism. Given leaders of the world's most populous authoritarian regime in China have embraced capitalism with the aim of shoring up the ruling party's legitimacy, understanding where and why political change has been headed in the city-state assumes an obvious wider theoretical and policy significance.

The Singapore case has led to a variety of explanations for the absence of a liberal democratic regime transition. In his influential book *The Third Wave*, Huntington (1991: 108) contended that the missing ingredient was one of political will, observing that 'a political leader far less skilled than Lee Kuan Yew could have produced democracy in Singapore'. Subsequently, explanations increasingly centred on the quality of political institutions. This approach has seen Singapore and other authoritarian regimes variously classified as a 'semi-democracy' or 'hybrid regime' because of the formal appearance of political competition through elections and other institutions (Case 2005). In this vein, Levitsky and Way (2002: 54) portray Singapore as a 'façade electoral regime' where 'electoral institutions exist but yield no meaningful contestation for power'. Such a characterization of the regime is descriptively accurate. However, it offers no particular insights into the determinants and dynamics of authoritarian rule in Singapore. This chapter is intended to redress this, both by making non-democratic institutions a focus of analysis in their own right and by examining political institutions in relation to the wider conflicts and alliances over state–civil society relationships inherent to capitalist development.

The institutional and ideological means by which authoritarian rule in Singapore is reproduced have changed significantly since the 1960s, as has the balance of interests served by the regime. None of this can be understood without analysing the way that capitalism has developed. As anticipated by early modernization theorists, economic development has indeed produced greater social diversity and new social interests that require a political accommodation. However, rather than leading to an irrepressible expansion of independent civil society, creative institutions within the state have been developed to facilitate expanded opportunities for political participation.

In what might be described as an evolving *consultative authoritarian regime*,[2] these new institutions traverse parliamentary and extra-parliamentary spheres to involve a range of individuals and groups in public policy discussion or feedback. At the same time, they exclude contestation with the ruling party and increasingly involve the development of non-democratic values of political representation. Such a direction is related to how the consolidation and expansion of state capitalism has enhanced the power of technocratic elites predisposed towards more bureaucratic and administrative techniques of political control and mobilization. While their emphasis on *consultation* is meant to limit the boundaries and conduct of political conflict, this is also informed by a view of politics as principally a problem-solving rather than normative exercise that can usefully harness relevant information and expertise.

Consultative authoritarianism, then, is distinguished from other forms of authoritarianism by the emphasis on state-controlled institutions to increase political participation. Political suppression and intimidation remain integral to these regimes. However, new social and economic interests generated by capitalist development are increasingly engaged through various creative mechanisms of consultation in an attempt to obviate greater demand for independent political space. In these particular authoritarian regimes, ideological emphasis on consensual politics is marked and consultative mechanisms are necessary to give substance and legitimacy to claims about more appropriate alternatives to liberal democratic change. Importantly, while consultative authoritarianism reflects growing sophistication in strategies of political control, perceived advantages in economic and social governance in the context of dynamic and globalized market systems can also be important considerations by ruling elites.

The discussion below begins by explaining the circumstances that gave rise to the emergence of consultative authoritarianism and then proceeds by examining, in turn, the parliamentary and non-parliamentary institutions through which new opportunities for political participation have been promoted. This will be followed by some observations about the implications of this analysis for understanding political regime dynamics more generally within Southeast Asia.

The core argument is that in Singapore new modes of political participation are shaping the inclusion and exclusion of different groups and individuals in the political process, favouring both functional and elitist conceptions of citizenship and representation as clear alternatives to a rights-based democratic politics. The social foundations of this sort of consultative authoritarianism have been laid by the particular dynamics of state capitalism in Singapore. Similar historical and geopolitical contexts of capitalism's development across Southeast Asia may also render emerging social and political forces in some parts of the region potentially vulnerable to new forms of state-sponsored political participation. However, the precise coalitions of interest associated with capitalist development in Singapore are not replicated elsewhere in Southeast Asia, suggesting limits to the possibilities of consultative authoritarianism in the region.

State capitalism and consultative authoritarianism

Consultative authoritarianism's foundations were laid in significant part by Singapore's particular state capitalist path taken after self-government. The PAP came to power in 1959 through an alliance of leftist and Chinese-educated nationalist forces controlling trade unions and student, cultural and ethnic organizations, on the one hand, and right-wing English-educated middle-class nationalists on the other hand. However, inherent tensions in this historical marriage of convenience became unmanageable in office and by July 1961 a breakaway faction formed the Barisan Sosialis (BS) or Socialist Front, stripping the PAP of grass-root networks and mass mobilization capacity. It is critical that the PAP's response was not just to exploit state power to harass and intimidate political opponents, but also to develop new bases of power and support to ensure the PAP's long-term electoral survival. This latter strategy generated a powerful new class of politico-bureaucrats and a form of state capitalism that rendered many Singaporeans directly or indirectly dependent on the state for access to economic and social resources, including housing, employment, business contracts and access to personal savings. This structural relationship has fostered vulnerability to political co-option and intimidation and constrained alternative social and economic bases from which challenges to the PAP can be mounted.

In response to the severing of links between the PAP and independent civil society organizations in 1961, the ruling party and state were effectively merged. In the process, policy formation became the preserve of the PAP executive in consultation with senior civil servants, diminishing the importance of wider party structures. Civil service appointments not only enabled the PAP to extend control over the state apparatus, but the upper echelons of the civil service soon became the standard route to political leadership (Worthington 2003). This state–party nexus in turn facilitated the development of grassroots para-political institutions and state-owned media through which PAP ideology was disseminated, while the state-sponsored and PAP-affiliated National Trades Union Congress (NTUC) emerged as pivotal to the ruling party's policy implementation and electoral support mobilization.

Consolidation and extension of the ruling party's power owes much to the flourishing of state capitalism in subsequent decades. A massive programme of public housing begun in the 1960s not only helped meet an urgent social need, it generated popular support for the PAP and afforded it a capacity for social and political engineering. These apartments, on ninety-nine-year leases from the government, enabled the PAP to control the racial composition of electorates and to discriminate in dispensing state infrastructure against electorates voting for opposition parties (Chua 1991; Chin 1997). Meanwhile, the state's initial economic roles were geared towards supporting industrialization via government departments and statutory bodies and essential infrastructure, but direct investment by government-linked companies (GLCs) dramatically escalated as the economy grew. GLCs not only consolidated their dominance over the commanding heights of the domestic economy but internationalized, becoming pivotal to the integration of state economic and political power. Here state holding company Temasek – whose chief executive officer Ho Ching is the wife of Prime Minister Lee Hsien Loong – and the Government of Singapore Investment Corporation (GIC) – chaired until early 2011 by Minister Mentor Lee Kuan Yew and then by his son the Prime Minister – have been major players. The former boasted an investment portfolio with a net market value exceeding US$120 billion in 2010 and the latter in charge of foreign reserves officially, and probably conservatively, declared on its website as 'in excess of US$100 billion' (http://www.gic.com.sg/aboutus.htm). Interlocking directorships and other arrangements avail the political executive of a capacity to exert direct and indirect influence over GLCs.

The state capitalist path was not simply a choice born out of functional economic imperatives: the PAP contained and circumscribed the domestic bourgeoisie's development as a matter of political strategy. Suspected links between elements of local business and oppositionists in the 1960s made the PAP weary of this class (Vischer 2007). Opportunities for the domestic bourgeoisie have thus been heavily conditioned by, and dependent on, articulation with state capitalism. Consequently, in contrast with what transpired in Taiwan and South Korea from the 1980s, there has been no concerted private sector challenge to the economic dominance of the state that could be exploited by democratic forces in Singapore. Meanwhile, much of the city-state's middle class is either employed in government departments, statutory bodies or GLCs, or indirectly derives its livelihood from servicing state capitalism through the provision of commercial, legal or other professional services.

The net effect of Singapore's brand of state capitalism is to limit the space for independent economic and social bases that could be harnessed by critics and opponents of the PAP even more so than under many other authoritarian regimes. This structural relationship helps explain not just the effectiveness of repressive legislation but also the growing propensity for, and vulnerability to, various forms of PAP state political and ideological co-option.

Therefore, by the early 1980s, the PAP leadership profile had narrowed acutely in favour of technical or managerial elites most useful to the economic interests of the state–party (Rodan 2008). One symptom of this absolute power of technocrats was an increasing shift in the techniques of political control towards legal and administrative means. Defamation suits, for example, became a preferred means for taming critics and opponents, while regulations covering licences and permits for public gatherings and disseminating political materials proliferated. Another symptom was the ushering in of a new phase of institutional and ideological reforms to promote increased opportunities for political participation. Importantly, this charted an expansion of the political space of the state – not civil society – and was grounded in a recognition that authoritarianism would need to be dynamic to endure in the face of the complex social changes that the city-state's dramatic economic development had experienced.

Against the background of a 12.9 per cent drop in government support in the 1984 general election, the PAP's younger technocratic leaders began an ideological and institutional reform campaign promoting state-sponsored political participation. Early in this project, Goh Chok Tong (Goh 1986: 7), Prime Minister between 1989 and 2004, asserted that:

> What a plural society like ours needs is a tradition of government which emphasizes consensus instead of division, that includes rather than excludes, and that tries to maximize the participation of the population in the national effort, instead of minimizing it.

Importantly, this sort of consensus politics is seen as functional for elite rule, helping to gather intelligence useful to the effective refinement and implementation of policy, a point Lee Hsien Loong (Lee 1999) has been explicit about: 'In a rapidly changing environment, much of the valuable up-to-date information is held by people at the frontline. Policy makers must draw on this knowledge to understand realities on the ground, and reach better solutions.' He reiterated this perspective on the eve of his ascension to Prime Minister, endorsing more civic political participation on the basis that: 'The overriding objective is to reach the correct conclusions on the best way forward' (Lee 2004). New forms of political participation, then, are meant not just to marginalize competitive politics by framing politics as a technical exercise; but also to render the one-party state more politically robust by developing new institutions incorporating citizens into preferred forms of conflict management.

These ideas, and the 1984 election results that precipitated them, surfaced in the context of a rapid social and economic transformation that exposed some of the limitations of existing structures of political co-option. The NTUC and grassroots Citizens' Consultative Committees (CCCs), for example, were constrained in their capacity to represent the interests of lower-income Singaporeans as material inequalities and living costs increased with capitalist development. The contradiction between elitist official rhetoric championing meritocracy and a dearth of opportunities for increasing numbers of middle-class professionals to exert an influence over public policy was also becoming apparent. Thus, new institutions have been developed creatively expanding the sites of participation, including through government parliamentary committees, public committees of enquiry led by government ministers, a public policy think tank and nominated members of parliament. These sites, however, represent an alternative to collective political action through independent civil society organizations (including opposition political parties) in favour of ideologies and processes intended to narrow the scope and nature of political contestation.

The discussion to follow focuses on two of the most significant such initiatives in consultative authoritarianism, one outside the parliamentary system and the other marking a modification to it. A host of mechanisms have been developed that allow for both individuals and groups to be involved in public policy and service delivery feedback and discussion forums and channels. As will be demonstrated, there is no shortage of public concerns about government policy directions that these mechanisms are designed to target. However, who can be involved or represented through these mechanisms, on what basis and for what purposes, is vital to the regime implications of this apparent opening up of politics.

Public feedback as administrative politics

The most significant non-parliamentary institution of consultative authoritarianism was launched in 1985 – the Feedback Unit (FBU) within the Ministry of Community Development. Its stated mission was to: receive and document for action suggestions from the public on national policies and problems; gather feedback on existing or impending government policies and their implementation with a view to improving them; ensure swift and effective responses by government departments to public suggestions and complaints; and help inform and educate the public about national policies and problems. The importance attached by the PAP to this institution was reaffirmed in 2006 when it was reviewed and renamed REACH – Reaching Everyone for Active Citizenry @ Home. REACH Supervisory Panel chairman and government member of parliament (MP), Amy Khor (2006), proclaimed that FBU's 'roles have to be enhanced, its reach widened and its channels of communication strengthened'. In the rationale for REACH, special emphasis was placed on the importance of greater engagement of younger Singaporeans and the need to exploit new media platforms to that end.

The direction of the REACH is broadly set by the Supervisory Panel, whose head (officially referred to as chairman) is appointed by the relevant minister, the current title of which is Community Development, Youth and Sports, with the concurrence of the Prime Minister. Not only is the chairman invariably a currently serving PAP MP, but so are many other members of the Panel. Since 2001, the non-PAP MP composition has increased but largely through the incorporation of people nevertheless belonging to the PAP establishment. In 2010, for example, the 25-person Panel included seven government MPs (including the chairman), five from the PAP-affiliated CCCs, six from GLCs and three from PAP-affiliated unions. The omission of opposition politicians and independent civil society activists from the Panel is precisely because the idea is to foster a 'consensual' rather than competitive conception of, and framework for, politics.

Who can be involved in these processes, over what matters and how depends on the purpose and nature of the particular channel of political participation involved. Where channels are intended to gather information for the government to better understand public reaction to an existing or prospective policy or issue these can be quite open and inclusive. Yet where they are meant to solicit suggestions on policy improvement or policy initiatives, the process is more selective. By far the most frequent form of participation fostered through feedback channels is by individuals, but notional representation of groups and social categories is also actively sought. However, by constructing the social categories to be represented or by working closely with preferred existing groups, authorities have been able to shape this representation to achieve a fragmentation in the treatment of political issues and a disciplining of policy debate to choices and debates linked to the ruling party's agenda.

Online consultation channels, which account for the vast bulk of the feedback, have been especially significant in promoting individual forms of participation. Some of this feedback is solicited from the People's Forum database of over 7,000 registered respondents, matching the issue involved with demographic characteristics deemed of interest by REACH, a statutory body or a government department. Much of it, however, is generally open to the public.

One online channel involves e-Consultation Papers (eCPs) published by government departments and agencies and seeking either targeted or open expressions of views through SMS and email. Reactions from those affected by, or interested in, existing or proposed policies are sought. Another form of individual participation has been e-Polls, indicative polls surveying around 500 to 1,000 participants each time (Feedback Unit 2004:88). These are again driven by the issues or questions of interest to government ministries or agencies but target specific respondents. Some involve annual surveys such as on the budget, while others are conducted on wide-ranging policy issues as they arise, which has included marriage and procreation measures, racial integration in schools, and the White Paper on Terrorism. REACH's e-Townhall web-chat initiatives, chaired by MPs and other political appointments, have also been adopted to engage citizens following major government policy announcements. The inaugural such exercise in February 2007, for example, sought the public's views on the 2007 Budget Speech, which could be discussed in real time directly with the Minister of State for Finance and Transport, Lim Hwee Hua, and REACH chairman Amy Khor.

The Discussion Corner, referred to as the Discussion Forum under FBU, has been yet another avenue for individual participation. Unlike eCPs, all discussion here takes place on the REACH website and not on government department websites. Also, instead of asking for comments on specific policies and laws, the topics for discussion are typically more general and open-ended, although often requesting people's responses to certain facts, arguments or issues that REACH has effectively defined as a problem. The propensity of Singaporeans to emigrate, for example, was opened up for comment in August 2006. Through the General Feedback channel, there has also been in place for some time an avenue for individuals to make comments without prescribed categories or topics. Here citizens are linked to the relevant government departments that subsequently reply directly to the participant rather than engage in any public debate. Complaints or suggestions are, in effect, treated as technical or service quality issues to be dealt with privately.

Although online feedback may be more voluminous, live meetings are often more significant for policy education and influence. They are also more amenable to group involvement. One example is Dialogue Sessions, which were the first form of feedback introduced and remain a core medium. In 1986 there were fewer than 20, but by 2003 more than 60 for that year were organized (Feedback Unit 2004: 35). These are generally small and informal, involving pre-policy and post-policy consultations. Some topics are initiated by REACH, others by ministries. Annual topics include the Pre-Budget and the National Day Rally Speech Dialogue Sessions, but mostly these meetings address issues as they are deemed relevant at the time and have included SARS, the threat of terrorism, low wage workers, gambling, and proposed smoking bans, for example. Most meetings – chaired by two Supervisory Panel members, one of whom is a PAP MP – are in principle open to the general public but in practice this is largely through invitations to select members of the People's Forum and what REACH refers to as 'strategic partners': 'organisations the Unit works with to widen and deepen its reach to the people' (Feedback Unit 2004: 35, 37). This has involved groups already with a record of working co-operatively with the ruling party, such as: the NTUC; ethnic self-help groups MENDAKI, Chinese Development Assistance Council, Singapore Indian Development Association and the Eurasian Association; educational institutions; clan associations and chambers of commerce and industry.

A separate category of meetings that is less policy-driven is the Tea Sessions, also chaired by a PAP MP and one other Supervisory Panel member. These are far less frequent, usually held twice a year, but participants have a greater opportunity to raise issues that concern them. Importantly, though, the way that REACH conceptualizes social sectors has an impact on the participation and content of meetings. Tea sessions are broken up into one or other of 14 discrete groups of Singaporeans, including students, youths, women, professionals, ethnic communities, 'heartlanders', small and medium enterprises, and multinational corporations. Observations from participants themselves suggest that this compartmentalization of issues conditions discussions in the Dialogue and Tea Sessions (Feedback Unit 2005a: 10).

The most significant channel in terms of demonstrable policy influence is the Policy Study Workgroups (PSW) or what was referred to during the FBI period as Feedback Groups, established in 1997 by then Prime Minister Goh. These groups, chaired by people from the private or social sector, undertake in-depth policy studies and submit proposals to government at annual conferences. The proposals, embodying arguments and evidence drawn from a range of consultations under the workgroups' auspices, are subsequently published with responses from the relevant ministry or agency. The potential and limitations of such political participation are illustrated by a comparison of the differing fortunes of proposals emanating from the previous Health and Political Development Feedback Groups.

In response to recommendations from the Health Feedback Group, the Health Minister announced in early 2006 that Singapore's national healthcare financing system would be reformed. This would enable larger withdrawals from individual medical insurance accounts to cope with expensive outpatient treatments that the accounts could not previously be used for (Khaw 2006). The Health Ministry also responded positively to a number of the Group's recommendations on ways to manage the threat of chronic diseases (Feedback Unit 2005b). In explaining the Group's impact, its chairman Lee Kheng Hock (Lee 2006) emphasized that he saw the work of his group as 'trying to bring an issue to the top of the in-tray' rather than changing the course of government policy.

By contrast, the Political Matters and Media Feedback Group (subsequently renamed the Political Development Feedback Group) hit a brick wall with its 2002 Recommendations for Best Practices in Political Governance for Singapore. The document called for an independent and transparent electoral commission to level the political playing field, transparency and accountability for GLCs, measures to ensure legal and judicial impartiality, reforms to foster freedom of association and greater access to the media for opposition parties. This was one exercise where opposition political party and independent civil society activists were discernibly involved in the consultations. In his evaluation of the fortunes of the Best Practices recommendations, the Supervisory Panel chairman at the time, Wang Kai Yueng (Wang 2006), pointed out that, since there was no ministerial priority accorded to political reform, the chances of any departmental bureaucrats embracing the paper were always slim.

Clearly, these various mechanisms of state-sponsored consultation through REACH are designed to steer political participation as much as possible away from open debate about the objectives and content of public policy towards the more limited exercise of helping to improve or implement PAP government policy. In this respect, it is possible to point to various concrete outcomes from consultation. Crucially, though, the highly compartmentalized way in which different groups and individuals are consulted also militates against the formation of political coalitions around, and indeed beyond, specific sectoral or policy issues. Moreover, these consultative mechanisms embody a technocratic conception of politics rooted in a Weberian bureaucratic rationality which seeks to convert political problems into issues of administrative delivery and efficiency. Politics is, in effect, administratively incorporated into the state (Jayasuriya and Rodan 2007: 787–9; Rodan and Jayasuriya 2007). Here notions of representation are grounded not in citizenship rights but in the rationality of the public policy process.

This is an important shift in the nature of authoritarian political rule that cannot be fully appreciated by the transition theory problematic of whether or not these institutions are functional or dysfunctional in democratic terms. The question is instead whether or not this shift in political rule will be effective in accommodating Singaporeans' aspirations for political participation and avail the PAP of new foundations for regime legitimacy.

Nominated members of parliament

Another initiative in this new form of political rule involves the introduction of nominated members of parliament (NMPs). This institution highlights the complex layering possible under consultative authoritarianism, sometimes superimposing new modes of political participation on existing ones. In providing political participation not just for individuals in their own right and as members of state-conceived social categories, but also as members of independent NGOs, this institution is especially significant for its attempt to politically co-opt these organizations. This societal incorporation thus combines with administrative incorporation to expand the political space of the state (Jayasuriya and Rodan 2007: 783–5).

NMPs are appointed by the President for terms of up to two-and-a-half years on the advice of a Special Select Committee appointed by parliament. In contrast with elected MPs, they cannot vote on money bills, bills to alter the Constitution or motions of no confidence in the government. However, they can speak on these issues and vote and speak on any other bills and motions. In explaining the need for NMPs, Prime Minister Goh sought to address what he saw as a public misconception that the PAP was closed to alternative points of view on policy. The legislation altering the Constitution referred to 'independent and non-partisan views' in the selection criteria for NMPs (Ho 2000: 90). Significantly, though, Goh made mention not only of the value of incorporating talented people with special expertise in the professions, commerce, industry, social services and cultural domains, but also of sections of society currently under-represented in parliament, including women.

Since the first two NMP appointments in 1990, the scheme has expanded significantly by 2011 to involve 57 different people and a total of 76 appointments (some NMPs serving more than one term). In an attempt to capture the chief characteristics and dynamics of the various NMP appointments since the beginning of the scheme in June 1990 through to the eleventh parliament ending in April 2011, Table 8.1 identifies these on the basis of interest groups or

Garry Rodan

sectors. The individuals involved can generally be depicted as principally belonging to one or other interest group or sector, but many straddle these categories. This would appear to be a strategy by the parliamentary select committee responsible for the appointments to simultaneously incorporate or address different target interest groups and sectors.

One of the striking themes has been a sustained bias towards inclusion of people from the professions and academia (27.8 per cent), with medical and legal professionals especially prominent. In addition to being appointed in their own right, academics and professionals have often been appointed as notional representatives of women or ethnic minorities, or as champions of environmentalism or social welfare. In this way, the link between formal educational credentials and public policy expertise is reinforced at the same time as functional groups are politically incorporated. This evidences elitist and functional premises of the PAP's technocratic ideology.

The most heavily 'represented' single category of NMPs has involved the business sector (34.4 per cent). Especially significant is the repeated incorporation of senior past or present figures from within peak employer and business bodies. Singapore's increasing exposure to economic globalization has brought continuing challenges for the private sector. The consolidation and expansion of GLCs has not been without its critics from the local business community either.

As the PAP has more vigorously embraced economic globalization in recent decades, material inequalities have widened significantly in Singapore, testing trade union officials' ability to represent workers' interests to the government. Increasingly exorbitant ministerial and senior civil servant salaries justified in elitist terms have only compounded working-class resentment about rising inequalities. Representation of the NTUC in NMP appointments is thus a symbolic statement to counteract the idea of NTUC impotence.

Appointments in the three categories in Table 8.1 of 'Women', 'Societal' and 'Ethnicity' traverse areas involving embryonic civil society organizations. The number of appointments incorporating 'representatives' of these organizations has not been high, but their strategic significance for attempted state political co-option has. Thus, the appointment of orthopaedic surgeon Kanwaljit Soin to the eighth parliament was a conspicuous attempt to encourage activists within the moderate but independent feminist Association of Women for Action and Research (AWARE) towards direct engagement within a PAP-controlled institution. Soin did much to give the NMP scheme credibility, dominating parliamentary question time and occasionally

Table 8.1 Single and multiple categorization of NMPs by sector

Parliament	NTUC	Academia	Professionals	Business	Women	Societal	Ethnicity	Youth
11th	2	3 (1)	1 (1)	5 (2)	(4)	3 (2)	1 (3)	3 (3)
10th	2	2 (2)	3 (2)	7 (3)	(8)	2 (3)	(3)	2 (2)
9th	2	1	3 (2)	5 (2)	(4)	2	1 (3)	
8th	2	2	1 (3)	3 (2)	1 (1)	(2)	1 (2)	
7th			1	1 (1)				
Sub-totals	8 (0)	8 (3)	8 (8)	20 (9)	1 (17)	6 (5)	3 (11)	5 (5)
	12.0%	12.90%	14.52%	33.87%	1.61%	11.29%	4.84%	8.06%
Total	8	11	17	31	18	14	14	10
	6.50%	8.94%	13.82%	25.20%	14.63%	11.38%	11.38%	8.13%

Notes:
Bracketed figures refer to the additional cross-categorizations of NMPs.
Note also that some NMPs have been appointed in more than one parliament so they are counted for each parliament but only once for the sector they are deemed to 'represent' within that parliament. Hence, while the total number of appointments is 68, this translates into 62 sectoral categorizations.

shaping public debate, as in 1995 when she introduced a private member's bill – the Family Violence Bill. Although this was defeated, Soin (1999) reflected that:

> The media took up the subject of family violence in an earnest and responsible way and gave it a great deal of coverage, and this contributed to increased general awareness of the issue ... Also the government made amendments to the Women's Charter and these incorporated many of the principles and concepts of the aborted Family Violence Bill.

She has not only endorsed the NMP scheme in view of the existing limits to political space, but also maintains that: 'Even if a bipartisan system should eventually evolve here, there will still be a role for non-partisan NMPs to add another perspective to issues' (Soin 1999).

Another AWARE president, Braema Mathiaparanam, based her application around foreign domestic labour advocacy. Braema was also foundation President of Transient Workers Count Too (TWC2), an organization that was officially registered in 2004. Issues facing migrant workers have received remarkably little attention from opposition parties. The Nature Society of Singapore (NSS) has been recognized too through the appointment of orthopaedic surgeon Geh Min – the first female president of the NSS and a past president of AWARE. Like AWARE and TWC2, while not a radical organization, NSS's independence and comparative activism from the late 1980s posed a question about the adequacy of existing structures of political co-option on issues of potential appeal to Singapore's expanding middle class.

The other attempted co-option of an independent organization has involved the Association of Muslim Professionals (AMP), established in 1991 out of frustration with Mendaki – the officially sanctioned council representing ethnic Malays and controlled by Malay PAP MPs. PAP tolerance of AMP independence is in part a function of ruling party preference for problems of socio-economic disadvantage being viewed through an ethnic rather than a class prism. AMP chairman Imram bin Mohamed was among the 1994 NMP appointments, a move attempting to reinforce this ethnic framework of analysis.

Changing PAP perceptions of political challenge are also reflected in appointments loosely referred to in Table 8.1 as 'Youth'. Appointments have included Eunice Olsen – a television show host, volunteer youth worker, part-time musician, 2000 beauty queen and winner of the 2006 Singapore Youth Award – as well as Patricia Soh-Khim Ong – a PhD in mechanical engineering and the recipient of the 2004 Singapore Youth Award for Science and Technology – and Siew Kum Hong – a lawyer and political blogger. Each emanating from a different social milieu, collectively these and other similar appointments highlight the PAP's attempt at some form of political accommodation to the rapidly growing electoral weight of Generations X and Y voters.

After two decades, the NMP scheme is now embedded. But do NMPs see themselves as representatives? And, if so, how? Towards answering these questions interviews were conducted with NMPs from the ninth and tenth parliaments, revealing that NMPs variously see themselves as representing people, interests and/or ideas.

The NMP who saw himself most unambiguously in a representative role was Edwin Khew, whose application was jointly sponsored by the Singapore Manufacturers' Federation (SMF) (of which Khew was President) and the Singapore Business Federation (SBF). According to Khew (2007), people within the SMF in particular were of the view that 'the interests of manufacturing weren't well represented in parliament'. He established groups of major business leaders within the SMF and the SBF to chair various committees to receive and review input from the business community. These groups were conversant with the routine of parliamentary procedures and schedules, and thus ensured recommended questions were supplied two weeks before any parliamentary sitting.

By contrast, Geh Min (Geh 2006) asserted that she represented 'environmental issues and interests' and other issues neglected by the parties. In parliament she raised such issues as the illegal wildlife trade and animal rights. Geh explained that she regularly received solicited and unsolicited feedback from NSS members and others in her personal network but there was no routine process of consultation. According to her: 'The luxury of being an NMP is bringing up issues that are relevant but won't win many votes, such as issues of interest to the NSS, which enjoys niche support' (Geh 2006). Goh Chong Chia, a professional architect who was also an NMP in the ninth parliament, echoed this perspective. Nominated by a professional body, Goh (2006) saw himself 'representing views not readily expressed in parliament by either the PAP or the opposition', emphasizing how 'NMPs are not beholden to anyone and are not seeking re-election from a constituency, they are at liberty to pursue those interests'.

Meanwhile, Siew Kum Hong saw himself 'representing a specific segment of the population – 'young, late 20s, English-educated, Western in outlook, fairly liberal, Internet savvy' (Siew 2007), while Eunice Olsen (2007) conceded that technically she cannot represent anybody but that she 'would like to represent the thoughts of the youth' in particular and that her role in the media and her music afforded informal opportunities to gauge youth issues. Academic lawyer Thio Li-Ann (Thio 2007) saw herself representing constitutional matters and human rights issues, with absolutely no claim to consulting anyone on the matters she raised in parliament.

Clearly few of the respondents have at their disposal developed structures of feedback and consultation to facilitate engagement with large numbers of citizens. Yet through the Select Committee it is clear that the PAP has been fostering the idea of NMPs as representatives. What appears to matter to the government, though, is that NMPs conform in some way with those elements emphasized in Edmund Burke's (1996) 1774 account of representatives: substantive virtue and expert knowledge. That expert knowledge, though, may increasingly extend beyond technical expertise to include a good feel for views and aspirations among sections of the population not adequately incorporated into the PAP state through other means.

Overall, the NMP record of tangible policy impact is unimpressive. Just one piece of legislation initiated by an NMP has been approved in parliament – Walter Woon's Maintenance of Parents Bill in 1994 – and a mere handful of other pieces of legislation have been NMP-initiated. Nevertheless, the numbers of people seeking appointments or accepting nominations for appointment rises. Why?

Soin's view that NMPs afford at least some opportunity for greater political engagement without the risks associated with formal political opposition is likely shared by others. However, a recurring theme from NMP interviews was the assertion that the scheme also enabled issues to be raised that are not taken up with any seriousness, if at all, by political parties. Included here are environmentalism, feminism, gay rights, treatment of foreign workers, urban design and constitutional reform issues. These might be described as middle-class or socially progressive issues, which neither the ruling party nor the opposition parties can easily embrace without risk of alienating the socially conservative Chinese-speaking working class, or so-called 'HDB Heartlanders'. The technocratic approach to politics fostered by the PAP through the NMP scheme thus affords these issues legitimacy not readily available through the existing parties.

Yet the prospects of broad coalitions across classes around issues of social inequalities and social justice are further dampened by the fragmentation and compartmentalization of political debate encouraged by the NMP scheme. First, the scheme promotes the idea of politics as a set of rational public policy deliberations and choices where it is the logical power of argument, rather than the force of political alliances and collective action, that offers best prospects.

Second, issues to be represented are not only, in effect, shaped by the Select Committee, but individuals and social organizations are drawn into a process of atomization as they each work away on their respective specific policy ideas or concerns.[3]

Conclusions and implications for analysing other regimes

Understanding the political regime in Singapore requires more than scrutiny of the democratic credentials of its political institutions. Those credentials have been suspect for many decades. Yet the political regime has been anything but static, undergoing significant changes in the attempt to accommodate new social forces and contain tensions associated with the city-state's path of capitalist development. In particular, with the ushering in of consultative authoritarianism and its associated active citizenship, political participation is of heightened importance to the process by which contestation is actually contained. This includes new structures and notions of representation meant to limit politics to exercises in the governance of problem solving rather than more explicit debate and challenge over larger normative choices. Through state-sponsored and state-defined groups, fragmented political engagement is fostered as an attractive alternative to independent collective action, which continues to be heavily circumscribed and scrutinized by authorities.

As we have seen through the brief examinations of REACH and NMPs, new forms of state-sponsored political participation have met with a degree of acceptance – especially among business and professional classes. This cannot be explained without reference to the particular way that state capitalism has been consolidated in Singapore, which has enhanced not only the power and homogeneity of a class of politico-bureaucratic ruling elites, but also the direct and indirect dependence of citizens on the state controlled by these elites. The blocking of independent political space and the vulnerability to overtures of creative state-sponsored alternatives in political participation are intimately related.

The implications of the above analysis extend to the study of authoritarian regimes within and beyond Southeast Asia. Developments in Singapore suggest the possibility of far more creative institutional and ideological potential among authoritarian regimes than hitherto countenanced by transition theorists. In Singapore there has been an explicit shift towards consultative authoritarianism, but to differing degrees similar initiatives can be found in China and Vietnam, for example (He 2006; Jayasuriya and Rodan 2007). However, the crucial point is that not all authoritarian regimes are inclined towards or capable of moving in this direction, and it is only by linking political institutions with wider political economy dynamics that we can begin to understand some of the divergent paths of authoritarian rule. The state capitalist trajectory of Singapore under the PAP, dominated by a powerful class of technocrats, is not a general feature of authoritarian rule and may be an ideal foundation for consultative authoritarianism. The question to ask is: what sorts of coalitions and interests are being consolidated or challenged as capitalist development transforms the economies and societies of other authoritarian regimes? The answer to this has a considerable bearing on the extent and nature of change to political institutions.

On this basis, there are significant points of intersection between Singapore's experience and those of various post-authoritarian regimes in Southeast Asia where democratic transitions are being attempted. This includes a shared legacy of Western support for repressive governments to shore up capitalism during the Cold War. Consequently, civil societies have often had to be built from low bases and in a context of late industrialization under globalized capitalism less conducive to strong, independent trade unions linked to reformist political parties, as was typical of the route democracy took in Britain and Western Europe. In the Philippines, Thailand and

Indonesia, for example, political avenues for the middle class have been limited owing to the absence of independent, cohesive working-class organizations and peak employer groups with which to form alliances.

Not coincidentally, middle-class support for democracy has not been readily incorporated into political movements or parties – not simply because of deficient political institutions but because the historical and geopolitical context of capitalist development has influenced the character of civil society and the relationships between its component elements (Rodan and Jayasuriya 2009). Arguably this renders these social forces in Southeast Asia potentially more amenable to various forms of state-sponsored political participation – some of which may have resonance with Singapore's consultative authoritarianism.

Nevertheless, the capacity or inclination for following the Singapore model elsewhere in Southeast Asia is also constrained by the absence of comparable coalitions between technocratic and political elites on the one hand and the complete suffocation of civil society on the other – both of which are products of a specific form of state capitalism. Consequently, initial steps towards consultative authoritarianism in Vietnam have some way to go before they approximate the scale and character of what has been described above of Singapore. To get to that point, amongst other things, state power would have to first be controlled by an unequivocally technocratic and rationalist elite coalition capable of crafting structured state dependence into a force for systematic political co-option. Here Vietnam and China face similar challenges in any attempt to emulate the Singapore case: keeping business and professional interests under the tent of a cohesive and mutually reinforcing set of power relationships of state power. The scale and complexity of market transformations in these larger countries are more conducive to pockets of middle-class and private sector interests that may contest or complicate the comprehensive institutionalization of rationalist and market functionalist ideologies evident in Singapore – the ideal model of consultative authoritarianism. The degree to which working classes can be mobilized through state-controlled trade unions and complementary forms of political participation is also unlikely to match that in the city-state.

Notes

1 Research for this essay was supported by Australian Research Council funding for a Discovery Project (1093214), 'Representation and Political Regimes in Southeast Asia', for which the author is grateful.
2 The term 'consultative authoritarianism' has recently been used by He Baogang and Stig Thøgersen (He and Thøgersen 2010) to characterize tendencies in contemporary China. It was used much earlier by H. Gordon Skilling (1970) in his work on political change in communist systems and subsequently drawn on by Harry Harding (1987) to characterize post-Mao political reform in China. Harding (1987: 2000) contended that consultative authoritarianism 'increasingly recognises the need to obtain information, advice, and support from key sectors of the population, but insists on suppressing dissent, cultivating its vision of public morality, and maintaining ultimate political power in the hands of the Party.'
3 For a fuller discussion of NMPs see Rodan (2009).

References

Burke, E. (1996) 'Speech at the conclusion of the poll 3 November 1774', in Warren M. Elofson with John A. Woods (eds) *The Writings and Speeches of Edmund Burke, Volume III: Party, Parliament, and the American War 1774–1780*, Oxford: Clarendon Press, pp. 63–70.
Case, W. (2005) 'Southeast Asia's hybrid regimes: when do voters change them?' *Journal of East Asian Studies* 5 (2): 215–37.

Chin, J. (1997) 'Anti-Christian Chinese chauvinists and HDB upgrades: the 1997 Singapore general election', *South-East Asia Research* 5 (3): 217–41.

Chua Beng-Huat (1991) 'Not depoliticized but ideologically successful: the public housing program in Singapore', *International Journal of Urban and Regional Research* 15 (1): 24–41.

Diamond, L., M. Plattner, Yun-han Chu and Hung-mao Tien (eds) (1997) *Consolidating the Third Wave Democracies: Regional Challenges*, Baltimore, MD: Johns Hopkins University Press.

Feedback Unit (2005a) 'Youth Connect Workshop Report', Feedback Unit, Singapore: Ministry of Community Development and Sports.

——(2005b) *Annual Conference of Feedback Groups, 29 January 2005, Pan Pacific Hotel Singapore: Speeches, Transcripts, Ministries' Replies*, Singapore: Ministry of Community Development and Sports.

——(2004) *Building Bridges: The Story of Feedback Unit*, Singapore: Feedback Unit, Ministry of Community Development and Sports.

Geh Min (2006) Interview, Singapore, 6 November.

Goh Chok Tong (1986) 'A nation of excellence', address at the Alumni International Singapore, 1 December, Singapore Ministry of Communications and Information.

Goh Chong Chia (2006) Interview, Singapore, 6 November.

Harding, H. (1987) *China's Second Revolution: Reform After Mao*, Washington, DC: Brookings Institution.

He Baogang (2006) 'Participatory and deliberative institutions in China', in E. Leib and Baogang He (eds) *The Search for Deliberative Democracy in China*, Houndmills: Palgrave Macmillan, pp. 175–96.

He Baogang and Stig Thøgersen (2010) 'Giving people a voice? Experiments with consultative authoritarian institutions in China', *Journal of Contemporary China* 19 (66): 675–92.

Ho Khai Leong (2000) *The Politics of Policy-Making in Singapore*, Singapore: Oxford University Press.

Huntington, S. (1991) *The Third Wave: Democratization in the Late Twentieth Century*, Norma: University of Oklahoma Press.

Jayasuriya, K. and G. Rodan (2007) 'Beyond hybrid regimes: more participation, less contestation in Southeast Asia', *Democratization* 14 (5): 773–94.

Khaw Boon Wan (2006) '2006 speeches: Annual Conference of Feedback Groups', 21 January, Pan Pacific Hotel, Singapore; available at: www.moh.gov.sg/corp/about/newsroom/speeches/details.do?id=35553298 (accessed 16 November 2006).

Khew, Edwin (2007) Interview, Singapore, 26 July.

Khor, Amy (2006) 'Feedback Unit's 21st anniversary dinner speech', 12 October, Pan Pacific Hotel, Singapore; REACH website, available at: www.reach.gov.sg/Default.aspx?tabid=141 (accessed 1 December 2006).

Lee Hsien Loong (1999) 'Speech by Deputy Prime Minister Lee Hsien Loong at the Administrative Service dinner and promotion ceremony', 29 March, Mandarin Hotel, Singapore; available at: www.singapore 21.org.sg/speeches_290399.html (accessed 4 October 2006).

——(2004) 'Speech by Deputy Prime Minister Lee Hsien Loong at the Harvard Club of Singapore's 35th anniversary dinner', 6 January; available at: http://unpan1.un.org/intradoc/groups/public/documents/APCITY/UNPAN015426.pdf (accessed 27 October 2006).

Lee Kheng Hock (2006) Interview, Singapore, 9 November.

Levitsky, S. and L. Way (2002) 'The rise of competitive authoritarianism', *Journal of Democracy* 13 (2): 51–65.

Olsen, Eunice (2007) Interview, Singapore, 14 May.

Rodan, G. (2008) 'Singapore "exceptionalism"? Authoritarian rule and state transformation', in J. Wong and E. Friedman (eds) *Political Transitions in Dominant Party Systems: Learning to Lose*, New York: Routledge, pp. 231–51.

——(2009) 'New modes of political participation and Singapore's nominated members of parliament', *Government and Opposition* 44 (4): 438–62.

Rodan, G. and K. Jayasuriya (2007) 'The technocratic politics of administrative participation: case studies of Singapore and Vietnam', *Democratization* 14 (5): 795–816.

——(2009) 'Capitalist development, regime transitions and new forms of authoritarianism in Asia', *Pacific Review* 22 (1): 23–48.

Siew Kum Hong (2007) Interview, Singapore, 17 May.

Skilling, H.G. (1970) 'Group conflict and political change', in Chalmers Johnson (ed.) *Change in Communist Systems*, Stanford, CA: Stanford University Press, pp. 215–34.

Soin, Kanwaljit (1999) 'Woman doctor in the house', *Singapore Medical Journal* 40 (4); available at: www.sma.org.sg/smj/4004/articles/4004ia5part2.html (accessed 30 April 2008).

Garry Rodan

Thio Li-Ann (2007) Interview, Singapore, 16 May.
Vischer, S. (2007) *The Business and Politics of Ethnicity: A History of the Singapore Chamber of Commerce and Industry*, Singapore: Singapore University Press.
Wang Kai Yueng (2006) Interview, Singapore, 9 November.
Worthington, R. (2003) *Governance in Singapore*, London: RoutledgeCurzon.

9

VIETNAM

The ruling Communist Party and the incubation of 'new' political forces

Martin Gainsborough

Introduction

Vietnam has been ruled in its entirety by the Vietnamese Communist Party since the country was reunified shortly after the end of the American war in 1975. Since that time, the Party has sought to prevent independent political parties from forming while also trying to keep other forms of social organization or popular expression under wraps.[1] Nevertheless, politics has not stood still, in part because of changes permitted by the Party but also because of the consequences of marketization and international integration which have led to social change and the emergence of new political forces. The latter can reasonably be said to include a more powerful business elite – still with close ties to the state even if in some cases it is operating under a 'private sector' label – a richer and more assertive middle class, and recently, new opposition groups and independent trade unions, the latter still illegal and of questionable influence in the greater scheme of things (Cheshier 2010; Gainsborough 2010: 9–24; Hayton 2010: 113–34; Wells-Dang 2010).

In terms of characterizing these 'new' political forces, the key point is that we need to be extremely sceptical of the 'triumph of the private sector' kind of arguments which are some-times advanced to explain change in Vietnam. Instead, the story is one of the emergence of new business interests – and their associated family members – *from within the state sector*, and generally speaking *continued close ties between this elite and the state* – as an essential condition of operating successfully. A similar caution is needed when assessing new forms of middle-class activism often associated with the growth of non-government organizations or so-called civil society. Yes, there is increased outspokenness and some pressure for new forms of political expression, but aside from isolated dissident elements most people are content to operate within the one-party context. Consequently, it is important to understand that the epithet 'new' needs to be understood circumspectly.

Against this backdrop, most accounts of Vietnamese politics today have adopted a narrative of change with caveats. In many respects, such an approach seems self-evidently reasonable. However, such approaches are not without weakness. This chapter argues that Vietnam scholars need to be much clearer and more precise about what has changed and what has not, about the direction of change, and about how we explain the diverse outcomes we observe. In terms of diversity of outcome, I am particularly thinking of the fact that while many of the old Party elite have made the transition into the reform era, not everyone has. To try and shed light on these issues, I shift the focus in this chapter onto what I regard as the fundamental building blocks of Vietnamese politics understood as the importance of relationships in Vietnamese politics; the close connection in people's minds between public office and money-making; the importance of patronage; uncertainty as an instrument of rule; and political paternalism. Understanding these often enduring economic and political relationships, I argue, is crucial if we are to move towards a deeper understanding of Vietnamese politics, including properly contextualizing the emergence of 'new' political forces, including opposition forces.

The chapter is structured as follows. I first look at how Vietnamese politics has conventionally been analysed. This also serves to orientate the reader in relation to some of Vietnam's key political landmarks. I then critique the existing literature before setting out my approach. I am calling my approach a 'patronage' approach to politics to contrast it with some of the other approaches used to analyse Vietnamese politics, which are discussed below. However, to be clear, this is not a cultural, behavioural or modernization theory approach. I am using a patronage approach to shed light on the mechanics of how the ruling elite has metamorphosed over the last two decades so that while it has many things in common with the past, it is not identical with it. This applies to both how the elite is constituted ('its character') and some of its outlooks, although I would not wish to exaggerate the latter. Having set out my approach, I then look at its implications, both for how we characterize change (and continuity) in Vietnamese politics and for how we understand it. Finally, I conclude.

Vietnam politics: a review

Most discussions of Vietnamese politics today are constructed around a narrative of reform (*doi moi*) embodying a sense that reform has been important in the trajectory the country has taken. Reflecting this, it is actually quite difficult to talk about politics in Vietnam today without invoking a 'reform' discourse.[2] Leaving aside what 'reform' is or when it began, most studies typically make reference to the Sixth National Communist Party Congress held in 1986, which although largely associated with economic reform also included a critique of the existing political system. Adopting an institutional approach, Carlyle Thayer captures this best when he quotes from the Political Report produced for the Sixth Congress. The Political Report highlights a range of issues but it is most notable for its drawing attention to poor coordination between different elements of the party-state along with a tendency by Party officials to operate outside of the law and ride roughshod over electoral procedures:

> there exist in our society some abnormal phenomena, that is, a lack of coherence between the party, the state and the people ...
>
> In many cases, party committees at various levels run the whole show, doing the work of state bodies. The selection of people into elected bodies in many places is done in a forcible manner ...
>
> As our party is now in power, all cadres whatever positions must live and work in strict compliance with the law ... No-one is allowed to make use of their power and influence to infringe on the law.
>
> *(Sixth Congress Political Report, cited in Thayer 1992: 113–14)*

It is this critique – set out at the Sixth Congress – which is generally seen to have set in train formal moves by the Party to build a state 'ruled by law', to strengthen the role of the country's legislature, the National Assembly, and to clarify the relationship between the Party and the government. These issues all remain current to this day, although how exactly the Party views 'rule of law' or the correct relationship between the state and its citizens is an open question.

Continuing in this vein, discussions of Vietnamese politics often make mention of the Seventh National Party Congress held in 1991. It is at the Seventh Congress that the Party is viewed as having decisively turned its face against political pluralism, losing a politburo member, Tran Xuan Bach in the process, apparently because of high-level disagreements on the issue (Womack 1997: 84). As the Political Report to the Seventh Congress stated:

> we reaffirm our will to constantly broaden socialist democracy; but to promote democracy in the right direction and successfully, this process should be properly led ... Pursuing extreme liberal demands, practising democracy without linking it with order and discipline or without sufficiently taking into consideration the political and social situation, would [not] only prevent good intentions about the promotion of democracy being successful, on the contrary, this would lead to consequences harmful to the people's interests.
>
> *(Communist Party of Vietnam 1991: 104)*

The Seventh Congress occurred in the context of the collapse of Communism in Eastern Europe and the former Soviet Union. It was also not long after popular protests in Tiananmen Square in China in 1989. Given economic difficulties in Vietnam, pressure on Hanoi to change course politically was intense at this time both internally and externally. However, having resisted the clamour for change in 1991, opposition to multiparty rule has been the Party's big non-negotiable ever since. In an interview with *Time* magazine in 2002, reported by Vietnam News Agency, the then Party General Secretary, Nong Duc Manh, was quoted as saying that Vietnam would *never* have need for opposition parties (cited in Gainsborough 2002: 706).[3] Thus, whenever the Party talks about the need for more democracy – as it often does – it is with the conception of it in a one-party context. For example, when the former Politburo member and one-time National Assembly chairman Nguyen Van An spoke in 2009 about future ways to develop democracy in Vietnam, he gave as examples the direct election of the Party General Secretary by the National Party Congress, the direct election of local People's Committee chairmen by voters, and the Politburo and Party Central Committee listening 'attentively' to the government and National Assembly (VietnamNet Bridge 2009).[4]

Since the early 1990s, politics in Vietnam has been analysed in large part against the backdrop of the position adopted by the Party at the Seventh Congress but also in relation to the reform agenda pursued by the government in conjunction with the international donor community, which has been more active in Vietnam since the 1990s. Consequently, the issues which have received scholarly attention have largely although not exclusively tracked the government-donor agenda, including public administration reform (Painter 2005), grassroots democracy (UNDP 2006), the role of the National Assembly in politics (Salomon 2007), media freedom (McKinley 2009), corruption (Vasavakul 2008) and 'civil society' (Kerkvliet et al. 2008).

Key debates amongst Vietnam scholars have focused on the extent to which Party authority is being eroded (Dixon and Kilgour 2002; Fforde 2005; Gainsborough 2007b; Thayer 2009a), whether politics in Vietnam is in fact more participatory than is suggested by its authoritarian label (Dang Phong and Beresford 1998; London 2009; Wells-Dang 2010), and how much emphasis to put on the state as opposed to society in analysing change (Kerkvliet 1995, 2005). Thayer (2009b) has sought to shift the analysis more firmly onto opposition groups, including independent labour and religious groups, arguing that their study has been marginalized in mainstream approaches. While this may well be the case, how important such groups are to the broad direction Vietnam is travelling is debated (Hayton 2010: 113–34; Wells-Dang 2010). Again, what we see here, therefore, are largely institutional approaches in which the debate focuses on whether institutions are changing or whether participation is real.

Vietnam politics reconsidered

I divide my critique of the approaches noted above into three areas: assessing the balance between continuity and change, being clear about the direction of change, and explaining the outcomes we observe. I first look at how scholars have captured the balance between continuity and change.

Change versus continuity

On close examination, it is evident that Vietnam scholars have often struggled to pin down precisely what has changed and what has not. This is particularly the case with some of the more timeless features of Vietnamese politics – what I referred to at the beginning of the chapter as the building blocks of Vietnamese politics, namely the importance of relationships; the close connection in people's minds between public office and money-making; the importance of patronage; uncertainty as an instrument of rule; and political paternalism – which, given the field's preoccupation with change, even change with caveats, can easily get lost.[5] Also, in relation to the usual debates about Vietnamese politics, it can often feel as if scholars are arguing about whether the glass is half empty or half full. A good example would be the question of whether the National Assembly has emerged as a more authoritative institution in the reform era and, if so, the extent to which these changes have occurred (Salomon 2007, Malesky and Schuler 2008, London 2009). Moreover, there is again a sense in which the key building blocks of politics are not sufficiently acknowledged

The direction of change

It is not just that Vietnam scholars have had trouble pinning down what has changed and what has not, there is also a lack of precision in the existing literature regarding how to characterize change (i.e. change to what?) and also over how we account for the various outcomes we observe.

Looking at how we characterize change first, there is a danger – particularly in the context of a widening of the political space like that which is occurring in Vietnam – that we inadvertently start to view change through liberal eyes. This is in part a consequence of the heavily normative nature of much international donor community activity in Vietnam since the 1990s, notably its so-called governance programmes (World Bank 2010). A tendency to view Vietnamese politics through a liberal lens also bears resemblance to the old transition paradigm whereby change is assessed in terms of whether it brings a country closer or further away from liberal democracy, with other 'end-states' ignored.[6] Of course, Vietnam is not immune to external influences, but however it may look on the surface the influence of liberal democracy is still skin deep. But once again this raises the question of change to what? My argument is that while certain members of the elite have fallen and others prospered over the last two decades – for a variety of quite specific political and economic reasons – the underlying political culture and its associated ways of behaving politically have remained firmly non-liberal in Vietnam, notwithstanding the pluralist rhetoric which sometimes accompanies Vietnamese politics today. In this sense, I view Vietnam's politics as being remarkably similar to countries like Indonesia, Cambodia or Singapore, granted some subtle but important distinctions in terms of the character of the state.

The characterization of change by mainstream scholarship is also not as robust as it could be because of a tendency to view politics in Vietnam in zero sum terms such that one actor or group's loss is seen as another's gain. This is evident in relation to discussions about whether Party authority is being eroded but it also can be seen in relation to discussions about the rise of 'civil society' and the activities of opposition groups. In reality, politics is much more fluid than this. Moreover, while the Party may lose ground in one area, this does not mean it is losing ground in all areas.

Explaining outcomes

In terms of explaining the outcomes we observe, the tendency in the existing literature would be to emphasize the way in which old 'pre-reform' political forces, understood as Party interests or those close to the old planned economy, have managed the transition into the new era. This would be seen partly as a consequence of the Party remaining in power and partly because of the way in which the market emerged out of the plan (Fforde and de Vylder 1996). Relevant here is the way in which there was a distinct pecking order under the old state subsidy system – with privileged members of the elite receiving preferential treatment and hence being able to start accumulating capital even under the plan. Reflecting this, many of the new business interests which emerged in the 1990s had their origins firmly in the state sector, including privately registered firms (Gainsborough 2003: 16–39; Cheshier 2010). That said, it is not simply a case of old elites transitioning smoothly into the new era. Some people have fallen spectacularly. Most have had to reinvent themselves in order to survive, and not everyone has been successful (Gainsborough 2003: 16–39, 78–97). A dynamic account of politics needs to be able to make sense of this diversity, explaining why some people have prospered in the new era and why others have not. Most existing accounts do not do this very well. For instance, frequently the rise or fall of politicians and other elite members is attributed to differences over policy (the classic 'reformers' vs 'conservatives') when in fact it is much more determined by struggles for control over limited state and other resources, ranging from state budget money to foreign investment and international donor finance. Disputes are sometimes dressed up in policy terms but this is usually a cover for more Machiavellian-inspired jockeying (Gainsborough 2007a).

It is in response to these weaknesses that the chapter proceeds.

Key building blocks of Vietnamese politics

One assessment of the different approaches to the study of policy-making processes at the leadership level in Vietnam is provided by Thaveeporn Vasavakul (1997). She identified three competing approaches: the factional power approach; the collegial/collective leadership approach; and the sectoral approach. The factional approach, which is still the most influential approach among scholars of Vietnamese politics, sees differences among Party leaders as being driven by individual/factional interests grouped around policy differences. The collegial/collective leadership approach argues that Party leaders have a shared sense of the national interest but disagree over the means to achieve them. The sectoral approach, meanwhile, sees 'interest group' politics at work in Vietnam arguing that a politician or an official's geographical or 'sectoral' base is key to understanding elite policy-making, *not* patronage or support for a particular Party boss (Vasavakul 1997: 81–3).[7]

While there are problems with all three approaches, they are useful in focusing our attention on the essential building blocks of Vietnamese politics. In light of Vasavakul's review, we can ask the following questions. First, is it appropriate to talk in terms of factions in respect of Vietnamese politics, are sectors better, or are neither appropriate? Second, what is the role of personalities or patronage in politics – seemingly rejected as being important by the sectoral approach? Third, is it possible to point to a certain commonality of outlook amongst Vietnam's elite as the collegial/collective leadership approach suggests? Finally, is it helpful to view politics as being about disputes over rival policy positions, or the means to achieve them, as all three approaches do?

In order to answer these questions, I now turn to my alternative 'patronage' approach to Vietnamese politics, working through the five key building blocks I identified earlier in the chapter. As will be seen, my approach places heavy emphasis on interests as the key determinant of outcomes.

Relationships

Relationships (*quan he*), or who you know, are crucial in Vietnamese politics. It is not that some people are in relationships (e.g. the political elite) and others are not. Everyone is in them. It is just that some relationships run closer to the top or are better at unlocking doors. Who you know is crucial to getting things done. This is the case in all spheres of life, ranging from securing a job to running a business, ensuring the best for your children, managing relations with your local police and getting medical treatment. As Vietnamese people will tell you: when they get sick they think about who they know.

Relationships are also important as a source of protection. It is in this context that political umbrellas (*o du*) are important in Vietnam. Umbrellas extend from the political centre downwards, with a central umbrella generally regarded as better than a local one (Gainsborough 2007a: 17). Being known to have a good umbrella means that people are less likely to hassle you. As a director of an equitized company in northern Lao Cai told me, explaining how he navigated the province's predatory business environment: 'people are still wary of me because I am a member of the Party and used to work at a former state enterprise' (cited in Gainsborough 2009: 269).

When I talk about relationships, I am not thinking about hard and fast 'factions' and certainly not factions linked to distinct policy positions (i.e. the factional power approach). In Vietnam, as in much of Southeast Asia, elites hang loose to policy. Being too clearly identified with a particular policy position is potentially dangerous. Moreover, it restricts freedom of movement and prevents opportunism in terms of going after resources, particularly financial resources (Gainsborough 2010: 7). Instead, when I talk about relationships I am imaging a loose configuration of personalities with relationships forming – and re-forming – around such things as shared commercial interests, blood or marital ties, shared home town or province, time served together, perhaps in the war, in the bureaucracy or overseas, and past obligations and debts.

That relationships are so important in Vietnam reflects the fact that things do not happen because of the impartial application of rules ('rule of law'). Rather, it is who you know which influences what you get such that we can say that while it would be mistaken to say there is no rule of law, how it is interpreted and applied is profoundly influenced by who you are.

Public office and personal advancement

A second key building block of Vietnamese politics is the strong connection in people's minds between public office, making money and other forms of personal advancement (Gainsborough et al. 2009: 377–427). As with who you know, holding public office gives you status and in turn a degree of protection. However, holding public office also gives you access to resources along with opportunities to do business and levy fees – many of which are illicit or informal. When you hold public office in Vietnam people will want to know you for what you can do for them, and officials can charge for their services here too. Moreover, it is well understood that a percentage of money raised will end up in one's pocket or an institutional account.

That this is how it works can be seen from the fact that people are prepared to pay to obtain public office despite the fact that the formal salary is low. This only makes sense if officials expect to be able to recoup their investment through other means (Transparency International 2006, Salomon 2008).

Patronage

The third key building block of Vietnamese politics is an outgrowth of the previous two, namely the importance of patronage. Patronage in the form of access to jobs, money, resources and favours is both dished out and received, leading to a constant round of mutual obligation and debt (*no*). From the perspective of the person in a position to hand out patronage, looking after those in your circle – otherwise known as nepotism – is the ethically right thing to do. Indeed, it would be bad form not to. It also serves to get things done and to create a circle of people on whom the patron can rely.

From the perspective of those on the receiving end of such largesse it is important to nurture one's relationship with one's patron by showing them appropriate deference or giving them gifts. Importantly, this can include passing a portion of one's illicit earnings upwards to the person to whom you owe your job, or who sits above you in the hierarchy. Once again, this is the ethically right thing to do (Gainsborough *et al.* 2009: 410–11). Failure to transfer a portion of one's illicit earnings upwards – not the obtaining of such earnings in the first place – is considered deviation from the norm and hence corrupt. It is often in this context that we see the prosecution of corruption cases in Vietnam (Gainsborough 2003: 78–97).

Patronage is important all the time in Vietnam but it particularly comes to the fore in the run-up to the National Party Congresses when key positions are circulated (Gainsborough 2007a). Reflecting this, scholars have noted a spike in public investment in the two years prior to a Party Congress, with a decline thereafter (Abrami *et al.* 2008).

Uncertainty as an instrument of rule

A fourth key building block of Vietnamese politics is uncertainty as an instrument of rule. Rules in Vietnam are notoriously unclear. However, the system works against them being clarified. Here, it is useful to recall the strong connection in people's mind between public office and money-making. For those who hold office, a lack of clarity over the rules pertaining to their behaviour provides scope for discretion in the interpretation of the rules, which in turn creates opportunities for making money. This includes levying fees to provide routine administrative services. It also includes fining people for alleged transgressions, which are easy to commit or for someone to say you have committed, when the rules are impossible to make sense of in the first place. For those who have to run the gauntlet of the bureaucracy, this further underlines the importance of being well connected.

Rule by uncertainty is also used to discipline those seen as stepping out of line in a more overtly political sense. This is evident in relation to Vietnam's emerging civil society, organized labour and dissidents. In relation to the labour market, regulations governing the right to strike are so confusing and Kafkaesque that it is said to be next to impossible to call a strike while keeping within the rules. This provides the state with the means to throw the book at workers if it deems their activity is unusually threatening, or they wish to make an example of them. From the perspective of workers, this means they are never quite sure what the consequences of their actions will be, which tends to act as a constraint on their behaviour (Kim 2005).

Political paternalism

The fifth and final building block of Vietnamese politics relates to what I call political patern-alism. In Vietnam, as in many Confucian-influenced cultures, politics is strongly paternalistic and elitist. This has implications for what is viewed as the 'correct' relationship between the state and its citizens, or the rulers and ruled. At root, and in stark contrast to the West, there is implied strong belief that the goodwill and high moral capacity of those in authority, rather than the institutional checks and balances favoured in the liberal tradition, will ensure power is restrained. Such views run deep in Vietnam: they are not simply held by those in power in Vietnam but are part of the cultural mindset of all the country's citizens. This includes, one suspects, many of those formally opposed to the Party.[8]

The continued relevance of this cultural mindset can be seen in relation to the importance of 'family', or who your parents are, in Vietnamese politics – documented in detail in one's *ly lich* or curriculum vitae. It is also evident in the perennial discussion about whether the country's leaders must be Party members or whether talent or moral stature is more important (Gains-borough 2007a: 4). Interestingly, emphasizing an underlying political paternalism in Vietnamese politics gives some credence to the collective leadership approach, although not in the way it has been conventionally understood.

We now look at the implications of a patronage approach to politics both for how we characterize change in Vietnam and how we understand it.

Understanding change in Vietnamese politics

In the previous section, I set out what I regard as the key building blocks of Vietnamese politics identified as the importance of relationships in Vietnamese politics; the close connection in people's minds between public office and money-making; patronage; uncertainty as an instru-ment of rule; and political paternalism, arguing that these have not received as much attention in mainstream scholarship as they ought to. Once these building blocks are understood, a number of things fall into place, which makes for a deeper and more informed view of Vietnamese politics. I now set this out.

The first point to make is that we are now in a position to be much clearer about the balance between change and continuity in relation to how people behave and think politically, since it is evident that while certain things have changed during the reform era others have stayed the same. More than this, we are able to be precise about what has changed and what has not – a weakness, it was suggested, with existing scholarship. Here, a distinction between surface and deep 'change' would appear to be useful since it is evident that much of what is commonly identified as 'change' in Vietnam over the last two decades is in fact relatively superficial. This includes large swathes of what is usually identified as 'reform' as pursued via the government-donor agenda. Meanwhile, the fundamental underpinnings of Vietnamese politics – the importance of relationships, the strong connection between public office and money-making, patronage, the use of uncertainty as an instrument of rule, political paternalism – which all predate the reform era, have changed very little.

Building on this, we can also be clearer about the direction of change in Vietnam such that based on the account of politics offered here we are now much less likely to inadvertently view Vietnam's transition through liberal eyes. Being clear about the importance of relationships in Vietnamese politics, for instance, puts us in a stronger position to be able to interpret the Party's 'rule of law' agenda. Certainly, the idea that who you know is important in getting things done flies in the face of impartial applications of rules. An approach to politics which places heavy emphasis on the moral capacity of those who rule also raises question about the extent to which those in power *are* seen as needing to operate according to the same rules as everyone else.

Being clear about the close connection in people's minds between public office and personal advancement, or the importance of patronage in politics, sheds a very different light on the idea of corruption and what exactly corruption is in the Vietnamese context. By definition, corruption is deviation from an established norm, but if exploitation of public office for private gain is the norm, corruption must be something else. This is certainly missed in all the usual discussions of corruption in Vietnam.

A focus on political paternalism is helpful in making sense of the Party's deep unease with 'civil society' or indeed any form of organization which operates outside of Party-controlled structures. It also raises profound questions about what the government thinks it is doing when it pursues a public administration reform agenda with the international donor community, given the heavy emphasis in this agenda on liberal checks and balances, which as we have seen the Party is still deeply ambivalent about.[9] It also makes it easier to understand how elections to Party or government positions, including the National Assembly, are much more seen as an occasion when voters confirm the intrinsic merit of the leadership rather than a competitive contest between alternatives. At the same time, a focus on political paternalism makes it easier to understand (although not condone) the Party's tendency to treat dissidents harshly. Human rights derive from buying into this paternalistic political mindset. Failure to do so means you surrender your rights.[10]

The approach I have advocated in this chapter is also helpful when it comes to explaining the diverse outcomes we observe. On the one hand, being attentive to the importance of relationships in politics, the close connection between public office and personal advancement, and patronage, make it relatively straightforward to understand why many of the old elites have managed to make the transition into the new era. On the other hand, we can also see why the transition has not been straightforward, with certain members of the elite falling by the wayside and almost everyone having to reinvent themselves. Part of this has to do with the predatory nature of politics as different actors vie for ascendancy. This too forms an important part of a patronage approach to politics. However, it also has to do with the *way* in which the political system reinvents itself such that while power has a tendency to reproduce itself, it constantly has to make adjustments in order to survive. This also makes sense in relation to the approach to politics set out here.

The way in which Vietnam's political system works to reinvent itself while constantly having to make adjustments comes across clearly in relation to how public administration reform (PAR) has played out in practice. Part of the PAR agenda, which embodies a classic international donor-inspired programme of governance reforms, has involved closing down parts of the bureaucracy. However, while certain offices have been closed, new ones have sprung up in their place (PAR Steering Committee 2006: 8–9). The PAR agenda has also involved trying to clarify administrative procedures, including civil servant job descriptions, but here again progress has been slow at best. While this is often puzzling to outsiders, such difficulties make perfect sense when one considers the centrality of money-making in respect of public office, since closing down government departments or clarifying job descriptions strikes at the heart of the discretionary behaviour on which officials depend to supplement their income and hence must be opposed.

That the PAR agenda has been resisted largely successfully comes across very clearly if one looks carefully at media coverage of difficulties encountered by businesses or citizens seeking to navigate the bureaucracy. Leaving aside the perpetual hype about 'streamlined' administrative procedures, it is noteworthy how many of the same complaints heard in the 1990s about

Table 9.1 Trends in public sector employment, 1995–2008 (million persons)

1995	1996	1997	1998	1999	2000	2001	2002	2003	2004	2005	2006	2007	2008
3.1	3.1	3.3	3.4	3.4	3.5	3.6	3.8	4.0	4.1	4.0	3.9	4.0	4.1

Source: General Statistics Office (2010).

difficult, time-consuming and costly procedures continue to be heard today. All that has changed is that the practices which make navigating the bureaucracy so difficult have shifted from one area to another as various offices and certain kinds of activities are shut down (Malesky 2008; Gainsborough *et al.* 2009). Trends in public sector employment since the 1990s, which have been uniformly upwards despite the PAR agenda, tell a similar story (see Table 9.1). However, it is a story of a particular kind of political economy, where the close association between public office and money-making is a key part of it, and where with this dynamic at work the system constantly works to reinvent itself, thereby subverting PAR-like initiatives aimed at streamlining the state. This is quite a different kind of interpretation from a 'reformer' vs 'conservatives' (or even an entrenched corruptors or dispensers of patronage vs reformers interpretation) since based on the reading offered here all members of the elite are seeking to enrich themselves, largely if not exclusively by leveraging off their public position.

Conclusion

In this chapter, I have argued that Vietnam scholars need to be clearer and more precise about what has changed and what has not, about the direction of change (change to what?), and about how we explain diverse outcomes. In particular, I have argued that we need to be careful not to inadvertently view change in Vietnam through liberal eyes, which I have suggested is a danger as the political space in the country widens and given the heavily normative character of much international donor activity, including the tendency of Vietnamese elites to adopt the language of reform without internalizing the substance. I also suggested that what the Vietnam field needs is a *dynamic* account of politics, which can explain not just the perpetuation of elite power but also its disruption and metamorphosis.

In response, I have put forward a 'patronage' approach to politics centred on the importance of relationships in Vietnamese politics; the close connection in people's minds between public office and money-making; patronage; uncertainty as an instrument of rule; and political paternalism, arguing that putting these things centre-stage is essential if we are to move forward on the issues I have highlighted, specifically the mechanics of elite change and non-change. In light of my analysis, I have argued that much of what is identified as change in Vietnam – notably around the government-donor 'reform' agenda – is quite superficial and that looking at the key building blocks of Vietnamese politics it is evident that much has remained the same. An emphasis on these key building blocks also brings the essentially non-liberal nature of Vietnamese politics into sharper focus and makes elite ambivalence towards groups and individuals operating outside Party-controlled structures more understandable.

In terms of explaining the outcomes we observe – i.e. both the continuation of existing power, its disruption and its metamorphosis – I have emphasized the way in which power in Vietnam's political system (the actual not formal system) has a tendency to reproduce itself but that in the face of predatory and acquisitive behaviour on the part of other actors in the system, power is naturally adaptive. That said, while members of the elite are constantly seeking new ways to maintain the link between public office and making money, this is occurring in a context in which political paternalism remains deep-rooted.

The result is that we finish with an account of Vietnamese politics which stresses the system's underlying resilience. In some ways, it might be said that this sits uncomfortably with those accounts which emphasize the way in which the ruling Party is struggling to maintain its authority. However, it is worth questioning this. On the one hand, the Vietnamese Communist Party will not always rule Vietnam and certainly will not to do so unchallenged, but on the other hand whoever is at the helm will inherit a state dominated by the key characteristics I have identified. Thus, while the faces may change in terms of who inhabits Vietnam's elite ranks, much of their practice and outlook presently remains the same.

Notes

1 See Vasavakul 2001, 2003, for a discussion of the formal mechanisms through which this occurs.
2 See Gainsborough 2010 for a critical look at the invoking of 'reform' as a window on Vietnam's politics.
3 The original interview by Kay Johnson (2002) phrased Nong Duc Manh's stance towards opposition parties more circumspectly as '[not] for the moment'. See Johnson 2002.
4 The People's Committee chairman is currently elected by the People's Council, which is itself directly elected by popular vote. At the Tenth Party Congress, a straw poll of all delegates to the Congress was taken on the post of Party General Secretary although final voting lay with the Central Committee. See Abrami et al. 2008.
5 To be clear, the point is that the building blocks I refer to have not received the attention they ought in analyses of Vietnam politics because they sit uncomfortably with the standard 'change' discourse which has accompanied the so-called reform years. See Gainsborough 2010 for an extended analysis of this point.
6 See Jayasuriya and Rodan 2007 for a critique of the transition approach.
7 A sectoral base refers to whether an official has a Party or government background, is from the military, or has a technocratic or business background. Note, it could be argued that a patronage approach is integral to a collegial or sectoral approach. However, this point is not made in the Vietnam literature where the three different approaches to elite policy-making are seen as distinct.
8 The point I am making here is it important to look beyond the headline statements of opposition groups to the Party to try and uncover their underlying world view, not assuming that it is necessarily liberal.
9 The answer favoured here is that what we have seen is a largely pragmatic response by Vietnam's political elite, much less a signing up to the donor-inspired reform agenda. See Gainsborough 2010: 157–76.
10 Bound up with this paternalism is also a form of organic philosophy where there is no possibility of diverging from ideological or institutional mainstreams, although strictly speaking the latter need not be paternalistic.

References

Abrami, R., E. Malesky and Yu Zheng (2008) 'Accountability and inequality in single-party regimes: a comparative analysis of Vietnam and China', Harvard Business School Working Paper.
Cheshier, S. (2010) 'The new class in Vietnam', unpublished thesis, University of London.
Communist Party of Vietnam (1991) Seventh National Congress: Documents, Hanoi: Vietnam Foreign Languages Publishing House.
Dang Phong and M. Beresford (1998) Authority Relations and Economic Decision-Making in Vietnam: An Historical Perspective, Copenhagen: NIAS Publications.
Dixon, C. and A. Kilgour (2002) 'State, capital and resistance to globalisation in the Vietnamese transitional economy', Environment and Planning A 34: 599–618.
Fforde, A. (2005) 'Popular authority seeking power?' Asian Survey 45 (1): 146–52.
Fforde, A. and S. de Vylder (1996) From Plan to Market: The Economic Transition in Vietnam, Boulder, CO: Westview Press.
Gainsborough, M. (2002) 'Political change in Vietnam: in search of the middle class challenge to the state', Asian Survey 42 (5): 694–707.

——(2003) *Changing Political Economy of Vietnam: The Case of Ho Chi Minh City*, London and New York: Routledge.

——(2007a) 'From patronage to "outcomes": Vietnamese Communist Party congresses reconsidered', *Journal of Vietnamese Studies* 2 (1): 3–26.

——(2007b) 'Globalisation and the state revisited: a view from provincial Vietnam', *Journal of Contemporary Asia* 37 (1): 1–18.

——(2009) 'Privatisation as state advance: private indirect government in Vietnam', *New Political Economy* 14 (2): 257–74.

——(2010) *Vietnam: Rethinking the State*, London and New York: Zed Books.

Gainsborough, M., Dang Ngoc Dinh and Tran Thanh Phuong (2009) 'Corruption, public administration and development: challenges and opportunities', in Jairo Acuna-Alfaro (ed.) *Reforming Public Administration Reform in Vietnam: Current Situation and Recommendations*, Hanoi: National Political Publishing House.

General Statistics Office (2010) *General Statistics Office of Vietnam*, official website; available at: www.gso.gov.vn/default_en.aspx?tabid=491 (accessed 26 April 2010).

Hayton, B. (2010) *Vietnam: Rising Dragon*, New Haven, CT and London: Yale University Press.

Jayasuriya, K. and G. Rodan (2007) 'Beyond hybrid regimes: more participation, less contestation in Southeast Asia', *Democratization* 14 (5): 773–94.

Johnson, K. (2002) 'We don't want to keep secrets anymore', 22 January; available at: www.time.com/time/printout/0,8816,195506,00.html# (accessed 26 April 2010).

Kerkvliet, B. (1995) 'Village–state relations in Vietnam: the effect of everyday politics on decollectivization', *Journal of Asian Studies* 54 (2): 396–418.

——(2005) *The Power of Everyday Politics: How Vietnamese Peasants Transformed National Policy*, Ithaca, NY: Cornell University Press.

Kerkvliet, B., Nguyen Quang A and Bach Tan Sinh (2008) *Forms of Engagement Between State Agencies and Civil Society Organizations in Vietnam: A Study*, Hanoi: VUFO-NGO Resource Centre Vietnam.

Kim, Jee Young (2005) 'Making industrial conflict public: patterns of newspaper coverage of strikes in Vietnam', Paper presented at Centre d'Etudes et de Recherches Internationales (CERI) and Institut d'Etudes Politiques de Paris (Science Po), 9–10 December.

London, J. (2009) 'Viet Nam and the making of market-Leninism', *Pacific Review* 22 (3): 375–99.

McKinley, C. (2009) *Media and Corruption: How Has Vietnam's Print Media Covered Corruption and How Can Coverage Be Strengthened?* Hanoi: United Nations Development Programme.

Malesky, E. (2008) 'The Vietnam Provincial Competitiveness Index: measuring economic governance for private sector development. 2008 final report', Vietnam Competitiveness Initiative Policy Paper No. 13, Hanoi, Vietnam Chamber of Commerce and Industry (VCCI) and United States Agency for International Development's Vietnam Competitiveness Initiative (VNCI).

Malesky, E. and P. Schuler (2008) 'Paint-by-numbers democracy: the stakes, structure, results, and implications of the 2007 Vietnamese National Assembly elections', Journal of Vietnamese Studies 4 (1): 1–48.

Painter, M. (2005) 'The politics of state sector reforms in Vietnam: contested agendas and uncertain trajectories', *Journal of Development Studies* 41 (2): 261–83.

PAR Steering Committee (2006) 'Report on the Review of the Implementation of the First Phase (2001–5) of the PAR Master Programme (2001–10)', Report No. 01/2006/BC-BC-CCHC, 27 April, Hanoi.

Salomon, M. (2007) 'Power and representation at the Vietnamese National Assembly: the scope and limits of political *doi moi*', in S. Balme and M. Sidel (eds) *Vietnam's New Order: International Perspectives on the State and Reform in Vietnam*, New York and Basingstoke: Palgrave Macmillan, pp. 198–216.

——(2008) 'The issue of corruption in recruitment, appointment and promotion of civil servants in Vietnam', Note for the 3rd Anti-Corruption Dialogue, Hanoi, June.

Thayer, C.A. (1992) 'Political reform in Vietnam: *doi moi* and the emergence of civil society', in R. Miller (ed.) *The Developments of Civil Society in Communist Systems*, Sydney: Allen and Unwin.

——(2009a) 'Political legitimacy of the one-party state: challenges and response. Vietnam: political overview', paper presented at Vietnam Update 2009, Australian National University, Canberra, 19–20 November.

——(2009b) 'Vietnam and the challenge of political civil society', *Contemporary Southeast Asia* 31 (1): 1–27.

Transparency International (2006) *National Integrity Systems, Country Report, Vietnam*; available at: www.transparency.org/news_room/latest_news/press_releases_nc/2006/2006_11_21_nis_vietnam (accessed 26 April 2010).

UNDP (2006) *Deepening Democracy and Increasing Participation in Viet Nam*, UNDP Viet Nam Policy Dialogue Paper 1, Hanoi: United Nations Development Programme and Vietnam Academy of Social Sciences.

Vasavakul, Thaveeporn (1997) 'Sectoral politics and strategies for state and party, building from the VII to the VIII Congress of the Vietnam Communist Party (1991–96)', in A. Fforde (ed.) *Ten Years after the 1986 Party Congress*, Political and Social Change Monograph 24, Canberra: Australian National University, pp. 81–136.

——(2001) 'Vietnam: *doi moi* difficulties', in John Funston (ed.) *Government and Politics in Southeast Asia*, Singapore: Institute of Southeast Asian Studies, pp. 372–410.

——(2003) 'From fence-breaking to networking: interests, popular organisations, and policy influences in post-socialist Vietnam', in B. Kerkvliet, R. Heng and D. Koh (eds) *Getting Organized in Vietnam: Moving in and Around the Socialist State*, Singapore: Institute of Southeast Asian Studies, pp. 25–61.

——(2008) 'Recrafting state identity: corruption and anti-corruption in *doi moi* Vietnam from a comparative perspective', paper presented to 'Rethinking the Vietnamese State: Implications for Vietnam and the Region', Vietnam Workshop, 21–22 August, City University of Hong Kong.

VietnamNet Bridge (2009) '"Entrust heavy responsibilities to innovators", former NA Chairman urges', 20 August; available at: http://english.vietnamnet.vn/interviews/2009/08/864361/ (accessed 26 April 2010).

Wells-Dang, A. (2010) 'Political space in Vietnam: a view from the rice roots', *Pacific Review* 23 (1): 93–112.

Womack, B. (1997) 'Vietnam in 1996: reform immobilism', *Asian Survey* 37 (1): 79–87.

World Bank (2010) 'Vietnam Development Report 2010: modern institutions', Joint Donor Report to the Vietnam Consultative Group Meeting, Hanoi, 3–4 December.

SECTION III
Markets and governance

10

POLITICS, INSTITUTIONS AND PERFORMANCE

Explaining growth variation in East Asia

Richard Doner

Introduction

The World Bank's 1993 report, *East Asian Miracle*, was significant not only for highlighting the outstanding economic performances of the region's market economies, but also (albeit half-heartedly) for attributing this performance to strategic interventions by state agencies in consultation with private actors. The report also signalled intra-regional complexity, noting performance differences between the four Newly Industrializing Countries (NICs – South Korea, Singapore, Taiwan and Hong Kong) and four members of the Association of Southeast Asian Nations – Indonesia, Malaysia, Thailand and the Philippines (henceforth the ASEAN-4).

These differences suggested qualms by both the Bank and other observers as to the generalizability of the NICs' experience even to regional neighbours. This scepticism focused not so much on the benefits of the NICs' interventionist policies, although doubt about such benefits was widespread among mainstream economists. The core problem was rather that effective implementation of such policies required institutional qualities – typically labelled 'developmental states' – that are rare in the developing world (Pack 2000a: 64). By implication, the weaknesses of the otherwise high-performance ASEAN-4, at least relative to the NICs, reflected weaker institutions. This assertion raises several questions central to East Asian development and the particular position of the more developed ASEAN economies within the region's growth:

- How strong is the causal link between institutions and growth performance in the region? Later in this chapter I confirm this relationship by comparing institutional capacities in the NICs with those in the ASEAN-4, especially Malaysia and Thailand, the two most successful ASEAN countries and thus those most likely to match the NICs' development performance.
- How do we account for intra-regional variation in institutional capacity? I propose a political approach to the origins of such variation in which the pressures and opportunities facing political leaders is more important than their autonomy.
- What are the implications of such variation for sustained growth in the ASEAN-4? The last section of this chapter highlights the risks of what have been labelled 'middle-income traps' facing Malaysia and Thailand as they struggle with problems such as rising entry barriers to

participation in global production networks, organizationally and politically weak labour, low business demand for indigenous technological skills, and high external dependence. The final section of the chapter briefly reviews the political bases for sustained growth.

Explaining variation in East Asian development: policies and institutions

To assess the actual impact of developmental states, it is useful to begin by tracing the ways in which the concept emerged from the striking – and surprising – performance of the East Asian NICs. Viewed in retrospect, the NICs are best understood as what John Gerring calls 'extreme cases' (Gerring 2007: 89), cases with extreme values on an outcome and/or explanatory variable of interest. Their utility derived not from their position vis-à-vis an existing theory, but rather from the fact that their values were distant from the mean of a given distribution in the absence of a clear theory (Gerring 2007).[1] Initial interest in the NICs resulted from awareness of their impressive growth, not an understanding of the sources of that growth. Such an understanding emerged only subsequently as scholars looked closely into the actual policies and mechanisms through which this growth occurred. It was largely work by these scholars that gave rise to the concept of the developmental state.[2]

The first part of this section reviews the NICs' performance relative to the ASEAN-4, especially Malaysia and Thailand. I then turn to two sets of explanations for intra-regional variation: policies and institutions. I highlight the particular challenges of developmental policies and the need for effective institutions to implement such policies. But as noted above, my emphasis is less on institutional forms than on capacities. As institutional forms, developmental states can be understood as organizational complexes in which coherent and independent bureaucratic agencies engage with organized private sectors to spur national economic transformation (see Doner *et al.* 2005). Although a useful starting point, this emphasis on institution as a form glosses over possible variation in the organizational design of public and private actors, as well as their coordination; it includes outcomes in the definition; it is largely silent as to the actual capacities of these complexes; and it says nothing about institutional origins.

Performance variation

Growth in the NICs was impressive, in part because their income levels grew and their economies became more diversified, i.e. they moved from agriculture to industry and greatly expanded the range of manufactured goods and exports. But other countries have done the same thing.[3] Equally if not more important was the NICs' success in upgrading: They (1) moved from lower to higher value-added processes, products, functions and sectors; (2) this movement involved local linkages, i.e. increasing inputs – both material and technological – from indigenous firms; and (3) this shift was largely efficient in that locally produced goods met price, quality and delivery standards of global value chains.[4] In other words, the NICs were able to reconcile diversification and indigenously based industrial deepening with export competitiveness.

Growth has also been impressive in the ASEAN-4. Per capita GDP has risen consistently, with even the 1997 Asian Financial Crisis constituting only a brief pause in these countries' decades-long growth (*Economist* 2009). Turning specifically to Malaysia and Thailand, both are middle-income countries, with Malaysia higher up in this bracket than Thailand (see Table 10.1). Malaysia and Thailand compare favourably even with the East Asian NICs when it comes to growth, exports, capital formation and manufacturing.[5] Both countries have also diversified impressively as reflected in the decline of primary products in total exports, the expanding range of agricultural products, the growth of mid- and high-technology products, especially

Table 10.1 Income groups: East Asia

Country	Income group (1)	GNI (nominal 2008 (2)	GNI PPP 2008 (2)
South Korea	high	$20,560	$28,120
Taiwan	high	$17,230[1]	$27,122[2]
Singapore	high	$34,760	$47,940
Hong Kong	high	$31,420	$43,960
Malaysia	upper-middle	$6,970	$13,740
Thailand	lower-middle	$2,840	$5,990
China	lower-middle	$2,770	$6,020
Indonesia	lower-middle	$2,010	$3,830
Philippines	lower-middle	$1,890	$3,900
Vietnam	low	$890	$2,700

Notes:
[1] Based on World Bank classification: low income, $975 or less; lower-middle income, $976–$3,855; upper-middle income, $3,856–$11,905; and high income, $11,906 or more.
[2] World Development Indicators database, World Bank, 1 July 2009.

electronics, and, in the case of Thailand, automotive exports. Exports have been impressive, and they have been especially important for Thailand since the 1997 economic crisis, increasing from around half to almost three-quarters of GDP (see Table 10.2). Not coincidentally, this economic growth has also had significant 'human development' benefits (UNDP 2007: 2; NEAC 2010; Yusuf and Nabeshima 2010: 16).

However, upgrading in the ASEAN-4 has lagged the NICs. Success in expanding the medium- and high-technology exports record is marred by limited local inputs, high trade dependency and, in some cases, de-nationalization. The high trade deficit characteristics of mid- and high-tech industries and the general lack of indigenous suppliers in industries such as Malaysia's semiconductors and Thailand's disk drive and automotive production indicate that

Table 10.2 East Asian export of goods and services as percentage of GDP

	South Korea	China	Thailand	Indonesia	Malaysia	Philippines	Singapore	Vietnam[1]
1996	28	20	39	26	92	41	—	36 (1990)
1997	32	22	48	28	93	49	—	
1998	46	20	59	53	116	52	—	
1999	39	20	58	36	121	51	—	
2000	41	23	67	41	120	55	—	
2001	38	23	66	39	110	49	191	
2002	35	25	64	33	108	50	193	
2003	38	30	66	30	107	50	212	
2004	44	34	71	32	115	51	225	
2005	42	37	73	34	117	48	238	70
2006	43	40	73	31	117	47	246	
2007	46	42	73	29	110	43	231	

Source: World Bank, World Development Indicators
Note:
[1] Cited in Kohli 2009: Table 5.

local producers account for little of the value in most mid- and high-tech industries (Doner 2009: 9–11, 35–7; Yusuf and Nabeshima 2009; NEAC 2010). As Rasiah notes, 'Domestic policies ... have only favoured structural widening ... the entire export-oriented sector has not developed import-replacing linkages' (Rasiah 2003: 60). The result has been a sort of dualism in which manufacturing is 'often disembodied from the rest of the national economy' (Jomo 2001: 14). Thus, a 2005 World Bank report on Thailand concluded that 'high tech exports ... [were] ... a misleading indicator of technological performance' (World Bank 2005: 98) with Thailand remaining an assembler, not a manufacturer or designer. Malaysia's electronics sector certainly includes some technologically impressive firms, but these are generally locked into original equipment manufacturing (OEM) relationships that prevent the firms from developing their own brands and increasing margins (NEAC 2010). Yusuf and Nabeshima go so far as to conclude that 'No Malaysian manufacturing firm has established itself as a major contract ... supplier of a product or a service with an expanding international market' (Yusuf and Nabeshima 2009: 140). Growth has been, in other words, largely driven by factor accumulation, especially capital investment, often by foreign producers, not productivity improvements based on local technological capacities (Yusuf and Nabeshima 2009). Lall describes Thailand as having a dynamic export growth based on the relocation of labour-intensive activities away from the older NICs and Japan, but a very shallow technological base (Lall 1992). Uchida and Cook provide a more fine-grained analysis, suggesting that, in the ASEAN-4, trade specialization in high-tech industries 'do[es] not have corresponding technological specialization' (Uchida and Cook 2005: 718).These weaknesses are more broadly reflected in the comparative rankings in productivity and technology competencies as well as other indicators of infrastructure capacity and human capital.

It is worth noting that differences in initial levels of local technology and scientific knowledge do not account for these variations in development performance (see Uchida and Cook 2005; Schiller 2006). Nor are these differences attributable to a lack of awareness of or interest in technology and upgrading on the part of Malaysian and Thai policy makers. Both countries have proclaimed the need to improve local technology, initiated plans to deepen local linkages, and aimed to link industrial deepening with export promotion (see Jomo 2001). These attempts have generally fallen short. This judgement is not to minimize the significance of these countries' achievements in income growth, poverty reduction and economic diversification. It is not to deny the presence of exceptional cases in which some degree of upgrading has occurred (discussed below). Nor is it to deny the fact that these achievements were the result of deliberate interventions. Indeed, they confirm Rodrik's argument that scratching the surface of any non-traditional export success stories will reveal various kinds of 'interventions lurking beneath the surface' (Rodrik 2007: 109).

The differences between the NICs and the ASEAN-4 are nonetheless important, and they are reflected in the growing literature on the dangers of Malaysia and Thailand finding themselves stuck in middle-income traps between low wage producers and highly skilled innovators (see Gill and Kharas 2007; Yusuf and Nabeshima 2009). What accounts for this intra-regional variation?

Policies

An answer to this question emphasizing 'policy' is a useful, albeit incomplete, point of departure. Scholars have gone well beyond the view of economic policy as an undifferentiated category to highlight a range of policy interventions distinguished by the scope of coverage and degree of selectivity.[6] At the broadest level, *functional* policies refer to those measures 'designed to improve the efficiency of market operations' (e.g. general monetary and fiscal policy, financial supervision, openness to foreign investment and trade, and physical and social infrastructure). A second category includes *horizontal* (Kaplinsky 2005: 241) policies 'aimed at remedying generic market failures, without favouring particular activities or sets of activities over others' (Lall 2000: 23). Such policies include worker training, openness to foreign technology, export promotion, and non-targeted incentives for R&D to complement competitive market processes. With these kinds of policies, dynamic firm practices and performances are presumed to occur through competitive emulation (Pack 2000b: 87).

But there is cause for scepticism about the process of competitive imitation. Some have argued that productivity gains are 'too time-consuming for most private firms to underwrite without government support, the amount and duration of support depending on the industry' (Amsden 1994: 632). This perspective highlights the benefits of selective measures, commonly labelled 'industrial policies,' i.e. interventions that directly influence resource allocations to particular sectors in order to improve sector-specific competencies, to raise their productivity, and to influence their relative importance within the economy (Wade 1990; Amsden 2001; Rodrik 2007: 100). Such measures might include sector-specific tariff protection or (even better) export incentives; training schemes; foreign investment incentives; financial subsidies; and/or specialized infrastructure, such as agricultural or manufacturing extension.

Performance differences between the NICs and the ASEAN-4 do not track neatly to the presence or absence of horizontal and/or selective interventions. Malaysia and Thailand have devoted significant resources to the promotion of both cross-sectoral competencies and sectors such as textiles, steel, autos, electronics, tourism, rubber and sugar (Rock 1995, 2000; Doner 2009; Ritchie 2010). As suggested above, the results have been decidedly uneven in the ASEAN countries: there has been much more success at promoting sectoral emergence and expansion than at facilitating technologically advanced inputs from local producers, despite on-going concerns about competitiveness, productivity, and technology. Explaining these persistent weaknesses requires recognizing, first, the particular challenges of upgrading policies; second, the kinds of institutional capacities required to address such challenges; and therefore, third, the fact that different development tasks 'demand' different policies and capacities.

Development policies can be understood as collective action problems in which individual firms' costs and benefits do not match those of an entire sector or country. Such problems can be differentiated along at least three dimensions: first, the numbers of participants whose engagement is necessary to policy implementation; second, the amount and nature of information required; and third, distributional implications, i.e. who gains and who loses over what periods of time from the policy's implementation. Other things being equal, policies aimed at upgrading require the participation of more actors, a mastering of more information, and an ability to manage more losers than do policies aimed at diversification. To be sure, diversification as structural change involves accumulating and investing capital in new activities, such as a steel mill, that hold uncertain returns but require a variety of complementary resources (Rodrik 2007). But it is easier to find the capital for the construction of a steel mill than to run it at levels of price, quality and delivery attractive to downstream steel users, such as auto manufacturers (Waldner 1999).

This is the case in large part owing to the central role of innovation, i.e. a process or product new to a firm or group of firms, and associated technology in upgrading. The absorption and diffusion of technology is difficult, involving not passive waiting for external flows, but rather an endogenous, cumulative learning process in which local producers recognize the value of new information, assimilate it and apply it to commercial ends (Cohen and Levinthal 1990). The market imperfection and failures inherent in this process are especially daunting. In addition to capital market failures, uncertain returns, and the need for complementary assets, technology development exhibits long gestation periods, involves an extensive degree of tacit learning through trial and error, and frequently implies significant losses as well as gains.

These translate into significant information requirements. Even if formally codified, the ability to internalize new knowledge requires trial and error: 'even when the production techniques used in the advanced countries are transparent to outsiders, their transfer to new economic and institutional environments typically require adaptations with uncertain degrees of success' (Hausman and Rodrik 2002: 4). This is because the technology is new to the firm, and in part because the knowledge is being applied and must be adapted to a context different from that in which it was originally developed. Absorbing and disseminating technology is thus typically not only a technical process but also a site-specific one for which most developing country firms have little experience or clear templates. Since it is characterized by such complexity and uncertainty, improvements in productivity and technology also require the involvement of multiple actors in a process of collective problem-solving and the 'co-production' of essential inputs, such as technical training, through on-going deliberation (Schrank 2011).[7] This iterative discovery process requires that firms (and farms) engage with many partners, including competitors, upstream producers, buyers, equipment suppliers, service providers, public research institutions, universities, and relevant state agencies. Together, these actors constitute 'networks of innovation' or 'national systems of innovation' (see Intarakumnerd *et al.* 2002).

The need for interaction between two sets of actors, downstream and upstream producers, also highlights potential distributional conflicts. For example, the establishment of synthetic fibre production constitutes structural change in a country whose economy has traditionally relied on agriculture and light manufacturing. But in upgrading, the resulting fibre must be attractive in terms of price, quality and delivery to midstream spinners, weavers and dyers, and to downstream garment producers. Improving upstream production is not always easy; indeed, it is inconsistent with the process of rent transfer from finished-goods producers to the intermediate-input producers more typical of structural change in developing countries. This particular distributive tension is most obvious in the case of trade liberalization that threatens upstream producers. But the efficiency pressures of upgrading translate into other potential losses, such as the potential for under-performing firms or sectors to lose investment incentives.

Problems in each of the above three areas have been evident in Southeast Asian development efforts. The Thai Board of Investments, for example, has attempted to shift its focus from jobs and foreign exchange earnings to local linkages, technology spill overs and local innovation. Yet such efforts have run up against the need to understand the varying technological properties of specific industries, the logistical and strategic concerns of multinational businesses, and the rapidly evolving international investment environment (Felker and Jomo 2003; Thailand Development Research Institute 2009). Thai firms also suffer from weak network linkages: a comparative analysis of Southeast Asian firms found a strong association between innovation activities and extra-firm cooperation, with Bangkok-based firms ranking lowest on both dimensions, Singaporean firms highest, and Penang in the middle (Berger and Revilla Diez 2003). Especially problematic are university–industry linkages to promote technical competencies required by locally based producers. Finally, unresolved upstream–downstream conflicts plague Thailand's sugar, textile and rubber sectors, and as noted earlier both Malaysia and Thailand have had significant difficulty in promoting upstream suppliers for autos and electronics (Doner 2009; Doner, Intarakumnerd and Ritchie 2009).

In sum, differences in policies and policy objectives are not correlated with performance outcomes. How then do we explain the significant variation between the NICs and ASEAN-4 with regard to development?

Institutions

The answer to this puzzle typically involves institutions, especially those associated with developmental states. As noted, such states are cohesive, expert and independent bureaucratic agencies systematically engaged with ('embedded in') organized private sectors to spur national economic transformation[8] (see Woo-Cumings 1998; Doner *et al.* 2005). But this emphasis on specific organizational forms and linkages suffers from several potential flaws: first, while NICs do share core institutional features,[9] they also exhibit differences in their modes of public–private ties, the degree and nature of private sector organization, and the relative influence of lead agencies (Wong and Ng 2001). Second, the weaknesses of Malaysia's Economic Planning Unit and Thailand's National Economic and Social Development Board demonstrate the fallacy of assuming that the official presence of self-proclaimed developmentalist institutions, such as 'pilot agencies', actual translate into the capacity to implement policies[10] (Stubbs 2009: 8). Finally, the performance variation between the NICs and the AEAN-4 does not correspond well to differences in bureaucratic expertise, independence, cohesion and probity. David Kang, for example, has argued that 'Korea and the Philippines both had extensive corruption that permeated the normal politics of elections, economic policy making, taxation, and the day-to-day running of the country' (Kang 2002: 64, 20).[11]

The key differences lay more in the degree to which corruption was hived off in Korea, allowing Park Chung-Hee 'to meet his patronage requirements and still seek economic efficiency' (Kang 2002: 64). The critical point here is that, under this bifurcation, cronyism and corruption were pervasive in areas such as construction but were largely absent from both macroeconomic policy and real sector upgrading.[12] In Marcos' Philippines, there was little bifurcation: all parts of the economy were up for grabs. The Thai and Malaysian states both exhibit bifurcation. But the technocratic side of these arrangements has operated largely to ensure cautious macroeconomic policy and to facilitate the operations of multinational corporations whose increasing dominance of manufacturing exports has been a key source of jobs and foreign exchange. Conversely, various combinations of cronyism, corruption and fragmentation have been more common, not simply in non-tradables such as construction and telecommunications, but even more importantly in parts of the real sector dominated by local producers. A largely hands-off approach characterizes foreign-dominated parts of the real sector in both countries (Uchida and Cook 2005: 706).

Put differently, whereas in Korea and Taiwan state agencies pushed and worked with local producers to combine industrial deepening with export-level competitiveness, their Malaysian and Thai counterparts have left manufactured exports largely to foreign producers while either protecting or ignoring indigenous firms. None of this is to minimize the export dynamism of Thailand in, say, autos, textiles and sugar, and of both countries in electronics and rubber. Indeed, it is in recognition of these accomplishments that these countries merit the label of 'intermediate states' characterized by very uneven bureaucratic coherence, pervasive clientelism in public–private relations, and extensive factionalism within the private sector (Evans 1995).[13] It is rather to emphasize the fact that, unlike the middle-income trap–prone Malaysia and Thailand, institutions in the East Asian NICs were able to encourage growing competitiveness through technology development and innovation on the part of indigenous producers. Here, it is important to recall that promoting local technology development and innovation involves significant challenges: the need to coordinate multiple actors, to master new kinds of information, and to manage distributional conflicts. The key question is: what kinds of institutional *capacities* are necessary to overcome such challenges?

Three sets of capacities merit note.[14] First, consultation helps diverse actors to gain information about each other's preference, interests and capacities with regard to a particular issue. Second, credible commitments, to compensate losers through selective benefits and/or to sanction defectors, help reduce actors' tendencies to free ride and/or to renege on agreements. This issue of credibility is especially important given the risks inherent in public support for local producers. As numerous authors have emphasized, measures such as tariff protection, subsidized loans, special access to inputs, specialized infrastructure investments, and training programmes are necessary for overcoming the market failures inherent in undertaking new activities and in the absorption and dissemination of new technology; but they carry significant risks of inefficient rent accumulation. Given such risks, the challenge is making rents conditional on performance (Amsden 1989). Doing so requires monitoring actors' actual behaviour: 'Without monitoring, there can be no credible commitment' (Ostrom 1990: 45).[15]

The argument is certainly not that such capacities are ubiquitous and pervasive in the NICs but absent in the best-performing members of the ASEAN-4. It is rather that these capacities are much more widespread in the real sectors of the former than in the latter. Space limits prohibit a review of the extensive evidence for this contention (Amsden 1989, 2001; Wade 1990; McKendrick et al. 2000). Instead, consider variation in a key element of local upgrading efforts – namely, promotion of technology spill overs from foreign to indigenous producers. As noted, success in this area requires understanding the varying technological properties of specific industries, the logistical and strategic concerns of multinational businesses, and the rapidly evolving international investment environment. It also requires developing the location-specific assets, especially local technical skills, through which such spill overs can occur. For example, research has demonstrated that foreign investment enhances skills in countries relatively well endowed with skills when foreign investment begins (de Velde and Xenogiani 2007).

Malaysia and Thailand have been significantly less active than the NICs in promoting FDI spill overs and in developing the human resource base for absorption of such spill overs (see, for example, Mardon 1990; McKendrick et al. 2000). The Malaysian and Thai approach is one of 'passive FDI-dependent learning' (Yusuf and Nabeshima 2009: 159, n. 1) that has engendered little of the learning assumed to flow from the presence of foreign producers. It is worth emphasizing that this lack of spill overs is not primarily a function of deliberate obstruction by foreign investors but rather cross-national variation in the capacities to take full advantage of FDI. For example, spill overs from the same foreign disk drive producers exhibited significant cross-national variation, with the strongest results in Singapore and weakest in Thailand. The variation was a function of differences in national institutional capacities (McKendrick et al. 2000). In contrast to Singapore's active supplier development programmes, Thailand's Board of Investments has lacked basic information on the shifting needs of key investors (Thailand Development Research Institute 2009). Similarly, Malaysia's 'lack of institutional development to stimulate structural upgrading has confined much export expansion to low value-added activity, even those involving technology-intensive industries' (Rasiah 2003: 66).[16] In fact, Malaysia's government did not approve a framework for long-term industrial upgrading until the mid-1990s, over twenty years after the launch of electronics production in Malaysia (Henderson and Phillips 2007: 88). These weaknesses are mirrored by those in technical training.[17]

In sum, the NIC–ASEAN differences in economic performance are a function of variation in institutional capacities. How then do we explain this institutional variation?

Institutional origins

Economists typically explain institutions governing market transactions as choices by private actors to enhance their mutual welfare. In fact, institutions ultimately arise from the rough-and-tumble of elite politics (Moe 1984; Knight 1992; Bates 1995). But politicians are typically motivated by securing their own power through institutions that channel largesse to key constituencies, often economic elites interested in easy profits through speculation and rent seeking. Why would political leaders expend resources to provide the kinds of public goods necessary for economic competitiveness, even as they might reserve some sectors for patronage? Why would Park Chung-Hee or Lee Kuan Yew see good economics – constant improvements in efficiency and productivity – as good politics, whereas Ferdinand Marcos used the Philippine institutions for the enrichment of himself and a small group of cronies, and whereas Thai leaders, including Field Marshall Sarit, generally protected technocrats in the Bank of Thailand and Finance Ministry while opening parts of the real sector to favouritism and corruption and others to multinationals?[18]

One answer is that they could. Put differently, some combination of 'weak society' and state autonomy allowed leaders to adopt the long time horizons necessary for investments in com-petitiveness-supporting institutions (Stubbs 2009: 6). Although plausible in some cases, the autonomy argument has important limitations. Autonomy seems to be neither a necessary nor sufficient condition for the creation of institutional strength. Consider the facts: first, the Philippine state under Marcos 'became both more coherent and more autonomous from social interest groups'; second, Thai military leaders enjoyed significant autonomy from politically weak Sino-Thai business; and finally, the relationship between Park Chung-Hee and Korean business was less one of state autonomy than one of 'mutual hostages' (Kang 2002: 64).[19]

The autonomy argument also leads to a neglect of the claims facing political leaders and the resources available to satisfy such claims. These can be understood through the concept of 'systemic vulnerability' or the simultaneous interplay of popular pressures for welfare improve-ment, external security threats, and scarce resource endowments. External threats and popular pressures constitute claims on resources. Where such resources are scarce and pressures are high, political elites will attempt to build growth-promoting institutions to generate needed resources. Thus, the availability of institutional capacities depends on the ways in which resource claims and resource availability influence the calculus of national political elites and the concentration of political authority through which elites operate. At its most basic, the argument is thus that external threats and internal pressures have been more moderate and resource-based revenues more available in the ASEAN-4 than in the NICs (Doner et al. 2005). Although this approach builds on other scholars' attribution of ASEAN–NIC differences to resource constraints and to external security threats,[20] it is distinctive in integrating these factors with domestic pressures. However, it is important to address three potential challenges to the approach. These involve resource constraints in the NICs; variation in vulnerability, and the role of politics.

Resource constraints in the NICs?

The large amounts of US military and economic aid to Taiwan and South Korea, as well as the spikes in prices of key commodities for Singapore and Malaysia, raise questions as to whether the NICs suffered from resource constraints. Indeed, Richard Stubbs contends that this contention reflects an attempt to 'shoehorn the … (developmental state) … into a specific theoretical model, neglects what actually happened on the ground and is consequently seriously flawed' (Stubbs 2009: 8). This charge usefully highlights the difficulties of specifying levels of resource constraints necessary to stimulate institutional development.

But the charge misses two related points. The relative value of accessible resources depends on the claims on those resources: the more intense external and domestic pressures – and such pressures were significant for Korea, Taiwan and Singapore – the more sensitive political leaders will be to uncertainty in resource access. And leaders, especially in South Korea and Taiwan, were far from confident in their access to such resources. Solid US support for Korea in the

1950s began to wane in the 1960s:[21] In the early part of the decade, just as North Korea 'was recovering faster than, and beginning to pose a genuine threat to, the South' (Kang 2002: 38–9) the US was growing impatient with South Korea's slow, stumbling development efforts and clearly intended to reduce economic assistance, even as Washington's attention was shifting to Vietnam. By the late 1960s, as the US began withdrawing almost half of its military forces from Korea under the 'Nixon Shock', it was clear that the US commitment to Korea's defence 'was waning ... and the Park regime was forced to cast about for new directions ... The Korean focus on heavy industry and chemical manufacturing in the 1970s was largely a result of Park's perception of the deteriorating international situation' (Kang 2002: 38–9).

A combination of security pressures and resource constraints was also key to the emergence of institutional strengths in Taiwan. The country's shift to a 'development-orientation' was facilitated by growing export markets and foreign investment; and while US aid to Taiwan tapered off, the island benefited significantly by exporting goods to US-financed procurement in Vietnam. But what initially provoked a move to more developmentalist institutions was 'a crisis within Taiwan's budget and foreign trade sector ... caused by US aid cuts and the government's growing defence expenditure' (Nordhaug 1998: 141) in the late 1950s. Military requirements declined in the 1960s as Taiwan abandoned plans to retake the mainland after the US refused to finance such an effort. But if the country abandoned 'offensive militarism', development strategy was still influenced by intensifying security concerns: The country's heavy-industry drive, along with major reforms of the educational and R&D systems, reflected the need to address the 'Nixon Shock' of improved relations with the PRC and the end of free military aid to Taiwan.

Vulnerability: a dichotomous variable?

A more serious problem with the 'systemic vulnerability' approach is its implied dichotomy, i.e. the NICs were highly vulnerable and thus developed strong institutions, whereas the ASEAN-4 were not vulnerable and developed weaker institutions. It is true that pressures on elites in Malaysia and Thailand, as well as in Indonesia and the Philippines, were significantly less severe than those encountered by Taiwan, Korea and Singapore.[22] But the Southeast Asian countries have faced a variety of pressures whose intensity has varied cross-nationally, temporally and, to a degree, cross-regionally, thus justifying a more ordinal approach to vulnerability. An appreciation of the range of variation has the added benefit of increasing the number of observations through which to assess the overall contention that increased vulnerability stimulates institutional strengthening. Consider the following:

Temporal variation: crises and truncated reforms in Thailand and Malaysia[23]

The 1980s debt crises and the 1997 Asian Financial Crisis stimulated significant institutional strengthening in both countries. Thailand, for example, responded to the 1980s debt crisis not only with significant macroeconomic reforms but also with a corporatist-like, technocrat-led public–private sector consultation and the establishment of a Restructuring Committee designed to address problems of real sector competitiveness. Similarly, in response to the 1997 financial crisis, the government undertook an ambitious effort to raise industrial productivity (in addition to financial sector reform). Again, this took the form of a corporatist-like set of consultations, the Industrial Restructuring Programme, designed to involve business and government officials upgrade 13 sectors via some eight sets of measures ranging from product design to equipment modernization to labour skills. Both the 1980s Restructuring Committee and the post-1997 IRP were eventually abandoned. The 1980s effort was dropped as a combination of devaluation and a flood of East Asian FDI inflows stimulated a growth of labour-intensive and natural resource exports. A similar dynamic occurred after 1997: pressure for productivity improvement dropped with a devaluation-induced jump in exports and significant financial inflows through IMF and ADB support, as well as $1.5 billion from Japan's Miyazawa Fund.

Malaysia was hit less hard by the 1997 Asian Financial Crisis, in part owing to Prime Minister Mahathir's adoption of heterodox policies, especially avoiding IMF borrowing and imposing capital controls. What bears emphasis, however, is that Malaysia's ability to pursue this strategy was based on access to funds from the national oil company, Petronas, the Employee Provident Fund and the Japan Export Bank. A further advantage was the size and the 'dispensability' of Malaysia's foreign workforce. Migrants, who staffed many of the worst hit sectors, especially construction, left Malaysia, allowing the country to export much of its unemployment.

Place-specific variation: the case of Penang

Contrasts *within* Malaysia also demonstrate the impact of different degrees of vulnerability. Rajah Rasiah and others have documented the fact that Penang, unlike Malaysia's other two regional states where electronics is important, has developed the institutional capacity for facilitating upgrading by local electronics producers, especially suppliers to multinational semiconductor firms (Doner and Hershberg 1999; Rasiah 2000; Henderson and Phillips 2007). The key institution, the Penang Development Corporation, emerged under conditions of relative scarcity and internal political pressure:

> The problems of economic decline (associated with the collapse of Georgetown's entrepot functions) were compounded by the fact that, as the principal location for political mobilization among the Malaysian Chinese, Penang was not a state favoured by a *Bumiputera* (Malay)-dominated federal government. The consequence was that the Penang government had to look to the state's internal resources to help drive economic development. The institutional key to this was the PDC.
>
> (Henderson and Phillips 2007: 86)

Cross-national, sector-specific variation: automobiles in Thailand and Malaysia

From a relatively similar size to Malaysia at the end of the century, Thailand's auto industry has since become the region's automotive hub and dwarfed that of Malaysia in vehicle production and exports, in parts production and exports, and in trade balance.[24] A significant part of these differences can be attributed to policy choices: whereas Malaysia's auto industrialization strategy initially opted for extensive national ownership and high levels of protection,[25] Thailand has relied on foreign producers, reduced protection in favour of export incentives, facilitated automotive clusters, and pursued scale economies through special incentives for 1-ton pick-up trucks and, subsequently, for fuel-efficient eco-vehicles. At one level, these policies themselves reflect differences in ethnic politics. Malaysia's auto project was part of a broader, heavy industry effort to strengthen the technical and entrepreneurial of ethnic Malays, whereas Thai auto strategy had neither an ethnic component nor, after 2000, much of an emphasis on local ownership, including in parts production. But Malaysia's sustained commitment to an inefficient national project has been facilitated directly by its support from Khazanah, the government investment fund, which holds 42 per cent of Proton's equity, and less directly by petroleum, which accounts for around 40 per cent of government revenue. In Thailand, on the other hand, there has been neither state ownership of auto producers nor public subsidies for any particular brand. Instead, key public policies – cluster development, promotion of pick-up trucks and eco-cars, and export incentives – have been driven by acute government sensitivity to the need for foreign exchange earnings and job creation.[26]

Intra-national, cross-sectoral variation: rubber in Malaysia[27]

Unlike Malaysia's inefficient auto industry, its rubber industry has grown, diversified and upgraded. Until the late 1980s, Malaysia was the world's largest producer and exporter of natural rubber. Its subsequent decline to number three was a function in part of expanding rubber cultivation in Thailand and Indonesia, and in part a function of Malaysia's own deliberate shift to oil palm. But other features of Malaysian rubber are equally impressive. One is its effective linkage development: the country has expanded (downstream) production of rubber-related manufactured goods, especially condoms and medical gloves, of which it is the world's second and first largest producer respectively. Malaysia has also developed a vibrant capital goods industry supplying rubber and rubber products producers. Second, the country has been the source of key innovations in the production and processing of natural rubber, as well as in the production of rubber-based manufactures.[28] Promoting this impressive performance have been a network of stable, efficient government institutions operating in fairly close contact with both rubber producers and downstream firms.

How do we explain this impressive performance, especially relative to Malaysia's auto industry? Some of the answer has to do with the legacy of rubber production and research initiated under British colonialism. But equally – if not more – important have been two sets of pressures. First, the rubber industry has been a very important source of revenue for Malay farmers, a critical political constituency[29] (see, for example, Rudner 1970). Second, rubber has played a critical, albeit declining, role as a foreign exchange earner for Malaysia. Although rubber's contribution to GDP declined from 25 per cent in 1950s to around 10 per cent in the mid-1970s, rubber exports still yielded between 20 and 25 per cent of total export earnings. As such, the industry was a critical source of the country's initial five-year plans. By the 1990s, natural rubber exports had fallen and rubber manufactures were only 3.4 per cent of total manufactured goods (NEAC 2010: 48–9). But these levels have been important, especially after the 1997 crisis when, in the words of a Malaysian Rubber Board engineer, rubber and palm oil 'saved the day'.

In sum, vulnerability can be more or less systemic. But the cases of variation reviewed above demonstrate that even increasing degrees of vulnerability typically translate into institutional shifts.

Where's politics?

The systemic vulnerability account of institutional origins attributes the preferences of political leaders to structural factors such as security threats and resource constraints. But the ability to translate those preferences into institutions and policies depends in part on more proximate political arrangements through which leaders act. A useful way to frame such arrangements is 'veto players', i.e. actors with the capacity to block changes to the status quo by virtue of their positions as government officials or members of governing coalitions.[30] A core contention of this approach is that larger numbers of veto players make decisions more credible by impeding quick changes, whereas a small number of veto players allows for more decisive action.

Although recent work has challenged this dichotomy on the grounds that multiple veto players may actually promote agreements to change policies (see Scartascini et al. 2008), it is clear that multiple veto players often do impede or disrupt effective changes in policies and institutions. A stark illustration comes from Thailand, where the long-serving director of a public–private automotive institute attributed the difficulty of establishing an R&D organization to the fact that he has had to work with – and attempt to educate as to the importance of R&D for local auto producers – 14 Ministers of Industry in 11 years (author interview, July 2010).[31]

Again, however, it is useful to push back the causal chain and explore the possibility that the number of veto players is not static and 'exogenous' but rather itself affected by vulnerability pressures. There is indeed evidence that intense pressures can lead to a reduction in the effective number of players, thus facilitating both decisive action (the Thai case) and an increase a single veto player arrangement, thus facilitating more credible action (the Singapore case) (Doner, Hicken and Ritchie 2009). This is not to argue that political institutions, whether constitutions or coalition structures, are easily modified. It is rather to note that the relatively rare cases of significant institutional reform often occur during 'tough times' that influence more proximate political arrangements.[32]

The economic and political challenges of sustainable growth in Southeast Asia

I have argued that growth in the ASEAN-4, especially Thailand and Malaysia, has been uneven. The ASEAN countries have experienced income growth, improved general welfare and significant economic diversification. But relative to the East Asian NICs, they have not moved into higher value-added activities based on indigenous technology and linkages. I have argued that this unevenness reflects not policies but institutional capacities, and that these capacities are in turn a function of different kinds and levels of constraints and opportunities facing political leaders. Put more simply, I have attempted to flesh out the 'political will' that influences development efforts. What does all mean for the future of Southeast Asia's most dynamic economies? What are their prospects for avoiding middle-income traps?

On the positive side, the ASEAN countries' impressive rebound from the 2008 recession reflects significant strengths (*Economist* 2009). Since the 1997 Asian Financial Crisis, these countries have improved financial supervision, maintained diversification efforts and continued to enjoy the fruits of resource-, labour- and assembly-based exports. But these strategies, including their positive results, portend much less positive outcomes in the longer term. In this (admittedly speculative) conclusion, my goal is to synthesize key factors that will influence broader development prospects in Southeast Asia.

I do so by exploring the nature of today's globalization and the ASEAN countries' strategies for engaging in it. My basic contention is that, first, globalization confronts the ASEAN countries with a new set of challenges and, second, that their development strategies have both intensified these challenges and imposed constraints on their abilities to overcome them. I have already alluded to one obstacle in effective ASEAN responses: the ability of Malaysia and Thailand to ride out crises through reliance on natural resource and assembly activities effectively reduces pressures on elites to develop such capacities.

Below, I focus on the institutional strengths required to benefit from rapidly changing and dis-integrated global production networks, and the weakening of domestic coalitions necessary for an effective response to such conditions. Labour's capacity to exert pressure and support for indigenous upgrading is weak, as is that of domestic business, while foreign producers can avoid contributing to indigenous capacities. At least two possible problems emerge from these conditions: a low skill equilibrium trap; and political tension whose expression varies by country.

Compressed development

Understood as functionally integrated but globally dispersed production systems, today's globalization differs in some key ways from the external pressures and opportunities facing the NICs in the 1970s and 1980s. One key way is that development pressures under today's globalization are more 'compressed' in at least two respects.[33] First, stages and shifts (in production technology, social relations and attitudes) that, in the past, occurred over a century and a half in the UK, some 50 years in Japan, and a few decades in the NICs, are now even further compacted and, in some cases, simultaneous. The implications of this are significant. With technology rapidly changing, developers such as Malaysia and Thailand must become even more effective learners. And as technological change has involved even more actors (e.g. producers, advanced users, universities), these countries must become better collaborators, both internally and externally. Put in terms of the framework presented earlier, development today requires an ability to master new kinds of information, to coordinate even more numerous partners, and thus to muster greater institutional capacities.

Second, countries such as Malaysia and Thailand have fewer if any opportunities to develop complete, national production structures (i.e. upstream, midstream and downstream) in industries that also have the potential to be globally competitive. Japan and the NICs could focus on emulating and learning from all aspects of an existing global industry without actually being engaged at the global level, at least in initial stages. But the global production networks in which Malaysia and Thailand are engaged, especially those such as electronics and autos, are disintegrated and globally dispersed, even if highly organized. As a result, these countries 'must find ways to participate, add value, and *specialize*' (Whittaker *et al.* forthcoming: 2, emphasis in original). This has some significant benefits: global networks offer access to complementary resources for countries with limited capital and indigenous technology. But it also means a reduction in opportunities for domestic value creation through linkages while compelling firms to battle for rents in specific but shifting export niches.

As highly open economies,[34] the ASEAN countries are especially exposed to these pressures which, combined with the rapidity of technological change and stringent product standards, only intensify the need for institutional capacities noted earlier. Yet the obstacles to linkage development, especially upstream linkages, undermine the dense input–output linkages identified by Robert Wade (2006) as being importance coalitional bases for sustained growth. Exacerbating this problem has been the ineffectiveness of Malaysian and Thai efforts at linkage development (noted earlier).

'Societal weakening' – the case of labour

Under today's globalization, low costs can coexist with high quality and prompt delivery. Indeed, 'to maintain or advance their position' in global networks, 'suppliers have to engage in a balancing act between maximising quality (to meet buyers' standards) and minimising costs/prices' (Barrientos *et al.* 2010: 11). Some firms respond by adopting the 'low-road' approach of low wages and poor working conditions, often through total reliance on casual or informal workers. Others opt for the 'high road' of improving working conditions and wages. A hybrid approach is increasingly common: firms simultaneously employ a more skilled, formal workforce and a lower skilled, more informal workforce at the same site.[35] This is the case, for example, in Thailand's dynamic auto industry where, especially after the 1997 crisis when employers focused on the need for flexibility, many firms adopted hybrid systems of simultaneously employing permanent and temporary workers (Archanun *et al.* 2010: 107–9).

More broadly, the use of such contingent employment has expanded in Southeast Asia. The phenomenon is especially pronounced in Thailand, where roughly two-thirds of the workforce operates in the informal sector (Brown 2004: 100; Pasuk and Baker 2008). Informality in Malaysia and Thailand has been further encouraged by access to large numbers of migrant workers – mostly external in the Malaysian case, and both external and internal in the Thai case. This fragmentation of the workforce has depressed wages, reduced business incentives for investing in skill upgrading, and contributed to varying but troublesome levels of income inequality and overall insecurity.[36] It has also been a factor in the organizational and political weakening of labour in Thailand and, to a lesser degree in Malaysia[37] (Brown 2004: 89). Peter Wad, for example, argues that the

> increasing use of contract workers in the Malaysian auto industry over the past two decades increases numerical flexibility for the employers but it also puts a downward pressure on workers in terms of increased employment insecurity and lower wages, aggravated by low levels of union organization among contract workers due to misinformation and negative attitudes to unionism among immigration authorities and employers. Retrenchment benefits are also low even in the unionized sector with collective agreements. This rising flexibilization of the labour market without adding social security measures adds to the institutional weakening of trade unions in Malaysia created by tight and tightening labour laws together with employers' anti-union attitudes and practices. The cross-pressure spills over into preventing employment improvements ... And it is *testified by the low skilling of the auto industry's workforce.*
>
> (Wad 2009a: 20, emphasis added)

As suggested in the above quote, deliberate government policies have contributed to labour's weakness as well. Caraway's recent survey of labour rights in East Asia found Malaysia at the lower end of the spectrum and Thailand in the middle for individual rights, and both scoring among the lowest with regard to collective rights (i.e. union formation, collective bargaining and the right to strike). Especially striking is Caraway's puzzlement over the fact that Thailand's weak record on collective labour rights is closer to the more authoritarian states of China, Laos, Malaysia and Singapore than the (now) more democratic South Korea, Taiwan and the Philippines (Caraway 2009: 177).[38]

At least three non-mutually exclusive explanations for labour's weakness in Thailand merit further research. One involves Thailand's traditionally low level of labour organization mobilization, at least relative to Malaysia. Another is that Thailand's aggressive strategy of export promotion in general and reliance on foreign producers and global production networks, especially in higher-technology manufacturing, encouraged political leaders, including those in elected governments, to focus largely on keeping wage levels low relative to regional competitors (see, for example, Lawler and Suttawet 2000: 231–2). Finally, Kurtz's (2009) argument that contemporary economic liberalization raises barriers to and incentives for collective action for labour and other popular sectors may be especially relevant to highly liberalized Thailand.

As important as its source are the consequences of labour weakness. In addition to its deleterious impact on the quality of democracy, organizationally and politically weak labour may constitute an obstacle to the technology- and innovation-based upgrading so important for sustained growth. This assertion is based on evidence of the developmental benefits of labour inclusion and cross-class collaboration in the small states of Western Europe, Japan and Singapore.[39] Such inclusion seems to have at least three specific benefits. First, it can help to provide compensation and security helpful in maintaining broad political consensus in the face of tough economic

Richard Doner

adjustments (Katzenstein 1985: 29–30). Second and related, it can contribute to risk-hedging institutions, such as insurance, that allow workers to make long-term, albeit somewhat risky investments in education and training (Brooks and Merola 2010). Finally, as reflected in Wad's call for 'productivity alliances' in Malaysia's auto industry, labour's inclusion can 'raise productivity and innovation by mobilizing workers with hands-on knowledge and workplace experience about the state of automotive production' (Wad 2009a: 22).

Weak business demand for skills

The preceding discussion noted the need for risk-hedging institutions for workers to invest scarce resources in education and training. But these decisions also depend on a clear demand for improved skills on the part of business. Such demand is often in short supply in Southeast Asia. One reason for this is the technological weakness of *indigenous* business due to past protection, to the impact of the 1997 financial crisis, to the tremendous difficulties of meeting the standards of global production networks, and to the lure of involvement in less challenging non-tradable goods and services[40] (Archanun 2006: Ch. 8). But there are also problems with demand from *multinational* producers. Given their access to global suppliers, these firms can dispense with the resource-consuming efforts to promote skill-based domestic suppliers. In industries such as electronics and autos, these firms tend to be capital intensive. Thus, electrical and mechanical and mechanical machinery and automotive goods account for over a third of Thailand's exports but employ well under 5 per cent of the labour force (World Bank 2010). And where foreign firms do need to expand the supply of skilled labour, the temptation is to develop training programmes in-house and on-the-job rather than to contribute to industry-wide or public provision of such training services.

This combination of factors often results in a 'low-skill equilibrium trap' in which workers are reluctant to invest in training and education because of a shortage of available positions, but businesses are reluctant to upgrade, i.e. by investing in more skill-based activities, because of a shortage of skilled personnel.[41] Even where there is private sector demand for broader skills, the supply response is often weakened by bureaucratic and political fragmentation.[42]

Export-based vulnerability

A last challenge to sustained growth has to do with extensive reliance on export markets. With Thai exports as a percentage of GDP rising from 48 per cent before the 1997 crisis to 73 per cent in 2007, a recent World Bank report noted with some alarm that 'The Thai economy runs on a single engine: external demand' (World Bank 2010: 1).[43] Malaysia's external reliance is even more extensive, with exports and imports of goods and services amounting to over 100 per cent of GDP (Asian Development Bank 2010a: 209–13). On the positive side, these figures reflect Thai and Malaysian success in sectors ranging from autos to textiles to rubber. But they obviously also highlight significant national vulnerability to exogenous shocks. In one sense, Malaysia and Thailand are well positioned to expand domestic demand by virtue of their growing middle classes: owing to their GDP growth, the two countries are among the five Asian countries with the largest middle classes by population shares (Asian Development Bank 2010b: 6).[44] There are, however, obstacles to further growth in middle-class and overall domestic demand. One, noted earlier, is the danger of jobless or wageless growth in manufacturing. A second problem is the under-provision of a key source of socio-economic stability – education – due to the low skill equilibrium and politically induced fragmentation in education institutions noted earlier. A third, in the case of Thailand, is the fact that some 40 per cent of workers are still in agriculture, a sector vulnerable to natural and exogenous demand shocks. Indeed, Thailand seems especially vulnerable with a relatively small middle class (under 9 per cent of the population) (World Bank 2010: 70).

Politics and sustainable growth

Several authors, noted above, argue that economic development, especially more technologically demanding levels, require broad, domestic political support. Such coalitions can facilitate compensation for difficult economic adjustments and provide security for risky investments. What are the prospects for such supportive political coalitions in the middle-income countries of Southeast Asia? No overall answer is possible, but several factors noted earlier in this chapter suggest grounds for pessimism, but not despair.

First, neither Malaysia nor Thailand has experienced high levels of post-WWII popular mobilization that could have laid the bases for labour's subsequent organization and political inclusion. Such mobilization did occur in semi-democratic Singapore.[45]

Second, the high degree of Malaysian and Thai exposure to globalization has contributed to a weak and embattled domestic capitalist class, a small and politically marginalized formal working class, a white-collar working class conscious of dependence on global forces, and, especially in the Thai case, a high percentage of the working population remaining in declining agriculture or surviving in the urban informal sector (Pasuk and Baker 2008: 80). Third, natural resource endowments and access to migration-inflated labour supplies lessen pressures on Malaysian and Thai political elites to follow China and the East Asian NICs in actually nurturing growth coalitions.[46]

Yet while poverty has declined significantly in both countries, inequalities have persisted and insecurities endure, in part as a function of high external dependence. Will such conditions result in the kinds of popular mobilization that might promote greater labour inclusion and prompt political leaders to undertake productivity-related measures, including institutional strengthening?[47] In the case of Malaysia, the impact of such mobilization will likely be moderated by petroleum-funded side payments and ethno-religious expression. More developmental results might emerge in Thailand, where rural–urban inequality has already helped fuel a significant populist movement whose leader – Thaksin – initially committed himself to productivity-enhancing policies and institutional reforms.[48] Granted, this commitment was superficial, reflecting a typical populist combination of personalize leadership and intra-elite divisions. But the movement has already provoked a stronger elite commitment to social insurance that can further encourage popular political participation.[49] If combined with weak external demand and/or natural resource shocks, such elite responses and popular participation could lead to the actual implementation of Thaksin's productivity promises.

Notes

1 Such cases are thus not 'outliers,' since there is no existing theory from which they diverge.
2 On the developmental state, see Johnson (1982), Amsden (1989), Haggard (1990), Wade (1990). More recent scholarship includes Woo-Cumings (1998) and Kohli (2004).
3 For useful reviews of growth patterns, see Pritchett (1998) and Amsden (2001).
4 Most concepts of economic upgrading emphasize dimensions of value added (product, process, function and chain). For a fuller review, including related scholarship on upgrading, see Doner (2009: 7–8).
5 For specific data on comparative economic performance, see 'Higher Education and Thailand's National Innovation System,' a draft report for the World Bank's Regional Study on Higher Education, by Richard Doner, Patarapong Intarakumnerd and Bryan Ritchie (2009).
6 Unless noted, this taxonomy draws on Kaplinsky (2005: Ch. 8) and Lall (1992, 2000).

7 Lee and Kim (2009) argue that technical training, and related institutions, is especially important for middle-income countries, whereas secondary education is important for lower-income countries.

8 This definition overlaps with the institutional and relational components listed by Stubbs (2009: 5–6).

9 See Table 1 in Doner *et al.* (2005).

10 See the useful review of this fallacy by Haggard (2004: 62).

11 On the benign impact of certain types of corruption in Thailand, see Doner and Ramsay (2000).

12 On Taiwan, see Fields (1997).

13 On the strengths of Thailand relative to the Philippines and Indonesia, see Doner (2009).

14 See a review of the extensive literature in new institutional economics as synthesized in Doner (2009: Ch. 3).

15 Haggard (2004: 68) summarizes the point:

> Governments must define the objectives of the rent in terms of some discernible market failure or externality, monitor rent recipients, and credibly commit to withdraw rents for non-compliance or non-performance ... If governments cannot credibly signal their willingness to revert to a market equilibrium, or some other punishment strategy for non-compliance, then firms will exploit the government.

It should be noted that some policies are inherently more conditional. On export diversification, see Schrank and Kurtz (2005).

16 Rasiah lumps Thailand and Malaysia together, along with Indonesia, as relying on 'labour-intensive items, mainly import-processing non-resource-intensive exports' (Rasiah 2003: 65, italics added). On the labour-intensive nature of Malaysia's electronics industry see Uchida and Cook (2005: 713).

17 On Malaysia, see NEAC (2010); on Thailand, see Doner, Intarakumnerd and Ritchie (2009); and for cross-national comparison, see Ritchie (2010).

18 Of course, Thai macroeconomic policy underwent politicization beginning in the late 1980s (Thitinan 2001).

19 Kang attributes this mutual vulnerability to degrees of concentration, i.e. 'a relatively coherent state but also a small number of powerful interest groups' (2002: 17). But this emphasis on size is at odds with the importance of small and medium-sized firms in Taiwan; it fails to 'endogenize' the private sector, i.e. the possibility that political leaders can influence the size of local firms; and it ignores the problems of upgrading often encountered by highly diversified, albeit large, business groups.

20 On resource constraints, see Rasiah (2003: 66) and Booth (1999: 311). On security threats, see Stubbs (2009: 9).

21 The argument also draws on Woo-Cumings (1998).

22 Pressures on Singapore's leaders included a wave of labour unrest in the late 1940s; its expulsion from Malaysia and consequent loss of a domestic market and access to natural resources in 1965; Malay–Chinese racial riots in 1964; and Britain's 1967 decision to accelerate military withdrawal by 1971 (Doner *et al.* 2005: 347).

23 This section draws especially on more extensive discussions in Doner (2009: Ch. 4) and especially Doner 'The 2008–9 Financial Crisis and export-oriented economies: challenges of sustainable growth', paper prepared for a workshop on 'The Global Impacts of the Financial Crisis', Cornell University, 31 October 2009.

24 Malaysia's motor vehicle production in 2000 was 284,000 vehicles, Thailand's 325,000. In 2007, Malaysia's total had risen to 413,000 compared to 1,193,000 for Thailand. Malaysia's auto vehicle exports were worth $105 million in 2000 and $209 million in 2006, compared to Thai totals of $1.6 billion in 2000 and $6.6 billion in 2006 (Wad 2009b: Tables 2, 3, 4). This section also draws on Doner (2009: Ch. 7) and Ravenhill (2009).

25 In fact, local ownership has deteriorated: only one significant assembly, PROTON, has stayed in business.

26 Interviews with Thai government officials, Bangkok, July 2010. On the impact of oil revenues in the Indonesian auto industry, see Doner (2009: Ch. 7). Figures on Malaysian petroleum revenues from NEAC (2010: 129).

27 Unless noted, information in this section is based on interviews conducted with Malaysian glove producers, officials of the Malaysian Rubber Board, and private researchers in Kuala Lumpur (July 2010).

28 Such innovations include the development of 'block rubber'; the use of gas stimulants for higher tap yield; DNA research on latex allergies; glove production process modification; and new compounds for more environmentally efficient rubber products.

29 This factor also emerged in interviews conducted in July 2010.
30 'Effective' number of veto players is a function of those with formal veto authority and the divergence of preferences among such actors. See Tsebelis (2002) and Cox and McCubbins (2001). For an application to Southeast Asia see MacIntyre (2003).
31 This is not surprising given the fact that, from 1979 to 2001, Thailand underwent 25 governing coalitions and 43 cabinet reshuffles (Chambers 2006: 13)
32 On path-dependent impact of socio-economic structures, see Kurtz (2009).
33 This discussion of 'compressed development' is drawn from Whittaker et al. (forthcoming).
34 An indicator of exposure to dis-integrated global value chains is a country's value of total trade in intermediate manufactured goods. Malaysia and Thailand, as well as the Philippines and Indonesia, are among the top 12 developing countries on this dimension (Whittaker et al. forthcoming: Table 1).
35 The concept of 'informality' has become less clear as employers have adopted a range of approaches to reduce costs and increase flexibility. Following the ILO, informality is defined here to include (1) self-employed; (2) wage workers in insecure and unprotected jobs (unregistered, casual, temporary); and (3) household workers. The second category appears to be especially important as 'increased reliance on contract employment, widespread non-enforcement of employment law, and increased legislative encouragement of irregular and part-time work, alongside structural relocation of workers through status reclassification, have effectively casualized formal sector employment itself' (Deyo forthcoming, emphasis added). Deyo proposes the term 'contingent' labour, which includes casualization (short-term, often informal work) and contract labour (temporary work with relatively clear terms of employment, although the length of employment may vary).
36 On the impact of informality and migration in Malaysia, see, for example, NEAC (2010: 50–1), Turner (2005), Tham and Liew (2004). On Thailand, see, for example, Huguet and Sureeporn (2005). On inequality, see, for example, Gill and Kharas (2007: 30), UNDP (2007).
37 Labour in Malaysia has historically been much more organized than in Thailand. But Malaysian labour has become increasingly decentralized and enterprise-based since the late 1980s (Wad 2004: 237–8).
38 Note that Thailand's rating on the legal right to form unions was the lowest of all democracies, and Malaysia's was equal to that of Singapore and lower than Cambodia's (Caraway 2009: 167).
39 On the growing role of the National Trade Union Congress in Singapore's response to globalization, see Yuen and Lim (2000).
40 The significant weakening of indigenous firms in Thai auto associations was clear in author interviews conducted in Bangkok, July 2010.
41 This trap seems to be pervasive in Latin America (Schneider and Karcher 2010).
42 On the pathologies of Thailand's training institutions, see Doner, Intarakumnerd and Ritchie (2009).
43 Figures from World Bank Development Indicators. Indonesia and the Philippines exhibit much less external reliance, with exports 29 per cent of Indonesian GDP and 43 per cent of Philippines GDP.
44 Unless otherwise noted, this discussion draws on Asian Development Bank (2010b).
45 On Singapore, see Lau (2003). The mobilization animating the Malayan 'Emergency' (1948–60) was limited to ethnic Chinese, especially in rural areas.
46 On the creation of growth coalitions, see especially Gallagher and Hanson (2009).
47 See Boix (2008) for an argument that inequality encourages civil strife, although he also argues that fixed assets, not a key feature of Southeast Asian economies, encourage strife.
48 For a review of Thaksin's (unfulfilled) commitments, see Doner (2009: 125–39).
49 On the Abhisit government's efforts to mimic Thaksin's populist policies, see *Bangkok Post*, various issues. On the contribution of social insurance to political participation and further distribution, see Brooks and Merola (2010).

References

Amsden, A. (1989) *Asia's Next Giant: South Korea and Late Industrialisation*, New York: Oxford University Press.
——(1994) 'Why Isn't the whole world experimenting with the East Asian model to develop?' *World Development* 22 (4): 627–33.
——(2001) *The Rise of 'The Rest': Challenges to the West from Late-Industrializing Economies*, Oxford: Oxford University Press.
Archanun Kohpaiboon (2006) *Multinational Enterprises and Industrial Tans formation: Evidence from Thailand*, Cheltenham: Edward Elgar.

Archanun Kohpaiboon, Pisut Kulthanavit, Prasert Vijitnopparat and Nognuch Soonthocnchawakan (2010) 'Global recession, labour market adjustment and international production networks: evidence from the Thai automotive industry', *ASEAN Economic Bulletin* 27 (1): 98–120.

Asian Development Bank (2010a) 'Asian development outlook', Manila.

——(2010b) 'Key indicators 2010: the rise of Asia's middle class', Manila.

Author interview (2010) Conducted jointly with Patarapong Intarakumnerd, Bangkok, 12 July.

Barrientos, S., G. Gereffi and A. Rossi (2010) 'Capturing the gains: economic and social upgrading in global production networks', Working Paper 2010/03; available at: www.capturingthegains.org/publications/workingpapers/ (accessed 3 August 2010).

Bates, R.H. (1995) 'Social dilemmas and rational individuals: an assessment of the new institutionalism', in J. Harriss, J. Hunter and C. Lewis (eds) *The New Institutional Economics and Third World Development*, New York: Routledge, pp. 27–48.

Berger, M. and J. Revilla Diez (2003) 'Technological capabilities and innovation in Southeast Asia – empirical evidence from Singapore, Penang (Malaysia) and Singapore', paper presented at the Creating, Sharing And Transferring Knowledge: The Role of Geography, Institutions and Organizations DRUID Summer Conference, Copenhagen.

Boix, C. (2008) 'Economic roots of civil wars and revolutions in the contemporary world', *World Politics* 60 (3): 390–437.

Booth, A. (1999) 'Initial conditions and miraculous growth: why is Southeast Asia different from Taiwan and South Korea?' *World Development* 27 (2): 301–21.

Brooks, S. and V. Merola (2010) 'Unequal democracy: the politics of insecurity in developing countries 1800–19860', paper presented at 2010 Meeting of the American Political Science Association.

Brown, A. (2004) *Labour, Politics and the State in Industrializing Thailand*, London: Routledge.

Caraway, T.L. (2009) 'Labour rights in East Asia: progress or regress?', *Journal of East Asian Studies* 9: 153–86.

Chambers, P. (2006) 'Factions, parties, and the durability of parliaments, coalitions, and cabinets: the case of Thailand (1979–2001)', unpublished ms.

Ching, Y. (2000) 'Globalization, labour market deregulation and trade unions in Singapore', in C. Rowley (ed.) *Globalization and Labour in the Asia-Pacific Region*, London: Frank Cass.

Cohen, W.M. and D.A. Levinthal (1990) 'Absorptive capacity: a new perspective on learning and innovation', *Administrative Sciences Quarterly* 35: 569–96.

Cox, G.W. and M.D. McCubbins (2001) 'Institutional determinants of economic policy', in S. Haggard and M.D. McCubbins (eds) *Presidents, Parliaments and Policy*, Cambridge: Cambridge University Press.

de Velde, D.W. and O. Morrissey (2004) 'Foreign direct investment, skills, and wage inequality in East Asia', *Journal of the Asia Pacific Economy* 9 (3): 348–69.

de Velde, D.W. and T. Xenogiani (2007) 'Foreign direct investment and international skill inequality', *Oxford Development Studies* 35 (1): 83–104.

Deyo, F.C. (forthcoming) *Reforming Asian Labor*, Ithaca, NY: Cornell University Press.

Doner, R. (2009) *The Politics of Uneven Development: Thailand's Economic Growth in Comparative Perspective*, New York: Cambridge University Press.

——(2010) 'The politics of economic upgrading in export-oriented Southeast Asia,' paper presented at 'The Second East Asian Miracle? The Political Economy of Asian Responses to the 1997–98 and 2008–2009 Crises', workshop organized by the Japan International Cooperation Agency Research Institute (JICA-RI), Tokyo, 20–21 September.

Doner, R. and E. Hershberg (1999) 'Flexible production and political decentralization: elective affinities in the pursuit of competitiveness?', *Studies in Comparative and International Development* 34 (1): 45–82.

Doner, R. and A. Ramsay (2000) 'Rent-seeking and economic development in Thailand', in Mushtaq Khan and K.S. Jomo (eds) *Rents, Rent-Seeking and Economic Development: Theory and Evidence in Asia*, Cambridge: Cambridge University Press, pp. 145–81.

Doner R., B.K. Ritchie and D. Slater (2005) 'Systemic vulnerability and the origins of developmental states: Northeast and Southeast Asia in comparative perspective', *International Organization* 59 (2): 327–61.

Doner, R., A. Hicken and B.K. Ritchie (2009) 'The political challenge of innovation in the developing world', *Review of Policy Research* 26 (1–2): 151–71.

Doner, R., P. Intarakumnerd and B.K. Ritchie (2009) 'Higher education and Thailand's national innovation system', draft report for the World Bank, East Asian Project on Higher Education, East Asian Regional Study.

Economist (2009) 'On the rebound', 15 August: 69.

Evans, P. (1995) *Embedded Autonomy: States and Industrial Transformation*, Princeton, NJ: Princeton University Press.

Felker, G.B. and K.S. Jomo (2003) 'New approaches to investment policy in the ASEAN 4', in K.S. Jomo (ed.) *Southeast Asia's Paper Tigers*, London: Routledge.

Fields, K. (1997) 'Business organization in Korea and Taiwan', in B. Schneider and S. Maxfield (eds) *Business and the State in Developing Countries*, Ithaca, NY: Cornell University Press, pp. 122–51.

Gallagher, M and J.K. Hanson (2009) 'Coalitions, carrots, and sticks: economic inequality and authoritarian states', *PS: Political Science and Politics* 42 (4): 667–72.

Gerring, J. (2007) *Case Study Research: Principles and Practice*, New York: Cambridge University Press.

Gill, I. and H. Kharas (2007) *An East Asian Renaissance: Ideas for Economic Growth*, Washington: World Bank.

Haggard, S. (1990) *Pathways from the Periphery*, Ithaca, NY: Cornell University Press.

——(2004) 'Institutions and East Asian growth', *Studies in Comparative International Development* 38 (4): 53–81.

Haggard, S. and R. Kaufman (2008) *Development, Democracy, and Welfare States*, Princeton, NJ: Princeton University Press.

Hausman, R. and D. Rodrik (2002) 'Economic development as self-discovery', Kennedy School, Faculty Research Working Paper – RWP02–023 (March).

Henderson, J. and R. Phillips (2007) 'Unintended consequences: social policy, state institutions and the "stalling" of the Malaysian industrialization project', *Economy and Society* 36 (1): 78–102.

Huguet, J. and Sureeporn Punpuing (2005) *International Migration in Thailand*, Bangkok: International Organization for Migration.

Intarakumnerd, P. Pun-arj Chairatana and Tipawan Tangchitpiboon (2002) 'National innovation system in less successful developing countries: the case of Thailand', *Research Policy* 31 (8–9): 1445–57.

International Labour Organization (2007) 'The contribution of migrant workers to Thailand: towards policy development', prepared by Prof. Philip Martin, University of California (Davis) for the International Labour Organization (ILO), Bangkok.

Johnson, C. (1982) *MITI and the Japanese Miracle: The Growth of Industrial Policy, 1925–1975*, Stanford: Stanford University Press.

Jomo, K.S. (2001) 'Growth and structural change in the second-tier Southeast Asian NICs', in K.S. Jomo (ed.) *Southeast Asia's Industrialization: Industrial Policy, Capabilities and Sustainability*, New York: Palgrave, pp. 1–30.

Kang, D. (2002) *Crony Capitalism: Corruption and Development in South Korea and the Philippines*, New York: Cambridge University Press.

Kaplinsky, R. (2005) *Globalization, Poverty and Inequality*, Cambridge: Polity.

Katzenstein, P. (1985) *Small States in World Markets: Industrial Policy in Europe*, Ithaca, NY: Cornell University Press.

Knight, J. (1992) *Institutions and Social Conflict*, New York: Cambridge University Press.

Kohli, A. (2004) *State-Directed Development: Political Power and Industrialization in the Global Periphery*, Princeton, NJ: Princeton University Press.

——(2009) 'Nationalist vs dependent capitalist development: alternate pathways of Asia and Latin America in a globalized world', *Studies in Comparative International Development* (December) 44 (4): 386–410.

Kurtz, M. (2009) 'The social foundations of institutional order: reconsidering war and the "resource curse" in Third World state building', *Politics and Society* 37 (4): 479–510.

Lall, S. (1992) 'Technological capabilities and industrialization', *World Development* 20 (2): 165–86.

——(2000) 'Technological change and industrialization in the Asian newly industrializing economies: achievements and challenges', in Linsu Kim and R.R. Nelson (eds) *Technology, Learning and Innovation: Experiences of Newly Industrializing Countries*, Cambridge: Cambridge University Press, pp. 13–68.

Lau, A. (2003) *A Moment of Anguish: Singapore in Malaysia and the Politics of Disengagement*, Singapore: Eastern Universities Press.

Lawler, J.J. and C. Suttawet (2000) 'Labour unions, globalization and deregulation in Thailand', in C. Rowley and J. Benson (eds) *Globalization and Labour in the Asia-Pacific Region*, London: Frank Cass.

Lee, Keun and Byong-Yeon Kim (2009) 'Both institutions and policies matter but differently for different income groups of countries: determinants of long-run economic growth revisited', *World Development* 39 (3): 533–49.

MacIntyre, A. (2003) *The Power of Institutions: Political Architecture and Governance*, Ithaca, NY: Cornell University Press.

McKendrick, D., R.F. Doner and S. Haggard (2000) *From Silicon Valley to Singapore: The Competitive Advantage of Location in the Hard Disk Drive Industry*, Stanford, CA: Stanford University Press.

Mardon, R. (1990) 'The state and the effective control of foreign capital: the case of South Korea', *World Politics* 43 (1): 111–37.

171

Moe, T.M. (1984) 'The new economics of organization', *American Journal of Political Science* 28 (4):739–77.

National Economic Advisory Council (NEAC) (2010) *New Economic Model for Malaysia*, Kuala Lumpur: NEAC.

Nordhaug, K. (1998) 'Development through want of security: the case of Taiwan', *Forum for Development Studies* 1: 129–61.

Ostrom, E. (1990) *Governing the Commons: The Evolution of Institutions for Collective Action*, Cambridge: Cambridge University Press.

Pack, H. (2000a) 'Industrial policy: growth elixir or poison?' *The World Bank Research Observer* 15 (1) (February): 47–67.

——(2000b) 'Research and development in the industrial development process', in Linsu Kim and R.R. Nelson (eds) *Technology, Learning and Innovation: Experiences of the Newly Industrializing Economies*, New York: Cambridge University Press, pp. 69–94.

Pasuk Phonpaichit and C. Baker (2008) 'Thaksin's populism', *Journal of Contemporary Asia* 38 (1): 62–83.

Pholphirul, P. (2010) 'Economic contributions of migrant workers to Thailand', *International Migration* 48 (5): 174–202.

Pritchett, L. (1998) 'Patterns of economic growth: hills, plateaus, mountains, and plains', Policy Research Working Paper Series 1947, World Bank.

Rasiah, R. (2000) 'Politics, institutions and flexibility: microelectronics transnationals and machine tool linkages in Malaysia', in F. Deyo, R.F. Doner and E. Hershberg (eds) *Economic Governance and the Challenge of Flexibility in East Asia*, Boulder: Rowman and Littlefield.

——(2003) 'Manufacturing export growth in Indonesia, Malaysia and Thailand', in K.S. Jomo (ed.) *Southeast Asian Paper Tigers? From Miracle to Debacle and Beyond*, London: RoutledgeCurzon.

Ravenhill, J. (2009) 'The lure and challenges of the automobile industry', unpublished MS, Australian National University.

Ritchie, B. (2001) 'Innovation systems, collective dilemmas, and the formation of technical intellectual capital in Malaysia, Singapore, and Thailand', *International Journal of Business and Society* 2 (2): 21–48.

——(2010) *Systemic Vulnerability and Sustainable Economic Growth: Skills and Upgrading in Southeast Asia*, Cheltenham: Edward Elgar.

Rock, M. (1995) 'Thai industrial policy: how irrelevant was it to export success?' *Journal of International Development* 7 (5): 745–57.

——(2000) 'Thailand's old bureaucratic polity and its new semi-democracy', in Mushtaq Khan and K.S. Jomo (eds) *Rents, Rent-Seeking and Economic Development*, Kuala Lumpur: Cambridge University Press, pp. 182–206.

Rodrik, D. (2007) *One Economics, Many Recipes*, Princeton, NJ: Princeton University Press.

Rudner, M. (1970) 'The state and peasant innovation in rural development: the case of Malaysian rubber', *Asian and African Studies* 6: 75–96; reprinted in David Lim (ed.) (1975) *Readings on Malaysian Economic Development*, Kuala Lumpur: Oxford University Press, pp. 321–31.

Scartascini, C., E. Stein and M. Tommasi (2008) 'Veto players, intertemporal interactions and policy adaptability: how do political institutions work?', Inter-American Development Bank Working Paper 645 (August).

Schiller, D. (2006) 'The potential to upgrade Thai innovation system by university-industry linkages', *Asian Journal of Technology Innovation* 14 (2): 67–92.

Schneider, B. and S. Karcher (2010) 'Complementarities and continuities in the political economy of labour markets in Latin America', *Socio-Economic Review* 8 (4): 623–51.

Schrank, A. (2011) 'Co-producing workplace transformation: the Dominican Republic in comparative perspective', *Socio-Economic Review*, doi: 10.1093/ser/mwr008.

Schrank, A. and M. Kurtz (2005) 'Credit where credit is due: open economy industrial policy and export diversification in Latin America and the Caribbean', *Politics and Society* 33 (4): 671–702.

Shafer, M. (1994) *Winners and Losers: How Sectors Shape the Developmental Prospects of States*, Ithaca, NY: Cornell University Press.

Stubbs, R. (2009) 'Whatever happened to the East Asian developmental state? The unfolding debate', *Pacific Review* 22 (2): 1–22.

Thailand Development Research Institute (2009) Comments from Seminar on Politics and the State in Economic Upgrading, Bangkok, 28 January.

Tham Siew-Yean and Liew Chei-Siang (2004) 'Foreign labour in Malaysian manufacturing: enhancing Malaysian competitiveness', in Abdul Rahman Embong (ed.) *Globalisation, Culture and Inequalities: In Honour of the Late Ishak Shari*, Bangi: Penerbit UKM, pp. 253–74.

Thitinan Pongsudhirak (2001) 'Crisis from within: the politics of macroeconomic management in Thailand, 1947–1997', PhD dissertation, London School of Economics.

Tsebellis, G. (2002) *Veto Players: How Political Institutions Work*, Princeton, NJ: Princeton University Press.

Turner, D. (2005) 'Malaysia's regime of labour control and the attempted transition to a knowledge based economy: the problematic role of migrant labour', *Review of Indonesian and Malaysian Affairs* 39 (2): 45–68.

Uchida, Yuichiro and P. Cook (2005) 'The transformation of competitive advantage in East Asia: an analysis of technological and trade specialization', *World Development* 33 (5): 701–28.

United Nations Development Programme (UNDP) (2007) *Thailand Human Development Report 2007: Sufficiency Economy and Human Development*, Bangkok: UNDP.

Wad, P. (2004) 'Transforming industrial relations in the Malaysian auto industry', in R. Elmhirst and R. Saptari (eds) *Labour in Southeast Asia: Local Processes in a Globalised World*, New York: Routledge, pp. 235–64.

——(2008) 'The development of automotive parts suppliers in Korea and Malaysia: a global value chain perspective', in R. Rasiah, Y. Sadoi and R. Busser (eds) *Multinationals, Technology and Localization: Automotive and Electronics Firms in Asia*, London: Routledge, pp. 47–64.

——(2009a) 'Automotive industry in Malaysia: evolution and impact of global crisis', Working Paper 278, Geneva, International Labour Office.

——(2009b) 'The automobile industry of Southeast Asia: Malaysia and Thailand', *Journal of the Asia Pacific Economy* 14 (2): 172–93.

Wade, R.H. (1990) *Governing the Market*, Princeton, NJ: Princeton University Press.

——(2006) 'The case for open-economy industrial policy', paper for PREM conference on the Institutional Foundation of Growth, World Bank, April, Washington, DC, and GRIPS seminar, May, Tokyo.

Waldner, D. (1999) *State Building and Late Development*, Ithaca, NY: Cornell University Press.

Whittaker, D.H., Tianbiao Zhu, T. Sturgeon, Mon Han Tsai and T. Okita (forthcoming) 'Compressed development', *Studies in Comparative International Development*.

Wong Poh-kam and Chee-Yuen Ng (2001) 'Rethinking the development paradigm: lessons from Japan and the four Asian NIEs', in Wong Poh-kam and Chee-Yuen Ng (eds) *Industrial Policy, Innovation and Economic Growth*, Singapore: Singapore University Press

Woo-Cumings, M. (1998) 'National security and the rise of the developmental state in South Korea and Taiwan', in H. Rowen (ed.) *Behind East Asian Growth*, New York: Routledge, pp. 319–40.

World Bank (1993) *The East Asian Miracle: Economic Growth and Public Policy*, Washington, DC: Oxford University Press.

——(2005) 'Thailand: investment climate, firm competitiveness, and growth', 30 August, Bangkok.

——(2008) *Thailand Economic Monitor* (April) Bangkok.

——(2010) *Thailand Economic Monitor* (June) Bangkok.

Yuen Chi Ching and Lim Ghee Soon (2000) 'Globalization, labour market deregulation and trade unions in Singapore', in C. Rowley and J. Benson (eds) *Globalization and Labour in the Asia Pacific Region*, London: Frank Cass, pp. 154–83.

Yusuf, S. and K. Nabeshima (2009) *Tiger Economies Under Threat: A Comparative Analysis of Malaysia's Industrial Prospects and Policy Options*, Vol. 566, Washington, DC: World Bank.

——(2010) *Tiger Economies Under Threat: A Comparative Analysis of Malaysia's Industrial Prospects and Policy Options*, New York: Cambridge University Press.

11

DONORS, NEO-LIBERALISM AND COUNTRY OWNERSHIP IN SOUTHEAST ASIA

Andrew Rosser

During the 1990s and early 2000s, much of the scholarly and policy-oriented literature on aid effectiveness suggested that aid had done little to promote economic growth in developing countries or had had a positive impact on growth only in countries that had 'sound' policies and institutions (Dollar and Pritchett 1998; Burnside and Dollar 2000; Easterly 2006). At the same time, several scholars produced evidence to suggest that policy conditionality had been ineffective in promoting economic policy reform in developing countries – in one influential study, for instance, Dollar and Pritchett (1998) found that conditionality did not guarantee that reforms would be carried out, or be successful or sustainable once they were. The result was a new consensus that policy conditionality needed to be reduced or even abandoned in favour of greater country ownership of aid programmes if aid was to become more effective in promoting economic growth in developing countries. In March 2005, this new consensus led to donor governments and the international financial institutions (IFIs) – that is, the World Bank, the International Monetary Fund (IMF), and the regional development banks – (hereafter referred to collectively as 'donors') signing the *Paris Declaration on Aid Effectiveness* (hereafter the *Paris Declaration*) along with a host of leading development NGOs and governments from many aid recipient countries. This declaration lists country ownership as the first of five key principles of aid effectiveness, the others being alignment, harmonization, managing for results and mutual accountability. It also outlines a series of measures aimed at realizing the principle of country ownership (and the other principles) in practice and sets specific related targets for donors and aid recipient countries to achieve within specified timeframes (OECD-DAC 2005). In September 2008, the signatories to the *Paris Declaration* reiterated their support for greater country ownership at the 3rd High Level Forum on Aid Effectiveness in Accra, Ghana, and committed to further measures aimed at realizing this principle in the *Accra Agenda for Action* (OECD-DAC 2008a). Indeed, the *Accra Agenda for Action* arguably gave greater prominence to the notion of country ownership, noting that it was the international development community's 'first priority' with regards to aid effectiveness.

The purpose of this chapter is to examine the way in which this principle has informed donor strategies for engaging with developing countries, in particular within Southeast Asia. It is argued that there is a conflict between donors' expressed commitment to country ownership and the political imperative they face to promote neo-liberal policies in developing countries. Plans for country ownership in reality confront the influence that business and security interests in donor countries have over donor aid policies and the imperative that this generates for

Western governments and the IFIs (whose governing bodies are dominated by these governments) to pursue market outcomes. A key challenge for donors has thus been to work out a compromise between these competing agendas. To illustrate this inherent conflict and to explore the nature of the emerging compromise, I examine two current donor strategies from the Southeast Asian region: the World Bank's strategy for engaging with Indonesia for 2009–12 and the Asian Development Bank's (ADB) strategy for engaging with fragile states (which was formulated in 2007). Between them, these strategies suggest that donors have subordinated the principle of country ownership to that of promoting neo-liberal forms of governance where the two have been in conflict, indicating that the emerging compromise is one that favours the interests of business and security elements in donor countries over concerns about aid effectiveness.

In presenting this argument, I begin by examining the nature of the country ownership principle as outlined in the *Paris Declaration* and *Accra Agenda for Action* and the way in which it conflicts with the neo-liberal agenda. I then examine the way in which this conflict has been resolved in the World Bank's strategy for engaging with Indonesia and the ADB's strategy for engaging with fragile states. The final part of the chapter considers the implications of this outcome for development trajectories and the effective use of aid within the Southeast Asian region.

Country ownership and neo-liberalism

The *Paris Declaration* formally defines country ownership as aid recipient countries exercising 'effective leadership over their development policies, and strategies and coordinat[ing] development actions' (OECD-DAC 2005: 3). This, in turn, it states, requires aid recipient countries to 'exercise leadership in developing and implementing their national development strategies through broad consultative processes'; 'translate these national development strategies into prioritized results-oriented operational programmes as expressed in medium-term expenditure frameworks and annual budgets'; and 'take the lead in coordinating aid activities at all levels' (OECD-DAC 2005: 3). For their part, donors are expected to 'respect partner country leadership and help strengthen their capacity to exercise it' by making increased use of recipient countries' systems and procedures and employing national strategies and objectives in the design and evaluation of their aid programmes rather than their own strategies and objectives (OECD-DAC 2005: 3). Similarly, the *Accra Agenda for Action* envisages aid recipient country governments exercising 'stronger leadership' in developing and implementing development policies to 'achieve their own economic social and environmental goals' and donors supporting them by 'respecting' their 'priorities, investing in their human resources and institutions, making greater use of their systems to deliver aid, and increasing the predictability of aid flows' (OECD-DAC 2008a: 1).

Between them, these various requirements envisage a shift away from project-based forms of aid towards programme-based forms of aid such as general budget support, sector budget support and sector-wide approaches on the grounds that the latter give governments in developing countries greater control over how aid is used. Indeed, the sections of the *Paris Declaration* that deal with alignment explicitly require donors to make increased use of recipient country public financial management and procurement systems and to assess development performance against targets established in national strategies rather than donor strategies and objectives. The *Accra Agenda for Action* – which was formulated following an OECD survey that found that the international development community was unlikely to meet many of the targets specified in the *Paris Declaration* and particularly those related to ownership (OECD-DAC 2008b) – outlines a number of further measures to promote recipient country ownership. These include:

developing country governments working more closely with parliaments, local authorities and civil society organizations in preparing national development strategies; donors supporting efforts to increase the capacity of stakeholders within government and civil society to contribute to discussions on aid and development; donors using aid recipient country systems as the first option in relation to activities managed by the public sector; and donors developing strategies for strengthening rather than undermining aid recipient country systems when use of these systems is not feasible (OECD-DAC 2008b).

The principle of country ownership fits uncomfortably with the neo-liberal agenda that has constituted development orthodoxy for more than three decades. Neo-liberalism has been defined as 'a theory of political economic practices that proposes that human well-being can best be advanced by liberating individual entrepreneurial freedoms and skills within an institutional framework characterized by strong private property rights, free markets, and free trade' (Harvey 2005: 2). Accordingly, supporters of neo-liberalism seek to 'maximis[e] the reach and frequency of market transactions, and ... bring all human action into the domain of the market' (Harvey 2005: 3). In policy terms, this has meant promoting the policies of the so-called Washington Consensus: fiscal discipline, tax reform, trade liberalization, foreign direct investment liberalization, deregulation, interest rate liberalization, privatization, exchange rate liberalization and secure property rights (Williamson 1990). Since the mid-1990s, the neo-liberal agenda has shifted slightly as it has become increasingly concerned with promoting 'good governance' and enhancing the role of civil society in the development process, a shift that has given rise to the so-called 'post-Washington Consensus' (PWC). But this shift has been made in a way that has preserved an emphasis on a central role for market forces in the development process. On the one hand, the promotion of good governance and the role of civil society has been geared towards creating the political and social conditions necessary for market-oriented reform rather than a more democratic development process (Jayasuriya and Rosser 2001). On the other hand, the notion of good governance itself has been understood largely in terms of market-based models of public sector management such as the new public management (NPM). This model calls for such market-based reforms as privatization, the introduction of competition within the public sector and between the public and private sectors, and the improvement of public services via the introduction of service charters and stronger processes of performance audit and assessment (Minogue 2002: 134).

The principle of country ownership conflicts with this agenda in two ways. First, it implies that development strategies should emerge organically from aid recipient countries' own specific contexts rather than be constructed on the basis of external templates, even if the latter are widely viewed as superior in some technical respects – as Zimmermann (2008) has put it, it implies that development strategies should be 'home-grown' as well as 'home-owned'. Much recent work on the political economy of development has suggested that where poor countries have successfully pursued 'home-grown' development strategies these have tended to be characterized by strategic forms of state intervention in the economy rather than the pursuit of neo-liberal policies. The principal examples in this respect are South Korea, Taiwan and Singapore (Amsden 1989; Rodan 1989; Wade 1990), although Chang (2003) among others has shown that the use of strategic forms of state intervention was also a feature of the experiences of early industrializers such as England, France and Germany. The implication of the country ownership principle – and in particular the idea that development strategies should be home-grown – is that if today's poor countries are to achieve development success, they cannot afford to be limited to the policy options prescribed by the neo-liberal agenda.

Second, the principle of country ownership implies weaker political pressure on aid recipient countries to adopt neo-liberal policies. As numerous scholars have pointed out, donors have long used their structural leverage – that is, the leverage they have had by virtue of their control over scarce and mobile investment resources (Winters 1996) – to pressure governments in aid recipient countries to adopt neo-liberal policies, in particular, via the use of conditionality in loan agreements and selective approaches to aid allocation that reward countries that adopt these policies (see, for instance, Buira 2003 and Hout 2004). The principle of country ownership implies that donors should desist from using this leverage in order to facilitate aid recipient country leadership of the development process, in doing so reducing the political pressure on the latter countries to pursue neo-liberal policies. Indeed, it implies that donors have no legitimate role to play in developing country policy-making processes at all – rather, these processes should be the sole preserve of domestic actors such as parliamentary representatives, civil servants and civil society activists.

To be sure, the agenda outlined in the *Paris Declaration* and *Accra Agenda for Action* does not constitute a complete break with the era of neo-liberal conditionality and donor-driven development agendas. Most importantly, the way in which the principle of country ownership is operationalized in the *Paris Declaration* reinforces donor leverage over the development process. The *Paris Declaration* requires that progress vis-à-vis the country ownership principle be measured in terms of whether or not aid recipient countries have established 'operational development strategies'. As Zimmermann (2008: 1) has pointed out, these strategies can be seen as 'code for the poverty reduction strategy papers (PRSPs) demanded of governments by the World Bank and International Monetary Fund', most of which are drafted with donor participation, assessed by donors for quality and hence heavily influenced by neo-liberal ideas (see also Booth 2008: 2 and Eurodad 2008). But the principle of country ownership, as distinct from the way in which it is operationalized, clearly conflicts with the neo-liberal model for the reasons that I have outlined above. Indeed, the fact that donors have watered down this principle by operationalizing it in a way that favours the neo-liberal agenda merely serves to illustrate the tensions that it poses.

The fact that the principle of country ownership conflicts with the neo-liberal agenda has created a contradiction for donors inasmuch as, while the effectiveness of aid in promoting development – and hence its legitimacy and public support – hinges to a significant extent on the ability of donors to surrender leadership over the development process to aid recipient countries, it is politically inconceivable for them to simply abandon their commitment to neo-liberalism. The point here is that the neo-liberal orientation of donors' aid policies reflects the interests of politically powerful elements in donor countries. On the one hand, it reflects the interests of big business in these countries (Diven 2001; Lancaster 2007). As I have argued elsewhere in relation to the Australian case (Rosser 2008), although big business has often been 'relatively disengaged' on aid policy issues – reflecting the fact that its prime interests lie in areas of policy such as industrial relations, trade, finance, fiscal, investment and tax – it has nevertheless had clear interests in relation to aid policy. In particular, it has seen aid policy as a useful way of opening up business opportunities in developing countries and increasing the profitability of existing investments in these countries. At the same time, it has exercised enormous influence over aid policy by virtue of its structural leverage over the state, the lobbying activities of business representative organizations (which at times have focused explicitly on aid policy issues), and the fact that aid policy-making processes have typically occurred within the executive arm of government, effectively excluding progressive NGOs and development experts from participation in the aid policy-making process.

On the other hand, the neo-liberal orientation of donors' aid policies also reflects a belief within military and foreign policy establishments in donor countries that neo-liberal reform is necessary to address the security risks that aid recipient countries – in particular, those classified as 'fragile states' – pose to donor countries. The views of military and foreign policy establish-ments have long been an important driver of aid policy in donor countries – indeed, Lancaster (2007: 25) has suggested that aid would probably not exist today, or at least not be as sizeable in financial terms as it currently is, were it not for the fact that the both the US and the Soviet Union found aid to be a useful way of achieving geo-strategic objectives during the Cold War. In recent years, military and foreign policy establishments in donor countries have increasingly argued that poor governance in fragile states is one of the key causes of global security threats such as organized crime, terrorism, illegal immigration and Weapons of Mass Destruction threats, and that fragile states therefore need to improve the quality of their governance systems via the adoption of 'appropriate' policies and institutions as defined by neo-liberalism (Cammack et al. 2006: x). For instance, as Hameiri (2008, 2009) has illustrated, this thinking was a clear part of Australia's approach to engaging with fragile states in the South Pacific during the Howard years. The Howard government, he argues (2009: 358), sought to manage 'the potential risks posed by state fragility and failure in Australia's near region through programs designed to transform the domestic governing apparatuses of neighbouring states' in accordance with the NPM and the neo-liberal agenda more generally. Such a transformation was seen as functional to the management of these risks, he suggests, because state fragility itself was construed – indeed defined – in terms of the ability of the state to provide the policy and institutional arrangements – the structures of governance and public administration – that facilitate market-led development (Hameiri 2008: 364).

With such powerful interests promoting the adoption of neo-liberal aid policies, govern-ments in donor countries have had little option but to fall into line, in relation to both their own respective national aid programmes and those of the IFIs, the governing bodies of which they dominate.[1] A key challenge for donors has thus been to find a way of resolving the tension between the country ownership principle and the political imperative that they face to promote neo-liberal reform in aid recipient countries. The donor strategies examined below suggest that they have done so in a manner that has subordinated the principle of country ownership to the dictates of the neo-liberal agenda and, in turn, a concern with aid effectiveness to business and security interests in donor countries.

The World Bank's strategy for engaging with Indonesia

The World Bank has had a long-standing engagement with Indonesia and a particularly close one since the mid-1960s when Suharto's 'New Order' government came to power. Throughout this period, it has consistently sought to influence the country's economic and social policies and in particular to promote neo-liberal policy and institutional reform (Robison 1986; Winters 1996; Rosser 2002). Its various country reports and strategy documents have – as the Bank itself has recently acknowledged in relation to its 2003–7 *Country Assistance Strategy* for Indonesia – been 'agenda-setting' documents (World Bank 2009: 11) while the projects and programmes it has funded have been aimed at shaping this agenda in the specific areas in which they have been implemented. In endeavouring to influence the country's economic and social policies, the Bank has been able to exploit its structural leverage as well as that of the donor community more generally.[2] Aid has at no point accounted for more than 6 per cent of Indonesia's Gross National Income (GNI) since the late 1960s and for most of this period has been below 2 per cent (Rosser 2006: 62). But the country has nevertheless needed access to aid to support specific initiatives and to assist at times of economic crisis, most notably following the collapse of international oil prices in the mid-1980s and the Asian economic crisis in the late 1990s. The Bank was able to exploit these needs to promote dramatic deregulation of the finance sector and to a lesser extent trade and investment sector deregulation and privatization in the 1980s in particular (Rosser 2002).

The Bank's 2009–12 *Country Partnership Strategy* (CPS) for Indonesia suggests that it intends to make a break with this approach, reflecting the international donor community's newfound concern with promoting country ownership of the development process. Instead of trying to set the policy agenda, it says, the Bank will henceforth 'strongly align behind and help implement the Government's own reform priorities' (World Bank 2009: 11). This in turn, it says, will require the Bank to focus its support on government strategies, objectives and programmes, as outlined in the government's medium-term development plans, annual plans and state budgets; and use Indonesia's systems and procedures as much as possible, including by co-financing slices of government budgeted priority programmes (World Bank 2009: 12). Underlying this strategy, it suggests, is recognition that 'successful institutional change in a large, diverse, dynamic and democratic, middle-income country such as Indonesia tends to be government-initiated and led' – in other words, country-owned (World Bank 2009: 11).

At the same time, however, the CPS incorporates a selective approach to the allocation of aid between sectors and areas within Indonesia that arguably undermines country ownership. Under this selective approach, the Bank will not engage in all sectors and areas but will focus on those 'that are *significant* for Indonesia's stakeholders, where there remain *vital needs,* in which reform *opportunities* arise, where there is unambiguous *demand* from Indonesia's key stakeholders, and where the [World Bank Group] will have the *capacity* to deliver' (italics in original) (World Bank 2009: 11). The reference to sectors and areas 'in which reform *opportunities* arise' is particularly important for our purposes because it suggests that the Bank intends to continue using its leverage to promote neo-liberal reform notwithstanding its commitment to follow the government's leadership. Indeed, the Bank is quite transparent about this, noting at one point that in supporting the implementation of the government's policies and programmes, it 'intends to leverage relationships and investments to bring about broad-based policy, institutional and systemic reforms' and select activities 'on the basis of their contribution to strengthening Indonesia's institutions and systems, particularly those of the public sector' (World Bank 2009: 10–11). In essence, the Bank is indicating that it will choose to support only those government policies and programmes that are consistent with its neo-liberal agenda or which it thinks it can transform to fit this agenda.

The Bank has for a long time been opposed to Indonesian government initiatives associated with the radical populist and nationalist traditions in Indonesian economic thinking, both of which call for extensive state intervention in the economy.[3] While the former set of ideas had little impact on government policy during the New Order years, the latter set of ideas was highly influential during the oil boom period, leading to the pursuit of a state-led industrialization strategy (Robison 1986). Since the fall of the New Order, nationalist ideas have taken a back seat because the government has lacked the resources to finance large-scale industrial projects. But radical populist ideas have become increasingly influential, as (now elected) politicians have sought to mobilize votes from the lower classes (Rosser *et al.* 2005). In adopting a selective approach to the allocation of aid between sectors and areas within Indonesia, the Bank has sought to ensure that it is not forced, by dint of commitment to the principle of country ownership, to fund and support policies that embody these ideas.

This approach has had significant implications for the sectoral structure of the Bank's lending programme in Indonesia. For instance, while the CPS indicates that education will be among the Bank's 'core engagements' between 2009 and 2012, it relegates health to the category of 'other engagements areas', noting that no new investments are currently being considered for this sector. The Bank is again quite transparent about its reasons for treating these sectors differently. In education, the CPS notes, the Bank has developed a 'close relationship' with the government ministries responsible for this sector, the Ministry of National Education and the Ministry of Religious Affairs (World Bank 2009: 21), reflecting their shared commitment to school-based management and other neo-liberal education policies (Irawan *et al.* 2004). In health, however, the Bank and the Ministry of Health have been at loggerheads, reflecting former Health Minister Siti Fadillah Supari's nationalistic approach to health policy – she is a self-styled opponent of neo-liberalism and the international organizations that promote it (Bari 2009) – and her pursuit of costly universal health care reforms.[4] Accordingly, the CPS states that further Bank support for health sector activities is contingent upon 'government counterparts and stakeholders' in that sector 'demonstrat[ing] a clear commitment to addressing critical governance and institutional challenges' (World Bank 2009: 23) – in other words, shifting from a nationalistic to neo-liberal approach.

In essence, then, the CPS suggests that while the Bank's commitment to country ownership is not simply rhetorical, it is clearly subordinate to its commitment to neo-liberalism. To the extent that country ownership does not prevent the Bank from pursuing its long-standing practice of promoting neo-liberal reform in Indonesia, it is willing to allow some level of country ownership. But where the two agendas come into conflict, the Bank has decided to sacrifice country ownership.

The ADB's strategy for engaging with fragile states

The ADB was founded in 1966 in order to promote economic development, poverty reduction and regional cooperation within the Asian region. Like the World Bank, it provides various forms of assistance to developing countries including loans, technical assistance, grants, guarantees and equity investments. Over half of this assistance has been used to fund infrastructure projects such as roads, airports, power plants, and water and sanitation facilities, with projects related to the environment, regional cooperation and integration, financial sector development and education also being key areas of activity. This assistance is funded in large part out of the ADB's ordinary capital resources, with the remainder coming from special funds. The membership of the ADB reaches across the Asia-Pacific region and includes both developed and developing countries. However, the US and Japan are the dominant members in terms of the influence that they exercise over the ADB's policies and activities. Each accounts for 15.571 per cent of the ADB's total subscribed capital, giving them a powerful voice within the Bank's Board of Governors and Board of Directors. At the same time, Japanese nationals have dominated management positions within the Bank, particularly the presidency with all eight ADB Presidents so far having been Japanese (ADB n.d.a, n.d.b; Dent 2008: 768). Some scholars have argued that Japan's prominent role in the ADB has imbued the ADB with 'Japanese developmentalist thinking and ideology … in contrast to the market-liberal reformist approach of the World Bank and … IMF' (Dent 2008: 768–9). However, the influence of the US, Japan's own recent shift towards neo-liberalism at home (Beeson 2007) and the fact that the ADB raises much of its funding on international capital markets (a key champion of neo-liberal policies) have ensured that the ADB's approach to development policy has – in recent years at least – differed little from that of the World Bank and IMF. Much recent commentary on the ADB's strategies has accordingly emphasized their conformity to the neo-liberal agenda (Cruz-del Rosario 2008).

In dealing with fragile states, the ADB has operated mainly through the Asian Development Fund (ADF), one of the ADB's special funds. The ADF was established in 1973 to provide grants and loans at concessional rates to the ADB's poorest member countries and in this respect is very similar to the International Development Association (IDA), the concessional lending arm of the World Bank. Not all ADF-eligible countries are formally classified by the ADB as fragile states – or 'weakly performing countries' (WPCs) to use the ADB's preferred term. But to the extent that the ADB has released information about its classifications, a number of ADF-eligible countries appear to have been classified as fragile states, including two in Southeast Asia: Timor Leste and Lao Peoples' Democratic Republic (ADB 2007: 11).

The ADB's approach to fragile states is 'grounded' in its annual performance-based allocation (PBA) exercise (ADB 2007: 10). The PBA exercise seeks to create an incentive structure that encourages poor countries (in particular those deemed to be fragile states) to improve their policies and institutions by directing ADF resources to those that have 'appropriate policies and institutions' (as interpreted by the ADB) and 'the ability to use ADF funds effectively' (ADB 2007: 10). The ADB assesses the appropriateness of countries' policies and institutions through the Country Performance Assessment (CPA) process which scores countries in relation to five criteria:

(i) the quality of [a country's] macroeconomic management, (ii) the coherence of its structural policies, (iii) the degree to which its policies and institutions promote equity and inclusion, (iv) the quality of its governance and public sector management, and (v) the performance of the ADF loan portfolio in the country.

The first four of these criteria are assessed using the World Bank's Country Policy and Institutional Assessment (CPIA) questionnaire and guidelines. The CPIA rates low-income countries on the basis of 20 equally weighted criteria that fall into four broad categories: economic management; structural policies; policies for social inclusion; and public sector management and institutions (Alexander 2004: 17).

The use of the CPIA invests the ADB's approach to engaging with fragile states with a strong neo-liberal orientation. The World Bank (2007: 1) argues that the CPIA provides an objective measure of how 'conducive' a country's policy and institutional framework is to 'fostering poverty reduction, sustainable growth, and the effective use of development assistance'. However, its assessment criteria are broadly consistent with the neo-liberal agenda, in particular its currently dominant expression in the form of the 'post-Washington consensus' (PWC) (Carroll 2007: 133; van Waeyenberge 2009). The criteria that make up the CPIA emphasize the importance of deregulated markets, conservative macroeconomic and fiscal policies, and public administration and other institutional structures that provide transparency and accountability, all of which are elements of the PWC. In essence, it constitutes a device for measuring how closely a country adheres to the neo-liberal model.

The ADB argues that its fragile states strategy is governed by a concern to maximize the effectiveness of its aid by supporting and nurturing country ownership (ADB 2007: 14). It further argues that donors need to 'take context as the starting point', the first of the OECD's principles of good international engagement in fragile states, and to calibrate action and analysis 'to particular country circumstances' (ADB 2007: 7), both ideas that are consistent with the country ownership principle. However, by disciplining fragile states that stray from the neo-liberal pathway, the PBA system arguably undermines the country ownership principle. Rather than permitting the governments of fragile states to exercise leadership with respect to their development strategies, it effectively punishes them if they fail to adopt neo-liberal policies and institutions by denying them access to the ADF's concessional resources, as the ADB (2007: 10) itself acknowledges: 'Given that PBA is based on performance assessment, WPCs are likely to receive progressively lower allocations as performance deteriorates.' It is hard to see how such an approach 'supports' and 'nurtures' country ownership, as the ADB claims.

Implications for development trajectories and aid effectiveness

This chapter has suggested that there has been a conflict between donors' expressed commitment to country ownership, as evidenced by their signing of the *Paris Declaration* and the *Accra Agenda for Action*, and the political imperative they face to promote neo-liberal policies in developing countries, with the result that they have made only a half-hearted attempt to promote country ownership of the development process in developing countries and those in Southeast Asia in particular. The two donor strategies examined in the chapter – the World Bank's strategy for engaging with Indonesia for 2009–12 and the ADB's strategy for engaging with fragile states – suggest that where these two agendas have been in conflict with one another, donors have subordinated the principle of country ownership to that of promoting neo-liberal policy and institutional reform.

What are the implications of this for development trajectories in developing countries and in particular those in Southeast Asia? Does it mean that these countries will be locked into a neo-liberal path to development – or underdevelopment if, as some have argued, these policies are detrimental to development (see, for instance, Chang and Grabel 2004)? And what does it mean in terms of the effective use of aid within the region?

There can be little doubt that donors' continued promotion of neo-liberal policies and institutions increases structural pressure on aid recipient countries to adopt and implement these policies and institutions. While aid has shrunk considerably as a proportion of global capital flows over the past few decades, donors nevertheless continue to have considerable structural power in their own right, particularly in aid dependent countries. At the same time, they have been able to leverage the structural power of other controllers of mobile capital (e.g. financial investment houses, hedge funds, international lenders, footloose manufacturers), whose policy agenda is broadly similarly to theirs. However, donors and other controllers of mobile capital are not as powerful as some writers – particularly those who operate from a dependency theory perspective – assume. For instance, numerous studies on the politics of economic reform in Southeast Asia have suggested that domestic political and social forces in developing countries that are opposed to neo-liberalism have often had the ability to successfully counter pressure from donors and other mobile capital controllers for neo-liberal reform because of their occupancy of the state apparatus or close connections to those who occupy the state apparatus. In particular, it is argued that politico-bureaucratic elements who occupy the state apparatus and their corporate clients have been able to block or hijack economic reform processes at either the policy-making or implementation stages, leading to the perseverance of oligarchic systems of capitalism in which political authority remains concentrated in the hands of a small number of politico-business groups (Rosser 2002; Robison and Hadiz 2004; Rodan et al. 2006). Such outcomes have prevailed even in weak and fragile states where the structural power of donors is greater than in other developing countries because of these states' relatively high need for aid, with Cambodia being perhaps the best Southeast Asian example in this respect (Hughes 2006). Indeed, the World Bank's acceptance of government leadership in the Indonesian case can be seen as recognition by donors of the limits of their structural leverage as a force for promoting neo-liberal reform – why not express support for the notion of government leadership if you have no hope of achieving donor leadership? The consequence in terms of developing countries' development trajectories is to leave significant scope for the persistence of forms of capitalism that vary from the neo-liberal model and, in the Southeast Asian context in particular, take an oligarchic form.

In terms of aid effectiveness, the implication of donors' decisions to privilege neo-liberalism over country ownership is that aid will only play a significant role in promoting development in

Southeast Asia to the extent that (i) aid recipient countries within the region choose to pursue neo-liberal policies independently of donor pressure – in other words, on the basis of a home-grown development strategy; *and* (ii) such policies are actually geared towards the achievement of development goals and not simply the short-term rent-seeking agendas of politico-bureaucratic and business elites. In the absence of these conditions, donors will find either that their attempts to promote neo-liberal reform are stymied by resistance from powerful domestic groups who have an interest in pursuing an alternative home-grown approach, or that they produce the sorts of perverse reform outcomes that contributed to the Asian economic crisis of the late 1990s – for instance, deregulated financial markets without the accompanying regulatory reforms required to ensure proper prudential supervision and regulation. Southeast Asia's long history of contesting neo-liberal reform suggests that these conditions are unlikely to be met but rather, as indicated above, that the region will remain characterized by oligarchic forms of capitalism. In this context, aid programmes driven by neo-liberal imperatives will cut against the grain, undermining country ownership and the emergence of the home-grown alternatives that, as the *Paris Declaration* indicates, are now widely viewed as holding the key to development and the effective use of aid.

Notes

1 On the role of donor countries in the governance of the World Bank and International Monetary Fund, for instance, see Woods (2000).
2 The Bank has long been the 'lead donor' in Indonesia in the sense that it has had more extensive engagement with the Indonesian government over policy issues than any other donor and has played a leading role at the joint government–donor meetings associated with the Inter-Governmental Group on Indonesia (IGGI)/Consultative Group on Indonesia (CGI). For instance, prior to the disbandment of the CGI in the mid-2000s, its annual country reports on Indonesia were always prepared in the lead-up to these meetings and were a key input into them.
3 On the nature of these traditions, see Chalmers and Hadiz (1997).
4 Interview with a World Bank official in the health section of the Jakarta office, Jakarta, October 2009. The Bank voiced its concerns – diplomatically, of course – about Siti Fadillah Supari's universal health scheme plans in Rokx *et al.* (2009).

References

ADB (Asian Development Bank) (n.d.a) *Fighting Poverty in the Asia Pacific*, Manila: ADB.
——(n.d.b) *Asian Development Bank Profile*, Manila: ADB.
——(2007) *Achieving Development Effectiveness in Weakly Performing Countries (The Asian Development Bank's Approach to Engaging with Weakly Performing Countries)*, Manila: ADB.
Alexander, N. (2004) 'Judge and jury: the World Bank's scorecard for borrowing governments', *Social Watch*: 17–23; available at: www.unpan1.un.org/intradoc/groups/public/.../UNPAN018179.pdf, (accessed 27 May 2010).
Amsden, A. (1989) *Asia's Next Giant: South Korea and Late Industrialization*, New York: Oxford University Press.
Bari, S. (ed.) (2009) *Kumpulan Wawancara Siti Fadillah Supari: Berkiblat Kata Hati Menggeser Tapal Batas Dunia*, Yogyakarta: SFS Fans Club and Lembaga Kajian Islam, dan Sosial.
Beeson, M. (2007) 'Competing capitalisms and neoliberalism: the dynamics of, and limits to, economic reform in the Asia-Pacific', in K. England and K. Ward (eds) *Neoliberalization: States, Networks, People*, Oxford: Blackwell, pp. 28–47.
Booth, D. (2008) 'Aid effectiveness after Accra: how to reform "the Paris Agenda"', Briefing Paper 39, Overseas Development Institute.
Buira, A. (2003) 'An analysis of IMF conditionality', in A. Buira (ed.) *Challenges to the World Bank and IMF: Developing Country Perspectives*, London: Anthem Press, pp. 55–90.
Burnside, C. and D. Dollar (2000) 'Aid, policies, and growth', *American Economic Review* 90 (4): 847–68.

Cammack, D., D. McLeod, A. Rocha Menocal with K. Christiansen (2006) *Donors and the 'Fragile States' Agenda: A Survey of Current Thinking and Practice*, London: Overseas Development Institute.

Carroll, T. (2007) 'The politics of the World Bank's socio-institutional neoliberalism', unpublished thesis, Murdoch University.

Chalmers, I. and V.R. Hadiz (eds) (1997) *The Politics of Economic Development in Indonesia: Contending Perspectives*, London: Routledge.

Chang, H. (2003) *Kicking Away the Ladder: Development Strategy in Historical Perspective*, London: Anthem.

Chang, H. and I. Grabel (2004) *Reclaiming Development: An Alternative Economic Policy Manual*, London and New York: Zed Books.

Cruz-del Rosario, T. (2008) 'Regionalism, governance and the ADB: a Foucauldian perspective, Centre on Asia and Globalisation, Working Paper 003, National University of Singapore.

Dent, C. (2008) 'The Asian Development Bank and developmental regionalism in East Asia', *Third World Quarterly* 29 (4): 767–86.

Diven, P. (2001) 'The domestic determinants of food aid policy', *Food Policy* 26: 455–74.

Dollar, D. and L. Pritchett (1998) *Assessing Aid: What Works, What Doesn't, and Why*, New York: Oxford University Press.

Easterly, W. (2006) *The White Man's Burden: Why the West's Efforts to Aid the Rest Have Done So Much Ill and So Little Good*, New York: Penguin

Eurodad (2008) *Turning the Tables: Aid and Accountability Under the Paris Framework*, Brussels: Eurodad.

Hameiri, S. (2008) 'Risk management, neo-liberalism and the securitisation of the Australian aid program', *Australian Journal of International Affairs* 62 (3): 357–71.

——(2009) 'The region within: RAMSI, the Pacific Plan and new modes of governance in the South Pacific', *Australian Journal of International Affairs* 63 (3): 348–60.

Harvey, D. (2005) *A Brief History of Neoliberalism*, Oxford: Oxford University Press.

Hout, W. (2004) 'Political regimes and development assistance: the political economy of aid selectivity', *Critical Asian Studies* 36 (4): 591–613.

Hughes, C. (2006) 'Cambodia', *IDS Bulletin* 37 (2): 67–78.

Irawan, A., Eriyanto, L. Djani and A. Sunaryanto (2004) *Mendagangkan Sekolah*, Jakarta: Indonesia Corruption Watch.

Jayasuriya, K. and A. Rosser (2001) 'Economic orthodoxy and the East Asian crisis', *Third World Quarterly* 22 (3): 381–96.

Lancaster, C. (2007) *Foreign Aid: Diplomacy, Development, Domestic Politics*, Chicago, IL and London: University of Chicago Press.

Minogue, M. (2002) 'Power to the people? Good governance and the reshaping of the state', in U. Kothari and M. Minogue (eds) *Development Theory and Practice: Critical Perspectives*, Houndmills: Palgrave, pp. 117–35.

OECD-DAC (2005) *Paris Declaration on Aid Effectiveness: Ownership, Harmonisation, Alignment, Results and Mutual Accountability*, Paris: OECD High-Level Forum, 28 February–2 March; available at: www.oecd.org/document/18/0,3343,en_2649_3236398_35401554_1_1_1_1,00.html (accessed 3 September 2008).

——(2008a) *Accra Agenda for Action*; available at: www.accrahlf.net/WBSITE/EXTERNAL/ACCRAEXT/0,contentMDK:21690826~menuPK:64861649~pagePK:64861884~piPK:64860737~theSitePK:4700791,00.html (accessed 4 February 2009).

——(2008b) *2008 Survey on Monitoring the Paris Declaration: Making Aid More Effective by 2010*, Paris: OECD.

Robison, R. (1986) *Indonesia: The Rise of Capital*, Sydney: Allen and Unwin.

Robison, R. and V.R. Hadiz (2004) *Reorganising Power in Indonesia: The Politics of Oligarchy in an Age of Markets*, London: Routledge.

Rodan, G. (1989) *The Political Economy of Singapore's Industrialization*, London: Macmillan.

Rodan, G., K. Hewison and R. Robison (eds) (2006) *The Political Economy of South-East Asia: Markets, Power and Contestation*, Melbourne: Oxford University Press.

Rokx, C., G. Schieber, P. Harimurti, A. Tandon and A. Somanathan (2009) *Health Financing in Indonesia: A Reform Road Map*, Washington, DC: World Bank.

Rosser, A. (2002) *The Politics of Economic Liberalisation in Indonesia: State, Market and Power*, Richmond: Curzon.

——(2006) 'Indonesia', *IDS Bulletin* 37 (2): 53–66.

——(2008) 'Neo-liberalism and the politics of Australian aid policy-making', *Australian Journal of International Affairs* 62 (3): 372–85.

Rosser, A., K. Roesad and D. Edwin (2005) 'Indonesia: the politics of inclusion', *Journal of Contemporary Asia* 35 (1): 53–77.

van Waeyenberge, E. (2009) 'Selectivity at work: country policy and institutional assessments at the World Bank', *European Journal of Development Research* 21 (5): 792–810.

Wade, R. (1990) *Governing the Market: Economic Theory and the Role of Government in East Asian Industrialization*, Princeton, NJ: Princeton University Press.

Williamson, J. (1990) *Latin American Adjustment: How Much has Happened?*, Washington, DC: Institute for International Economics.

Winters, J. (1996) *Power in Motion: Capital Mobility and the Indonesian State*, Ithaca, NY: Cornell University Press.

Woods, N. (2000) 'The challenge of good governance for the IMF and World Bank themselves', *World Development* 28 (5): 823–41.

World Bank (2007) *Country Policy and Institutional Assessments: 2007 Assessment Questionnaire*; available at: http://siteresources.worldbank.org/IDA/Resources/CPIA2007Questionnaire.pdf (accessed 9 February 2009).

——(2009) *Investing in Indonesia's Institutions for Inclusive and Sustainable Development*, Washington, DC: World Bank.

Zimmermann, F. (2008) *Home-Owned and Home-Grown: Development Policies That Can Work?* Policy Insights No. 71, Paris: OECD Development Centre.

12

THE JUDICIALIZATION OF MARKET REGULATION IN SOUTHEAST ASIA

*John Gillespie**

Introduction

Judicialization – the shift towards governance through legal rules, legal professionals and judicial power – offers promising insights into the architecture of regulatory systems and the complex processes through which they are being transformed (or not) in Southeast Asia. It is important to understand whether courts are acquiring discretionary power at the expense of the executive in Southeast Asia, because for decades developmental states in this region have relied heavily on executive power to order markets (Jayasuriya 2004).

This chapter investigates whether, in promoting politically neutral courts in Southeast Asia, international donor agencies are privileging one version of judicialization over other possible models that allow courts more flexibility in applying the law. It focuses in particular on attempts in Indonesia and Vietnam to create a constitutional court with powers to check state intervention in the marketplace. This analysis is used to assess what types of judicialization are suited to the fragmented markets and polycentric regulatory conditions found in Indonesia and Vietnam.

Southeast Asia has a complex history of judicialization. In most countries in the region judicialization reached a zenith during the nineteenth century when colonial authorities attempted to extend central control over military, criminal and economic activities (Hooker 1975). With few exceptions, other areas of social interaction such as family and inheritance relationships remained embedded in relational matrixes that bound clans and villages together with personal and primarily sentimental relationships. Following de-colonization, the power of judges relative to other state regulators has followed three basic patterns. In Malaysia and Singapore, judicial power, especially in the administrative and civil rights arenas, slowly declined as the developmental state gained momentum (Lee 2004). Subject to periodic reversals, and starting from a low base, judicialization in the Philippines (Pangalangan 2004) and Thailand (Munger 2009) has increased across all fronts. As we shall see, in Vietnam and Indonesia the story is somewhat different. Post-colonial regimes at first actively dismantled colonial legal systems and then, more recently, began building them up again. Before examining these stories in more detail, it is necessary to explain the concept of judicialization in more depth.

Judicialization and different models of economic regulation

Judicialization is a broad term that covers different types of regulatory phenomena, each with its own distinctive development implications (Dowdle 2009). The literature discussing judicialization in

Asia is dominated by two tropes. The first is that Southeast Asian countries are developmental states in which high-performing bureaucrats use grants of discretionary power to plan the economy (Hira 2004). Rather than directly determining market outcomes, they guided markets towards certain outcomes. Debate continues about whether this portrait accurately depicts the interaction between the states and markets, but most commentators agree that overall the bureaucrats played a decisive role in selecting economic winners and courts played a comparatively minor regulatory role.

By the late 1990s, and especially following the East Asian Financial Crisis in 1997, developmentalism lost some of its appeal. As the corruption cases against Soeharto and other state regulators mounted, a consensus emerged that, along with factors such as volatile global capital, crony capitalism played a major role in the crisis (Wade 1998). International donor agencies, especially the World Bank and IMF, which were never comfortable with the developmental state, led the charge in advocating the 'rule of law' to remedy the problems (Kennedy 2006).

The second dominant trope, which has been promoted strongly by international development agencies such as the World Bank and United Nations Development Programme, called on governments in the region to develop politically neutral legal apparatus (especially courts) to promote social cohesion, co-operation and stability, and above all else to check executive power with universal legal rules (Trebilcock and Daniels 2008: 1–28). This variation of 'rule of law' was modelled closely on an Anglo-American template that placed judicialization and judicial review at the pinnacle of the regulatory system (Trubek and Santos 2006).

In formulating legal development programmes, international donor agencies such as the World Bank and Asian Development Bank were strongly influenced by modernization theory, then in vogue among development theorists, which drew on a reductive reading of Weber that stripped away the nuance and focused on his pronouncements about the role of 'rational' legal systems in the emergence of modern capitalism. In this view, the rule of law reforms in Southeast Asia could be instrumentalized by transplanting U.S. or European institutions and substantive law ('international best practice'). Law became a positivist instrument to engineer social change.

International donors during the 1980s and 1990s sought to correct earlier failures, which they believed had underestimated the self-interest of recipient states. For example the World Bank depicted the states as the source of all economic problems. Instead of an instrumentalized Weber they prescribed neo-liberalism. They aimed to roll back the state and placed their faith in markets to produce development objectives. These neo-liberal policies became known as the 'Washington Consensus'. They aimed to streamline regulatory procedures, maintain small budget deficits, broaden the tax base, end state subsidies, allow the market to set interest rates, liberalize trade and foreign investment, privatize state-owned enterprises, abolish impediments to foreign direct investment, and guarantee secure property rights. They also regarded judicial neutrality as a prerequisite for effective courts and economic reform (Jayasuriya and Rosser 2001).

When deregulation did not produce the desired economic growth, donors turned to New Institutional Economics, which offered a more nuanced account of development without fundamentally disrupting neo-liberal objectives. By the mid 1990s, the state was no longer considered predatory and venal, but 'the key institution to ensure that the market functions properly' (Harrison 2004). By the late 1990s donors ceased talking about macroeconomic fundamentals and instead spoke of 'governance' and the importance of 'good governance'. They advocated post-Washington consensus reforms in which the private economy no longer entirely dominated and other objectives such as human rights and poverty alleviation gained prominence (Newton 2008). What remained unchanged in the policies was belief in the capacity of 'neutral' courts to protect property rights and stimulate economic development.

187

That international donor agencies presented governments in Southeast Asia with an historically contingent judicial model is revealed by briefly reviewing the development of judicialization. In pre-modern England and America the judiciary was the main constitutional agency used to formulate regional policies (Skowronek 1982). The legislature and executive lacked the organizational capacity to gather information and formulate regulatory policies at the provincial level – their power was remote from the everyday decisions made by most people. The absence of central power, coupled with judicial powers to draw from historical cases – the precedent powers – gave courts an unparalleled capacity to develop policy and regulate local affairs in areas left unregulated by the central state. Far from being politically neutral, courts were actively engaged in policy development in sensitive political areas.

The politically neutral courts currently promoted by international donor agencies only began to emerge with the development of the welfare state and administrative bureaucratization in post-World War I Europe and America (Majone 1994). Central administrative organs needed to expand in size and competency and began to more actively oversee local governance. At the same time industrialization and marketization increasingly harmonized and standardized markets (Jessop 2001). This in turn increased the capacity of bureaucrats to apply central regulations uniformly across the nation – a development that is now termed the 'regulatory state'. As integrated markets flattened regional difference, there was less need for courts to flexibly apply policy at the local level and the preferred role of courts changed from active policy makers to politically neutral agencies applying legislative rules – the 'rule of law' model promoted by international development agencies.

More recently there is evidence that shifting consumer demand and global production chains are fragmenting markets in industrialized countries (Deyo *et al.* 2001). As a result the harmonized and standardized regulatory environments that supported the 'rule of law' model are eroding. As ideas, standards and practices from the rest of the world begin to flow into western communities, central state rules and precepts that for generations constituted a 'rule of law' may no longer provide viable solutions to local problems. It is possible that as these local regulatory environments become more complex and opaque, the role of judges will change from the neutral arbiters preferred by the 'rule of law' model to the more proactive policy makers of the past. In these circumstances courts will need to engage more actively with local constituencies to craft legal solutions that fit local probes. All this suggests that in promoting politically neutral courts in Southeast Asia, international donor agencies are privileging one version of judicialization that evolved under particular regulatory conditions in Europe and the United States over other possible models that allow courts more flexibility in applying the law. The case studies considered below explore whether different types of judicialization are more suited to the fragmented markets and polycentric regulatory conditions found in Indonesia and Vietnam. But first it is useful to set the scene by briefly considering the colonial legacy of judicial rule in Southeast Asia.

A brief review of judicialization in Southeast Asia

Formal courts and professional lawyers played a marginal role in pre-colonial Southeast Asia, but colonization excited a rapid period of judicialization (Hooker 1975). Yet even at the height of colonization, courts and imported western legality co-existed in an uneasy alliance with pre-colonial governance systems – creating a type of legal pluralism (Hooker 1978; Lev 2000: 13–32). The central legal regime, replete with the trappings of western legal systems, applied to Europeans and the small indigenous urban elites, while a highly decentralized regulatory system applied to the vast majority of the population who lived in rural villages. Even in Thailand, which escaped direct colonial rule, the state adopted a Law on the Organization of Court in 1908 that established a European-style judicial system in Bangkok, while leaving pre-modern rule in rural areas largely intact (Hooker 1978: 565–8).

For specifics about judicialization under colonial rule, consider Vietnam. Like other colonizing powers (for example the Dutch in the East Indies), the French colonial authorities used the central legal system primarily to maintain social order and serve colonial commercial interests (Osborne 1969: 78–9). Imported commercial laws (including contracts, land titling, *hypotheques* and company laws) were needed to regulate transplanted capitalist institutions. Since imported commercial law only applied to Europeans and assimilated Vietnamese, incongruities with indigenous commercial practices were considered irrelevant.

With the exception of the criminal code, French laws rarely touched the lives of most Vietnamese. Only a small number of Vietnamese ever elected to submit disputes to French law, and even then only for family or inheritance disputes (Young 1979: 772). French-appointed village chiefs filtered central laws and administrative edicts through pre-modern traditional and neo-Confucian precepts (Grossheim 2004: 55). Most conflicts were mediated by village elders, neighbourhood and merchant associations and family hierarchies that operated outside the juridical orbit (Nguyen Duc Nginh 1993: 352–5). Officially mediated conflicts exposed disputants and by extension their families and village to loss of proper virtue and not infrequent demands for bribes.

At the close of the colonial era, well-developed judicial systems flourished throughout Southeast Asia in colonial urban centres, while in the rural periphery village regulation only interacted with the criminal courts. Following independence, the new governments in many countries, with the exception of Malaysia, Singapore and the Philippines (Hooker 1975: 143–58; Pangalangan 2004), sought to discredit colonial rule and stamp their authority over the legal system. It became fashionable to speak of post-colonial law, for example *hukum revolusi* (revolutionary law) in Indonesia, which emphasized bureaucratic regulation at the expense of judicial review (Lev 2000: 215–44).

With some limited exceptions, in general the power of courts to check executive regulation of the economy rapidly declined in post-colonial societies. Nowhere was this more noticeable than in Vietnam, where the court system became a tool of socialist instruction (Nicholson 2007: 124–37). Although not as extreme as in Vietnam, the executive in other Southeast Asian states quickly gained the upper hand. Malaysia and Singapore, for example, began the post-colonial period with a judiciary that was prepared to check bureaucratic power. But judicial jurisdictional and discretionary powers to review the executive were slowly restricted at the same time that political processes imbued the courts with a sense of judicial restraint (Lee 2004: 235–44; Lin 2009: 302–6). Intriguingly it is courts in Indonesia, one of the first countries to suppress judicial review, that are now showing considerable progress towards the judicialization of governance.

It is difficult to neatly summarize the trajectory for judicialization in Southeast Asia, because the regulatory conditions vary considerably across the region, and also within countries. For example, judicial powers may rapidly expand in the commercial area, but decline or remain static in politically sensitive areas such as administrative or civil rights law. The following studies from the region illustrate this important dynamic.

Constitutional courts in Indonesia

Constitutional courts are a growing global phenomenon. The power to declare legislation, and in some cases government and political decisions, unconstitutional has spread around the world and by 2005 over three-quarters of world states had adopted some type of constitutional review (Horowitz 2006). Much of the current enthusiasm for constitutional courts in Southeast Asia is attributable to the high-profile judicial reforms in Japan, Korea and Taiwan (Ginsburg 2003). For example, since its introduction in 1987, the Constitutional Court in Korea has heard over 10,000 cases – making it one of the most active constitutional courts in the world (Chan Jin Kim 2006).

The recent emergence of active constitutional courts in Thailand and Indonesia challenges the notion that this type of judicialization is most likely to emerge in economically developed countries such as those found in North East Asia (Butt 2006; Ginsburg 2009). By the end of 2008 the Constitutional Court (*Mahkamah Konstitusi*) in Indonesia had handled 156 review cases concerning seventy-four different laws (Ginsburg 2009). The next section examines a series of constitutional cases in Indonesia to assess the capacity of the Constitutional Court to compete with the executive in shaping economic policy.

Establishing the Indonesian Constitutional Court

In 2001 the MPR (or People's Consultative Assembly), Indonesia's highest legislature, amended the 1945 Constitution to establish a constitutional court (Harman 2007). Although law reformers for decades had argued for this court, it was not until the *reformasi* period following the fall of President Soeharto in 1998 that a window of opportunity arose (Ellis 2007). Members of the MPR were reacting against the policy of *integralism* that emerged during the Soeharto period that elevated a politicized notion of the public good above the law. After decades of abuse by the Soeharto regime, the normally divided parties in the MPR formed a consensus about the need to prevent legislative and executive agencies from violating constitutional norms and principles (Kawamura 2003). They concluded that constitutional guarantees are meaningless without an independent body with powers to review the constitutionality of legislation and executive action (Ellis 2007).

To the surprise of many observers, the newly established Constitutional Court quickly showed that it was prepared to reinterpret government policy. For those with longer memories the Court's tenacity was not unprecedented (Lev 2000). At the zenith of the Soeharto regime, the Administrative Court amazed commentators by ruling that a minister had acted unlawfully in cancelling the publishing permit of *Tempo* – a magazine that dared to criticize state policy. The question is whether the new Constitutional Court of the post-Soeharto era would become a core component of the regulatory framework.

Reinterpreting government economic policy

At the height of the East Asian Financial Crisis in 1998 the Indonesian government agreed to privatize some key industries, such as water and electricity supply, in return for financial support from the IMF (McLeod 2000). A wide array of NGOs and other social organizations opposed the conditions attached to these loans, arguing that privatization was likely to increase fees and reduce services for the rural poor.

Groups of concerned citizens and NGOs petitioned the Constitutional Court to decide whether government privatization policies were compatible with the preamble and article 33 of the Constitution. These provisions were originally enacted in 1945 to give the government powers over key economic sectors to curb market behaviour that might exploit the economically vulnerable. The petitioners asked the Court to infer from the Constitution a general principle that legislation should 'protect all Indonesians and their native land' and to order the government not to privatize key service industries.[1] This issue struck at the heart of very powerful interests and would test the political viability of the new court.

The Electricity Privatization Case

Implementing the conditions imposed by the IMF's loan, the DPR (House of Representatives) in 2002 enacted Law No. 20 on Electricity Supply to privatize the generation and supply of electricity. Later that year a group of NGOs representing rural associations petitioned the Constitutional Court to strike down the law. They argued that electricity generation is a key economic sector and the Constitution requires the government to maintain control (*dikuasai*) to protect the rural poor. Displaying a remarkable degree of assertiveness, the Court decided in 2004 to annul the Electricity Law 2002 and reinstate the Electricity Law No. 15 of 1985. This Soeharto-era law gave the government a monopoly over electricity generation. The Court reasoned that the Electricity Law 2002 was inconsistent with 'the soul and spirit of Article 32 (2)'. It went on to conclude that electricity generation is essential to the Indonesian economy and the lives of the people and should remain under government control.

Using its powers to examine witnesses, the Court compelled state officials to answer the claims made by the NGOs that private competition would disadvantage the rural poor by concentrating electricity supply in wealthy urban areas. It also took evidence from expert witnesses that seemed to rebut government claims that privatization and competition invariably produce greater efficiencies that drive prices down and advantage the poor.

The Court was especially concerned with the provisions in the Electricity Law 2002 that 'unbundled' the generation of electricity by allowing private companies to compete with the established state-owned generators. It viewed privatization as a threat to state-owned companies because private, especially foreign-owned, companies were in a better position to attract inexpensive international capital and compete in open markets. The Court inferred from article 33 a general principle that gave the Indonesian people power to maintain 'state control' over 'important branches of production'.

In defiance of the Court's ruling the government issued Regulation No. 3 2005 that gave private enterprises rights to generate electricity. Part A of the Regulation makes its intention clear: 'In the framework of increasing the availability of electricity for the public interest, the roles of state owned enterprises, regional state owned enterprises, the private sector, community groups and individuals must be increased.' The Court could not strike down the regulation because it lacked constitutional power to review subordinate legislation issued by the executive. Meanwhile the Supreme Court refused to use its powers of review to strike down the regulation as unconstitutional and the private generation and supply of electricity commenced soon after the regulation was promulgated (Assegraf 2006).

A few months later the Court ruled on the constitutionality of Law No. 22 on Oil and Gas Exploration and Law No. 7 on Water Resources 2004, both sought to privatize key service sectors (Setianto 2005; Mova Al'Afghani 2006). The Court struck down Law No. 22 because it allowed widespread privatization in oil and gas exploration, but upheld the Water Resources Law 2004 on the grounds that it only permitted partial privatization. By requiring majority state ownership, the Law ensured that the government maintained 'control' over an 'important branch of production'.

It is possible to identify a range of political, legal and economic reasons for the expansion of judicial power in Indonesia. As previously noted, the MPR had a political motive for giving the Constitutional Court broad-ranging review powers. After decades of flagrant executive abuses and bureaucratic corruption under the Soeharto regime, a consensus emerged that a body removed from politics should oversee executive powers. The 'rule of law' model with its politically neutral courts seemed to offer a solution. Yet by any measure the Court's decision to overrule a highly sensitive economic policy developed by the executive goes well beyond conventional understandings of politically neutral courts. To explain this excursion into policy making, it is necessary to look beyond a textual reading of the privatization cases, and examine the political and social context in which the judgments were made.

The Court took aim at the authoritarian character of *integralism* – the doctrine that animated Soeharto's developmental state. First they stressed that in the post-Soeharto era citizens (not just state officials) have the right to participate in policy making by challenging the constitutionality of government legislation. Then they acted on this principle by finding constitutional constraints on the executive's powers to privatize key industries and pursue a neo-liberal deregulatory agenda.

The Court also questioned the legitimacy of the conditions attached to the IMF bailout. They constructed a narrative from witness statements suggesting that the IMF's conditions were tainted by duress, because the government accepted them when Indonesia faced bankruptcy and was in no position to reflect the will of the people. Never far below the surface was the concern that privatization gave transnational corporations access to key industries without an obligation to protect the most socially vulnerable.

In addition, the Court used legal reasoning to transform a political and economic dispute between the government and NGOs about privatization into a legal contest framed according to constitutional doctrine. The wide press coverage and popular support for constitutional review legitimized the use of legal processes to resolve an otherwise intractable political and economic dispute (Stockmann 2007: 63). From this perspective, the Court has strengthened and expanded the role of law in resolving economic and social problems – and in the process it has promoted judicialization.

To some extent the Court's inability to constitutionally compel the government to follow its rulings was off-set by its expressive power (Metz 1994). The very act of reviewing legislation influenced the way people think about laws and constitutional constraints over executive power. Although meanings are given to laws in multiple sites inside and outside the formal legal system, the Court is now understood to play a special role in determining the meaning of laws. It enabled NGOs to harness this expressive power to campaign against neo-liberal privatization and prevent the government from abandoning the rural poor to market forces.

In some respects the Court resembles the politically neutral judicial agencies promoted by international donor agencies. It resisted government pressure by allowing citizens to check the unconstitutional exercise of state power. But it has attracted considerable criticism (Butt and Lindsey 2009: 278–86) for overstepping its powers in formulating economic regulatory policy. Critics claim that it became a political actor, departing from the 'rule of law' script, dictating in detail what legislatures and executives must or must not do, blocking the popular will and arrogating power that it was never intended to exercise.

The Indonesian case is by no means unusual. Other newly established constitutional courts in transitional societies, such as the Hungarian Constitutional Court, have been, by western liberal standards, extremely assertive in directing the legislature and executive (Lane Scheppele 1999: 81–7). One reason for this behaviour is that newly established constitutional courts in developing societies, unlike their counterparts in mature constitutional societies, need to fill a policy void left vacant by decades of authoritarian rule. In this sense the Court in Indonesia may be seen to act like courts in pre-industrial Europe in exercising considerable policy-making powers in fragmented and opaque regulatory conditions generated by Indonesia's private oligarchies. If the state agencies gain the upper hand and develop universal standards and policies to explain and solidify legislation, the Constitutional Court may voluntarily limit its discretionary powers.

Judicialization in Vietnam

Having recently emerged from decades of isolation from global capitalism and the 'rule of law' model, it is unsurprising that judicialization has taken a different turn in Vietnam from non-socialist Southeast Asia. During the period of high socialism (1954–86), the party and state primarily ruled through administrative fiat and campaigns led by party-controlled mass organizations (Ginsburgs 1979). The state did not pay attention to building a legal and judicial system until after *doi moi* (renovation) reforms in 1986 (Gillespie 2006: 62–7, 87–102; Sidel 2009: 5–30).

There is a long history in Vietnam of citizens using petitions to 'complain and denounce' (*giai quyet khieu nai to cao*) administrative abuses.[2] What is comparatively recent is the notion that public officials are, at least in principle, legally accountable for their actions. Plans to establish administrative courts with powers to review executive action were opposed by some party cadres who were appalled at the prospect of submitting to legal actions brought by ordinary citizens (Gillespie 2009: 218–21). As it turned out they had little to fear. On the rare occasions that courts rule against state officials, judges have been unable to enforce their decisions. Against this failed attempt to judicialize administrative governance, it is instructive to consider current debates about establishing a constitutional court – the next wave of judicialization in Vietnam.

Debating a constitutional court

Party leaders raise two main objections to establishing a constitutional court. The first is legalistic and offers no real political obstacle to change (Voice of Vietnam 1992). According to the Soviet 'unity-of-powers' (*tap trung quyen luc*) doctrine that was imported into Vietnam during the 1960s, the National Assembly (NA) is placed at the apex of constitutional power. Only the NA has the authority to interpret the Constitution. The doctrine does not contemplate a Montesquieuean 'separation of powers' with checks and balances among the state institutions, because this would give inferior state branches, such as the courts, powers to review the constitutionality of superior-level legislation.

The second objection is more substantive as it ponders whether constitutional courts might constrain communist power. Senior party leaders recall the historical socialist concern that capitalists may use courts as 'coercive tools to exploit other classes' (Vo Tri Hao and Ha Thu Thuy 2008: 25). They wonder whether 'exploiters' such as foreign investors and domestic capitalists will use a constitutional court to undermine core socialist values embedded in legislation such as preserving the leading economic role for state-owned enterprises. In their view judicial review has the potential to disrupt the socialist project and check party leadership of the state, outcomes that party leaders will not seriously consider.

The group of legal academics at the National University and Institute of State and Law, who advocated the establishment of a constitutional court, respond with three main arguments (Tran Ngoc Duong 2008: 34–8). First, they claim that the status quo is not working because in fifty years the NA has not once interpreted the Constitution. Second, the NA is not the appropriate body to perform this role. If NA delegates both formulate legislation and then review the constitutionality of their own decisions, they are acting as both 'player and umpire' (Bui Xuan Duc 2007: 10–18). Third, they argue that the Constitution needs to reflect the changing role of law in society. In the command economy only party and state officials needed to understand and interpret the law, whereas in the mixed-market economy citizens and corporations maintain horizontal legal relationships and have a direct stake in the legal system. Private actors need a court to strike down unconstitutional laws (Author interview 2006a).

Reforms aiming to establish a constitutional court form part of the broader law reform agenda. For the present, party leaders seem receptive to arguments promoting a constitutional court to reduce inconsistencies among superior and subordinate legislation issued by the executive (Sidel 2009: 270–10). This envisages a co-ordinating function for the Constitution. They are much less sympathetic to a 'rule of law' project that would give citizens powers to challenge the constitutionality of policies underlying legislation or to circumscribe party powers with laws.

Although the party is clearly uncomfortable with giving judges powers to interpret and unify laws on a national scale, it actively supports agencies that exercise quasi-judicial powers to resolve sensitive social issues. For example, government agencies throughout Vietnam call in the Government Inspectorate (Thanh Tra Chinh Phu), a state investigation agency, to resolve intractable complaints about administrative abuse (Editing Group 2007).[3] Their method of resolving these 'hard' cases is well illustrated by disputes about the compensation paid by the government for land compulsorily acquired for new infrastructure developments (Nguyen Van Thanh and Dinh Van Minh 2004: 83–100). As Vietnam rapidly industrializes, state authorities are increasingly acquiring land for new factories, roads and government buildings. In some instances government inspectors have uncovered malfeasance by state land officials – clear legal violations. More typically, however, complaints relate to policy matters such as inadequate compensation values set by provincial authorities or other factors that do not directly violate the law.

The inspectorate soon exhausts legal resources in resolving these complaints and turns to 'reason and sentiment in carrying out the law' (ly va tinh trong viec chap hanh phap luat) – a decision-making practice that formulates outcomes without technically and rigidly applying the law (Author interview 2006b). In land compensation cases the inspectorate must balance at least three competing policy interests: claims for more compensation by citizens, the local government's desire to preserve the state budget and the national interest served by investment projects. They appeal to hop ly (reasonableness), backed by a mix of political, moral and legal norms, to persuade local authorities and complainants to compromise. Although the outcomes aim for situational justice, they may eventually form the basis for crafting a universal set of principles that could apply to other cases.

A striking feature about this system is the ineffectiveness of law in resolving grievances. Law is only decisive where government officials have clearly acted outside their authorized powers. In 'hard' cases that are not directly addressed by the law, the inspectorate is encouraged by the party to intervene, even if this means expanding their powers well beyond the categories of complaint that the state is prepared to legally recognize. In this way inspectors act like judges in pre-industrial England; they formulate local-level policy in areas where the uniform state laws are too inflexible to provide plausible solutions.

What is instructive about Vietnam is that judicialization is proceeding, but not in the ways envisaged by international donor agencies promoting the 'rule of law' model. In Vietnam's fragmented and opaque political and economic landscape, it is unrealistic to expect uniform central laws to provide authoritative solutions throughout the country. Because courts are expected to find legal solutions to cases, they are comparatively ineffective in resolving difficult cases that require the interpretation of legislative policy. With the exception of certain civil law complaints, the number of court cases has plateaued (Nicholson 2007: 260–6). Some commentators (Do Thi Ngoc 2001) believe that after an initial enthusiasm for judicialization, both the government and public have lost faith in the capacity of a centralized and professionalized judiciary to deliver just outcomes.

To check executive power, the party has given other state agencies such as the Government Inspectorate quasi-judicial powers to resolve cases without strictly applying the law. Whether this is a sign of de-judicialization or finding new and more appropriate forms of judicialization is debatable. What is clear, however, is that Vietnam is unlikely in the short to medium term to follow Indonesia and Thailand in establishing constitutional courts with broad-ranging policy powers.

Conclusion: assessing the prospects for judicialization in the region

Courts are only one means of resolving disputes and addressing social tension and even in western countries they are generally the forums of last resort. The current promotion of courts by international development agencies as the panacea for moderating the excesses of developmental states seems to ignore the historical relationship of courts to other legal, social and economic institutions. The standardized markets and well-established commercial laws in Singapore and Malaysia are compatible with the 'neutral' law-bound courts promoted by international donors. This type of judicialization is most pronounced in the commercial arena where the courts are encouraged by the state to follow the 'rule of law' model and preserve property rights. The political elite are, however, reluctant to give courts review powers that may confine their political agendas within constitutional limits. As mentioned earlier, Kanishka Jayasuriya labels this type of narrow commercial judicialization 'economic constitutionalism' (Jayasuriya 1999: 119–21).

In contrast, a political culture is evolving in Indonesia and Thailand that seems to tolerate citizens using courts to check the constitutionality of government intervention into the marketplace. But strong opposition to this strand of liberal legality remains and it is perhaps premature to declare the success of this mode of judicialization. In the case of Indonesia the Constitutional Court filled a policy vacuum following the fall of the Soeharto regime and it may progressively lose power as the legislature and especially the executive regain authority. In Thailand the Constitutional Court prospered by serving the interests of the elite military and political networks standing behind the Democracy Party (Munger 2009). Whether the courts in Indonesia and Thailand can leverage the legitimacy they have generated to counteract political moves against them remains unclear. The situation in Vietnam more closely resembles the 'economic constitutionalism' in Malaysia and Singapore than the more liberal constitutionalism permitted in Indonesia and Thailand. Judicialization is slowly increasing in civil relationships in Vietnam, although courts are still unable to reliably protect commercial property rights against state and even private interference. But courts have not been given the political authority to meaningfully review the government's regulatory powers, and attempts by the state to push sensitive cases into the courts have resulted in aggrieved parties venting their frustration in the streets. As a result, the party is experimenting with investing government agencies, such as the Government Inspectorate, with quasi-judicial powers to flexibly resolve intractable disputes. These agencies function like courts in pre-industrial England because they formulate policy in areas the state cannot effectively regulate with central laws. Given the profound regional differences and opaque markets in Vietnam it may take decades before courts can use standardized central laws to compete with bureaucratic intervention in the marketplace.

Taking different pathways, courts and quasi-judicial agencies have made inroads into the power of bureaucrats to regulate the market in Southeast Asia. But this type of judicialization has not necessarily followed the 'rule of law' model promoted by international development agencies. Rather than becoming politically neutral in every social sphere, courts and quasi-judicial agencies in some social arenas openly enlist political support to counteract pushback by executive bodies and powerful private interests. Indeed, the history of court reform suggests that independence from politics is not necessarily the most effective way to foster judicialization (Friedman 1998: 333, 394–5). Judgments create winners and losers. Attacks on judicial agencies

195

from the executive are inevitable, especially during their vulnerable inception period. Since judicial agencies lack the 'purse and the sword' to defend themselves, to some extent they must rely on politics to expand into areas regulated by bureaucrats.

Notes

* The author gratefully acknowledges funding support from ARC discovery grant DP0985927.
1 See Constitutional Court Decision No 5/2003 reviewing Law No. 32/2002 on Broadcasting (the Broadcasting Law case).
2 *Hoang Viet Luat Le* Nguyen Dynasty 1815, article 380.
3 Law on Complaints and Denunciation 2004.

References

Assegraf, R. (2006) 'Judicial reform in Indonesia 1998–2006', in *Reforming Laws and Institutions in Indonesia: An Assessment* IDE-JETRO 2007; available at: www.ide.go.jp/English/Publish/Asedp/pdf/074_02.pdf (accessed 18 January 2008).

Author interview (2006a) 'Nguyen Dan Dung', Faculty of Law, Hanoi National University, June.

——(2006b) 'Nguyen Van Kim', Deputy Director Legal Department, Thanh Tra Chinh Phu (Government Inspectorate), Hanoi, October.

Bui Xuan Duc (2007) 'Ban Ve Mo Hinh Bao Hien o Viet Nam: Tu Giam Sat Boi Quoc Hoi Chuyen Sang Tai Phan Bang Toa An Hien Phap' [Discussion on the model of constitutional protection in Vietnam, from supervision by the National Assembly to judgment by Constitutional Court], *Tap Chi Luat Hoc* 8: 10–18.

Butt, S. (2006) 'Judicial review in Indonesia: between civil law and accountability? A study of constitutional court decisions 2003–6', unpublished thesis, University of Melbourne.

Butt, S. and T. Lindsey (2009) 'The people's prosperity? Indonesian constitutional interpretation, economic reform, and globalization', in J. Gillespie and R. Peerenboom (eds) *Regulation in Asia: Pushing Back on Globalization*, London: Routledge, pp. 270–95.

Chan Jin Kim (2006) 'Constitutional review in Korea', *Korean Journal of International and Comparative Law* 34: 29–71.

Deyo, F., R. Doner and E. Hershberg (eds) (2001) *Economic Governance and the Challenge of Flexibility in East Asia*, Lanham, MD: Rowman and Littlefield.

Do Thi Ngoc (2001) 'Tong Hop Cac Noi Dung Co Ban Cua Hoi Thao "Van Hoa Tu Phap"' [Major contents of the conference 'Judicial Culture'], *Thong Tin Hoa Hoc Phap Ly* 7: 13–32.

Dowdle, M. (2009) 'On the regulatory dynamics of judicialization: the promise and perils of exploring "judicialization" in East and Southeast Asia', in T. Ginsburg and A. Chen (eds) *Administrative Law and Governance in Asia: Comparative Perspectives,* London: Routledge.

Editing Group (2007) 'Project for Establishment of Administrative Tribunals in Vietnam', unpublished paper, Hanoi, 13 March.

Ellis, A. (2007) 'Indonesia's constitutional change reviewed', in R. McLeod and A. MacIntyre (eds) *Indonesia: Democracy and the Promise of Good Governance*, Singapore: Institute of South East Asian Studies, pp. 24–33.

Friedman, B. (1998) 'The history of the countermajoritarian difficulty, Part One: The road to judicial supremacy', *New York University Law Review* 73: 333–95.

Gillespie, J. (2006) *Transplanting Commercial Law Reform: Developing a 'Rule of Law' in Vietnam*, Aldershot, UK: Ashgate.

——(2009) 'The juridification of administrative complaints and review in Vietnam', in T. Ginsburg and A. Chen (eds) *Administrative Law and Governance in Asia*, London: Routledge, pp. 205–29

Ginsburg, T. (2003) *Judicial Review in New Democracies: Constitutional Courts in Asia*, Cambridge: Cambridge University Press.

——(2009) 'Constitutional afterlife: the continuing impact of Thailand's postpolitical constitution', *International Journal of Constitutional Law* 7 (1): 83–105.

Ginsburgs, G. (1979) 'The genesis of the people's procuracy in the Democratic Republic of Vietnam', *Review of Socialist Law* 5: 187–201.

Grossheim, M. (2004) 'Village government in pre-colonial Vietnam', in B.J. Tria Kerkvliet and D.G. Marr (eds) *Beyond Hanoi: Local Government in Vietnam*, Singapore: Institute of Southeast Asian Studies, pp. 54–89.

Harman, B. (2007) 'The role of the constitutional court in Indonesian legal reform', in *Reforming Laws and Institutions in Indonesia: An Assessment* IDE-JETRO 2007; available at: www.ide.go.jp/English/Publish/Asedp/pdf/074_02.pdf (accessed 18 January 2009).

Harrison, G 2004 *The World Bank and Africa: the Construction of Governance States*, London: Routledge.

Hira, Anil (2004) 'Governance crisis in Asia: developing a responsive regulation', in M. Ramesh and M. Howlett (eds) *Deregulation and its Discontents*, Cheltenham: Edward Elgar, pp. 13–25

Hooker, M.B. (1975) *Legal Pluralism: An Introduction to Colonial and Neo-Colonial Law*, Oxford: Clarendon Press.

——(1978) *A Concise Legal History of South East Asia*, Oxford: Clarendon Press.

Horowitz, D. (2006) 'Constitutional courts: a primer for decision makers', *Journal of Democracy* 17 (4): 125–37.

Jayasuriya, K. (1999) 'The rule of law and governance in the East Asian state', *The Australian Journal of Asian Law* 1 (2): 107–23.

——(ed.) (2004) *Asian Regional Governance: Crisis and Change*, New York: RoutledgeCurzon.

Jayasuriya, K. and A. Rosser (2001) 'Economic orthodoxy and the East Asian crisis', *Third World Quarterly* 22 (2): 381–96.

Jessop, B. (2001) 'Regulationist and autopoeticist reflections on Polanyi's account of market economics and the market society', *New Political Economy* 6 (2): 213–32.

Kawamura, K. (2003) 'Politics of the 1945 Constitution: democratization and its impact on political institutions in Indonesia', IDE Research Paper No. 3, Institute of Developing Economies (IDE-JETRO) September; available at: www.ide.go.jp/English/Publish/Papers/pdf/03_kawamura.pdf (accessed 18 January 2009).

Kennedy, D. (2006) 'Three globalizations of law and legal thought: 1850–2000', in D. Trubek and A. Santos (eds) *The New Law and Economic Development: A Critical Appraisal*, Cambridge: Cambridge University Press, pp. 19–73.

Lane Scheppele, K. (1999) 'The new constitutional court', *East European Constitutional Review* 8: 75–97.

Lee, H.P. (2004) 'Competing conceptions of rule of law in Malaysia', in R. Peerenboom (ed.) *Asian Discourses of Rule of Law*, London: Routledge, pp. 225–49

Lev, D. (2000) *Legal Evolution and Political Authority in Indonesia: Selected Essays*, The Hague: Kluwer Law International.

Lin, J. (2009) 'The judicialization of governance: the case of Singapore', in T. Ginsburg and A. Chen (eds) *Administrative Law and Governance in Asia: Comparative Perspectives*, London: Routledge, pp. 287–312.

McLeod, R. (2000) 'Soeharto's Indonesia: a better class of corruption', *Agenda: A Journal of Policy Analysis and Reform* 7 (2): 99–112.

Majone, G (1994) 'The rise of the regulatory state in Europe', *Western European Politics* 17: 77–101.

Metz, E. (1994) 'A new social constructionism for sociolegal studies', *Law and Society Review* 28: 1243–65.

Mova Al'Afghani, M. (2006) 'Constitutional court's review and the future of Water Law in Indonesia', *Law, Environment and Development Journal* 2 (1): 1–18.

Munger, F. (2009) 'Globalization, investing in law, and the careers of cause lawyers – taking on rights in Thailand', *New York Law School Law Review* 53: 745.

Newton, S. (2008) 'Law and development, law and economics and the fate of legal technical assistance', in J. Arnscheidt, B. Van Rooij and J. M. Otto (eds) *Lawmaking for Development: Explorations into the Theory and Practice of International Legislative Projects*, Leiden, Netherlands: Leiden University, pp. 23–52.

Nguyen Duc Nginh (1993) 'Markets and villages', in Pham Huy Le (ed.) *The Traditional Village in Vietnam*, Hanoi: Gioi, pp. 315–68.

Nguyen Van Thanh and Dinh Van Minh (2004) *Mot So Van De Ve Doi Moi Co Che Giai Quyet Khieu Kien Hanh Chinh O Viet Nam* [Some issues about renovating mechanisms for solving administrative complaints in Vietnam], Hanoi: Nha Xuat Ban Tu Phap, pp. 76–147

Nicholson, P. (2007) *Borrowing Court Systems: The Experience of Socialist Vietnam*, Lieden: Martinus Nijhoff.

Osborne, M. (1969) *The French Presence in Cochin China and Cambodia: Rule and Response (1859–1905)*, Ithaca, NY: Cornell University Press.

Pangalangan, P. (2004) 'The Philippines "People Power" constitution, rule of law, and the limits of liberal constitutionalism', in R. Peerenboom (ed.) *Asian Discourses of Rule of Law*, London: RoutledgeCurzon, pp. 371–84.

Setianto, B. (2005) 'Chaotic conflict of constitutional court ruling on Water Resources Law', *International NGO Forum on Indonesian Development Newsletter* 6.

Sidel, Mark (2009) *The Constitution of Vietnam: A Contextual Analysis*, Oxford: Hart.

Skowronek, S. (1982) *Building a New American State: The Expansion of National Administrative Capacities, 1877–1920*, New York: Cambridge University Press.

Stockmann, P. (2007) *The New Indonesia Constitutional Court*, Jakarta: Hanns Seidel Foundation Indonesia.

Tran Ngoc Duong (2008) 'Doi Moi Can Ban Ve Nhan Thuc Cung Nhu To Chuc Thuc Hien Viec Giai Thich Chinh Thuc Hien Phap Luat va Phap Lenh O Nuoc Ta Nuoc Ta Hien Nay' [Basic renovation of consciousness and implementing the official interpretation of the constitution, laws and ordinances in Viet Nam], *Tap Chi Nghien Cuu Lap Phap* 3: 34–8.

Trebilcock, M. and R. Daniels (2008) *Rule of Law Reform and Development: Charting the Fragile Path of Progress*, Cheltenham: Edward Elgar.

Trubek, D. and A. Santos (eds) (2006) *The New Law and Economic Development: A Critical Appraisal*, Cambridge: Cambridge University Press.

Vo Tri Hao and Ha Thu Thuy (2008) 'Nhung Van De Ly Luan Cua Viec Thanh Lap Tai Phan Hien Phap o Viet Nam' [Theoretical issues about establishing the Constitutional Court], *Tap Chi Nghien Cuu Lap Phap* 4: 23–26.

Voice of Vietnam 1992 'Vo Chin Ong report to the National Assembly', 25 March, in FBIS-EAS-92–060, 27 March.

Wade, R. (1998) 'The Asian debt-and-development crisis of 1997–?: causes and consequences', *World Development* 26 (8):1535–53.

Young, S. (1979) 'Vietnamese Marxism: transition in elite ideology', *Asian Survey* 19 (8): 770–9.

13

GLOBAL CAPITALISM, THE MIDDLE CLASS AND THE SHAPE OF THE NEW MEGA CITIES OF THE REGION

Chua Beng Huat

On 3 April 2010, in Bangkok, Thailand, the United Front for Democracy against Dictatorship (UDD), better known as the 'Red Shirts', consolidated the main camp of their mass street protest from the by now conventional symbolic locus of political protest of Ratchadamnoen Road, where they had been for more than a month, to the upscale or upmarket shopping and hotel district, Ratchaprasong. It is somewhat ironic that the Red Shirts were largely from the provincial rural poor in the north and northeast of the country, drawing resonance and support from the urban poor and other rural migrants to the city that fill the lower rungs of the urban service economies. The UDD's protest was to force the existing government, a coalition led by the Democratic Party, to resign and call fresh elections, on the grounds that the government was not popularly elected but had come to power on a parliamentary vote, after the duly elected government was dissolved by an act of the Constitutional Court.

This shift of protest venue from the location of historical political weight to the international financial and consumption and entertainment centre of the city replicates similar development elsewhere in Southeast Asia: for example, in the case of the People Power movement in Manila, discussed later in the chapter. The shift in the symbolic loci of power is itself a reflection of the transformation of the city from one which is defined by an industrial production economy to one increasingly determined by global financial capital and the service industry economy, in which the city government plays an entrepreneurial role in making the city commercial edifices to cater to both this rising middle class and the globally mobile, not only tourists but also expatriate managers and their families. The urban economy of the capital city is thus transformed into one that is dominated by the economy of real estate of corporate mega-structures and high-price condominiums and of consumption with its shopping and entertainment complexes. Illustrative of this transformation is obviously Singapore, followed by Kuala Lumpur and Bangkok and increasingly Jakarta. The shift of symbolic venue of political protest in Bangkok is symptomatic of this larger and deeper transformation of the urban economy of the capital cities of Southeast Asia. The concerns of this chapter are the social, cultural and political consequences of this economic transformation.

Red Shirts in Bangkok

Bangkok's symbolic locus of protest has been, hitherto, along Ratchadamnoen Road. Until the military coup in 1932 which replaced the kingdom with a modern state, Ratchadamnoen Road was 'a "royal road", alongside which palaces, temples and public buildings were located, not a road to be lined with shops, workshops or residences of common people' (Evers and Korff 2000: 85). After the coup, the road was widened and reconfigured.

> The palaces lining the road were transformed into public buildings. The royal palace became the parliament building. At the northern end was a big square for military parades overlooked by the parliament building. The straight street was lined by the ministries ... In the centre of 'central' Ratchadamnoen Avenue was the democracy monument ... At the end of the street was the Ministry of Justice, the Ministry of Defense, the city pillar [guardian angel of the city], Sanam Luang [ceremonial field for cremation of kings and queens] and the newly founded University of Politics and Ethics: Thammasat University.
>
> *(Evers and Korff 2000: 85)*

From its inception as the royal procession road to the more recent building of the Democracy Monument and placement of institutions of the new 'democratic' nation, this road was meant to be the symbolic locus of political and administrative power. Dialectically, it could not avoid also becoming the contested site for revolts and protests for change. The place was marked, for example, by the 1976 killing of university students, protesting the return to Thailand of a deposed military dictator, who had been removed three years earlier by mass protests against the military regime initiated by university students. The 1973 uprising has been retrospectively interpreted by many analysts of Thai politics as the event that marked the emergence of the 'political middle class' in Thailand (Ockey 1999: 237–40). In 1976, the students began their protest demonstrations at Sanam Luang, subsequently moved into the grounds of Thammasat University. On 6 October, right-wing paramilitary groups led by Thai military and police attacked the students, killing, it was officially reported, 46 students and providing the excuse for the military coup that removed the fledgling democratic government. Abiding by the political history of the city, the Red Shirts also initially sited the main camp of the two demonstrations locations in Ratchadamnoen Road, around the Democracy Monument.

As mentioned above, the Red Shirts decamped from Ratchadamnoen and consolidated their presence at Ratchaprasong district, the area of global capitalist consumerism. This is the district of upscale department stores and luxury shopping malls – Central, Gaysorn Plaza, Isetan, Zen, Erawan Bangkok, Peninsula Plaza. It is also a district where upscale global chain hotels are found – Grand Hyatt, Four Seasons and Intercontinental. The area is also connected to the Siam shopping district, which includes Siam Square, the most popular teenage hangout. Many of the large and upscale shopping malls in the Siam district are built on land leased from the Thai Royal Family, through the Crown Property Bureau. The two areas together constitute the high-end shopping district for both the Thai middle and upper classes and international tourists.

Obviously, the shift was aimed at exacting maximum disruption to the city's service economy. But it also had huge symbolic significance. With the best of the world's consumer goods enticingly displayed in the plate-glass windows and the upscale restaurants and bars in the international hotels, Ratchaprasong condenses different semiotic meanings for different Thai social classes: first, the good life that comes with financial success of the rising middle class fostered by rapid national economic growth; second, the aspirations of those who are working or struggling but have yet to attain the good life; and, finally, a constant reminder to the working poor of their material deprivation. To the last group, Ratchaprasong symbolizes the wealth and power of the elite in Bangkok, against whose continued domination in national political power the protesting Red Shirts raged. The occupation of Ratchaprasong was to hit the rich and the aristocracy where it hurts most. It disrupted profit flow from their businesses and disrupted their pleasure of consumption; most upper middle-class and wealthy Bangkok residents considered it dangerous to venture into the demonstration area. Indeed, some who were opposed to the Red Shirts had opined that they would be quite undisturbed if the latter would continue to hold their mass camp in the Democracy Monument area, as it is not a place of necessity to them.[1] It was the perfect symbolic and material target in what had come to be called 'a class war' in Thailand in which the poor Red Shirts were revolting against the Bangkok ruling elite.

Yet one needs recall that the tactical manoeuvres of occupying financially important locations rather than locations of symbolic political significance to effect maximum pressure on extant government had previously been used by the class enemy of the Red Shirts, the People's Alliance for Democracy (PAD), or the 'Yellow Shirts'. The PAD was a coalition of monarchist and anti-democratic elites, supported largely by the Bangkok-based middle class, who realized that their absolute political dominance was slipping away, after Thaksin Shinawatra came to power by mobilizing the votes of the demographically significant rural poor. In 2006, PAD's mass street protests resulted in the coup that ousted Thaksin. When the subsequent 2008 election was won by the new party of Thaksin the PAD returned with street protests. These began at the Democracy Monument on Ratchadamnoen Road, followed by the occupation of Government House. However, in their final push to oust the duly elected government, the PAD mass rally occupied and shut down the two airports in Bangkok, including Suvarnabhumi International Airport. A day after the shutting down of the airport, the Constitutional Court dissolved the three parties which formed a coalition of the elected government. The PAD decamped the next day. Here again, we see that the mass protest rallies had begun in the symbolic Democracy Monument and Government House but were finally effective only with the occupation of the international airport, the gateway to the city for global business travel and the global tourist dollars that flow into the national economy. Ironically, the wealthy organizers behind the PAD had disrupted its own economic interests while it threatened the national economy. This instance thus challenges any simple conclusion that occupation of financially important locations by the Red Shirts is a 'class war' between the poor and the rich.

The two protest movements clearly demonstrate that locations which are loaded with political symbols of historical significance have not been entirely replaced, since the demonstrations began at these historical sites. Rather, new locations of symbolic power, emerging out of globalization of capital city economies, are now being added. In many instances, such new locations of financial and consumption power have proved to be much more efficacious in effecting social and political change as politics of the present economic condition displaced the politics of decolonization and nation building of the past. The movement of the Red Shirts into the Ratchaprasong district has its parallels elsewhere in Southeast Asia. It recalls the People Power 2 demonstrations in the Philippines in 2001 and the failed coup by a group of disgruntled military officers in 2003. In the first instance, 'Ayala Avenue, the road that runs through the heart of Makati's business and commercial district, was a major site for protests' (Shatkin 2005: 597); in the second instance, '296 soldiers of the Armed Forces of the Philippines (AFP) occupied a section of the Makati CBD' (Shatkin 2005: 598) for 19 hours. The addition of the financial and commercial areas as symbolic locations of political contests is succinctly summarized by Shatkin: 'symbols of history and national origin [are] being challenged by new sites that symbolize the global function of the city, and people's perception of the role of the global economy in the country's destiny' (2005: 599).[2] The political symbolic shifts in Bangkok and Manila clearly reflect and are driven by a general trend in the changes of the political economy of cities not only in Southeast Asia but everywhere in the age of rapid capitalist globalization. In Jakarta in 1973, the Malari riots spread all over the city but were heavily concentrated in Jalan Thamrin and often aimed at the offices of big companies.

Marketing cities

The rise in importance of financial and consumer power in the capital cities is a consequence of the demands placed on urban governments in the current phase of global capitalism. The progressive concentration of production into selective emerging economies around the world, including the People's Republic of China (PRC), involved a general deindustrialization of large cities. To improve their revenue streams, 'urban governments had to be much more innovative and entrepreneurial, willing to explore all kinds of avenues through which to alleviate their distressed conditions and thereby secure a better future for their population' (Harvey 1989: 4). According to Harvey this shift to 'entrepreneurialism' had been taking place in the US and Britain since the 1970s global recession and as a general tendency became visible by the mid 1980s. The same tendency also became noticeable in the early 1990s in the capital cities of Southeast Asia, although developments were temporarily disrupted during the 1997 regional financial crisis and its aftermath. This belated development is indicative of the convergence of urban development patterns between Southeast Asian capital cities with developed nations, which began with the new international division of labour that saw the relocation of industrial production to the region since the 1960s, as part of the globalization process (Dick and Rimmer 1998). The city as an entrepreneur is necessitated by the need to capture the increasingly globally mobile flows of capital, such as multinational knowledge-based enterprises in finance, media and communications, entertainment, software and bio-pharmaceuticals, and people, which includes not only executives and professionals who service the multinational enterprises but also, as a source of a city's revenue, globe-trotting tourists.

Several significant consequences follow if a capital city is successful in attracting enterprises, talents and tourists. First, consumption instead of production will be the mainstay of the city's economy. Second, the shift to consumption-based economy is part of the larger shift of employment base towards the service sector which, as has already been observed in global cities (Sassen 2001), has a tendency of developing a pattern of employment in which a very large number of low-income service industry labour, often made of undocumented migrant workers from underdeveloped regions of the world, serves a small number of very high-income earners. For cities in emerging economies, such as the Southeast Asian countries, it is always the capital cities that are engaged primarily in this entrepreneurialism. Third, the economic growth and employment opportunities for professionals and the administrative workforce contribute significantly to the expansion of the local middle class. Finally, low-end service sector employment opportunities are regionalized in that the jobs at this level are filled by migrant labour, legal and illegal, drawn from lesser developed neighbouring countries.

Manila typifies this development driven by globalization of capital. As Shatkin (2005: 590–1) observes:

> First the city has emerged as a 'command and control' centre for the country's integration into the global economy. The Makati central business district, built and managed by the Ayala Land Corporation, contains 90 percent of the headquarters of the top 1000 companies in the country and about 80 percent of headquarters of multinational corporations.

Second, 'Metro Manila is a centre for consumption, more significantly, the growth of the Filipino middle class that has increased disposable income and a strong penchant to consume'; third, 'The concentration of hotels, transportation infrastructure, travel agencies and amenities in Metro Manila means that a disproportionate amount of economic benefits of tourism accrue to the capital'; finally, 'Metro Manila has emerged as a city of labour export ... with more than 90 percent of OCW (Overseas Contract Workers) recruitment agencies located in Metro Manila.'

With perhaps the exception of Singapore and Kuala Lumpur, which are importers of contract workers from the region, this description of Metro Manila would fit any of the capital cities in Southeast Asia. The fullest expression of these features is to be found in Singapore due to its being a city-state.

Finance, shopping and art

In the competition to be a desired location for global capital, talents and tourists, a city must demonstrate that it has all the accoutrements that the globalized leisure and consumer industries can offer within its boundaries, to enable any successful globe-trotting professional and his/her family members to tailor their respective preferred 'lifestyle' (Cronin and Hetherington 2008: 2). Concurrently, to properly house the multinational enterprises and local service industries that support the former's operations, such as lawyers, accountants, public relations and media communications professionals, commanding structures of corporate architecture must be constructed to reflect the 'power' of the enterprises. To house the senior executives and professionals that work in these enterprises, luxurious accommodations in strategic locations with ready access to all the consumption facilities must be built. The consumption facilities must themselves be housed in distinctive iconic buildings as 'cathedrals of desire' with gleaming plate-glass windows that attract the eyes but keep the bodies of mass market shoppers out. All these land use demands which in aggregate constitute the physical and infrastructure aspects of urban development render the planning office of the city government into a meeting and negotiating ground, as well as the office of governance, for a wide range of agents with competing interests and agendas. The outcomes of such negotiations determine the land use pattern, built forms, metonymic visual representations of the city and its overall spatial configuration. What makes Singapore an exemplary illustration of this process is that, as a city-state, the entire island can be, and has been, conceptualized by the planning office as a single planning unit (Chua 1997: 27–59), which makes it easy to read the city, even by ordinary users of the city.

The iconic picture that the publicity offices of the Singapore government use to represent its triumphal economic success story is the waterfront of tall, metallic grey and glass modernist corporate buildings. The current business district, known as the 'Golden Shoe' (Chua 1989) has absorbed and expanded the boundaries of the original central business district established at the founding of Singapore in 1819. The 'creative destruction' of capitalism in erasing the past to make room for the new was a recurrent phenomenon in this sector of the city; since the early nineteenth century, the commercial buildings that face the sea, which are always among the largest edifices of each era, have stood for no more than thirty years before being demolished to begin a new cycle of construction, when the land prices would have appreciated and new building technologies are available to intensify the land use with even bigger and taller buildings.

The only trace of the British colonial past of this area is the miniaturized façade of the department store for Europeans, John Little. The reduced and reproduced façade stands as the entrance to a mass rapid transit station. During the early 1970s, John Little relocated to Orchard

Road, just as this road was emerging as the new shopping and five-star international hotel district. However, its high social status, sustained by its colonial heritage in the days when department stores were few and reserved primarily for the small White community and rich and Anglicized locals, has also been radically reduced. Still selling predominantly the same household goods, it stood insignificantly until it was demolished in late 2000 in a street of new shopping malls designed by celebrity architects, with trendy if cryptic names, like ION, designed by Pritzker Prize Laureate, Zaha Hadid, parading the highest fashion and luxury merchandises of global brands. The success of the tourism and consumption industries is reflected in the report that in the global recession year of 2008, 937,000 Chinese from the PRC spent 2.4 billion Singapore dollars shopping; this is but a tiny fraction of 60 billion Singapore dollars the Chinese tourists had spent worldwide in that year (*Sunday Times Singapore*, 9 May 2010). And they are second when it comes to spending in Singapore, following in the wake of Indonesian tourist-shoppers.

John Little's insignificant presence in Orchard Road, the premier shopping district for the local middle class and tourists alike, is a condensed representation of the radical transformation of Singapore from a decaying port city dependent on regional commodity trade until the 1950s, into an important node in the network of global cities and a model of rapid economic growth that globalized finance and knowledge-based industries can bring to a selected location. As for the port, once an important symbol that inspired literary and other modes of aesthetic expressions because it determined a significant part of local culture and everyday life, it is still there but evokes no symbolic or cultural resonance in the artistic or mundane mindscape of contemporary Singaporeans, although it is among the busiest ports in the world and remains one of the most important state monopolies. Its symbolic significance has been replaced by Orchard Road, the preferred location for the staging of national public events, except for the annual National Day Rally.

Along the Singapore river-front by the financial district, the old shophouses have been 'conserved' – in actuality rebuilt replicas of the old – and occupied by bars and restaurants. On the opposite river bank is the beginning of the 'arts and culture' district. Here, the colonial edifices have a different fate from John Little. The buildings both grand and small that housed government departments have been renovated to their past glory as part of the national architectural heritage and re-used as museums and art galleries; for example, the Empress Palace, which was once the citizenship department, is now the Asian Civilization Museum, sitting in an expanse of green field and on a well-shaded lot, a place for repose from the financial district. The Museum has as its tenants and as a source of revenue the trendy Bar Opiume and the Indochine Restaurant for Thai cuisine, where the denizens of the financial district gather after work. The Old Parliament House has also become the Art House, with a quaint rickety screening room for art-house movies. The old City Hall and the Supreme Court buildings, both European neo-classical buildings constructed in the 1920s, the unanticipated twilight of the British Empire in Southeast Asia, are under restoration and renovation to become the Singapore National Art Gallery. Across the road from these buildings, sited on reclaimed land, is the iconic Esplanade Theatres on the Bay, housing a 1,800-seat concert hall with state of the art acoustics, built at the cost of 600 million Singapore dollars. The Theatres building, fashioned like two enlarged, compound eyes of a fly, is now an iconic metonymic image of Singapore.

The construction of these precincts that concentrate particular economic and cultural activities – 'media, art museums, iconic buildings, and leisure spaced like cafés, boutiques, and bars' – are part of the city's 'symbolic economy', 'where cultural images are made, marketed, and most visibly consumed' (Zukin 2008: xi). This symbolic economy is part of the general process of a city's attempt to 'brand' and market itself to the world. In Singapore, as in other cities, all these place-making activities, which have transformed spaces into places of strong identities as locations of intense social and cultural activities and are using them to market the city to the target users (Chang and Huang 2008: 228), are executed with unequal partnership between the government and the private sector, in which the government bears the cost and private sector reaps the benefits minus tax (Harvey 1989: 7).

Social costs of the entrepreneurial city

Property anxieties

While the middle class in Southeast Asian capital cities are undoubtedly benefiting from the economic globalization of their respective cities, this is not without its costs. Two areas of middle-class anxieties are observable. First is the increasing sense of perceived or real social and public insecurities, as the newly developed condominiums are surrounded by informal settlements of the urban poor. In cities such as Manila, where local governments do not have the capacity to keep encroachment of public spaces in check, all public spaces are vulnerable to occupation by informal settlements, which is itself a mode of 'privatization' of public spaces. 'For example, the impressive buildings that house the congress and the Supreme Court in the National Government Center stand incongruously in the midst of Southeast Asia's largest informal settlement' (Shatkin 2005: 594). Meanwhile the middle class, in fear of the perceived dangers surrounding them, move into different levels and modes of 'self-imprisonment'. Generalizing from their observations of developments in Jakarta since the 1960s, Dick and Rimmer concluded that, 'Gated residential communities, condominiums, air-conditioned cars, patrolled shopping malls and entertainment complexes, and multi-storeyed offices are the present and future world of the insecure middle class in south-east Asia' (Dick and Rimmer 1998: 2317).

Self-excluded from the perceived chaotic and insecure public spaces, the cocoons in which the upper middle class reproduce their daily life, from apartments to cars to shopping complexes, become more and more opulent, perhaps to make the social exclusion more tolerable. Thus, the home reflects the same excess of decoration and use of expensive building material as that of the shopping complexes, generating business for the interior design companies, another emergent service sector.

Second, all the real estate developments in office and commercial, residential buildings and entertainment venues, engendered real estate as a major sector of the economy. Real estate becomes an avenue of potential investment and speculation for high returns, not only for large developers but also for individual middle-class investors. Regional transnational real estate developers are ubiquitous in Southeast Asian capital cities; a short list includes Lippo Land (Indonesian), Capital Land (Singapore), City Development Limited (Singapore), Ayala Corporation (Philippines), Genting (Malaysia). These real estate developers ranked among the top transnational enterprises (Haila 2000). All these companies are diversified real estate developers in office, commercial and residential developments.

At the individual level, the ready coming and going of international companies and executives from one city to another does not encourage multinational enterprise to invest in their own buildings. They choose instead to rent both office spaces and residential units for their high-salary international executives; an expatriate pay package for assignment in Asia would include a hefty housing component. In an urban economy populated by multinational enterprises, there is therefore a high demand for upscale rental housing and offices. Rental properties, particularly upscale condominiums, have become a new avenue for investment and speculation by middle-class individuals with surplus cash. In cities like Singapore, the attractiveness of such investment is enhanced by several financial factors: (i) the very high rates of private savings and thus high level of cash liquidity create a low interest environment for borrowing money;

(ii) rental return from expatriate tenants will generally cover at least the interest component of the investment, while it accumulates capital gains; (iii) while income from rent is taxed, capital gains on sale of the house is tax free, making investment in rental housing very attractive. Little wonder that ownership of rental housing is a common phenomenon among the Singaporean middle class.

Obviously, investments in rental housing chase up housing prices. Take as an example the rapid recovery of the real estate sector in Singapore after the global financial crisis of 2008–9. The International Monetary Fund reported that housing prices rebounded very quickly in the second half of 2009 in East Asia, including Singapore. In Singapore, 'the proportion of real estate loans to total bank lending … was close to 80 percent in Q4 2009'; 'capital inflows have further fuelled property price increases' as 'foreigners and companies accounted for 12.5 percent of third-quarter purchases in 2009'. It noted that many purchasers, local and foreign, have been buying 'in the expectation of price appreciation, rather than simply for dwelling purposes'. The IMF warned that 'the region's booming real estate markets may pose risks to financial stability in the future', as banks are 'increasingly vulnerable' to price correction and 'the widely anticipated rate hikes … will increase burden on household balance sheets' (all quotes from *The Business Times*, 22 April 2010). However, by mid 2010 the Singapore government's measures to cool down the real estate market had successfully slowed down price increases and rental prices increasing as the global economy appeared to be stabilizing and multinational companies brought back their international expatriate executives.

The ever increasing prices of housing intensify the anxieties of those among the middle class who are aspiring or struggling to own their first home. These are predominantly younger families and individuals, who do not stand to inherit the second house or flat that their parents owned as rental housing. Hesitation and fear of purchasing at the 'wrong' time in the market plagues such first-time buyers, as the real estate bubble builds up quickly and deflates equally quickly. The aggregated anxieties for home ownership create an atmosphere of fear of being left without owning a home. The resulting competition among would-be home owners further pushes up prices. All of these contribute to the speedy build-up of a financial bubble, waiting to be burst. Ironically, while the bursting of the bubble may translate into financial hardship for individual investors who cannot hang on to the house, it also spells opportunities for those waiting in the queue for their first home and those with deep pockets for investments to buy in. The cycle continues, and with each cycle the peak price tends to be higher than the last, moving the desired house further into the horizon of affordability for the struggling families and individuals. Each successive cohort of new home buyers is obviously victim to the 'success' of the entrepreneurial effort of the urban government. Even in Singapore, where the government, having as good as monopolized housing provision through its national public housing programme, and had been able to 'guarantee' that housing is affordable to up to 90 per cent of the residential population, housing price inflation has necessitated radical changes in public housing home-ownership policy. In the past decade, owners of public housing flats had been allowed to own private housing units for a source of rental income. However, the rapid rise in housing prices in spite of continuing uncertainties in the global economy after the 2008–9 global recession has compelled the Singapore government to disallow owners of public housing flats to concurrently own other properties, at home and abroad, as of 30 August 2010.

Effects on low-income citizens

The planning and infrastructure development for sites of finance and consumption are executed by the planning department of the urban government. Not only are the high capital construction costs of cultural facilities, such as concert halls and museums, paid by the public purse, so too are the ongoing subsidies on the operational costs of these institutions; for example, the Esplanade Theatres on the Bay in Singapore is subsidized to the tune of about 30 million Singapore dollars annually.[3] These public expenditures are, of course, justified as necessary for the benefits of the citizens, especially in generating employment. However, any promise of generalized sharing of the cultural facilities among all citizens is illusory, as the cultural facilities and the upscale shopping complexes are, in practice, zones of exclusion of low-income individuals, whose only access to these places are as low-end employees, from front-line retail sales person to waiters and waitresses and cleaning crews. Yet the illusion is palpable even among the low-income citizens, who take pleasure in the modernity of 'their' city vicariously (Huang 2004). The taxi driver in Shanghai could have been speaking for all taxi drivers in Southeast Asian capital cities when he said, 'Now in Shanghai we can see everything but we also know that we cannot have it. So in comparison to before, we know there is a lot out there, but we cannot have it' (quoted in Davis 2005: 186). If the objects of desire are not financially attainable, they are 'visually available', actual material deprivation is sublimated, suppressing the fact of inequality of income and access, if only temporarily. In more general terms, 'Many of those at the margins – excluded for many reasons, but most immediately because they do not have any money – nevertheless show a fascination with the culture codes associated with the wealth and power of the new [rich]' (Young 1999: 57).

Indeed, a general tendency of a service industry economic growth is to generate greater income inequality. In Singapore, the most successful globalized economy in Southeast Asia, income inequality has been intensifying between high-income professionals and those who have access to managerial jobs in multination corporations, and low-income groups, who face stagnant wages or even declines in real income; the Gini Coefficient exceeded 0.5 in 2006. As the economy grows in the service-led economy, the unofficial poverty line was also raised in 2009 from 1,500 to 2,000 Singapore dollars per month, which is a small fortune for the working class in the rest of Southeast Asia. Furthermore, growth in/through consumerism generally increases the cost of living, as prices of commodities are pegged to middle-class affordability levels (Chua and Tan 1999). This reduces the consumption capacity of the lower income groups for daily necessities, as they struggle to meet the rising cost with their proportionally ever reducing income, thus further impoverishing the low-income citizens and the poor.

In housing, the effect of gated housing estate development is plain to see in many Southeast Asian capital cities, in which the new high-rise condominium blocks are surrounded by low-rise informal settlements. The concrete, glass and steel of the high-rise blocks stand in stark contrast to the housing of impermanent, often, found material, such as wooden panels, palm thatch, plastic and canvas sheets. The general environment of these informal settlements varies greatly, from being relatively well serviced with utilities and sanitation to open sewers and almost total lack of other utilities. In such settlements, all open spaces are vulnerable to encroachment and privatization by some residents. Indeed, it can be argued that it is these surroundings that partly drove the middle class into their gated communities.

Significantly, if the low-income and poor citizens were housed in modern concrete blocks, the face of the city in question would be completely transformed, shifting it from an 'Asian' mega city congested with informal settlements to a modern city of the first world. Such is the case with Singapore, with the low income and the poor well hidden in high-rise blocks in planned public housing estates, where more than 80 per cent of citizens and permanent residents make their homes. To the untrained eye, the blocks of one- and two-room flats, the smallest flats offered by the public housing authority, the Housing and Development Board, are no different from the rest of the blocks that house the better-off, including high-income families, as the income ceiling for eligibility for 99-year leasehold housing has been raised to

8,000 Singapore dollars per month. Furthermore, all residents in the estate are served by the same public services and amenities, thus homogenizing that part of daily life that is reproduced within the housing estate and reducing the visibility of income inequality. Singapore therefore does not show its underbelly to the world; indeed, it is common for young middle-class individuals to believe that there is no poverty in a 'homogenously' middle-class Singapore. Few citizens or visitors would see homelessness in Singapore. This public visual impression of the absence of poverty is an important contributing element in the marketing of Singapore to the world of enterprise, talents and tourists.

Conclusion

Since the 1960s, with the transfer of capital and exporting of low-end industries and jobs from developed countries to the region, Southeast Asian economies have been progressively integrated into global capitalism. The employment opportunities generated by the multinational companies for professional and managerial staff have engendered a new middle class.[4] After some four decades of continued economic expansion, albeit at different rates in different countries, the economies in each country can be said to have 'normalized', in contrast to the rapid expansion of the economy during the early years of industrialization. This has enabled those who were among the first to grasp the opportunities made available to consolidate their class and wealth positions. Rapid and widespread upward mobility is a thing of the past. Those who are still in the lower income strata will find it increasingly difficult to break through to the higher financial position. As globalization intensifies, low-wage production industries are pushed out of the city – in the case of Singapore, pushed out of the city-state completely. Cities begin to compete for financial and service industries, such as the operational headquarters of multinational enterprises and knowledge-based, high-technology industries, such as media and communications and bio-pharmaceutical, and chase after the global tourist dollar. These processes bring the Southeast Asian city closer and closer to the development that had been taking place in developed nations; the most developed of Southeast Asian cities, such as Singapore, begin to acquire similar spatial and visual characteristics to those of global cities in developed nations. The landscape becomes dominated by modern tall buildings congested into a financial district, housing the managerial functions and international executives of multinational companies; shopping districts which are identifiably different for different classes of local and foreign consumers; architectural heritage buildings and districts, renovated and restored, are reused as museums and art galleries – all to make the city an enticing place, as the Singapore government puts it, 'to live, work and play' for the globally mobile talented and the rising local middle class, who are well served by the local working class and low-wage migrant workers. The social and spatial transformations of the Southeast Asian capital cities are only distinguishable from those in developed countries by the remaining tropical architecture and settlement patterns of the lower income and poor citizens in the city. When such tropical traces are completely erased, as in Singapore, there is no longer an Asian city but a global city, struggling to establish an identity through its iconic buildings that are designed by the same coterie of celebrity architects on hire to all the global cities in the world.

Note

1 I owe this observation to Michael Montesano.
2 People Power 1 against President Marcos, in 1986, had occupied historically significant sites, namely the Rizal National Park and the Mendiola Bridge that lead to Malacanang Palace, the presidential residence (Shatkin 2005: 595–6).

3 At the time of writing, May 2010, the exchange rate is approximately 1 US dollar to 1.35 Singapore dollars.
4 This process has been very well explored in the six-volume book series, *New Rich in Asia*, under the general editorship of Richard Robison and David Goodman.

References

Chang, T.C. and S. Huang (2008) 'Geographies of everywhere and nowhere: place-(un)making in a world city', *International Development Planning Review* 30 (3): 227–48.

Chua Beng Huat (1989) *The Golden Shoe: Building Singapore's Financial District*, Singapore: Urban Redevelopment Authority.

——(1997) *Political Legitimacy and Housing*, London: Routledge.

Chua Beng Huat and Tan Joo Ean (1999) 'Singapore: where the middle class sets the standard', in M. Pinches (ed.) *Culture and Privilege in Capitalist Asia*, London: Routledge, pp. 137–58.

Cronin, A.M. and K. Hetherington (2008) *The Consuming Entrepreneurial City: Images, Memory and Spectacle*, London: Routledge.

Davis, D. (2005) 'Urban consumer culture', in M. Hockx and J. Strauss (eds) *Culture in Contemporary China*, London: Routledge, pp. 183–98.

Dick, H. and P.J. Rimmer (1998) 'Beyond the Third World city: the new urban geography of Southeast Asia', *Urban Studies* 35 (12): 2303–21.

Evers, H.D. and R. Korff (2000) *Southeast Asian Urbanism: The Meaning and Power of Social Space*, Singapore: Institute of Southeast Asian Studies.

Haila, A. (2000) 'Real estate in global cities: Singapore and Hong Kong as property states', *Urban Studies* 37 (12): 2241–56.

Harvey, D. (1989) 'From managerialism to entrepreneurialism: the transformation in urban governance in late capitalism', *Geografiska Annaler* 71B (1): 3–17.

Huang, M.T. (2004) *Walking between Slums and Skyscrapers: Illusions of Open Space in Hong Kong, Tokyo and Shanghai*, Hong Kong: Hong Kong University Press.

Ockey, J. (1999) 'Creating the Thai middle class', in M. Pinches (ed.) *Culture and Privilege in Capitalist Asia*, London: Routledge, pp. 230–50.

Sassen, S. (2001) *The Global City: New York, London, Tokyo*, Princeton, NJ: Princeton University Press.

Shatkin, G. (2005) 'Colonial capital, modernist capital, global capital: the changing political symbolism of urban space in Metro Manila, the Philippines', *Pacific Affairs* 78 (4): 577–600.

Young, K. (1999) 'Consumption, social differentiation and self-definition of the new rich in industrializing Southeast Asia', in M. Pinches (ed.) *Culture and Privilege in Capitalist Asia*, London: Routledge, pp. 56–85.

Zukin, Sharon (2008) 'Foreword', in A.M. Cronin and K. Hetherington (eds) *The Consuming Entrepreneurial City: Images, Memory and Spectacle*, London: Routledge.

SECTION IV
Civil society and participation

14

THE LIMITS OF CIVIL SOCIETY

Social movements and political parties in Southeast Asia

Edward Aspinall and Meredith L. Weiss

Beginning in the late 1980s, peaking in the 1990s and continuing into the 2000s, both scholars of Southeast Asia and reformers in the region enthused about the democratic potential of civil society (for example, Budiman 1990; Uhlin 1997; Clarke 1998; Alagappa 2004). They imagined civil society, commonly defined as the realm of associational life between family and state, as a site where ordinary Southeast Asian citizens were organizing autonomously, carving out democratic space, and challenging the legitimacy of authoritarian regimes. Scholars and activists alike pointed to the enormous range of associations – human rights, environmental and women's groups, non-governmental organizations (NGOs) of various stripes, growing labour and farmers' organizations, to name just a few – that were emerging across the region. These organizations were apparently flourishing in conditions as diverse as post-Marcos Philippines and Suharto's Indonesia, and even sending out shoots in the infertile soil of Lee Kuan Yew's Singapore and the yet more desert-like conditions of military-ruled Burma (Kyaw 2004) or the one–party state of Vietnam (Kerkvliet *et al.* 2003).

Both the patterns of civil society organization that arose in the 1980s and 1990s in Southeast Asia, and the enthusiasm for such organization, were in large part a product of the nondemocratic regimes then dominating the region. Suppression of or limitations on opposition political parties led many middle-class reformers to look to alternative means of exercising political influence, often within radically decentred and loosely coordinated civil society sectors. Many of these reformers also sought to expand democratic space and promote political reform. In countries like Indonesia, Thailand and the Philippines, it was this combination of diversity and reform potential that made civil society resemble, in the eyes of its supporters and advocates, an engine of democratic change.

The prevalence of the civil society model as a strategy to oppose, or at least survive under, authoritarianism, was encouraged by wider regional and even global trends of political and ideological change. For example, emerging enthusiasm for the civil society model in part reflected the efforts of a post-Marxist left to seek new ways to advance agendas of popular empowerment and social justice while avoiding both the risks of repression and authoritarian tendencies they saw as coming with Leninism. Equally important was the rise of a new spirit of classical liberalism which understood the major division in society, not as one between antagonistic social classes, but as that between a society struggling for greater autonomy and an over-reaching state. This liberal vision in turn received both intellectual and financial succour from the advanced capitalist countries, with an array of both non-governmental and governmental agencies from the 1980s increasingly willing to support NGOs and other civil society organizations throughout the developing world, including Southeast Asia. Much of this support was channelled toward the promotion of alternative development models – farmer cooperatives, micro-credit schemes, alternative technology and the like – but especially from the 1980s, there was increasing support for groups working on more politically sensitive issues, such as human rights or environmental protection, land disputes and even labour rights. A major shift occurred in the 1990s, as donor governments, such as that of the United States, began to develop democracy-promotion programmes that supported civil society groups in some countries. Even the major international development agencies such as the World Bank began to incorporate support for civil society into their programmes, packaging it as 'participation in development' and support for 'good governance'.

As a result of these converging trends, for a brief moment reformers in Southeast Asia became enamoured of a new model of alternative politics that put civil society, popular empowerment and people's participation front and centre. In fact, however, and viewed more than a decade on, what is perhaps most striking about the shape of civil society and the social movements that populate it across Southeast Asia is its variety. This variety, in turn, substantially reflects the variety of political regimes in the region. Regimes in Southeast Asia run the gamut from military authoritarian to approaching liberal democratic. All these polities share some degree of space, however controlled or curtailed, for social movements of various forms. How these movements and their component social movement organizations (SMOs) figure into the polity, though, differs greatly. Indeed, we may categorize the region's regimes less by regime type per se than by the nature of their civil societies: those with a 'legitimate civil society', a 'controlled and communalized civil society' (which may be difficult to distinguish fully from the state) or a 'repressed civil society' (Alagappa 2004). Southeast Asian states with legitimate civil societies include post-1998 Indonesia, the Philippines, and Thailand – this category is the broadest one, although few of its members would be termed liberal democracies. States with controlled and communalized civil societies include Malaysia and Singapore. States in the region with repressed civil societies include Burma and Vietnam. Importantly, civil society may be legitimate without being terribly strong or internally unified.[1]

That diversity *within* civil society is critically important, affecting not just component organizations' core legitimacy, but their ability to bridge social sectors, percolate new ideas about society and politics, and either sustain or challenge the domination of state-supporting norms. SMOs are embedded within, and moulded by, prevailing structures of power, however much some of them deploy their clout to change those structures. In other words, civil society is as much an arena for the reproduction of social inequality as it is a site from which that inequality is challenged. Moreover, like other component parts of the polity, SMOs may logically span the ideological and tactical gamut: state-supporting to state-challenging, xenophobic to liberal, operationally murky to fully transparent.

Given these fundamental premises, one of the most consistent and noteworthy developments across the region is a new recognition of the limits of the civil society approach to political change, coupled with renewed attention to political parties as the other key set of vehicles for popular mobilization. Social movements and parties, analysts and activists increasingly find, complement each other, but are not interchangeable: political parties have a mandate and scope SMOs lack; SMOs enjoy flexibility and mutability that coherent parties cannot achieve. In particular, in countries in which there is a real space for democratic contestation through elections, we see a range of former civil society activists engaging or re-engaging with political parties as a means of directly contesting for governmental power. In the region's more democratic polities, at least, increasing numbers of SMO activists, independently legitimate thanks to their earlier engagement in civil society, but frustrated with the limitations on what they can achieve there, have entered formal politics. This pattern does not mean that the civil society model is no longer relevant. SMOs still not only function as important training grounds and recruitment pools for political parties and bureaucracies, but also offer information campaigns, policy lobbying, and more. Yet no longer in democratizing polities do they tend to assume the role of political opposition or see a need for real detachment from the state, as is more often the case under conditions of authoritarianism. In short, experience thus far suggests that civil society's much-touted democratizing influence is not only less certain, autonomous or decisive than its boosters suppose, but also tends to become even less so as democracy settles in. SMOs still can and do play a role in the more democratic states of Southeast Asia, but the position and potential of civil society should be understood differently in the context of different alternative channels for popular engagement and policy influence.

We trace these trends with reference to two core cases: Indonesia and Malaysia. These two states have experienced distinct sociopolitical patterns over time and represent a range of political possibilities. Indonesia has navigated among multiple regimes; early on its social movement organizations were tied closely to parties, but when parties were emasculated under authoritarian rule, they developed quite separately. In recent years, as Indonesia has democratized, some SMO activists have increasingly moved from civil society toward party-based engagement. Malaysia, in contrast, has a history of less radical disjunctures in regime type, and a long-standing stable of core opposition parties, participating consistently in a competitive electoral authoritarian polity. As in Indonesia, early SMOs helped to found Malaysia's early political parties, then faded to the background. Yet in Malaysia, too, coinciding with the invigoration of the civil society model across the region, SMOs regained prominence in the 1980s as a distinct force, largely unconnected to the world of political parties and elections. More recently, SMO-based activists and agendas have even significantly revitalized formal opposition politics, possibly at real cost to those SMOs. Guiding this comparison are questions on the links and disjunctures between formal and informal politics in Southeast Asia; we thus conclude by asking what the relationship between SMOs and more formal political structures are, and when and how these relationships change.

Civil society's colonial and postcolonial origins

The origins of contemporary Southeast Asian civil societies and the associations and social movements that populate them lie mostly in the early decades of the twentieth century, when an array of educational, self-help, sectoral and political associations came into being in the colonies and semi-colonies that constituted the region. Many such organizations aimed to advance the interests of a single community; many were defined by the politics of nationalism and anti-colonialism. The communist left and, more broadly, ideals of social egalitarianism and revolutionary mobilization of the lower classes, were also important influences across the region.

In the Netherlands East Indies, the first three decades of the twentieth century saw the establishment of Indonesia's first modern organizations, some of which continue to exercise influence to this day. Muhammadiyah (established 1912) and Nahdlatul Ulama (established 1926), for example, are still the country's largest Islamic organizations. Viewed schematically, these decades saw the birth of two distinct traditions of mass organization. On the one hand, some of the earliest organizations exhibited an elitist preoccupation with 'uplift', concentrating on an educational and service mission designed to bring 'natives' into the modern era and equip them with the knowledge and skills to benefit from it. Groups like Budi Utomo ('Noble Endeavour'), formed in 1908 and conventionally the first modern organization in Indonesian history, focused on improving the lot of the Javanese *priyayi* class of colonial administrators, while Muhammadiyah strove to promote the new 'modernist' Islamic principles then emanating from the Middle East, by which Muslims were encouraged simultaneously to return to the early ideals of their faith and engage with modern science and education.

A second tradition of organization emphasized popular unity, struggle and mobilization. This tendency was first embodied in Sarekat Islam (Islamic Union), a mass movement which blossomed in the second decade of the twentieth century, and rapidly took on anti-colonial, egalitarian and revolutionary impulses. When splits between communists and more conservative Muslims weakened Sarekat Islam in the early 1920s, and after an abortive communist revolt was repressed by the Dutch in 1926–7, the nationalist movement became the main locus of this new emphasis on anti-colonial unity, even as it struggled to survive in the face of repression from the colonial state.

Just as the Japanese occupation of 1942–5 ended Dutch colonial control, the ensuing revolutionary struggle for independence (1945–9) founded the new republic in a riotous profusion of popular organization. During the revolution, a proliferation of political parties, mass organizations and armed groups contended for power and strove to assert their sometimes very different visions of a new social and political order. Indonesia thus entered its period of postcolonial nation-building in the 1950s with a highly mobilized and organized society, where expectations of the material and other benefits that would ensue were very high. The deep politicization and organization of Indonesian society in the 1950s and 1960s took the form of '*aliran* politics', a term introduced by Clifford Geertz (1959, 1960). One feature of the *aliran* pattern was its communal foundation; another was the fusion of party and social movement organizations that underpinned it, with each major party (those of traditionalist Muslims, modernist Muslims, secular nationalists and communists) 'being surrounded by a set of voluntary social organizations formally or informally linked to it … An aliran is more than a mere political party, certainly more than a mere ideology; it is a comprehensive pattern of social integration' (Geertz 1959: 37).

Thus, Indonesia was not only a highly organized society, with a dense fabric of associational life, it was also deeply divided. Despite internal divisions of wealth and power, the different *aliran* asserted fundamentally different visions of the future, with the Indonesian Communist Party (PKI) and its microcosmos of affiliated mass organizations in particular threatening to upset the prevailing social order in a way that most other forces were determined to prevent. These contests came to a head in 1965–6 when the army and its civilian allies rallied against the left, wiping out the PKI, killing some 500,000 people in the process, and setting the scene for the military-dominated Suharto regime.

As in Indonesia, the roots of contemporary Malaysian civil society may be traced to the burgeoning of associational life in the early twentieth century. Then, faced with urbanization, intercommunal disparities and imminent independent sovereignty, a range of groups formed, oriented around communal progress, religion, minority rights and more, populating a new sort of public sphere (see Milner 1991). Even more so than in the Netherlands East Indies, these associations tended to follow the lines of ascriptive (racial or religious) identities. An array of clubs developed for sports, recreation, literature and similar issues, alongside more politically oriented organizations. In the latter category were groups that made representations to the British colonial government on policy matters, as well as ones that focused on cultivating race-consciousness and nationalism, especially among Malays, or on community development, self-determination, labour and group rights among the Chinese and to a lesser extent, Indian, communities. At the time, such organizations were really the only avenue for political participation, expression and community-building.[2] Given such factors as Malaysia's less tempestuous quest for independence, the slow development of a pan-Malayan national identity and the deeply vertically stratified structure of colonial society, this early associational life was substantially less fractious and mass-based than in Indonesia in the same period – despite, for instance, similar experience of military training and mobilization under Japanese wartime occupation.

While political parties, many of them successors to SMOs, formed across society in the early post-war period, the most successful of them were elite-led and communal in orientation. Malays were the most prone to shift their efforts from civil society to parties, particularly the United Malays National Organisation (UMNO) and Pan-Malayan Islamic Party (Parti Islam SeMalaysia or PAS). To a greater extent than for other communities, colonial rule had nurtured the Malay elite, not only through structures of partial indirect rule through peninsular sultans, but also through such institutions as the Malay Administrative Service. That integration with the colonial and developing postcolonial state fostered a deeper convergence between early SMOs and political parties among Malays. Among elites from other communities as well as the multiracial radical left, this shift toward political society was neither so pronounced nor so feasible. For instance, the British had left Chinese Malaysians (then about half the population) somewhat more autonomous and less well incorporated into the state bureaucracy, and vernacular education, the crux of much Chinese community organizing, remained largely outside the purview of the state. Largely as a result of this positioning, Chinese Malaysians remained heavily invested in civil society, even after the launch of largely communal political parties. And the adamantly anticommunist British banned the Malayan Communist Party, a policy the postcolonial regime sustained upon independence in 1957. The radical left found rough going in civil society as well; laws introduced in the late colonial and early postcolonial period (inspired by the cold war but enduring well beyond) required official registration for all sociopolitical organizations, allowed preventive detention of suspected troublemakers (particularly by way of the still-controversial Internal Security Act), and otherwise curbed civil liberties.

As the state developed and strengthened after independence, Malaysian social movements initially lost steam; civil society remained enervated through the 1970s. Still, a subset of religious, education-related and other SMOs sustained engagement, alongside 'public intellectuals', mass-based religious movements, trade unions and perennially out-of-office opposition political parties, which tended to align more with and function more like SMOs than parties.[3] Both states, then, ended the transitional period after independence with a mix of SMOs and institutionalized political parties, although the crux of power had by then shifted definitively toward the postcolonial state in both.

Social movements and civil society under increasingly authoritarian states

Again, viewed rather schematically, and not without some irony, we may say that civil society as a sphere of political organization and opposition separate from political parties came into its own in both countries in large part as a by-product of the strengthening of their respective states. But it did so just as those states grew strong enough to suppress or preclude further development of the social movements therein. Of the two countries which are our focus, it is again Indonesia which presents the more dramatic case. Suharto's 'New Order' regime explicitly aimed if not to bring an end to the mass politicization of the early post-colonial period, then at least to domesticate that energy and harness it to the state. The regime's military leaders, and the civilian intellectuals around them, formulated a political vision which depicted the 'irrationality' of the masses and their enthralment to 'primordial' sentiments as obstacles to economic development and social modernization (Liddle 1973). This vision became the intellectual foundation for the regime's policies of depoliticization, by which it proscribed organizations that it saw as threatening its interests and corralled most others into a network of corporatist organizations that it controlled (Reeve 1985: 115–18). By the early 1970s, Indonesia had gone from being a country in which mass organizations proliferated and dominated the public political stage, to one in which the army and bureaucracy were the dominant forces and social movements were increasingly suppressed (even if public protest occasionally broke out in more or less violent eruptions).

The government banned the old mass organizations of the left, and tried especially hard to prevent autonomous organization among lower-class groups, implementing a 'floating mass' policy limiting political party operations in rural areas, and establishing a government-controlled trade union body as the 'sole representative' of workers. The major non-leftist political parties were not banned, but there was massive government intervention into their internal structures to ensure that compliant leaderships controlled them and in 1973 they were forced to fuse into two tame non-government parties. Many other organizations, ranging from youth groups to journalists' or peasants' associations, some of which had previously been affiliated to parties and some of which had been independent, suffered a similar fate: they were shepherded into peak bodies controlled by government appointees. The government was less ambitious when it came to controlling religious organizations, whose leaders had claims to scriptural authority that was necessarily beyond the government's ken, but state officials nevertheless closely monitored preachers and religious groups to ensure that they did not criticize the government or attempt to mobilize against it. In this climate, although a large number of (non-leftist) organizations survived, their leaders learned quickly how to accommodate to the regime's rules, speak its language, and avoid overtly challenging it. Some pockets of relative autonomy persisted, such as on university campuses which became redoubts of anti-government protest, but even here the government ultimately cracked down in the late 1970s, adopting a 'Normalisation of Campus Life' policy which greatly constrained student councils and the student press. By the early 1980s, on the surface at least, the New Order regime ruled over a political scene in which a varied civil society survived, but with its autonomous organizational capacity all but eviscerated.

Yet the New Order's attitude to social organization was not one of unrelenting hostility. On the contrary, its developmentalist vision in many respects drew on the elitist preoccupation with uplift and improvement that had been one important strand within Indonesian associational life from the early twentieth century. As a result, organizations such as Muhammadiyah, which ran a large network of schools, universities, hospitals and other social services, were able not only to survive but even to secure some government support for their activities. The preoccupation with development provided fertile ground for the rise, from the early 1970s, of non-governmental organizations (NGOs) as a new mode of civil society organization. Professional organizations of staff and volunteers, rather than mass associations of members and supporters, a defining feature of these groups in Indonesia was that most claimed to be oriented to development (Billah 1994), thus justifying themselves in terms of the regime's own meta-narrative. At the same time, NGOs also flourished because they forged connections with international sources of political influence and, crucially, funding. Most Indonesian NGOs received funds from overseas, either from the major US philanthropic bodies and agencies or from European church-based and development agencies, or, eventually, from the overseas development agencies of major western governments. By 1996, the government estimated that there were 8,000 such bodies in Indonesia, most of them working in areas like consumer protection, micro-credit, health care and alternative technology (Aspinall 2005: 87).

In conditions through the 1980s and 1990s in which other avenues of anti-government political expression – especially political parties – were constrained, the NGO sector became an important niche for critical and socially engaged middle-class activism. Several key institutions, such as the Legal Aid Institute (LBH) and the environmental network Walhi, engaged in sometimes audacious anti-government activism, widely promoted ideas of human rights and social justice, and critiqued the regime and its ideas. By the early 1990s, LBH was proclaiming that it sought to become a 'motor of democratization' and NGO intellectuals and activists promoted a vision of 'civil society' as an arena of counter-hegemonic struggle against the dominance of the New Order state (Aspinall 2005: 86–115).

In fact, although NGOs played an important role in delegitimating the New Order, their mobilizational potential was limited, not only by the regime's restrictions on independent organization, but also by their own status as professional organizations of middle-class staffers seeking career security and advancement. During the 1990s, a new generation of more militant anti-regime activists emerged on campuses and elsewhere, often deriding the NGOs for their conservatism (Eldridge 1995: 39–40), and the first stirrings of independent organization emerged in areas like the labour union sector (Hadiz 1997). When the final crisis of the regime came in 1998, following the external shock of the 1997 Asian financial crisis, it was groups with the ability to mobilize on the streets with a minimum of formal organization – notably students – who led the protest wave in favour of Reformasi that eventually undermined the cohesion and will of the regime and forced Suharto from office. NGOs and similar SMOs had played an important role in undermining the ideational foundations of authoritarian rule and promoting ideas of liberalism and democratic rule in the public sphere, but lacked the organizational weight to directly lead anti-regime mobilizations.

In Malaysia, the shift from open and competitive democratic rule to a more restrictive 'semi-authoritarian' system was neither so dramatic nor so bloody as in Indonesia. Dramatic changes took place in the early 1970s, as after nearly two years' suspension of parliamentary government (1969–71), a bigger, broader governing coalition (the National Front, BN) pared back space for speech, association and opposition broadly. However, the years of Mahathir Mohamad's premiership (1981–2003) were especially defining; he brought the executive front and centre in governance, pressed an adamant (and largely successful) developmental agenda that renewed and redirected regime legitimacy, and combined simple repression with more innovative efforts (for instance, state-led Islamization) to quash or outbid opponents. As Mahathir consolidated his position through the 1980s, new waves of SMOs – women's groups, Islamist groups, human rights groups, workers' groups, community development groups, and more – took shape or shored up their position to exploit perceived windows of opportunity, to press new issues onto the government's agenda, or in response to perceived threats to associational activity and civil liberties.

Particularly as developmentalism – including 'money politics' and an overarching pragmatism (extending to a drive to co-opt those forces potentially useful to the state) – settled in, social movements diverged more significantly from formal politics than previously. While civil society-based movements retained a degree of influence upon the political order, activists tended to remain outside the increasingly centralized developmental state. For instance, championship of Islamist values and policies among Muslim SMOs, starting largely with Muslim student organizations, pressed government and opposition parties to prioritize Islam as an increasingly central element of state policies and party platforms. Similarly, advocacy efforts by Chinese educationist organizations, particularly the United Chinese School Teachers' and School Committees' Association (Dong Jiao Zong), kept issues of Chinese education and minorities' cultural rights alive.

In this period, too, the tide of NGOs sweeping the region reached Malaysia. Kicking off this trend was the Consumers' Association of Penang (CAP), launched in 1967; together with a growing array of partner organizations, CAP brought issues not just of consumers' protection, but also environmentalism and critical approaches to development, to public prominence. The civil liberties advocacy organization Aliran Kesedaran Negara (Aliran, National Consciousness Movement), established in 1977, is generally considered to have been the next modern NGO. Other advocacy-oriented organizations followed, for instance one important subset of organizations concerned with human rights and another focused on women's rights specifically, such as the All Women's Action Society (AWAM), Women's Aid Organization, and Sisters in Islam. Many of these groups became increasingly skilled at lobbying both government and opposition parties in addition to more diffuse consciousness-raising, public education and service delivery. Given Malaysia's soon comparatively high level of development as well as state restrictions on and barbs about foreign manipulation, financial support from overseas was less important to Malaysian NGOs than those elsewhere, although some SMOs did accept external funding. Also in dramatic contrast to Indonesia, where the party system was very weak, most of these organizations liaised more comfortably with opposition parties than with the increasingly dominant state, even if state subsidies, as for provision of domestic violence shelters or HIV/AIDS outreach services, supported a number of SMO-led initiatives. Moreover, NGO representatives served on government boards related to environmental, consumers', health, women's and other issues, and many of the highest profile social movement campaigns centred around lobbying for policy changes. Such efforts required close interaction with the ruling coalition. Indeed, the establishment during this period of a National Human Rights Commission and the enactment or fortification of legislation on issues such as domestic violence or consumers' protection may plausibly be traced to SMOs' agitation on these concerns.[4]

However much democracy-promoters lauded this new vibrancy in civil society, the space accorded social movements remained closely curtailed, nor did such activism signify real openness to more institutional engagement. Echoing a preference also clearly articulated in Singapore during the same period, the Malaysian government asked that activists organize in parties rather than in SMOs: the former could be effectively, legitimately defeated at the ballot box (especially given the imperfect fairness of Malaysian elections), while the latter were harder to deal with. In 1981, to encourage a more clear distinction between politically engaged and so-called 'friendly' NGOs, the government introduced amendments to the Societies Act that would require all 'political' societies – defined as ones that issued public statements – to register as such within a specified period and be subject to special constraints. A mass ad hoc campaign by SMOs won repeal of the amendments two years later. In an oblique nod to the political influence of advocacy-oriented SMOs, the regime famously labelled several of these groups, along with two opposition parties, 'thorns in the flesh' in a 1986 attack (Gurmit 1984, 1990; Means 1991: 194, 198–9).

The government attempted to keep such critical activities in check. Sporadic crackdowns, or at least the plausible threat of them, became the norm. Paramount among these attacks was 1987's Operasi Lalang, which saw the arrest of over 100 activists and politicians for alleged Marxist tendencies, many of them under the Internal Security Act (ISA). These arrests deterred some potential supporters from joining SMO campaigns, but also spurred new forms of protest and attendant organizations. For instance, human rights group Suara Rakyat Malaysia (Voice of the Malaysian People) formed out of a support group for ISA detainees and their families in the late 1980s.

Various factors fed SMOs' gains in numbers and prominence between the 1970s and 1990s. After 1970, government affirmative action policies encouraged the expansion of the middle classes and facilitated Malays' access to higher education; both a growing middle class and rising rates of education are generally positively correlated with civil societal activity. At the same time, rapid urbanization brought individuals from all ethnic and religious groups into close proximity, sparking social dislocation, but also causing or aggravating problems such as pollution, traffic congestion and a lack of affordable housing and amenities. All these conditions might spur political engagement. At the time, however, institutionalized political space was shrinking. Under Mahathir, UMNO grew more dominant within the BN coalition, policy-making became an increasingly top-down process, and opposition parties could make limited headway, particularly at the federal level; where they did secure gains, particularly at the state level, they did so largely through appeals to Islam rather than, for instance, class-based platforms as earlier when the left was stronger.

Moreover, social movement activism yielded significant gains only in some issue areas. For instance, persistent, broad-based initiatives against laws such as the ISA, Printing Presses and Publications Act, and Universities and University Colleges Act have failed time and again, and environmental activists have only sometimes been able to press a conservationist agenda; SMO-coordinated campaigns to forestall construction of massive dams, to preserve areas from logging and deforestation, or to stall ill-advised hill projects or road and bridge development, for example, have been similarly unsuccessful. The strength of social movements in this period, then, was not only itself curbed by depoliticizing norms and laws and a relatively impervious state, but also may have said more about citizens' lack of faith in official avenues for political engagement than their expectation of real influence through civil society.

By the 1990s, and again in an obvious parallel to developments in Indonesia, experience of SMO activism was starting to solidify a sense of entitlement among citizens to participate in the policy process and in political affairs more broadly, even if without real expectation of success. Even critical government and media discourse about NGOs raised awareness of these organizations and what they do. The state's implicit or explicit sanctioning of certain groups, devolution of certain social welfare tasks to voluntary organizations, and apparent need to crack down at times to curb overly potent and widespread social activism belied Mahathir's insistence on the need for an authoritative, strong state. Matters came to a head when Mahathir ousted his deputy, Anwar Ibrahim, from the government and party in 1998. Anwar used his case to rally thousands of Malaysians, frustrated with a lack of accountability, transparency and probity in government, to join a broadly inclusive social movement, dubbed Reformasi in tribute to the Indonesian movement of the same name earlier in the year, for thoroughgoing reforms of state institutions and policies. At this point, as apparent vulnerabilities in the incumbent regime shifted political opportunity structures, the scope and orientation of social movements entered a new phase. Centred on calls for political liberalization and the extension of a range of civil and political rights, the Reformasi movement united two poles traditionally segregated in Malaysia, one loosely leftist and the other Islamist. Coalition-building moved front and centre, both within civil society and between opposition political parties and SMOs. Moreover, activists from the latter started to grant far greater priority to electoral politics, whether directly by joining or launching campaigns, or indirectly by offering intellectual ballast and models.

An unprecedented proportion of Malaysian civil society engaged in Reformasi activism, either postponing or restyling issue-based advocacy and other specific interest agendas to foreground questions of democratization and systemic reform. The developing movement brought together groups organized around human rights, women's rights, indigenous people's rights, the environment, Islam, Christianity, labour and more, first in issue-oriented coalitions of opposition parties and NGOs, and then in a specifically electoral coalition dominated by political parties, the Barisan Alternatif (BA, Alternative Front). The BA aimed to organize the gamut of advocacy groups, mass Islamic organizations, labour unions, public intellectuals and students, as well as all the major opposition political parties in one encompassing coalition to oust Mahathir and reform the political order. At no point previously had the boundary between SMOs and parties been so permeable; activists moved readily between the two, gauging strategically how best to pursue their objectives amid a complex process of political bargaining and protest. For instance, while a limited number of SMO activists had stood as opposition party candidates in the past, the 1999 elections saw a new approach: a coalition of women's SMOs ran their own candidate as part of the BA slate (Martinez 2003). Environmental and other single-issue candidates were considered, too. More broadly, the participation of SMOs in an electoral campaign lent experience in intercommunal coalition-building (given past campaigns over rights violations and other issues), helped with targeted civic education, offered expertise in election and parliamentary monitoring, and vouched for the credibility and plausibility of the opposition platform. However much such engagement might seem to represent institutionalization of a democracy-supporting function for SMOs, more contingent dimensions of personal charisma, organizational capacity and new opportunities for civic education and mobilization offer far greater explanatory leverage, in terms both of whose agendas prevailed then and of long-term implications for civil society.

Social movements and political parties: towards re-engagement?

These patterns of increasing social movement activism and narrowing space between civil society and political society continued to accelerate from the late 1990s on, although with variation between the two countries and over time. After 1998, when the authoritarian regime of President Suharto collapsed, Indonesia experienced a period of reinvigorated social movement activity, reminiscent – at least in terms of raw political energy – of earlier phases of Indonesian history. Especially in the first two or three years of political transition, a vast array of new movements and organizations came into being. The range of groups involved is so diverse as to defy easy summary, but ranged from ethnonationalist movements and indigenous people's groups in peripheral regions to new lobbying groups of employers and business in Jakarta, from new gay and lesbian alliances to transnational Islamist groups, from anti-corruption watchdog organizations in the provinces to ethnic militias trying to control protection rackets in Jakarta or other cities. At the same time, government – which in short order was transformed into a lively multi-party democracy – became more open to input and pressure from social movements and NGOs, especially when it came to legislative reform. Importantly, this period also saw signs of re-engagement by activists in social movements and civil society with political parties, as many of them tried to make the transition from lobbying and pressure group politics to direct engagement in the contest for government power.

One early sign of social movements' re-engagement with political parties came within weeks of the fall of Suharto, when some of the old large *aliran*-based religious organizations sought to re-establish their links with the worlds of party and parliamentary politics. In particular, Muhammadiyah leaders sponsored the formation of PAN (National Mandate Party) and Nahdlatul Ulama sponsored the formation of PKB (National Awakening Party), both of which became important second-tier parties. Yet the 1950s pattern of a 'pillared society', where associational life cohered around political parties engaged in zero-sum conflict, did not revive. The absence of a powerful revolutionary left and abandonment by most Islamic parties of their earlier Islamic state goals meant the party system now lacked the centrifugal dynamic of the earlier decade (Mietzner 2008). More fundamentally, with few exceptions, a lasting legacy of the New Order was that the nexus between political society and civil society was broken and most societal organizations of note were no longer formally or informally aligned with political parties, but free-floating.

Indeed, in some ways, the new pattern of associational activity resembled the image of a diverse and energetic civil society, hemming in and challenging the state on all sides, that had been previously cherished by liberal reformers. Certainly, there was now a diverse range of groups that lobbied for reforms and tried to constrain state activity. This was evident, for example, in the labour sphere, where trade unions proliferated and had perhaps 10 million members five years after the 1997–8 crisis (Quinn 2003: 26, cited in Manning 2010: 157) and large street mobilizations by workers have succeeded in pressuring the government to withdraw revisions to labour legislation viewed as disadvantageous by unions (Manning 2010; see also Caraway 2004: 34–9, Ford 2009: Ch. 7). Above all, however, this pattern was evident in the newfound political influence of NGOs, advocacy organizations and think tanks, which used public pressure through the media or direct lobbying to effect legislative and even constitutional reform in a host of areas, such as the introduction of new anti-corruption laws and agencies, gender mainstreaming policies and laws on domestic violence, the establishment of crucial new democratic institutions such as direct presidential elections and a Constitutional Court, to name a few.

The resemblance between this pattern and the liberal model was itself no accident, but a result of activists' increasing integration in transnational networks, their growing reliance on financial support from developed country donors and, more broadly, growing globalization of politics. In the years following the fall of Suharto, international donors provided huge funding to Indonesian civil society, significantly affecting its shape. Donors like USAID pumped tens of millions of dollars into democracy programmes that, especially early on, largely aimed to build civil society capacity and advocacy. NGOs that flourished and built media profiles and public influence were those that were best able to adapt their discourse and priorities to those of the international agencies, even if this was a process that was fraught with tension and generated many resentments (Sinanu 2010). As the new democratic system settled into place, major donors increasingly shifted to supporting civil society activity that would improve government capacity, especially in policy formulation and service delivery, further contributing to a taming of the early unruly aspects of civil society (Aspinall 2010). Overall, the one place where the goal of a 'strong civil society' continued to be articulated most forcefully was, ironically, in the policy documents of donors.

Yet in certain crucial respects, this new decentred civil society proved to be very weak. Despite the tremendous energy and variety of groups pursuing reform and social justice agendas, NGOs and related groups were unable significantly to affect the basic composition of the ruling elite. The core institutions of state power continued to be dominated by elements of the oligarchic forces that had governed during the New Order (Robison and Hadiz 2004). Even as reforming NGOs saw elements of their political programme embodied in legislative and even constitutional change, they were largely unable to challenge the predatory dynamic that lay at the core of the polity, by which the oligarchy accessed and distributed state resources in the interests of primitive accumulation and power maintenance. Overall, a mood of impotent hostility to the new ruling elite and its corrupt practices emerged in activist circles, accompanied by frank acknowledgments by civil society activists of the limits of their own influence (Prasetyo et al. 2003). An 'anti-party' mood was another result, in which both the wider public and social activists in particular viewed political parties as fundamentally self-interested and corrupt (Johnson Tan 2002).

Another result of the impasse facing the liberal civil society model was an attempt by many individual social movement activists to become directly involved in government, and thus have influence on policy levers from within rather than simply trying to pressure from without. They did this by standing for election to legislatures as party representatives, a trend which became apparent in 2004 but was even stronger in the 2009 elections (McRae 2009). Rather than liberal or democratic reformers establishing a party of their own to contest elections (as had been tried in a few cases in early post-Suharto elections, but achieved abysmally low results), these activists joined mainstream parties as individual candidates. Some individuals, like former student and People's Democratic Party (PRD) activist Budiman Sudjatmiko, achieved some success and a level of influence in established parties (in Sudjatmiko's case, in PDI-P, the Indonesian Democratic Party-Struggle), but more of them failed to be elected (as was the fate, for example, of noted labour activist, Dita Indah Sari). At the time of writing, there is little evidence that the entry of former activists into parliament and the parties is having a significant impact on the tenor of mainstream politics. Rather, it appears to be a means by which a layer of former activists in anti-government social movements are being absorbed into the ruling elite. Such a pattern seems to confirm that the still substantially oligarchic state continues to control access to real power and influence.

Malaysia differs from Indonesia in that there was no democratic breakthrough comparable to the 1998 collapse of the Suharto regime. Indeed, Malaysia's Reformasi challenge of that year proved to be abortive. Yet at the same time, engagement of SMO activists in parties has continued to accelerate. SMOs reprised the collaborative approach they had pioneered in 1998 especially for the 2008 general elections, when regime weakness – this time under Prime Minister Abdullah Ahmad Badawi – again made political opportunities seem favourable for institutional involvement. This time, the combined opposition made unprecedented gains, far surpassing their performance in 1999. Civil societal activists contributed substantially to that achievement by helping to craft unifying platforms; serving as candidates themselves (in far greater numbers, and with greater success and impact, than previously, although as in Indonesia, individual activists had stood for election under various parties also in 1999 and 2004); and ratcheting up both the excitement and the quality of the campaign through protest, media and other activities. In the process, they kept their own core issues, from corruption to sustainable development, on the table. Explained one longtime activist and previous women's movement candidate, the late Zaitun Kasim, at the time, 'We can't leave politics to politicians … it is too important … We campaign on issues that the mainstream political parties will not touch' (quoted in Kuppusamy 2008).

The fact that SMO activists see such potential in electoral politics implies a shift in the timbre of the regime: activists apparently perceive it to be more open than during Mahathir's more autocratic heyday. Moreover, their election not only brought new voices and issues to parliament, but suggested new trends in political participation and empowerment, including the politicization of younger voters via online channels (many linked with SMOs or sympathetic to social movement campaigns) and a growing climate of both critical and constructive discourse. That said, however feasible it is for social activists to enter the electoral fray, those elected tend to lack policy-making experience.

Indeed, however informed by activists' calculations of how best to achieve their ends, the drift from SMOs to political parties comes at a potential cost, both for civil society and for the political system overall. In Indonesia the flow from civil society organizations to political parties has been only a trickle, but in Malaysia activists' focus on elections has taken useful leaders from alternative roles in civil society, added an overt partisan slant to SMOs, and reduced the resources available for impartial post-election policy and performance monitoring. In Malaysia, checks and balances are already weak, especially after years of executive centralization under Mahathir. The sort of democracy these activists themselves tout demands mechanisms for accountability, which could be further enervated by so many key SMO activists joining electoral politics. Even so, critical SMOs do still retain a clear vision of the distinction between social movements and parties. The civil society-based People's Parliament initiative, for instance, established a Citizen Think Tank blog and Representative Watch Committees shortly after the elections 'to help "our MPs" function the way they are supposed to' and to make sure 'the new kids on the block … don't go the way of Barisan' (quoted in Shahanaaz 2008). Moreover, the migration of social movement activists to parties brings into relief the unevenness with which advocacy-oriented NGOs, mass Islamist organizations and other SMOs are distributed across society: most clearly, the bulk of 'NGO candidates' contested in urban areas (especially Selangor, the federal territory of Kuala Lumpur, and Penang), reflecting where their base was strongest.

Overall, however, electoral politics and the actual practice of governing remain distinct from social movement mobilization – the same sort of gulf that leaves many social movement activists feeling politically impotent and suspicious of political parties in Indonesia. Starting even in the comparatively repressive Mahathir years, SMOs have had discernible influence upon certain policy agendas and outputs and activists from civil society have recently come to reprise the organic connections with political parties that marked the late colonial and early postcolonial period. And yet SMOs still face different opportunities, challenges and incentive structures than political parties. For instance, the former are more likely to rely on donor funds than state machinery, and are often better able to focus on issues apart from the communal alignments on which electoral support still tends to rest. SMOs, in short, cannot substitute for political parties in Malaysia or Indonesia, nor can they enjoy the same sort of power, but they do represent an enduringly, and increasingly, important supplement to parties.

Conclusion

Empirical evidence from across 'third wave' states of SMOs' mobilization for democracy, both encouraged and rewarded by (sometimes naïve) donor support, has cultivated a general sense of civil society's liberalizing potential. A strong civil society, the argument goes, makes for a strong democracy. In the background of this view is frequently a Tocquevillean vision in which a strong civil society is one that is dense but decentred, consisting of an array of organizations that hem in the state on every side, each mobilizing distinct constituencies and lobbying in favour of diverse and particularistic interests, but coming together when necessary to achieve common goals. In the Southeast Asian context, questions of regime change and good governance have especially piqued scholarly attention to this vision of civil society and to social movements, particularly given the centrality of such movements in both successful and failed regime transitions, not only in Indonesia and Malaysia in 1998, but also for instance in the Philippines in 1986 and Burma in 1988.

Our analysis of Malaysia and Indonesia provides reasons for caution. On the one hand, Southeast Asia does provide evidence for the political salience of civil society and social movements. The recent histories of both countries illustrates that Southeast Asia is not a political arena where only oligarchs and capital have free rein, but is one where activists and organized masses can at times also have real political agency and impact. However, it would be naïve to reproduce uncritically the celebratory tone of much of the early civil society literature. Trends in the last decade or so in both Malaysia and Indonesia reveal that social movement activists themselves find civil society to be in some respects a limited arena of political struggle, and are thus pulled toward engagement in political parties, electoral competition and attempts to win state power, with varying degrees of success in both countries. Moreover, it is to a large degree the very features of the civil society arena that conform with the liberal vision – the particularism of most civil society organizations, their lobbying orientation and professionalism, the weaknesses of their linkages to political parties and to mass constituencies – which tend to limit their ability to bring about more thorough-going political change. Indeed, it is not too far a stretch to say that it is the limits of the civil society model that have helped to produce limited democracies in Indonesia and Malaysia, and in other Southeast Asian countries. The simultaneous near-hegemony of neoliberal capitalism in the region since at least the 1980s, and the more recent trend toward securitization amid the global 'war on terror', likely magnify these tendencies by exalting the roles of stable states and markets above those of potentially disruptive social forces.

Moreover, in analytical terms, the focus on regime change has blinkered understandings of social movements: analyses have looked far more to NGOs and other SMOs' potential as drivers of democracy rather than to their own internal democracy, or to the modes in which they mediate between the rural/agrarian or urban/industrial grassroots, the middle classes and elite decision-makers. In this view, it makes sense to view civil society not merely as a political agent that may transform the state, but also as an arena where ideas about political and social order are popularized and where, in a Gramscian sense, bourgeois hegemony is achieved (Hedman 2007). In a similar vein, SMOs may be viewed not merely as counterweights to government but also as agents of governmentality, in the Foucauldian sense of the process by which individual subjects come to internalize dominant social and political norms, and to discipline and regulate their own behaviour (e.g. Bryant 2002; Li 2007). NGOs not only discipline the state, but also discipline citizens, especially subordinate groups, to accommodate themselves to emerging democratic political systems and liberal economic orders. And civil society itself is a domain of inequality: NGOs and other social movement organizations discipline client groups and are themselves disciplined by funding agencies and socio-political contexts. Such an understanding does not devalue social movements, but embeds them within the structures of power and hierarchy that infuse society, rather than merely positioning them as outside of, and counterposed to, the state.

Notes

1 On this variety, see for instance Rodan (1997).
2 On this early period, see especially Tham (1977); Firdaus (1985); Roff (1994); Heng (1996); Tan (1997).
3 Chua Beng Huat explains that faced with an immovable incumbent (in the case to which he refers, the Singapore's People's Action Party, although Malaysia's BN fits the pattern), 'opposition parties have in fact to campaign primarily on issues with identifiable constituencies, such as the poor, rather than with the generalized interests of seizing state power' (Chua 1995: 197).
4 Weiss and Saliha (2003) survey several of the most prominent of these movements.

References

Alagappa, M. (ed.) (2004) *Civil Society and Political Change in Asia: Expanding and Contracting Democratic Space*, Stanford, CA: Stanford University Press.
Aspinall, E. (2005) *Opposing Suharto: Compromise, Resistance, and Regime Change in Indonesia*, Stanford, CA: Stanford University Press.
——(2010) *Assessing Democracy Assistance. Indonesia: The Perils of Success*, Madrid: FRIDE.
Billah, M.M. (1994) 'Peta Ornop di Indonesia', Circle for Participatory Social Management (CPSM), Seri Monografi 02/94, Jakarta.
Bryant, R. (2002) 'NGOs and governmentality: "consuming" biodiversity and indigenous people in the Philippines', *Political Studies* 50: 268–92.
Budiman, A. (1990) *State and Civil Society in Indonesia*, Clayton, Vic.: Monash University, Centre of Southeast Asian Studies.
Caraway, T. (2004) 'Protective repression, international pressure, and institutional design: explaining labour reform in Indonesia', *Studies in Comparative International Development* 39 (3): 28–49.

Chua B.-H. (1995) *Communitarian Ideology and Democracy in Singapore*, New York: Routledge.

Clarke, G. (1998) *The Politics of NGOs in South-East Asia: Participation and Protest in the Philippines*, New York: Routledge.

Eldridge, P.J. (1995) *Non–Government Organisations and Democratic Participation in Indonesia*, Kuala Lumpur: Oxford University Press.

Firdaus Haji Abdullah (1985) *Radical Malay Politics: Its Origins and Early Development*, Petaling Jaya: Pelanduk Publications.

Ford, M. (2009) *Workers and Intellectuals: NGOs, Trade Unions and the Indonesian Labour Movement*, Singapore: National University of Singapore Press.

Geertz, C. (1959) 'The Javanese village', in G. W. Skinner (ed.) *Local, Ethnic and National Loyalties in Village Indonesia*, Yale University Cultural Report Series, New Haven, CT: Yale University Press, pp. 34–41.

——(1960) *The Religion of Java*, New York: Free Press of Glencoe.

Gurmit, Singh K.S. (1984) *Malaysian Societies: Friendly or Political?*, Petaling Jaya: Environmental Protection Society Malaysia and Selangor Graduates Society.

——(1990) *A Thorn in the Flesh*, Petaling Jaya: Gurmit Singh K.S.

Hadiz, V.R. (1997) *Workers and the State in New Order Indonesia*, London: Routledge.

Hedman, E.-L.E. (2007) *In the Name of Civil Society: From Free Election Movements to People Power in the Philippines*, Honolulu: University of Hawai'i Press.

Heng P.K. (1996) 'Chinese responses to Malay hegemony in peninsular Malaysia 1957–59', *Tonan Ajia Kenkyu [Southeast Asian Studies]* 34 (3): 32–55.

Johnson Tan, P. (2002) 'Anti-party reaction in Indonesia: causes and implications', *Contemporary Southeast Asia* 24 (3): 484–508.

Kerkvliet, B.J.T., R.H.K. Heng and D.W.H. Koh (eds) (2003) *Getting Organized in Vietnam: Moving in and around the Socialist State*, Singapore: ISEAS.

Kuppusamy, Baradan (2008) 'Politics – Malaysia: civil society leaders enter election fray' Inter Press Service, 13 February; available at: http://ipsnews.net (accessed 4 July 2008).

Kyaw Yin Hlaing (2004) 'Burma: civil society skirting regime rules', in M. Alagappa (ed.) *Civil Society and Political Change in Asia: Expanding and Contracting Democratic Space*, Stanford, CA: Stanford University Press, pp. 390–418.

Li, T.M. (2007) *The Will to Improve: Governmentality, Development, and the Practice of Politics*, Durham and London: Duke University Press.

Liddle, R.W. (1973) 'Modernizing Indonesian politics', in R.W. Liddle (ed.) *Political Participation in Modern Indonesia*, Yale University Southeast Asia Studies Monograph Series No. 19, New Haven, CT: Yale University Press, pp. 177–206.

McRae, D. (2009) 'Seeking representation', *Inside Indonesia* 97; available at: http://insideindonesia.org/content/view/1214/47/ (accessed 3 April 2010).

Manning, C. (2010) 'The political economy of reform: labour after Soeharto', in E. Aspinall and G. Fealy (eds) *Soeharto's New Order and its Legacy: Essays in Honour of Harold Crouch*, Canberra: ANU E Press, pp. 151–72.

Martinez, P. (2003) 'Complex configurations: the Women's Agenda for Change and the Women's Candidacy Initiative', in M.L. Weiss and Saliha Hassan (eds) *Social Movements in Malaysia: From Moral Communities to NGOs*, London: RoutledgeCurzon.

Means, G.P. (1991) *Malaysian Politics: The Second Generation*, Singapore: Oxford University Press.

Mietzner, M. (2008) 'Comparing Indonesia's party systems of the 1950s and the post-Suharto era: from centrifugal to centripetal inter-party competition', *Journal of Southeast Asian Studies* 39 (3): 431–53.

Milner, A.C. (1991) 'Inventing politics: the case of Malaysia', *Past and Present: A Journal of Historical Studies* 132: 104–29.

Prasetyo, S.A., A.E. Priyono and O. Törnquist (eds) (2003) *Indonesia's Post-Soeharto Democracy Movement*, Jakarta: Demos.

Quinn, P. (2003) 'Freedom of association and collective bargaining: a study of Indonesian experience 1998–2003', Working Paper, ILO, Geneva.

Reeve, D. (1985) *Golkar of Indonesia: An Alternative to the Party System*, Singapore: Oxford University Press.

Robison, R. and V.R. Hadiz (2004) *Reorganizing Power in Indonesia: The Politics of Oligarchy in an Age of Markets*, London and New York: RoutledgeCurzon

Rodan, G. (1997) 'Civil society and other political possibilities in Southeast Asia', *Journal of Contemporary Asia* 27 (2): 156–78.

Roff, W.R. (1994 [1967]) *The Origins of Malay Nationalism*, second edition, Kuala Lumpur: Oxford University Press.

Shahanaaz Habib (2008) 'Fighting for the right to speak', *The Star* (Malaysia), 18 May.

Sinanu, F. (2010) 'Everyday politics of global civil society: a study of relationships between local and international NGOs in Indonesia', unpublished PhD dissertation, Australian National University.

Tan L.E. (1997) *The Politics of Chinese Education in Malaya 1945–1961*, Kuala Lumpur: Oxford University Press.

Tham S.C. (1977) *The Role and Impact of Formal Associations on the Development of Malaysia*, Bangkok: Friedrich-Ebert-Stiftung.

Uhlin, A. (1997) *Indonesia and the 'Third Wave of Democratization': The Indonesian Pro-Democracy Movement in a Changing World*, Richmond: Curzon Press.

Weiss, M.L. and Saliha Hassan (eds) (2003) *Social Movements in Malaysia: From Moral Communities to NGOs*, London: RoutledgeCurzon.

15

DECENTRALIZATION AND DEMOCRACY IN INDONESIA

Strengthening citizenship or regional elites?

Henk Schulte Nordholt

Because Soeharto's authoritarian New Order regime (1966–98) was highly centralized, political observers focused their attention almost exclusively on the political centre, where more than 70 per cent of the money of the national economy circulated. Developments in the regions, often depicted as a passive periphery, were by and large ignored. However, after the fall of President Soeharto the relationship between the centre and regions changed fundamentally. From 1999 onwards a transition from authoritarian rule to electoral democracy was accompanied by administrative decentralization.

These changes did not come out of the blue nor were they unique for Indonesia. Since the 1980s centralized states across the world were seriously undermined by both neoliberalism and the fall of the Berlin Wall. In the western world a belief in the welfare state had given way to the acceptance of privatization while the end of the Cold War meant an end to the socialist state and the necessity to support authoritarian regimes in the so-called Third World. The assault on the centralized state was supported by an unlikely alliance of agencies including the World Bank, which believed that less state would result in more and better markets, and by NGO activists who considered the state as a repressive institution which had to be counterbalanced by democratic forces based in civil society.

In Eastern Europe and throughout Africa processes of administrative decentralization resulted in various degrees of regional autonomy. In Indonesia both regional autonomy and democracy were also at the heart of political change and were expected to enhance good governance and strengthen the role of civil society. This chapter aims to evaluate these optimistic expectations and investigate the extent to which local elites were able to capture and harness the local state.

The rapid implementation of a dependent decentralization

Because Indonesia suffered seriously from the monetary crisis in Asia which haunted the region from 1997 onwards, it had to accept the terms under which the International Monetary Fund (IMF) was willing to provide a loan of US$43 billion. Decentralization was a key demand because the IMF wanted to dismantle the centralized authoritarian state and the obstacles to markets embedded in it. There were, however, also domestic motivations to move quickly towards regional autonomy. After Soeharto's demise the ruling (state-sponsored) Golkar party had become the target of widespread criticism. This was, in particular, the case in Java where the monetary crisis had a serious impact on living standards and the new political party of Megawati Sukarnoputri, PDI-P, appealing to popular sentiment, rapidly gained ground. Thus, in order to survive the 1999 elections Golkar had to consolidate its position in the so-called Outer Islands. Outside Java the effects of the crisis were less serious but resentment against Javanese domination was widespread. In order to harness these sentiments Golkar overnight turned into an enthusiastic supporter of decentralization (Schulte Nordholt and van Klinken 2007).

Between April 1999 and January 2001 reforms aimed at regional autonomy were implemented with remarkable speed and without major disturbances. Ironically, it was from the outset a top-down operation. The plan was designed by a small group of high-level bureaucrats who were trained in public administration at American universities and maintained close links with international agencies ideologically committed to decentralization. In April 1999 the national parliament, still populated with old New Order politicians, accepted Law 22/1999 on Regional Autonomy without much discussion, even though the regions had not been consulted. The centre itself had made an end to more than three decades of centralized rule (Schulte Nordholt and van Klinken 2007).

Decentralization in Indonesia involved a process of administritive devolution, which involved the actual transfer of extensive formal administrative and political authority to lower levels of government. From now on elected parliaments in provinces, districts and municipalities would choose their own administrator and decide their own budgets. Districts and municipalities were primarily responsible for a wide range of administrative tasks. Strictly speaking, the central government was only responsible for national security and defence, foreign policy, fiscal and monetary matters, macroeconomic policy, justice and religion. Districts and municipalities were responsible for infrastructure, healthcare, trade, agriculture, industry, investment, environmental and land issues, education and culture.[1] Because the new autonomy was located at the district level, the power of provinces, a larger administrative unit, was dismantled, apparently to exclude the possibility of separatism based on various ethnic or historical allegiances.

Yet regional autonomy was not accompanied by the rise of local political parties. The law on political parties from that same year allowed only national parties to participate in the election, which initially gave national party bosses a considerable say in regional affairs. Seen from this perspective, decentralization was a divide-and-rule strategy, permitting administrative fragmentation, but guaranteeing ultimate control by the centre.

While Law 22/1999 was drafted by the Ministry of Interior, the accompanying Revenue Sharing Law (25/1999) was made by the Ministry of Finance and revealed the extent to which regional autonomy would still depend on the centre. The law stipulated that 25 per cent of the net domestic revenue would be channelled to the regions, 90 per cent of which had to be allocated to districts and municipalities. This implied that the central state would remain in control of 75 per cent of the state revenues. The central government maintained its grip on 80 per cent of the income tax, the value-added tax, import and export duties, and foreign aid.

Budgets of districts and municipalities consisted of a lump sum (the so-called *Dana Alokasi Umum*, DAU) which accounted on average for 80 per cent of the total revenue at the district level. Apart from these funds the government could allocate special funds, which accounted for 10 per cent of the said DAU.

Regions were allowed to raise their own income in the form of special taxation but these remained on the whole minor revenue sources. Only resource-rich regions profited considerably from the new law because they were allowed to keep 15 per cent of oil, 30 per cent of gas and 80 per cent of logging, mining and fishing revenues. This also implies that the central state kept 85 per cent of the oil and 70 per cent of the gas revenues. Only a few districts like Badung in South Bali (income from tourism) and Kutai Kertanegara in East Kalimantan (oil, gas and mining revenues) were, in financial terms, autonomous. Although decentralization had reduced the imbalance between centre and region as a whole, imbalances between rich and poor regions increased, because the richest regions now had access to fifty times more revenue than the poorest. Fiscal decentralization was therefore by and large synonymous with an uneven subsidized autonomy.[2]

The regional autonomy laws were implemented with considerable speed. Within twenty months the salaries of 2.1 million state employees were transferred from the national payroll to local budgets, and hundreds of laws, regulations and procedures had – ideally – to be adapted or abolished. Given the fact that many districts lacked sufficient capacity to meet the demands of this massive operation and provinces were no longer allowed to play a coordinating role, it was a small miracle that the implementation occurred without major disasters. Part of the explanation for this is that, for the majority of the population, their daily lives and economic activity did not depend too much on the government. Moreover, many things remained centralized, despite the new measures. For instance, decisions on the school curriculum and standards for exams were still made in Jakarta, while many administrators still continued their old habit of visiting Jakarta for consultations. This ambiguous situation produced a dependent form of autonomy.

Administrative involution

An unexpected effect of decentralization was the separation of provinces and districts, causing a rapid increase in the number of administrative units. Seven new provinces were carved out of the existing twenty-seven, bringing the total to thirty-three (excluding East Timor which became independent as a result of the popular vote in September 1999). At the same time the number of districts and municipalities increased from 300 in 1998 to no fewer than 440 in 2005. This process was called *pemekaran*, or flowering, and occurred mainly outside Java. By redrawing district borders new administrative units were created with exclusive access to government funding and potential for attracting lucrative contracts to build brand new administrative centres. This administrative involution was mainly driven from below by the combined interests of bureaucrats, politicians and business elites. By mobilizing ethnic sentiments and promising to bring government closer to the people these interests sought both local and national support for the creation of new districts. Because the national parliament had to approve the establishment of new districts, it goes without saying that this process involved intensive lobbying and transfers of money from district elites into the pockets of politicians in Jakarta. The 'costs' of a new district ranged from 1.5 to 3 billion Rupiah (US$150,000–300,000 based on the exchange rate at the time).

Sometimes the making of new provinces was stimulated by electoral motives and patronage networks in Jakarta. The small province of Gorontalo was, for instance, created in 1999 with the support of President Habibie, whose father came from that area. *Pemekaran* created uneven outcomes: the new province of Gorontalo had 800,000 inhabitants whereas the province of East Java counted 35 million people. Although *pemekaran* was an unplanned outcome of decentralization, it was not unique. Similar processes occurred also in Eastern Europe after the fall of the Berlin Wall, and in Africa. Moreover, because of the territorial command structure of the Indonesian army, the establishment of new districts caused not only an increase of local administrative bureaucracies but also an expansion of the military presence at the district level as it sought to build parallel structures.

An interesting example of *pemekaran* from above occurred in Papua. Under the presidency of Abdurrahman Wahid (1999–2001) when province was granted special autonomy in 2001.

This implied amongst other things that the province was entitled to keep 80 per cent of its mining revenues and 70 per cent of its oil and gas incomes. A special council (the Majelis Rakyat Papua, MRP) representing various interest groups, was to be established, which had to be consulted by the government on important matters. However, in 2003 President Megawati created the new province of West Papua and a series of new districts without consulting the MRP. By creating the new administrative units her own party, PDI-D, tried to challenge the power monopoly of Golkar in Papua. At the same time this move also increased internal discord among Papuans, which diverted them from unified national aspirations. On their part the armed forces had maintained a special mandate in Papua and the creation of this and other new districts strengthened their position even further.[3]

Contrary to neoliberal expectations that decentralization would reduce the size of the state, regional autonomy in Indonesia produced *more state* at the regional level while it brought not only government but also the military closer to the people.

The fight for regional power

The demise of Soeharto's New Order and the transition towards decentralization and democratization were accompanied by unprecedented civil warfare in West and Central Kalimantan, Central Sulawesi and the Moluccas. These so-called communal conflicts were fuelled by religious and ethnic sentiments, and caused 10,000 casualties and 1.3 million refugees (van Klinken 2007: 4).

Initially three sets of explanations were heard at the seminars in Jakarta where activists and academics met to discuss the sudden eruptions of regional violence. The first emphasized culture as the decisive factor, pointing at the 'primordial' nature of the conflict between Dayak and Madurese in Kalimantan. Perceived ethnic characteristics, such as 'Madurese are prone to violence', and 'Dayak are deep down still head hunters', were often employed to explain the violence. This perspective obscured human agency but represented the view of the 'civilized' centre looking down upon the backwardness and irrational cultural behaviour in the margins of Indonesia.

Another Jakarta-biased explanation maintained that violence in the regions was orchestrated by the armed forces and the Soeharto family who used the unrest to serve their own political interests at the national level. This approach denied the relevance of local agency. Although external influences had an impact on local conflicts, notably in the case of military interventions in Maluku, they were not decisive.

Finally, attempts have been made to explain the violence in economic terms as rebellions by underprivileged groups, like the Dayak who rebelled against the exploitation of their natural resources, or, as in Ambon, as a confrontation between immigrants and locals. The problem with this approach is that it does not explain why violence only occurred in particular places and not where similar economic and ethnic differences existed, and why these conflicts only took place at a particular moment in time.

In a convincing comparative analysis Gerry van Klinken (2007) contends that regional violence occurred during a period in which the power of the central state had temporarily weakened. Owing to the economic crisis, Jakarta was no longer able to invest in regional economies. As a result local elites no longer felt rewarded and protected by their superiors in the capital, while decentralization and democratic elections were on their way but the precise rules and regulation were not yet clear. This caused unrest and fear among regional elites but also offered them new opportunities. Under these circumstances, communal tensions turned into violent conflicts in West and Central Kalimantan, Central Sulawesi and the Moluccas.

According to van Klinken (2007) violence erupted in provincial towns, which had over the past decades experienced a rapid but state-dependent economic growth in combination with a high level of immigration. The result was an economy that depended to a large extent on state investments and government employment, and an urban environment that was highly diverse in terms of religion and ethnicity. Contrary to classic modernization sociology, which argues that religious and ethnic differences fade away as a result of modernization, these differences increased.

Under these highly volatile circumstances, urban elites tried to seize power in order to control flows of money and to dominate the changing political arena at the regional level. The leading actors during the conflicts were, according to van Klinken, influential urban politicians-cum-bureaucrats with good connections to local business people. In their efforts to gain regional power they mobilized their ethnic and/or religious constituencies. In Poso and the Moluccas escalating violence added to this momentum as well.[4]

Gradually violence came to an end in 2001–2 because participants were exhausted and the central government was thereby eventually able to intervene. Interestingly, none of those who had initiated the fighting had succeeded in gaining powerful positions. In Central Kalimantan one of the main protagonists of Dayak interests was defeated during elections for the governorship. In West Kalimantan and Central Sulawesi contending parties created separate districts for themselves, while in many regions a district head from one group chose a representative from the other group as his deputy.

Adat, aristocracy and regional identity politics

The communal conflicts had shown the ugly face of religious and ethnic identity politics in Indonesia. However, decentralization did not always coincide with violence, but throughout the archipelago there was an increase of exclusive identity politics at the regional level. Sometimes these were expressed in terms of *adat*, or customary law, elsewhere old aristocratic families tried to make a comeback.

Under colonial rule, *adat* law had become a tool in the hands of conservative Dutch administrators who wanted to contain the spread of Islam and nationalism by emphasizing the special character of separate regions in the archipelago. *Adat* was in this context used as an antidote to national unity and political mobilization. After independence *adat* lost its momentum, and under the New Order it was further marginalized into the domain of folklore. However, after Soeharto had stepped down, there was a widespread revival of *adat* consciousness because it was seen as a moral alternative for the corrupt New Order regime and a device to reclaim land that had been confiscated by the state (Davidson and Henley 2007). In 1999, the Alliance of Adat Communities in Indonesia (AMAN, Aliansi Masyarakat Adat Nusantara) was established by NGOs which claimed to represent deprived *adat* communities. Their 'traditional rights' were phrased in modern terms like 'grass roots', 'bottom up' and 'empowerment'. The notion of '*adat* community' resembles the term 'indigenous people' but this equation turned out to be problematic. Moreover, the notion of '*adat* community' presumes a homogeneous ethnic group and denies the impact of urbanization, migration and state institutions, also raising the question of who actually belongs to such a community and who is seen as an outsider. The emphasis on *adat* creates the opportunity to exclude migrants and tends to increase gender differences within these 'communities' (Schulte Nordholt 2008a: 149–51). Often, urban-based intellectuals spoke on behalf of these communities and claimed to represent their interests. These were sometimes caught up in the corruption that became such a part of the new local politics (Eindhoven 2007).

Just like *adat*, the position of regional aristocracies was firmly rooted in the late colonial state when the Dutch established a system of indirect rule in which the local nobility had to provide colonial authority with a familiar 'traditional' face. After independence most aristocrats lost political power and influence because they were seen as conservative allies of the colonial regime. After the fall of Soeharto, especially in areas outside Java descendants of old ruling families saw new opportunities to restore their former status. The moral bankruptcy of the New Order and the new regional autonomy opened the door to revive former sultanates and small kingdoms (*kerajaan*) which represented a nostalgic longing for the good old days when people supposedly lived in harmony under the benign leadership of local rulers. Corruption and the abuse of power, which had been intrinsic to indirect rule, were erased from this romantic picture of the past (Schulte Nordholt 2008a: 151–3).

Adat and aristocracy are alternative sources of authority, but it remains unclear how they fit into modern democracy. While some descendants of former rulers were used by ambitious administrators to give local culture more profile and stimulate tourism, others, like the Sultan of Ternate, had political ambitions of their own. In this case, the Sultan's attempt to become governor of the new province of the North Moluccas was not built on a reconciliation of conflicting parties under traditional leadership but involved becoming part of political conflicts and resulted in a humiliating defeat.

Thus, across the archipelago, decentralization encouraged the rise of identity politics. In Bali the so-called Ajeg Bali (Resilient Bali) movement aimed to defend Balinese culture vis-à-vis perceived outside threats. It gained widespread support and took an anti-Muslim turn by emphasizing the exclusive Hindu character of Balinese culture (Schulte Nordholt 2007). In the new province of Riau, in the other hand, efforts to emphasize an aristocratic Malay identity turned out to be problematic because of the many Chinese and other migrants, while the proximity of Singapore offered a potentially attractive model of modernity to counter appeals to tradition. Appeals to local culture were also offset by the national Jakarta-based television culture while the high modernity of Singapore was felt to be intimidating (Faucher 2007).

The irony of the Ajeg Bali movement and similar movements elsewhere in the archipelago is that they tend to stress their regional authenticity in a very similar *Indonesian* way through strikingly identical seminars where local identities are formulated through a mixture of old colonial concepts phrased in post-New Order bureaucratic language. The focus on regional autonomy and local identity politics tended to emphasize ethnic and religious differences. As a result a broader discourse on a common *Indonesian citizenship*, which presumes equality under the rule of law, was obscured.

Decentralizing corruption

Decentralization did not automatically result in good governance, partly because there was, at the district level, a general lack of administrative expertise. As noted earlier, international institutions like the World Bank saw decentralization primarily in technocratic terms and emphasized 'capacity building' to improve the quality of regional government. In doing so they ignored the entrenched nature of regional interest groups and their involvement in on-going power struggles (Hadiz 2003; Schulte Nordholt and van Klinken 2007: 15–18). Regional autonomy was, moreover, also characterized by a decentralization of corruption and other bad habits from post-New Order Jakarta.

Regional government was perhaps weak in administrative terms, but far from powerless. For their business activities traders and entrepreneurs needed formal licences and permissions from the local state and this opened the door for a variety of lucrative 'private–public' arrangements in which bureaucrats, politicians, the security forces and businessmen participated. The establishment of new provinces and districts (*pemekaran*) involved the building of new administrative centres where similar connections between politicians, bureaucrats and businessmen proved to be very profitable. These informal arrangements were made in the shade of the formal state and resulted in a privatization of public goods and an institutionalization of private interests (Robison and Hadiz 2004). The new province of Banten, for example, was to a large extent the project of a wealthy contractor with good connections in the upper world of Golkar and the criminal underworld of *jawara*. His daughter was elected by the provincial parliament as vice-governor but soon succeeded the governor, who was convicted for corruption (Masaaki and Hamid 2008; see also below). In the new province of Bangka-Belitung the mining and smuggling of tin became a source of income for the new provincial and district administrators in collusion with entrepreneurs, gangsters, the police and the navy (Erwiza 2007).

In this context rain forests became the main victims of regional autonomy. Initially, decentralization allowed district administrators to issue logging permits for small plots of land. This happened on a large scale, and it accelerated deforestation and the accumulation by local administrative-cum-business elites while the armed forces received protection money. From 2002 onwards the national Ministry of Forestry tried to reclaim its central authority, but in many regions large-scale corruption prevailed (McCarthy 2007; Morishita 2008).

Owing to the continuation of the so-called territorial system the Indonesian army maintained a powerful position at the district level. However, since the army and police were separated in 1999, the police service had to create its own sources of income (from gambling, prostitution and drug trafficking). This resulted sometimes in violent confrontations with the army over the control of profitable parts of the black economy (ICG 2002; Kingsbury and McCulloch 2006: 214).

From 2001 to 2005 it was clear that regional parliaments were emerging as hotbeds of corruption and had a strong bargaining position vis-à-vis the administrators. Because parliaments elected the new administrators, candidates running for office had to pay large sums of money in order to win the majority of the votes. These elections were often accompanied by violence and intimidation on the part of thugs affiliated with the main contenders (Hadiz 2003; Hidayat 2007; Schulte Nordholt 2007: 43–51). Because political parties distrusted each other military factions played a key role in many provincial and district parliaments during the election of governors and district heads. In 2002 and 2003 (retired) military officers became governors of Jakarta, West, Central and East Java, North Sumatra, Lampung and East Kalimantan (Mietzner 2009: 233).

Once elected, district heads and mayors faced regular confrontations with their parliaments in order to get their budget proposals and annual accountability reports approved. There is substantial evidence that such approvals often involved the transfer of large sums of money. Moreover, the bargaining power of parliaments over the executive was strengthened by their right to impeach administrators.

It can be reasonably argued that the vast majority of the 17,000 members of regional parliaments in Indonesia did not primarily represent the interests of their constituents. Instead, they considered themselves, at one level, to be part of a government that ruled by *fiat*. They enjoyed considerable privileges like cars, houses and regular visits to faraway places.

The impact of direct elections

Soon after the implementation of regional autonomy it became evident that the relationship between parliaments and administrators, had to be reviewed. In general, corrupt parliaments kept administrators hostage by forcing them to pay large amounts of money in order maintain their official positions. When in 2002 a constitutional revision opened the way for direct presidential elections, the national parliament decided that direct elections should also be held for governors, mayors and district administrators. This resulted in the revised Regional Autonomy Law no. 32 of 2004 (Schulte Nordholt 2008a: 234–7; Mietzner 2009: 345–9; Buehler 2010).

The new law strengthened the position of the governors, mayors and other administrators and reduced the power of regional parliaments. Direct elections gave administrators a stronger popular mandate and reduced the corrupt backroom practices of buying votes in parliaments. Administrators were no longer obliged to deliver an annual accountability report, meaning that parliaments lost another source of income. Moreover, under the new law, parliaments lost their right to impeach administrators and could only ask the Minister of Interior to do so, which reduced the number of impeachment cases considerably. Administrators, on the other hand, enjoyed more autonomy in financial and administrative matters. Districts heads also obtained a firmer grip on village administration, while village democracy was no longer mentioned in the law. At the provincial level, the position of the governors was somewhat strengthened. They received more coordinating responsibilities and remained strategic financial brokers because government funds were channelled through their offices to districts and municipalities.

From June 2005 onwards direct elections for regional administrators (*Pilkada*) were held throughout Indonesia. Between June 2005 and June 2007, 285 district heads and mayors, and fifteen new governors were elected. Initially, candidates had no experience with direct elections. In the first year 40 per cent of the incumbent administrators who ran for re-election suffered a defeat. It became clear that, apart from money politics, the evidence of administrative competence was also a necessary precondition for re-election. Moreover, candidates with a military background almost disappeared from the scene. Through a change in the Constitution military representatives lost their seats in national and regional parliaments and further military officers on average did not have enough funds to run for office.

Old-fashioned civil and military bureaucrats without popular support were replaced by new administrators who could mobilize large sums of money to finance their campaign. Still, 36 per cent of the new administrators consisted of government bureaucrats, who apparently had access to government funds and other forms of institutional support, while 28 per cent of the new administrators were entrepreneurs who could finance their own campaign. Candidates campaigned together with a running mate. Many successful pairs consisted of an experienced bureaucrat and a wealthy businessman, combining bureaucratic connections and capital.[5]

Direct elections raised the costs of campaigning considerably. Instead of the strategic bribing of a limited number of politicians (50 per cent plus one) district- and province-wide campaigns had to be funded. These generally involved advertisements in newspapers and on local television, banners, t-shirts, mass meetings with popular artists and, if necessary, street rallies for which participants received two to three US dollars each. On average the costs of a campaign at the district level were 1.5 million US dollars. Direct elections enhanced electoral democracy but limited the number of candidates at the same time.

It was not only corrupt parliaments, but political parties as well that hindered the development of regional democracy. Apart from Aceh, where local parties are permitted, in the rest of Indonesia only national parties may participate in regional elections. Because political parties tend to spend their funds primarily on national elections they are unable to support the large number of regional elections. Moreover, government subsidies for political parties were seriously reduced in 2005. Therefore, national party bosses tried to use regional elections as a means to make money. Local candidates had to pay political parties large sums of money in order to receive support to run for office or to obtain an eligible place on a party list.[6]

Candidates running for the position of district head had to pay party bosses in Jakarta up to US $200,000.

In order to reduce the grip of political parties on the regional electoral process, an amended Regional Autonomy Law (no. 12/2008) allowed independent candidates to run for office. This weakened the bargaining position of political parties, because party bosses were now under pressure to attract popular candidates to run for office under the banner of their party.

Important changes also occurred in elections for regional parliaments. Under Election Law no. 3, from 1999 constituents could only vote for a party. Each party selected its own list of candidates. But according to Law no. 12 from 2003 people could choose a party and select for themselves a particular candidate nominated on the official party list. The new Election Law no. 10 from 2008, followed by a decision of the Constitutional Court from December 2008, abolished the ranking order of the party lists. All these measures were intended to reduce the power of party bosses to collect money in exchange for a strategic place on the list. Now anyone on the list who obtained enough votes could be elected. This measure had unintended consequences because everyone started to campaign for him or herself, while competition between people on the same list was as serious as between candidates from different parties. It also meant that everybody had to pay his or her own campaign, as a result of which campaign costs skyrocketed.

By and large regional elections ran smoothly after 2005. The voter turnout is high, campaigns are not violent, and elections are fair. In that sense electoral democracy has taken root in Indonesia. Moreover, ethnic and religious cleavages no longer feature prominently in the elections, due to processes of *pemekaran*, which have resulted in a degree of ethnic or religious segregation, and because candidates are generally forced to mobilize constituencies beyond their own ethnic or religious group.

Administrators have strengthened their position, and electoral process is successful, but does that imply good governance and a democratization of administrative institutions?

Contested leadership

In general regional autonomy has not generated good governance. Owing to exposure in the media and pressure by external donors and critical constituencies during elections, and threatened by anti-corruption agencies from Jakarta, administrators are forced to invest more money in public health, education and infrastructure. However, the quality of service delivery has not improved and most local governments are unable to develop coherent and effective projects, while 80 per cent of local business continues to pay bribes (Buehler 2010).

Incidental success depends very much on a few exceptionally well-performing administrators. In December 2008 *Tempo* magazine presented, under the telling title 'A few good men', portraits of ten regional administrators with an admirable track record. They were argued to be 'clean', i.e. not corrupt, and able to improve public services. In a similar vein a Dutch newspaper wrote about the district head of Lebak in Banten. It had been exactly 150 years earlier, in 1859, that Multatuli (Eduard Douwes Dekker) had published his famous novel *Max Havelaar* in which the corrupt practices of the district head of Lebak at the time were exposed. One and a half centuries later the present district head, Haji Mulyadi Jayabaya, led a Multatuli revival in Lebak: the main road and a big auditorium are named after Multatuli. For the populist district head, there were clear advantages in supporting Multatuli, as a symbol of the eradication of corruption, and the promotion of free education and good governance (Vlasblom 2009). The examples of these 'few good men' clearly suggest that the performance of the vast majority of the district administrators is less impressive.

Despite the strengthening of their position, the new regional administrators in Indonesia must be distinguished from the system of 'bosses' that prevails in the Philippines. Nor do they generate new regional dynasties. In the Philippines, regional strongmen 'enjoy a monopolistic position over coercive and economic resources within their respective bailiwicks: long term mayors who ran their municipalities as their private fiefdoms, … [and] … governors … built up political machines and business empires that spanned entire districts or provinces' (Sidel 2004: 56). Instead, local power in Indonesia should be characterized by much more fluid clusters of bureaucrats, politicians and businessmen (Sidel 2004: 69). Most regional administrators in Indonesia are dependent on state funding, and vulnerable to electoral changes and judicial investigations.

The career of Chasan Sochib in West Java is a case in point. As already mentioned above, he had made a fortune in the construction business through his close relations with Golkar leaders and high-ranking military officers. He also had access to a wide network of criminal gangs which could be mobilized during elections. In 2000 he supported the establishment of a separate province of Banten and, in 2001, manoeuvred his daughter into the position of vice-governor. When the governor was arrested for corruption she succeeded him. Meanwhile her father ruled the new province from behind the scenes and allegedly said: 'I am actually the Governor General' (Masaaki and Hamid 2008: 125; see also Hidayat 2007). In 2006 his daughter was elected as governor but despite broad support by Golkar and PDI-P and extensive vote buying, she won the elections with only a very small margin. It turned out that the popularity of the 'ruling family' was rapidly declining because 'the governor' had failed to deliver the concrete benefits sought by his supporters.

Another example of family rule can be found in South Sulawesi (Buehler 2007; van Klinken 2008). Yasin Limpo came from an aristocratic family. In the 1950s he established a career in the army, and then switched to a civilian career in the provincial administration in the 1960s. Besides several business activities he also headed the boy scouts in South Sulawesi, which provided an opportunity to mobilize mass support for Golkar. His sons and daughters were also active in business and in politics. His son, Shahrul Yasin Limpo, started his career in the regional bureaucracy; he became district head in 1994 and was re-elected in 1999. Despite the fact that he was arrested in 2001 for drug abuse, in 2002 he successfully ran for the position of vice-governor of South Sulawesi. In November 2007 he challenged the incumbent governor and won the direct elections for the governorship of South Sulawesi with a very narrow margin. His victory was heavily contested. The defeated former governor appealed to the Supreme Court in Jakarta, accusing his opponent of ballot-rigging. The Court ordered a re-vote in several districts, which was refused by the local election committee. In the meantime local government was paralysed and the President appointed a caretaker, while Vice-President Yusuf Kalla, who comes from South Sulawesi, interfered as well. Eventually a re-count of the ballots, not a new vote, in the disputed districts confirmed the victory of Shahrul Yasin Limpo. The position of both the Limpo family and Chasan Sochib and his family is still strong but not uncontested. Within the system of direct elections even the most powerful families struggle to succeed.

Anti-corruption investigations threaten the continuity of the new regional power holders as well. Between 2002 and 2006, seven governors, sixty-three districts heads, and over a thousand members of regional parliaments were under investigation (Masaaki and Hamid 2008: 111–12). The number of convicted persons was less impressive, though. *Tempo* (2008) recorded that in 2007 sixty-one administrators were convicted, while in 2008 according to Buehler (2010) only twenty persons were actually detained.

A major anti-corruption case resulted in the arrest of Syaukani, the strongman of Kutai Kertanegara in East Kalimantan in 2007 (Evaquarta 2010). Kutai Kertanegara is one of the richest districts in Indonesia, possessing large amounts of oil, gas, coal and timber. During the New Order Syaukani had made a bureaucratic career in Golkar and had become Speaker in the district parliament. In 1999 he was elected as district head and became the chairman of the prestigious national association of district heads, APKASI. Due to the large revenues which flowed into the local government after regional autonomy had been implemented, he was able to build and finance a wide and powerful network of patron–client relationships. He ran for governor in 2008. However, an investigation by the national Corruption Eradication Commission (KPK) revealed that he had embezzled large sums of local revenue. In 2007 he was arrested, and instead of being elected as governor in 2008 he was sentenced to six years' imprisonment. Interestingly, Syaukani was convicted despite efforts by Vice-President Yusuf Kalla to rescue him. East Kalimantan possesses a concentration of natural resources and therefore it is understandable that it would be the target for a range of high-ranking power holders in Jakarta. Syaukani had hoped for support from national Golkar bosses like Yusuf Kalla. However, rather than Golkar, it was the Partai Demokrat of President Susilo Bambang Yudhoyono which took over control in East Kalimantan (Morishita 2008).

Looking back at these recent developments one may conclude that political leadership at the regional level still commonly seeks extra-legal funding for political success but is at the same time vulnerable vis-à-vis external anti-corruption investigations and critical constituencies. There are few indications that electoral democracy will soon lead to a fundamental democratization of government institutions.

Patronage democracy and weak citizenship

Regional autonomy and electoral democracy have to a large extent blurred the boundaries between state and society (Barker and van Klinken 2009). This embeddedness is partly the consequence of a variety of collusive networks connecting bureaucrats, politicians, businessmen and the armed forces. But it has also to do with the nature of elite–commoner relationships.

If 'bossism' is not the right term to describe this new political situation, 'patronage democracy' is perhaps a better concept to identify the main dynamics in regional politics. Seen from the perspective of patrons, 'patronage democracy' is very much embedded in local social settings with 'local elites who derive their power mainly from the state, and who relate with their constituency through clientelistic practices ... while their constituency identifies itself mainly in localist, often communalist terms' (van Klinken 2009: 145). Since patronage democracy combines patron–client relations with electoral democracy it puts greater emphasis on the bargaining power of clients vis-à-vis their patrons, while at the same time clients prefer to maintain unequal relationships with powerful patrons (Simandjuntak 2010). This patronage democracy is not transitory but permanent.

The extent to which one can categorize regional patrons as a class is open to debate. In abstract terms this is certainly true. In this respect, Rodan and Jayasuriya (2009) point at the resilient alliance of the middle class and state which allows for a certain form of democracy but modifies this to the extent that the middle classes are able to protect their own interests against challenges from distributional alliances. But once we try to identify in greater detail who actually belongs to the regional (middle) class of patrons and how permanent this class is, the picture becomes far more complicated and less stable. Smart and well-connected entrepreneurs might move in, while bureaucrats who lost their grip on networks and funds can drop out. In her study on the island of Sumba Jacqueline Vel uses the term 'political class' to identify those who dominate regional politics and control access to economic and financial resources of the state, which also includes people without a formal position like relatives of officials and retired administrators (Vel 2008: 16). Seen from this perspective, class seems to be a rather open category.

For those who expected that regional autonomy would result in good governance, substantive democracy and a strong civil society, the saddening conclusion is that, despite fair elections and judicial investigations, most corrupt administrators are simply replaced by other corrupt administrators. Reforms have brought change and the composition of the ruling elites has changed as well, but at the same time central features of the old system have firmly remained in place (Robison and Hadiz 2004).

Patronage democracy gives clients more bargaining power vis-à-vis patrons, but erases the possibility of a strong and relatively autonomous civil society. It not only reproduces unequal relationships between patrons and clients but excludes, by its very nature, solidarity among clients in terms of class. Clients prefer patronage democracy because it can deliver more than the weak and unreliable rule of law of an abstract nation-state. Moreover, patron–client networks are often embedded in ethnic and religious terms and specific regional settings, which emphasize difference instead of facilitating an overarching solidarity. Although political parties advocate national unity they are not interested in a fundamental discussion of what it means to be Indonesian. Nor do most NGOs, which are still primarily single-issue organizations (Schulte Nordholt 2008b). We may therefore conclude that, together with the rainforests, the idea of a shared Indonesian citizenship is the main victim of regional autonomy.

Notes

1 Law 22/1999 also granted village councils more influence in local affairs.
2 Ironically, despite the alleged danger of separatism, the provinces of Aceh and Papua were granted special autonomy (Laws 18 and 21/2001). Aceh would receive 80 per cent of the oil and gas revenues; see for Papua below.
3 Members of the elite corps Kopassus were involved in the murder of Papua leader Theys Elvay in November 2001.
4 John Sidel (2006) has offered an alternative analysis of these communal conflicts. He concentrates on religious aspects and presents a metanarrative of modernist and radical Islam wanting to expand political influence. In doing so he ignores the ethnic violence in Kalimantan.
5 Of the new administrators, 22 per cent were professional politicians, 8 per cent retired military, and only 6 per cent were activists or civil society leaders (Mietzner 2009: 345–9).
6 Law 32/2004 stipulated that candidates running for office needed the support of parties which had received 15 per cent of the seats or the votes during the last elections. The elections for governor in South Sulawesi in 2007 and in North Moluccas in 2008 ended in conflict because defeated parties rejected the results. Eventually the Constitutional Court in Jakarta had to make a final decision in these matters.

References

Barker, J. and G. van Klinken (eds) (2009) *State of Authority: The State in Society in Indonesia*, Ithaca, NY: Southeast Asia Program Cornell University.
Buehler, M. (2007) 'Rise of the clans: direct elections in South Sulawesi', *Inside Indonesia* 90.
——(2010) 'Decentralisation and local democracy in Indonesia: containing the public sphere', unpublished manuscript.
Davidson, J. and D. Henley (eds) (2007) *The Revival of Tradition in Indonesian Politics: The Development of Adat from Colonialism to Indigenism*, London and New York: Routledge.
Eindhoven, M. (2007) 'New colonizers? Identity, representation and government in the post-New Order Mentawai Archipelago', in H. Schulte Nordholt and G. van Klinken (eds) *Renegotiating Boundaries: Local Politics in Post-Suharto Indonesia*, Leiden: KITLV Press, pp. 67–89.
Erwiza, E. (2007) 'Deregulation of the tin trade and the creation of a local shadow state: a Bangka case study', in H. Schulte Nordholt and G. van Klinken (eds) *Renegotiating Boundaries: Local Politics in Post-Suharto Indonesia*, Leiden: KITLV Press, pp. 177–201.

Evaquarta, R. (2010) 'Corrupting politics', *Inside Indonesia* 99.

Faucher, C. (2007) 'Contesting boundaries in the Riau Archipelago', in H. Schulte Nordholt and G. van Klinken (eds) *Renegotiating Boundaries: Local Politics in Post-Suharto Indonesia*, Leiden: KITLV Press, pp. 443–57.

Hadiz, V.R. (2003) *Decentralization and Democracy in Indonesia: A Critique of Neo-institutionalist Perspectives*, Working Paper 47, Hong Kong: City University of Hong Kong.

Hadiz, V.R. and R. Robison (2005) 'Neo-liberal reforms and illiberal consolidations: the Indonesian paradox', *Journal of Development Studies* 41: 220–41.

Hidayat, S. (2007) '"Shadow state?" Business and politics in the province of Banten', in H. Schulte Nordholt and G. van Klinken (eds) *Renegotiating Boundaries: Local Politics in Post-Suharto Indonesia*, Leiden: KITLV Press, pp. 203–24.

ICG (International Crisis Group) (2002) *Tensions on Flores: Local Symptoms of National Problems*, Indonesia Briefing, Jakarta/Brussels: International Crisis Group.

Kingsbury, D. and L. McCulloch (2006) 'Military business in Aceh', in A. Reid (ed.) *Verandah of Violence: The Background to the Aceh Problem*, Singapore: Singapore University Press pp. 199–224.

McCarthy, J. (2007) 'Sold down the river: renegotiating public power over nature in Central Kalimantan', in H. Schulte Nordholt and G. van Klinken (eds) *Renegotiating Boundaries: Local Politics in Post-Suharto Indonesia*, Leiden: KITLV Press, pp. 151–76.

Masaaki, O. and A. Hamid (2008) 'Jawara in power, 1999 – 2007', *Indonesia* 86: 109–38.

Mietzner, M. (2009) *Military Politics, Islam, and the State in Indonesia: From Turbulent Transition to Democratic Consolidation*, Singapore: ISEAS.

Morishita, A. (2008) 'Contesting power in Indonesia's resource-rich regions in the era of decentralization: new strategy for central control over the regions', *Indonesia* 86: 81–107.

Robison, R. and V.R. Hadiz (2004) *Reorganizing Power in Indonesia: The Politics of Oligarchy in an Age of Markets*, London and New York: RoutledgeCurzon.

Rodan, G. and K. Jayasuriya (2009) 'Capitalist development, regime transitions and new forms of authoritarianism in Asia', *Pacific Review* 22 (1): 23–47.

Schulte Nordholt, H. (2007) *Bali. An Open Fortress 1995–2005. Regional Autonomy, Electoral Democracy and Entrenched Identities*, Singapore: National University of Singapore Press.

——(2008a) *Indonesië na Soeharto. Reformasi en restauratie*, Amsterdam: Bert Bakker.

——(2008b) 'Identity politics, citizenship and the soft state in Indonesia: an essay', *Journal of Indonesian Social Sciences and Humanities* 1: 1–21.

Schulte Nordholt, H. and G. van Klinken (eds) (2007) 'Introduction', in H. Schulte Nordholt and G. van Klinken (eds) *Renegotiating Boundaries: Local Politics in Post-Suharto Indonesia*, Leiden: KITLV Press, pp. 1–29.

Sidel, J. (2004) 'Bossism and democracy in the Philippines, Thailand and Indonesia: towards an alternative framework for the study of "local strongmen"', in J. Harriss, K. Stokke and O. Törnquist (eds) *Politicising Democracy. The New Local Politics of Democratization*, Basingstoke: Palgrave Macmillan, pp. 51–74.

——(2006) *Riots, Pogroms, Jihad Religious violence in Indonesia*, Ithaca, NY: Cornell University Press.

Simandjuntak, D. (2010) 'Who shall be raja? Patronage democracy in North Sumatra', unpublished thesis, University of Amsterdam.

Tempo (2008). 'A few good men: ten regents and mayors are our figures of 2008', *Tempo*, 23–29 December.

van Klinken, G. (2007) *Communal Violence and Democratization in Indonesia: Small Town Wars*, London/New York: Routledge.

——(2008) 'Indonesian politics in 2008: the ambiguities of democratic change', *Bulletin of Indonesian Economic Studies* 44 (3): 365–81.

——(2009) 'Patronage democracy in provincial Indonesia', in O. Törnquist, N. Webster and K. Stokke (eds) *Rethinking Popular Representation*, Basingstoke: Palgrave Macmillan, pp. 141–59.

Vel, J. (2008) *Uma Politics: An Ethnography of Democratization in West Sumba, Indonesia, 1986–2006*, Leiden: KITLV Press.

Vlasblom, D. (2009) 'De regent van Lebak 150 jaar later', *NRC Weekblad*, 24 December.

16

THE POST-AUTHORITARIAN POLITICS OF AGRARIAN AND FOREST REFORM IN INDONESIA

John McCarthy and Moira Moeliono

Indonesia is among the 'world's top three exporters' of coal, natural gas, and natural rubber. It is now the top world producer of crude palm oil and hosts 'the world's largest gold mine and second-largest copper mine' (ALB Legal News 2009). Indonesia is also widely seen as subject to an environmental tragedy, with attention principally focused on the loss of vast areas of forest cover each year. Criticisms of natural resource management also converge on environmental and distributional justice concerns (McCarthy and Warren 2009). Following the collapse of the Suharto regime in 1998, state planners confronted widespread resource conflicts and 'illegal' resource use practices inherited from decades of authoritarian rule. At the same time, donor agencies advocated policies that would further the pursuit of the Millennium Development Goals and the reduction of greenhouse gas emissions associated with rapid deforestation. State planners and donors have sought to address these problems, by means of legal changes to natural resource rights and benefit sharing, developing more integrated environmental policy and a more participatory state, and utilizing private–public arrangements and market mechanisms to reduce deforestation.

Initially, it seemed that these reforms would transform state institutions and practices of resource control. However, the transition has proved much more problematic. In this chapter we seek to understand the reasons why this is the case. Advocates of policy change may presuppose that changes to policy and institutional arrangements can remake environmental practices. However, we do not assume that the underlying political economy – associated with a particular structure of property rights – that underpins resource outcomes can be so easily transformed. By examining change in terms of the workings of institutions and the way these are shaped and influenced by embedded power relationships, we analyse the unresolved dilemmas faced by environmental reformers.

We begin by considering the theoretical arguments shaping our discussion. We then examine the political processes at play in the system through an analysis of the law-making process before considering four case studies. First, we discuss attempts to decentralize natural resource management, to make decision-making more responsive and to develop a more 'participatory' state, thereby leading to a more legitimate and just sharing of benefits from the resource sector. Second, we consider attempts to overcome the fragmented planning and decision-making process by creating a more integrated national environmental policy framework. Third, we analyse initiatives to initiate 'Agrarian Reform' and 'Forest Revitalization' before, fourth, considering the initial policies for 'Reducing Emissions from Deforestation and Degradation'

(REDD). Finally, we draw some conclusions regarding the nature of institutional transformation over the last decade.

Preliminary considerations

The last decade witnessed the widespread advocacy of 'environmental governance' approaches that involve moving away from state-centred approaches (Lemos and Agrawal 2006). Changes in the political and ideological landscape clearly created pressure to push back regulation. The state had often been portrayed as inflexible, inhibiting innovation, and only able to provide high-cost solutions. Further, critics characterized the state in industrializing countries as lacking law enforcement capacity and hence at best able to provide low levels of regulatory compliance. Regulatory agencies were seen as embedded in governance structures that are captured by business elites. This justified a search for alternatives to state 'command and control approaches'. These include more flexible, performance-based and co-operative mechanisms and policy tools that reflect the wider popularity of market-based policy instruments, including decentralization, self-regulation by corporations, using market incentives and external state-sponsored enforcement mechanisms. The assumption was that a suite of new policy instruments would provide greater effectiveness and efficiency over traditional command and control approaches (Gunningham 2009; Rooij 2010).

However, the state continues to be seen by most actors as the key actor for pursuing the 'common good' or 'public interest' in the environment. It is assumed a state requires certain attributes and capacities to work as an 'actor' dedicated to promoting the 'collective good' and to managing environmental problems, capacities not readily attained by states in developing country contexts. The mandate of particular state environmental agencies exists in tension with the role the state also plays as the promoter of development plans – expanding resource exports through maximizing the extraction and production of resources. Even where well-crafted environmental policies exist, all too often this conflict of interest within the apparatus of the state itself weakens the capacity of state environmental agencies to ensure effective environmental outcomes.

In contrast to the view of the state as some kind of benign 'leviathan' – of the state as a set of public institutions expressing 'the power of the people as it acts on its behalf' (Mackenzie 2009: 52), the state is elsewhere seen as a set of agencies dependent upon and advancing the economic, social and political power of particular social actors and interests (Leftwich 2000). This later perspective is particularly relevant to understanding the evolution and implementation of state policy that touches upon the use of contested and extremely valuable natural resources. As an alternative to seeing the state as a coherent actor, the central locus of power, we may view the state as part of a 'multi-faceted, complex assemblage of interlocking and interwoven power relations that extend within its borders and beyond its boundaries' (Mackenzie 2009: 73).

The currency of these latter perspectives coincides with a shift in viewpoint regarding how 'governing processes' are analysed. As Adger and Jordan (2009: 11) argue, 'analysts have seized on the term governance to try and capture important phenomenological changes in the processes of governing'. For our purposes governance refers to 'the framework and institutional structures by which rules are set and implemented' (Nadvi 2008: 324). The term has been used to describe perceived changes in state–society relationships following the perceived roll back of the state due to a range of encompassing changes sometimes associated with 'neoliberal' reforms – deregulation, privatization and decentralization, along with the increased scale of capital movement around the world, the distribution of production across global production networks ('globalization') and the increased salience of corporations. Analysts have posited a shift in power to alternative actors and levels. As states are viewed as less able to address pressing global problems or regulate the source of key problems, states are seen to be 'changing and adapting in the face of new challenges and experimenting with more elaborate forms of relations with society' (Bell and Hindmoor 2009: 21). With governments needing to 'develop and maintain close relationships with a range of non-state actors to achieve policy aims' (ibid.) the state is seen to take on more of an 'enabling' role, establishing the regulatory framework, 'steering' the administrative and institutional context, and adopting 'hybrid, multilevel and cross-sectoral' approaches (Lemos and Agrawal 2006).

At the same time, the term 'governance' has also been used normatively by those critical of state intervention (Adger and Jordan 2009). Supporting a shift towards market-based policy instruments, they argue this will provide for more efficient ways to allocate resources and regulate outcomes. Hence a dominant interpretation of sustainable development has emerged that assumes that environmental governance can materialize through market processes, the application of market-based instruments, and the use of the state to mobilize social actors and generate the incentives for dealing with key environmental problems. However, the nature, extent and effectiveness of the changes associated with 'governance' remain contested, with the state in so many ways still remaining central to environmental outcomes.

This chapter points to the limitations of theoretical arguments that work around the problems in the regulatory state and the political economy. While new policy instruments appear to offer greater effectiveness and efficiency over traditional 'command and control' approaches, in the Indonesian context we argue that the same political economy and institutional context that forestalled earlier state-centred approaches affects attempts to pursue these policy narratives. To be sure, at particular moments, social movements, donors and reformist elements within the state appear to have successfully advocated new policy narratives.[1] However, seemingly disaggregated political processes have accumulated over time to shape how these new narratives are taken up, demonstrating the continued potency of domestic corporations and their allies within the state who resist reform. In other contexts, successful reform initiatives have required a mutually empowering convergence of pro-reform actors inside the national government, donor agencies, NGOs and social movements. To be effective, where such coalitions are able to mobilize sufficient political capital to drive reform, they must overcome resistance. In this way they may create the 'enabling environment' required to facilitate the collective action that is critical to 'providing leverage and voice to underrepresented people' (Fox 2007: 140). In the absence of such an 'enabling environment', we conclude, in many respects the success of Indonesia's environmental reformists has remained largely figurative.[2]

Before proceeding further to discuss the importance of the transition for environmental governance in Indonesia, we will now briefly outline Indonesia's contested institutional arrangements.

The institutional setting

The New Order period bequeathed a three-fold heritage. First, as in any bureaucratic system, the state divided management problems into components and designed legal-institutional arrangements for each part (Rhodes 1997). Thus, Indonesian state agencies developed different roles and mandates for aspects of land tenure, resource-use decision-making and spatial planning.

In the early decades of the Indonesian Republic the Basic Agrarian Law, 5/1960 provided a single framework for dealing with land issues in Indonesia. However, in 1967 the New Order developed a forestry law and set up a parallel, vertically integrated set of legal and institutional arrangements for lands classified as 'forest areas' (Afiff et al. 2005). Since then land has been distinguished as either 'forestry' or 'non-forestry', a distinction that remains at the core of natural resource policy. With 70 per cent of Indonesia's land area (130 million hectares) classified as forest area, the New Order shifted key natural resource management responsibilities to the jurisdiction of the Ministry of Forestry (MoF). Nonetheless the National Land Agency carries out land administration, with responsibility for issuing land titles and land-use permits, collecting land taxes and administering long-term leases on state land in non-forestry areas under the jurisdiction of the agrarian law. Meanwhile, other land-using sectors such as mining, agriculture and estate crops have their own laws and administrative rules developed according to specific aims and agendas. While these are poorly integrated with each other and often mutually contradictory, they provide opportunities for these agencies to maximize commercial returns in their sectors. At the same time, the Environmental Ministry (KLH) is responsible for key policy-making and coordination responsibilities, working as an agency sympathetic to the environmental concerns of NGOs, social movements and international donors.

Building on colonial precedence, under the New Order a legal–political nexus crystallized that correlated with a particular structure of property rights in natural resources that has proved to be long enduring. This property rights system emerged in the following way. First, the MoF allocated vast areas to timber concessions, facilitating the capture of the very extensive forest resources by a coalition of actors close to the regime. Second, the MoF set aside large areas for nature protection. Third, the MoF oversaw a system of enclosure and land conversion. Corporate actors wishing to develop a plantation could apply for land concessions (HGU) that would involve excising areas out of the 'forestry estate' for plantation development – long-term leases on what would remain state land. Alternatively, they could apply for a timber plantation concession to enclose 'forest land' as a timber plantation.

The post-Suharto era inherited a natural resource sector dominated by an oligarchy of domestic corporations that had been succoured by the nexus of power and influence converging around the apex of the New Order state. Following the turmoil of the financial crisis and the end of the Suharto regime, the oligarchy controlling the timber sector reconstituted itself, retaining large degrees of control of corporations with concessions extending over very large swathes of the landscape.[3] While these corporations earlier focused on accumulation from timber extraction, with the exhaustion of the timber from natural forests, they have expanded into capital intensive products like pulp and paper and oil palm (Gellert 2004). These activities require control of extensive areas of land. With ambitious plans for expansion, this has entailed rapid, large-scale conversion of land into timber and oil palm plantations, especially post-1998. These elites – interpenetrating with the politico-bureaucratic structures within parties, the parliament and the state – largely thrive on the surpluses derived from commodity exports in the resource sector. These domestic actors collectively constitute powerful networks capable of forestalling the initiatives of pro-reform actors within the state as well as social movements and NGO coalitions. Alternatively, they can work with international corporations that may have little direct role in politics but may still use their 'financial influence in politics solely for specific and particularistic purposes' (Moore 2001: 311).

The fall of President Suharto in 1998 marked a shift towards a more democratic, decentralized and market-oriented political economy. During the rather chaotic transition period known as *reformasi*, villagers occupied contested state lands and plantations while vibrant grass-roots social movements advocated the reform of agrarian and forest laws (Lucas and Warren 2003; Peluso *et al.* 2008). With greater space for the articulation of aspirations under a multi-party system, a new legislature responded to volatile pressures from across the archipelago by decentralizing areas of administration and bringing in a new system of general elections. However, a key question here is: to what degree has democracy improved the prospects for environmental management? Has it improved resource management, and if so, for what reasons?

In the decade since Suharto's fall, none of the political parties has obtained a majority. Each president's survival has been seen to depend upon continued investment in balancing conflicting interests to maintain a governing coalition with fractious parties, forming 'rainbow cabinets' to accommodate short-term political interests, ostensibly to form a majority in the legislature. With no one coalition within national decision-making networks completely dominating the scene, various interests compete to promote their policy agendas. Party leaders endorse and support potential cabinet candidates interested in controlling sectoral agencies to advance their own or their party's political interests through extracting rents from administrative control over natural resources, rather than adhering to a policy direction set by a president or a political party (*Tempo* 2004: 73). These dynamics clearly limit the ability of state actors to formulate considered policy decisions and to make them binding across state agencies.

A number of authors have argued that effective states tend to emerge from interaction; bargaining and exchange between state apparatuses and other local groups with the requirement for internal institutional coherence. A critical element to state capacity here lies in the ability of the state to develop a high degree of autonomy from powerful interests (Evans 1995; Moore 2001). In the Indonesian case, the absence of this kind of autonomy coalesces with the fragmented nature of political coalitions to affect outcomes. Robison and Hadiz (2004: 8) have argued that

> attempts to dismantle the system of state controlled rents underpinning Indonesia's corporate moguls and to reform strategic gate keeping institutions have floundered as new political rulers found that the need to control patronage and secure off-budget was central to success in the new system of parliamentary power.
>
> *(Robison and Hadiz 2004: 8)*

To understand how this works, we will now discuss the politics of environmental law-making.

The law-making process

Policy formulations that relate to natural resources continue to be contested by those who wish (more or less) to retain the arrangements and patterns of resource control that prevailed in the New Order period. NGOs, social movements and pro-reform actors within the state wish for a new dispensation that better accommodates their interests or reformist ideals. Hence, as law-making processes are particularly revealing regarding the forces at work, we discuss the administrative and political dynamics at play. To understand the manner in which the law-making process takes place, we will now consider drafting processes, the process of consultation in law-making, the capacity of the legislative, and the role of special interests in the process.

Before an Act of Parliament or law (*undang-undang*) is passed, a rather diffuse set of discussions tend to occur involving the party caucus (*fraksi*) and committee system within the People's Representative Council (*Dewan Perwakilan Rakyat* or DPR). While the majority of laws are drafted by the relevant ministries, special committees within the DPR dominate the decision-making process. With 'discussion usually confined to the particular committee with responsibility for that policy area and the ministry or agency concerned' (Sherlock 2010: 8), once consensus is reached among the caucus leaders and government representatives in the relevant committee meetings, the bill moves through a ceremonial presentation to the plenary session of the DPR before passing to the president to be signed. The domination of the committee system – with closed door deals between caucus leaders – provides an 'important instrument of oligarchic control and avoidance of transparency and public accountability' (Sherlock 2010: 9).

This means that public consultation and discussion of key laws may be deliberately mini-mized. For instance, APKESI, the Association of District Governments, complained that during the revision of the key regional government law (UU 22/1999), there was very limited public consultation, and they were unable to obtain a draft of the law (Suharyo 2000). Although decentralization remained one of the key reforms of the post-Suharto period, the parliament slipped through a new law in 2004 with very little public scrutiny – during the interregnum after the presidential and legislative elections and before the formal swearing in of the new legislature and the Susilo Bambang Yudhoyono (SBY) administration.

This lack of transparency and openness in drafting processes can have serious consequences. Where a range of ministries are not involved, let alone the wider public or regional stake-holders, new regulations may lack wider legitimacy. Consequently, laws may be in a state of constant revision. Where they are revised quickly, the process sets in motion a new round of coordination issues as they come into conflict with other existing administrative arrangements.

At the same time the diffuse system can also open up possibilities for representation, public consultation and the presentation of other perspectives. For instance, in early 2007 the Ministry of Public Works (PU) brought a draft of its spatial planning legislation to the DPR. Although a network of academics interested in improving the draft law had been unable to affect the ministry's internal draft, they were able to influence the new law through the party caucuses involved in the committee discussion processes (Author interview 2007).

At other times, public pressure has affected law-making in particularly interesting ways. For example, during the heated political climate of post-1998, a coalition of NGO groups[4] successfully lobbied for the creation of a Consultative Assembly Decree (TAP 9/2001). Passed by the nation's highest legislature, the National Consultative Assembly (MPR), this decree called for the review of all tenure and natural resource-management laws and regula-tions (Lucas and Warren 2003). However, in the face of resistance from key sectoral interests (as described below), this decree remained symbolic, with follow-up legislation notably lacking.

As in other legislatures around the world, compromises between the different actors striving to affect the outcome need to be ironed out. As the approval and review processes in the DPR tend to be driven by particular timetables, consensus positions tend to be arrived at quickly at the climax of the legislative process. This can lead to ambiguity in legal formulations.

Sectoral departments have the privilege of preparing key implementation rules – Govern-ment Regulations (*Peraturan Pemerintah*) and Presidential Decisions (*Keputusan Presiden*) – that are meant to iron out these ambiguities. The long delays in crafting these regulations in many cases create serious impediments to implementing framework laws. Further, the internal departmental committees that draft the regulations are not required to consult the DPR. As a result, many regulations contradict other regulations or even sectoral laws. Where these reg-ulations are resisted in remote districts that have long-standing land tenure regimes and practices of resource use, or by regional governments whose interests oppose them, they become difficult to implement.[5]

Critics have long questioned the capacity of the DPR for processing new bills and the speed at which it works. In 2004, the key decentralization law (Law 22/1999) was revised (as dis-cussed above), reiterating the requirement set out in the earlier 1999 law that sectoral laws, including forestry laws, need to be brought into line with decentralization law.[6] In 2007, almost ten years after the reform period commenced, key legislation including a new environment and mining law inherited from the New Order period had yet to be revised.

The DPR Secretariat's capacity for legal review and public consultation is constrained by the level of funding for public participation and support for personnel. Insufficient funds (less than

US$10,000) are allocated from the National Budget to draft a bill. These funds are expected to cover all costs, including planning, hiring expert consultants, policy research, organizing public consultations and holding a series of public meetings.[7] Problems with the research capacity within the DPR and other institutions involved in legal drafting affect the capacity of those involved in the process. This makes the process dependent on funding and expertise from outside the DPR. It also affects the ability of legislators to access the type of technical information that would ensure that policy-making is well informed. Where sound analysis is absent, the policy formulations that the laws contain can be unrealistic and therefore ignored or re-interpreted during implementation.

Consequently, although parliament (DPR) has formal responsibility for proposing, writing, reviewing and approving framework laws, certain actors, typically a government department working with a private sector lobbying group or sponsor, subsidize the costs of passing a particular law by providing money and other benefits to parliamentarians and others in return for their support for the particular draft law or regulation. This ensures that special interests can readily affect the legal drafting, approval and review processes in the DPR committee system. Indeed, it is an 'open secret that large amounts of money continue to change hands ... during deliberations on legislation, especially if it concerns traditionally lucrative areas' (Sherlock 2010: 11).

For example, the 2007 investment law (UU Penanaman Modal 2007) was passed quickly with support from the powerful economic ministries without wide consultation, even though it controversially overrode key clauses in the agrarian law regarding access to land, granting foreigners control over land for as long as 90 years (Down to Earth 2007). This occurred at a time when 'some of Indonesia's most influential and politically connected companies' had 'refocused their business strategies and are joining hands with foreign investors to push forward the government's multi-billion dollar ambition to transform the country into the world's leading biodiesel producer' (Guerin 2007). Together with the new investment law, new government initiatives included policies to simplify arrangements for land-use permits and plant-licensing procedures. A coalition of NGOs later opposed the law in the constitutional court on the grounds that it gave too much power to investors, had serious implications for the environment and could lead to social conflict (Tempo Interaktif 2007).

Each sectoral department has a bureau for legislative affairs whose remit includes reviewing draft legislation (such as implementing regulations and decrees) to ensure its consistency within the larger legal framework of the sector before sending it out. The State Secretariat has a legal function to study proposed laws and regulations and ensure their consistency with other laws. If the Secretariat finds that a proposed regulation is not consistent with higher laws, the drafting department or DPR is legally obliged to redraft it. However, significant problems continue to occur,[8] suggesting that the state agencies responsible for overseeing the consistency of the legal system – the Directorate General for Legal Matters within the Department of Justice and Human Rights – have not prevailed. A shift in this direction is troublesome given the power that oligarchic interests can bring to play in law-making. The nexus of senior politicians and business leaders with key stakes in the resource sector – together with a legislative process 'particularly supportive of cabalistic or oligarchic control' – supports the continuation of the existing political economy of resource control (Sherlock 2010: 1).

It is not always possible to locate 'the smoking gun' – evidence of where this cabalistic control is at work. Nonetheless, as the following case studies illustrate, using various informal political alliances and political investments, the network of interests is able to shape outcomes – taking action to ensure particular reform issues are put on or off the agenda for discussion.

The dynamics of reform: three cases

Decentralization and the governance of resources

Within the environmental governance lexicon, decentralization emerged as the main policy tool for achieving better local participation in resource governance through enhanced accountability and representation. The agenda entailed remaking sub-national institutions, enhancing their discretionary authority, and reworking the political system in order to better process political demands from below. The idea here was that regional governments are closer to regional populations. As they are more readily accountable locally, they can more readily 'bridge' the national and the local through locally derived forms of accountability and representation (Schönwälder 1997). Replacing less effective command and control by using community governance as a social arrangement for sustainability, decentralization, along with enhanced participation, co-management and community forestry initiatives, formed part of a suite of initiatives to improve environmental governance.

In Indonesia decentralization reforms along these lines emerged during the period of political insecurity following the collapse of the New Order regime as an effort to make the system of governance more legitimate in the face of regional demands. This entailed a struggle between reformist elements and those with investments in the status quo, that was played out in the contest over the nature and direction of decentralization during its formulation and implementation following 1999 (McCarthy 2004).

The Ministry of Home Affairs was the main state agency responsible for overseeing the decentralization process, with oversight of the drafting of various decentralization laws and implementing regulations. However, the ministry faced significant challenges incorporating sectoral interests, including key agencies responsible for natural resource governance, such as the Ministries of Forestry, Mining, and Public Works, BAPPENAS and the National Land Agency. Across all sectors, central government agencies were slow to release guidelines, directions, training and supervision, at least in part because they were reluctant to come to terms with their reduced power and privileges under decentralization.

While the districts had gained significant areas of authority under the new dispensation, they were nevertheless required to follow higher-level laws, which were often contradictory and not backed up by clear guidelines and minimum service standards. Under the concept of *Pengawasan represif* (repressive control) in Law 22/1999 and its implementing regulations, the Ministry of Home Affairs could cancel errant regional regulations. Yet there was no systematic way to keep track of and review regional regulations. Where districts were seen as being errant, the process of mediation and discussion between central and regional governments was often long (Author interview 2004c). For some time the Ministry of Home Affairs tended to take a soft, conciliatory approach when regional regulations were out of line with higher-level regulations (Author interview 2004b).

The struggle between those who would support a new dispensation and those interests at the centre with large investments in the natural resource regime inherited from the New Order period remained unresolved. Further, decentralization enhanced the position of sub-national actors – including local state-based actors and interest groups. At the height of the *reformasi* period, the state needed to accommodate these actors if it was to be seen as more responsive and more adaptable to regional and local needs and hence attain more local legitimacy (McCarthy 2008). However, over time the underlying struggle over state control of resources became apparent in the contradictions between the framework forestry law and the regional government laws (Barr *et al.* 2006). Earlier, at the height of demands for reform, the MoF issued several regulations giving districts limited authority over forest resources, including the right to issue small-scale timber licences. In many districts, this led to excess exploitation, with local timber networks marketing timber directly into the timber value chains outside the control of the Ministry of Forestry. Later the ministry countered with a new implementing regulation (PP 34/2002) that curtailed the power of districts to issue permits and levy taxes, in effect allowing the MoF to regain central authority over timber licences and revenues in the name of a clamp down on 'illegal logging'.

In many respects the decentralization process amounted to a contest over resources and power played out as a dispute over legal authority over natural resources. This contest remains unresolved, with an unclear division of authority over forestry functions heightening the uncertainty of the institutional arrangements for natural resource management. Within this frame-work, parallel, overlapping and conflicting sets of rules governed the same areas of authority, leading to conflicts and creating short-term incentives for overexploitation (McCarthy 2004). The rather chaotic situation was ultimately used to justify the withdrawal of discretionary authority from local governments over natural resources and the return to the more centralized forms of resource control. This was finally confirmed under the new regional government law (Law 32/2004).

In parallel with the decentralization reforms, reformers attempted to create a more integrated natural resource framework.

Developing an integrated national policy framework

The advocates of sustainable development – including environmental NGOs, donor agencies, and reformist actors within government (particularly the State Ministry for the Environment and the National Planning Agency) – have argued for replacing fragmentary sector-by-sector approaches that are unable to deal with complex environmental problems with more integrated, sustainable approaches. This entails achieving greater coherence and integration within and among sectors and institutions as well as integration across different levels of governance (Brown 2009). Yet, as elsewhere, the idea of integration faces significant challenges from the underlying political–economy.

As noted earlier, in 2001 the nation's highest legislature, the National Consultative Assembly (MPR) issued a decree (TAP MPR No. 9/2001) effectively calling for the integration of Indonesia's natural resource policy framework. Social movements in collaboration with refor-mers within the state took up this opportunity, seeking to integrate tenure arrangements with spatial planning and forest tenure arrangements. During the next few years an ongoing struggle emerged as the State Ministry for the Environment (KLH), the National Land Agency and the key planning agency BAPPENAS, each supported by a network of NGOs, have championed different conceptualizations of how a framework for resolving the conflicting legal arrangements pertaining to natural resources might work.[9]

From the time of the former president, Abdurahman Wahid (administration 1999–2001), the Environmental Ministry (KLH) oversaw a working group, including NGOs concerned by the government's fragmented and overly sectoral approach to natural resources management, to formulate a new natural resources management law[10] in response to TAP MPR 9.[11] Faced with the complex labyrinth of existing laws on natural resource management, advocates of the reform were unable to show how they would integrate existing laws. Opponents argued that the introduction of a new legal subsystem would only complicate matters further. Interestingly, this draft law gives explicit consideration to protecting the resource rights of indigenous people, a proposal that the resource sector and other ministries found unacceptable (Author interview 2004a).

Following the direction set by the TAP MPR, the president passed a decree (Presidential Decree 34/2003) providing for the need to revise the basic agrarian law. Consequently, the National Land Agency prepared a draft for a new framework 'agrarian resources law' (*RUU Sumber Daya Agraria*). In the drafting process, the most significant input came from NGO members of the Consortium of Agrarian Reform. Given the National Land Agency's exclusive drafting process, there was little cross-sectoral support for its proposed reform. The draft land law languished for some time and was revised again by the new head of the National Land Agency under the new SBY administration, before being shelved after failing to achieve support in parliament (DPR). Tenure issues proved highly emotional, and there was always the spectre of conflict hanging over proposed tenure reforms. With the opposition of powerful interests at work, particularly the great domestic corporate empires with large investments in the sector, the president remained extremely cautious about the issue of agrarian reform.

In these deliberations, actors such as the large business groups involved in commercial logging, oil palm plantations and other resource intensive activities and their allies within the resource sector ministries (such as MoF) demonstrated their entrenched power through their ability to forestall reforms – such as to the agrarian and forest laws. Clearly it was not in the MoF's interest to have the National Land Agency or the State Ministry for the Environment developing a framework that might reduce the status of the forestry law and the authority of the ministry over the state-owned forest estate. The MoF showed very little interest in such efforts and worked to retain its administrative control over areas mapped as 'forestry estate' (Setiawan 2007). At the same time, other agencies had distinct interests in decisions about the management of state forest lands.[12]

A conflict over the question of whether rich mineral deposits found within protected forest areas should be exploited demonstrated the processes at work. After a protracted dispute, in which DPR members confessed to receiving payments for supporting a new mining regulation (Tempo 2004; Tempo Interaktif 2004), the president issued a decree early in 2004 allowing mining in protected forest areas.[13]

In the meantime, Indonesia's policy framework for natural resources remained contradictory. As the former Minister of the Environment Emil Salim noted, 'now every ministry has its own framework law. It all becomes chaotic, just like a forest of laws' (*Republika* 2006). The legal ambiguity maximized the discretionary power of those making decisions in the natural resource sector.

'Agrarian Reform' with 'Forest Revitalization'

During this period donor reports in support of the Millennium Development Goals (MDG) argued that more extreme poverty tends to be found among populations living in forest areas. Donor programmes linked the achievement of the MDGs in halving poverty and ensuring environmental sustainability with the role of forests in poverty alleviation, focusing on improving policies, institutions and processes, including those pertaining to forest community rights (Asia Forest Network n.d.). As the largest landlord in the country, the MoF needed to respond to this agenda.[14]

During the 2004 election, Susilo Bambang Yudhoyono, the current president, also made a campaign pledge regarding agrarian reform. Most of Indonesia's poor still reside in rural areas, with overall poverty continuing to increase at a greater rate in these areas.[15] To address this pressing problem, in 2005 the president of Indonesia launched a medium-term plan that included ambitious targets to reduce poverty, including in the countryside. This encompassed a programme of 'revitalization of agriculture, fisheries and forestry' (RPPK) as well as 'Agrarian

Renewal'. To this end the president strengthened the authority of the National Land Agency through a Presidential Regulation, *Perpres* No. 10/2006. The administration also decided that the National Land Agency would begin a programme to distribute some 12 million hectares, most of which were unproductive or deforested state forest lands (Down to Earth 2007).

While 'agrarian reform' is usually understood to involve the reform of a country's agrarian system, in this case reform meant the limited redistribution of parcels of land. Activists campaigned against what they termed 'pseudo-agrarian reform', arguing that this land redistribution failed to address the structural problems that are the underlying causes of poverty (Peluso *et al.* 2008). Policy discussions tended to emphasize individual property rights without providing a coherent legal framework for dealing with existing 'informal' and 'customary' rights held by the majority of the rural population. Yet the discussion of land reform raised great expectations, especially among civil society organizations that have long seen land distribution as a means of dealing with poverty (Lucas and Warren 2003; Affif *et al.* 2005).

The process, however, faced some serious obstacles. First, property rights in areas mapped as state forests remained subject to the forestry law (No. 41/1999). While the law recognized the existence of customary rights, these rights were defined in a narrow sense as communal rights of access subject to a set of rigidly defined conditions.[16] The MoF remained unwilling to consider more permanent and secure property rights beyond various limited use rights in the forestry estate.[17]

Second, it is no simple matter to redistribute up to 12 million hectares in the absence of basic information regarding existing 'informal' rights and eligibility of individuals for receiving land. Villagers occupied large areas of this land that fell within the boundaries of village territories. In many formerly uninhabited areas, where the MoF had little real capacity to control access, areas had been occupied or used for many years. At the same time entrepreneurs and large corporate interests had obtained permits (*ijin lokasi*) from district and provincial governments over many areas. This created a system of overlapping land entitlements within areas formally mapped as state forest.

Third, the highly differentiated policy process described earlier, with each resource sector making decisions within separate policy 'silos', haunted the planned reforms. Alongside the National Land Agency's plans, the Department of Agriculture's plantation revitalization plan[18] set out to develop 2 million hectares of agricultural land. Meanwhile, the Department of Energy and Mineral Resources launched a biofuels initiative. Both initiatives involved very large investments and ambitious plans to make new areas available.

In other countries forestry agencies have sought to re-appropriate resources following radical decentralization programmes (Ribot *et al.* 2006). In Indonesia, the MoF, which had yet to relinquish formal control over 'forest land', formulated a number of new policies, known as 'Forestry Revitalization'.[19] It included a more socially acceptable property-rights system in areas that might otherwise be redistributed under 'Agrarian Renewal'.

The MoF attempted to re-establish control in three ways: by setting up Forest Management Units (*Kesatuan Pengelolaan Hutan* – KPH), delineating their areas of operation, and establishing functional managing organizations. A new implementing regulation (PP 38/2007) strengthened the ministry's control, reducing district governments to providing technical considerations once a Forest Management Unit is designed and established under a management plan approved by central government (Ngakan *et al.* 2007). In response to demands for more socially responsible approaches, MoF had long experimented with 'social' and 'community' forestry initiatives granting local people various roles and rights with forest product commodities. It launched a new iteration of these policies under regulation PP 6/2007.[20]

The community forestry policy would now grant a long-term (35-year) lease to villagers, who would obtain formal use rights in areas that villagers had already occupied. This initiative remained controversial among some NGOs supporting agrarian reform as it was seen to extinguish customary claims over the land (Peluso *et al.* 2008). It also effectively restricted land uses to the type of activity determined by the official classification of forest function under the forestry law, and set clear limits on the type of intercropping to be allowed. In this way, MoF would convert its de facto loss of control over particular areas without adjusting its legal authority over the land by, for instance, granting more secure individual title.[21]

The Indonesian government classified 53.9 million hectares of the state forestry estate as 'degraded forest' (Ministry of Forestry 2007). The MoF developed a new 'people's plantation forest' scheme in these areas, ostensibly to improve the productivity and the ecology. Adapting the 'nucleus-plasma' model where corporations controlled core plantation units (the 'nucleus') and smallholders farmed surrounding areas (*plasma*) under contract, the scheme fitted with the private–public–social 'partnership' favoured in policy circles. By recruiting villagers to supply raw material for the pulp and paper industries, pulp and paper producers would obtain access to local labour, extending their economies of scale, while diffusing conflicts with local landowners by including their 'participation' in the production process. At the same time MoF would extend its control, setting strict guidelines regarding the species local villagers might grow and the conditions under which they might grow them. The scheme provided for the expansion of private timber plantations by a further 3.6 million hectares while rolling out people's plantation forests over 5.4 million hectares in areas that were considered to be currently unproductive and 'free' from formal tenurial rights (Dirjen Bina Produksi Kehutanan n.d.). In these ways MoF and their partners, having withstood the tide of reform, now reasserted their agendas within the forestry estate.

Reducing Emissions from Deforestation and Degradation (REDD)

By this time market-based mechanisms had emerged as the central strategy for dealing with deforestation. The idea here is that loss of forest 'is associated with the fact that conventional market systems undervalue ecosystem services in everyday decision making'. The application of market-based approaches, such as Reducing Emissions from Deforestation and Degradation (REDD) approaches, intend to 'correct this market failure and change undesirable behaviours' (Portela *et al.* 2010: 12). The idea here is a simple one. Forests should be given a monetary value, and financial rewards introduced for reducing forest-based emissions. While the environmental services derived from forests were not valued in the past, the idea is that markets will place a value on the carbon locked up in forests, creating large incentives for conserving forests as carbon sinks. As one report argued, only carbon markets will deliver enough funds for effective climate change mitigation efforts (Griffith 2007).

During 2007, reports on Indonesia's contribution to climate change pointed to the large-scale carbon emissions linked to forest fires, peat drainage and land clearance by oil palm plantation owners. Factoring in these emissions, a 2007 report listed Indonesia as the world's third-leading producer of greenhouse gases (UNEP *et al.* 2008) with the majority of these emissions coming from deforestation. This placed Indonesia at the heart of global discussions regarding REDD. Despite various reservations among social movements and NGOs (described below), REDD in Indonesia is accepted as an opportunity to improve forest governance. NGOs see it as a way to clarify the tenure and property rights system in forest areas, BAPPENAS as a way to improve coordination and MoF as a means to re-establish control and improve management.

The literature supporting market-based mechanisms argues that clear property rights are critical, ensuring that an exchange can be made between the supplier of the good (the landowner) and those who demand it (the buyer of the credit) (Portela *et al.* 2010). However, most forest lands are not yet demarcated and in many places remain 'fuzzy'. As one commentator noted: 'Identifying who should receive compensation as well as negotiating transparent and effective payment arrangements, is at best challenging especially with ambiguous land use rights and government jurisdiction in Indonesia' (Lang 2010).

Although discussions focus on ways to recognize the rights of local people, REDD has to proceed in the absence of a legal framework that offers secure property rights to village land-owners. At the same time, those with formal tenurial rights may obtain the main share of REDD funds, rather than those with 'informal', de facto rights. The fear is that REDD could allow the market to define rights in an uncompromising manner (Poffenberger and Smith-Hanssen 2009). If so, the benefits will exclusively flow to industrial and corporate interests, supporting the formalization of land rights in a fashion that bypasses local 'customary' authority structures and those unable to assert *de jure* rights. At the same time, actors interested in forest conservation are using the market approach, establishing companies investing in restoration concessions in the hope of gaining income from REDD.[22]

The participation of communities is seen as critical to controlling the local forces driving deforestation. The benefits to communities from REDD could include the strengthening of tenurial rights under national law and international agreements, increased revenues and grants for community development and forest management, and empowering local communities in multi-tiered agreements (Poffenberger and Smith-Hanssen 2009: 4). However, in the past resources have flowed out from forest areas mapped within village boundaries, with local villagers left looking on. NGOs and social movements continue to demand that forest zoning processes and legal property categories be reworked to incorporate local customary and territorial rights in a way that reduces the scope for land speculation and land grabbing (Gené and Aliadi 2009). However, to date they have been unsuccessful.

With the large domestic firms supporting the extension of large-scale extractive and agricultural industries into new areas, it remains unclear whether REDD can offer sufficient immediate incentives to prevent forest conversion. According to some studies, oil palm development offers higher yields than REDD. One study suggested that over 30 years, oil palm development would yield $3,800 – $9,600 per hectare net present value while REDD would offer only $614 – $994 per hectare (Poffenberger and Smith-Hanssen 2009: 2). To be sure, carbon prices could increase. Yet it remains unclear how REDD 'projects alone will halt the expansion of oil palm and road networks in the region surrounding a REDD project'. With vulnerable lowland forests remaining open to plantation development, this increases the 'likelihood that deforesta-tion might be displaced from the REDD project areas to forests' outside the project area ('leakage'), 'simply because the demand for agricultural products won't go away' (Lang 2010).

Discussions of market-based mechanisms also argue that effective legal and regulatory frame-works, supported by monitoring and enforcement, are critical. However, the problems of competition between agencies, overlapping responsibilities and roles, and the lack of clarity regarding authority and accountability remain unresolved. This problem was demonstrated when the president established a National Council on Climate Change (DNPI). Chaired by the president, the council includes 17 ministers with key natural resource and economic portfolios. However, recent reports noted that the new agency remained 'institutionally weak' due to its unclear responsibilities and functions, its lack of status vis-à-vis the ministries, and its poor budget (Satriastanti 2010). More recently, coordination has been mandated to the presidential-led agency for monitoring and control of development (UKP4) with the key agencies within the bureaucracy – BAPPENAS, KLH and the MoF – again sidelined (*Jakarta Post* 2010).

Since 2007 a new legal regime has been emerging, once again with 'persisting areas of uncertainty and overlap'.[23] The MoF prepared its guidelines for REDD implementation through regulations drafted by ministerial committees, with, according to critics, 'little involvement of civil society' (Anderson and Kuswardono 2008: 7). The new regulations supported the reassertion of MoF control over the 'forestry estate' in a number of respects. For instance, they sustained the assumption that the MoF has the authority to issue licences in the forestry estate, establishing ministerial control over the issuing of licences (IUP). With 'tight Ministerial control over VERs' (Verified Emission Reductions), carbon offset credits in the voluntary carbon markets, 'VER certificates would be sold directly to buyers or through [the] Carbon Exchange as approved by the Minister' (Devine 2009). Further, REDD projects in the regions would only proceed under central government authority. The MoF would assert its control over REDD projects, including an element of the revenues derived from them, 'regardless of whether the funding is private or public' (Anderson and Kuswardono 2008: 6).[24]

The outcomes of individual REDD projects will largely be determined by who controls them, how much revenue they generate, who benefits from REDD funds, and how the money is spent (Poffenberger and Smith-Hanssen 2009). A range of actors have emerged who seek to benefit from the sale of forest carbon credits, including forest agencies overseeing projects, local government with responsibilities for planning, NGOs involved in implementation, and universities carrying out research.

Conclusion

Viewing the state as a 'multi-faceted, complex assemblage of interlocking and interwoven power relations' (Mackenzie 2009: 73), this chapter has followed the seemingly disaggregated processes that have accumulated over time to shape reform. Over the last decade social movements, NGOs and pro-reform actors within the state, at times working together with donor agencies and foreign NGOs, have dedicated themselves to reforming elements of natural resource governance. These reforms have led to some positive changes: information is more readily available and many actors are more knowledgeable; some community rights have been recognized and legal opportunities have become available. While some services have improved, anti-corruption campaigns have made oligarchic actors more careful. However, as we have seen, powerful oligarchic interests counter these movements by influencing strategic political decisions regarding which governance reforms should be followed, how far they should proceed, or through selective implementation of the policies advocated by donor agencies. These elliptical processes typically occur in departmental and parliamentary committee rooms removed from the public gaze. Further, since the inception of decentralization, processes in the back rooms of regional parliaments have become more important, ensuring that oligarchic groups need to make larger political investments in regional and local governments and financial investments in local community development through various corporate social responsibility initiatives.

The key problem is that addressing the underlying issues would require interventions in the production and the property systems. This necessarily runs up against the dominant forces and processes at work in the political economy. If it is to occur, more encompassing reform of the resource sector requires political struggles over power and resources. In the absence of a strong, broad-based social or political movement able to challenge oligarchic power in the resource sector, the degree to which advocacy can lead to substantial shifts in laws, institutions and modes of resource control remains at best uncertain.

While different actors within the pro-reform constituency advocate particular policy narratives or reform agendas, over time these efforts have articulated with international environmental policy to shift state policy discourse (Peluso et al. 2008: 379). In many cases such efforts have reshaped the assumptions underlying state practices, yet to date they have not shifted the underlying structures. Meanwhile, the oligarchy of domestic corporations and dynastic politico-bureaucrats has continued to aggressively pursue new opportunities as they become available, such as for new oil palm and timber plantations, including the large-scale food estates currently being developed in Papua (*Jakarta Globe* 2010). By fusing public–private power and utilizing significant economic investments in the resource sector in parallel with political investments in the policy-making process, powerful networks of power and interest with investments in resource sectors set the boundaries for environmental reform, in many cases conceding to the rhetorical demands of reformist elements while ensuring that the application of environmental governance approaches remains largely figurative.

Notes

1 For example, see Lucas and Warren (2003).

2 This is not to deny that, in particular cases, pro-reform coalitions have had some achievements. For instance Burung Indonesia (formerly Birdlife) gained support in establishing the Hutan Harapan restoration concession in Jambi. Restoration concessions have been adopted in official regulations and several other companies have become interested. Further, World Agroforestry (ICRAF) developed models for recognizing community property rights and agroforestry systems on state forest land in Krui. Although Krui's precedent was never repeated, several districts have recognized 'customary forests' (*hutan adat*) and the rights of local people to manage them. While 'community forestry' (*hutan kemasyarakatan*) has yet to contribute a great deal to the devolution of forest areas into community hands, the Ministry of Forestry continues to experiment with 'village forests' (*hutan desa*) (Warta Tenure no. 5, April 2008, P.14/Menhut-II/2010) and 'community plantations' (*hutan tanaman rakyat*) (Warta Tenure no. 4, February 2007; *VetoNews* 15 November 2010).

3 See Oil Palm HQ (2009: 9). They are estimates based on publicly available information. In many cases accurate land bank figures are not publicly available

4 For example, the Forum for Communication in Community Forestry, the Consortium of Agrarian Reform, the Alliance of *Adat* Communities (AMAN).

5 *PeraturanPemerintah* No. 2/2008 concerning State Revenues from the Utilization of Forestlands for Non-forestry Development.

6 Article 237, Law 32/2004.

7 DPR staff member, personal communication.

8 Recent examples: PP 10/2006 vs UU 32/2004 and UU Capital Investment.

9 The new spatial planning law specifies that spatial planning remain a ministerial responsibility. As the head of BAPPENAS does not have full ministerial status, at present spatial planning remains the responsibility of the Ministry of Public Works.

10 RUU *PengelolaanSumberdayaAlam,* draft bill on natural resources management.

11 *PokjaOrnop* PSDA, NGO working group on natural resources management.

12 For instance, since decentralization local governments wish to exert more control over state forest lands. This is particularly the case in East Kalimantan where some newly created districts, which have up to 70–90 per cent of their district classified as state 'forest land', wish to rezone areas of land to 'free up' space for developing mining and oil palm activities. Indeed, East Kalimantan's spatial plan (*tata ruang*) is yet to be integrated with central government spatial plans and forestry plans. With large areas of forest already converted to other uses, East Kalimantan has wanted to convert another two million hectares of forest land for other purposes, a move resisted by the Ministry of Forestry (Author personal communication 2007–8; *Kaltim Pos* 2010)

13 To be sure, reform-minded people in the bureaucracy have advocated for key changes. For instance, Djamaluddin, Suharto's last Minister for Forestry, experimented with community forestry, allowing for new community-based property rights approaches to be applied in Krui, Lampung, primarily because he was open to such experiments (DTE, June 2002). However, later ministers had much stronger political party profiles. In the absence of a strong coalition, the efforts of reform-minded officials are hardly noticeable. Meanwhile the continued expansion of agriculture and mining has continued. For instance, in February 2010 a new regulation (PP 24/2010) was promulgated allowing for mining in protected forests (*Kompas* 2010).

14 As we will discuss later, since 2004 the government has promoted more 'people-oriented' forest management schemes such as 'village forests', 'community plantations' (*hutan tanaman rakyat*) and community forestry (*hutan rakyat*).

15 The majority of the rural population outside of Java lives on or near state forest lands. About 48.8 million people live on state forest land, and about 10.2 million of these are considered to be poor (Wollenberg *et al.* 2004).

16 For an overview, see Contreras-Hermosilla and Fay (2005).

17 This is inferred from the various ways MoF tries to accommodate communities: HKM, Htdesa, PHBM all only grant use rights. Since the early 1990s this has only entailed granting some 200,000 hectares of the 130 million hectares of the forest estate (Ditjen RLPS dan BPK 2008).

18 *Revitalizasi Perkebunan* [Plantation Revitalization].

19 *RevitalisasiKehutanan* [Forestry Revitalization].

20 For reasons of space we will limit our comments here to people's plantation forest initiatives.

21 Interview, MoF.

22 E.g. see BirdLife Global Forest Conservation Programme (2008).

23 Government regulation on forest planning, management and use (PP 6/2007) and a series of MoF decisions (PerMenHut P.68/Menhut-II/2008; PerMenHut P.30 /Menhut-II/2009; KepMenHut P.36/Menhut-II/2009).

24 At the time of writing these regulations are still in a process of revision.

References

Adger, W.N. and A. Jordan (2009) 'Sustainability: exploring the processes and outcomes of governance', in W.N. Adger and A. Jordan (eds) *Governing Sustainability*, Cambridge: Cambridge University Press, pp. 1–31.

Afiff, S., N. Fauzi, G. Hart, L. Ntsebeza and N. Peluso (2005) 'Redefining agrarian power: resurgent agrarian movements in West Java, Indonesia', Working Paper, Center for Southeast Asia Studies, UC Berkeley; available at: www.escholarship.org/uc/item/7rf2p49g (accessed 27 July 2010).

ALB Legal News (2009) 'Indonesia 2009'; available at: http://asia.legalbusinessonline.com/alb-special-reports/indonesia-2009/36703 (accessed 3 September 2009).

Anderson, Patrick and Torry Kuswardono (2008) *Report to the Rainforest Foundation Norway on Reducing Emissions from Deforestation and Degradation in Indonesia*, Jakarta, September; available at: www.lifemosaic.net/climatechange2.php (accessed 29 July 2011).

Asia Forest Network (n.d.) 'Asia regional exchange on forest sector contribution to the UN MDG'; available at: www.asiaforestnetwork.org/pub/pub75.pdf (accessed 10 June 2010).

Author interview (2004a) Official from *BAPPENAS* [National Development Planning Agency], 5 April.

——(2004b) Official from *BAPPENAS* [National Development Planning Agency], 13 April.

——(2004c) Official from Ministry of Home Affairs, 12 April.

——(2007) Eman, Institut Pertanian Bogor, 12 May.

——(n.d.) *MoF*.

Author personal communication (2007–8) 'Dirjen Baplan' on the occasion of several meetings on East Kalimantan's spatial plan.

Barr, C., I.A.P. Resosudarmo, A. Dermawan and J. McCarthy (eds) (2006) *Decentralization of Forest Administration in Indonesia*, Bogor: CIFOR.

Bell, S. and A. Hindmoor (2009) *Rethinking Governance: The Centrality of the State in Modern Society*, Melbourne: Cambridge University Press.

BirdLife Global Forest Conservation Programme (2008) 'The Harapan Rainforest Initiative, Sumatra'; available at: www.birdlife.org/action/ground/sumatra/Harapan%20Summary%20Document.pdf (accessed 28 June 2009).

Brown, K. (2009) 'Governance, government and the pursuit of sustainability', in W.N. Adger and A. Jordan (eds) *Governing Sustainability*, Cambridge: Cambridge University Press, pp. 32–53.

Contreras-Hermosilla, A. and C. Fay (2005) *Strengthening Forest Management in Indonesia through Land Tenure Reform: Issues and Framework for Action*, Washington, DC: Forest Trends; available at: www.forest-trends.org/documents/files/doc_107.pdf (accessed 20 June 2010).

Devine, L. (2009) 'REDD+ opportunities and challenges in Indonesia. Structuring Indonesian REDD+ projects and compliance with national regulations'; available at: www.unredd.net/index.php?option=com_docmanandtask = doc_downloadandgid = 1010andItemid = 53. (accessed 3 August 2010).

Dirjen Bina Produksi Kehutanan (n.d.) 'Pembangunan Hutan Tanaman Rakyat (HTR)'; available at: www.walhikalsel.org/downloads/PEMBANGUNAN%20HUTAN%20TANAMAN%20RAKYAT-Kalsel.pdf (accessed 4 June 2009).

Ditjen RLPS dan BPK (2008) *Eksekutif Data Strategis Kehutanan tahun 2007*, Indonesia: Kementerian Kehutanan Republik Indonesia.

Down to Earth (2002) 'Forest, people and rights', DTE Special Report, June 2002.

——(2007) 'New investment law is not pro-poor', *Down to Earth Newsletter*: 73.

Ekawati, Arti (2010) 'Massive Papua food estate to serve as nation's bread basket launched', *Jakarta Globe*, 11 August.

Emila and Suwito (2007) 'Hutan Tanaman Rakyat (HTR) Agenda baru untuk pengentasan kemiskinan?', *Warta Tenure* 4; available at: www.wg-tenure.org/file/Warta_Tenure/Edisi_04/Warta_Tenure_04e.pdf (accessed 28 February 2007).

Evans, P. (1995) *Embedded Autonomy: States and Industrial Transformation*, Princeton, NJ: Princeton University Press.

Fox, J. (2007) *Accountability Politics: Power and Voice in Rural Mexico*, New York: Oxford University Press.

Gellert, P.K. (2004) 'Oligarchy in the timber markets of Indonesia: from Apkindo to IBRA to the future of the forests', in B. P. Resosudarmo (ed.) *The Politics and Economics of Indonesia's Natural Resources*, Singapore: Institute of Southeast Asian Studies, pp. 145–61.

Gené, E.I. and A. Aliadi (2009) 'The Ulu Masen REDD demonstration activity: challenges at the policy and implementation levels'; available at: www.rsis.edu.sg/nts/Events/climate_change/session3/concept%20paper-Enrique%20Ibarra%20Gene.pdf (accessed 4 July 2010).

Griffith, T. (2007) 'Seeing "RED"? "Avoided deforestation" and the rights of Indigenous Peoples and local communities', Forest Peoples Programme; available at: www.forestpeoples.org/documents/ifi_igo/avoided_deforestation_red_jun07_eng.pdf (accessed 24 June 2010).

Guerin, B. (2007) 'A who's who of Indonesian biofuel', *Asia Times*, 23 May.

Gunningham, Neil (2009) 'Environment law, regulation, governance: shifting architectures', *Journal of Environmental Law* 21 (2): 179–212.

Jakarta Post (2010) 'Kuntoro Mangkusubroto chairs REDD+ task force', 24 June.

Kaltim Pos (2010) 6 November.

Kompas (2010) 'Tambang Tertutup di Hutan Lindung', 11 March.

Lang, C. (2010) 'Interviews about Ulu Masen, Indonesia: a REDD-labelled protected area', *REDD Monitor*, 20 January.

Leftwich, A. (2000) 'States of underdevelopment', in *States of Development: On the Primacy of Politics in Development*, Cambridge: Polity Press, pp. 71–104.

Lemos, M. and A. Agrawal (2006) 'Environmental governance', *Annual Review of Environment and Resources* 31: 297–325.

Lucas, A. and C. Warren (2003) 'The state, the people, and their mediators: the struggle over agrarian law reform in post-New Order Indonesia', *Indonesia* 76: 87–126.

McCarthy, J.F. (2004) 'Changing to gray: decentralization and the emergence of volatile socio-legal configurations in central Kalimantan, Indonesia', *World Development* 32 (7): 1199–1223.

——(2008) 'Shifting resource entitlements and governance reform during the agrarian transition in Sumatra, Indonesia', *Journal of Legal Pluralism* 55: 65–122.

McCarthy, J.F. and C. Warren (2009) 'Introduction', in C. Warren and J. McCarthy (eds) *Locating the Commonweal*, London: Routledge.

Mackenzie, I. (2009) *Politics: Key Concepts in Philosophy*, London: Continuum.

Ministry of Forestry (2007) 'Majalah Kehutanan Indonesia', Edisi I; available at: www.dephut.go.id/informasi/mki/07I/07IEditorial.htm (accessed 28 May 2009).

Moore, M. (2001) 'Political underdevelopment: what causes "bad governance"?' *Public Management Review* 3 (3): 385–418.

Nadvi, K. (2008) 'Global standards, global governance and the organization of global value chains', *Journal of Economic Geography* 8: 323–43.

Ngakan, P.O., A. Achmad and K. Lahae (2007) 'Implikasi perubahan kebijakan otonomi daerah terhadap beberapa aspek di sektor kehutanan: studi kasus di kabupaten Luwu utara, Sulawesi selatan', Center for International Forestry Research, Bogor.

Oil Palm HQ (2009) 'The world's top 15 listed palm oil planters'; available at: www.palmoilhq.com/PalmOilNews/the-worlds-top-15-listed-palm-oil-planters/

Peluso, N., S. Afiff and N. Rachman (2008) 'Claiming the grounds for reform: agrarian and environmental movements in Indonesia', *Journal of Agrarian Change* 8 (2–3): 377–407.

Poffenberger, M. and K. Smith-Hanssen (2009) 'Forest communities and REDD climate initiatives', *AsiaPacific Issues* 91, Honolulu, HI: East–West Center.

Portela, R., K.J. Wendland and L.L. Pennypacker (2010) 'The idea of market-based mechanisms for forest conservation and climate change', in C. Streck, R. O'Sullivan, T. Janson-Smith and R. Tarasofsky (eds) *Climate Change and Forests: Emerging Policy and Market Opportunities*, London and Baltimore: Chatham House and Brookings Institution Press.

Republika (2006) 'Emil Salim: RUU Tata Ruang Punya Kelemahan Besar yang Membahayakan'; available at: www.republika.co.id/ (accessed 22 March 2006).

Rhodes, R. (1997) *Understanding Governance: Policy Networks, Governance, Reflexivity, and Accountability*, Buckingham: Open University Press.

Ribot, J., A. Agrawal and A. Larson (2006) 'Recentralizing while decentralizing: how national governments reappropriate forest resources', *World Development* 3411 (11): 1864–86.

Robison, R. and V.R. Hadiz (2004) *Reorganising Power in Indonesia: The Politics of Oligarchy in an Age of Markets*, London: Routledge.

Rooij, Benjamin van (2010) 'Greening industry without enforcement? An assessment of the World Bank's pollution regulation model for developing countries', *Law and Policy* 32 (1): 127–52.

Santosa, S.J. (2008) 'Palm oil boom in Indonesia: from plantation to downstream products and biodiesel', *Soil, Air, Water* 36 (5–6): 453–65.

Santoso, H. (2008) 'Selamat Datang Hutan Desa?', *Warta Tenure 5*; available at: www.wg-tenure.org/html/wartavw.php?id=45 (accessed 30 April 2008).

Satriastanti, F.E. (2010) 'Climate council budget questioned by lawmaker', *Jakarta Globe*, 19 January.

Schönwälder, G. (1997) 'New democratic spaces at the grassroots? Popular participation in Latin American local governments', *Development and Change* 28 (4): 753–70.

Setiawan, U. (2007) 'Relevansi Program Pembaruan Agraria Nasional di Kawasan Kehutanan', in Emila and Suwito (eds) *Proceeding Roundtable Discussion: Permasalahan Tenurial dan Reforma Agraria di Kawasan Hutan dalam Perspektif Masyarakat Sipil, Bogor 29 November 2007*, Working Group on Forest Land Tenure, Bogor, Indonesia, pp. 111–16.

Sherlock, S. (2010) 'The parliament in Indonesia's decade of democracy: people's forum or chamber of cronies?', in E. Aspinall and M. Mietzner (eds) *Problems of Democratisation in Indonesia: Elections, Institutions and Society*, Singapore: ISEAS

Suharyo, W. (2000) 'Voices from the regions: a participatory assessment of the new decentralization laws in Indonesia', *Working Paper 2*, Jakarta: UNSFIR.

Tempo (2004) 'Bagi-bagi Kursi Menteri', 5 September: 23.

Tempo Interaktif (2004) 'Suap Demi Sahnya Perpu Tambang?', 23 July.

——(2007) 'Mahkamah Konstitusi Sidang Perdana Uji Materi Undang-undang Pananaman Modal', 2 August.

UNEP, GEF and Global Environment Centre and Wetlands International (2008) 'Assessment on peat lands, biodiversity and climate change', Global Environment Centre, Kuala Lumpur, and Wetlands International, Wegeningen.

VetoNews (2010) 15 November; available at: www.vetonews.com/ (accessed 15 November 2010).

Wollenberg, E., B. Belcher, D. Sheil, S. Dewi and M. Moeliono (2004) 'Why are forest areas relevant to reducing poverty in Indonesia?', *CIFOR Newsletter* 4 (December).

SECTION V
Violence and state authority

17

TACKLING THE LEGACIES OF VIOLENCE AND CONFLICT

Liberal institutions and contentious politics in Cambodia and East Timor

Caroline Hughes

Since the 1990s, the plight of peoples and states emerging from conflict has become a central focus of humanitarian and development policy. The opportunity to settle a series of civil wars, following the end of the Cold War, through United Nations peacekeeping operations, gave rise to a new industry in peace-building and post-conflict reconstruction, incorporating multilateral and bilateral aid agencies, international non-governmental organizations, private contractors, and academic researchers and consultants. Southeast Asia hosted two such operations, each ground-breaking at their respective times: in Cambodia from 1992 to 1993 and in East Timor from 1999 to 2002.

As relatively small countries which were inaccessible for decades during their respective wars, most of the contemporary scholarly writing on Cambodia and East Timor has come from the perspective of comparative evaluations of international policies for peace as practised in these two cases. Each of these operations has generated a considerable literature, much of which is written from the perspective of international relations or by staff members or consultants working for international peace operations. The two cases are regularly included in comparative volumes about peace-building, state-building and post-conflict reconstruction. Such comparative evaluations considerably outweigh the country-specialist literature, so that contemporary understandings of Cambodian and Timorese politics are heavily influenced by models from the literature on comparative intervention.

Within international relations, the literature on politics and policy in post-conflict states has tended to fall into two camps. In the 1990s and early 2000s, the vast majority of writing on this subject was problem- and policy-oriented, interrogating case studies in order to elicit 'lessons learned' for international organizations and aid agencies. Since 2004, a more critical literature has emerged on peace-keeping and state-building in post-conflict states, which draws on political theory, international relations and development studies for its theoretical innovations. This literature covers a spectrum of approaches, but agrees on the central proposition that previous mainstream policy debates over international intervention in states suffering and emerging from conflict uncritically both reflected and promoted particular aspects of liberal dogma, with deleterious results for the aims of peace, justice and development. In this chapter, I discuss these contending approaches, in the light of the theoretical schema provided in the introduction to this handbook, and in the light of the experience of the two Southeast Asian case studies, Cambodia and East Timor.

The purpose of this discussion is to challenge the assumptions of liberal institutionalist models, and the policies and practices in aid to post-conflict states which have resulted from these models, and to offer an alternative to existing critiques of liberal institutionalism, from the perspective of political economy. Political economy approaches possess explanatory power with regard to three aspects of post-conflict politics that have been inadequately conceptualized within the mainstream literature: the relationships of post-conflict states to global power structures and the impact of this on local politics; the role of local culture(s) in the politics of local response to international intervention; and the implications of these for the politics of local resistance to international strategies of internationalization. It is argued here that, as such, political economy offers an alternative from the over-determinism of either culturalist or Foucauldian approaches that have been prominent in the critical literature on post-conflict states.

International policy and local politics in post-conflict countries: post-Cold War frameworks

Liberal triumphalism and the UN in Cambodia

Liberal triumphalism in the early 1990s, following both the collapse of the Soviet Union and the expulsion of the Iraqi army from Kuwait, prompted a 'new interventionism' (Mayall 1996) designed to construct a new world order (Bush 1990) that could facilitate 'better standards of life in larger freedom' (Boutros-Ghali 1995). United Nations Secretary–General Boutros Boutros-Ghali defined a new form of international policy which he termed 'peace-building' and which formalized a transformation in the conception of peace, from Cold War approaches oriented towards the monitoring of ceasefires, to post-Cold War 'complex political settlements' to promote peace via the establishment of institutions to maintain security, development, justice and democracy. In 1993, a United Nations General Assembly resolution defined peace-building as 'sustained cooperative efforts by the United Nations to deal with the underlying economic, social, cultural and humanitarian causes and effects of conflicts in order to promote a durable foundation for peace' and 'the creation of a new environment to forestall the recurrence of conflicts' (United Nations General Assembly 1993). As such, it ushered in a new era of international intervention in the internal functioning of states and societies in post-conflict contexts.

The term 'peace-building' was initially coined by Johan Galtung, the radical founder of the International Peace Research Institute in Oslo. Galtung's work was radical in proposing a structuralist analysis of violence and peace in which the violence perpetrated by agents was regarded as linked to structures of oppression and power which cause misery, hardship and inequality. Galtung coined the term 'peace-building' to refer to activities which tackled structures promoting violence rather than simply acts of violence (Galtung 1985). This terminology was appropriated by Boutros-Ghali in his report to the Security Council entitled *An Agenda for Peace*, produced in 1992. In this document, Boutros-Ghali called for 'comprehensive efforts to identify and support structures which will tend to consolidate peace and advance a sense of confidence and well-being among people' (Boutros-Ghali 1995: 61).

In Boutros-Ghali's version, ideals of the liberal democratic peace and Galtung's theories of structural violence were amalgamated in such a way that authoritarianism specifically, rather than, for example, the liberal international economic order, was regarded as the structure that led to oppression. The promotion of national institutions to foster liberalism, democracy and capitalist development in all countries were, in fact, conceived as the solution to structural violence: as Boutros-Ghali described it, 'the transformation of deficient national structures and capabilities and ... the strengthening of new institutions' to promote 'social peace' as well as 'strategic or political peace' (Boutros-Ghali 1995: 62). This prescription was in line with the Kantian liberal peace thesis, revisited as the Cold War wound down by liberal scholars of international relations such as Michael Doyle, that liberal republics were unlikely to fight one another, and indeed would form an expanding pacific union (Doyle 1986), and it placed the onus for reform on the national rather than the international or global level. Similar attitudes emerged within the foreign policies of Western states in the same period, particularly oriented towards approaches of 'democratic enlargement' aimed at the countries of the former Soviet bloc. Boutros Boutros-Ghali articulated a vision of a new international order characterized by 'democratic principles at all levels of existence': but this was anchored on the vision of a community of democratic national states. The right to intervene to reorient national institutions towards the Kantian ideal was mooted; but the international order itself remained organized around state sovereignty rather than cosmopolitan democracy.

In a globalizing world, the state-centrism of such approaches to conflict has been the subject of surprisingly little controversy. The presumption that the right kind of national institutions can effectively oversee successful integration into global and regional economic orders from what is clearly, for the vast majority of post-conflict countries, an extremely disadvantaged starting point has been barely questioned, let alone challenged. Robert Cox's observation, that the role of the state in the South in a globalizing world is increasingly that of a 'transmission belt' reproducing values and norms that serve the interests of the liberal and capitalist developed world at the expense of the poor, is pertinent to the question of the ideologically charged nature of post-conflict reconstruction policies for promoting democracy and justice through the creation of new institutions of state war-torn countries (Cox 1995; Duffield 2001).

The period of post-Cold War United Nations interventionism from 1989 to 1994 occurred in this ideological milieu. Practices reflecting the liberal democratic ideal developed incrementally from one mission to the next; however, the Cambodian mission, at its time the most ambitious and overtly political mission ever, illustrated the explicitly Kantian link that was drawn at this time between the promotion of human rights and representative democracy and the achievement of peace. In the early post-Cold War period, there was an assumption that action to end violence, restrain authoritarian leaders and award the population at large a say over their future would lead to the flowering of liberal democracy almost automatically. Thus the literature on peacekeeping interventions focused primarily on the securing of peace deals and the keeping of elites on board, rather than on the longer-term institutionalization of liberal democracy. Rational choice theorists sought to model the conditions under which civil wars began and ended using game theory and concepts of opportunity costs, producing models for efficient conflict management and predicting negotiating strategies by combatants in peace processes (see Mason and Fett 1996). Such work was particularly associated with the *Journal of Conflict Resolution*, a journal published by the Peace Science Society (International) based at Pennsylvania State University, and focusing on quantitative and scientific analysis of conflict and peace. A contending approach to understanding the way that peace deals were secured focused on using historical case studies of 'success' and 'failure' to generate typologies and categorization schema to inform future policy (see Bertram 1995; Stedman 1997; Francis 2000; Stedman *et al.* 2002). This approach focused in particular on actors and incentives, regarding external interveners as 'custodians of peace' (Stedman 1997) which can act to alter incentives and motivate compliance.

The operation of UNTAC in Cambodia reflected this thinking. The mission incorporated components intended to restrain abusive and authoritarian state agencies; to promote human rights and freedom of choice via elections and the concern to preserve freedom of informed choice via a United Nations radio station and 'a neutral political environment conducive to free and fair general elections' (United Nations 1991). Support for electoral campaigning was regarded as the key to allowing the supposedly war-weary Cambodian population to vote for the peace and the new constitutional order that was portrayed as self-evidently in their best interests.

There was a long-term aspect to the UNTAC operation, enshrined in the Paris Agreement's provisions for a new constitutional order characterized by liberalism, the free market, democracy and respect for rights. However, the difficulties of organizing the first step on this path – the 1993 elections – in the face of the return of one party, the Khmer Rouge, to insurgency, meant that UN peacekeepers left rapidly after the elections, before the situation could deteriorate further. This unseemly retreat was criticized both by components within UNTAC (UNTAC 1993) and by the peacekeeping literature subsequently, as betraying the potential for long-term peace-building efforts that could have planted liberalism more firmly in Cambodia's somewhat unpromising soil. However, the UN's actions in this regard reflected not only a fairly accurate assessment of the extent to which Cambodia's political elite was prepared to tolerate further international action to promote a new liberal order, but also the experience of UN peacekeepers in Angola, where a return to warfare after UN-sponsored elections caused more death and suffering than the initial conflict the elections were supposed to resolve, and in Somalia, where American attempts to bring justice to Dodge City led to ignominious flight. This pattern of failure to move from the securing of tenuous peace deals to the institutionalization of democracy was borne out in subsequent years, when the collapse of international arrangements for elections in Rwanda led to genocide in 1994; and elections in Bosnia and Kosovo brought extremist parties to power.

From democratic peace to the imperative of modernization: East Timor and international authoritarianism

The situation in the mid-1990s, in which international policy-makers faced a set of post-peace-mission countries from Cambodia to Bosnia in which security had improved but liberal democracy had not emerged, led to a revision of the democratic peace thesis (see Snyder and Mansfield 1995) and a shift in perspectives related to international peacekeeping and peace-building. Increased attention on the question of whether war-torn societies could be brought to conform with liberal aspirations over the long term prompted greater focus on an institutionalist approach to peace-building, later reconceptualized as a process of state-building, in which international interveners would not merely referee a founding contest over who rules, but seek to implant institutions that could continue to ensure security and manage contests over who rules into the long term. This understanding of intervention persisted into the post-11 September world, following George W. Bush's emphasis on weak and failing states as a major threat to the United States in the context of the War on Terror.

The introduction of the 'long term' into conceptions of peace-building was also facilitated by greater interest in development agencies and international financial institutions in post-conflict reconstruction. The United Nations experienced difficulty in the 1990s in meeting its peace-keeping commitments, and continually suffered from the unwillingness of member states to properly fund peacekeeping operations. From the mid-1990s, however, such well-financed agencies as the World Bank and the United Nations Development Programme began to define a mandate for themselves in terms of post-conflict reconstruction and state-building, offering an opportunity to relieve the financial burden on the UN Department of Peacekeeping Operations, and the prospect of more or less open-ended intervention in the form of state-building and institutionalization. As Ben Reilly comments, strategies of institutionalization require a willingness to 'invest substantial time and money in an open-ended process of social and political development' (Reilly 2002: 123–4).

The distinction between short-term peace negotiations and long-term peace building was formalized by Oliver Ramsbotham in 2000. Ramsbotham defined five aspects of peace-building, and identified tasks to be completed over the short-term, medium-term and long-term with respect to each. The aspects concerned were: military and security; political and constitutional; economic and social; psycho-social including transitional justice and reconciliation; and international integration. In each aspect, immediate short-term tasks such as securing a ceasefire, holding a founding election, providing humanitarian relief, and promoting trust between former adversaries could be performed by UN peacekeepers, while longer-term tasks, including the establishment and maintenance of new institutions for providing security, representative governance, the rule of law, economic development and restorative justice would be taken on by indigenous actors supported by external agencies.

Focus on building institutions offered a solution to the key problem encountered by peace interventionists in the mid-1990s: how to deal with populations that did not emerge from civil wars as fully formed liberals. The experience of so-called 'new wars' of the mid-1990s, in which apparently atavistic ethnic conflicts were portrayed as reaching new levels of brutality in places such as Rwanda, Sierra Leone, Chechnya and the Balkans, challenged the presumption of liberal universalism inherent in the Agenda for Peace. Terms such as 'the new barbarism' were coined to describe culturalist theses such as that of Robert Kaplan in his infamous article 'The coming anarchy' (Kaplan 1994).

Institutionalism offered a theory of change that could save the liberal peace. As Ben Reilly describes it:

> Because institutions structure the routines of behavior in which political actors engage, they are crucial elements, over the longer term, in helping to build a moderate and sustainable political culture, in which routines of cooperation and accommodation come to be accepted as the norm rather than the exception.
>
> *(Reilly 2002: 137)*

As such, institutions supply not only a means to manage actors and their incentives, but also to transform them into peaceable liberals.

Within the institutionalist camp, further debates emerged over the role and nature of international action. Followers of John Paul Lederach advocated grassroots approaches focused on the restoration of relationships rather than the satisfaction of interests (Lederach 1997). Concerned with such issues as emancipation and transformation, this approach suffered from the problem that it was vague on the question of what international interveners could actually do, opening the door to potentially open-ended international engagement in grassroots community activities. This approach contrasted with the centralized and top-down approach of the United Nations which focused on state-building and the rapid formation of governments which could quickly shoulder responsibility for imposing order. In a review of post-conflict reconstruction published in the *Washington Quarterly* in 2002, Hamre and Sullivan articulated the US position on this question on the eve of intervention in Afghanistan and Iraq:

> The goal, during the short to medium run, is to build a minimally capable state, not to build a nation or address all the root causes that imperil peace. Those goals involve a longer term process that is beyond the scope of what external actors can achieve or lead; actors within the country itself must do so.
>
> *(Hamre and Sullivan 2002: 90)*

The rise of institutionalism within peacekeeping coincided with the emergence of institutional approaches to development more broadly. The impact of the new institutional economics within the World Bank, and the shift to 'good governance' models of development assistance from the mid-1990s, allowed a convergence between multilateral approaches to security and development, freed up billions of dollars for spending on post-conflict state-building, and provided an answer to the dilemmas of how to organize continued international supervision. Once immediate issues of security had been dealt with, Bank lending and conditionality offered a vehicle via which post-conflict state-building could continue to be monitored and influenced, even once peacekeepers had withdrawn.

The Bank's approach to post-conflict reconstruction has regarded this essentially as an economic rather than a political problem. The most prominent body of analysis emerging from the Bank is the work of Paul Collier's team at Oxford, who used statistical correlations to define conflict as a problem of under-development, and post-conflict reconstruction as a process of integration into the global economy as a means to secure economic growth. In 1998, the World Bank defined post-conflict reconstruction as follows:

> Post-conflict reconstruction has two overall objectives: to facilitate the transition to sustainable peace after hostilities have ceased and to support economic and social development. Economic recovery depends on the success of this transition and on the rebuilding of the domestic economy and restoration of access to external resources.
>
> *(World Bank 1998: 4)*

Under the influence of the new institutional economics, the Bank has pursued the building of institutions for governance from a perspective heavily influenced by a concern to better integrate post-conflict economies into regional and global orders, rather than primarily as a means to promote political accommodation amongst former combatants. This perspective was articulated in Francis Fukuyama's 2004 book *Statebuilding*, which employed public choice theory to argue that states in conflict-prone countries should be encouraged to become stronger but smaller, in order to facilitate the simultaneous promotion of market-oriented development and security to facilitate this. The increasingly central concern for state-building, as opposed to peace-building more broadly conceived, reflected, first, the influence of the new institutional economics emerging from the international financial institutions in the late 1990s and subsequently the security concerns associated with 'weak states' following the attacks that took place in the United States on 11 September 2001.

By the end of the 1990s, then, a key debate focused on the scale and scope of the intervention required for state-building. Roland Paris's (2004) critique of what he called 'the quick-and-dirty style of peace building that prevailed for much of the 1990s' represented the most influential rejection of the Kantian approach to electoral based solutions, and was articulated from the perspective of modernization theory. It extended also to encompass a critique of neo-liberal approaches such as Hamre and Sullivan's (2002), which regarded state-building in minimalist terms, and prioritized construction of a free market over entrenchment of state institutions. For Paris, both political and economic liberalization in a context of weak or non-existent institutions of state promote instability, because they permit the emergence of inequality, corruption and dispossession in the economic sphere, in turn promoting mass mobilization, demagoguery and, potentially, violence in the political sphere. Paris supports market democracy as a long-term objective, but draws on the work of Samuel Huntington and others to argue that the way to achieve this is via a strategy he calls Institutionalization Before Liberalization. This implies not only that rapid transitions to free markets might be destabilizing, but that 'authoritarian solutions for war-shattered states should not be rejected out of hand' (Paris 2004: 179). In particular this implies that weak institutions cannot effect social transformation: a long period of international trusteeship or tutelage to achieve effective administration and governability within society is necessary *before* opening the way to democratic self-rule.

The United Nations Transitional Authority in East Timor (UNTAET), established in 2000 following the tumultuous departure of the Indonesians and the successful disarmament of paramilitaries by the International Force for East Timor, reflected some of this thinking. On arriving in a country whose infrastructure had been largely destroyed and whose cadre of government officials had largely left for good, UNTAET conceived of itself as building a new state from scratch on a blank slate (Surkhe 2001; Chesterman 2005). Concerned to ensure the construction of the best possible institutions, UNTAET in fact was reluctant to consult or include the Timorese population in this process at all. UNTAET pursued a rigidly top-down approach, maintaining international control over the process of state-building for as long as possible, and prioritizing, as Roland Paris recommends, institutionalization over political liberalization.

Paris wrote approvingly of the UNTAET mission in East Timor, regarding it as illustrating 'how much can be accomplished ... when international agencies devote time and resources to rebuilding institutional structures in war-torn lands and carefully manage the movement towards democratization' (Paris 2004: 221). However, other writers, including former members of the UNTAET mission itself, wrote less approvingly of this manifestation of authoritarian liberalism in the Timorese context. Jarat Chopra, for example, resigned from his position as head of district administration in UNTAET in protest at the excessively top-down orientation of UNTAET, and its failure to give meaningful power or resources to local levels of government (Chopra 2002). Subsequently, an incipient conflict emerged between UNTAET and the World Bank, as the World Bank sought, through its Community Empowerment Programme, to provide funding and micro-credit facilities to swiftly constituted village development committees to promote local-level reconstruction in a manner that challenged UNTAET's highly centralized approach.

The World Bank's apparently 'bottom-up' approach was noted approvingly by a number of authors critical of the authoritarianism inherent in Paris's (and UNTAET's) approach. However, the World Bank's differences with UNTAET reflected less a concern to unleash collective action on the part of the poor in the name of democracy than a belief that the swift mobilization of entrepreneurial energies at the local level, via household micro-credit loans and small-scale rehabilitation of roads and markets, would boost economic growth. This was seen by the Bank as a more urgent priority than the shoring up of authoritative regulatory institutions at the Centre.

In fact, mobilization of the poor via this scheme was made difficult by the fact that the Community Empowerment Programme was based upon an extraordinary system in which funding was provided to elected committees which represented a variety of constituencies specified by the Bank – 'women' and 'youth', for example – but which specifically excluded existing local-level leaders, many of whom had emerged from the resistance movement and were genuinely respected opinion leaders within their villages. This unusual system reflected World Bank concern about the potential for 'elite capture' of the programme by unelected local leaders of various sorts. However, to a great extent this concern was either undermined by local politics, or itself undermined the utility of the programme. Subsequently, a World Bank evaluation of the programme found that this attempt at engineering new forms of political representation and leadership in Timorese villages had failed dismally: committees worked where they bowed to the informal oversight of existing village leaders. Where they attempted to work independently of existing leaders, as the Bank had envisaged they should, they were usually ineffective (see Hughes 2009b).

This example serves to illustrate wider critiques of Paris's thesis of 'under-institutionalization' in post-conflict societies: the idea that the key problem for post-conflict countries is their lack of institutions of governance. As the experience of the Community Empowerment Programme suggests, a lack of institutions is very rare in any human community: even where formal institutions may have collapsed under the weight of armed conflict, informal institutions or ad hoc community arrangements invariably emerge quite swiftly to provide a level of order and predictability in human relations. The blank slate upon which liberal institutions can be drawn does not exist: new formal institutions promoted by Paris's authoritarian interveners will need to come to an accommodation with pre-existing structures of authority and power.

Paris tackles this point obliquely in his comments on civil society. He argues that civil society within a post-conflict state will be characterized by a range of actors. These can be divided into 'good' actors, e.g. amongst political party leaders and civil society groups which advance the cause of moderation and peace, and 'bad' actors, which inflame hatred, often along ethnic lines, and seek to spoil peace processes. The task of international administrators is to distinguish between these groups, encouraging the good and discouraging the bad, *before* allowing the local population to take control of its own destiny via democratic processes and a move to free market relations. Paris admits that this requires a level of intervention, resources and, possibly, coercion, which international interveners have heretofore been unwilling to sustain. However, he argues that it offers the only prospect for the emergence of well-socialized liberal states (Paris 2004).

Critiques of the liberal institutionalist position

Critical recognition of the difficulty of using post-conflict institution-building to re-engineer relations of power and authority in post-conflict societies in a liberal direction has been widely recognized. Criticisms have taken three different forms. David Chandler focuses on the deformities in local politics produced by excessive international control of the institution-building process. Chandler regards the peace-building project as a form of 'empire in denial': the fact that interveners, in intrusive operations of international trusteeship such as the one mounted in Kosovo, retain real political power in their own hands and exclude local actors from this, entails that incentives for local actors to pursue political accommodations are removed or significantly reduced. For Chandler, the kind of authoritarian intervention that Paris has in mind has deleterious political effects which make the liberal project ultimately unrealizable, because it precludes the engagement of autonomous actors in bargaining with one another in pursuit of their interests (Chandler 2006).

A second approach, associated in particular with Oliver Richmond, is equally trenchant in its critique, but is founded on a specifically culturalist rejection of the possibility of an authoritarian road to liberalism. Richmond points out the internal inconsistencies in a liberal authoritarian position, but he regards the necessity of its failure as resulting not from internal contradictions in the project per se, but from a lack of liberal characteristics in post-conflict populations. He attributes this lack to the fact that most civil wars take place in non-Western countries with non-liberal cultural heritage. Consequently, Richmond characterizes Paris's peace-building approach, with particular reference to the Cambodian experience, as 'liberal hubris' destined to founder on the shoals of cultural resistance (Richmond and Franks 2007). In so doing, he draws upon the work of David Roberts, who has argued that politics in Cambodia since the United Nations intervention of 1991–3 has essentially reverted to type: to a model of neo-patrimonialism that is embedded in a Khmer culture which, despite devastating warfare and unimaginable destruction and upheaval, has persisted largely unchanged since pre-colonial times (Roberts 2001). Similarly, some analysts of East Timorese politics have called for a more enthusiastic embrace, on the part of both international interveners and political elites in Dili, of traditional systems of village rule (see Hohe 2002).

A third critique emerges from Foucauldian approaches current in development studies more broadly. This approach critiques the liberal internationalist project as depoliticizing: displacing opportunities for political action altogether via the substitution of administrative practices imposed through disciplinary techniques of power (see Harrison 2004; Gould 2005). Thus the form of change envisaged by Paris as a civilizing process of habituation to institutions of just governance is recast as a deadening process of discipline and rationalization. This is regarded as quite possibly successful in achieving more efficient administration but as problematic in that it betrays the possibility of emancipation. The shrinking of the political sphere disenfranchises the poor, even as they benefit from improved government services; and there is a danger that deep and potentially unbridgeable rifts may emerge between elites who have internalized Western rationalities and local societies which remain steeped in local practices and cultures. This undermines the state–society relationship and with it the potential for democratic forms of accountability or representation.

The latter critique has been more frequently applied to Africa than to case studies in South-east Asia, for two reasons. First, the so-called 'donor community' in Cambodia and Timor have exhibited less consensus in their operations than in some parts of Africa and have been less influential in the context of a more successfully capitalist region. The relative importance of donors such as Japan and, latterly, China vis-à-vis Western liberal donors has been greater. In Cambodia, regional investors such as Taiwan, Malaysia and South Korea have also been significant in determining policy. East Timor has successfully appealed for solidarity aid from Latin American donors such as Brazil and Cuba. Consequently, the donor–government relationship is more diverse than in parts of Africa, and the Foucauldian portrayal of aid as relentless discipline is less convincing. Perhaps more significantly, outcomes in both Cambodia and East Timor have not conformed to liberal rationalities. Although market relations and consumerist attitudes have become entrenched in urban Cambodia in particular, via policies which have encouraged a predatory form of capitalism, there has, arguably, not been an accompanying shift towards Western-style, liberal approaches to policy-making.

Among these different critiques, there has been surprisingly little emphasis on political economy. Political economy approaches encourage emphasis upon the changing nature and functions of the state in a globalizing world, and the way this reflects both politics – conceived as international, transnational and local coalitions of social forces – and economics – conceived as the changing nature of global and regional markets. Political economy provides its own take on the debates outlined above. First, with respect to the mainstream thesis of liberal institutionalism, political economists regard the nature and functioning of political institutions as determined by contentious social forces produced by international and local relations of production. Although institutions, once established, may exert an effect by structuring the political strategies of political coalitions in the short term, institutions ultimately reflect rather than determine distributions of power among contending class-based coalitions. Consequently, contrary to the predictions of liberal institutionalists, institution cannot of themselves produce the forms of liberal democratic political action that international peace-builders hope to see: they only do so if in alignment with supportive political coalitions emerging from various types of class formation.

This attribution of causality opens the prospect of economic determinism and a retreat into the teleologies of 1960s modernization theory; however, analyses of the empirical record suggest not only a degree of local variation in the ways in which class formations structure political coalitions and hence institutions (Bellin 2000), but also a historical trajectory in the current era of globalization which calls into question long-documented correlations between capitalist development, the emergence of the middle class, and liberal democracy (Jayasuriya 2005). As such, attention to structure no longer entails awaiting the emergence of an enlightened middle class to lead the march for democracy: rather, it suggests the need for fresh analysis of the kinds of global structures within which contemporary post-conflict states are inserted, and a reassessment of the correlations of the past in the light of this.

Furthermore, from a perspective of Marxist political economy, liberal institutions are seen as promoting particular relations of property and production, designed to both uphold and disguise unequal distributions of resources and power. As such, institutionalization is reconceptualized, less as a process of taming the state of nature in order to provide equal opportunity for all, as Paris asserts, and more as a process of stabilizing elites and limiting possibilities for contestation of their power. As such, a political economy critique questions not only the power of implanted institutions in post-conflict settings but also the normative import of the kind of institutions generally promoted by interveners.

Second, political economy emphasizes the interconnection in the contemporary world between the most war-ravaged country and the modern global economy, and this militates against awarding too much explanatory power to the notion of war-torn states as prone to cultural stasis and mired in pre-modernity. Cultural norms are regarded from a political economy perspective as changing in response to the operations of power. Social traditions are seen as offering a repertoire of images and practices to which power-holders may make ideological appeals; but as relations of power within society change as a result of economic transformation, those social traditions that are not useful to political coalitions will be submerged, while those that remain useful for mobilizing support will be continually reasserted and reinvented (Hobsbawm and Ranger 1992). While appeals to culture and authenticity are frequently an important aspect of post-conflict political rhetoric, this reflects creative and selective use of existing or remembered repertoires of contention by interested coalitions, rather than an inability to depart from traditional practices by unconscious pre-political propagators of groupthink (see Scott 1985).

Third, while the Foucauldian critique offers profound insights into strategies of power inherent in the operations of the international aid agency, it has less to say about the significant degree of resistance to those strategies that appears in the empirical record on the ground. Foucauldian critiques work best in contexts where the rationalizing and disciplinary functions of aid modalities and institutions have been successful in penetrating organs of state. Yet the history of post-conflict reconstruction from Cambodia to Afghanistan has been a history, predominantly, of failure. While the power and influence of international interveners in post-conflict states is undoubtedly a force to be reckoned with, it is by no means irresistible, as the tendency on the part of liberal theorists to advocate ever more extensive and longer-term intervention in order to achieve 'success' suggests. Arguably the inadequate theorization of the record of contention and effective resistance to liberal policies has prompted the retreat into a rather superficial culturalism notable among critics of the liberal peace.

Political economy approaches have been influential in the past fifteen years in understanding the causes and dynamics of civil wars, but have been far less prominent in examining trajectories of post-conflict development. The remainder of this chapter examines post-conflict reconstruction and state-building in Cambodia and East Timor from a political economy perspective, with the aim of rearticulating the relationship between institutions, culture, class and resistance in a manner which better explains the successes and the failures of international policy in these countries. In so doing, a model of post-conflict institution-building is put forward which denies the adequacy of a generic suite of international peace-building policies due to the importance of context-specific concatenations of local, transnational and international actors. Moreover, this model portrays the relationships between these actors as shifting, contested and infused with power relations which determine policy outcomes. This contestation is not the consequence of defence of the national against a rapacious international sphere, although political rhetoric frequently characterizes it as such, but a consequence of the ways in which ideologies of national identity and cultural tradition are mobilized in support of political and economic strategies on the part of different social groups. Because of this, each post-conflict situation is markedly different from the next.

Having said this, common features are discernible, particularly within the operations of the international aid industry, within which inter-organizational networking, policy transfer and cross-country transplantation of projects and programmes is not only generally practised but encouraged and rewarded by key organizations. Thus while contexts differ markedly, policies may be quite similar, offering bases for comparison and for eliciting generalities. The conclusion of this chapter will be that in Cambodia and East Timor, although the context differed sharply in many respects, similar international policies produced similar political problems, although these elicited quite different political responses.

Building institutions in Cambodia and East Timor

There were important differences of scope and ambition in the nature of the UN operations that oversaw the initial impetus towards a new institutional order in Cambodia and East Timor, in 1992–3 and 2000–2 respectively. However, the longer-term nature of engagement in post-conflict reconstruction by Western and multilateral donors in these two countries has been rather similar. In each case, the concern has been to promote a threefold conception of good governance. This has comprised: security, in the form of monopoly of violence by the state and the institution of a reasonably stable system of government; development, in the form of repair and extension of infrastructure, the institution of a private property regime, and the widening availability of opportunities for investment, trade, and access to credit; and social investment, in the form of provision of public services particularly in health and education. These three priorities, of state-building, development of markets and provision of services, reflect the influence of neo-liberal approaches. There has been a relative neglect of the more emancipatory model of positive peace as combining social justice and reconciliation, as favoured by radical peace theorists such as Galtung and Lederach. Aside from some limited experimental forays into the field of social capital on the part of development agencies in the late 1990s, the promotion of peaceful social relationships has been largely delegated to a mixture of non-governmental organizations, religious and cultural groups, and mental health professionals.

Although different aid agencies are associated with different strategies and priorities, a powerful consensus that the ultimate aim of post-conflict reconstruction is to provide a suitable environment for free market, private sector-led growth has entailed that approaches to security and government and social investment have been heavily market-oriented. A declining interest on the part of international donors and diplomats in democracy and civil rights has been notable, particularly in the Cambodian context, where concerns for stability drove a significant shift away from support for the democratic aspirations of the 1991 Paris Peace Agreements over the course of the 1990s. In particular, there has been little sympathy on the part of international aid agencies and donors for collective action in support of social justice in Cambodia. The staggering inequality of resource distribution which has emerged in Cambodia over the past twenty years has been regarded as an issue of contracts and property rights which needs to be tackled through the establishment of institutions and regulations to govern entrepreneurship, rather than an issue emerging from drastic inequalities in the distribution of power among social classes. In East Timor, also, the United Nations Transitional Authority was widely criticized for its heavily top-down orientation, and its failure to institute either effective forms of local politics or inclusive mechanisms for consultation, setting an anti-democratic example which was continued by the first elected Timorese government from 2002 to 2007. The sufferings of the population in the aftermath of the violence of 1999 and subsequent economic slump were subordinated, in international policy-making, to the imperative of establishing transparent government procedures for reducing fiduciary risk to donors, resulting in a state that had difficulty spending its budget in the midst of appalling economic hardship.

For political elites in post-conflict countries, the challenge of post-conflict politics focused on erecting a new political order that maintains the power and privilege of a ruling and/or capitalist class, while facilitating the flow of aid and eliciting a degree of support from the struggling population. The neo-liberal cast of international policy-making partly assists them in this, since it has a demobilizing effect on coalitions of the poor, muting their demands and channelling their participation into atomizing processes such as secret ballots and heavily policed development committees. However, the same effect also cripples politics by imposing limits on either populist or redistributive strategies for legitimation of the new regime.

The argument in this chapter is as follows: in post-conflict settings, international policy has focused on demobilizing not only armed groups, but many kinds of collective action in the interests of stability and a conception of peace as public order. There has been a suspicion of indigenous leaders, regarded as tainted by their association with the war effort, and consequently an attempt to bypass or dismantle local political coalitions, in favour of more individualistic forms of participation. This has been accompanied by a heavy emphasis on market-oriented forms of economic participation, such as regimes of property rights and micro-credit, designed to stimulate household entrepreneurship.

The liberal political institutions that oversee this new order are consequently disabled from the outset. They do not operate as effective arbiters of political contention, because they are disconnected, often quite deliberately, from existing coalitions pursuing particular types of political action. The mode of operation of these institutions, furthermore, is frequently heavily constrained by international prescriptions, training, funding conditions and oversight: this can limit the means available to them of establishing meaningful connections with groups of the poor.

To the disappointment of institutionalists, there is little evidence from Cambodia and East Timor so far that, over time, either elites or the poor become 'habituated' to new forms of political action in which these institutions become 'the only game in town'. The combination of demobilization of political coalitions of the poor, and promotion of individualistic, entrepreneurial action in the economic sphere, militates against the evolution of such institutions into effective organizers of political contestation. Rather, there tends to be a retreat into existing, often informal, modes of political action via existing state or non-state structures that circumvent liberal institutions. Such modes of action include, in the Cambodian and Timorese contexts, appeal to patrons, offering of bribes, and reinvention of traditional practices, for example for dispute resolution. Often, international aid donors have ended up endorsing such practices, in the light of the evident failure of formal institutions.

This has the effect of further atomizing the poor, trapping them in local and personalist political institutions, promoted as 'customary' but backed by international aid hierarchies. This changes the relations of interdependence between leaders and followers within villages, while simultaneously undermining the promise of democratic representation via such institutions as opposition parties, trade unions and elected parliaments. Other types of institution – particularly institutions that have pre-existing support bases that can be maintained outside the purview of international interveners – may find opportunities to gain strength from the dysfunctionality of liberal representative structures: beneficiaries in the context of Cambodia and East Timor have been the Cambodian People's Party (CPP) and the Catholic Church, respectively. Both of these represent broad-based but hierarchical institutions; both propagate rigid codes of behaviour incorporating powerful norms of loyalty, respect and quiescence in the face of superiors; and both link their own standing and internal organization to heavily interested portrayals of custom, culture and national identity. These institutions have supplied (different) answers to the problem of the failures of neo-liberal institutionalism, and have provided crucial support to the post-war order in their respective countries, in a manner which has made each of them central to political life. However, neither has offered avenues of emancipation to the poor. This chapter proceeds by providing examples of failures of liberal institutionalism in Cambodia and East Timor, and a brief analysis of the ways in which these failures contributed to the expansion in power and influence of the CPP and the Catholic Church respectively.

Failed liberal institutions in Cambodia: the natural resource regime

The natural resource regime in Cambodia offers a key example of the way in which market-oriented policies worked to weaken coalitions of the poor and to strengthen the power of the elite in a manner which ultimately undermined liberal institutions set up to regulate the sector, while strengthening non-liberal institutions that were politically successful but repressive vis-à-vis the poor. This analysis covers two key areas of natural resource management: forestry and land. In both sectors, post-conflict reconstruction entailed the erection of a regime for awarding use and property rights as a means to stimulate and regulate economic production. However, these regimes did not result in a level playing field for entrepreneurial activity by Cambodians: rather, they resulted in the concentration of power and resources in the hands of a violent and powerful political elite, which has consistently used land and forestry resources as a means to reward supporters and to generate political slush funds. Arguably, this was because the individualizing thrust of the regime established in collaboration between the Cambodian government and donors such as the World Bank worked to undermine the kind of collective action by the poor that would have been necessary to win a more equitable distribution of resources.

Cambodia emerged from the Cold War with large areas of almost pristine tropical forest. The forest contained valuable hardwoods much in demand from the global garden furniture industry and also provided resources for forestry communities. Although the figures for the amount of forest cover that has been lost in Cambodia over the past twenty years are politically contentious and based upon estimates rather than hard data, there is widespread agreement that forest cover has both declined markedly and been degraded rapidly (FAO 2002).

The history of Cambodia's post-war use of its forest resources can be divided into two: in the period of the 1990s, forestry comprised the largely unregulated and competitive stripping of forests by different sections of the elite as a means to fund military and political campaigns. As Philippe Lebillon has argued, stripping of forest assets in the 1990s was an important aspect of the strategy for encouraging the defection of insurgent commanders in the mid-1990s, following the United Nations peacekeeping force's failure to sustain the ceasefire in 1993. Award of rights to cut and export logs was contested throughout this time: from 1994, the government introduced a concession system of licences and permits for logging but this was extensively violated. International donors pressured the government to maintain formal and regulated control of a potentially valuable industry in the face of repeated scandals in which various logging interests were discovered to have paid large bribes to politicians in return for permission to break moratoriums and export large quantities of wood. However, the significance of discretionary control over logging permits for the stabilization of the political elite, the growth of political parties, and the exertion of civilian control over the military during this period entailed that little progress was made in regulating the industry until after the 1998 elections, when the political situation in Cambodia became more settled.

From 1999 a new regulatory regime was erected, with significant input from international donors. Powers to award concessions were centralized, cutting provincial-level government out of the process. New rules required concessionaires to submit Sustainable Forest Management Plans and Environmental and Social Impact Analyses to the Department of Forestry and Wildlife. A Forest Crimes Monitoring Unit was established to monitor compliance, and the entire system was to be overseen by an independent monitor appointed by the government. The international NGO, Global Witness, which had a long record of research and activism on the forestry sector in Cambodia, was appointed to the independent monitor's position.

However, this new institutional regime ultimately proved unsuccessful in either promoting the environmental sustainability of logging practices, or in redistributing benefits to the poor. The centralization of powers to award concessions and moves to cancel concessions already awarded to concessionaires deemed to be logging irresponsibly placed a great deal of power into the hands of the prime minister, who used this power to concentrate the logging industry into the hands of his own family members and most loyal supporters. The Department of Forestry and Wildlife was not galvanized as a result of its increased powers to tackle forest crimes. The Department was widely regarded as a conduit by which bribes and kickbacks were directed in Cambodian People's Party coffers, and its staff members in its twenty-three provincial offices tended to leave forestry planning to the concessionaires. Similarly, police and military in forestry areas tended to moonlight as security guards for logging companies, entailing a significant compromise in their ability or willingness to arrest perpetrators of forest crimes. The independent monitor, Global Witness, did make strenuous efforts to promote better oversight of the sector, releasing a series of critical reports detailing the failures of the new institutions. At the same time, a network of forestry activists began to emerge, with assistance from non-governmental organizations based in Phnom Penh, which began to mobilize in protests and advocacy around the new institutional regime, particularly in relation to forest crimes and the overstepping, by concessionaires, of the boundaries of their contracts. As such, institutionalization of a regulatory regime for logging appeared to be developing connections to collective action on the part of the poor, in a contestation over distributions of resources which could potentially confront some of Cambodia's most powerful families with some of its poorest.

This was short-lived, however. In December 2002, a group mobilized by the Forestry Network gathered outside the Department of Forestry and Wildlife in Phnom Penh, calling for an opportunity to feed into Environmental and Social Impact Analyses which were at the time in the process of being submitted to the Department by logging concessionaires. The protest was peaceful, but attracted the wrath of the police, who charged the crowd with electric batons. In the confusion, there were rumours that a protestor had been killed. The next month, Global Witness was sacked as the independent forest monitor, and a new monitor was appointed in the shape of a Swiss firm that had no activist history or aspirations. Members of Global Witness were threatened and attacked, and international Global Witness activists were denied visas to enter the country. At the same time, the Cambodian government engaged in a wider clampdown on protest activity in Phnom Penh, directed particularly at labour unions, but also encompassing any attempts to protest on environmental issues. The brief window of opportunity for the poor to directly challenge the government over the spoils of logging revenues closed. Subsequently, although a new Forestry Law was passed in 2002, the forest regulatory regime was able to be overridden at low political cost by powerful industry actors. Forestry has continued to operate as a source of fast cash for the ruling party, although this may soon come to an end as the forests disappear for good (see Global Witness 2007; Cock 2007; also Hughes and Conway 2003; Hughes 2007).

A similar story can be told with respect to distribution of land. In 1989, land reform distributed property rights to land to the tillers, in a popular move designed to boost the credibility of a teetering regime following the Vietnamese army's withdrawal and the decline in Soviet bloc aid. A Department of Land Titling was created to supply deeds of ownership to Cambodian farmers, and property rights were further clarified by the subsequent passage in 1992 of a Land Law. Progress on land titling was, however, slow: most farmers did not apply for official title, relying for their security of tenure on unofficial recognition of their land ownership by local authorities.

Following the 1993 elections, and particularly towards the end of the 1990s, as stability was better assured, population growth placed more pressure on existing distributions, and land values began to rise, land became a hotly contested issue in Cambodia. As in the forestry sector, a political elite concerned to stabilize its position allowed well-connected individuals, in the parties and in the military, to grab land with impunity. Lack of records, unresolved disputes lingering on from the pre-collectivization era, and a willingness to respond to bribery on the part of the courts and the Cadastral Commission permitted wealthy and powerful individuals to prevail over the poor. Such individuals also benefited from a wave of distress sales, as poor farmers, lacking irrigation, access to healthcare and with poor links to profitable markets, suffered the effects of drought and sickness. Sales of land to foot the bill for healthcare costs were particularly widespread. Land security was also used by local authorities to ensure voter support for the Cambodian People's Party during election campaign periods in 1998, 2002 and 2003: stories were frequently reported of opposition party supporters being threatened with dispossession if they failed to support the CPP. These various factors resulted in a sharp increase in inequality of land-holdings over the course of the 1990s, in contrast to a relatively equitable distribution in 1989.

In 2001, a Land Law was passed, intended to better regulate the sector and provide more accessible mechanisms for resolution of lingering land disputes. This was followed in 2002 by a Land Management and Administration Project (LMAP), supported by a variety of donors under the leadership of the World Bank, and intended to translate the provisions of the law into a more efficient regulatory regime for property rights. LMAP was initially planned to run for five years, but was subsequently extended until 2009. During this time, LMAP established new local cadastral commissions and oversaw the issue of more than a million land titles.

The project was cancelled in 2009, however, following criticisms from activist NGOs supporting land rights in Cambodia, and following three years of an unprecedented wave of violent evictions of poor people from their homes, particularly in the north-western provinces close to the Thai border and in the capital of Phnom Penh. Criticism of the project pointed to the fact that the project was designed to avoid areas that were envisaged by the government as 'development zones' or in which the status of the land was unclear – precisely the areas, in fact, where land tenure was most insecure. In these areas, LMAP's avoidance of getting involved opened the way to rapid and violent dispossession of the poor.

Like the Forest Crimes regime, the LMAP project focused on a deep fault line of contention over post-conflict distribution of resources in Cambodia. Like the forestry regime, the LMAP project drew back from areas where this political contention broke out into collective action, as poor communities mobilized to try to defend their houses from police bulldozers. The LMAP project pointed to the large number of relatively uncontroversial titles awarded as evidence of success, thereby prioritizing the establishment of as wide as possible a regime of property ownership over support for empowerment of coalitions of the poor in concrete battles over distributions of resources. As such, the project had little effect on the most valuable pieces of land in the most highly contested areas: most of the land titles issued were for relatively low-value rural farmland in areas where customary claims by individual families were already quite strong and reasonably well respected in any case. The project did provide guarantees that the subsistence-farming poor in many areas would be able to continue subsistence farming; however, by avoiding the more rapidly developing and highly contested parts of the country, the project allowed economic growth, in the form of the rise of agro-industry and private urban property developments, to operate resolutely in the interests of the rich.

In both of these cases, international policy was justified in terms of promoting economic growth through the strengthening of institutions that could provide equal protection of property rights, including the property rights of the poor. However, in both cases this backfired. In part this was certainly because of the political manoeuvring of the elite, which sought to privilege the interests of key regime supporters in the military, initially, and subsequently within the community of Cambodian tycoons that donated to party campaign funds, and consequently worked to undermine efforts to ensure the equal application of the law to rich and poor alike.

Estimates of the Gini coefficient for inequality in Cambodia illustrate the relationship between political manoeuvring and the success of the property rights regime, reflecting three phases in Cambodia's political development over the post-conflict period. Rapid increase in inequality, measured as an increase in the Gini coefficient from 0.35 to 0.39 between 1993 and 1997, reflected the use of Cambodia's assets by political elites to cement the loyalty of the military, of business and of defecting insurgents. This was followed by a period from 1998 to 2004 in which inequality stayed more or less constant and poverty declined, following the end of the war, and a period of institutionalization during which the Cambodian People's Party retook power and sought to build its legitimacy both internationally and at home. The Forestry and Land Laws were passed during this period and the forest crimes and land titling regimes established. From 2004 to 2007, inequality surged again to an estimated Gini coefficient of 0.43 (World Bank 2007; Guimbert 2009) as the economic boom brought a new strategy of dispossession of the poor in urban areas and in areas of agro-industrial land concessions, even while some of the profits were redistributed in the form of development spending in villages in the rural heartland.

The predatory use made of the property rights regime to advance the interests of the rich at the expense of the poor should not exculpate these regimes themselves. In part, the liberal vision of equality of opportunity for an entrepreneurial poor failed because the individualistic form of the regimes erected undermined the capacity for the poor to mobilize in their own defence: a rigidly administrative approach and a failure to appreciate the necessity for collection action in support of the poor entailed that the elite could get away with a predatory approach. In fact, it is arguably the case that over the past decade in particular, the willingness of the government to erect these kinds of weak regulatory regimes has encouraged a tendency on the part of Western donors to ignore the rapid decline in the tolerance of political rights to collective action in Cambodia. In donor policies, institutions are promoted as a substitute for rights to collective action; yet without the possibility for collective action on the part of the poor, institutions are unlikely to ever achieve any kind of authority over the actions of the political elite. The result has been that inequality has increased dramatically, not only during the period of unregulated asset-stripping that characterized natural resource management in the 1990s, but also during the period of apparent institutionalization in the 2000s. This massive accumulation of resources in the hands of a tiny elite represents arguably the most striking characteristic of Cambodia's post-war political and economic trajectory.

Failed liberal institutions in East Timor: local government

A further example of failed liberal institution-building is to be found in efforts to construct local government in East Timor. The top-down orientation of UNTAET and the failure of the Community Empowerment Programme have already been described. Following UNTAET's handover of power to the elected FRETILIN government in May 2002, severe problems of legitimation emerged from the difficulties the government faced in promoting its own legitimacy in Timor's villages, in the light of the approach to state-building urged upon it by its international donors.

Top-down strategies for state-building saw intense focus on the establishment of national ministries and a national parliament, but far less attention to the empowerment of local levels of government. Following the 1999 crisis, most villages had reorganized themselves rather quickly, informally electing or appointing new leaders at the *aldeia* (hamlet) and *suco* (village) level, many of whom had previously been members of local organizing committees of the clandestine resistance movement. These leaders were recognized by international donors and national government to the extent of becoming interlocutors for various humanitarian assistance and development projects; however, they were not paid a salary or given a budget to spend on their activities. At the sub-district and district levels, administrators were appointed from the centre and given salaries, offices and a staff to work with; however, they too had no discretionary budgets to spend on development projects. Although at district and *suco* level, leaders formulated plans and lists of needs in terms of development and rehabilitation, the funding for these was dependent upon bidding for projects from international NGOs or from central funding schemes like the Community Empowerment Programme and its successor, the UNDP-organized RESPECT programme. District administrators were expected to keep tabs on the various organizations running development projects in their districts, but their means for monitoring progress were in fact very limited. At the same time, the competitive nature of funding entailed that for each funded project there were many development plans that remained on the drawing board, unrealized. During fieldwork conducted in 2005 in the districts of Liquica and Manatuto, village leaders expressed their disillusionment with a situation in which they were expected to spend their own time and resources mobilizing villagers to participate in development planning, but were given no guarantee of success. Discontent with this situation emerged from three sources. First, villagers and village leaders interviewed compared the situation unfavourably with the relative plethora of funding for development schemes and public works under the later years of Indonesian rule. In the later years of the Suharto era, under the auspices of various 'hearts and minds' programmes, a model of development was adopted that focused heavily on public works and infrastructure development providing paid opportunities for labour for villagers, provision of development goods such as livestock, and subsidized purchasing of Timor's main crops of rice and coffee. Following the departure of the Indonesians, infrastructure had been destroyed, the rice and coffee industries collapsed, opportunities for labour dried up, and development goods were replaced by stringent emergency rations.

A second source of discontent was the lack of attention paid by the government to instituting mechanisms for consultation or communication between villages and central government. The winner of the 2001 elections, FRETILIN, was a party that enjoyed a high profile as the party of resistance, both within East Timor and internationally. However, in organizational terms it barely existed beyond the Central Committee. While tens of thousands of Timorese identified themselves as FRETILIN supporters, the party had no functioning structures at local level; a number of self-organized FRETILIN groups existed in different places and among different constituencies, but these represented a problem in themselves since their ideas and aspirations frequently conflicted with those of the Central Committee, and many groups resolutely resisted their own subordination to central party control. In terms of providing a means by which the government could mobilize coalitions of supporters behind a national policy platform for reconstruction, the party worked very poorly indeed.

This problem was exacerbated by what has often been termed the 'unrealistic expectations' of the Timorese people. While there is no data concerning what, in fact, the Timorese people did expect from their new government in terms of development outcomes, fieldwork conducted towards the end of FRETILIN's first term in 2005 indicated that the rhetoric of total mobilization employed by the resistance persisted into the post-independence era. This rhetoric had focused heavily on ideals of active participation and equality: ideals which were interpreted by the new government as entailing a spirit of self-help and self-reliance among villages in the independence period, but which were interpreted by villagers, conversely, as entailing an equal share of the millions of dollars in reconstruction aid which were apparently flowing into the country but not reaching the village level.

The crux of the problem was the inability of the model of development initiated to facilitate the spending of much needed development assistance. During the early post-independence period, East Timor was heavily aid-dependent and suffering from a catastrophic economic collapse in its key industries. Both unemployment and poverty climbed to extremely high levels. However, government institutions were unable to respond, to the extent that the government consistently failed to spend its own budget, even in this climate of overwhelming need.

Mechanisms for budget execution were established within the East Timorese government by UNTAET; following independence, the World Bank took a lead role, via its Transitional Support Programme, in assisting the government to manage, monitor and report back to donors on the expenditure of funds. The Transitional Support Programme was based in the Ministry of Finance and Planning, resulting in heavy centralization of oversight of government spending. Although not a programme that incorporated conditionalities per se, the Transitional Support Programme was funded on a yearly basis by a variety of donors, and it was understood that failures to ensure sufficient transparency in budget execution could result in donors withdrawing from the scheme.

As it happened, the consensus among various reviews of this programme was that transparency of budget execution was very high, and fiduciary risk to donors, consequently, very low, an outcome that initially prompted donors to rate the Transitional Support Programme a success (ITAD 2008). However, the trade-off for this, as a number of reviews also noted in the 2002–6 period, was that high levels of control stifled the ability to delegate resources and spend money in a timely fashion: on average over the period between 2003/4 and 2005/6 the Timorese government managed to spend only 60–70 per cent of its yearly budget (ITAD 2008: 24). A review by the Japanese International Cooperation Agency in 2004, for example, stated:

> The GOTL has instituted a sound system of financial controls to manage funds, where decision making is centralized and fiduciary risks are minimal. This provides a measure of comfort to donors. But donors are also interested in seeing that funds are steadily expended. When a financial system is highly centralized the result is poor budget execution which has been the case in Timor-Leste.
>
> (Beasley et al. 2005: 30)

An independent evaluation review by the World Bank itself following the 2006 violence downgraded the assessment of the success of the Transitional Support Programme, commenting:

Timor-Leste performs well on fiduciary accountability, but this comes at a high cost to service delivery … Budget execution is very slow … due to heavy centralization of expenditure management, tight expenditure and procurement controls, weak capacity in ministries, and poor communication between the MPF (Ministry of Planning and Finance) and line ministries.

(World Bank 2006: 9–10)

There was little progress made in this matter between 2002 and 2006, reflecting a concern within the government of East Timor that Timor's small size and relative lack of importance in the eyes of many major donor countries meant that continued aid flows were dependent upon good performance and keeping corruption at bay. These concerns were also a significant issue in the context of Timor's troubled negotiations with Australia over ownership of large oil resources in the Timor Sea. Most commentators agreed that the oil clearly belonged to Timor, and Australia had gained control over it largely through its nefarious dealings with Jakarta during the years of the Indonesian occupation. However, although not figuring in formal negotiations, the idea of the difficulty of managing oil resources and the dangers of 'natural resource curse' hung over the proceedings. An implicit backdrop to the oil negotiations was the view that Australia could not responsibly give Timor its oil back until it had proved it had the institutions to manage such a potentially dangerous developmental resource (Hughes 2005a).

At the same time, donors enthusiastically lobbied the Timorese government to commercialize the status of various other public goods, particularly electricity and public housing. These were particularly urban concerns: in rural areas, there was more concern with the re-establishment of free health and education services, and in these areas the government did make good progress in re-establishing infrastructure and boosting access, in part by abolishing fees. However, urban areas were the areas in which FRETILIN lost support heavily during its first term, and where unrest eventually broke out in 2006, and these areas suffered most from policies designed to promote the commercial viability of utilities as a move towards privatization.

With respect to electricity, infrastructure was badly damaged during the 1999 violence, and almost all senior management and technical staff were Indonesian and left after the ballot. The electricity supply had been state-owned, heavily subsidized and not very efficient. Only 20 per cent of households were estimated to be connected to the National Grid. The challenges following 1999 were to repair and rehabilitate infrastructure; make electricity supply more cost-effective and self-financing; and initiate a major rural electrification campaign to support human, rural and private sector development. A particular need was building the technical and management capacities of staff.

UNTAET began this task, creating a state-owned company, Electricidade de Timor Leste (EdTL). Under UNTAET, electricity was provided free to the population, but in 2001 laws were passed determining pricing and billing practices, as a step towards commercialization of EdTL. A Basic Law for the National Power System was passed in May 2003, which awarded management autonomy to EdTL, limiting the government's role to that of a regulatory authority. The aim was to phase out subsidies to EdTL, rendering power supply on the existing grid self-financing, as a prelude to privatization through a long-term concession contract in the future. The Power Sector Action Plan envisaged an international public tender for a twenty-year Build Operate Transfer contract on all EdTL's operations – production, distribution and commercialization. In 2004, interim management of EdTL was contracted out to a private management company from Macau, which was supposed to improve EdTL's technical and financial performance.

A significant aspect of this commercialization drive was the installation of prepaid meters into customers' homes in Dili and the surrounding areas, in order to improve revenue collection.

This was a tumultuous process, met with considerable resistance by customers, and in one case Power Authority personnel were attacked. The government launched a publicity campaign to try to promote customer compliance with the new measures, including enlisting the help of its neglected local authority chiefs. The use of local authority chiefs to pressure customers into accepting prepaid meters allowed the acceleration of the programme, according to a World Bank report; however, it placed further pressure on village chiefs already feeling that their legitimacy and authority was in question thanks to the lack of attention paid to awarding them resources and facilities (World Bank n.d.).

Similarly, families who moved into housing that had been abandoned by departing Indonesian officials, following the violence and destruction of 1999, found themselves being charged increasing rates of rent by the government after independence, regardless of their financial circumstances and ability to pay. This drive by the government to raise money from its impoverished population through these kinds of service fees represented a regressive revenue-raising regime, in a climate where many families had been suddenly plunged into severe poverty. It had a chilling effect on the legitimacy of the state-building drive over which the government was presiding (Hughes 2005b).

While this agenda was heavily donor-driven, the FRETILIN leadership that emerged after 1999 had much to gain from it. Amongst the top leaders, returnees from exile in Portugal, Lusophone Africa and Australia were heavily represented, and these individuals had the most slender links with the population at home, having been away for decades. The imperative of demobilizing the population through building up the centre at the expense of the villages appeared to the leadership group as viable means of shoring up their own authority over the party and the country, given the difficulties of imposing their own authority on a population that regarded themselves, and not the FRETILIN leaders, as having won the war. The FRE-TILIN government's approach to nation-building might well be described as 'anti-populist' in that it forged an alliance with donors, and focused on meeting donor demands for transparency, rigour and commercial viability, at the expense of building mechanisms for communicating with supporters in the villages. As a result, it alienated swathes of the population who just a few years before had enthusiastically backed the resistance of which FRETILIN was a part. Over the first four years of independence, beyond the walls of government offices, support for the government fell away dramatically, even as donors praised the government's state-building process. Arguably, this climate of disaffection produced the fertile conditions for the rioting and instability of the period from 2006 to 2007.

Successful institutionalization: the Cambodian People's Party and the Catholic Church

In both Cambodia and East Timor, international policy for promoting liberal institutions and markets dovetailed with elite strategies for securing post-war patterns of power and privilege to produce a situation in which the poor faced increasing hardship and limited opportunities for political representation. The outcome, however, has been quite different in the two countries. In East Timor, the result of the failures of the FRETILIN government to remain in tune with popular aspiration led to the resignation of Prime Minister Alkatiri amid rioting and violence in Dili; in Cambodia, by contrast, stability has increased and the CPP government, led by Prime Minister Hun Sen, has become increasingly popular.

The answer to this apparent paradox lies in the way that the Cambodian People's Party forged and promoted its own coalitions of political support, in a manner which ultimately allowed the party to represent itself as the party of the poor, despite the mass dispossession over which it presided for twenty years. The party's ability to achieve this was through circumvention of efforts at liberal institutionalization, facilitated by a willingness to tolerate, even encourage, the institutionalization of mass corruption at all levels of the state apparatus.

Over the period of the 1990s, the Cambodian People's Party fought off its rivals, the royalist movement and the insurgent Khmer Rouge, through a mixture of intimidation, co-optation and outbidding. This was achieved by taking control of the military and using the massive profits generated by, for example, logging and the skimming of aid budgets to buy off rivals and opponents. By the end of the 1990s, few serious elite opponents to the CPP remained, and the party shifted its approach to the eliciting of public support through strategies of mass patronage, paid for in part by the same profits and in part by new sources of revenue, in particular large donations given by increasingly wealthy Cambodian tycoons, eager to curry favour with the new government. A new party–business alliance developed over the boom years of 2002 to 2007, in which well-connected businessmen could secure preferential treatment by state officials in return for making party donations. By donating US $100,000 to a CPP-sponsored development project, a businessman could earn himself the legal award of the title of *Okhna* – an honorific which signalled to any state official with whom the *Okhna* might subsequently deal that this was a person who should be treated with deference and respect owing to his political connections. *Okhnas* can be found dominating activity in all areas of economic life in contemporary Cambodia, running sugar plantations on economic land concessions; awarded control of special economic zones; and in possession of monopoly licences for the import of such profitable goods as petrol, pharmaceuticals and Western brands of liquor. *Okhnas* dominate the Cambodian Chamber of Commerce and the Private Sector Forum, both organizations which have the ear of the prime minister and advise him on a wide range of policies from investment to trade to agriculture.

Meanwhile the money donated by *Okhnas* pays for party campaigning across the country, to the extent that party-donated development funds to local government outstrip state development budgets by two or three to one (Craig and Kimchoeun 2011). Party ceremonies in which politicians attend the opening of new schools, temples, roads and irrigation schemes are a regular feature of rural life and of the nightly television and radio news. These kinds of populist campaigns have dramatically increased the popularity of the Cambodian People's Party and the prime minister across the heavily populated heartland of the central rice plains. They are less effective in the border and highland areas where *Okhna* investment schemes in plantation agriculture disrupt village livelihoods; and in Phnom Penh where property development companies have driven a mass eviction campaign over the past five years.

The phenomenon of the rise and rise of the Cambodian People's Party has been explained in the main with reference to a presumed authoritarian tendency in Khmer culture. Indeed, the party itself, in its ostentatious patrimonialism, its vast temple-building programme, and its exaggerated deployment of hierarchical honorifics and rituals associated with a monarchical past, has promoted this explanation. However, the party's success can equally be explained as the outcome of a fortuitous symbiosis between Cambodian elite interests and the orientations of liberal intervention, which has been effective in demobilizing the poor while failing utterly to constrain the predatory instincts noted in early stages of capitalist development in many countries across the world. The successful creation of markets for land, labour and natural resources has been accompanied by the design of policies and institutions which focus on individual rights rather than collective action, in a manner that cripples the possibility of the emergence of a counter-movement, and allows any sign of protest or agitation to be swiftly crushed. Liberal donors have collaborated in this process, in the name of economic growth and political stability.

In the case of East Timor, it is not yet clear whether a similar phenomenon will emerge. However, it is noteworthy that as the crisis of 2006 was building, and in its aftermath, the Catholic Church emerged as a key political player. The Church organized mass demonstrations against the FRETILIN government in 2005 over the issue of religious education. The demonstrations lasted nineteen days and gathered thousands of protestors from across the country in an entirely peaceful show of support for the Church outside the Timorese parliament in Dili. This impressive show of mobilization not only dealt a severe blow to the legitimacy of the government, but illustrated the power of the Church to bring together coalitions of support in a manner which future governments would have to reckon with. It is noteworthy that in the 2007 elections, Jose Ramos-Horta ran, successfully, for the presidency with no party organization behind him, but with the backing of the Church.

While the Church does not appear likely to step overtly into Timorese politics, its emergence as a powerful actor in defence of its own interests is significant. Democratic politics as promoted by international donors and the Timorese political elite has not produced new representative organs that can project the voice of the poor into national political debate. The Church thus appears in sharp relief as one of the few organizations in the country that can organize collective action, and finds itself in a powerful position as a result. While the Church may be viewed, optimistically, as an organ of civil society and therefore as an inhibitor of authoritarian tendencies in government, its status as a representative institution of the poor is equivocal. It is widely regarded as a symbol of Timorese identity and as a product of the resistance; yet its ideology is highly conservative and as such it is hard to see the Church as a vehicle for an emancipatory politics.

Conclusion

In both Cambodia and Timor, the institutions that have thrived and strengthened in a post-reconstruction era were institutions that had, or were able to acquire, independent and discretionary sources of finance, a relatively tightly organized network of officers, an organizational presence across the country, and strong claim to authority based upon ideological appeals to culture and identity. These institutions have in neither case turned out to be particularly liberal in their policy objectives, but they have shown the significance of the ability to mobilize grassroots populations through a mixture of rhetoric and patronage. Arguably, the growth in strength and stature of these organizations in a post-conflict period has occurred because of the weakness of liberal institutions implanted by post-conflict interveners.

The weakness of liberal institutions, in turn, emerges from the internal contradiction in the liberal peace-building project. The literature has supplied a number of different interpretations of this contradiction: the contradiction between using authoritarian means to promote liberal ends; the contradiction between implanting Western institutions on non-Western cultures; and the contradiction between practices of empire in a rhetoric of liberation. There has been relatively little discussion, however, of the fact that liberal institutions in a post-conflict setting, although they espouse to some extent the rhetoric of a level playing field for entrepreneurial self-betterment on the part of the population, are in fact intended, as in all liberal countries, to provide the basis for the emergence of market competition in which the fittest will outperform the weakest, leading to the emergence of wider inequalities in distributions of resources. The emergence of such inequalities happens rapidly and obviously, and may often occur in direct contradiction to political ideals of fraternity and equality that tend to be favoured by parties emerging from conflict.

The cases discussed above suggest that a real problem for liberal interveners is the tension between the atomizing individualism inherent in the forms of liberal organization promoted in post-conflict societies, and the requirement of collective action at the grassroots to promote the interests of the poor during the inevitable post-conflict struggle over distributions of resources. Liberal institutions, although frequently advanced as vehicles through which the poor can acquire voice and impose accountability on governments, in fact work poorly in promoting the interests of the poor, and channel the political energies of the poor into forums where they are only indirectly represented, and in which they are disadvantaged by exclusionary discourses and rules of procedure. The demobilizing thrust of liberal interventionism, regarded as necessary to end the violence of warfare, in fact demobilizes the poor far more than it demobilizes their rulers, opening the way to alienation and impoverishment in a context of rising inequality resulting from global economic integration, or to the award of significant advantage to organizations that can adopt a populist stance. The latter is likely to promote greater stability, as in the case of Cambodia, but at the expense of ideals of democracy and liberal progress. The former, as in East Timor in 2006, is likely to promote escalating social and political tension.

References

Beasley, A., J. Malick, A. Melnyk and S. Mizuta (2005) *Program Assistance: The Democratic Republic of Timor-Leste, Country Case Study*, Tokyo: Japanese International Cooperation Agency; available at: www.mofa.go.jp/policy/oda/evaluation/2004/timor.pdf (accessed 20 July 2010).

Bellin, E. (2000) 'Contingent democrats: industrialists, labour and democratization in late developing countries', *World Politics* 52 (2): 175–205.

Bertram, E. (1995) 'Reinventing governments: the problems and perils of United Nations peacekeeping', *Journal of Conflict Resolution* 39 (3): 387–418.

Boutros-Ghali, B. (1995) 'An agenda for peace: preventive diplomacy, peacemaking and peace-keeping', report of the Secretary-General pursuant to the statement adopted by the Summit Meeting of the Security Council, 31 January 1992, UN Doc. No. A/47/277-S/24111, 17 June 1992, reprinted in Boutros Boutros-Ghali, *An Agenda for Peace 1995*, New York: United Nations.

Bush, George Sr (1990) 'Toward a new world order', speech to Joint Session of Congress, Washington DC, 11 September 1990; available at: www.uni-leipzig.de/ral/gchuman/documents/allgemein/Reader Sommerschule/US-President%20Bush%20on%20new%20world%20order%201990.pdf (accessed 20 July 2010).

Chandler, D. (2006) *Empire in Denial*, London: Pluto Press.

Chesterman, S. (2005) *You the People: The United Nations, Transitional Administration, and State-building*, Oxford: Oxford University Press.

Chopra, J. (2002) 'Building state failure in East Timor', *Development and Change* 33 (5): 979–1000.

Cock, A. (2007) 'The interaction between a ruling elite and an internationally promoted reform agenda: the case of forestry under the Second Kingdom of Cambodia, 1993–2003', unpublished thesis, La Trobe University.

Cox, R. (1995) 'Critical political economy', in B. Hettne (ed.) *International Political Economy: Understanding Global Disorder*, London: Zed Books.

Craig, D. and P. Kimchoeun (2011) 'Party financing of local investment', in C. Hughes and Kheang Un (eds) *Cambodia's Economic Transformation*, Copenhagen: NIAS Press.

Doyle, M. (1986) 'Liberalism and world politics', *American Political Science Review* 80 (4): 1151–69.

Duffield, M. (2001) *Global Governance and the New Wars: The Merging of Development and Security*, London: Zed Books.

Food and Agriculture Organization of the United Nations (FAO) (2002) 'National forest products statistics, Cambodia', in *An Overview of Forest Products Statistics in South and Southeast Asia*, Geneva: FAO; available at: www.fao.org/docrep/005/ac778e/AC778E09.htm (accessed 16 November 2010).

Francis, D.J. (2000) 'The tortuous path to peace: the Lome Accord and post-war peace building in Sierra Leone', *Security Dialogue* 31 (3): 357–73.

Fukuyama, F. (2004) *Statebuilding: Governance and World Order in the Twenty-First Century*, London: Profile Books.

Galtung, J. (1985) 'Twenty-five years of peace research', *Journal of Peace Research* 22 (2): 141–85.

Global Witness (2007) *Cambodia's Family Trees: Illegal Logging and the Stripping of Public Assets by Cambodia's Elite*, London: Global Witness.

Gould, J. (2005) *The New Conditionality: The Politics of Poverty Reduction Strategies*, London: Zed Books.

Guimbert, S. (2009) Presentation, World Bank Country Office Retreat, Siem Reap, 28 May.

Hamre, J.J. and G.R. Sullivan (2002) 'Toward post-conflict reconstruction', *Washington Quarterly* 25 (4): 85–96.

Harrison, G. (2004) *The World Bank and Africa: The Construction of Governance States*, Abingdon: Routledge.

Hobsbawm, E. and T. Ranger (eds) (1992) *The Invention of Tradition*, Cambridge: Cambridge University Press.

Hohe, T.(2002) 'The clash of paradigms: international administration and local political legitimacy in East Timor', *Contemporary Southeast Asia* 24 (3): 569–89.

Hughes, C. (2005a) Field notes, Dili, April–July.

——(2005b) Field notes, Liquica.

——(2007) 'Transnational networks, international organizations and political participation in Cambodia: human rights, labour rights and common rights', *Democratization* 14 (5): 834–52.

——(2009a) *Dependent Communities: Politics and Aid in Cambodia and East Timor*, Ithaca, NY: Cornell Southeast Asia Program.

——(2009b) '"We just take what they offer": community empowerment in post-war Timor-Leste', in E. Newman (ed.) *New Perspectives on Liberal Peace Building*, Tokyo: United Nations University Press.

Hughes, C. and T. Conway (2003) 'Understanding pro-poor political change: the policy process Cambodia', Overseas Development Institute Working Paper, August.

ITAD (2008) *Evaluation of the Timor Leste Country Programme, 2003–2008*, Dublin: Irish Aid; available at: www.dci.gov.ie/Uploads/East%20Timor.pdf (accessed 20 July 2010).

Jayasuriya, K. (2005) 'Beyond institutional fetishism: from the developmental to the regulatory state', *New Political Economy* 10 (3): 381–8.

Kaplan, R. (1994) 'The coming anarchy: how scarcity, crime, overpopulation, tribalism and disease are rapidly destroying the social fabric of our planet', *The Atlantic Monthly*, February.

Lederach, J.P. (1997) *Building Peace: Sustainable Reconciliation in Divided Societies*, Washington, DC: United States Institute of Peace.

Mason, T.D. and P.J. Fett (1996) 'How civil wars end: a rational choice approach', *Journal of Conflict Resolution* 40 (4): 546–68.

Mayall, J. (1996) *The New Interventionism 1991–1994: The United Nations Experience in Cambodia, Former Yugoslavia and Somalia*, Cambridge: Cambridge University Press.

Paris, R. (2004) *At War's End: Building Peace after Civil Conflict*, Cambridge: Cambridge University Press.

Ramsbotham, O. (2000) 'Reflections on United Nations post-settlement peace building', *International Peacekeeping* 7 (1): 169–89.

Reilly, B. (2002) 'Post-conflict elections: constraints and dangers', *International Peacekeeping* 9 (2): 118–39.

Richmond, O. and J. Franks (2007) 'Liberal hubris? Virtual peace in Cambodia', *Security Dialogue* 38 (1): 27–48.

Roberts, D. (2001) *Political Transition in Cambodia 1991–1999: Power, Elitism and Democracy*, New York: St Martin's Press.

Scott, J.C. (1985) *Weapons of the Weak: Everyday Practices of Peasant Resistance*, New Haven, CT: Yale University.

Snyder, J. and E. Mansfield (1995) 'Democratization and the danger of war', *International Security* 20 (1): 5–38.

Stedman, S.J. (1997) 'Spoiler problems in peace processes', *International Security* 22 (2): 2–53.

Stedman, S.J., D. Rothschild and E. Cousens (2002) *Ending Civil Wars: The Implementation of Peace Agreements*, Boulder, CO: Lynne Rienner.

Surkhe, A. (2001) 'Peacekeepers as nation builders: the dilemmas of the UN in East Timor' 8 (4): 1–20.

United Nations (1991) *Agreement on a Comprehensive Political Settlement on the Cambodia Conflict*, Article 6, Paris: UN.

United Nations General Assembly (1993) 'An agenda for peace', General Assembly Resolution, UN document A/RES/47/120, 20 September 1993; reprinted in B. Boutros-Ghali, *An Agenda for Peace 1995*, second edition, New York: United Nations.

UNTAC Human Rights Component (1993) *Final Report*, Phnom Penh: UNTAC.

World Bank (n.d.) *Ensuring Public Access to Information and Strengthening Civil Society*, Washington, DC: World Bank; available at: http://siteresources.worldbank.org/INTTIMORLESTE/Resources/Strengthening-Institutions-Civil-Society-8.pdf, (accessed 16 November 2010).

——(1998) *Post-Conflict Reconstruction: The Role of the World Bank*, Washington, DC: World Bank.

——(2006) *Country Assistance Strategy for the Democratic Republic of Timor-Leste for the Period FY06–FY08*, Dili: World Bank.

——(2007) *Sharing Growth – Equity and Development in Cambodia*, Phnom Penh: World Bank.

18

TESTING THE BOUNDARIES OF THE STATE

Gangs, militias, vigilantes and violent entrepreneurs in Southeast Asia

Ian Wilson

On 23 November 2009 a convoy of 57 men and women were stopped at a roadblock in the southern Philippines by an armed agent of a local warlord, together with a number of local police. On their way to register Esmael Mangudadatu as a candidate for the elections for governor in the province of Maguindanao in the southern Philippines, the group, which included Mangudadatu's wife, were taken to a remote area and brutally killed and their bodies buried in a mass grave. Those behind this unprecedented and audacious act of political violence were linked to the Ampatuan clan, a powerful family which had held sway over Maguindanao since the late 1990s (ICG 2009). The killings were apparently intended as a warning to Mangudadatu, the only other significant challenger to the rule of the head of the clan and governor of Maguindanao, Andal Ampatuan Sr. This outrage presented the Arroyo government with a grievous dilemma. It had been reliant upon the clan to secure votes for the president and patronage from Manila had allowed them to develop their power unchecked. The massacre reflected their sense of impunity. Extreme even by the standards of the Philippines, where political violence and murder is endemic around election times, the murders brought to the attention of the country and the world the existence of well-armed groups operating outside the law and prepared to use extreme violence with state funding and consent.[1] Subsequent raids by the Philippines military on the compound of the Ampatuan clan during a week-long state of emergency uncovered a massive weapons cache.[2]

Unlike the Abu Sayyaf or Moro Liberation Front, the Ampatuan clan were not insurgents, separatists or an organized crime syndicate, but local powerbrokers and ostensibly elected officials who had been allowed to build their extra-legal authority with the knowledge, support and funding of the central government in Manila under the pretext of combating insurgents, in return for political support. In a country with one of the longest histories of electoral democracy in Southeast Asia, the Maguindanao incident poses a number of questions regarding the relationship between privatized violence and democratic states in Southeast Asia, some of which will be explored in this chapter. Some of the most critical include: what does the existence of privatized violence tell us regarding the nature and limits of state power and the specific trajectories of democratization in the region, and to what extent is the proliferation of gangs and privatized violence the product of other broader processes such as urbanization, social inequality, economic disparity?

Drawing upon examples from Indonesia, the Philippines and East Timor this chapter will argue that forms of organized non-state and privatized violence in Southeast Asia, such as organized gangs, vigilantes and militias, have exerted and continue to exert a considerable influence in the region, eroding and undermining state power and legitimacy by operating within gaps created by its 'patchiness' and yet at the same time often being integral to the consolidation and maintenance of particular configurations of power. However, while they are frequently sponsored or mobilized by governments and elite interests, such as in Maguindanao, it will be argued that the continued existence of groups of armed young men throughout Southeast Asia cannot be attributed solely to their occasional 'usefulness' to state or elite interests, but are also a product of far broader structural forces operating on a regional and global scale that are, in many instances, beyond the immediate control of the state. This includes in particular the staggering explosion in urbanization in the region and resultant patterns of poverty, informality and social exclusion, together with a range of negative impacts of globalization and the entrenchment of unconstrained markets. For the residents of crowded slums and poor neighbourhoods in cities such as Jakarta, Manila, Phnom Penh and Bangkok, the state, unable or unwilling to either control or support burgeoning urban populations, often exists largely as a symbolic presence rather than a quotidian one. With little in the way of basic public infrastructure, law enforcement or social welfare, various other forms of informal social organization and 'order' emerge within these communities, such as gangs, local strongmen, vigilantes and other forms of territorial-based groups employing forms of coercion.

Another factor is the dynamics of democratization itself. It was initially expected that the introduction of decentralized forms of electoral-based democratic politics and donor-funded 'good governance' reforms throughout the region would increase public participation, accountability, transparency and efficiency in the political process. It was assumed this would, in turn, reduce the conditions believed to produce non-state violence-wielding groups. However, in many instances it has resulted in their proliferation and diversification. In part this can be accounted for by the somewhat haphazard, corrupt and partial manner in which reforms have been implemented, together with the resilience of predatory political elites who have reconfigured themselves in accord with the new socio-political dynamics. This power of adaption is also at the core of gang life. As Dichiara and Chabot (2003: 78) argue, gang formation, organization and change are both 'reactive and proactive to social forces and the gang members' perceptions of social reality'. Far from being static entities, gangs respond to the material, social and political constraints in which they are immersed in a variety of often contradictory ways. Despite their diversity, command over territory lies at the heart of the life of organized gangs and violent entrepreneurs, be it a bus terminal, neighbourhood, rural village or sector of the underground economy. This has intersected in equally diverse ways with localized contestations of power via the ballot box in the context of increased political decentralization and implementation of electoral democracy throughout the region. Democratic process has seen violent entrepreneurs become central players as powerbrokers, contestants for formal power themselves, or as parallel forms of order with whom legitimate power holders must attempt to negotiate, co-opt, contain or eliminate, promises of the latter being a frequently deployed populist tactic. Less recognized, it has also seen gangs in particular developing into forms of street-level opposition, and resistance by marginalized groups and communities. As Sassen has noted, 'street level politics makes possible the formation of new types of political subjects that do not have to go through the formal political system' (Sassen 2003: 13).

The classic Weberian definition of the state identifies one of its defining characteristics as the 'territorial monopoly over the legitimate use of physical force' (Weber 1964: 154). However, a complete monopoly over force by the state, legitimate or otherwise, remains more an ideal than a lived reality. Michael Taylor has argued that states never fully possess an actual monopoly over force even if they may claim it. According to Taylor (1982: 5), what a nominally functional state does constitute is 'a concentration of force and the attempt by those in whose hands it is (incompletely) concentrated to determine who else shall be permitted to employ force and on what occasions'. Charles Tilly (1975: 62) also avoids any mention of legitimacy or mono-polization in the use of force in his definition of the state, identifying it simply as an entity 'controlling the principal means of coercion within a given territory'. What both authors sug-gest is that once the principal means of force has been brought under effective control, which in the case of most nation-states involves the military and police, other violence-wielding groups can potentially be managed or contained through a combination of negotiation, sub-contracting, incorporation, suppression or elimination.[3] In this context 'legitimacy' emerges as a product of struggles to construct and dominate a particular form of social and political 'order', and to define and control the authority of the state. Challenges facing the state in establishing an effective monopoly over the use of force in a given territory are limited not only to practical logistics, but also to the emergence of contesting 'legitimacies'. In Indonesia, for example, fracturing of patron–client relationships between political elites and criminal networks in the post-New Order period has seen former regime henchmen repackage themselves in a variety of guises, such as religious vigilantes, ethnic empowerment organizations, local security providers and 'supporter groups' of politicians and political parties, all of which assert particular claims to legitimacy in the use of force and a monopoly over various forms of rent extraction.

Yet the presence of such groups, which has been almost constant in many parts of the region since colonial times, cannot be explained in and of itself as a manifestation of state failure to monopolize force, 'governance voids', or either a still ongoing and partial process of democratic transition or opportunities presented by democracy itself. As the gang researcher John Hagedorn (2008) has argued, gangs and groups of armed men are a permanent fixture of urban landscapes globally, be it in advanced and transitional democracies, authoritarian regimes or fragile states. In Indonesia and the Philippines in particular, the failure of the promise of democratic decen-tralization to bring economic prosperity to rural areas has seen a constant stream of migration into national and regional capitals, putting increased pressure on limited infrastructure and expanding already overcrowded urban slums and poor neighbourhoods. Often with minimal effective state presence in terms of basic infrastructure or services, gangs, vigilantes and local militias have emerged as a significant form of informal governance, a source of social welfare and identity and group solidarity for youth in these marginalized communities and the informal economy from which they etch out a living, and continue to remain one of a limited number of options available. This increases where the presence of the state is felt in largely negative terms or by its absence, such as in forced evictions, police corruption and brutality or a lack of health or education facilities. According to statistics compiled by UN Habitat in 2001, in Southeast Asia approximately 57 per cent of the population now live in urban centres, of who 28 per cent reside in communities identified as slums (UN Habitat 2007). As of 2010, urbanization rates in the region continue to rise steadily, with 50 per cent of Indonesia's total population residing in urban areas; the figure in the Philippines is 66 per cent. Of these, 23 per cent and 44 per cent respectively live in slums.[4] In megacities such as Jakarta and Manila formal sector employment has also continued to contract, with the overwhelming majority making a living from the informal or underground economy.[5] Drawing on the findings of the UN Habitat report, Koonings and Kruijt (2009: 21) identify the close correlations that exist globally between 'poverty, inequality, exclusion, youth unemployment and living in slum cities, the incidence of violence and crime and the possibility of victimization by state and non-state armed actors'. Drawing upon Mike Davis's influential work on the global proliferation of slums,

Hagedorn suggests that the corollary to this 'planet of slums' is 'a world of gangs' (Hagedorn 2008: 3).

Relations with the state: bottom up or top down?

In his comparative study of the relationship between protection rackets, organized criminal groups and political elites, the criminologist Schulte-Bockholt (2006: 25) has argued that during periods of 'crisis of hegemony', political elites regularly form alliances with organized crime, gangs and other violent non-state groups as a means of consolidating elite interests when instability or upheaval threaten to alter existing power relations. Examples of this can be found throughout history in a diverse range of socio-political settings, from alliances between the mafia and Christian Democrats in post-WWII Sicily to Yakuza collaboration with right-wing nationalists in 1930s Japan, and numerous instances in Latin America in which drug lords have joined forces with military dictatorships to fight left-wing rebels and suppress pro-democracy movements.[6] Southeast Asia is also replete with similar elite–criminal alliances, such as collaboration between organized criminal networks and the New Order state in Indonesia, right-wing cults and the Aquino government in the Philippines or the military junta and *chao pho* godfathers in 1960s Thailand.[7]

According to Schulte-Bockholt's theory, a 'strong state', be it a democracy or a dictatorship, will generally endeavour to eliminate or co-opt alternate sources of protection and violence in order to circumvent the possibility of their transformation into sources of instability (Schulte-Bockholt 2006: 18). However, during a period of 'crisis' when elites believe their interests to be under threat, such as during a period of rapid transition or socio-political upheaval, they will often seek to form alliances with organized crime, gangs, etc., in order to suppress counter-hegemonic forces (Chantornvong 2000: 26). In order to remain in power, elites incorporate potentially disruptive sub-hegemonic groups such as gangs within their networks of economic advantage. In these circumstances the interests of predatory states and violent entrepreneurs dovetail. Elites require the localized coercive power of organized crime and gangs, while for the groups themselves alignment with elite interests can be an avenue for further integration within the central structures of domination and power. Schulte-Bockholt contends that both frequently share crucial sets of interests, i.e. the suppression of organized labour and dependence upon forms of extra-legal rent seeking. Despite the historical alignment of organized racketeering, criminal groups and violent entrepreneurs with repressive regimes, Schulte-Bockholt (2006: 35) contends that such criminal–elite alliances are not characteristic of particular types of political organization or historical periods and can be just as easily found in formal well-functioning democracies. What can alter significantly is the power dynamics of the relationship, the capacity of the state to effectively manage these relationships, and the relative ability and space within which these groups can operate, including in ways which may threaten or challenge elite and state interests.

Schulte-Bockholt's argument is a compelling one and resonates with a long and complex history of elite–criminal/private violence alliances in the region. However, the current dynamics found in Indonesia and the Philippines in particular are different from those outlined by Schulte-Bockholt in a number of ways. Most importantly, elites are not as easily able to use state power to repress or remove violent entrepreneurs with the same degree of efficiency as, for example, during Suharto's New Order or the Marcos regime. As a result violent entrepreneurs, who are frequently called upon by local elites to harass and suppress counter-hegemonic forces such as a revitalized labour movement, anti-corruption activists or political rivals, have been able to use their prime instrumentality in the establishment and preservation of particular configurations of power to become equal and at times dominant partners in these alliances, rather than merely 'hired goons'. This miscalculation on the part of local elites regarding the changed nature of political dynamics has aided, perhaps unwittingly, in the evolution of these organizations and networks into significant constellations of social power. This has particular relevance to Southeast Asian states such as Indonesia, the Philippines and East Timor, where the introduction of regional autonomy, political decentralization and competitive electoral politics at the local level has resulted in new spaces for engagement and the exercise of influence by individuals who emerge from (but do not represent the interests of) groups previously largely excluded from the political process.

Another aspect of Schulte-Bockholt's argument that becomes problematic when applied to democratic Southeast Asian states is that it doesn't adequately address the significant diversity of organized non-state violence-wielding groups, with Schulte-Bockholt adopting a somewhat reductionist view of criminal racketeers as essentially primitive forms of totalitarian states. They preside over predatory and reactionary forms of organization which ultimately seek to impose repressive socio-political orders, and which only become ideological 'by adapting to the world view prevalent in the elite structures into which they integrate' (Schulte-Bockholt 2006: 22). As Jankowski (2003: 191) has pointed out, there has often been a failure to differentiate criminal groups and gangs from other types of collective behaviour and organization or recognize the extent to which they are influenced by the larger structures within which they operate. Contemporary research in Southeast Asia has shown that in practice the distinctions between gang, militia, vigilante, protection racketeers or state agent are often at best arbitrary, with the realities involving complex networks of intertwined sets of interests, goals and identities that shift and morph in accord with changing social and political dynamics. The work of Brown and Wilson (2007) and Kreuzer (2009) on the southern Philippines, for example, has demonstrated the porous and constantly shifting line between local warlords, organized criminal gangs, religious militants and counter-insurgent vigilantes. John Sidel (1999) has argued compellingly that despite strong democratic credentials local 'bossism', which blurs the line between formal and informal political power, is an entrenched and persistent feature of politics in the Philippines that shows few signs of abating. In Indonesia, ethnic-based gangs have simultaneously been advocates for the urban poor, racketeers, hired thugs for political and economic elites, civilian police auxiliaries and in a number of instances a recruitment pool for terrorist networks. Religious vigilantes such as the Defenders of Islam Front (Front Pembela Islam, or FPI) for example, whose activities over the past decade have oscillated between criminal racketeering, political opportunism and Islamist militancy, have been a thorn in the side of attempts by the Jakarta administration to impose the rule of law. They have also been useful allies for politicians pursuing conservative social agendas.

Similarly, despite its comparatively small population of only around one million, the fledgling state of Timor Leste has, as James Scambary (2009) has shown, been plagued by a bewildering array of gangs, militias and martial arts groups motivated by as divergent interests as political ambition, mystical beliefs, responses to grinding poverty and a desire and need for identity, social solidarity and 'respect' in a fractured post-conflict society. Like Indonesia and the Philippines, while some East Timorese gangs are more clearly 'outlaws', others have close links to major political parties and elements of the military and police, with most sitting somewhere in between (TLAVA 2009). With these blurring of categories and interests, not only between types of non-state groups but also between state agents and the groups themselves, ambiguities emerge regarding their direction as either top down or bottom up: are we seeing a proliferation of agents of political elites or groups easily instrumentalized to defend their interests, predatory and essentially criminal groups exploiting lapses and gaps in state authority, or grass-roots responses to 'crises of hegemony', not of elites, but of marginalized and disaffected social groups?

As mentioned previously, the massive expansion of urban populations in the region has been marked by informality not just in the economic sphere but also in 'governance'. High levels of unemployment and endemic poverty all contribute to large pools of what criminologists have described as 'groups of unsupervised youth'. Because of economic and social pressures these groups often come under the supervision of organized crime and gangs or act as recruitment pools for religious vigilantes and ethnic and nationalist militias as well as politicized thugs and state auxiliaries. As Hagedorn (2008: 49) has stated, 'while the underground economy may become a solution to the gang members' problem of survival, religious, ethnic or communal identity becomes the solution to the problem of meaning'. Gangs and similar forms of organization are a reaction from 'alienated, angry and well-armed young men' often immersed in an intractable reality of poverty and social exclusion (Hagedorn 2008: 3). Part of the success of religious militants, vigilantes and ethnic militias in recruiting urban youth has been the provision of a 'cause' that intersects with, rather than contradicts, more instrumentalist concerns. For example, despite an ostensive concern with enforcing a conservative religious morality, the FPI draws its membership almost entirely from poor urban youth who usually have little in the way of religious background or commitment (see Wilson 2008). The apparent 'hypocrisy' of the group, so often noted by media commentators, is in reality the disjunction that emerges between the pragmatism of rank and file members and the more ideological and politically opportunistic motives of the group's leadership (Wilson 2008).[8] The social existence of these communities is marked by what Bayat (2007: 580) has referred to as 'informal life', which is 'characterised by autonomy, flexibility, and pragmatism, where survival and self-development occupy a central place'. For the urban poor, ideological commitment, for example to Islamic militance, is something that 'requires certain capacities (time, risk-taking, money) that the disenfranchised often lack' (Bayat 2007: 588). Hence they tend towards giving contingent support to a diverse and eclectic range of political or social movements only so long as these core instrumentalist objectives are advanced in some way. In a similar vein, paramilitaries and militia groups linked to local political parties or elites (such as the political party Satgas in Indonesia) also answer the need for pragmatic answers to material deprivation together, with the potential for social mobility and advancement. Elite backing provides a competitive advantage in territorial contestations for control over limited resources. Just as elites approach these disenfranchised groups in pragmatic terms, the reverse is also the case. With the exception of standing 'private armies' such as those of the Ampatuan clan, discussed earlier, arrangements between local gangs, violent entrepreneurs and elites are generally informal and on an 'as required' basis (Camacho et al. 2005). Fervent loyalty is largely absent, with allegiances frequently shifting based upon strategic and practical considerations.

Insofar as gangs, vigilantes and militias are commonly defined by their use of violence and criminality, they also come overwhelmingly from the social and economic underclass. Processes such as decentralization, the broadening and consolidation of the electoral process and regional autonomy have provided not only a new socio-political reality but also a new discursive framework, in which gangs, vigilantes and violent entrepreneurs may articulate and stake territorial claims based upon communal identities, populist rights claims of marginalized social groups and critiques of the state, rather than vertical lines of political patronage and defence of elite ideology and interests. The outcomes are also not necessarily entirely malevolent, reactionary or self-serving. This interplay between attempts to address the material needs of the group (which can include but is not limited to criminal behaviour) and the pursuing of previously inaccessible avenues for the realization of the aspirations of members has resulted in significant increases in

Ian Wilson

membership despite the existence of numerous other formal organizations, such as political parties. Here the work of Brotherton on the transformation of organized gangs in the United States towards what he describes as 'street organizations', 'the transitional stage between a gang and a social movement', provides an alternate theoretical framework for understanding how gangs, vigilante groups or militias can be *simultaneously* violent defenders of predatory interests and sources of criminality, while also vehicles for proactive social and cultural resistance by politically and socially marginal communities (Brotherton 2007: 252).

In this respect it is important to recognize some of the more benign and even socially ben-eficial aspects of these groups for those involved. These often include the provision of jobs, livelihoods and basic services for members and the community which are otherwise not pro-vided or accessible. As will be discussed later, ethnic militias in Jakarta such as the Betawi Brotherhood Forum (Forum Betawi Rempug, or FBR) offer free legal aid, job training and ambulance services to members and their families, services which, despite some improvements in public service delivery to the poor in Indonesia's capital, are still largely inaccessible. Simi-larly, while engaging in criminality and social conflict, organized gangs in post-independence East Timor, such as 7–7 and Slebor, also provide opportunities for work, albeit limited, in a country with unemployment rates ranging between 30 and 50 per cent for 20–29-year-olds (TLAVA 2009: 2). Even from the neo-liberal perspective of free markets as the necessary pre-condition for development, Sidel (2004: 66) has argued that, rather than being 'hallmarks of backwardness and obstacles of capitalist development', local strongmen have in fact been 'front line agents of capitalist development' and economic growth.

With these issues in mind, the following brief examples from the Philippines and Indonesia are not meant as comprehensive overviews of either of these countries, something that is clearly beyond the scope of this chapter, but rather snapshots, each of which illustrates some of the complexities and contradictions in regard to the dynamics that exist between non-state violence-wielding groups, political elites and the state, and what this can potentially tell us regarding the nature and limits of state power.

Mis-managing a monster: vigilantes and the state in the Philippines

The Philippines has one of the longest histories of electoral-based democracy and sovereign state building in the region, with the first elections for a lower house Philippines Assembly held in 1907 and the first fully elected president in 1935 (Kreuzer 2009: 47). Despite this, non-state and private groups using violence have been a persistent feature of the political landscape (Kreuzer 2009: 48). One particular manifestation of this has been vigilante groups. Much earlier than the Maguindanao massacre, the Philippines state had already been accused of creating their own 'monster' in the 1980s through the formation of civilian vigilante groups, known as CVOs (Civilian Volunteer Organizations). Beginning in 1982 under President Marcos, civilian vigilantes became an integral element of counter-insurgency strategies against communist insurgents as well as MNLF and later MILF rebels in the country's south. However, it wasn't until after the overthrow of the Marcos regime by the People Power revolution of 1986 and the rise of Corazon Aquino to the presidency that these groups began to proliferate and gain in strength and influence. By 1989 the number of vigilante groups was estimated at being anywhere up to 640 nationally (Hedman 2000: 130). A number of these groups, such as the right-wing cultists in the Divine Missionaries of Christ or the street gangs of Alsa Masa, already existed. Others sprang up independently, both as a local response to an upsurge in crime and communist insurgent violence, and as vehicles for criminal opportunists seeking to benefit from the climate of upheaval. The altering of the constitution in 1987, which ordered the abolition of private armies and unauthorized armed groups, also saw many private armies of local clans simply relabel themselves as CVOs or, through informal relationship with local military, gain the status of state-sanctioned militias known as Civilian Armed Force Geographical Units (CAFGU) (Camacho *et al.* 2005: 16).

As Kowalewski (1996: 63) has argued, state-mobilized vigilante groups are less a reflection or extension of the state than they are a 'political mirror-image of dissident groups'. In circumstances of relative stability these same groups could be considered a potential destabilizing force. Vigilantes are partners of the state only insofar as they are able to be effectively harnessed towards particular ends. This brings with it a number of both risks and benefits for the state. The most likely dangers are those of losing control, or of these vigilantes otherwise transforming into counter-hegemonic forces. The benefits include the ability to pursue aggressive and violent pogroms towards dissidents at arm's length and to temporarily co-opt criminal networks. Violent excesses can be disavowed with far greater ease than if they were carried out by the military or police. Many of the members of these vigilante groups consisted of petty criminal networks and gangs, impoverished slum dwellers and poor peasants, together with a bizarre menagerie of local millenarian and religious cults. According to Kreuzer (2009: 55), prior to the advent of the counter-insurgency strategy of the 1980s, 'bottom–up' vigilante organization was a relatively rare phenomenon. It was with the collapse of peace talks and cease-fire between insurgents and the new Aquino government that pre-existing networks of criminal and privatized violence were able to reconfigure themselves in ways more immediately conducive to the interests of the state.

President Aquino used the rhetoric of people power together with the threats posed by insurgents to legitimate the empowering of reactionary, predatory and criminal groups. As Kreuzer (2009: 55) states:

> vigilantes provided crucial services in the elite's efforts for a restorative reframing of the vague ideology of empowerment underlying People Power at a time when the traditional elites were fighting to divert the emancipatory impetus for reform and reconstruct the old order where they had reigned supreme.

This valuable service, of suppressing perceived threats to entrenched interests, was not without consequences. Patronage provided by local elites, the military and the police saw some groups quickly transform into effectively autonomous units. With the injection of funding, weapons and a loose mandate, vigilante groups such as the cultist Tadtad (infamous for dismembering its victims and consuming their livers), Kuratong Baleleng, Ilaga and Alsa Masa conducted a bloody reign of terror, imposing localized forms of extra-legal 'order' and rent extraction and carrying out beatings and extrajudicial executions with virtual impunity (Hedman 2000). Hedman (2000: 126) argues that under the rubric of post-Marcos democratization the state was able to use the 'redistribution' of legitimate violence to these reactionary and criminal groups as a substitute for broader democratic structural reforms. The result was beneficial to both the state and local elites on two fronts: not only did the vigilantes succeed in tackling the upsurge in insurgent violence, but in the process they managed to effectively terrorize the entire population, dampening any impetus towards greater democratic reforms. Gangs, extreme cults and vigilante groups provided the state with proxies to carry out its dirty work with enough distance from state authorities to allow it to disavow excesses, while at the same time extolling them as a manifestation of people's empowerment.[9]

However, while the more overt face of brutal vigilantism as insurgent violence in Davao City and other urban centres declined, those involved by no means disappeared. Some were absorbed into the private armies of local bosses and warlords such as the Ampatuan clan, described by

Sidel (1999: 19) as 'predatory power brokers who achieve monopolistic control over both coercive and economic resources within given territorial jurisdictions or bailiwicks'. The central government, in particular under the presidency of Gloria Arroyo, turned a blind eye, partly through the ability of such forces to secure votes for government parties, albeit through coercive and violent means. Others, still using the cover of being a CVO, have morphed into kidnap ransom gangs; the Tadtad has remained active while the Alsa Masa and Kuratong Baleleng network splintered into a mixture of protection racket gangs and crime syndicates as well as rumoured 'anti-crime' death squads for Davao City's mayor, Rodrigo Duterte (Camacho *et al.* 2005: 18). Despite the vigilante atrocities of the 1980s and 1990s, and more recently the Maguindanao massacre of 2009, in August 2010 the Philippines military, under the directive of recently installed President Benigno Aquino III, has aided in the revival of the Alsa Masa, in a renewed campaign against the communist New People's Army.[10] Having helped create – or, more accurately, empower – a 'monster', the Philippines state has been unable to effectively manage it. As Schulte-Bockholt suggests, in a period of 'crisis of hegemony' the state seeks alliances with criminal and violence-wielding groups to help protect its interests (Schulte-Bockholt 2006: 26). However, in the case of the Philippines, as Kreuzer (2009: 59) contends, this patron–client relationship has not been a 'benign bond furthering mutual interest'. Periodic state clientelism in dealing with insurgents, securing electoral support or fighting 'crime' has in fact deepened the entrenchment of criminal groups, wielders of privatized violence and local bosses who are now in possession of a seemingly unassailable 'gatekeeper' role, leaving the state with few options other than to turn to them again.

From state agent to 'voice of the oppressed': gangs in post-New Order Jakarta

The trajectories in Indonesia have been somewhat different from those in the Philippines. Even in the colonial period, the Dutch had used gangs and groups of local strongmen and criminals as crucial sub-contracted agents. Nationalists sought to recruit them, as one of the few sources of organized violence outside of colonial control, into the independence struggle and to integrate them into the embryonic Indonesian armed forces.

During the thirty-two years of Suharto's New Order regime, it was able to exercise a significant degree of control and organization over informal groups. At times when groups were perceived to be moving beyond effective state control and threatening to coalesce into potential 'structural threats', the New Order reasserted its power brutally and unambiguously. Fearful of a local equivalent of the Yakuza or Mafia, state agencies under the directive of Suharto took action to atomize these networks and re-establish a dependent relationship (*Tempo* 1982). The most dramatic of these measures was what came to be known as the 'Mysterious Shootings' killings (Penembakan Misterius, or Petrus) of the 1980s, during which several thousand alleged petty criminals and gangsters were summarily executed, including networks aligned to potential rivals to Suharto.[11] The possibility that the cultivation of criminal networks by political elites and the military could result in rival power bases as much as it could bolster state power was managed by Suharto by encouraging rivalries and power struggles between groups. In this way the kind of entrenched warlordism and bossism found in the Philippines and Thailand was avoided.

This control, however, was by no means absolute. As Barker (2007: 90) has pointed out, one of the enduring myths of state power during the New Order was its omnipotence. The image often presented is one of a pyramidal and unified structure in which the thousands of sub-components, including *preman* (a thug or gangster) and state-backed militias, worked together as part of a giant cohesive whole (Barker 2007: 90). The reality was, however, far more complex and fragmented, and in many instances groups would pursue divergent interests to the state, or even on occasions stand in defiance of state authority. The situation was one of a constant tension, where a multitude of actors employed violence and coercion under the guise of the state and its symbols, only kept in check by the capacity of the state apparatus to apply shock therapy, brutally cracking down when considered necessary. This was no longer the case in the post-New Order environment.

The post-1998 advent of democratic reforms produced both newfound freedoms to organize and the fragmenting of previous clientelist networks and the state capacity to monopolize force. This resulted in an explosion of ethnic militias, street gangs, religious vigilantes, private security providers and politically aligned paramilitary groups (Robison *et al.* 2008). Former regime henchmen repackaged themselves in a variety of guises suited to the new socio-political dynamics, while for thousands of unemployed youth involvement in the plethora of new gangs, militias, paramilitaries and political party security wings brought with it opportunities not only for sources of income, but also for social mobility. Previously uncontested localized monopolies over turf and rent extraction were challenged, often violently. Even those groups most closely identified with the previous regime, such as Pemuda Pancasila, sought to distance themselves from their past and repackage themselves as an independent group, going so far as to establish their own political party.[12]

Gangs, ethnic militias and vigilante groups now vary considerably in terms of their ideological and political orientation and affiliation, just as members vary from hardened gangsters to unemployed university graduates, urban poor and informal sector workers. Many urban-based groups still draw much of their membership from this growing *preman* underclass of unemployed or underemployed youth, which continues to expand owing to the pressures of rapid urbanization and the inability of the formal economy to provide adequate numbers of jobs. As during the New Order, these new gangs are often involved in racketeering, illegal economies, violent entrepreneurship and vigilantism, both as a service supplied to a ready market for forms of intimidation and as an imposed coercive relationship within their immediate community.

Yet as Hagedorn (2008) has observed, as much as gangs 'feed' from the informal economy and poor communities, they are also a part of them and at times act in their defence. In Jakarta, gangs and ethnic militias have resisted evictions of slum dwellers, demanded 'tax' from businesses for community projects, pressured chain stores to employ locals and lobbied politicians to improve health facilities. In lieu of adequate state services, successful gangs are often major community benefactors commanding a loyalty which frequently confounds and frustrates both law enforcement agencies and developmentalist NGOs. This dimension of gangs and militias is often overlooked in studies of contemporary Indonesian politics, which generally categorize them as either manifestations of criminality and deviance, reactive responses to poverty, or the sub-contracted violent defenders of the interests of political and economic elites, a reactionary and predatory manifestation of 'uncivil society' (Hadiz 2003: 607). While these characterizations are not without degrees of truth, they fail to fully account for or critically examine the complexity and altered dynamics of the post-1998 period. It is now not uncommon to find the co-existence of seemingly contradictory ventures within a single gang: semi-organized criminal behaviour as a response to material deprivation, forms of proto-political organization and consciousness that seeks to identify and address what are believed to be the structural causes of this deprivation, patron–client relationships with political elites and intimidation, and also pro-active engagement with local communities.

The FBR, for example, is one of the largest gangs in Jakarta with a membership of approximately 80,000. Emerging out of inter-ethnic gang conflicts in Cakung, East Jakarta in 2002, its branches have spread throughout Greater Jakarta, operating protection rackets pressuring businesses, vendors and clubs to make 'donations' to it under the rationale of empowering the indigenous Betawi population. The FBR has had numerous flirtations and short-lived alliances with elites and political parties. In an effort to gain privileged access to job training facilities it co-operated with former governor Sutiyoso in harassing urban poor activists. When its hopes weren't realized the alliance ended. It has also given support to political parties such as the Islamist PKS, the Democrat Party of current president Susilo Bambang Yudhoyono and the National Wakening Party. After the death of the FBR's founder, Fadloli el-Muhir, in 2009, the leadership fell to his nephew, Lufti Hakim. Young and university educated, Hakim clearly felt less bound to the patron–client politics game of his predecessor and has sought to radically reform the group's purpose, practice and politics:

> Effectively there is no real political opposition in Indonesia such as we see in Europe or the US. The parties are solely concerned with securing power, and not in representing a con-stituency. What we want is direct participation and representation, not simply to be mobilized on behalf of such-and-such a party.
>
> *(Author interview 2009)*

Hakim severed formal alliances with political parties, instead instructing members to vote according to their own convictions.

The extortion of business as a means of subsidizing the group still continues, but now co-exists with more systematic and lawful lobbying for them to formally employ FBR members. In addition to this, the FBR have provided job training and 'entrepreneurial spirit' training schemes for members. Despite these attempts at reform, however, petty crime – in particular demanding protection money from vendors – is a core source of money for many FBR mem-bers. Attempts to minimize the reliance of members upon crime have also not been without internal conflict, with some more seasoned gangsters within the group resenting attempts to open its doors too widely, fearing it may threaten their own power and territory. By the same token, many smaller gangs have affiliated with the FBR for the very reason that its name brings a degree of protection from larger rivals and in some cases the police. As a concession to public anger over inter-gang violence Hakim has taken the previously unheard-of step of expelling members involved. He has also continued lobbying the Jakarta administration for anti-crime measures that seek to tackle what the group argues is its fundamental cause: lack of employ-ment. Since 2001 the administration has periodically conducted city-wide 'anti-preman' campaigns ostensibly aimed at breaking up street gangs and racketeers. With stretched resources, endemic corruption within the police force and a lack of political will, the overwhelming target of these raids has been unsupervised youths, beggars, street vendors and street children, prompting the FBR to state that they were in fact less a war against preman than a 'war against the poor', and that 'the real criminals are the ones in ties, sitting in parliament and government offices, not people struggling to feed their families' (Author interview 2009). What we see with the changes in groups such as the FBR is that, no longer content to serve as merely the disposable foot soldiers of elites, some members of the *preman* underclass are seeking 'legitimate' political ave-nues in order to represent their own interests and find concrete resolutions to the structural problems in which they are immersed. By engaging in a degree of self-organization, providing tangible services in the communities in which it is based, and defending *preman* not as criminal thugs but as a social and economic underclass, the group has expanded its constituency well beyond its beginnings in the street gangs of East Jakarta.

As Masaaki and Rozaki (2006) have pointed out, non-state violence in Indonesia has occur-red and continues to do so not because the state necessarily condones it, though it often has. It is due to the fact that the state and its component parts have been unable to prevent the existence of non-state violence and, more crucially, have relied and continue to rely upon it to consolidate its own power and defend its interests. However, despite not having the same long history of electoral democracy and state building as the Philippines, Indonesia has not seen anything near the same levels of violence and disruption as its neighbour. While a number of gangsters have made the transition to politician and parliamentarian, this has not resulted in the kind of entrenched bossism or proliferation of private armies and attendant bloodshed as in Maguindanao. As Buehler notes, the performance of these 'gangster politicians', such as Bangkit Sitepu in North Sumatra, have been decidedly uneventful, and several have lost seats in subsequent elections, quietly disappearing from the public view (Buehler 2009). There are a number of reasons for this, which can be explained by the nature of state power and politics in both the New Order and post-New Order. One is the 'success' of Suharto's New Order in preventing the emergence and consolidation of powerful local bosses or clans able to entrench themselves as local gatekeepers. There is no Indonesian equivalent of an Ampatuan clan. In this regard, Suharto's divide-and-rule stratagem has left at least one positive legacy in the post-New Order period.

Buehler also identifies the lack of a significant history of violent feuds between oligarchic clans such as in the Philippines. The more decentralized nature of electoral politics in Indonesia, where there are between three and ten parliamentary seats available per electoral district compared with one in the Philippines, means that in effect less is up for grabs, making a resort to violence appear an unnecessary risk (Buehler 2009).[13] Also unlike the Philippines, where there is potential for repeated consecutive terms, Indonesia has imposed a cap of a maximum of two five-year terms.[14] These same factors have facilitated the entry of previously excluded actors, such as institutionalized gangs, religious vigilantes and militias. Yet despite continuing instances of street-level intimidation and coercion, these constraints have, in the Indonesian context, had the effect of moderating rather than exacerbating the potential for an escalation of violence. Finally, while flows of funds from the central government have increased the possibilities for corruption and the distribution of favours at the local level, it has also reduced the 'competitive pressure on local elites' that may result in the use of physically coercive strategies (Buehler 2009).

In conclusion, there are a number of key points which can be taken from this discussion. Increasing urbanization, economic disparity, social inequality together with the attendant growth of slums and retreat of the state in the provision of essential services all mean that gangs and other formations of 'armed young men' will remain a feature of the social and political landscape in Southeast Asia into the foreseeable future. The persistence of non-state violence-wielding groups cannot be reduced solely to problems of governance, inadequate law enforcement or the patronage or clientelism of political elites. Such groups, irrespective of their ideological or political orientation, provide networks of solidarity, identity and opportunities to fulfil material needs in the context of socio-economic environments where there is often a paucity of options. Finally, and in a more comparative sense, the existence of organized non-state groups using violence is not the unique preserve of the developing world or particular kinds of regimes; long-established and otherwise well-functioning democracies are as prone to the proliferation of non-state violence-wielding groups as 'fragile' or post-authoritarian states.

Notes

1 The massacre, in which thirty journalists were killed, was according to the ICG 'the biggest single death toll of journalists ever in a single incident anywhere in the world' (ICG 2009).
2 According to the ICG this included mortars, rocket launchers and assault rifles (ICG 2009).

3 This includes mercenaries, bandits and irregular armed forces that have so often been crucial to the formation of nation-states (see Davis and Pereira 2003).

4 While the urban population figures are for 2010, the percentage of slum dwellers is based on 2001 figures.

5 In 2001 Blunch *et al.* cited a figure of 77.9 per cent for the proportion of the Indonesian urban work force located in the informal sector, compared with 66.9 per cent in the Philippines and 51.4 per cent in Thailand (Blunch *et al.* 2001). In 2008 it was estimated that as many as 60 million out of Indonesia's workforce of 97 million worked in the informal sector (Khalik 2008).

6 See, for example, the various contributors in Koonings and Kruijt (2004).

7 On the *chao pho* see Chantornvong (2000).

8 This 'hypocrisy' is apparent between the FPI's ostensive 'anti-vice' stance and evidence that members extort money from clubs, bars and gambling dens.

9 A similar situation can be seen in Thailand, where the insurgency in the south together with organized drug trafficking has been used by the government as the rationale for the establishment of civilian paramilitaries and vigilante units. (See McCartan 2010.)

10 The group has been renamed Alsa Lumad, the Lumad being indigenous peoples in the southern Philippines (Olea 2010).

11 In particular, those of Ali Murtopo, an architect of New Order ideology, who was considered at the peak of his influence in the late 1970s a potential challenger to Suharto for the presidency.

12 On the history of the Pemuda Pancasila, see Ryter (1998).

13 Another important factor is the relative dearth of availability of firearms in comparison to the Philippines, making physical conflict, when it occurs, potentially less bloody.

14 What this cap has done, however, is increase efforts to establish family dynasties via the election of the children or close relatives of the incumbent. Examples include the districts of Tabanan and Jembrana in Bali, as well as Banten in West Java.

References

Author interview (2009) *Lufti Hakim*, Jakarta, 16 August.

Barker, J. (2007) 'Vigilantes and the state', in T. Day (ed.) *Identifying with Freedom: Indonesia after Suharto*, New York: Berghahn Books, pp. 87–94.

Bayat, A. (2007) 'Radical religion and the habitus of the dispossessed: does Islamic militancy have an urban ecology?' *International Journal of Urban and Regional Research* 31 (3): 579–90.

Blunch, N.-H., C. Sudharshan and R. Dhushyanth (2001), 'The informal sector revisited: a synthesis across space and time', World Bank Social Protection Discussion Paper Series No. 0119, Washington, DC: World Bank.

Brotherton, D. (2007) 'Towards the gang as a social movement', in J. Hagedorn (ed.) *Gangs in the Global City: Alternatives to Traditional Criminology*, Chicago, IL: University of Illinois Press, pp. 251–72.

Brotherton, D. and L. Barrios (2004) *The Almighty Latin King and Queen Nation: Street Politics and the Transformation of a New York City Gang*, New York: Columbia University Press.

Brown, L. and P. Wilson (2007) 'Putting crime back into terrorism: the Philippines perspective', *Asian Criminology* 2: 35–46.

Buehler, M. (2009) 'Suicide and progress in modern Nusantara', *Inside Indonesia* 97; available at: http://insideindonesia.org/content/view/1217/47/ (accessed 24 September 2010).

Chantornvong, Sombat (2000) 'Local godfathers in Thai politics', in R. McVey (ed.) *Money and Power in Provincial Thailand*, Singapore: Nordic Institute of Asian Studies, pp. 53–73.

Camacho, A., M. Puzon and Y. Ortiga (2005) 'Children and youth in organised armed violence in the Philippines: contextualisation, personal histories and policy options', Children and Youth in Organised Armed Violence Project, Philippines Country Report; available at: www.coav.org.br/publique/media/Report%20Filipinas.pdf (accessed 9 April 2009).

Davis, D. and A. Pereira (eds) (2003) *Irregular Armed Forces and their Role in Politics and State Formation*, Cambridge: Cambridge University Press.

Dichiara, A. and R. Chabot (2003) 'Gangs and contemporary urban struggle: an unappreciated aspect of gangs', in L. Kontos, D. Brotherton and L. Barrios (eds) *Gangs and Society: Alternative Perspectives*, New York: Colombia University Press, pp. 77–94.

Hadiz, V.R. (2003) 'Reorganizing political power in Indonesia: a reconsideration of so-called democratic transitions', *Pacific Review* 16 (4): 591–611.

Hagedorn, J.M. (2008) *World of Gangs: Armed Young Men and Gangsta Culture*, Minneapolis and London: University of Minnesota Press.

Hedman, E.-L. (2000) 'State of siege: political violence and vigilante mobilization in the Philippines', in B. Campbell and A. Brenner (eds) *Death Squads in Global Perspective: Murder with Deniability*, New York: St Martins Press, pp. 125–52.

ICG (International Crisis Group) (2009) 'The Philippines: after the Maguindanao massacre', Asia Briefing No. 98, 21 December.

Jankowski, Martin Sanchez (2003) 'Gangs and social change', *Theoretical Criminology* 7 (2): 191–216.

Khalik, A. (2008) 'Informal sector helping Indonesia cope in global downturn', *Jakarta Post*, 12 February.

Koonings, K. and D. Kruijt (eds) (2004) *Armed Actors: Organised Violence and State Failure in Latin America*, London: Zed Books.

——(eds) (2009) *Mega-cities: The Politics of Urban Exclusion and Armed Violence in the Global South*, London: Zed Books.

Kowalewski, D. (1996) 'Countermovement vigilantism and human rights: a propositional inventory', *Crime, Law and Social Change* 25 (1): 63–81.

Kreuzer, P. (2009) 'Private political violence and boss-rule in the Philippines', *Behemoth: A Journal on Civilisation* 1: 47–63.

McCartan, B. (2010) 'Justice deficit in southern Thailand', *Asia Times Online*, 27 January; available at: www.atimes.com/atimes/Southeast_Asia/LA27Ae01.html (accessed 3 July 2010).

Masaaki, O. and A. Rozaki (2006) 'Editors' introduction', in Okamoto Masaaki and Abdur Rasaaki (eds) *Kelompok Kerkerasan dan Bos Lokal di Era Reformasi* [Violent Groups and Local Bosses in the Reform Era], Yogyakarta and Kyoto: IRE Press and Center for Southeast Asian Studies.

Olea, R. (2010) 'In Davao, military uses vigilante groups against NPA', *Bulatlat*, 21 August; available at: www.bulatlat.com/main/2010/08/21/in-davao-military-uses-vigilante-groups-against-npa/ (accessed 9 September 2010).

Robison, R., I.D. Wilson and A. Meliala (2008) 'Governing the ungovernable: dealing with the rise of informal security in Indonesia', Asia Research Centre Policy Brief No. 1, June; available at: wwwarc. murdoch.edu.au/wp/pb1.pdf (accessed 3 July 2009).

Ryter, L. (1998) 'Pemuda Pancasila: the last loyalist free men of Suharto's order?' *Indonesia* 66: 45–74.

Sassen, S. (2003) 'Globalization or denationalization?' *Review of International Political Economy* 10 (1): 1–22.

Scambary, J. (2009) 'Anatomy of a conflict: the 2006–7 communal violence in East Timor', *Conflict, Security and Development* 9: 265–88.

Schulte-Bockholt, A. (2006) *The Politics of Organized Crime and the Organized Crime of Politics: A Study in Criminal Power*, Oxford: Lexington Books.

Sidel, J.T. (1999) *Capital, Coercion and Crime: Bossism in the Philippines*, Stanford, CA: Stanford University Press.

——(2004) 'Bossism and democracy in the Philippines, Thailand and Indonesia: towards an alternative framework for the study of "local strongmen"', in J. Harriss, K. Stokke and O. Tornquist (eds) *Politicising Democracy: The New Local Politics of Democratization*, Basingstoke: Palgrave Macmillan, pp. 51–74.

Taylor, M. (1982) *Community, Anarchy, Liberty*, Cambridge: Cambridge University Press.

Tempo (1982) 'Belum sampai tingkat mafia' [Not yet at the level of a mafia], 3 April.

Tilly, C. (ed.) (1975) *The Formation of Nation States in Western Europe*, Princeton, NJ: Princeton University Press.

TLAVA (Timor-Leste Armed Violence Assessment) (2009) 'Groups, gangs and armed violence in East Timor', Issue Brief No. 2, April.

UN Habitat (2007) 'Global report on human settlements 2007: enhancing urban safety and security', United Nations Settlement Programme, Earthscan, London.

Weber, M. (1964) *The Theory of Social and Economic Transformation*, trans. A.M. Henderson and T. Parsons, New York: Free Press.

Wilson, I.D. (2008) 'As long as it's *Halal*: Islamic *preman* in Jakarta', in G. Fealy and S. White (eds) *Expressing Islam*, Singapore: ISEAS, pp. 192–210.

SECTION VI
The region and the world

19

CONTESTED BORDERS, CONTESTED BOUNDARIES

The politics of labour migration in Southeast Asia

Michele Ford

Temporary labour migration is a contemporary global phenomenon driven by unequal economic relations within and between states, but also by conflict, repression and even natural disasters. Its strong historical precedents notwithstanding, international labour migration has been transformed in recent decades by the ease of transportation, which has enabled workers to travel between home and host country (and to second and third host countries) on short-term contracts. While clearly of benefit to capital both as a cheap form of waged labour and through the role that foreign domestic workers play in the reproduction of the local labour force, the presence of large numbers of temporary migrants presents a dilemma to host-country governments, which struggle to balance the demands of economic growth and the social implications of the decision to import 'second-class' workers. In an attempt to manage these risks, they seek to control flows of migrant workers – in many cases, strongly supported by local trade unions concerned with the welfare of their (local) members.

Southeast Asia, which encompasses key source and destination countries, offers a useful case study of the politics of temporary labour migration. The importance of foreign contract workers to the economic well-being of both groups of countries has led to contests within and between governments over questions of jurisdiction. While facilitating short-term migration, governments continue to frame foreign labour primarily as a migration or security issue. However, it has become increasingly obvious that large-scale temporary labour migration is of great consequence not only in terms of border controls, but also in terms of labour relations. Indeed, many of the social and political difficulties that have arisen around the rapid growth in this kind of migration have their roots in the ambiguous position of low-skilled foreign contract workers within the labour markets and industrial relations systems of the countries where they are employed.

This chapter examines the political economy of labour migration in the region, with a focus on its implications for collective action. It argues that the pivotal role of temporary labour migrants in Southeast Asia poses intellectual and practical challenges to the way we think about work, mobility and the nature and exercise of labour rights both by individuals and collectively. While temporary labour migration is a serious short-term threat to already weak trade unions in the region, internationally driven responses to the challenge it presents also offer hope of reinvention and renewal. If even only partially successful, attempts to broaden union constituencies and develop alliances across sectors and national boundaries stand to better equip trade unions to deal not only with temporary labour migration but with the other challenges to organized labour posed by neoliberalism.[1]

Contested borders

In recent decades, large-scale international temporary labour migration has been a key part of the economic and social experience of almost all Southeast Asian states. Within the political economy of the region, the position of temporary foreign workers is defined both by the landscape of capitalism and by the labour regimes embedded in them. Southeast Asia is dominated by developmentalist states that do not provide a comprehensive social safety net for their citizens – either because they are too poor to do so, or because they are ideologically opposed to state welfarism. When combined with strong disparities in the level of wealth between states and highly stratified labour markets within them, the lack of social security becomes an important push-factor, as poor Southeast Asian countries increasingly look to temporary labour migration as a means of alleviating pressure on their weak internal labour markets. High rates of unemployment and policy frameworks that favour mass temporary labour migration drive the citizens of countries of origin like Indonesia and the Philippines abroad to destinations in the Middle East and North Asia, and to wealthier countries within Southeast Asia itself. Once overseas, these workers provide an important source of foreign income. In the case of the Philippines, the national economy has come to be heavily reliant on remittances, which in the first quarter of 2010 alone contributed US$4.3 billion to national earnings (Bangko Sentral ng Pilipinas 2010). Although remittances represent a much smaller proportion of the overall economies of other major sending countries in the region, they make a significant contribution to foreign exchange earnings and a vital part of the economic infrastructure of the particular districts from which large numbers of workers migrate.

Wealthier economies in Southeast Asia rely heavily on these flows of foreign workers to support economic growth, providing cheap labour for manufacturing, construction and services without the burden of funding the reproduction of labour. Singapore and Malaysia – the main regional destinations for Indonesians, Filipinos and Thais, along with many South Asians – have extremely tight labour markets. Although Singapore also attracts significant numbers of highly paid foreign professionals, in both countries wage differentials between skilled and semi-skilled occupations generate strong demand in 'dangerous and dirty' industries like construction and dock work, but also for domestic workers and carers, whose presence permits middle-class women to outsource the work of the household in the absence of state-funded facilities for the care of children and the aged (see Ford 2010b). The other major destination country in Southeast Asia is Thailand, itself a labour exporter, which attracts migrant workers from poorer countries in the Mekong Subregion, including Laos and Cambodia, for much the same reasons, but also millions of Burmese.

The financial crisis of 1997 demonstrated the extent to which temporary labour migration has become a structural feature in the region. During the crisis, the governments of Malaysia and Thailand stepped up efforts to control numbers of temporary labour migrants by closer regulation of entry and the imposition of increasingly punitive sanctions against those found working without appropriate documents. In Malaysia, a total ban was imposed on new recruitment of foreign labour in August 1997, only to be lifted following protests by businesses and employers of domestic workers. Although re-imposed in January 1998 for workers in the manufacturing, construction and service sectors, the ban did nothing to slow flows of irregular migrant workers, and when it was again lifted in mid-1998, numbers of regular workers quickly recovered (Kanapathy 2004). The Thai government responded to the crisis by launching a campaign to deport migrant workers to create jobs for nationals – an initiative that also ultimately failed. In the Tak province near the Thai–Burmese border, for example, around 20,000 migrants were deported in the year 2000, but only 6,000 Thais had applied for the positions they vacated (Martin *et al.* 2006: 137–8). All the while, undocumented migrant workers continued to enter Thailand from other mainland Southeast Asian states.

On the one hand, continued flows of irregular labour migrants during and after the crisis exposed the weaknesses in the border controls of these countries. In the case of Malaysia, repeated deportation campaigns have done little to stop Indonesian labour migrants from Sumatra entering Peninsular Malaysia or workers from Kalimantan entering the eastern states of Sabah and Sarawak. Similarly, Thailand's long and porous land and sea borders with a number of poorer countries in the Greater Mekong Subregion make it difficult for Thai authorities to control border crossings, especially as corruption on both sides of Thailand's borders means that, even if detected, intending migrants have an opportunity to pay for safe passage (Ford 2006a, 2007). On the other hand, employers' vehement opposition to the bans of the late 1990s demonstrated the strength of demand for foreign workers even in times of significant economic hardship, suggesting that arguments about fluctuating demand generating a need for temporary – as opposed to permanent – foreign labour are greatly overstated.

This mismatch between pressures for intra-regional labour migration and governments' attempts to regulate flows of foreign workers for social and political reasons serves to exacerbate already high levels of undocumented labour. Irregular labour migrants find employment in many sectors of the economy in both east and west Malaysia, including the plantation sector, construction and services, but also in small to medium manufacturing in the industrial states of the west. In Thailand, unregistered migrant workers from Burma, Cambodia, Lao PDR and, to a lesser extent, China are found in a broad cross-section of occupations in the formal and informal economy. Singapore prides itself on its ability to keep irregular labour migrants out but, although it is more successful than its neighbours, there are nevertheless many who enter the city-state illegally for work. It is by definition impossible to accurately quantify numbers of irregular labour migrants in the region, but according to estimates they constitute up to 40 per cent of the total number of labour migrants in the region's eastern migration systems (Battistella 2002: 8).

The question of labour migration to Thailand, and to a lesser extent Malaysia, is further complicated by refugee flows. As neither country is signatory to the 1951 United Nations Convention relating to the Status of Refugees, the governments of Malaysia and Thailand do not differentiate between refugees and irregular labour migrants. Yet, in addition to the refugee camps along the Thai–Burma border, large numbers of Burmese refugees live and work in locations throughout Thailand. There is also an increasing presence of Burmese in Peninsular Malaysia – which for many years was a primary destination for Acehnese refugees – as well as a significant concentration of refugees from the southern Philippines in the eastern Malaysian state of Sabah. In many cases, the distinction between asylum seekers and economic migrants is blurred, as the lack of jobs at home is a primary motivation for some migrants from areas experiencing conflict. Thus, for example, while many activists argue that the flood of refugees to Thailand would slow if the political situation in Burma changed, others, like Denis Arnold, argue that even if the military regime were to fall, migration to Thailand would continue because employment prospects are so poor (Arnold 2006: 5–6). Many asylum seekers who have left their homes in fear of persecution also work in irregular situations, particularly in contexts where their refugee status is not recognized.

Contested boundaries

In the destination countries of Southeast Asia, the capacity of unskilled and semi-skilled labour migrants to access their labour rights depends in part on their location on a continuum of legality. Migrant workers' position on that continuum is determined by a complex range of systemic, yet contingent, definitions influenced by a multitude of factors beyond mode of entry and status on arrival, including geographical location, country of origin and sector of employment, along with the shifting terrain of ever-evolving government policies. Thus, even where foreign workers are 'legal', in many contexts the conditions of the short-term permits with which host-country governments issue them limit their activities, for example by determining the kind of work they may undertake or proscribing their right to join associations. However, temporary migrant workers are excluded from the formal industrial relations system not just because they are migrants. They are also excluded because of the sectors in which they work. Although immigrant and foreign workers constitute a significant proportion of the blue-collar formal sector workforce in some destination countries, most are employed on the fringes of the formal sector or in informal sector occupations, that are poorly integrated into state industrial relations mechanisms.

Unlike areas of law that draw on deeply held socio-cultural values or long-standing practice, the regulations governing labour migration are arbitrary, constantly defined and redefined as they are by competing legal systems and claims for departmental jurisdiction. As many scholars writing about labour migration have emphasized, the categories 'documented' and 'undocumented' are almost always fluid. Regular migrants may voluntarily enter into irregular status by breaching their visa conditions. However, they may also do so involuntarily because of changes within the regulatory framework or because regulations are framed in such a way as to give employers the power to jeopardize migrant workers' status, for example by failing to pay a levy, by confiscating travel documents or by forcing workers to do work not permitted under their visa conditions. Conversely, irregular migrants may be able to regularize their status through regularization programmes or by returning briefly to their home country, for example during an amnesty, before re-entering the host country with the appropriate documents, or by moving to a third country.

Governments in Southeast Asian source countries create the 'regular' channels through which low- and semi-skilled labour migrants must pass if they wish to be recognized, and play a role in determining the extent to which those regular channels are used. Although labour migration flows in the region are shaped to some extent by ethnicity and nationality, it is clear that class and skill have been the essential criteria underpinning host country decisions to seek to integrate some groups of foreign workers but not others. Unlike highly skilled professionals, unskilled and semi-skilled foreign workers do not have the bargaining power required to move freely in the international labour market. Instead, they are constrained by home and destination country policies and often punitive bilateral labour agreements reached with an eye to facilitating and controlling migrant labour flows rather than ensuring the safety and well-being of workers.

A striking characteristic of temporary labour migration in Southeast Asia is the detailed and precise way in which these host states categorize and deal with different groups of people seeking to work within their borders. Singapore, Malaysia and Thailand all have complicated formulas that differentiate between foreign workers on the basis of their mode of entry, but also their nationality and in some cases their gender. In Malaysia, regular labour migration is not only managed by sector and nationality, but also according to geographic location. As of March 2007, the national policy on foreign workers, which regulates labour migration in Peninsular Malaysia, permitted employment in export-oriented manufacturing and a number of non-export-oriented manufacturing industries. Under this policy, nationals of ASEAN countries were permitted to work on plantations and in manufacturing, services and construction, central Asians in manufacturing, services and construction, and Indians as restaurant cooks, high-voltage cable workers and on the plantations. In addition, Nepalese and Sri Lankan workers already employed in Malaysia could be replaced by workers of the same nationality where employment fell within specific parameters. In the eastern state of Sabah, only Filipinos and Indonesians could be employed, while in Labuan, employers could recruit Indonesians, Filipinos, Thais, Bangladeshis and Pakistanis.[2] At that time, there was no specified list of nationalities for recruitment in Sarawak, where a licence and employment quota must be obtained (Immigration Department of Malaysia 2007).

The supremacy of host countries' migration regimes does not go entirely unchallenged. Sending countries like the Philippines and Indonesia attempt – with varying levels of success – to influence the conditions under which their nationals work overseas through bilateral agreements and other mechanisms. Interests within the host country itself may also diverge. In Malaysia, for example, there are ongoing and quite public tensions between government departments concerned with labour and security (Pillai 1999; Turner 2005). Ultimately, though, the migration status of semi- and low-skilled labour sets the outer limits of the extent to which they are recognized by the host country as workers.

Yet while migration status determines who is recognized as a worker, it is not the only factor shaping access to host-country industrial relations processes and institutions. While generally (but not always) better off than their undocumented compatriots, even those who have entered a foreign country through official channels and continue to meet migration-related regulations seldom receive the same wages and enjoy the same conditions as locals doing the same job. Temporary migrant workers employed in the blue-collar formal sector workforce of wealthier countries in the region have at best conditional access to basic labour rights, including access to decent work, legal redress and the right to freedom of association. In addition, many migrant workers are employed in marginal formal sector occupations, or in the informal sector, which lies outside the scope of the formal industrial relations system altogether. Employed in private homes as domestic or care workers, the bulk of women moving for work within Southeast Asia are particularly far removed from industrial relations mechanisms. However, the informal sector also includes large sections of the construction industry, much of the service sector, and even parts of the manufacturing sector that rely on homeworkers or on outsourced labour – occupations that are effectively excluded from nationally and locally determined frameworks that set out and attempt to protect labour rights.

The limits of contestation

Despite its important international dimension, the international labour movement is essentially defined at the national and sub-national scales. As a result, like other industrial relations institutions, trade unions are ill-equipped to deal with the inherently transnational problem of temporary labour migration. Around the globe, trade unions have long been hostile towards migrant labour because of the threat foreign workers were seen to pose to the interests of 'locals' (Haus 1995; Nissen and Grenier 2001; Teicher et al. 2002), particularly when migrant labour flows increase or in times of economic hardship. In some contexts, trade unionists have recognized that this kind of protectionism is a problematic strategy. As Haus (1995) suggests, one of the reasons that US unions did not campaign for restricted immigration in the 1980s and early 1990s was that they realized that since they could no longer have control over who was employed in a particular industry they needed to be able to organize workers regardless of where they were born. Avci and McDonald (2000) make a similar argument with regard to British unions, observing that trade unions have become more concerned about their ability to organize workers rather than worrying about where those workers come from, as the bargaining position of organized labour weakens in the increasingly transnational context of the European Union.[3]

In Southeast Asia, however, systematic discrimination against temporary migrant labour on the part of the labour movement indicates that migration status continues to be more important to unions than foreign and local labour's shared experiences as workers. As a result, it has been migrant labour NGOs rather than trade unions that have most often responded to foreign workers' inability to access their labour rights. NGOs' efforts initially focused on service provision, driven by concern about the problems foreign workers experience as migrants. However, many NGOs in the Asian region have gradually moved from an exclusive focus on service provision and advocacy towards migrant worker organizing in the hope of tapping the transformative power of collective action to break down structures preventing foreign workers from exercising their labour rights.

During the course of this organizing work, migrant labour NGOs in northeast Asia became increasingly aware of the benefits to foreign workers of gaining access to local industrial relations mechanisms, and of their own institutional limitations in that domain – in short, recognizing that unions can play a role in the protection of foreign workers' labour rights, both through the national industrial relations system and in the international arena through the ILO, that NGOs simply cannot play. This awareness prompted key migrant labour NGO networks such as the Migrant Forum in Asia to attempt to recruit local trade unions throughout the Asian region to the migrant labour cause. Meanwhile, having acknowledged that trade unions' nationally based constituencies leave them ill-equipped to deal with emerging regional and global labour markets, in the early 2000s the international trade union movement began to encourage trade unions in other regions to become more proactive on migrant labour rights.

The convergence of interests between the international labour movement and regional migrant labour NGO networks created significant momentum for change, pushing Southeast Asian trade unions to develop proactive policies on temporary migrant labour. Responses to this pressure in the region have necessarily varied in line with local labour movements' different levels of conviction, degrees of commitment and capacity to promote change. In Thailand and Malaysia, there is a clear geographical dimension to trade unions' ability to represent migrants, since significant concentrations of foreigners live and work in isolated regions and migrant workers are not permitted to form their own unions (a restriction that also applies in Singapore). In Thailand, many Burmese workers are employed in purpose-built factories in the Thai–Burma borderlands, in regions which are of no interest to local trade unions. Large numbers of Indonesian migrant workers are employed on plantations in the eastern Malaysian state of Sabah, where local trade unions are particularly weak. Equally, reliance on local trade unions limits organizing along labour market lines, as most foreign workers are employed in poorly unionized sectors, or in peripheral parts of organized sectors. For example, in Singapore, although foreign maritime engineering workers employed by large companies like Keppel Shipyard can join a union, most foreign workers are employed by non-unionized sub-contractors. Third, internal politics and external constraints mean that local trade unions do not always offer benefits that are attractive to foreign workers, or have the capacity to protect recruits from being dismissed for having engaged in trade union activities.

Poorly resourced and extremely divided, Thailand's is the weakest of the destination country labour movements in Southeast Asia. It is no surprise, then, that migrant labour issues are a low priority even for unionists sympathetic to migrant workers. The Thai Labour Solidarity Committee (TLSC), which brings together peak bodies representing over 350 trade unions with 26 labour NGOs and other labour organizations has demonstrated a strong focus on migrant labour issues in its advocacy campaigns, arguing that migrant workers would be much less vulnerable to police persecution if they were part of a mainstream Thai union, and that Thai unionists have a duty to build solidarity amongst workers regardless of their background. In 2010, the State Enterprise Workers Relations Confederation joined with the TLSC and the Human Rights and Development Foundation to petition the United Nations Special Rapporteur on the Human Rights of Migrants for an urgent inquiry into a proposed nationality verification process for Burmese migrants in Thailand, with support from Global Union Federations, including Building and Wood Workers International and the International Federation of Chemical, Energy, Mine and General Workers' Unions. However, like much of Thai society, the majority of trade unionists continue to see foreign workers as outsiders who compete for Thai jobs, and Thai unions have been very slow to integrate migrant labour issues into their core union work. As a result, grassroots initiatives involving migrant workers remain very much the domain of NGOs like the Thai Labour Campaign and the MAP Foundation and grassroots migrant worker groups like the Mae Sot-based Yaung Chi Oo Workers Association and its rival, the Burma Labour Solidarity Organization.

Malaysia, the destination country with the largest, most established official labour migration programme in the region, has been a particular target for both NGO networks and the Global Union Federations. Partly as a result of this international pressure, the Malaysian Trades Union Congress (MTUC), which was previously hostile to migrant workers, revised its policy position. The MTUC has made efforts to reach out to migrant workers, appointing a full-time programme officer to deal with the foreign domestic worker question, seconding another staff member half time to deal with migrant workers in other sectors and providing legal support in selected cases concerning migrant workers through its industrial relations department.[4] Although support for these initiatives among member unions is patchy, as the public face of the Malaysian labour movement, the MTUC's pro-migrant worker rhetoric has had a significant impact in the public sphere.

There is some cooperation on migrant labour issues between the MTUC and the long-established migrant labour NGO, Tenaganita, which has been the principal force in both advocacy and service provision for migrant workers in Malaysia.[5] Grassroots organizing programmes have also been initiated by some national sectoral unions, particularly in the port, timber and plantation sectors. In the case of the Timber Employees Union Peninsular Malaysia, these initiatives have had significant support from Building and Wood Workers International, which encouraged the union to develop stronger links with its counterparts in sending countries and has funded a full-time organizing position for a Nepalese trade unionist to help recruit Nepalese workers in Malaysia. In a different kind of initiative, the Malaysian Liaison Council of Union Network International (UNI), another of the Global Union Federations, established a migrant labour help desk run by members of its 40 Malaysian affiliates to assist foreign workers who experience difficulties. The hotline, which initially targeted foreign domestic workers but then was expanded to cover other sectors, fields several hundred calls a month from documented and undocumented migrant workers. In an attempt to circumvent the government's policy on migrant labour unions, UNI has also sponsored the formation of an Indonesian-registered trade union called Unimig that organizes Indonesian workers in Malaysia.

Singapore's wealthy, service-oriented trade unions possibly recruit proportionally more temporary migrant workers than their counterparts in Malaysia. As all formal-sector workers are covered by Singaporean labour law, there is no basis on which companies may discriminate against temporary migrant workers; however, as in Malaysia, only unions in sectors with a concentrated migrant presence have migrant labour programmes.[6] In Singapore, semi- and unskilled foreign workers are concentrated in the shipping, building and construction, manufacturing and services sectors, including domestic work, hospitality and retail. The sectoral unions most active in organizing migrants are the Shipbuilding and Marine Engineering Employees' Union (SMEEU), the Singapore Organisation of Seamen (SOS) and the Building Construction and Timber Industries Employees' Union (BATU) – in the case of BATU and SOS, with strong encouragement from Building and Wood Workers International and the International Transport Federation respectively.

The National Trades Union Congress of Singapore (NTUC), which is closely aligned with the ruling People's Action Party, adopts a very positive public stance on documented migrant labour. In the face of rising concerns among Singaporeans about foreign workers, the NTUC has also moved to provide concrete services to foreign workers. The most significant of these measures has been the establishment in 2008 of a Migrant Workers' Centre, which provides services to foreign workers in crisis and conducts outreach programmes to assist foreign workers to integrate better into Singaporean society, such as English-language courses and cultural awareness seminars.[7] The NTUC also runs programmes to encourage employers to take a more responsible attitude towards their foreign employees. However, unlike the MTUC, whose migrant labour policy includes advocacy for the ratification of the International Convention on the Protection of the Rights of All Migrant Workers and Members of their Families, the NTUC follows the Singaporean government line, namely that ratification of the convention is not necessary as Singapore already has the capacity to ensure that foreign workers are protected.

Conclusion

When Southeast Asian migrant labour NGOs reached the limits of service provision, they followed the example of their Northeast Asian counterparts and began devoting more of their resources to organizing. It quickly became clear, however, that while informal groups and registered associations could provide support to migrant workers, their capacity to promote structural change was limited because they had at best peripheral status within national and international industrial relations forums and processes. In a region where no destination country permits migrant workers to form their own unions, this left them with little choice but to try to bring established trade unions to the table.

Local trade unions were in most cases at first reluctant to engage with an issue they saw to be at best peripheral and more often detrimental to the interests of local workers. This reluctance in part stemmed from prejudice, but also from the knowledge that it is logistically difficult to organize temporary migrant workers in any national context – let alone in ones characterized by punitive legal and industrial relations regimes and weak trade unions. Nevertheless, with encouragement and material support from the international labour movement, local trade unions in the region began to reposition themselves with regard to foreign workers, with peak union bodies in Thailand and Malaysia in particular having shifted a long way from the overt and hostile rhetoric they had favoured in the 1990s. Although accommodation of short-term foreign contract labour is necessarily far more difficult at the grassroots level, a number of significant examples of concrete programmes and strategies exist. In short, there has been a dramatic shift in the activist landscape, as trade unions begin to deal more seriously with the question of how to organize temporary foreign workers.

Even when combined with the ongoing campaigns of middle-class migrant labour NGO activists, it is important not to overstate trade unions' power to act as a foil to the industrial relations and immigration regimes that control and regulate foreign labour in any region, let alone in the developmentalist states of Southeast Asia. The national scale and sectoral biases of industrial relations mechanisms means that foreign workers' ability to join, and be represented by, a trade union is contingent on the intersection between their migration status and the location of their occupation in the labour market. The temporal limits of their contracts make them a poor investment for poorly resourced union organizers who are already overstretched. Nevertheless, the momentum generated by the confluence of NGO and international trade union interests, with its regional and global dimensions, has generated new ways to deal with the inherently transnational problem of temporary labour migration. Importantly for trade unions, it has also demonstrated their potential for better dealing with the other 'non-standard' workers who increasingly dominate all levels of the global production system. In doing so, it offers hope – albeit fragile – for the future of organized labour in Southeast Asia's developmentalist states.

Notes

1 This chapter was written as part of an Australian Research Council (ARC) Discovery Project entitled 'From Migrant to Worker: New Transnational Responses to Temporary Labour Migration in East and Southeast Asia' (DP0880081). The discussion presented here draws on Ford (2006b, 2007, 2010a) and on data collected in interviews conducted in the region between 2007 and 2010.
2 For a detailed discussion of these kinds of processes and their implications, see Ford (2010a).
3 See, for example, Fitzgerald and Hardy (2010) and Meardi (2008).
4 Another influential factor was a change in the MTUC's central leadership. The MTUC took much more sympathetic line on foreign workers after President Syed Shahir bin Syed Mohamud and General Secretary Rajasekaran were elected in 2005.
5 In recent years, several more NGOs have engaged with migrant labour issues in Malaysia. Most service-oriented and advocacy NGOs with an interest in migrant labour are affiliated with a national network of NGOs with an interest in migrant labour and refugee issues called the Migrant Working Group, formed in 2006. Besides Tenaganita, the network's members include the Women's Aid Organization, the National Human Rights Society, the Labour Resource Centre, Suara Rakyat Malaysia SUARAM, Amnesty International Malaysia, the Penang Office for Human Development, A Call to Serve, All Women's Action Society, Shelter, the Legal Aid Centre (Kuala Lumpur) and the Malaysian Bar Council. Other NGOs that have had contact with the network include Migrant Care and the National Office for Human Development.
6 Note, however, that not all companies allow the union to represent migrant workers in collective bargaining. Of the 45 companies in which the SMEEU has branches, only two have collective labour agreements that cover migrant workers. Both of these are foreign-owned companies, and both are in marine engineering, with relatively small workforces of around 500.
7 The centre was established in collaboration with the Singapore National Employers' Federation and with seed funding from the Singapore government.

References

Arnold, D. (2006) 'Capital expansion and migrant workers: flexible labor in the Thai–Burma border economy', unpublished Master's thesis, Mahidol University.

Avci, G. and C. McDonald. (2000) 'Chipping away at the fortress: unions, immigration and the transnational labour market', *International Migration* 38 (2): 191–207.

Bangko Sentral ng Pilipinas. (2010) *First Quarter 2010 OF Remittances Rise to US$4.3 Billion*; available at: www.bsp.gov.ph/publications/media.asp?id=2333 (accessed 3 July 2010).

Battistella, G. (2002) 'Unauthorised migrants as global workers in the ASEAN region', *Southeast Asian Studies* 40 (3): 350–71.

Fitzgerald, I. and J. Hardy (2010) '"Thinking outside the box"? Trade union organizing strategies and Polish migrant workers in the United Kingdom', *British Journal of Industrial Relations* 48 (1): 131–50.

Ford, M. (2006a) 'After Nunukan: the regulation of Indonesian migration to Malaysia', in A. Kaur and I. Metcalfe (eds) *Divided We Move: Mobility, Labour Migration and Border Controls in Asia*, New York: Palgrave Macmillan.

——(2006b) 'Migrant labor NGOs and trade unions: a partnership in progress?' *Asian and Pacific Migration Journal* 15 (3): 299–318.

——(2007) 'Advocacy responses to irregular labor migration in ASEAN: the cases of Malaysia and Thailand', Migrant Forum in Asia and the South East Asian Committee for Advocacy.

——(2010a) 'Constructing legality: the management of irregular labour migration in Thailand and Malaysia', in M. v.d. Linden (ed.) *Labour History Beyond Borders: Concepts and Explorations*, Leipzig: Akademische Verlagsanstalt.

——(2010b) 'Laboring practices: Southeast Asia', in S. Joseph (ed.) *Encyclopedia of Women and Islamic Cultures*, Amsterdam: Brill Online.

Ford, M. and N. Piper. (2007) 'Southern sites of female agency: informal regimes and female migrant labour activism in East and Southeast Asia', in J. Hobson and L. Seabrooke (eds) *Everyday Politics of the World Economy*, Cambridge: Cambridge University Press.

Haus, L. (1995) 'Openings in the wall: transnational migrants, labor unions, and US immigration policy', *International Organization* 49 (2): 285–313.

Immigration Department of Malaysia. (2007) *Semi-skilled and Unskilled Foreign Workers*; available at: www.imi.gov.my/eng/perkhidmatan/im_separa.asp (accessed 16 February 2007).

Kanapathy, Vijayakumari (2004) 'Country report: Malaysia: international migration and labour market developments in Asia: economic recovery, the labour market and migrant workers in Malaysia', paper presented at Workshop on International Migration and Labour Markets in Asia, Tokyo, 5–6 February.

Martin, P., M. Abella and C. Kuptsch. (2006) *Managing Labor Migration in the Twenty-First Century*, New Haven, CT: Yale University Press.

Meardi, G. (2008) 'Capital mobility, labour mobility, union immobility? Trade unions facing multi-nationals and migration in the EU', paper presented to the First Forum of the International Sociological Association, Barcelona, 5–8 September.

Nissen, B. and G. Grenier (2001) 'Union responses to mass immigration: the case of Miami, USA', *Antipode* 33 (3): 567–92.

Pillai, P. (1999) 'The Malaysian state's response to migration', *Sojourn* 14 (1): 178–97.

Teicher, J., Chandra Shah, and G. Griffin. (2002) 'Australian immigration: the triumph of economics over prejudice?' *International Journal of Manpower* 23 (3): 209–36.

Turner, D. (2005) 'Malaysia's regime of labour control and the attempted transition to a knowledge-based economy: the problematic role of migrant labour', *Review of Indonesian and Malaysian Affairs* 39 (1): 108–31.

20

TRADE POLICY IN SOUTHEAST ASIA

Politics, domestic interests and the forging of new accommodations in the regional and global economy

Helen E.S. Nesadurai

Introduction

Despite the importance of foreign trade to the growth performance of Southeast Asian countries, trade policy in the region has displayed a high degree of ambivalence between openness and protectionism even from the mid-1980s when most Southeast Asian governments embarked on what had then seemed a decisive shift towards economic openness. In fact, there appears to be some sort of dynamic equilibrium between trade liberalization and trade protectionism. This puzzle is part of broader political economy debates that query why reformers across much of Southeast Asia have found it difficult to overturn interventionist economic and trade policies, as well as the patronage-based networks so prevalent in the region, in favour of market-based economic systems and liberal trade policies. This chapter addresses this debate by examining two interlinked dimensions of trade policy: (a) the trade orientation of the national economy, or the degree to which the economy is formally open to exports and imports of goods and services as well as to investment given the close links between investment and trade; and (b) the institutional forms through which trade cooperation with other countries is conducted, whether through multilateral, regional or bilateral arrangements.

Adoption of protectionist trade policies in the midst of official liberalization rhetoric has been interpreted in much of the economics literature as policymakers and rulers simply lacking the political will to initiate liberal trade policies that will help enhance the efficiency of the economy and strengthen its growth prospects. A number of political economy studies have, however, attempted to unpack the notion of 'lack of political will' to show how the twists and turns of *domestic politics*, rather than economic structure alone, influence the trade policy choices of governments. The extent to which trade liberalization is politically possible in Southeast Asia is often shaped by protectionist demands from domestic business interests, sometimes acting through their respective business associations. More influential have been those corporate players closely linked to ruling elites through patronage networks or coalitions; politicians seek to favour these interests in order to maintain these mutually beneficial relationships (Islam and Chowdhury 2000). In other instances, constraints on how far liberalization can go are imposed by nationalist concerns with safeguarding domestic industries and firms, especially those regarded as strategic for the country. A number of scholars have suggested, however, that growing competitive pressures arising from a globalizing world economy will increasingly push policymakers to dismantle interventionist trade and economic policies and other institutional structures that had facilitated state direction of domestic economic activity (Maswood 2002: 32).

Yet the empirical evidence from Southeast Asia from the 1990s and into the first decade of the twenty-first century points to the co-existence of liberal and protectionist or interventionist trade policies. Governments do not necessarily move towards comprehensive trade liberalization in the face of market pressure or in accordance with the policy advice of international organizations like the World Bank.[1] While analyses of the determinants of liberal versus protectionist trade policies are helpful, the more salient question is not why trade liberalization *or* trade protectionism prevails but how the two are interrelated within the domestic political economy and in relation to the global market. The rest of this chapter addresses this issue, beginning with a brief discussion of the key features of trade policy in the region.

Trade policy in Southeast Asia: trade orientation and trade cooperation arrangements

Despite the historical importance of trade to Southeast Asia, trade policy in the region has never been unequivocally liberal in the post-colonial period. More often than not, a mixed trade policy regime has prevailed as governments used tariffs and other economic instruments to attain various national development goals. For much of the 1960s and 1970s, the resource-rich Southeast Asian economies relied on primary commodity exports to drive economic growth. But these states also adopted an import-substitution industrialization (ISI) strategy in line with the development policy wisdom of international institutions such as the World Bank at that time. However, the domestic industries established behind tariff walls under the ISI strategy often had to be supported by the wealth generated from primary commodity earnings, which cushioned the losses that inefficient domestic industries, particularly state-owned enterprises, were soon registering (Islam and Chowdhury 2000: 30). These loss-making domestic industries needed to be supported for a variety of political reasons, for instance to accommodate ethnic affirmative action policies such as in Malaysia, nationalist priorities in Indonesia and, more generally, the 'patrimonial and clientelistic links' between government and business that soon became pervasive in Southeast Asian states such as Malaysia, Indonesia, Thailand and the Philippines (MacIntyre 1994: 7).

The compensatory mechanism provided by primary commodity export earnings meant that economic reforms, including trade liberalization, could be postponed. It was only when primary commodity prices plummeted between 1982 and 1986 and Southeast Asian economies entered into recession that their governments began to seriously consider economic reforms (Islam and Chowdhury 2000: 30). While Singapore had already adopted an export-oriented industrialization (EOI) strategy since independence in 1965 and Malaysia had pursued a limited EOI strategy through free trade zones from 1970, the switch to EOI across Southeast Asia occurred in the mid- to late 1980s. By deregulating and opening up their economies, these governments sought to increase the competitiveness of their respective economies and restore growth. However, these same governments also chose to maintain protective tariff and non-tariff barriers to shield a range of domestic industries in both manufacturing and services. In fact, these two seemingly opposing dimensions of trade policy are inextricably linked. The booming performance of many liberalized manufacturing sectors had allowed governments across the region to offset, and therefore tolerate, the inefficiencies generated by other protected sectors in manufacturing as well as in services (Jayasuriya 2003: 202). Although the 1997–8 Asian financial crisis led to further liberalization of trade policy, protectionist arrangements continue as well.

Trade cooperation: the lure of preferential arrangements

The mid-1980s economic reforms common across much of Southeast Asia were driven by the unilateral policy decisions of national governments prompted by economic crisis (Islam and Chowdhury 2000: 30). Even though a number of reform programmes since then would continue to be driven by unilateral actions, Southeast Asian governments also committed themselves to multilateral liberalization through the GATT and later the WTO (Sally 2004). Multilateral liberalization, it was felt, would enhance global market access for Southeast Asian exports. However, their governments were unwilling to accept some of the new WTO agenda items, notably to liberalize investment rules, open up government procurement to foreign investors, and introduce competition policy; they also made limited offers on services liberalization. With no new global trade agreement concluded since the 1996 WTO Ministerial Meeting in Singapore, Southeast Asian states were left with unilateral action and preferential trade liberalization negotiated amongst a subset of states as the two main vehicles for securing market access abroad.

In fact, the Southeast Asian governments had already embarked on a preferential regional free trade agreement through the Association of Southeast Asian Nations (ASEAN) in 1992. They saw the ASEAN Free Trade Area (AFTA) as the instrument that would help their individually small states attract foreign direct investment (FDI) amidst the growing competition for foreign capital posed especially by China and other regional markets. These governments made ambitious liberalization commitments in AFTA unlike their more cautious stance in APEC (with Singapore being the exception).[2] Yet implementation problems later emerged when these very same governments reneged on these commitments as they sought to exclude or delay for varying periods of time politically important domestic sectors from regional liberalization, notably petrochemicals, agricultural commodities including rice, and automobiles (Nesadurai 2003a: 128–70). In 2003, following completion of the first phase of AFTA, ASEAN embarked on the ASEAN Economic Community project (AEC) with the aim of creating a single, integrated Southeast Asian market and production space by 2020. The AEC is also expected to encounter implementation problems as regional integration will require governments to address the politically more difficult 'beyond the border barriers' posed by domestic regulations and other non-tariff barriers (NTBs).[3]

Aside from regional liberalization arrangements such as AFTA and the AEC and to a lesser extent APEC, Southeast Asian states like Singapore, Thailand and Malaysia have also turned to negotiating other forms of preferential trading arrangements (PTAs), usually involving two states (bilateralism) or a group of states such as the Trans-Pacific Partnership (TPP) Agreement that involve nine economies.[4] Singapore and Thailand have been the most active proponents of bilateral PTAs, having respectively concluded ten and six agreements with other states or with other regional groupings like EFTA and BIMSTEC (Ravenhill 2009: 232–3). Malaysia has thus far concluded agreements with Japan and Pakistan and is negotiating bilateral agreements with five other states, including the US (Hoadley 2007; MATRADE 2010). The remaining Southeast Asian states have been far less active in negotiating bilateral PTAs (Ravenhill 2009: 232–3).

Bilateral arrangements have also involved cooperation on trade liberalization between ASEAN as a single bloc and a number of third countries. Thus far, five such agreements have been finalized, namely with China, India, South Korea, Japan and the Australia–New Zealand bloc.[5] The United States opted to negotiate bilateral free trade agreements (FTAs) with individual ASEAN countries through the Enterprise for ASEAN Initiative (EAI) because Washington anticipated difficulties in concluding a single, ASEAN-wide FTA that would be acceptable to the US Congress and to important US business groups. The first of such agreements was concluded with Singapore in 2003 while negotiations with Thailand and Malaysia have stalled over pharmaceuticals and domestic procurement respectively.

However, many of these new preferential trading arrangements, both regional ones like those under ASEAN and the various bilateral arrangements concluded thus far, tend to accommodate trade protection in the form of 'carve-outs' from liberalization in some sectors even while emphasizing the reduction of trade barriers in other sectors. Even the most 'WTO-plus' of these bilateral PTAs allow for pick-and-mix liberalization agendas that exclude politically sensitive sectors (Ravenhill 2009). Similarly, AFTA accommodates domestic political and economic sensitivities through its embrace of political negotiations and compromises in place of pre-determined rules and sanctions to drive implementation. Moreover, AFTA did not impose uniform liberalization schedules for individual products but allowed these to be determined unilaterally by member governments, in effect a form of variable geometry approach to regional liberalization that saw traders facing multiple bilateral PTAs rather than a single regional FTA (Ravenhill 2009: 226). The AEC has also adopted the principle of variable geometry through the 'ASEAN minus X' implementation formula where smaller subsets of ASEAN governments proceed to implement their commitments in particular areas of cooperation even if other members are unable to begin just yet.

In short, the Southeast Asian preference for mixed trade regimes that accommodate both trade liberalization and protection has also been worked into the new forms of preferential trade cooperation negotiated both amongst the Southeast Asian countries and between them and extra-regional states. What accounts for these trends in trade policy in Southeast Asia?

Patronage coalitions and trade policy in Southeast Asia

Although the specific contours of domestic state–society relations differ across Southeast Asia with its very diverse political systems and societies, two features common to the region are the central role played by the economy in politics and the close government–business relations embedded within patronage networks that shape a good many economic policy choices, including trade policy. Managed properly, the economy delivers economic prosperity to the country and its people at large, while it also helps governments achieve nationalist priorities as well as domestic distributive agendas. In internally divided societies that are characteristic of Southeast Asia, distribution matters, although the distributive imperative does not always follow income/wealth disparities but can be complicated by calculations based on affective criteria such as ethnicity. By channelling economic opportunities to selected domestic social groups through interventionist action rather than market forces, political elites aim to reduce the extent to which inter-group disparities and grievances undermine political order while shoring up their political legitimacy amongst groups whose support elites regard as vital. Similarly, nationalist priorities, usually aimed at privileging domestic over foreign businesses for strategic and security reasons or for reasons of national pride, rely on interventionist rather than market-based policies.

While trade policy in the region has, to some extent, been shaped by these nationalist and distributive concerns, the extensive patronage networks in the region mean that political elites also design economic policies to serve their own interests and those of allies or 'clients', usually domestic business elites. Although this does not mean that competitiveness concerns have not mattered in Southeast Asia, the point is simply that ruling elites have had to balance such imperatives with the need to ensure that selected groups, firms and individuals are able to secure private gains. The precise nature of trade policy choices will then depend on the composition of these dominant coalitions in the different Southeast Asian countries and how different ruling elites respond to competing demands from their key allies even as they respond to other, domestic priorities and external pressures from the global economy.

The relationship between state and business, although a central element in the political economy of Southeast Asia, differs across different states. In Singapore, for instance, even though foreign investors and state capital have traditionally been key sources of growth in the Singapore political economy, from the late 1980s domestic private capital, especially in services like banking and finance, became important not only to the growth prospects of the island economy: it was also co-opted into the ruling network of political/bureaucratic elites and state capital that dominated economic policymaking and governance in Singapore (Rodan 1993; Yeung 1999; Nesadurai 2003a: 116–18). In Indonesia, domestic capital, particularly ethnic Chinese capital, had always been an important part of the Indonesian political economy. However, the interests of state capital and indigenous Indonesian business interests were increasingly accommodated from the 1980s and 1990s as the government sought to minimize resentment against the ethnic Chinese conglomerates that had long enjoyed a close relationship with politically influential elites, including the military and then President Suharto (Schwarz 1999; Rosser 2003). In Malaysia, despite the crucial role of foreign capital in driving economic growth, the interests of domestic corporations became important to the extent that these are vital to the 'ethnic Malay capitalist project' and to the broader Malaysian economic nationalism championed by former Prime Minister Mahathir (Khoo 1995, 2000). This meant that the choice of economic policy was shaped by their potential impact on particular ethnic Malay corporate interests as well as the broader group interests of ethnic Malays. Although a limited number of non-Malay business interests would also be privileged in the interests of a broader Malaysian economic nationalism, the political legitimacy of the ruling coalition that had governed the country since independence in 1959 was, nevertheless, centred on securing and advancing ethnic Malay rights and special privileges in a multi-ethnic Malaysia (Lee and Nesadurai 2010).

To be sure, strong political leadership may be able to drive policy independently of vested interests. However, even leaders with a high degree of executive power are themselves located within particular domestic social and political contexts that circumscribe to different degrees their capacity and willingness to make policy choices that might undermine their private interests or the interests of groups linked to the political elite. More often than not, trade policy choices emerge out of the accommodations that political elites have had to forge with key business allies although strong leaders may stand a better chance of initiating policies that go against clientelist interests. Such accommodative processes also mean that competitive pressures on the domestic economy will not always result in a comprehensive or unequivocal policy response of liberalization. Political leaders are likely to try and find ways of offsetting the resulting losses faced by previously sheltered sectors or firms due to trade reform. Adept politicians supported by a capable state apparatus may be able to devise new forms of protectionism or develop new economic opportunities for their core support base even as they respond to external pressures.

Political leadership, vested interests and trade policy in Southeast Asia

Across Southeast Asia, economic recession was responsible for the initial set of unilateral reform measures adopted in the mid-1980s. Because the economic recession also worsened political cleavages within dominant coalitions and in broader domestic society, political leaders discovered considerable political will to embark on economic reforms, including trade liberalization.

Although protectionist pressures were present, these were muted both by the severity of the recession and by the capacity of the political leadership in the different countries either to deflect these protectionist demands or to rework domestic bargains in the ways outlined above.

The twin influence of crisis and strong political leadership is exemplified by the Philippines experience with trade liberalization, but only in the decade following the 1986 toppling of Philippine dictator Ferdinand Marcos. The severity of the mid-1980s crisis enabled the post-Marcos Administration of President Cory Aquino to push through a slew of economic and trade reforms in the late 1980s against opposition even from within her Administration, including from her Trade and Industry Secretary, Jose Concepcion, who was also a prominent business leader (Kraft 2007: 119–24). However, the reforms galvanized business interests opposed to trade liberalization to organize themselves as the Federation of Philippine Industries (FPI). Many of these business actors had emerged out of the ISI policy of the 1970s and had either developed strong links to political elites or were themselves part of the political elite that had diversified into business. They were not averse to using their political influence to shape trade policy. Although strong leadership would also help Aquino's successor, Fidel Ramos, initiate further trade reforms in the 1990s, the growing influence of protectionist business interests compelled the Ramos Administration to engage in 'traditional pork-barrel politics' – domestic accommodations with members of the Philippine political/business elite – to get reforms accepted (Kraft 2007: 104). Only in sectors dominated by business interests in favour of reforms could trade liberalization continue unhindered (Kraft 2007: 120–6).

The 1997–8 Asian financial crisis failed to usher in a new round of reforms in the Philippines, however. For one, the crisis was not as severe in the Philippines as in other parts of East Asia, which reduced pressure on the leadership to continue with economic reforms (Montes 1999). For another, President Joseph Estrada who presided over the country following his electoral win in 1998 was unable to exercise the kind of strong political leadership previously displayed by Presidents Aquino and Ramos to deal with protectionist demands now coming not only from political and business elites but also from non-elite social groups concerned about the effects of previous liberalization programmes on domestic unemployment, and from nationalists and leftists unhappy with the spectre of foreign control of the economy. Estrada's support base in the urban and rural poor coupled with the fragile legitimacy of his rule led the government to adopt populist policies and review tariff reductions, including those to which the Philippines had earlier committed under AFTA and the WTO. This pattern would continue during the tenure of Estrada's successor, Gloria Arroyo (Kraft 2007).

Clearly, a weak state and an equally weak political leadership is unable to rise above entrenched domestic interests, particularly those that are part of powerful politics–business coalitions in the country. Similarly in Indonesia, economic and trade policy reforms continue to be hostage to the political and business interests that are linked to the country's ruling elite. A recent development in the country illustrates the power wielded by these groups over policy and indeed over the future of reformist technocrats in government. The need to assuage powerful business and political elites who are part of his multi-party ruling coalition reportedly prompted President Yudhoyono in 2010 to transfer his reformist minister of finance to a World Bank post; the far-reaching reforms initiated by Sri Mulyani Indrawati had allegedly upset powerful business leaders, politicians and senior bureaucrats whose support the President could not afford to lose (*Jakarta Post*, 6 May 2010).

In Malaysia, the strong leadership exercised by Prime Minister Mahathir also helped push through a package of economic reforms in response to the mid-1980s economic crisis. Mahathir also adopted a set of new policies through which wealth and rents could be transferred to favoured individuals and firms, especially ethnic Malay business interests. Privatization, a new round of ISI in the heavy industries sector, services such as banking, finance and tele-communications, as well as the non-tradables sectors, notably construction, would help the political elite build coalitions with new groups in domestic society, principally an emerging class of ethnic Malay *private* business actors beholden to the dominant Malay political party, UMNO (United Malays National Organization) in the ruling Barison Nasional (National Front) coali-tion of political parties. A limited number of Malaysian–Chinese and Malaysian–Indian business leaders aligned with the ruling elite also benefited from these new policies. Since the late 1980s, these business interests constituted a valuable new support base for ruling politicians, often contributing funds for party and parliamentary elections (Gomez 1996). These new Malaysian conglomerates were also privileged because they were a key part of Prime Minister Mahathir's economic nationalist agenda aimed at nurturing internationally competitive Malaysian corporations.

In Malaysia, politics–business links have been permeated by ethnicity dynamics because the ruling government in multi-ethnic Malaysia had pledged to develop an ethnic Malay business class to offset perceived ethnic Chinese dominance of the economy following the 1969 race riots. This was a key goal of Malaysia's New Economic Policy (NEP) adopted in 1971 that also provided privileged access to employment, credit, education, scholarships, business and corporate ownership to ethnic Malays and other citizens deemed to be part of the *Bumiputera* (indigenous) category (Tori 1997: 212). The NEP was designed to also ensure that Malay political dom-inance, which had seemed in danger of being eroded by Chinese electoral gains in 1969, would be maintained through the control of economic resources by the Malay-dominated ruling elite and private Malay business interests. Although the NEP was replaced in 1990 with the National Development Policy and in 2010 by the New Economic Model, the goal of creating a Malay business class remains important for ruling Malay/UMNO politicians although it does not go uncontested by the Chinese and Indian ethnic minorities (Lee and Nesadurai 2010).

The political importance to the ruling elite in Malaysia of these new business allies would limit the extent to which trade reform could be undertaken in services and non-tradeables like construction where these groups dominated; a more open trade and investment regime could, however, operate in parts of the manufacturing sector where these corporations were less involved. Although the 1997–8 Asian financial crisis ushered in tariff reforms in sectors like automotive components as well as banking and finance, others like automobiles and govern-ment procurement would remain sacrosanct for a considerable period of time despite displaying losses and inefficiencies. Malaysia is only now considering a review of its government procure-ment policy in order to make progress on bilateral FTA talks with the US and to facilitate its participation in the Trans-Pacific Partnership negotiations. Improving relations with the US is a key goal of the current Prime Minister, Najib Tun Razak. However, the government has been careful to stress that the review would find ways to increase foreign participation in government procurement without marginalizing domestic, especially Malay/*Bumiputera* interests (*New Straits Times*, 1 May 2010).

How will Malaysian political elites work out a bargain that will be acceptable to both domestic groups and elite interests on the one hand and key foreign governments and foreign business interests on the other hand in a sector such as government procurement that has been central to the politics of patronage in Malaysia? The broader question for trade politics in Southeast Asia is how ruling elites can safeguard domestic political priorities and the interests of politically important domestic business interests that require protection from competition if, as some scholars argue, the structural logic of globalization means that global market competition makes neoliberal reforms inevitable. However, it should be noted that politically important domestic business interests are not always looking for protection of the domestic market. It all depends on their location within the domestic, regional and global market structures. In many cases, these businesses may be operating in export-oriented sectors that benefit from more open trade policies, or they may have outgrown an initial focus on the domestic market and are looking towards regional or global markets. Nevertheless, the point to consider is how policy-makers secure domestic interests and priorities if these run counter to the structural logic of globalization. The next section discusses how this structural logic overlooks the possibilities of *collective* agency that allow actors, even small developing states, to intervene in the global economy through inter-state cooperation so that politically valuable domestic economic arrangements, even if uncompetitive, can be sustained.

Trade cooperation: accommodating domestic interests

Economic cooperation arrangements are increasingly subject to bargaining by participating governments seeking accommodations on trade policy to ensure that their drive to gain market access abroad does not unduly undermine crucial national priorities and the interests of politically important domestic groups, including those of elite business interests. Governments, in fact, have tried to use external cooperation to help them delay or even avoid painful domestic adjustments through careful design of these agreements. In Southeast Asia, such dynamics have been especially evident in three areas: AFTA, ASEAN cooperation on investment and services, and the decade-old turn to bilateral PTAs.

Regional trade liberalization and domestic interests

The Southeast Asian governments in 1992 initiated AFTA to help them prevent foreign investment diversion from their economies. They planned to achieve this by reducing intra-regional tariffs and other internal barriers to the regional movement of goods and later services, thereby creating a single large geographical space (the regional free trade area) to which investors would consider (re)locating production. Although prompted by growing investor interest in large regional markets such as NAFTA and the Single European Market, their immediate concern was neighbouring China, a huge emerging economy with considerable wealth-generating potential that the Southeast Asian governments regarded as their main competitor for investments (Nesadurai 2003a: 78–98).

While the collaborative regional strategy made sense given global capital's 'regional logic', domestic reforms that would have made their respective economies more open to FDI would also have been an appropriate response that could have supplemented regional market creation. However, political elites were not prepared at that time either to offer investors additional investment incentives or to deregulate their respective economies to allow foreign investors more freedom in the domestic market. Despite the reforms of the mid-1980s, many Southeast Asian states, including Singapore, continued to maintain domestic restrictions on the operations of foreign investors. These ranged from equity limits to employment conditions, land owner-ship restrictions, performance conditions, and restrictions on which sectors' foreign investors could freely enter (Nesadurai 2003a: 78–98). Doing away with these regulations would have undermined both nationalist aspirations to nurture home-grown businesses and the bargains ruling elites had already forged with politically important domestic businesses. Instead, political elites hoped that providing investors with a large regional space in which to locate transnational production networks would be enough to keep foreign investors interested in Southeast Asia and, by extension, in their individual countries.

Perhaps that would have been sufficient if intra-regional liberalization had indeed been implemented as scheduled. Instead, a number of governments reneged on their original AFTA commitments in the mid-1990s, beginning with Indonesia backtracking on its earlier liberalization commitments. Indonesia raised tariffs on selected petrochemical products without any prior warning to its AFTA partners. It also unilaterally withdrew a number of agricultural items (cloves, wheat and sugar) from regional liberalization. The domestic business firms that operated in these sectors, all linked to friends and family of then Indonesian President Suharto or those that were linked to the powerful Indonesian armed forces, were able to get Indonesia's initial liberalization commitments overturned (Nesadurai 2003a: 128–50).

These actions reflect the unpredictable nature of policymaking in a country where two elite coalitions have competed with each other over how the economy is governed – the liberal technocrats comprising bureaucrats and ministers who subscribed to neoclassical economic and trade policy and the economic nationalists who believed in interventionist policies to chart Indonesia's national development and to help nurture indigenous Indonesian (*pribumi*) businesses to compete with the more successful Indonesian–Chinese conglomerates (Rosser 2003). Indonesian businesses were also able to influence policy, particularly through their links with Suharto and his family or the military. Ethnic Chinese corporate leaders also exercised a degree of influence over economic policy through their connection with Suharto. They were especially reliant on Suharto's patronage and his protection to safeguard their interests in a country where the ethnic Chinese were treated with suspicion; in return, they provided the funds Suharto needed for his favoured projects. The technocrats who had charted the 1980s reforms and who saw AFTA as a useful adjunct to domestic reforms were replaced in 1993 by nationalist-oriented policymakers who were opposed to regional liberalization for fear it would undermine domestic business interests and cause domestic dislocations for groups like farmers. The foremost of these nationalists were Ginandjar Kartasasmita and B.J. Habibie, who went on to become Indonesian President following Suharto's downfall in 1998. In fact, the ascendance of the nationalists in government had been the result of the upheavals caused by the relatively rapid pace and scope of the 1980s reforms initiated by the liberal technocrats (Schwarz 1999: 49–97).

Although governments in Southeast Asia did not always concede to the growing domestic clamour for protection from regional liberalization, they capitulated when politically influential firms or politically important sectors were involved. For instance, Malaysian trade officials withdrew automobiles from AFTA disciplines soon after the Asian financial crisis on the express instructions of Prime Minister Mahathir to protect the national car project, which served as the flagship for Mahathir's heavy industries programme and his economic nationalist agenda. In contrast, demands from automotive components manufacturers were not entertained, even though these demands predominantly came from ethnic Malay producers who had been nurtured under the country's Vendor Development Programme (Nesadurai 2003a: 146–50). For the national car company, Proton, to survive and become a competitive international player, it needed to source competitively priced high-quality automotive components from the international market rather than from the high-cost domestic component producers in the vendor programme as in the past. The nationalist priorities of a powerful political leader like Mahathir trumped even ethnic distributive priorities in this case.

Implementation problems such as these led to new accommodations among the members of ASEAN as they sought to prevent the collapse of AFTA. The resulting compromise involved the downward revision of original liberalization targets while new rules were adopted to make regional liberalization more transparent and predictable (Nesadurai 2003a: 158–70). By revising AFTA targets downwards, affected governments could, for an extended period, safeguard the livelihood of politically important non–elite constituencies, for instance rice farmers in Indonesia, Malaysia and the Philippines, who would have been unduly affected by cheaper rice imports, particularly from Thailand. They were also able to reassure politically influential domestic corporate players who had found the original liberalization schedule threatening. In turn, this compromise helped to sustain elite coalitions in these countries and their grip on domestic political power. Countries like Thailand that had lost in the short run from these compromises only gained over the longer run from the general commitment to continue with AFTA and from the new, stricter rules that also signalled to investors that regional liberalization remained on track.

The preference for political solutions to regional implementation problems is also evident in the ASEAN Economic Community (AEC) project initiated in 2003 and driven by the same FDI logic that drove regional market creation under AFTA. Leaders have supported flexible implementation in this project through the 'ASEAN minus X' principle, they have eschewed legalistic, third-party, non-discretionary implementation mechanisms in favour of mechanisms for consultation and mediation, they have retained a strong role for ASEAN officials in dispute settlement and they have ignored the potential of sanctions to address implementation problems (Hsu 2008: 75–8). By adopting a political approach to regional integration, ruling elites are accorded some breathing space should they need to accommodate nationally determined priorities and secure politically important business interests.

Nurturing domestic businesses: ASEAN and developmental regionalism

The Southeast Asian governments have also used regional cooperation more actively to nurture local entrepreneurs and firms by designing the 1998 ASEAN Investment Area (AIA) scheme to offer market access and national treatment privileges to ASEAN investors (both state and domestic private investors) ten years ahead of non-ASEAN investors, an approach to regional cooperation that I have elsewhere termed 'development regionalism' (Nesadurai 2003b). The partial protection accorded to domestic investors by the temporary investment privileges were expected to help these businesses grow and become globally competitive through initially exploiting scale economies and first-mover advantages in the larger ASEAN market.[6]

The developmental approach to regional investment liberalization had been spearheaded by Malaysian and Indonesian concerns in the mid-1990s that domestic/national firms would not be able to survive global competition should a liberal global investment regime be adopted that embraced the principles of national treatment and freedom of operation worldwide for all foreign investors. APEC, the WTO and the OECD had by this time already discussed the value of having just such a global regime. Although the OECD's Multilateral Agreement on Investment later failed, Southeast Asian governments believed that such a liberal FDI regime would come sooner rather than later and that they had to act fast to give domestic firms a chance to expand and exploit business opportunities in the ASEAN regional market before transnational corporations were given that privilege (Nesadurai 2003b). As already noted, foreign investors continued to face investment restrictions in Southeast Asia during the 1990s, especially in services where fairly restrictive FDI conditions prevailed. However, global recessionary pressures in 2001 meant that this 'developmental' approach to regional investment liberalization had to be temporarily overturned. Later, the 2008 ASEAN Comprehensive Investment Agreement (ACIA) accorded permanent national treatment and market access privileges to ASEAN-based *foreign* investors as well (AEM 2008). With Southeast Asian governments preoccupied with ensuring high growth rates, the 'FDI' logic of regionalism triumphed over its developmental logic.

However, what is of interest to this discussion is how regional investment liberalization was originally designed to allow Southeast Asian governments the space to secure national priorities and domestic business interests. A similar developmental logic operates in the Southeast Asian approach to services liberalization, which privileges regional liberalization before multilateral efforts (Hamanaka 2009). State-linked firms and politically important domestic private interests are important players in a range of service sectors, particularly telecommunications and banking and finance. For instance, despite the adoption of domestic reforms in its financial sector following the Asian financial crisis, Malaysia continues to restrict foreign participation in financial services both to increase the share of *Bumiputera*/Malay equity in this sector and, more generally, to enhance the growth of domestic providers of financial services (Sivalingam 2008: 398). Despite the influence of external market pressures, where governments are able to do so they continue to maintain illiberal arrangements for reasons of domestic expediency.

Preferential trading arrangements: the lure of à la carte bilateralism

Bilateral PTAs, as already noted, are fast becoming an instrument of trade cooperation in Southeast Asia. The stalling of multilateral liberalization at the WTO and the travails of ASEAN regional liberalization explain why Singapore and later Thailand turned to negotiating bilateral PTAs with a variety of extra-regional countries. Despite other motivations such as security, diplomatic status and foreign policy leverage, broadening market access for a country's exports and attracting foreign investors rank among the foremost reasons as to why governments invest considerable time and resources into negotiating bilateral PTAs (Hoadley 2007). Initially resistant to this trend, Malaysia, like other Southeast Asian countries, has also jumped on the bilateral bandwagon to ensure that its firms and exports are not disadvantaged in economies that have already concluded preferential arrangements with other partners, lending support to the idea of bilateral PTAs catalysing a 'domino' cascade of yet more bilateral PTAs.[7] A key feature of the new bilateralism is its tolerance of exclusions and selective rather than comprehensive liberalization agendas, thus allowing for 'liberalization without political pain' (Ravenhill 2003: 307).

For instance, Thailand's FTAs have favoured only selected industrial sectors such as electronics and information technology while maintaining protection in sectors in which domestic business interests dominate, such as textiles and clothing, finance and services. Likewise, Malaysia has resisted removing the protection accorded to the national car industry, other heavy industries and in selected service sectors while refusing to consider removing remaining FDI restrictions especially in services and allowing foreign companies access to government procurement contracts. Even Singapore managed to avoid conceding too much to US, Australian and New Zealand demands to remove interventionist practices in government procurement, to liberalize financial and other services and to reduce the extensive presence of government-linked corporations in the Singapore economy (Hoadley 2007). Clearly, these bilateral PTAs have not been employed to lock in domestic reforms that would dismantle illiberal domestic economic arrangements (Ravenhill 2003, 2009; Hoadley 2007).

In fact, such FTAs may actually *help maintain* the accommodative arrangements political elites have forged with domestic business elites while at the same time gaining market access abroad. Although major markets like the US and the EU may not be willing to tolerate the continuation of arrangements that could disadvantage American and European firms, an increasing number of 'permissive' FTAs negotiated with small non-traditional trading partners may still offer benefits to Southeast Asian countries if they help to diversify markets and develop new economic relationships worldwide. At the very least, bilateral PTAs offer some space for domestic political elites to rework domestic bargains while adjustments are made at a more measured pace. On the other hand, permissive PTAs could allow these illiberal arrangements to persist with changes made only at the margin provided there are no serious external economic or diplomatic pressures that compel more far-reaching domestic reforms. It is also easier to negotiate such tailor-made deals bilaterally, especially with countries that are not major powers, rather than multilaterally or even regionally. Because of the difficulties in accommodating the clashing domestic interests of a large group of countries, regional liberalization in settings with more than a handful of negotiating partners like ASEAN Plus Three and East Asia has not been possible while APEC's efforts in trade liberalization have been unsatisfactory. The stalemate at the WTO may have opened up space in the global political economy that Southeast Asian (and other) governments have exploited to develop new forms of trade cooperation arrangements that are more accommodating of domestic interests.

Conclusion: implications of Southeast Asia's elite accommodations

Trade policy in Southeast Asian countries has displayed a high degree of ambivalence, incorporating elements of trade liberalization and trade protectionism in some form of dynamic, accommodative equilibrium. Similar accommodations have also been evident in these countries' preferential trading arrangements, including regional liberalization schemes. Far from using these preferential arrangements, particularly the bilateral PTAs, to leverage domestic economic reforms, bilateral PTAs that exclude sensitive sectors and adopt a sectoral rather than comprehensive approach to trade liberalization are helping to sustain domestic patronage and other illiberal politico-economic arrangements in Southeast Asia. What often seems like policymakers and rulers lacking the political will to initiate and sustain liberal trade policies that will help place the economy on a sound footing is, in fact, the outcome of rational *political* calculations that go beyond purely economic imperatives.

However, such strategies are not without their costs. The accommodations that political elites have had to make in the past have generally excluded non-elite social groups like labour who have not enjoyed the same degree of access to political power as business and other elite actors (Deyo 1998). Not only are business actors valuable partners in the drive for growth and industrial development, they are also essential players in the patronage networks linked to political elites. Governments in many parts of Southeast Asia have in the past suppressed labour in order to deliver low-wage and docile workers for industrialization. These practices continue to date with labour groups not consulted on many issues that directly affect their well-being, including trade agreements (ATUC n.d.). The repercussions of such practices are clearly seen in Indonesia, where past exclusion of labour groups from elite bargains over economic and trade policy has made it far more difficult for today's policymakers to engage in some form of accommodation with labour groups that could facilitate the economic reforms needed to sustain jobs growth. The repression and even violence to which workers had been subjected under the Suharto regime for the best part of three decades has had the unfortunate effect of creating a labour backlash in the more open political conditions in post-Suharto, democratic Indonesia. Labour groups savour their new-found political voice, challenging and resisting official attempts at economic reforms, trade liberalization and external trade cooperation (*New Sunday Times*, 2 May 2010).

Similarly, Thailand is now suffering the consequences of institutionalized marginalization of the rural poor for a good part of the last three decades. The 'trickle-down' approach to economics long favoured by Thai technocrats has pitted the rural poor against metropolitan (Bangkok-based) political and business elites and the Thai middle classes (Phongpaichit and Baker 1995: 148; Songsamphan 2007: 36–7). Provincial politicians and provincial business interests have exploited these sentiments, exacerbating the social divide with an overlaying divide between the metropolitan elite and the provincial elite (McVey 2000; Chachavalpongpun 2010). These deep divisions in Thai society have found their most recent expression in the violent clashes that began in April 2010 in Bangkok between the Red Shirts (mostly poor and rural supporters of former Prime Minister Thaksin Shinawatra, deposed in a 2006 military coup) and the present Thai government. Despite his authoritarian tendencies and his alleged corrupt dealings, the rural poor have remained loyal to Thaksin, the first political leader who paid serious attention to their needs including by using part of his personal wealth, albeit to enhance his chances to win elections, which he did twice with rural support (Buruma 2010). Thaksin's economic and social programmes for the rural poor, although criticized as populist, have nevertheless struck a chord amongst this large but marginalized group. The entrenched class and elite divisions, and the tensions and struggles they have given rise to, are unlikely to be resolved anytime soon (Chachavalpongpun 2010).

To be sure, democratization has complicated trade politics in the region but the fault is not with democracy *per se* but with the kinds of elite politics that elide the problems faced by labour (such as in Indonesia) and the rural poor (as in Thailand) or that capitalize on the exclusion of these groups to win popular support. Posing the problem of trade politics in Southeast Asia in binary terms between trade liberalization (good) versus domestic protectionism (bad) also fails to address the distributional consequences of liberal trade policy and the continued exclusion of its invisible stakeholders from policy calculations. Sound trade governance must address the concerns of these non-elite groups and incorporate supportive social policies to address the inevitable social and economic dislocations that trade liberalization invariably generates. However, it will be rather more difficult to dismantle the patronage networks still common in the region. If ruling elites are able to design accommodative trade policies as they have done in the past, it may be possible for these illiberal patronage arrangements to continue.

Notes

1 Despite acknowledging that interventionist policies had played a role in East Asian development success, international organizations like the World Bank (1994), nevertheless, have called on policymakers to adopt economic liberalization and open trade policies, particularly since state interventions elsewhere have not always produced successful outcomes.
2 The contrast between APEC and AFTA is discussed in Nesadurai (2008).
3 Among the more common NTBs found in the region are licensing requirements, technical regulations, quotas, internal taxes, stipulations that traders use government-sanctioned insurance and shipping firms as well as restrictive government procurement policies (Austria 2004).
4 TPP negotiations have been conducted between Australia, New Zealand, Chile, Peru, Brunei, Singapore, Vietnam and the US. The Malaysian government announced in October 2010 that it will participate in these negotiations (*Bernama*, 6 October 2010).
5 Information from the website of the ASEAN Secretariat at: www.aseansec.org/20164.htm (accessed 10 May 2010).
6 The theoretical rationale for developmental regionalism is discussed in Nesadurai (2003a: 41–3). What is important for this discussion is the motivation and rationale for the project rather than whether such a policy was workable.
7 Baldwin (1997) first proposed the 'domino' theory.

References

AEM (2008) 'Joint Media Statement of the Fortieth ASEAN Economic Ministers (AEM) Meeting', 25–26 August, Singapore; available at: www.aseansec.org/21934.htm (accessed 29 June 2011).
ATUC (n.d.) *ASEAN Social Charter*, Malaysia: ASEAN Trade Union Council; available at: www.ASEAN-Social Charter.net (accessed August 2007).
Austria, M. (2004) *The Pattern of Intra-ASEAN Trade in Priority Goods Sectors*, Final Main Report submitted to the ASEAN–Australia Development Cooperation Programme; available at: www.aadcp-repsf.org/docs/03–006e-FinalReport.pdf (accessed 25 November 2005).
Baldwin, R.E. (1997) 'The causes of regionalism', *World Economy* 20 (7): 865–88.

Bernama (2010) 'Malaysia joins TPP negotiations', 6 October.

Buruma, I. (2010) 'The powerlessness of the powerful', *New Straits Times*, 9 May.

Chachavalpongpun, P. (2010) 'Confusing democracies: diagnosing Thailand's democratic crisis, 2001–8', in M. Caballero-Anthony (ed.) *Political Change, Democratic Transitions and Security in Southeast Asia*, London and New York: Routledge, pp. 34–52.

Deyo, F. (1998) 'Labour and industrial restructuring in Southeast Asia', in G. Rodan, K. Hewison and R. Robison (eds) *The Political Economy of Southeast Asia: An Introduction*, Melbourne: Oxford University Press.

Gomez, E.T. (1996) 'Electoral funding of general, state and party elections in Malaysia', *Journal of Contemporary Asia* 26 (1): 81–99.

Hamanaka, S. (2009) 'The building block versus stumbling block debate of regionalism: from the perspective of service trade liberalization in Asia', *Journal of World Trade* 43 (4): 873–91.

Hoadley, S. (2007) 'Southeast Asian cross-regional FTAs: origins, motives and aims', *Pacific Affairs* 80 (2): 303–25.

Hsu, L. (2008) 'The ASEAN Charter and a legal identity for ASEAN', in *The ASEAN Community: Unblocking the Roadblocks*, ASEAN Studies Centre Report No. 1, Singapore: Institute of Southeast Asian Studies, pp. 71–83.

Islam, I. and A. Chowdhury (2000) *The Political Economy of East Asia: Post-Crisis Debates*, Melbourne: Oxford University Press.

Jakarta Post (2010) 'SBY political deal may be behind Mulyani's exit', 6 May.

Jayasuriya, K. (2003) 'Introduction: Governing the Asia-Pacific – beyond the "new regionalism"', *Third World Quarterly* 24 (3): 199–215.

Khoo, B.T. (1995) *Paradoxes of Mahathirism*, Kuala Lumpur: Oxford University Press.

——(2000) 'Economic nationalism and its discontents', in R. Robison, M. Beeson, K. Jayasuriya and Hyuk-Rae Kim (eds) *Politics and Markets in the Wake of the Asian Crisis*, London: Routledge, pp. 212–37.

Kraft, H. (2007) 'The Philippines: democratization and trade liberalization', in *Political Transition and Economic Development in East Asia*, East Asian Development Network Research Report, Jakarta: CSIS Publishing, pp. 95–128.

Lee, H.G. and H.E.S. Nesadurai (2010) 'Political transition in Malaysia: the future of Malaysia's hybrid political regime', in M. Caballero-Anthony (ed.) *Political Change, Democratic Transitions and Security in Southeast Asia*, London and New York: Routledge, pp. 97–123.

MacIntyre, A. (1994) 'Business, government and development: Northeast and Southeast Asian comparisons', in A. MacIntyre (ed.) *Business and Government in Industrialising Asia*, Ithaca, NY: Cornell University Press.

McVey, R. (2000) 'Of greed and violence and other signs of progress', in R. McVey (ed.) *Money and Power in Provincial Thailand*, Singapore: Institute of Southeast Asian Studies, pp. 1–29.

Maswood, J. (2002) 'Developmental states in crisis', in M. Beeson (ed.) *Reconfiguring East Asia: Regional Institutions and Organizations After the Crisis*, London: RoutledgeCurzon, pp. 31–48.

MATRADE (2010) *Malaysia's Free Trade Agreements*, Malaysia External Trade Development Corporation; available at: www.matrade.gov.my/cms/content.jsp?id=com.tms.cms.section.Section_e6b0d410–17f000 010–13c913c9-ccfb4170 (accessed 10 May 2010).

Montes, M. (1999) 'The Philippines as an unwitting participant in the Asian economic crisis', in K. Jackson (ed.) *Asian Contagion: The Causes and Consequences of a Financial Crisis*, Boulder, CO: Westview Press.

Nagai, F. (2003) 'Thailand's FTA policy: from dual track policy to new Asian policy', in Siriporn Wajjwalku (ed.) *Japan–ASEAN Comprehensive Partnership: Asian Perspectives*, Bangkok: Thammasat University Press.

Nesadurai, H.E.S. (2003a) *Globalisation, Domestic Politics and Regionalism: The ASEAN Free Trade Area*, London and New York: Routledge.

——(2003b) 'Attempting developmental regionalism through AFTA: the domestic sources of regional governance', *Third World Quarterly* 24 (3): 235–53.

——(2008) 'Southeast Asia's new architecture for cooperation in trade and finance', in V.K. Aggarwal and Min Gyo Koo (eds) *Asia's New Institutional Architecture: Evolving Structures for Managing Trade, Financial and Security Relations*, Berlin and Heidelberg: Springer-Verlag, pp. 151–80.

New Straits Times (2010) 'Malaysia reviewing govt [sic] procurement policy', 1 May.

New Sunday Times (2010) 'Asians demand more money, jobs', 2 May.

Phongpaichit, P. and C. Baker (1995) *Thailand: Economy and Politics*, Kuala Lumpur: Oxford University Press.

Ravenhill, J. (2003) 'The new bilateralism in the Asia Pacific', *Third World Quarterly* 24 (3): 299–317.

——(2009) 'East Asian regionalism: much ado about nothing?' *Review of International Studies* 35 (Special Issue): 215–35.

Rodan, G. (1993) 'Reconstructing divisions of labour: Singapore's new regional emphasis', in R. Higgott, R. Leaver and J. Ravenhill (eds) *Pacific Economic Relations in the 1990s: Cooperation or Conflict?* Boulder, CO: Lynne Rienner, pp. 223–49.

Rosser, A. (2003) 'Coalitions, convergence and corporate governance reform in Indonesia', *Third World Quarterly* 24 (3): 319–37.

Sally, R. (2004) *Southeast Asia in the WTO*, Singapore: Institute of Southeast Asian Studies.

Schwarz, A. (1999) *A Nation in Waiting: Indonesia's Search for Stability*, St Leonards: Allen and Unwin.

Sivalingam, G. (2008) 'Financial reforms in an emerging economy: the case of Malaysia', *Economic Papers* 27 (4): 393–402.

Songsamphan, C. (2007) 'Political transition, economic development, changing political arena and democratic contestation', in *Political Transition and Economic Development in East Asia*, East Asian Development Network Research Report, Jakarta: CSIS Publishing, pp. 31–63.

Tori, T. (1997) 'The new economic policy and the United Malays National Organisation', *The Developing Economies* XXXV (3): 209–39.

World Bank (1994) *The East Asian Miracle: Economic Growth and Public Policy*, New York: Oxford University Press.

Yeung, H.W.-C. (1999) *Singapore's Global Reach: An Executive Report*, Singapore: Department of Geography, National University of Singapore.

21

SOUTHEAST ASIAN PERCEPTIONS OF AMERICAN POWER

Natasha Hamilton-Hart

9/11 was also good for Asia in that it created opportunities for new partnerships and coalitions, although it also put pressure on many of the governments in their bilateral relationship with the United States.

(Chan Heng Chee, Singapore Ambassador to the United States; Chan 2005: 94)

In the wake of the United States-led war on Afghanistan launched in October 2001, a largely transatlantic debate on global unipolarity escalated rapidly. The 2002 US national security doctrine reasserting claims of primacy and the right to launch pre-emptive war, an extra-territorial 'war on terror', and the invasion and occupation of Iraq starting in March 2003 provided further fodder for commentary. As these events dominated news headlines, critical analyses of American foreign policy and the unparalleled nature of American power proliferated. Nonetheless, in this period, Southeast Asian countries increased their cooperation with the US on issues ranging from counter-terrorism to military exercises and bilateral preferential trade agreements. Public perceptions of the US swung sharply to negative in Indonesia and Malaysia, but foreign policy elites across much of the region tempered criticism of post-2001 American foreign policy with beliefs in the positive and stabilizing role of the US.

This chapter asks why, despite some variation across the region, many members of the foreign policy community in Southeast Asia appear to view the US as a generally benign international power. The idea that the US is a benign power enjoys an intellectual lineage but, as shown in the first section of this chapter, it competes with intellectual traditions that have cast the US in a much more negative light. These more negative depictions do circulate in Southeast Asia, as shown in the second section here, but mostly outside of foreign policy circles. Societal views, therefore, have often been at odds with the generally cooperative and accommodating stance of Southeast Asian governments towards the US in the post-2001 period. The final section argues that acceptance (albeit with different degrees of enthusiasm) of American primacy by regional governments is based on a convergence between the regime interests of ruling groups and American priorities. Perceptions of the US in foreign policy circles reflect this convergence of interest but do not conceive of it in narrowly self-interested terms. Instead, their perceptions of the US are supported by a set of beliefs and narratives that have acquired the status of expert knowledge within foreign policy circles. Such beliefs warrant further analysis as essentially political and moral statements that reflect positional understandings of history and progress.

The United States as benign hegemon, fallen angel and rogue state

Substantively, most claims about the international role of the US were not new in the years after 2001, but some aspects of the debate were somewhat novel. As noted in one review, the term 'American empire' was back in use, and this time it was not restricted to long-term critics of the United States (Cox 2003). American empire now had its defenders (e.g. Ferguson 2004, Mallaby 2002), and even scholars who had largely stayed away from foreign policy controversies could write of an 'American imperium' (Katzenstein 2005). Perhaps inevitably, by the end of the decade the decline of American hegemony replaced American empire as a subject of discussion.[1] What any decline means, however, depends on how one assesses central features of American foreign policy. It is also worth recalling that the debate about US primacy dates back to the end of the Cold War (e.g. Lynn-Jones 1991); and a much longer tradition of scholarship on US hegemony deals with its leadership within the non-communist world since the end of World War II. The relative decline of the US and the contours of a world 'after hegemony' (Keohane 1984) have been discussed more than once since the early 1970s.[2] The opinions and analyses surfacing since 2001, therefore, are inevitably informed by longer experiences and images of the international role of the US.

Three distinct images of the US can be drawn out from the scholarly literature on US international primacy: the US as a benign hegemon, a fallen angel and as a rogue state. Broadly, these images also capture contending views of the US among policy elites and sections of the general public. The first image presents the US as a benign hegemon: a force for stability and prosperity, and a provider of public goods such as an open market, an international currency and a set of global institutions that provide a stable, rule-based system. Liberal variants emphasize the US as a democratic, self-restrained, consultative and multilateral power, which ultimately seeks 'rules for the world' rather than to 'rule the world' (Ikenberry 2004).[3] Others dispense with the idea that the US is particularly rule-based or consultative, but maintain that the benefits of American hegemony are shared widely, even if they are not universally welcomed (e.g. Ferguson 2004; Kagan 2006a, 2006b). For those who see the US as a uniquely liberal and restrained great power, the unilateralism of American policy after 2001 is either taken to be anomalous (e.g. Ikenberry 2004), or it is whitewashed in an attempt to defend American foreign policy in this period (e.g. Feinstein and Slaughter 2004). Consistent with this line of thinking, the world is not 'pushing back' against US primacy because most other countries either gain from it directly, or at least are not threatened by it.[4]

In the second image of the US, that of a fallen angel, many of the attributes of the benign hegemon are invoked, but the US is seen as having fundamentally deviated from its Cold War path of providing public goods for those under its sphere of influence (e.g. Mahbubani 2005). Depending on the explanation offered for this shift in US policy, predictions vary as regards the chances of the US recovering its leadership role. Particularly for structural realists and others who have argued that unipolarity invites its own demise, the rise of new great powers and increased balancing against the US is predicted. Indeed, several accounts detect signs of incipient balancing behaviour, such as 'soft balancing' or 'pre-balancing' and hedging.[5]

The third image of the US, as a rogue state and persistent offender, challenges the idea that the US was ever any kind of essentially benign international player. While admitting that certain clients have benefited from the international exercise of US power, its foreign policy is seen as unrestrained, unilateral and lawless – often with devastating effects on populations around the

331

world (e.g. Blum 2002; Chomsky 2003; Johnson 2000). In some versions, unfolding political change within the US, as empire unravels American democracy at home, marks a new era (Johnson 2004, 2006). In other versions, there is nothing new about the coercive and destructive aspects of American global power (Chomsky and Herman 1979). In both cases, the US is seen as having more than a public relations problem; and the actions that create antipathy date back to well before the presidency of George W. Bush and his 'neoconservative' advisers, even if they presented the world with a particularly unappealing face of American power (e.g. Ali 2002; Sardar and Davies 2002).

The debate about what the US is and what it does has presented very selective glimpses of how other parts of the world respond to the US. Critics of the US cite negative public opinion polls and non-state retaliation against the US (e.g. Johnson 2000), while defenders claim discontent is peripheral and transitory (e.g. Kagan 2006b). But overall, far more attention has been given to the United States than to the countries affected by it. There is a cluster of work on public opinion and social attitudes (e.g. Farber 2007; Katzenstein and Keohane 2007; Carlson and Nelson 2008) and some collections which present avowedly elite or non-representative views (e.g. Lennon 2002). Integrating analyses of what the US does with explanations of how other countries perceive and relate to it is a challenge for critics of US foreign policy in particular. They have extensively catalogued the negative consequences of American foreign policy and may well answer the question of 'why do people hate America' (Sardar and Davies 2002), but they do not give serious attention to the question of why, given these ample grievances, 'blowback' has been so limited.[6]

Perceptions of the US were returning to more positive levels even before the end of the George W. Bush presidency.[7] Indeed, only a short while afterwards – and in a context where most causes for grievance against the US remain fundamentally unaltered – positive views of the US were significantly higher than negative views in most major countries (BBC 2010). Further, as Katzenstein and Keohane note, not only is public opinion volatile, 'the consequences of anti-American views are more difficult to detect than one would think on the basis of claims made by the Left ... Superficial manifestations of anti-Americanism seem to have few systematic effects on policy' (Katzenstein and Keohane 2007: 11). For the structural realists who predict a return to balancing behaviour and the erosion of unipolarity, the question must be why signs of balancing against the US by great powers (and bandwagoning with such powers by smaller states) – to the extent they exist – have been so ambiguous and so late in coming. After all, the US clearly presented the world with the challenge of primacy at the beginning of the 1990s, and explicit claims to primacy have been made by every administration since then (Layne 2009: 148).

On the surface, the simplest explanation for why foreign policy elites in Southeast Asia (and in some other parts of the world) do not perceive US primacy as threatening is that it is indeed a benign hegemon. The divergence between popular opinion and elite views, in societies where it exists, could be attributed to elites being better informed. This explanation, however, ignores the political positioning and specific interests of those perceiving the US. This chapter argues that contending perceptions of American power reflect specific political, material and moral standpoints. Analyses of what kind of an international power the US is need to be rooted in an appreciation of the differential consequences of American actions for different social groups, classes and, in some cases, countries.

Southeast Asian divisions and contradictions

In the case of Southeast Asia, a region that has lived with American power since World War II, the behaviour of most governments presents more than a few anomalies for analyses that focus on the negative effects of American influence. For America's longstanding friends and allies in the region – essentially the non-communist early members of the Association of Southeast Asian Nations – at every juncture when it seemed as though the US might reduce its involvement in the region, the response has been to press for continued American presence and engagement. Thus the American military withdrawal from Vietnam in 1973 prompted foreign policy and defence establishments to express anxiety about whether the US would remain committed to the rest of the region (Tilman 1987). The end of the Cold War prompted a flurry of statements on the need for continued American engagement, and attempts to anchor it more firmly in the region through multilateral initiatives and increased bilateral cooperation (e.g. Acharya 2000). Two of the countries which suffered the destructive force of American military power in the years before 1973, Cambodia and Vietnam, increased cooperation with the US in the 1990s.

In the post-2001 era, American unilateralism appears to have created some 'unease' among Southeast Asian governments, but actual policies pursued by these governments were almost uniformly in the direction of greater cooperation with the United States – indeed, a lack of attention from the US figures prominently among the complaints voiced by governments and foreign policy elites (e.g. Yamamoto et al. 2001; Koh 2004, 2008; Mauzy and Job 2007). While post-2001 US security doctrine and practice have been subject to scholarly criticism, many of these critiques simultaneously detail increased cooperation with the US and the strengthening of American bilateral ties in the region, even as American policy undermined 'hopes for a more robust multilateral security order in Asia' (Acharya 2005: 224–5).

The greatest obstacle to increased cooperation, at least on the Southeast Asian side, stemmed not from elite-level strategic concerns about a unilateral and aggressive United States, but from elite calculations of public opinion (Capie 2004). Thus in Malaysia and Indonesia, the two countries where popular disaffection with the US was most widespread, political leaders did publicly state their opposition to the war on Iraq and criticize other aspects of American foreign policy, such as its support for Israel. However, this constraint produced echoes in elite-level rhetoric rather than a shift in strategic stance towards the US. In the rest of the region, polling data and other available measures of popular opinion suggest that majorities generally either approved or acquiesced to their governments' cooperation with the United States. In Malaysia and Indonesia, large street protests condemned US policy but there were no widespread boycotts of American products or firms.

The views of commentators and organized groups within Southeast Asian countries cover the full spectrum of opinion on the US as a global power. Some columnists and public intellectuals produced sharply critical analyses of the US as an imperial power, and decried the illegality and abuses associated with its post-2001 foreign policy. Thus in the Philippines, Renato Redentor Constantino's regular newspaper columns described the US as a habitual offender when it came to violating both sovereignty and human rights.[8] In Malaysia, one of the country's major English-language newspapers carried critical opinion pieces, and opposition groups and religious organizations also condemned US foreign policy.[9] Similar voices were raised in Indonesia.[10] Even in Singapore, a few articles in the state-controlled daily newspaper questioned the rationale for the invasion of Iraq, and at least one societal group later issued a call (on its own website) to bring the US to account for war crimes.[11]

Some public intellectuals and commentators struck a tone of disappointment and reproof rather than outrage, prefixing their criticisms with invocations of America's great and positive contributions, at least in the past.[12] Even the critical voices appearing in mainstream outlets rarely matched the stridency of many Western critics of US foreign policy.[13] While bookshops in Malaysia and Indonesia carried a large number of works denouncing the US as a criminal hegemon or terrorist empire, demand for this type of work was mostly met either by

333

well-known Western critics or – particularly in Indonesian bookshops – writers from the Middle East whose work had been translated from Arabic.[14]

The most critical views came largely from two distinct sources: established leftist writers and activists in the Philippines, and some 'hard-line' Muslim individuals and organizations in Indonesia and Malaysia.[15] Both these sources had established repertoires of criticism of the US, and were thus able to generate unequivocal analyses of the US as an inherently predatory power. Thus, for example, the open organization allegedly linked to the terrorist Jemaah Islamiah network, Majelis Mujahidin Indonesia, produced articles linking depredations of the US with Indonesia's own governing class, and others published trenchant criticisms.[16] More mainstream Islamic organizations voiced many criticisms of post-2001 US foreign policy, but leaders of the country's largest Islamic organizations expressly distanced themselves from groups identified as hard-line, associating them with religious conflict and intolerance.

In this situation, Southeast Asian governments had a relatively free hand to pursue cooperation agendas that suited them when it came to relations with the US, even if Malaysia and Indonesia were more circumspect. Singapore stands out as the most consistent and unequivocal in its support for US foreign policy in this period, backing the invasion of Iraq at the United Nations, increasing counter-terrorism cooperation, providing military facilities for the US, increasing bilateral military exercises, and sending a small non-combat unit to Iraq. It also concluded a bilateral preferential trade agreement with the US in 2003. Singaporean leaders did not question the grounds for the invasion of Iraq but vehemently took up the American claim that the invasion was justified as a response to the Iraqi weapons programme. Goh Chok Tong, for example, was reported in March 2003 as saying that, 'It is clear to everyone, unless that person wears blinkers, that this is a war to remove the weapons of mass destruction from Saddam Hussein' (quoted in Acharya 2005: 210). A mild newspaper commentary on the failure to find such weapons was condemned by the Foreign Minister's press secretary, who not only restated the official justification supporting the attack but took the occasion to capitalize on the saturation coverage of terrorism in the local media:

> Singaporeans cannot afford to strike postures fashionable with the oppositionist media in America and Britain at the expense of the security of Singaporeans. Should we have waited until the Jemaah Islamiah exploded bombs in Singapore before acting against it? Similarly, should the US have waited until all its critics were convinced before acting against Saddam? A small nation in terrorist-infested South-east Asia does not have this luxury of libertarian posturing.
>
> *(Tan 2003)*

No revision of opinion was forthcoming later, when the US was urged to stay the course in Iraq (Lee 2007).[17]

The US's treaty allies in the region, the Philippines and Thailand, also joined the 'coalition of the willing' in support of the war against Iraq. Thailand's early equivocation, which was rumoured to have been overcome with some arm-twisting of then Prime Minister Thaksin Shinawatra by American officials, appears to have been judged a fundamental mistake by foreign policy professionals. Thaksin himself overcame initial reluctance to support US policy as well as anger at American criticisms of his own human rights record, as he oversaw programmes of increased cooperation in military and security arenas, as well as pursuing a bilateral trade agreement with the US (Connors 2006; Rodan and Hewison 2006). The Philippines sent a small contingent to Iraq and invited US troops back to the country as 'advisers' in the fight against insurgency and terrorism in the south. The payoffs, in terms of increased military aid and anticipated benefits in terms of positioning for contracts in occupied Iraq, were widely noted (Tyner 2005; Reid 2006). The only sour point in relations was the President's decision to withdraw the Philippine contingent from Iraq earlier than scheduled owing to the kidnapping of a Filipino there. This move did provoke criticism from the US, but was taken in the context of a generally supportive, pro-American stance.[18]

In Indonesia and Malaysia, strongly negative views of American foreign policy expressed by social actors outside of the foreign policy community presented both constraints and opportunities for political leaders. The Indonesian Vice President in 2002, from an Islamic political party, was among many politicians who made critical public statements of the US, including labelling the US as the 'real terrorist' (quoted in Mauzy and Job 2007: 638). But quiet cooperation actually increased in this period, particularly after the terrorist attack in Bali in October 2002. While President Megawati was accused by opponents of being overly supportive of the US, she was defeated in the presidential elections of 2004, not by any of the political parties more critical of the US, but by her own former Security Minister, a retired army general who had longstanding friendly relations with the US and pursued these when in office. The domestic political advantages created by American foreign policy outweighed any negatives (Bourchier 2006; Hadiz 2006).

Malaysia's then Prime Minister, Mahathir Mohamad, made the strongest open criticisms of the US of any Southeast Asian political incumbent. In public speeches at the UN General Assembly in September 2003 and at the meeting of the Organization of the Islamic Conference (OIC) in October 2003, Mahathir accused the US of using the 'war on terror' to dominate the world. After stepping down from office, he joined sharply critical civil society groups in describing US policymakers as war criminals. However, his stinging criticisms of the US were interpreted by many members of the foreign policy community in Malaysia to reflect a mixture of his own well-known proclivity for combative anti-Western rhetoric and his desire to be seen as an independent spokesman for developing country interests, rather than an over-compliant friend of the US. Given the widespread popular Malaysian antipathy to American actions in its 'war on terror' and war against Iraq, the political motive for doing so was fairly apparent, especially given the way the Malaysian government had used the context to clamp down on its domestic political opponents (Nesadurai 2006). As noted by the head of a government-linked Malaysian institute, despite the criticisms, 'Malaysia's bilateral ties have improved significantly in the last two years' (Khadijah 2003: 99). Malaysia continued its established programme of military cooperation with the US and did not cancel exercises such as an annual military training programme, which continued as usual in the months after the invasion of Iraq.[19] Mahathir's eventual successor, Najib Abdul Razak, was supportive of increased cooperation with the US.[20]

Overall, the pattern of bilateral relations between the US and most Southeast Asian countries suggests that the governments of these countries are basically comfortable with US influence and presence. Notwithstanding bursts of criticism from outspoken leaders such as Mahathir and Thaksin, at a period when US unipolar preponderance at the global level was unprecedented and its foreign policy was attracting extraordinary levels of condemnation for being provocative, aggressive and unilateral, the main response from the Southeast Asian region was to increase cooperation and continue efforts to deepen engagement with the US. The implication is that these Southeast Asian governments have a preference for US hegemony. As concluded in a survey of post-2001 relations, 'American predominance and leadership continues to be acknowledged and valued generally in Southeast Asia' despite 'reduced comfort' due to the Iraq war and the Bush administration's 'style of conducting business'. Nonetheless, 'Southeast Asians by and large prefer US dominance' (Goh 2005: 192). Although not acknowledged explicitly, a hierarchical regional order led by the US appears to be accepted by most of Southeast Asia, just as it has been – albeit with some caveats – by China and Japan (Van Ness 2002).[21] The question this raises is: why are Southeast Asian governments inclined to see US hegemony in this light?

Supporting beliefs in the foreign policy establishment

A full explanation of the attitudes and actions of Southeast Asian governments in response to the US is beyond the scope of this chapter (Hamilton-Hart 2012). The short answer to the question of why most governments are happy to live with American hegemony is that they have benefited from it. As demonstrated in a number of accounts of the domestic political dynamics surrounding responses to post-2001 American foreign policy, US policy has allowed entrenched elite actors to strengthen themselves at the expense of domestic political opponents. Writing with regard to Singapore and Thailand, Garry Rodan and Kevin Hewison have shown that, 'the US-led War on Terror has created new opportunities for the consolidation, refinement and restoration of authoritarian practices' (Rodan and Hewison 2006: 106).[22] In turn, the American preoccupation with security issues after 2001 meant that the US moderated some of its previous demands for economic and political liberalization that had caused friction with Southeast Asian governments in the 1990s. In this way, the post-2001 period was one which saw increased alignment between, on the one hand, regime interests in Southeast Asian countries and, on the other, US interests in supporting governments that 'can deliver order, loyalty and security' (Robison 2006: 66).

Such benefits are rather different from those proposed in accounts of the US as a benign hegemon. However, while political leaders such as Thaksin, Macapagal-Arroyo and Mahathir undoubtedly realized the political and economic benefits of cooperating with the US in this period, this does not fully explain elite views of American hegemony. These views rest on a set of supporting beliefs, which underlie the conclusion that the US can be trusted to provide regional stability and security goods, at least more so than any other country. These beliefs are, from one perspective, self-serving. However, they are also informed by the particular set of informational and social cues available to members of the foreign policy community as relatively elite actors occupying (to varying degrees) insider roles in policy circles. This chapter's description of these supporting beliefs is based on a series of interviews with seventy-four members of the foreign policy community in six Southeast Asian countries – Indonesia, Malaysia, Singapore, the Philippines, Thailand and Vietnam – carried out between May 2007 and August 2009. This pool of interviewees consisted of serving and retired diplomats (twenty-five), other government officials (ten), think-tank personnel and academics linked to their country's foreign policy establishment (thirty-three), and journalists responsible for coverage of foreign news and national foreign policy (six).[23] While not necessarily representative, this sample provides a partial picture of beliefs circulating in the foreign policy communities of Southeast Asia.

A central belief supporting the acceptance of American hegemony is the idea that the US is a source of stability, security and prosperity. The chairman of a Singaporean foreign policy think-tank, the Singapore Institute of International Affairs (part of the influential 'track 2' network of ASEAN-ISIS think-tanks), even while suggesting that the US has not been living up to its values since 2001, concludes that:

> Most in Asia do not desire an end to US primacy. Indeed, US presence is what they have known, lived with, and largely prospered from over the past few decades. The overarching wish of Asian states is instead that the present hour of US primacy continues to provide stability and show benevolence for all, even in the face of post-9/11 exigencies and imperatives.
>
> *(Tay 2004: 128)*

This is the repeated assessment expressed in the reports of elite opinion and the writings of think-tank analysts and many government-linked academics. For example, writing in his capacity as rapporteur for Southeast Asian respondents, a prominent Singaporean diplomat noted that

> Southeast Asia appreciates the indispensable role which the United States has played in the maintenance of regional security and its positive role in spurring the region's rapid social and economic development ... Since the end of World War II, the US has provided Southeast Asia with a security umbrella that has been a stabilizing factor for the development of the region.
>
> *(Koh 2004: 35, 38)*[24]

My own sample of interviewees was more heterogeneous and qualified in their enthusiasm; nonetheless, four times as many people judged the US to play a necessary role in ensuring regional stability, as compared to the number who felt that the US was not necessary in this respect.[25]

The most commonly cited reason for why the US is necessary was the claim that it is needed to 'balance' against China, although most respondents took care to note that China is not a current strategic threat. In a statement made while then Deputy Prime Minister, Lee Hsien Loong asserted in 2002 that: 'Politically and strategically, the US is the only realistic player which can balance China' (Lee 2002). Lee Kuan Yew, still a cabinet member, continues to hold this opinion, reportedly stating in a speech in 2009 that the US would be

> the sole superpower for two or three more decades despite the fallout from last year's global crisis ... Beijing is neither willing nor ready to take on equal responsibility for managing the international system ... The size of China makes it impossible for the rest of Asia, including Japan and India, to match it in weight and capacity in about 20 to 30 years. So we need America to strike a balance.
>
> *(Quoted in* The Straits Times, *29 October 2009)*

The idea that a bipolar balance of power is a relatively stabilizing international distribution of power has a long heritage in international relations scholarship, but the assertion that American military engagement and force-projection capabilities in East Asia produce such a balance warrants attention. Not only does American military capacity dwarf that of any other power, it has also repeatedly and explicitly laid claim to exercising a preponderance of power in the region.[26]

For Southeast Asian leaders to admit openly to a preference for American predominance is rather uncomfortable given official proclamations of non-alignment and frequent public foreign policy statements calling for the region not to be dominated by any one power. Singapore leaders are exceptional in calling so openly for the US to play a 'balance', but their preferences resonate more widely within the foreign policy communities of other Southeast Asian countries.[27] While no-one wishes to live with US 'dominance' in the sense of being dictated to, a strategic predominance of power exercised by the US appears to be preferred by many. Identifying the US role as one of providing a stabilizing 'balance' offers a way of presenting the status quo in more palatable terms than to admit to preference for US predominance. In the interview sample for this chapter, almost all respondents agreed, when queried about the term 'balance', that the status quo actually represented an imbalance of power. Despite this, not only did a solid majority claim that US power was a positive and stabilizing force, only nine considered it to be destabilizing or potentially threatening.[28] Many respondents compartmentalized what they judged to be destabilizing actions of the US; for example, maintaining that while the

American 'war on terror' was misguided and had probably worsened the terrorist threat, overall the US played a stabilizing role. Only three respondents unequivocally considered the US to be a potential threat or source of instability, compared to fifty-two who stated explicitly that the US was either not a potential threat or was significantly less threatening than any alternative hegemonic power.

Reasons varied for seeing the US as a relatively benign, non-threatening hegemonic power. Some respondents pointed to domestic checks and balances in the American system of democracy, and several made reference to the good intentions and war-averse nature of the American population. Others referred to history, saying that the US had proven it was not an imperial or aggressive power interested in making territorial claims – or that even if this was not always the case, their own familiarity with the US (both personal and in a historical national sense) made it possible to trust the country. A third frequently cited explanation was the geographic distance of the US from Asia. These reasons were often put forward by respondents who, earlier in the interview, had criticized post-2001 US foreign policy for waging war without the authorization of the United Nations (in a region just as geographically distant from the US as East Asia), human rights abuses and other breaches of international law. While some did note the contradiction, this was commonly dealt with by making two ancillary judgements: first, that 2001 marked a turning point in US foreign policy (which was the expressed view of more than half of the sample); second, that such aberrational episodes would tend to self-correct.

In discussing whether American power was stabilizing, very few respondents took up the main points of criticism that had been levelled at US foreign policy in Asia in recent years. These criticisms include the US role in encouraging a more militarized and nationalistic Japan (McCormack 2004), the destabilizing dynamics of ballistic missile defence plans (Tow and Choong 2001) and its nuclear weapons policy (both development plans for battlefield nuclear weapons and its willingness to ignore disarmament commitments).[29] Indeed the major critiques of the 2002 US National Security Strategy and American handling of regional flashpoints such as Taiwan and North Korea (Gurtov and Van Ness 2005) were not raised by the overwhelming majority of respondents when discussing the issue of whether the US role in Asia was stabilizing or destabilizing. It is certainly possible to mount a defence of US policy on all these fronts (Christensen 2006), and to conclude, along with Singaporean Foreign Minister George Yeo, that 'Whatever others might say of the previous administration, from our perspective, US policy on East and South-east Asia under President George W. Bush was constructive and good for the region' (Yeo 2009).

The pattern of reasoning, however, was to work backwards from the conclusion that US power was non-threatening and stabilizing to whichever explanations were most readily available, bypassing the major points of possible contention. The explanations for seeing the US as non-threatening are all well known, and concur with much of the liberal scholarship that presents the US as a benign hegemon. In that sense, interviewees offered reasoned arguments supporting their judgements. However, these arguments require taking a perspective on both the present and the past that is highly positional and selective. First, it was clear that China – the most frequently cited source of potential future instability or uncertainty – was held to different standards compared to the US, in terms of both current policy and past actions. Second, in addition to seeing post-2001 US foreign policy as aberrational, historical events involving the US in East Asia were also bracketed. These include colonial rule in the Philippines, the conduct of the Philippine–American war, the World War II bombing of Japan, the Vietnam war and associated intensive bombing of Cambodia and Laos, and Cold War-era American interference in domestic conflicts, often in support of repressive ruling groups and military-backed governments. To the extent that these events were mentioned at all by interviewees (in response to a question about the historical role of the US in the region), those who saw them as mistakes but nonetheless perceived the role of the US positively were able to compartmentalize them, sometimes citing them as examples of how the American political system is capable of self-correcting policy errors over time.

These judgements make sense only if the casualties of American actions are allowed to fade into relative insignificance, or are accorded less significance than the benefits conferred by the US. This is the sense in which the 'stability' brought by the US needs to be understood. If not, it would be impossible to sustain the frequently heard statements that circulate without contention in foreign policy circles, such as the reported consensus view that: 'Since the end of World War II, Southeast Asia has regarded the United States as a security guarantor of the Asia-Pacific and welcomes its forward deployed military presence in the region' (Koh 2008: 39). The author, one of Singapore's most experienced and lauded diplomats, cannot be ignorant of the countries and peoples in Southeast Asia that manifestly did not welcome the US presence for the whole of this period, a time when millions of casualties were inflicted by American firepower. Not ignorance, then, but a moral and political trade-off lies behind this view of the United States, a trade-off that reflects the political and social positioning of members of the foreign policy community in Southeast Asia.

A degree of diplomatic politeness and reticence is of course to be expected from members of the foreign policy community. However, it is difficult to attribute clear positive statements to diplomatic caution. While some respondents (notably those in Vietnam) did appear to be somewhat constrained in expressing personal opinions on policy-related issues, many offered lively and outspoken critiques. The hypocrisy of American posturing on human rights, its over-militarized counter-terrorism policies, its tendency to see Southeast Asia through the lens of terrorism, and intrusive conditionalities calling for human rights or economic reforms were among the complaints raised. These echo public statements from members of the foreign community. US policy on Burma, for example, is criticized quite frankly in a number of statements.[30]

Given this willingness to offer criticisms on other issues, the indirect nature of many of the criticisms of post-2001 US policy is noticeable. In an eighteen-page summary of Southeast Asian views of the US in 2004, less than a year after the invasion of Iraq, only seven lines referred obliquely to 'disquiet in the region at some aspects of US policy. This is particularly true of its doctrine of pre-emptive strikes and the apparent disregard for the multilateral institutions', followed by the observation that 'The ongoing Israeli–Palestinian conflict, the pre-emptive war against Iraq, and the situation in Iraq have attracted considerable criticism against the US in Indonesia and elsewhere in the region' (Koh 2004: 39–40). This is consonant with a tendency to see US foreign policy as predominantly a Muslim problem, with Muslim sentiment 'complicating' bilateral relations (Goh 2005: 192) as governments were 'pressured by the ground' – with the advice to the US to brush up on its public diplomacy, 'to ensure you earn the goodwill you deserve' (Chan 2005: 97–8). This should not be taken as meaning that elite views in the region largely agreed with American foreign policy at this time. Many expressed disapproval of US policy; but prevailing professional wisdom was that personal objections should be over-ruled in favour of promoting bilateral relations with the US. As noted by the head of a Singaporean think-tank,

> For the majority of Asian states, despite some negative public opinion in many societies and perhaps private doubts, anti-Americanism has not been entrenched as state opinion. Asian leaders have instead responded quite promptly, whether as true allies or opportunistic ambulance chasers, to align their own agenda with that of the United States.
>
> *(Tay 2004: 122)*

Conclusion: The political and the professional

Beliefs about the United States expressed by members of the foreign policy community in Southeast Asia reflect a reading of the past and the present that is fundamentally shaped by the outcome of political contests in their own societies. US hegemony has been good for the anti-communist ruling elites who had consolidated their positions in non-communist Southeast Asia by the mid-1960s. The material benefits of alignment with the US during the Cold War were significant (Stubbs 2005), but defeated opponents and the excluded sections of society they represented have reason to contest a version of history bathed in the rosy glow of a benign American imperium. Tellingly, when asked whether post-2001 US foreign policy represented a turning point or aberration, the two groups of respondents who were most likely to disagree on this point were those from Vietnam and the Philippines. Not only are these the two countries which have faced the US as military adversaries, they are also the two in which the losing side of the great Cold War ideological and political rift continues to have a real presence. Vietnam, of course, remains officially communist, and its political elite is to some extent divided between 'old guard' elements and reformists leading the turn towards the US (Bolton 1999; Thayer 1999; Vuving 2006). And the Philippines is not only the one country in the region with an active communist opposition, its elite educational institutions have retained elements with left-wing sympathies. The other side of history, therefore, is much more visible within the Philippine nationalist mainstream than in most other countries of Southeast Asia.[31]

Notes

1 See Layne (2009) for a review of some recent works addressing this issue.
2 For an early sceptical review, see Strange (1987).
3 For the intellectual lineage of this assessment, see, for example Ikenberry (2000), Nye (1990), Ruggie (1993).
4 Examples include Brooks and Wohlforth (2008), Lieber and Alexander (2005), Walt (2002).
5 See Layne (2007) for a review of these arguments, and Ross (2006) for an application to Asia.
6 The foreign policy actions of the US are central to many of these grievances, but some also arise out of concerns over the influence of American culture or economic power. Such grievances have often registered most among sections of society outside of foreign policy elites.
7 As widely reported, international opinion polls showed plummeting support for the US from 2002, with majorities or pluralities in many countries, including several traditionally aligned with the US, judging American influence to be mostly negative. At the nadir of its standing in 2003–4, polls showed the US being identified as a greater threat to world peace than any other country. By 2006, however, opinions in several countries became more positive. See, for example, the survey data discussed in Katzenstein and Keohane (2007) and Carlson and Nelson (2008).
8 See Constantino (2006) for an edited collection.
9 For example, regular columns in *The Star* by associate editor Bunn Nagara (e.g. 4 January 2007). See also the discussion in Nesadurai (2006) and collected writings by a former editor of the *New Straits Times* (and former Malaysian representative to the UN) Abdullah Ali (Abdullah 2005).
10 See, for example, Riza (2004, 2006), as well as the discussion in Budianta (2007). Leaders of the two largest Islamic organizations in Indonesia also condemned American foreign policy. See, for example, *Jakarta Post* (2003).
11 The *Straits Times* reported on its own poll of elite opinion in Asia, which showed that most respondents disputed the US case for war on Iraq in the absence of a UN mandate (30 September 2002). A few of its columnists raised moderately worded criticisms of the war. Stronger criticisms were voiced by other Singaporeans. See, for example, Centre for Contemporary Islamic Studies (2004).
12 For example, Malaysia's Karim Raslan (Karim 2003), Indonesia's Jusuf Wanandi (2006a) and Thailand's Kavi Chongchitavorn (2006, 2008).
13 In addition to the authors cited above, left-leaning media outlets such as Britain's *Guardian* newspaper regularly carried articles from writers such as George Monbiot, Seumas Milne and others, whose views

on US foreign policy were far more hard-hitting from those written by columnists writing regularly for mainstream newspapers in Malaysia, Singapore or Indonesia.

14 Exceptions include books by a Malaysian – a former aide to Mahathir Mohamad – Chang (2005a, 2005b) and by an Indonesian journalist for the daily *Kompas*, Kuncahyono (2005).

15 For example, Sison (2003). There are many critical accounts of the US's historical actions in the Philippines widely available in bookshops.

16 For example, MMI (2004). See the review of MMI and Hizbut Tahir statements in Ahnaf (2006).

17 The lack of political contestation and consequent ability of leaders such as Lee Kuan Yew to ignore their critics is particularly pronounced in Singapore.

18 The reasons for the early withdrawal may have included the President's religiously inspired disenchantment with the war, as human suffering increased (Tyner 2005). However, the political rationale is also evident, given the enormous importance of overseas Filipino workers to the country. Popular attitudes favoured the decision to withdraw but also favoured the US military return to the Philippines, and public opinion polls showed solidly positive views of the US (Abinales 2006).

19 See, for example, the US Navy's report on its annual CARAT (Cooperation Afloat Readiness and Training) exercises with Malaysia in 2003 (Bane 2003).

20 In a 2002 speech made in his capacity as Minister of Defence, Najib Abdul Razak extolled the 'special relationship' between the US and Malaysia, and noted both the longstanding cooperation that existed between the two countries and increased cooperation since 2001 (Najib 2002).

21 See Lake (2007) for a discussion of international hierarchy more generally.

22 Hadiz (2006) makes a similar argument in relation to Indonesia. See also the contributions to Beeson (2006).

23 For scholars and think-tank personnel, the criterion for considering someone part of their country's foreign policy community was whether a person regularly took up one or more of the following roles: (a) participant in semi-official 'track 2' regional dialogues; (b) adviser to government on foreign policy issues; (c) paid foreign policy consultant to the government; (d) organizer of joint events or programmes with the foreign ministry; (e) instructor in professional training courses or study programmes for government officials. The rationale for including these respondents is that their stated beliefs can be taken as reflecting 'acceptable' views within the foreign policy establishment. The assumption is that if they regularly voiced 'unacceptable' views they would not remain engaged in regular interaction with foreign policy officials.

24 Similar language is used in the 2001 and 2008 Asia Foundation reports. See Yamamoto *et al.* (2001) and Koh (2008). See also See Seng Tan (2007), especially pp. 142–8, for an extended review of thinking in Southeast Asian foreign policy circles, presenting contrasting images of China and the US, as well as Kwa and Tan (2001), Goh (2005), Wanandi (2006b), Jawhar (1995). There is, of course, likely to be a pro-American bias in a group of respondents selected by the Asia Foundation.

25 Fifty-two respondents considered the US necessary in this respect; thirteen disagreed. The others were either equivocal or did not answer the question directly.

26 These claims to predominance are explicit in major official statements, such as the Quadrennial Defense Review, as well as other US military and security planning documents. This does not prevent claims such as the following in Southeast Asian foreign policy circles: 'America's security presence has ensured that Southeast Asia has not been dominated by any one power; a core objective US security strategy in the region' (Koh 2008: 39).

27 The memoirs of Lee Kuan Yew are littered with references to the essential, stabilizing role of the US as a security guarantor since World War II. He concludes with the necessity of maintaining a 'balance between the United States and Japan on one side and China on the other' (Lee 2000: 762), at no point addressing the imbalance of military power inherent in this arrangement.

28 Other respondents were not clear on this point, including a relatively high proportion of Vietnamese interviewees.

29 One of the few to criticize US nuclear weapons policy was Dewi Fortuna Anwar, an Indonesian member of the international Weapons of Mass Destruction Commission, a strong advocate of nuclear disarmament.

30 See, for example, the blunt statement by a serving ambassador that 'the US should not hold ASEAN hostage to Myanmar' (Chan 2005: 96–7) and critiques in Yamamoto *et al.* (2001) and Koh (2008). Several interviewees objected quite frankly to American intrusion on human rights issues, as well as disagreeing with many aspects of post-2001 foreign policy.

31 For example, the author of what was described as an exposé of 'American oppression, coercion and repression' had a prominent career in journalism and academia, and his book (Grego 2006) carried

endorsements from individuals with standing in government, politics, journalism and academia. On the pluralistic memories of the Philippine elite regarding the US, ranging from enthusiastic amnesia to critical nationalism, see Ileto (2005).

References

Abinales, P. (2006) 'The American empire and the southern Philippine periphery: an aberrant case?', in V. R. Hadiz (ed.) *Empire and Neoliberalism in Asia*, London: Routledge, pp. 156–68.

Acharya, A. (2000) *Quest for Identity: International Relations of Southeast Asia*, Oxford: Oxford University Press.

——(2005) 'The Bush doctrine and Asian regional order: the perils and pitfalls of preemption', in M. Gurtov and P. Van Ness (eds) *Confronting the Bush Doctrine: Critical Views from the Asia-Pacific*, London: Routledge, pp. 203–26.

Ahnaf, M I. (2006) *The Image of the Other as Enemy: Radical Discourse in Indonesia*, Chiang Mai: Asian Muslim Action Network and Silkworm Books.

Ali, T. (2002) *The Clash of Fundamentalisms: Crusades, Jihads and Modernity*, London: Verso.

Bane, J. (2003) 'Final phase of CARAT 2003 kicks off in Malaysia', Story No. NMS030724-05, 25 July, United States Navy; available at: www.navy.mil/search/display.asp?story_id=8671 (accessed 30 July 2003).

BBC (2010) 'Global views of United States improve while other countries decline', BBC World Service Poll, 19 April; available at: www.bbc.co.uk/pressoffice/pressreleases/stories/2010/04_april/19/poll.shtml (accessed 19 April 2010).

Beeson, M. (ed.) (2006) *Bush and Asia: America's Evolving Relations with East Asia*, London: Routledge.

Blum, W. (2002) *Rogue State: A Guide to the World's Only Superpower*, London: Zed Books.

Bolton, K. (1999) 'Domestic sources of Vietnam's foreign policy: normalizing relations with the United States', in C. Thayer and R. Amer (eds) *Vietnamese Foreign Policy in Transition*, Singapore: ISEAS, pp. 170–201.

Bourchier, D. (2006) 'The United States, Bush and Indonesia', in M. Beeson (ed.) *Bush and Asia: America's Evolving Relations with East Asia*, London: Routledge, pp. 162–78.

Brooks, S and W. Wohlforth (2008) *World Out of Balance: International Relations and the Challenge of American Primacy*, Princeton, NJ: Princeton University Press.

Budianta, M. (2007) 'Beyond the stained glass window: Indonesian perceptions of the United States and the war on terror', in D. Farber (ed.) *What They Think of Us: International Perceptions of the United States since 9/11*, Princeton, NJ: Princeton University Press, pp. 27–48.

Capie, D. (2004) 'Between a hegemon and a hard place: the "war on terror" and Southeast Asian–US relations', *Pacific Review* 17 (2): 223–48.

Carlson, M. and T. Nelson (2008) 'Anti-Americanism in Asia? Factors shaping international perceptions of American influence', *International Relations of the Asia-Pacific* 8 (3): 303–24.

Centre for Contemporary Islamic Studies (2004) 'American war crimes', press release, 26 May; available at: www.ccis.org.sg (accessed 28 May 2004).

Chan, H.C. (2005) 'George W. Bush and Asia: retrospect and prospect', in R. Hathaway and W. Lee (eds) *George W. Bush and East Asia: A First Term Assessment*, Washington, DC: Woodrow Wilson International Center for Scholars, pp. 93–8.

Chang, M. (2005a) *Brainwashed for War, Programmed to Kill*, Selangor: Thinker's Library.

——(2005b) *Future Fast Forward: The Zionist Anglo-American War Cabal's Global Agenda*, Selangor: Thinker's Library.

Chomsky, N. (2003) *Hegemony or Survival: America's Quest for Global Dominance*, New York: Metropolitan Books.

Chomsky, N. and E.S. Herman (1979) *The Washington Connection and Third World Fascism*, Boston, MA: South End Press.

Chongchitavorn, K. (2006) 'US changes tone and approach on ASEAN policies', *The Nation*, 24 April.

——(2008) 'US needs to overhaul agenda in Southeast Asia', *The Nation*, 25 February.

Christensen, T. (2006) 'Fostering stability or creating a monster? The rise of China and US policy toward East Asia', *International Security* 31 (1): 81–126.

Connors, M. (2006) 'Thailand and the United States: beyond hegemony?' in M. Beeson (ed.) *Bush and Asia: America's Evolving Relations with East Asia*, London: Routledge, pp. 128–44.

Constantino, R.R. (2006) *The Poverty of Memory: Essays on History and Empire*, Quezon City: Foundation for Nationalist Studies.

Cox, M. (2003) 'The empire's back in town: or America's imperial temptation – again', *Millennium: Journal of International Studies* 32 (1): 1–27.

Farber, D. (ed.) (2007) *What They Think of Us: International Perceptions of the United States since 9/11*, Princeton, NJ: Princeton University Press.

Feinstein, L. and A.-M. Slaughter (2004) 'A duty to prevent', *Foreign Affairs* 83 (1): 136–50.

Ferguson, N. (2004) *Colossus: The Price of America's Empire*, New York: Penguin.

Goh, E. (2005) 'The Bush administration and Southeast Asian regional security strategies', in R. Hathaway and W. Lee (eds) *George W. Bush and East Asia: A First Term Assessment*, Washington, DC: Woodrow Wilson International Center for Scholars, pp. 183–94.

Grego, F. (2006) *The American Blackmails on the Philippines and the World*, Manila: Congress Magazine Publishing.

Gurtov, M. and P. Van Ness (eds) (2005) *Confronting the Bush Doctrine: Critical Views from the Asia-Pacific*, London: Routledge.

Hadiz, V.R. (ed.) (2006) *Empire and Neoliberalism in Asia*, London: Routledge.

Hamilton-Hart, N. (2012) *Hard Interests, Soft Illusions: Southeast Asia and American Power*, Ithaca, NY: Cornell University Press.

Ikenberry, J. (2000) *After Victory: Institutions, Strategic Restraint, and the Rebuilding of Order after Major Wars*, Princeton, NJ: Princeton University Press.

——(2004) 'Illusions of empire: defining the new American order', *Foreign Affairs* 83 (2): 144–54.

Ileto, R. (2005) 'Philippine wars and the politics of memory', *Positions: East Asia Cultures Critique* 13 (1): 215–35.

Jakarta Post (2003) 'NU, Muhammadiyah leaders to tell Bush his policies aid terror', 22 October.

Jawhar, H. (1995) 'Southeast Asia and the major powers', *Pacific Review* 8 (3): 508–17.

Johnson, C. (2000) *Blowback: The Costs and Consequences of American Empire*, New York: Metropolitan Books, Henry Holt.

——(2004) *The Sorrows of Empire: Militarism, Secrecy, and the End of the Republic*, New York: Metropolitan Books, Henry Holt.

——(2006) *Nemesis: The Last Days of the American Republic*, New York: Metropolitan Books, Henry Holt.

Kagan, R.(2006a) 'Cowboy nation', *The New Republic Online*, 16 October; available at: http://carnegie endowment.org/publications/?fa=18796 (accessed 23 May 2010).

——(2006b) 'Still the colossus', *The Washington Post*, 15 January.

Karim, R. (2003) 'A view from Southeast Asia', *Foreign Policy* 137: 38–9.

Katzenstein, P. (2005) *A World of Regions: Asia and Europe in the American Imperium*, Ithaca, NY: Cornell University Press.

Katzenstein, P. and R. Keohane (2007) 'Varieties of anti-Americanism: a framework for analysis', in P. Katzenstein and R. Keohane (eds) *Anti-Americanisms in World Politics*, Ithaca, NY: Cornell University Press, pp. 9–38.

Keohane, R. (1984) *After Hegemony: Cooperation and Discord in the World Political Economy*, Princeton, NJ: Princeton University Press.

Khadijah, Md Khalid (2003) 'September 11th and the changing dynamics of Malaysia–US relations', *Asian Review* 16: 91–112.

Koh, T. (2004) 'Southeast Asia', in *America's Role in Asia: Asian Views*, San Francisco: The Asia Foundation.

——(2008) 'The United States and Southeast Asia', in *America's Role in Asia: Asian and American Views*, San Francisco: The Asia Foundation.

Kuncahyono, T. (2005) *Irak Korban Ambisi Kaum Hawkish*, Jakarta: Buku Kompas.

Kwa, C.G. and S. Seng Tan (2001) 'The keystone of world order', *Washington Quarterly* 24 (3): 95–103.

Lake, D. (2007) 'Escape From the state of nature: authority and hierarchy in world politics', *International Security* 32 (1): 47–79.

Layne, C. (2007) 'The unipolar illusion revisited: the coming end of the United States' unipolar moment', *International Security* 31 (2): 7–41.

——(2009) 'The waning of US hegemony – myth or reality?' *International Security* 34 (1): 147–72.

Lee, H.L. (2002) 'Speech by Deputy Prime Minister Lee Hsien Loong at the Fortune Global Forum on 12 November 2002'; available at: http://app.mfa.gov.sg/pr/read_content.asp?View,1657 (accessed 14 November 2002).

Lee, K.Y. (2000) *From Third World to First: The Singapore Story, 1965–2000*, New York: HarperCollins.

343

——(2007) 'The United States, Iraq, and the war on terror', *Foreign Affairs* 86 (1): 2–7.

Lennon, A. (ed.) (2002) *What Does the World Want from America? International Perspectives on US Foreign Policy*, Cambridge, MA: MIT Press.

Lieber, K. and G. Alexander (2005) 'Waiting for balancing: why the world Is not pushing back', *International Security* 30 (1): 109–39.

Lynn-Jones, S. (ed.) (1991) *The Cold War and After: Prospects for Peace*, Cambridge, MA: MIT Press.

McCormack, G. (2004) 'Remilitarizing Japan', *New Left Review* 29: 29–45.

Mahbubani, K. (2005) *Beyond the Age of Innocence: Rebuilding Trust Between America and the World*, New York: Public Affairs.

Mallaby, S. (2002) 'The reluctant imperialist', *Foreign Affairs* 82 (2): 2–7.

Mauzy, D. and B. Job (2007) 'US policy in Southeast Asia: limited re-engagement after years of benign neglect', *Asian Survey* 47 (4): 622–41.

MMI (Majelis Mujahidin Indonesia) (2004) 'Amerika, Polri, dan Ba'asyir', 6 May; available at: http://majelis.mujahidin.or.id (accessed 20 May 2004).

Nagara, B. (2007) *The Star*, 4 January.

Najib Abdul Razak (2002) 'US–Malaysia defense cooperation: a solid success story', speech at the Heritage Foundation, Washington, DC, 3 May; available at: www.heritage.org/Research/Lecture/US-Malaysia-Defense-Cooperation (accessed 20 May 2002).

Nesadurai, H. (2006) 'Malaysia and the United States', in M. Beeson (ed.) *Bush and Asia: America's Evolving Relations with East Asia*, London: Routledge, pp. 179–95.

Nye, J. (1990) *Bound to Lead: The Changing Nature of American Power*, New York: Basic Books.

Reid, B. (2006) 'Bush and the Philippines after S11', in M. Beeson (ed.) *Bush and Asia: America's Evolving Relations with East Asia*, London: Routledge, pp. 145–61.

Riza Sihbudi (2004) 'Dunia Islam vs Politik Amerika', 11 February; available at: http://majelis.mujahidin.or.id (accessed 3 May 2004).

——(2006) 'Dinamika dan Kecenderungan Politik Islam di Timur Tengah dan Dunia Muslim', *Jurnal Politika* 2 (1): 7–34.

Robison, R. (2006) 'The reordering of Pax Americana: how does Southeast Asia fit in?' in V.R. Hadiz (ed.) *Empire and Neoliberalism in Asia*, London: Routledge, pp. 52–68.

Rodan, G. and K. Hewison (2006) 'Neoliberal globalization, conflict and security: new life for authoritarianism in Asia?' in V.R. Hadiz (ed.) *Empire and Neoliberalism in Asia*, London: Routledge, pp. 105–22.

Ross, R. (2006) 'Balance of power politics and the rise of China: accommodation and balancing in East Asia', *Security Studies* 15 (3): 355–95.

Ruggie, J. (ed.) (1993) *Multilateralism Matters: The Theory and Praxis of an Institutional Form*, New York: Columbia University Press.

Sardar, Z. and M.W. Davies (2002) *Why Do People Hate America?* Cambridge: Icon.

Sison, J.M. (2003) *US Terrorism and War in the Philippines*, Philippines: Aklat ng Bayan.

Strange, S. (1987) 'The persistent myth of lost hegemony', *International Organization* 41 (4): 551–74.

Stubbs, R. (2005) *Rethinking Asia's Economic Miracle: The Political Economy of War, Prosperity, and Crisis*, Houndmills, Basingstoke: Palgrave Macmillan.

Tan, L.C. (2003) 'Singapore's support for action on Iraq prompted by wider concerns', *The Straits Times*, 11 June.

Tan, S.S. (2007) *The Role of Knowledge Communities in Constructing Asia-Pacific Security*, Lewiston, NY: Edwin Mellen Press.

Tay, Simon S.C. (2004) 'Asia and the United States after 9/11: primacy and partnership in the Pacific', *Fletcher Forum of World Affairs* 28: 113–32.

Thayer, C. (1999) 'Vietnamese foreign policy: multilateralism and the threat of peaceful evolution', in C. Thayer and R. Amer (eds) *Vietnamese Foreign Policy in Transition*, Singapore: ISEAS, pp. 1–24.

Tilman, R. (1987) *Southeast Asia and the Enemy Beyond: ASEAN Perceptions of External Threats*, Boulder, CO: Westview Press.

Tow, W.T. and W. Choong (2001) 'Asian perceptions of BMD: defence or disequilibrium?' *Contemporary Southeast Asia* 23: 379–400.

Tyner, J. (2005) *Iraq, Terror and the Philippines' Will to War*, Lanham, MD: Rowman and Littlefield.

Van Ness, P. (2002) 'Hegemony, not anarchy: why China and Japan are not balancing US unipolar power', *International Relations of the Asia-Pacific* 2: 131–50.

Vuving, A. (2006) 'Strategy and evolution of Vietnam's China policy', *Asian Survey* 46 (6): 805–24.

Walt, S. (2002) 'Keeping the world "off-balance": self-restraint and US foreign policy', in J. Ikenberry (ed.) *America Unrivalled: The Future of the Balance of Power*, Ithaca, NY: Cornell University Press, pp. 121–54.

Wanandi, J. (2006a) 'Strategic trends in East Asia', *Indonesian Quarterly* 34 (4): 345–52.

——(2006b) *Global, Regional and National: Strategic Issues and Linkages*, Jakarta: CSIS.

Wheeler, M. (2006) 'US and southern Thailand conflict', public seminar on 'Southern Violence and the Thai State', Bangkok, 18–19 August.

Yamamoto, T., P. Thiparat and A. Ahsan (2001) *Asia's Role in Asia: Asian Views*, San Francisco, CA: The Asia Foundation.

Yeo, G. (2009) 'Remarks by Minister for Foreign Affairs George Yeo in Parliament during Committee of Supply Debate on 6 February 2009'; available at: http://app.mfa.gov.sg/2006/lowRes/press/view_press.asp?post_id=474506/02/2009 (accessed 8 February 2009).

22

STATE POWER, SOCIAL CONFLICTS AND SECURITY POLICY IN SOUTHEAST ASIA

Lee Jones ★

> Do international relations precede or follow (logically) fundamental social relations? There can be no doubt that they follow. Any organic innovation in the social structure, through its technical–military expressions, modifies organically absolute and relative relations in the international field, too.
>
> *Antonio Gramsci (1971: 176)*

International Relations (IR) scholars reading the other chapters in this volume may well be struck by the stark difference between the way that they conceptualize state behaviour and the methods that scholars of domestic politics and political economy use to understand state power, regimes, violence, authority and governance. In much of the mainstream IR theory applied to Southeast Asia, the anarchic international system constitutes a sufficiently autonomous realm for the external behaviour of states to be analysed quite separately from the internal power relations that actually constitute those states. It thus becomes possible to explain, say, the security policy of Southeast Asian states in terms of their pursuit of 'national interests', or with reference to their 'identity' and interstate norms. While occasional references to domestic politics might be unavoidable, for many IR theorists, 'states' are simply the pre-given units of international politics and we do not need to probe their origins, evolution or underpinnings particularly deeply.[1] While the agenda of international security may have broadened elsewhere to encompass actors and referent objects beyond the state, in Southeast Asia scholars argue that 'the state remains the critical actor' (Caballero-Anthony 2008: 195) and 'securitisation has largely been a state-centric project' (Emmers and Caballero-Anthony 2006: 32).

This chapter argues that state-centric approaches of international security policies are rarely sustainable in practice and offer a very limiting perspective on the behaviour of Southeast Asian states. IR theories too often neglect the specific nature of state power revealed by scholars of domestic politics and political economy. Rather than adopting a 'top-down' view of security policy as being determined by anarchy, abstract 'national interests' or interstate norms, this chapter advocates a 'bottom-up' approach, showing how specific policies are shaped by the particular constellations of power and interests that underpin states. From this perspective, there are multiple contending sources of foreign and security policy. While the geopolitical and strategic agendas identified by IR scholars certainly do exist, they represent the ideas and interests of very specific groups, notably the technocracies of foreign ministries which are embedded within global community of foreign policy apparatchiks. To the extent that their ideas become state policy, however, this reflects their interests and not some general, immutable, 'national' interest. More to the point, there are other socio-political forces – classes, class fractions, business groups, ethnic and religious groups, other parts of the state apparatus, and so on – whose ideas and interests frequently clash with and may override those of foreign policy officials. What actually emerges in practice, therefore, reflects conflicts among these different forces as they struggle to impose their interests as *raison d'état*.

From this perspective, security policies can only be understood as 'the products of historical structures and processes, of struggles for power within states, of conflicts between the societal groupings that inhabit states and the interests that besiege them' (Lipschutz 1995: 8). As the other chapters in this volume show, Southeast Asia's late capitalist development has produced highly distinctive forms of state and regime, modes of social control, institutions, interests and alliances. If we accept that states are not simply 'ideal types', always and everywhere the same, but are necessarily shaped by the concrete conditions in which they develop, the distinctive nature of state power in Southeast Asia must logically find expression at the international level. Indeed, domestic social conflict is a vital explanatory factor for the forms taken by regional conflicts and cooperation.

The argument proceeds in three sections. The first briefly critiques the statism and methodological nationalism of existing IR theory before discussing the ways in which domestic struggles over state power condition foreign and security policies. The second section uses this approach to analyse the policies of states within the region towards Burma. The country's military dictatorship is frequently said to be generating serious security threats, yet neighbouring states seem curiously resistant to taking action against the regime. This only makes sense if we understand their policies as being shaped and influenced by various social and economic interests and agendas. The third section more briefly applies the same approach to analyse Southeast Asian states' policies on environmental degradation and border conflicts.

Rethinking regional security policy

Security studies have traditionally been the bailiwick of IR scholars. As an academic discipline, IR was founded on the notion that relations between states possess their own distinctive dynamics that can be analysed and theorized separately from states' internal relations. This was initially an analytical distinction, but it has increasingly hardened into an ontological one. States are often simply assumed to be coherent, fixed, sovereign units expressing 'national interests' or possessing their own 'identities', dispensing with the need to consider how they are constituted and whose interests they actually represent, and how this might condition their external relations. Domestic political struggles are usually referred to in an *ad hoc* and opaque fashion. This section briefly critiques this top-down approach, focussing on the two dominant theories used in Southeast Asian IR, realism and constructivism, and explains how social conflicts over state power actually influence states' foreign and security policies.

The deeply embedded statism of IR theory has expressed itself in all varieties of scholarship on the security of Southeast Asia. 'Realist' analysts are generally sceptical about interstate cooperation because of the anarchic nature of the international system. They emphasize the role of great powers and shifts in the 'balance' between them as the fundamental determinants of regional security (e.g. Leifer 1989; Jones and Smith 2006). Realists have sometimes explained international conflicts with reference to domestic developments. Michael Leifer, for example, argued that Sukarno's crusading, anti-imperialist foreign policy in the 1960s was driven by attempts to manage the rising power of the Indonesian left. However, he proceeds to present the apparent return to *realpolitik* under Suharto as the resumption of the state's autonomy from domestic vested interests, restoring the rational management of Indonesia's external relations (Leifer 1983). This explanatory strategy presents the influence of domestic struggles on foreign and security policy as occasional, extraordinary and aberrant, rather than as a constant and evolving dynamic.

Constructivist scholars have attempted to show how norms, ideas and culture can help mitigate the effects of international anarchy that realists foreground. They argue that Southeast Asian states have had an important influence on regional security order by enunciating norms of interstate conduct that have 'socialized' the member-states of the Association of Southeast Asian Nations (ASEAN), and even external powers, transforming their interests and identities (Acharya 2001; Johnston 2003). However, constructivists have reinforced the statism and methodological nationalism of IR theory by conceptualizing states as *de facto* persons, capable of having an 'identity' as well as 'interests' (Wendt 2004). Like realists, constructivists have referred fleetingly to domestic dynamics to explain events that interstate norms cannot, such as the founding of ASEAN (Acharya 2001: 49), or to account for policy divergences, which are often explained rather crudely with reference to countries being 'more' or 'less' democratic (e.g. McDougall 2001). However, the consequence of treating states as persons is that no systematic attention can be paid to their domestic constitution. Constructivists' failure to enquire critically into the nature of state power has led critics to argue that they play directly into elite hands by deflecting 'analytical attention away from both existing tensions among ASEAN states and internal divisions within their states that reflected unresolved ethnic and religious dissonance and opaque networks of corruption and patronage' (Jones and Smith 2002: 100).

After lengthy neglect, IR scholars have recently begun to recognise the importance of domestic dynamics, particularly given the clear impact of the upheavals unleashed by the 1997–8 Asian financial crisis on foreign and security policies in the region. Once committed to illiberal and authoritarian 'Asian values', regional states now proclaim their fondness for 'democracy', 'human rights' and 'good governance', indicating their desire to shift from an elite-driven to a 'people-centred' ASEAN by boosting civil society 'participation'. Scholars cannot but attribute this shift to the 'democratic moment' of the Asian financial crisis and particularly the democratization of Indonesia (Acharya 1999). Analysts now speculate on the possibility of 'participatory regionalism' and the use of ASEAN as a forum for democracy promotion (Acharya 2003; Emmerson 2007). Moreover, they are grappling with how to reincorporate these domestic dynamics into their theorizing of regional security (e.g. Emmerson 2009).

So far, however, attempts to achieve this are ahistorical and theoretically unsatisfying. Scholars often treat the influence of domestic power relations on security policy as something entirely new, rather than something new only to IR analyses. Jörn Dosch, for example, claims that the 'intertwinedness of international and national structures and processes ... did not seem to exist until very recently'. He explains this alleged novelty by referring to the greater 'regime accountability' caused by democratization, which has reduced 'state autonomy' in foreign policy (Dosch 2006: 71, 21–30). This wrongly assumes that authoritarian states can somehow sit in splendid isolation from their own societies, doing as they will, and that only democratic states can express societal interests. Indonesia's Suharto regime, for example, which Dosch claims was simply dominated by a tiny political elite, reflecting the Javanese culture of kingship, was actually based on the support of business elites, the professional middle classes, Islamists, anti-communist nationalists, traditional rural authorities and the army (Robison 1986). The emphasis on formal institutional change since 1997 neglects the possibility that the same socio-economic and political elites whose interests have long dictated Indonesian policy have reorganized themselves to capture these new, apparently democratic institutions (Robison and Hadiz 2004).

Focusing narrowly on institutions ignores the wider constellations of social and economic power in which political institutions always develop and which conditions their operation in practice, leading to rather naïve views of the impact of democratization. Scholars too often assume that democratization naturally produces a 'shift from a realist to a more liberal perspective' (Dosch 2006: 46). It is simply seen as a 'logical consequence of domestic political change that the … most democratic states in Southeast Asia … should have been driving forces in the quest for a regional commitment to democracy and human rights' (Dosch 2009: 84). However, as many political economists have demonstrated, formally democratic regimes can in fact harbour highly illiberal practices, suggesting that institutions matter less than the social forces mediated through them. Rüland's (2009) recent study of the Indonesian parliament's role in foreign policy, for example, suggests that democratization has given vent to highly nationalistic, chauvinistic forces, not liberal ones. Similarly, changes in ASEAN's institutions are seized upon to suggest that 'the closed black box of high policymaking inside ASEAN has finally been pried open' by civil society organizations (Caballero-Anthony 2009: 216–17). Yet studies of the domestic influence of such organizations suggest that they remain profoundly constrained by the power of entrenched political and economic elites, casting doubt upon ebullient assessments of their regional strength (Reid 2006).

This suggests that a different view of the state is necessary in order to properly grasp the implications of social conflict for state power and for regional security policy. Rather than being seen as neutral apparatuses or sets of institutions, states are better understood as expressions of power. Far from being autonomous from their societies, even the most authoritarian states are actually interpenetrated with them in complex ways (Poulantzas 1976; Jessop 2008). Social forces – understood as ethnic and religious groups and especially classes and class fractions – struggle against one another to impress their interests and ideologies as *raison d'état*. They use a variety of means to do so, cultivating relations with or even capturing parts of state apparatuses, or using their social and economic power to frustrate and undermine official policy and ensure that, in practice, it is their interests which are realized. Because the capacity of different social forces to achieve these ends varies enormously, and because different state forms afford starkly divergent opportunities for them to do so, state power 'reflects and essentially underpins the prevailing hierarchies of power embodied in the social order' (Hewison *et al.* 1993: 6).

As other chapters of this volume have explored, in Southeast Asia states have been captured by groups made dominant by the legacies of colonial rule, Cold War strategies and state-led economic development: principally, a highly illiberal, frequently predatory, oligarchic elite. This has influenced foreign and security policy in several ways. Dominant societal forces are often able to capture state apparatuses directly and use them instrumentally, shaping them to suit their own purposes. This both shapes the overall contour of foreign and security policy and produces specific policy outcomes. A particularly egregious example is tycoon-turned-politician Thaksin Shinawatra, who became Thailand's foreign minister in the mid-1990s and prime minister from 2001–6. In 1994, his company, ShinCorp, was reportedly involved alongside officers of Thailand's National Security Council in a failed coup attempt against Cambodian prime minister Hun Sen, which was designed to advance the business interests of Thaksin and his allies (Jones 2010: 488). Thaksin also used his ministerial roles to acquire lucrative contracts for ShinCorp's subsidiary, Sattel, in Burma; correspondingly, he always promoted a soft line towards Burma's military regime (Pasuk and Baker 2004: 213; McCargo and Ukrist 2005: 54–5). This sort of instrumental control of state policy by oligarchic interests helps explain why, as one analyst wryly remarks, 'nothing drives government policy in Southeast Asia like the smell of money' (Ott 1998: 73).

The interpenetration of state apparatuses with different, potentially oppositional social forces also leads to social conflicts being played out within states themselves, generating incoherence in security policy. In the early 1990s, for example, the Thai government officially ceased its support for the guerrilla movements it had sponsored in Cambodia during the Cold War. However, various military, bureaucratic and business elites had established lucrative relationships with the guerrillas, relying on their cooperation to dominate the cross-border, black-market trade in arms, gems, timber and other commodities. These forces lobbied vociferously against, and essentially ignored, government policy. Army and police units simply continued to work with the guerrillas in order to line their own pockets (Rungswasdisab 2006: 103–11). The ability of powerful interests to control how state apparatuses are used in practice thus led to official policy being completely undermined and for Thailand to violate United Nations Security Council embargoes designed to assist the Cambodian peace process.

The influence that oligarchic elites exercise within state apparatuses, the economy and society more broadly also enables them to constrain state policy even when they do not control governments directly. In 1997, for example, the Asian financial crisis led to the downfall of the oligarchic Chavalit government in Thailand and its replacement by the reformist, neoliberal Democrat Party, which is based largely in the Bangkok middle class. Despite the change in government, the new foreign minister cautioned that

> The task of balancing the interests between the more progressive and entrenched establishment interests is a delicate one. Foreign policy cannot get ahead of social factors. Foreign policy must reflect the domestic structure; must reflect the existing social structure altogether. If foreign policy is internally contradictory, the benefits gained would fall short of their potential. For example, if our policy of promoting human rights and democracy hurts the interests of our traders along the border, the policy will encounter domestic political resistance and be ultimately unsustainable.
>
> *(Surin 1998)*

'Social structure' thus operates as a constraint on official policy, even at a distance. This is not simply because governments fear electoral defeat, but because dominant social forces are able to condition whether and how state apparatuses actually perform their officially assigned functions.

The distinctive nature of state power in Southeast Asia thus powerfully affects state policy and its practical implications.[2] From this 'bottom-up' perspective it is insufficient to make only ad hoc references to domestic developments or focus solely on formal declarations or institutions to explain the scope and content of regional security policy. If we wish to understand state policy we need to understand the strategy and interests of the specific social forces implicated in a given issue area and analyse the ways in which these forces constrain and enable state managers to respond. We will now apply this approach to analyse regional policy towards Burma.

Regional policy towards Burma

Burma's military-dominated regime, which stands accused of repeated human rights abuses and of generating serious transnational security threats, has become a major international political issue over the last two decades. Liberal critics in the West and Southeast Asia often criticize ASEAN for tolerating rather than dealing forcefully with the threats the Burmese regime creates to regional security. The Association's non-interference principle is often cited to explain this reaction. In reality, ASEAN states have frequently violated non-interference when dealing with Burma. They have, for example, increasingly criticized the repression of opposition forces and have repeatedly sought a role to play in Burma's process of 'national reconciliation' (Jones 2008). 'Non-interference' is thus a weak explanation for their failure to respond to Burma as a security threat. Analysing how policy is embedded in broader processes and power relations at the national level provides a better guide to state behaviour. First, it shows that oligarchic business interests, in particular, shape the basic contours of Southeast Asian states' policies towards Burma. Some things which appear as 'transnational security threats' to the region's liberal non-governmental organizations (NGOs) and political parties are actually seen as lucrative opportunities by more powerful oligarchic forces. Parts of state apparatuses are even directly involved in exploiting these opportunities. Second, we can examine how social conflict transforms security policy and the state. When liberalizing forces took control of the Thai government in 1997, they adopted a much more hostile policy towards Burma, identifying transnational flows as security threats, and began reconfiguring the state to act against them. However, this was reversed when oligarchic forces recaptured the state. Third, we can explore how regional states deal with the dilemmas created when gaps emerge between the policies generated by oligarchic domination and the demands of important extra-regional states. Several regional states have created more space for liberal critics to attack Burma, yet the risk of this being used for domestic purposes means that the space is tightly policed.

'Threats' as oligarchic opportunities

Dominant oligarchic interests have been very influential in setting the basic contours of regional policies on Burma. While liberal political parties and civil society groups see transnational flows from Burma, such as refugees, as a challenge to regional security, the region's business oligarchs see them as a commodity to be exploited and thus refuse to 'securitize' them.

Liberal critics in the West and in Southeast Asia have identified various transnational flows produced by military domination in Burma as threats to international security, including high incidences of communicable diseases like HIV/AIDS, forced and illegal migration, and exports of illegal narcotics. An estimated 700,000 Burmese refugees reside in neighbouring countries, as many as two million illegal Burmese migrants live in Thailand, and up to 500,000 are in Malaysia (DLA Piper Rudnick Gray Cary 2005: 56; IOM 2008). Burma exported an estimated $123m-worth of opium in 2008, and around 700m methamphetamine tablets as recently as 2004 (UNODC 2008: 43; Devaney et al. 2005: 48). Drug addiction and closely correlated HIV-infection rates in neighbouring countries have steadily grown. ASEAN itself has discursively 'securitized' a number of related issues, in 2000 declaring the goal of a 'drug-free ASEAN' by 2015, issuing a declaration on the protection of migrants in 2005, and expanding regional cooperation to include the combating of HIV/AIDS and transnational crime. However, some Southeast Asian NGOs and liberal politicians argue that this response is merely rhetorical and ineffective. For them, these problems constitute security threats requiring robust, interventionist measures by the United Nations, ASEAN and/or other powers like China and India (see, for example, www.altsean.org, www.aseanmp.org).

The disjuncture between critical interpretations of these threats, ASEAN's official security discourse and what regional states actually do in practice can be explained via the nature of state power in Southeast Asia. Rather than dealing with Burma forcefully as a security threat, ASEAN governments have instead pursued a policy of 'constructive engagement'. Launched in the early 1990s, this policy aimed to transcend the frosty relations of the Cold War era to facilitate trade and investment, encourage pro-market reforms and minimize China's influence in Burma. Although the policy was initially devised by Thai foreign ministry officials with the explicit goal of promoting reforms in Burma, in practice the contours of constructive engagement were principally set by the requirements of ASEAN's business classes. The Burmese and Indochinese markets were seen as lucrative destinations for accumulated investment capital and a crucial source of raw materials to replace supplies exhausted by ASEAN's long economic boom. The displacement of Thailand's military regime in 1988 by an elected government comprising leading business oligarchs paved the way for these interests to be prioritized in foreign and security policy and for Bangkok to try to turn neighbouring 'battlefields into marketplaces' (Jones 2008: 273–5).

Rapprochement with Burma was pioneered by well-connected senior military officers and state-linked business elites looking to expand their corporate interests into Burma. Many of them were or became involved in politics, like General Chavalit Yongchaiyudh, who became Thailand's prime minister in 1996. Thai politico-business elites were followed by Malaysian investors, including the state oil company, Petronas, which sank $587m into twenty-five projects in Burma by 2001, and many Suharto cronies, who invested similar sums. These intimate connections between state and business elites ensured a cautious, non-confrontational approach towards the military regime. The political and economic reforms promoted by neighbouring states as part of 'constructive engagement' were limited to those compatible with this agenda and were commensurate with regional elites' own illiberal styles of domestic governance (Jones 2008: 273–4, 278).

Recognizing the social basis of constructive engagement enables us to understand why the negative externalities of military rule in Burma are apparently accepted with such equanimity by neighbouring states. The vast numbers of Burmese refugees and migrants in Malaysia and Thailand, for example, are widely seen by business leaders not as a security risk but as a source of cheap, exploitable labour. Malaysia's economy depends heavily on foreign labour, with over two million legal and up to a million illegal workers (perhaps half of them Burmese) supplementing the 11.3m-strong domestic workforce. NGO leaders allege that Burmese migrant workers were used to construct the federal capital at Putrajaya, and a recent investigation even alleged the direct involvement of senior state officials in the trafficking of Burmese migrants across the Thai border (Jones 2008: 285; US Congress 2009).

Thai manufacturing, agriculture and fishing is also dependent on the exploitation of predominantly Burmese migrants. The International Labour Organization estimates that migrant labour produces up to 6.2 per cent of Thailand's GDP, or $11bn per year (Martin 2007). As in Malaysia, elements of the Thai state, whatever official government policy may be, are interpenetrated by or identical to the forces enriching themselves through such exploitation. According to Kraisak Choonhavan (2008), the Democrat Party's deputy leader, the National Security Council believes that up to five million Burmese migrants live in Thailand and worries they may soon 'explode with discontentment and anger'. Yet northern businessmen are currently able to quash strikes by 'hir[ing] policemen to do the job of suppression' (Kraisak 2008). The non-governmental Labour Rights Protection Network also alleges the involvement of Thai soldiers in people-trafficking (Ellgee 2009). Senior military officers and their allies on both sides of the border have long been accused of involvement in the black-market trade in drugs, arms and other goods, and Thai army units have reportedly even been bribed by both the Burmese government and rebel groups to intervene in battles across the border (Lintner 1999; Maung 2001: 58, 50–2).

The social, economic and political dominance of illiberal business interests, and their interpenetration with state apparatuses, thus produces an approach towards Burma which tolerates, exploits or even welcomes, rather than securitizing, the transnational flows produced by military rule.

Social conflict reshapes security policy and states

Illiberal business interests have not always been able to simply impose their interests upon the state. Occasionally, especially in moments of crisis, liberalizing middle-class forces may impose their preferences as government policy. However, due to the interpenetration of state apparatuses with powerful interests opposed to their agenda, liberalizers often face significant resistance both inside and outside the state. Consequently, they are often compelled to reorganize state apparatuses to pursue their goals. However, the political economy of the region is so weighted against liberalizing political parties that they are often unable to hold power for long, except in alliance with oligarchic groups.

The opponents of constructive engagement tend to be drawn from the liberal section of the middle class, which derives little benefit from the policy and has long been hostile to the Burmese regime. However, because of their subordinate position, liberals have struggled to impose their reading of the situation onto their respective states. The most forceful attempt to do so occurred under the Democrat government in Thailand from 1997 to 2001. Following repeated seizures of Thai personnel and installations by Burmese dissidents in late 1999 and early 2000, the government sealed the border and cracked down on Burmese migrant workers, severely damaging northern business interests (Haacke 2006: 8). The government also reorganized the state apparatus, promoting anti-Burmese reformers to key positions in the army. The new chief of the Thai Army, General Surayud, identified Burmese drugs as the principal threat to Thailand's security in January 2000, and by May, the deputy foreign minister had reportedly backed military raids on drug factories inside Burma, blasting the regime for sheltering narco-traffickers. Surayud endorsed the idea the following month, and armed clashes between the two countries' armies began along the border (Tasker and Crispin 2000; Kavi 2001: 125). The Democrats also tried to dilute ASEAN's non-interference principle, pressing for ASEAN to send a troika of foreign ministers to berate Burma. Outraged oligarchs condemned this ruinous deterioration in bilateral relations, trying to topple Chuan's administration in a parliamentary no-confidence motion (Associated Press 1999).

Despite Surin's warning about the necessity of government policy reflecting the 'social structure' (Surin 1998), the Democrats over-reached the government's wider social limitations. They were soundly defeated by Thaksin Shinawatra's Thai Rak Thai (TRT) party at the 2001 elections, which restored both the oligarchic domination of Thai politics and business as usual with Burma. Thaksin promoted leading Thai oligarchs to cabinet positions, following the Thai Chamber of Commerce's advice to make General Chavalit defence minister and use him to improve bilateral relations (Snitwongse 2001: 201). Thaksin cracked down on Burmese dissidents inside Thailand, renounced Thailand's policy of sponsoring Burmese rebel groups to create a 'buffer zone' along the border, and drastically reorganized the state apparatus, sidelining anti-Burmese reformers in the army and installing his own cronies (Pasuk and Baker 2004: 184–7; McCargo and Ukrist 2005: 131–51). Burma reopened the border to trade and reactivated fishing concessions, while Thai government funds were used to facilitate new investments in Burma, with Chavalit's allies and Thaksin himself rushing to exploit fresh opportunities (Moncrief and Khiel 2002; McCargo and Ukrist 2005: 54–5). The Thaksin government also ended the Democrats' attack on Burma's sovereignty, emphasizing 'non-interference' to justify their new policy. Meanwhile, Thaksin harnessed public concern about narcotics, not to attack Burma but to wage a domestic 'war on drugs' in which over 2,700 people were extra-judicially killed, many of them allegedly local 'godfathers' who had resisted incorporation into TRT networks (McCargo and Ukrist 2005: 227). Thaksin only took a critical line towards Burma when a lucrative free trade deal with the US was threatened in the wake of an anti-opposition crackdown by the junta in 2003 (Jones 2008: 279).

These dramatic reversals in policy, and the reconfigurations of the state which accompanied them, clearly cannot be explained without reference to Thailand's domestic social conflict. Moreover, it is this conflict which determines the state's relationship to ASEAN's non-interference principle, rather than the norm which determines state behaviour.

The dilemmas of strategic liberalization

Challenges to business-friendly policies towards Burma do not merely emanate from the domestic field, however. Particularly since a resurgence of hard-liners in the Burmese regime since 2003, Western states have also applied a great deal of pressure on ASEAN. This has imperilled the external economic and political relationships from which dominant forces benefit. Several Southeast Asian states have therefore allowed more space for domestic critics of Burma, to enhance their standing in Western capitals. However, the risk of this space being exploited to demand *domestic* reforms means that it is often tightly policed. This illustrates that the degree of liberalization in foreign and security policies remains subject to broader structural constraints.

The widening of domestic space is clearest in the Philippines and Indonesia. Since the demise of the Suharto regime and its significant business interests in Burma, dominant groups in these two states have had little interest in defending the Burmese regime. Indeed, Indonesian elites have found playing up their liberal-democratic image a useful way of regaining Western aid in the wake of the Asian financial crisis, and of restating Jakarta's supposed right to lead ASEAN (Emmerson 2007; Rüland 2009). Indonesian legislators are thus happy to criticize military rule in Burma, and have been at the forefront of the ASEAN Inter-Parliamentary Myanmar Caucus (AIPMC) which campaigns for intervention in Burma. However, because many legislators are drawn from the old elite and benefit from widespread corruption, they have refused to support a similar caucus on 'good governance'. This shows that liberalizing forces are not automatically unleashed by democratization, but remain subject to broader structural constraints on state power (Jones 2009: 398–400).

More authoritarian regimes like those in Cambodia, Singapore and Malaysia have also granted space to critics of Burma from within their own parliaments to help burnish their 'democratic' credentials and distance themselves from the junta. However, the risk that liberalizing opposition parties might use this space to pursue a domestic agenda means that this space remains constrained and policed. Singapore, for instance, has strongly encouraged the AIPMC, but arrested opposition politicians and protest groups for staging their own independent demonstrations against Burma. Similarly, the Malaysian government has ensured that the AIPMC legislators' attacks on Burma do not go so far as to damage state-linked economic interests. They were allowed, for example, to criticize the regime in parliament, but not to pass a resolution calling for sanctions. As an opposition parliamentarian explains, since 'some of the MPs, or the government-linked corporations, like Petronas' retain investments in Burma 'we can't call for sanctions because this will hurt the investors from Malaysia' (Kok 2008). Consequently, even when political space is strategically relaxed, dominant forces can take steps to constrain its use, and entrenched political economy relationships still operate as a background constraint.

The 'social conflict' approach to analysing regional security policies has revealed why Southeast Asian states seem surprisingly indulgent of Burma. What appears as a 'threat' to some social groups may be a lucrative opportunity for others. What matters is less the nature and magnitude of the material flows across borders, but rather their relationship to the interests, ideologies and strategies of key social forces, and the power relations between these forces.

Implications for other issues: across and upon borders

The approach developed above can potentially help us understand a wide range of 'security' issues. Indeed, it can help shed light on why a region with many so-called 'non-traditional' security threats elicits so little practical cooperation to tackle these threats: the social forces that benefit from or even produce these threats may be too deeply entrenched, or the conflicts among them too severe, to permit such cooperation. This section indicates how the framework could be applied to analyse environmental governance and border conflicts.

Haze

Environmental degradation is widespread in Southeast Asia, and occasionally it is securitized. In particular, the annual 'haze' (smog) arising from Indonesian forest fires has become a major political issue. In the worst year, 1997, the haze had a greater impact than the *Exxon Valdez* disaster, affecting the health of seventy million people and costing an estimated $4.5bn (Glover and Jessup 1999). As with the Burma issue, this seems an objective 'threat' requiring decisive action, and certainly environmentalist NGOs make such claims. ASEAN states, which had been discussing environmental issues since 1990, also appeared to securitize the issue in their regional agreement on haze in 2003. However, this agreement remains unratified by the Indonesian parliament, and therefore offers no basis for Malaysia and Singapore, the worst-affected countries, to take action. The 2006 haze was almost as severe as that in 1997, suggesting that this problem is far from resolved.

The barrier to effective cooperation against this 'threat' is not, as IR scholars would again have it, ASEAN's non-interference principle. Rather, as Tay explains, it is 'certain agro-industrial firms, ambitious politicians, and venal officials who mutually benefit from cheaply burning off land to plant cash crops' in Indonesia, and the 'corruption and collusion between some of the large plantation firms that use fire and the officials who are supposed to control and suppress such illegal acts' (Tay 2009: 233). The Indonesian military – and perhaps the police – relies on illegal activities, including logging, to raise at least half of its operational costs, and powerful agri-business magnates are able to dominate state institutions and corrupt judicial outcomes at the local and even national levels (ICG 2001; Matthew and Van Gelder, 2002). It is thus unsurprising that the ASEAN haze agreement remains unratified and no decisive action has been taken against polluters.

Why are the Singaporean and Malaysian governments reluctant to take unilateral action against haze producers inside Indonesia? Partly, they are doubtless afraid of evoking a predictable, hostile response from the Indonesian state. However, they may also wish to avoid other repercussions that are not so clearly apparent. Indonesian ministers have called for Malaysia and Singapore, as the main export destinations for illegal timber, to help stem unlawful logging in Indonesia. Tay (2009) dismisses this as merely diversionary. However, this overlooks the fact that key agri-businesses involved in slash-and-burn operations, like Asia-Pacific Resources International Holdings Ltd (APRIL), are actually headquartered in Singapore and operate processing facilities in Malaysian Borneo (Matthew and Van Gelder 2002: 14–15). APRIL is just one of the many Indonesian businesses, led by one of the ethnic Chinese magnates who dominate the regional economy, which benefited hugely from state patronage under Suharto before relocating to Singapore to escape financial reckoning during the 1997 Asian financial crisis (Studwell 2007: esp. 163–7). It reminds us that a full explanation of transboundary 'security' issues is rarely complete without taking into account the complex and evolving transnational organization of economic, social and political power.

Border Conflicts

The 'social conflict' approach may also help in analysing more 'traditional' security issues, such as border disputes. Take, for example, the Thai–Cambodian border conflict, which has been raging since July 2008 and has involved vitriolic diplomatic exchanges, repeated incursions of Thai forces into Cambodia, and even armed clashes. Ostensibly, the dispute concerns a few square miles of scrubland adjacent to the Preah Vihear temple, which was granted to Cambodia by an International Court of Justice ruling in 1962. In fact, the conflict has virtually nothing to do with territory or border 'security' at all; its roots lie firmly in Thailand's domestic social conflicts.

The dispute emerged as part of an effort to topple the Thai government in 2008. The government was led by the People's Power Party (PPP), which won a plurality of votes in the first democratic elections following the military coup that overthrew the Thaksin government in 2006. The TRT had been forcibly disbanded but had simply reconstituted itself as the PPP and quickly seized power thanks to continued support from the rural poor. Consequently, the same forces that had opposed Thaksin in 2006 now lined up against the PPP. This alliance spanned the middle classes, big businessmen disgruntled at Thaksin's monopolization of lucrative opportunities, and the palace network, including politico-business and military and bureaucratic elites who resented Thaksin's growing encroachment on their turf (Connors and Hewison 2008).

These forces, led in parliament by the Democrats, began agitating against the government in a way which directly precipitated conflict with Cambodia. Using courts stuffed with anti-Thaksin judges during the military interregnum, they launched a series of highly politicized lawsuits against the PPP. In a so-called 'judicial coup', the courts first ruled that the PPP must disband due to electoral irregularities. The PPP simply reconstituted itself as Puea Thai and carried on. The courts then targeted individual ministers for prosecution, forcing the resignation of Prime Minister Samak Sundraravej over the hosting of a television cookery show. The border dispute began when Foreign Minister Noppadon Pattama supported Cambodia's bid for UNESCO recognition of Preah Vihear as a world heritage site. Democrat legislators (falsely) claimed that the government had thereby unconstitutionally alienated Thai territory, initiating another lawsuit. The constitutional court ruled in favour of the Democrat suit. Noppadon was forced to resign, and the government had to send politically unreliable troops to the border. Clashes were then inevitable.

The border conflict was thus triggered by the entirely opportunistic use of a long-dormant interstate dispute for purely domestic purposes. It has persisted because despite the Democrats having lured away a Puea Thai faction in December 2008, enabling them to finally dislodge their enemies and form a coalition government, the social conflict underpinning the country's political upheaval is far from resolved. The farmers, workers and oligarchs loyal to Thaksin are refusing to simply submit to the middle classes and elites clustered around the palace. On the contrary, this intense social struggle has produced open violence on the streets on several occasions, notably the massacre of 90 red-shirted protestors in April 2010. In opposition, Puea Thai has mimicked the Democrats' opportunistic use of Preah Vihear to advance their position in this conflict, attacking the Democrats in March 2009 for 'losing' 250 metres of territory by ignoring the construction of a new Cambodian road to the temple. Thus, troops remain stationed along the border, producing continued tensions and territorial violations. Reflecting what is really at stake at Preah Vihear, Cambodia's prime minister retaliated by appointing Thaksin as his economic adviser in November 2009. The border dispute is thus unlikely to end any sooner than the profound social conflicts in which it is firmly rooted in Thailand.

Conclusions

This chapter has argued that the roots of security policy in Southeast Asia are best sought not in the realm where abstract norms and national interests supposedly hold sway, but rather in the domestic social conflicts that shape state power and policy. The particular nature of the region's social and economic development has created powerful forces which are able to either directly capture or indirectly impose their wishes on the state, or organize themselves in ways that frustrate policy implementation or bend it to their interests. A proper understanding of international security issues is impossible without exploring their relationship to the strategies and interests of important societal groups. Many regional security issues are intractable precisely because they are rooted in obdurate social conflicts, or because they relate to particularly entrenched interests. To ignore this relationship inevitably produces naïve, technocratic policy prescriptions that have no realistic chance of being adopted, in the short term at least, given the social constraints faced by governments.

This in turn helps to explain why it is often so difficult to get states to sign up to instruments of global governance or to meet their obligations under such instruments. Take, for example, environmental governance, which is an increasingly important issue on the global security agenda and the focus of growing numbers of multilateral treaties and institutions. Issues like climate change, air pollution, forest depletion and species extinction are increasingly acknowledged in Southeast Asia's regional security discourse. However, the actual formulation and implementation of policies is filtered through dominant domestic interests. Regional states have long been in league with rapacious corporate interests, embracing porous borders and pursuing deregulation in neighbouring territories to help shift environmental exploitation into spaces where political mobilization around green issues is less effective (Pangsapa and Smith 2008). States are also reluctant to join and implement global accords around these issues because natural resources are often exploited by networks directly connected to politico-security elites who benefit from off-budget revenues and other collusive relationships (Talbott and Brown 1998; Smith *et al.* 2003). To the extent that environmental governance does occur it is likely to take an 'authoritarian' form which will reinforce dominant interests (Beeson 2010).

However, as we have seen, security policy is not simply an unfettered expression of the interests of dominant forces. Rather, states and their policies are contingent outcomes of struggles for power and control. As Thailand's relations with Burma and Cambodia show, social conflict can generate dramatic shifts in policy as competing groups reorganize the state to promote their ideologies and interests. The future of security policy in Southeast Asia will thus depend on the ongoing social, economic and political transformation of the region. In many key states, despite the persistence of oligarchic power, middle-class oppositional movements are becoming more influential, particularly in Indonesia, Thailand and Malaysia. Furthermore, they are beginning to organize themselves internationally, through bodies like inter-parliamentary caucuses on Myanmar and good governance (for legislators), and the ASEAN People's Forum (for NGOs). Growing popular disillusionment with government corruption, collusion and nepotism has doubtless compelled the creation of new national and regional institutions, and public commitments to liberal values.

However, new institutions and discourse do not automatically guarantee progressive outcomes. While institutions created to perpetuate oligarchic rule in a more 'legitimate' form can occasionally be exploited by reformists in unexpected ways (Rodan 2008), the risk of co-optation is ever-present. Rather than building up independent social bases to enhance their power, middle-class reformists have historically preferred to demand 'good governance' and technocratic rule merely to advance their own narrow interests, adopting explicitly *anti*-democratic insurrectionist strategies and expressing disdain for the 'backwards', corruptible masses (Thomson 2007). This strategy has led many reformists into deeply compromising alliances with entrenched, conservative forces (Reid 2006; Kitirianglarp and Hewison 2009). Even if this strategy was reversed, the region's entrenched political economy relationships so profoundly 'undermine cohesive, independent, collective political action' that real political transformation 'requires a transformation in the

357

political economy' (Rodan and Jayasuriya 2009: 43). Reformers are therefore necessarily playing a very long game.

Notes

* I am grateful to Richard Robison and Shahar Hameiri for their feedback on earlier drafts. This chapter draws extensively on my article 'Beyond Securitization: Explain the Scope of Security Policy in Southeast Asia', *International Relations of the Asia Pacific* (2011) doi:10.1093/irap/icr002 published online 19 March 2011.

1 There are of course important exceptions, notably Etel Solingen's often neglected liberal analyses of Southeast Asian regional cooperation (e.g. Solingen 2005). However, even Solingen's work remains limited by its reliance on ideal-typical coalitions which ill-fit the Southeast Asian context.

2 It is worth pointing out that while the specific detail here applies to Southeast Asian states, the general theoretical argument and analytical method is universally applicable, including to the 'great' powers. For example, US policy towards Latin America during much of the Cold War is arguably incomprehensible without taking into account the interests of American corporations like the United Fruit Company.

References

Acharya, A. (1999) 'Southeast Asia's democratic moment', *Asian Survey* 39 (3): 418–32.

——(2001) *Constructing a Security Community in Southeast Asia: ASEAN and the Problem of Regional Order*, London: Routledge.

——(2003) 'Democratization and the prospects for participatory regionalism in Southeast Asia', *Third World Quarterly* 24 (2): 375–90.

Associated Press (1999) 'Opposition launches censure motion against Thai government', 15 December.

Beeson, M. (2010) 'The coming of environmental authoritarianism', *Environmental Politics* 19 (2): 276–94.

Caballero-Anthony, M. (2008) 'Non-traditional security in Asia: the many faces of securitization', in A.F. Cooper, C.W. Hughes and P. De Lombaerde (eds) *Regionalisation and Global Governance: The Taming of Globalisation?* Abingdon: Routledge, pp. 187–209.

——(2009) 'Challenging change: nontraditional security, democracy, and regionalism', in D.K. Emmerson (ed.) *Hard Choices: Security, Democracy, and Regionalism in Southeast Asia*, Singapore: ISEAS, pp. 191–217.

Connors, M.K. and K. Hewison (2008) 'Introduction: Thailand and the "good coup"', *Journal of Contemporary Asia* Special Issue, 38 (1): 1–10

Devaney, M., G. Reid and S. Baldwin (2005) 'Situational analysis of illicit drug issues and responses in the Asia-Pacific region', Canberra, Australian National Council on Drugs; available at www.burnet.edu.au/freestyler/gui/files/rp12_asia_pacific_46f99d4df0c00.pdf (accessed 11 December 2009).

DLA Piper Rudnick Gray Cary (2005) *Threat to the Peace: A Call for the UN Security Council to Act in Burma*, New York: DLA Piper Rudnick Gray Cary.

Dosch, J. (2006) *The Changing Dynamics of Southeast Asian Politics*, Boulder, CO: Lynne Rienner.

——(2009) 'Sovereignty rules: human security, civil society, and the limits of liberal reform', in D.K. Emmerson (ed.) *Hard Choices: Security, Democracy, and Regionalism in Southeast Asia*, Singapore: ISEAS, pp. 59–90.

Ellgee, A. (2009) 'DKBA "involved in human trafficking"', *The Irrawaddy*, 18 December.

Emmers, R. and M. Caballero-Anthony (2006) 'The dynamics of securitization in Asia', in R. Emmers, M. Caballero-Anthony and A. Acharya (eds) *Studying Non-traditional Security in Asia: Trends and Issues*, Singapore: Marshall Cavendish, pp. 21–35.

Emmerson, D.K. (2007) 'Challenging ASEAN: a "topological" view', *Contemporary Southeast Asia* 29 (3): 424–46.

——(ed.) (2009) *Hard Choices: Security, Democracy, and Regionalism in Southeast Asia*, Singapore: ISEAS.

Glover, D. and T. Jessup (eds) (1999) *Indonesia's Fire and Haze: The Cost of the Catastrophe*, Singapore: IDRC/ISEAS.

Gramsci, A. (1971) *Selections from the Prison Notebooks*, trans. Q. Hoare and G.N. Smith, London: Lawrence and Wishart.

Haacke, J. (2006) 'Myanmar's foreign policy towards ASEAN: from success to failure?' paper presented at BISA conference, University College, Cork, Ireland, 19 December.

Hewison, K., R. Robison and G. Rodan (1993) 'Introduction: Changing forms of state power in Southeast Asia', in K. Hewison, R. Robison and G. Rodan (eds) *Southeast Asia in the 1990s: Authoritarianism, Democracy and Capitalism*, St Leonards, Australia: Allen and Unwin, pp. 2–8.

International Crisis Group (ICG) (2001) 'Indonesia: natural resources and law enforcement', *Asia Report* no. 29, ICG, Brussels.

International Organization for Migration (IOM) (2008) 'Situation report on international migration in East and South-East Asia', IOM, Bangkok; available at: www.iom-seasia.org/resource/pdf/iomsituationreport. pdf, (accessed 11 December 2009).

Jessop, B. (2008) *State Power: A Strategic–Relational Approach*, Cambridge: Polity.

Johnston, A.I. (2003) 'Socialization in international institutions: the ASEAN way and International Relations theory', in G.J. Ikenberry and M. Mastanduno (eds) *International Relations Theory and the Asia-Pacific*, New York: Columbia University Press, pp. 107–62.

Jones, D.M. and M.L.R. Smith (2002) 'ASEAN's imitation community', *Orbis* 46 (1): 93–109.

——(2006) *ASEAN and East Asian International Relations: Regional Delusion*, Cheltenham: Edward Elgar.

Jones, L. (2008) 'ASEAN's albatross: ASEAN's Burma policy, from constructive engagement to critical disengagement', *Asian Security* 4 (3): 271–93.

——(2009) 'Democratization and foreign policy in Southeast Asia: the case of the ASEAN inter-parliamentary Myanmar caucus', *Cambridge Review of International Affairs* 22 (3): 387–406.

——(2010) 'ASEAN's unchanged melody? The theory and practice of "non-interference" in Southeast Asia', *Pacific Review* 23 (4): 477–500.

Kavi C. (2001) 'Thai–Burma relations', in *Challenges to Democratization in Burma – Perspectives on Multilateral and Bilateral Responses*, Stockholm: International Institute for Democracy and Electoral Assistance, pp. 117–29.

Kitirianglarp, K. and K. Hewison (2009) 'Social movements and political opposition in contemporary Thailand', *Pacific Review* 22 (4): 451–77.

Kok, Teresa (2008) *Interview*, Kuala Lumpur, January.

Kraisak Choonhavan (2008) *Interview*, Bangkok, January.

Leifer, M. (1983) *Indonesia's Foreign Policy*, London: Allen and Unwin.

——(1989) *ASEAN and the Security of Southeast Asia*, London: Routledge.

Lintner, B. (1999) *Burma in Revolt: Opium and Insurgency since 1948*, Chiang Mai: Silkworm Books.

Lipschutz, R.D. (1995) 'On security', in R.D. Lipschutz (ed.) *On Security*, New York: Columbia University Press, pp. 1–23.

McCargo, D. and P. Ukrist (2005) *The Thaksinization of Thailand*, Copenhagen: NIAS Press.

McDougall, D. (2001) 'Regional institutions and security: implications of the 1999 East Timor crisis', in A. Tan, and J.D.K. Boutin (eds) *Non-traditional Security Issues in Southeast Asia*, Singapore: IDSS, pp. 166–96.

Martin, P. (2007) *The Contribution of Migrant Workers to Thailand: Towards Policy Development*, Bangkok: ILO.

Matthew, E. and J.W. Van Gelder (2002) 'Paper tiger, hidden dragons 2: April fools', Friends of the Earth, London; available at: www.foe.co.uk/resource/reports/april_fools.pdf (accessed 20 June 2011).

Maung Aung Myoe (2001) *Neither Friend nor Foe: Myanmar's Relations with Thailand since 1988 – A View from Yangon*, Singapore: IDSS.

Moncrief, J.S. and G. Khiel (2002) 'Art for politics' sake', *The Irrawaddy*, January.

Ott, M.C. (1998) 'From isolation to relevance: policy considerations', in R.I. Rotberg (ed.) *Burma: Prospects for a Democratic Future*, Washington, DC: Brooking Institution Press, pp. 69–83.

Pangsapa, P. and M.J. Smith (2008) 'Political economy of Southeast Asian borderlands: migration, environment, and developing country firms', *Journal of Contemporary Asia*, 38 (4): 485–514.

Pasuk P. and C. Baker (2004) *Thaksin: The Business of Politics in Thailand*, Copenhagen: NIAS.

Poulantzas, N. (1976) *State, Power, Socialism*, London: New Left Books.

Reid, B. (2006) 'The Arroyo government and "civil society" participation in the Philippines', in G. Rodan and K. Jayasuriya (eds) *Neoliberalism and Conflict in Asia after 9/11*, Abingdon: Routledge, pp. 180–201.

Robison, R. (1986) *Indonesia: The Rise of Capital*, Sydney: Allen and Unwin.

Robison, R. and V.R. Hadiz (2004) *Reorganising Power in Indonesia: The Politics of Oligarchy in an Age of Markets*, New York: RoutledgeCurzon.

Rodan, G. (2008) 'Accountability and authoritarianism: human rights in Malaysia and Singapore', *Journal of Contemporary Asia* 39 (2): 180–203.

Rodan, G. and K. Jayasuriya (2009) 'Capitalist development, regime transitions and new forms of authoritarianism in Asia', *Pacific Review* 22 (1): 23–47.

Rüland, J. (2009) 'Deepening ASEAN cooperation through democratization? The Indonesian legislature and foreign policymaking', *International Relations of the Asia-Pacific* 9 (3): 373–402.

Rungswasdisab, P. (2006) 'Thailand's response to the Cambodian genocide', in S. Cook (ed.) *Genocide in Cambodia and Rwanda: New Perspectives*, New Brunswick, NJ; London: Transaction Publishers.

Smith, J., K. Obidzinski, S. Subarudi and I. Suramenggala (2003) 'Illegal logging, collusive corruption and fragmented governments in Kalimantan, Indonesia', *International Forestry Review* 5 (3): 293–302.

Snitwongse, K. (2001) 'Thai foreign policy in the global age: principle or profit?' *Contemporary Southeast Asia* 23 (2): 189–212.

Solingen, E. (2005) 'ASEAN cooperation: the legacy of the economic crisis', *International Relations of the Asia-Pacific* 5(1): 1–29.

Studwell, J. (2007) *Asian Godfathers: Money and Power in Hong Kong and South-East Asia*, London: Profile Books.

Surin P. (1998) 'Thailand's foreign policy during the economic and social crises', speech at Thammasat University, Bangkok, 12 June 1998.

Talbott, K. and M. Brown (1998) 'Forest plunder in Southeast Asia: an environmental security nexus in Burma and Cambodia', *Environmental Change and Security Project Report* 4: 53–60.

Tasker, R. and S. Crispin (2000) 'Flash point', *Far Eastern Economic Review* 163 (22) (1 June): 24–6.

Tay, S.S.C. (2009) 'Blowing smoke: regional cooperation, Indonesian democracy, and the haze', in D.K. Emmerson (ed.) *Hard Choices: Security, Democracy, and Regionalism in Southeast Asia*, Singapore: ISEAS, pp. 219–39.

Thomson, M.R. (2007) 'The dialectic of "good governance" and democracy in Southeast Asia: globalized discourses and local responses', *Globality Studies* 10 (4): 1–21.

United Nations Office on Drugs and Crime (UNODC) (2008) 'Opium poppy cultivation in South East Asia', New York, UNODC; available at: www.unodc.org/documents/crop-monitoring/East_Asia_Opium_report_2008.pdf (accessed 11 December 2009).

US Congress (2009) *Trafficking and Extortion of Burmese Migrants in Malaysia and Southern Thailand*, Washington, DC: US Government Printing Office.

Wendt, A. (2004) 'The state as person in international theory', *Review of International Studies* 30 (2): 289–316.

INDEX

Abdillah of Medan 80n12
Abdullah, Ali 340n9
Accra Agenda for Action (OECD-DAC, 2008) 174, 175, 177, 182
adat law 233–34
administrative devolution 230
administrative involution 231–32
Afghanistan, wake of war in 330
agency, limitations on 14
Agrarian Law (1960) in Indonesia 244–45
agrarian reform in Indonesia 242–43, 251–53
agricultural exports 7
aid effectiveness: development trajectories and 182–83; implications of donor decisions 182–83; literature on 174
Alliance of Adat Communities in Indonesia (AMAN) 233
Almonte, Jose 109
American power, perceptions of 4, 330–42; acceptance of US primacy 330–31, 332; Afghanistan, wake of war in 330; American hegemony, decline of 331; American imperium 331; anti-Americanism, superficial manifestations of 332; benignity of US power, 330–31; bilateral relations, patterns of 335–36; bipolar balance of power, notion of 337–38; causalities of American actions, reticence over 339; China as source of instability 338–39; commentators, opinions of 333–34; contradictions on 332–36; cooperation agendas, pursuit of 334; democratic system in US, checks and balances in 338; divisions on 332–36; foreign policy establishment, supporting beliefs in 336–39; geographic distance of US from Asia 338; images of US in literature of primacy 331–32; Indonesia, negative views of social actors in 335; international role of US, claims about 331; Malaysia, negative views of social actors in 335; negativity of US power 131–32, 330–31; organized groups, opinions of 333–34; personal responses 340; popular opinion, divergence

between elite views and 332; post-2001 US policy, indirect nature of criticisms of 339; professional responses 340; stability and prosperity, belief in US as source of 336–37, 338; treaty allies 334–35; trust in US benignity 338; unilateralism of US policy 331, 333; volatility of opinion 332
Anglo-American law template 187
anti-Americanism, superficial manifestations of 332
anti-colonialism 28–29
Anti-Corruption Commission in Indonesia 74–75
Anwar Ibrahim 221
Aquino, Corazon 47, 99, 105, 107, 108, 109, 112, 113, 117n22, 294, 295, 320
Aquino III, Benigno S. 'Noynoy' 97, 107, 112, 113, 114, 115n1, 116n16, 296
Aquino Sr., Benigno 61, 102
aristocracy in Indonesia 233–34
Arroyo, Gloria 94, 110, 111, 112, 117n22, 117n23, 296, 320
Asia-Pacific Export Community (APEC) 317, 324, 326
Asia-Pacific Resources International Holdings Ltd (APRIL) 355
Asian Development Bank (ADB): Country Performance Assessment (CPA) 181; neo-liberalism, institutional reform and 175; strategy for engagement with fragile states 180–81
Asian economic crisis (!997–98) 3, 34, 35, 72, 84, 153, 178–79, 183; debates on interpretation of politics of Southeast Asia 11, 13
Asian economic crisis (1997–98): growth variations, market capitalism and 160–61; market regulation, judicialization of 187
ASEAN Free Trade Area (AFTA) 317–18
Asian populism, wave of 84
Association of District Commissioners (APKESI) in Indonesia 247
Association of Muslim Professionals (AMP) in Singapore 129

361

quantitative methodologies 16

radical decentralization in Indonesia 71
Rajasekaran, General Secretary 313n4
Ramos, Fidel 99, 109, 110, 113, 320
Ramos-Horta, Jose 284
Rasyid, Yunus 80n12
Ratchadamnoen Road, Bangkok 199, 200, 201
rational choice theory: debates on interpretation
    of politics of Southeast Asia 6, 16; violence and
    conflict, tackling legacies of 265
Reaching Everyone for Active Citizenry
    (REACH) in Singapore 124–25, 126, 127, 131
Reagan, Ronald 6, 16
real estate developments, global capitalism and
    205–6
Red Shirts in Thailand 199, 200–202; mass
    mobilization of 91–92, 93
reduction of emissions from deforestation and
    degradation (REDD) 242–43, 253–55
reform, imperatives in Philippines 113–15
reform dynamics in Indonesia 249–55, 255–56
reformasi in Indonesia 72–73, 219, 245–46, 249–50
regime presentation powers of Macapagal-Arroyo
    in Philippines 111–12
regional autonomy laws in Indonesia 230–31
regional identity politics in Indonesia 233–34
regional power in Indonesia, fight for 232–33
regional security policy 347–50, 356–58
regional special taxation in Indonesia 230–31
regional trade liberalization, domestic interests and
    322–24
regularized migration channels 308
relocation of power in Thailand, early opposition
    to 87
rent-seeking activities in Philippines 98
rental housing, investment in 206
representational structures in Philippines 97
representatives, Burke's account of 130
repressed civil society 214
resentment of oligarchy in Thailand 84–85
resources: constraints on NICs 159–60;
    governance of 249–50
reunification in Vietnam, Communist Party rule
    and 135
Revenue Sharing Law (1999) in Indonesia 230
revolutionary wars 8
Royal Powers, royal prerogative and 88

Salim Group in Indonesia 71
Samak Sundraravej 356
Sarit, General (later Field Marshall) 7, 159
service economy, protest and disruption of
    200–201
Shinawatra, Thaksin 11, 12, 15, 35, 48, 71, 83,
    84, 94n5, 95n9, 169n48, 169n49, 201, 327,
    334, 335, 336, 349, 353, 356; bureaucratic

resentment against 88; electoral victory 88–89;
    populism of 87–88; power relocation, demands
    for 87; rise of 85–86, 93, 94; state power, social
    conflict and security policy 349; threat to old
    oligarchy, perception of 87, 89, 93;
    transformation from modernist to populist
    87–88, 93–94Siew Kum Hong 129, 130
Shinawatra, Yingluck 94
Singapore 2, 7, 9, 12, 16; authoritarian legalism in
    62; civil oligarchy in 61; civil society, social
    movements and political parties 213, 214; civil
    society organizations in 35; Corrupt Practices
    Investigation Bureau (CPIB) 63; corruption,
    dealing with 63; 'Golden Shoe' business district
    in 203–4; independence for 62; investment
    constraints on oligarchs 62–63; legal strength of
    63; legal system in 63–64; National Trades
    Union Congress of (NTUC) 312; oligarchs and
    oligarchy in 54–55, 61–64, 65n10; paranoia and
    fear at birth of 62; People's Action Party (PAP)
    63, 64; resource access for 159–60;
    service-oriented trade unions in 311; Singapore
    Youth Award 129; state interventionism in 176;
    student movement in 33; total defense posture
    in 62–63
Sitepu, Bangkit 299
skills, weak business demand for 166
Sochib, Chasan 238
social costs of entrepreneurial cities 205–8
social democracy: capitalism and 8–9; demise of 6
social movement organizations (SMOs) 12–13,
    214–15, 217, 219–20, 221–22, 224–25, 226;
    susceptibility to co-option 14
social structure, official policy and 350, 353
socialism, rise of 30–31, 31–32
societal weakening, labour and 164–66
socio-economic transformations 25
Soeharto 71, 74, 75, 187, 190, 192, 229, 232, 233
    see also Suharto
Soh-Khim Ong, Patricia 129
Soin, Kanwaljit 128, 129, 130
Sondhi Limthongkul 89, 90, 91
South Korea 3, 9; competitiveness of 157;
    populism in 94; resource access for 159–60;
    state interventionism in 176
Sri Mulyani Indrawati 320
stability and prosperity, belief in US as source of
    336–37, 338
state power, social conflict and security policy 4,
    346–58; Asia-Pacific Resources International
    Holdings Ltd (APRIL) 355; Association of
    South-East Asian Nations (ASEAN) 348, 349,
    351–52, 355; border conflicts 355–56; Burma
    in context of social conflict and reshaping of
    security policy 352–53; constructive
    engagement with Burma 351–52; constructive
    engagement with Burma, opposition to 353;